CLASSICS OF WESTERN THOUGHT

VOLUME IV

The Twentieth Century

CLASSICS OF WESTERN THOUGHT

Under the General Editorship of
Thomas H. Greer
Michigan State University

   I **The Ancient World** THIRD EDITION
      Edited by
      Stebelton H. Nulle
      Michigan State University

  II **Middle Ages, Renaissance,
     and Reformation** THIRD EDITION
      Edited by
      Karl F. Thompson
      Michigan State University

 III **The Modern World** THIRD EDITION
      Edited by
      Charles Hirschfeld
      Late of Richmond College,
      The City University of New York
      and
      Edgar E. Knoebel
      Michigan State University

  IV **The Twentieth Century**
      Edited by
      Donald S. Gochberg
      Michigan State University

CLASSICS OF
WESTERN
THOUGHT

The
Twentieth
Century

VOLUME IV

Edited by   **Donald S. Gochberg**
Michigan State University

HARCOURT BRACE JOVANOVICH, INC.
New York   San Diego   Chicago   San Francisco   Atlanta

Foreword

The twentieth century has brought an explosion of ideas in all fields of knowledge, an eruption beyond the scale of any similar happening in any previous century. As one might expect, the written expressions of these ideas are amazing in both their variety and their quantity; and thus, selecting the "best" of the century's written works is extremely difficult. As the editor of this book, Donald Gochberg has nevertheless attempted the "impossible"—to draw together, from many types of writing, representative and "classic" documents of the twentieth century.

The models for this new anthology are the three earlier volumes in the established Classics of Western Thought series: *The Ancient World; Middle Ages, Renaissance, and Reformation;* and *The Modern World.* The third volume contains documents from the last four centuries; however, scale and spatial considerations permit it only a limited number from the twentieth century. Thus, though the three earlier volumes are well suited to the broad time-span of most courses in Western civilization or in humanities, they do not offer sufficient material for courses devoted exclusively to *contemporary* history or ideas.

Responding to the needs in such courses, Professor Gochberg not only has selected writings of this century exclusively but has focused his attention upon those published after 1950. Thus, as the fourth volume in the Classics of Western Thought series, *The Twentieth Century* duplicates no materials in the preceding volumes and may be used either in conjunction with them or independently. Whichever use is chosen, it is my belief that the book will be of great help to teachers and students who wish to become more conversant with the valuable ideas of their own exciting century.

Thomas H. Greer

Preface

This new volume, the fourth in the Classics of Western Thought series, offers a representative selection of the leading ideas of the twentieth century—as expressed, chiefly, in the West. Each of the preceding volumes in the series covers a number of centuries and, for the most part, presents its selections in chronological order. The selections in this volume, however, are arranged topically. The titles of the seven sections into which they are divided—the result of a thematic analysis of hundreds of the century's writings—reflect some of the period's major concerns and should help to make the intellectual relationships among the selections easily discernible. In addition, the major clashes or concurrences of the various writers in each section are discussed in brief biographical/critical headnotes to the selections. (Dates of publication cited in the headnotes normally indicate the first appearance of the work in a book printed in the English language.)

As the selections show, the twentieth century has been a time in which humanity has been nearly strangled by totalitarianism (Section I) and continually subjected to the omnipresent, potentially dehumanizing force of technology (Section II). In an attempt to avoid domination by the technology they themselves created, contemporary humans seek to re-establish a harmonious relationship with their natural environment (III). When unable to find that harmony with nature, or among themselves, many feel unfulfilled and out of place in their own lives (IV). Some people turn to the ancient solace of religion, frequently finding it intellectually inadequate or stylistically changed beyond recognition (V). Dozens of competing new movements in other areas of life—education, literature, art, music, and politics, for example—leave some people wondering whether the "old standards" still convey any authority. Indeed, even the traditional consciousness of one's own identity is often challenged (VI). Inevitably, looking over the history of their turbulent century, many individuals attempt to reassert control over their destiny by predicting, and thereby influencing, the future (VII).

Of course, no simple thematic scheme can do justice to the complex range of ideas expressed in the volume's selections. It is hoped, however, that the topical arrangement will suggest the many radical transformations of thought that have occurred during the present century. These new thoughts are here presented in literary forms almost as varied as the ideas they communicate: poems, novels, plays, short stories, essays, memoirs, proverbs, historical treatises, scientific discourses, political and artistic manifestoes, religious proclamations, and social analyses.

Additional literary works, some readily available in paperback editions, can be used in conjunction with this volume. For example, a reading of Kafka's *The Trial,* Orwell's *1984,* or Beckett's *Waiting for Godot* will provide the reader of this volume with a fuller treatment of the theme of personal alienation than is provided by the selections alone. Also the reading of an appropriate narrative text—such as Thomas H. Greer's *A Brief History of Western Man,* which was designed for use with this series—will help to provide the historical setting for the ideas set forth in the selections.

As the century progresses, so will its intellectual expression. Thus it is expected that this volume will soon require changes. The readers' comments on the selections and their suggestions for future editions will be welcomed. Above all, it is hoped that the readers' confrontations with the important ideas presented in these selections will aid in the general raising of consciousness necessary for a successful human passage into the *twenty-first* century.

Donald S. Gochberg

Contents

III Man and Nature

IV The Human Malaise

VII Prospects and Portents

I
Totalitarianism

1

Bruno Bettelheim

Behavior in Extreme Situations:
Coercion

*Bruno Bettelheim (1903–   ), a practicing psychoanalyst, was one of the
many Europeans who directly experienced the trauma of the Nazi concentration camps. During his years as a student at the University of Vienna, his
interests were initially aesthetic, and, for a time, he combined majors in literature and art history. But, influenced no doubt by the intellectual prominence
of Sigmund Freud and his followers in Vienna, Bettelheim eventually
switched to psychoanalysis, considering it a way in which he might contribute to the creation of a stable and free Austrian society amidst the social and
economic collapse that followed the First World War. He earned a doctorate
in that field in 1938, the year in which Hitler annexed Austria. Arrested by
the Nazis and transported to Germany as a political and racial prisoner, Bettelheim spent over a year at forced labor in the concentration camps at
Dachau and Buchenwald. Fortunately, as the Second World War had not
quite begun, Americans who knew of his pioneering work with emotionally
disturbed children were able to use their influence to secure Bettelheim's
release. He then immigrated to the United States. Now living in Chicago,
he has for many years been the director of a leading residential school for disturbed children.*

*In all of his published works Bettelheim has applied the techniques of psy-
choanalysis to the clarification and solution of social problems, using as major
sources of original data both his work in the psychological rehabilitation of*

Reprinted with the permission of Macmillan Publishing Co., Inc. from chapter 4,
"Behavior in Extreme Situations: Coercion," of *The Informed Heart: Autonomy in a
Mass Age* by Bruno Bettelheim, © The Free Press, a Corporation, 1960.

children and his sojourn in Nazi concentration camps. He has contributed significant studies on such subjects as the dynamics of prejudice, veterans' problems, the psychoanalysis of fairy tales, and child-rearing in the cooperative communal environment of the Israeli kibbutz.

An essay written by Bettelheim soon after his release from the concentration camps, "Individual and Mass Behavior in Extreme Situations," became required reading for all American military officers in Europe during the Second World War. Among his further reflections on oppression is The Informed Heart: Autonomy in a Mass Age *(1960), from which the following selection is taken. Using the camps as the most extreme of many examples, Bettelheim documents in this work the conflict between individual autonomy and the conformist pressures of modern mass society. The concentration camps were, he contends, vast laboratory instruments for shattering individual egos, instruments that in many cases achieved their purpose. He firmly believes that this destruction of the autonomous self was a calculated and systematic political program throughout the totalitarian regime of the Nazis. Indeed, the reactions of many inmates in the camps foreshadowed the general tendency of contemporary individuals, even in comfortable and essentially benevolent societies, to psychologically relinquish their identities in the face of subtly coercive social pressures. Only the "informed heart" guided by an autonomous mind, says Bettelheim, enables the individual to retain true personality and genuinely humane values. The concentration camps were an aspect of a continuing attack upon the liberal values of the Enlightenment, such values as individual freedom, reason, tolerance, and human progress. These were values that most of the educated upper-middle classes, among whom Bettelheim matured, had assumed to be inviolable. Indeed, he warns, what "the German concentration camps taught about the influence of the environment on man remains a lesson we need to comprehend . . . as an example of the very nature of the coercive mass state."*

. . . it is now common knowledge that prisoners suffered extreme deprivation and were deliberately tortured. Suffice it to review here the minimum facts: prisoners were clothed, housed and fed in total inadequacy; they were exposed to heat, rain, and freezing temperatures for as long as seventeen hours a day, seven days a week. Despite extreme malnutrition, they had to perform hardest labor. Every single moment of their lives was strictly regulated and supervised. They had no privacy whatsoever, were never allowed to see a visitor, lawyer, or minister. They were not entitled to medical care; sometimes they got it, sometimes not, but if they did it was rarely administered by medically trained persons. No prisoner was told why he was imprisoned, and never for how long. . . .[1]

. . . the Gestapo had several varied, though related purposes. One major goal was to break the prisoners as individuals, and to change them into a docile mass from which no individual or group act of resistance could arise. Another purpose was to spread terror among the rest of the population, using prisoners both as hostages and intimidating examples of what happened if you did try to resist.

In addition, the camps were a training ground for the SS. There they were taught to free themselves of their prior, more humane emotions and attitudes, and learn the most effective ways of breaking resistance in a defenseless civilian population; the camps thus became an experimental laboratory in which to study the most effective means for doing that. They were also a testing ground for how to govern most "effectively"; that is, what were the minimum food, hygienic, and medical requirements needed to keep prisoners alive and fit for hard labor when the threat of punishment took the place of all normal incentives; and what was the influence on performance when no time was allowed for anything but hard labor, and the prisoners were separated from their families. This use of the camps as experimental laboratories was later extended to include the so called "medical" experiments, in which human beings were used in place of animals.

By now the German concentration camps belong to the past. We

---

[1] In 1942, three years after my release, the policy of mass extermination was instituted and all camps were classified into three groups. Type I camps were basically forced labor camps where prisoners were deprived of mobility, and maximum work was extracted from them; otherwise these camps were fairly livable and the prisoners had considerable latitude in arranging their lives. Type II camps were more or less of the type in which I spent a year; both Dachau and Buchenwald became Type II camps when this classification went into effect. Type III camps were extermination camps where no effort was made to modify personality since their only purpose was to exterminate prisoners as efficiently as possible.

   Thus most of what follows pertains to Dachau and Buchenwald at the time of my imprisonment (1938–39) when all camps were a combination of what were later separated into Type II and III camps. *"Muselmänner,"* for example, were present in the camps at that time and my discussion of their behavior is based on personal observation. [Footnotes in this selection are all by Bettelheim. *Ed.*]

cannot be equally certain that the idea of changing personality to meet the needs of the state is equally a thing of the past. That is why my discussion centers on the concentration camp as a means of changing personality to produce subjects more useful to the total state.

These changes were produced by subjecting prisoners to conditions specially suited to the purpose. Their extreme character forced the prisoners to adapt themselves entirely and with the greatest speed. In order to analyze the process it may be broken down into several stages. The first stage centered around the initial shock of being imprisoned, the journey to the camp, and the prisoner's first experiences inside it. The second stage comprised the adaptation to the camp situation in a process that changed both the prisoner's personality and his outlook on life. . . .

Why I Began to Study the Prisoners

. . . not detached curiosity, but vital self interest induced me to study my own behavior and the behavior I noticed around me. To observe and try to make sense out of what I saw was a device that spontaneously suggested itself to me as a way of convincing myself that my own life was still of some value, that I had not yet lost all the interests that had once given me self respect. This, in turn, helped me to endure life in the camps. . . .

Thus my interest in trying to understand what was going on psychologically is an example of a spontaneous defense against the impact of an extreme situation. It was individually conceived, was neither enforced by the SS nor suggested by other prisoners, and was based on my particular background and training. Although at first I was only dimly aware of this, it was meant to protect me from a disintegration of personality I dreaded. . . .

While some prisoners were reticent, most were more than willing to talk about themselves, because to find someone interested in them and their problems helped their badly shaken self esteem. Talking at work was not permitted; but since practically everything was forbidden and punished severely, and since the guards were so arbitrary that prisoners who never broke a rule fared no better than those who did, all rules were broken whenever there was some chance of getting away with it.

Every prisoner was confronted with the problem of how to endure degrading work for from twelve to eighteen hours a day. Just about the only relief was to talk, whenever the guards did not prevent it. Though much of the day one was far too exhausted or depressed to make conversation, there were times for it at work, though it was forbidden, or else during the short lunch period or after work in the barracks, when it was permitted. Most of this time had to be used for resting or sleeping, but those who had not given up all interest in living felt a need for some conversation. . . .

Shortly after coming to this country, within a few weeks after my release, I began to put some of my memories down on paper. I hesitated for almost three years to interpret them, because I felt that my anger about the camp experience would interfere with objectivity. By then I thought I had reached as objective an attitude as I could ever expect to reach, so I began to prepare the manuscript for publication.

The difficulty of observing and analyzing mass behavior when the reporter is part of the group seems obvious: so is the task of observing and analyzing oneself when there is nobody around to check and correct. It is still more difficult to remain objective when one discusses experiences which, by their very nature, arouse the strongest emotions. I hope that full awareness of these limitations has helped me to avoid at least the most obvious pitfalls.

TRAUMATIZATION

The Shock of Imprisonment

Sudden personality changes are often the result of traumatic experiences. In discussing the impact of the camps on the prisoners, the initial shock of being torn away from one's family, friends and occupation and then deprived of one's civil rights and locked into a prison, may be separated from the trauma of subjection to extraordinary abuse. Most prisoners experienced these two shocks separately, because they usually spent several days in a local prison where they were relatively unharmed, before being transported to the camp.

Their "initiation" to the concentration camp, which took place while on transport, was often the first torture prisoners had ever experienced and was, for most of them, the worst torture they would be exposed to either physically or psychologically.

Whether and how much the initial shock was experienced as severe trauma depended on the individual personality. But if one wishes to generalize, the prisoners' reactions can be analyzed on the basis of their socio-economic class and their political sophistication. Obviously these categories overlap, and they, too, are separated only for the purposes of discussion. Another factor of importance was whether a prisoner had ever been in prison before, either as a criminal or for political activity.

Non-political middle class prisoners (a minority group in the concentration camps) were those least able to withstand the initial shock. They were utterly unable to understand what had happened to them and why. More than ever they clung to what had given them self respect up to that moment. Even while being abused, they would assure the SS they had never opposed Nazism. They could not understand why they, who had always obeyed the law without question, were being persecuted. Even now, though unjustly imprisoned, they dared not oppose their oppressors even in thought, though it would have given them a self respect they were badly in need of. All they could do was plead, and many groveled. Since law and police had to remain beyond reproach, they accepted as just whatever the Gestapo did. Their only objection was that *they* had become objects of a persecution which in itself must be just, since the authorities imposed it. They rationalized their difficulty by insisting it was all a "mistake." The SS made fun of them, mistreated them badly, while at the same time enjoying scenes that emphasized their position of superiority. The group as a whole was especially anxious that their middle class status should be respected in some way. What upset them most was being treated "like ordinary criminals."

Their behavior showed how little the apolitical German middle class was able to hold its own against National Socialism. No consistent philosophy, either moral, political, or social, protected their integrity or gave them strength for an inner stand against Nazism. They had little or no resources to fall back on when subject to the shock of imprisonment. Their self esteem had rested on a status and respect that came with their positions, depended on their jobs, on being head of a family, or similar external factors. . . .

Eventually they could not help realizing their abysmal change in status. Since to them this was tantamount to a total loss of self respect, they disintegrated as autonomous persons. For them, imprisonment alone was often enough to start the process and carry it quite some length. For instance, the several suicides that took place in prison and during the transport were mostly confined to this group.

Nearly all of them lost their desirable middle class characteristics, such as their sense of propriety and self respect. They became shiftless, and developed to an exaggerated extent the undesirable characteristics of their group: pettiness, quarrelsomeness, self pity. Many became depressed in an agitated way and complained eternally. Others became chiselers and stole from other prisoners. (Stealing from, or cheating the SS was often considered as honorable as stealing from prisoners was thought despicable.) They seemed incapable of following a life pattern of their own any more, but copied those developed by other groups of prisoners. . . .

Initiation to the Camps

Usually the standard initiation of prisoners took place during transit from the local prison to the camp. If the distance was short, the transport was often slowed down to allow enough time to break the prisoners. During their initial transport to the camp, prisoners were exposed to nearly constant torture. The nature of the abuse depended on the fantasy of the particular SS man in charge of a group of prisoners. Still, they all had a definite pattern. Physical punishment consisted of whipping, frequent kicking (abdomen or groin), slaps in the face, shooting, or wounding with the bayonet. These alternated with attempts to produce extreme exhaustion. For instance, prisoners were forced to stare for hours into glaring lights, to kneel for hours, and so on.

From time to time a prisoner got killed, but no prisoner was allowed to care for his or another's wounds. The guards also forced prisoners to hit one another and to defile what the SS considered the prisoners' most cherished values. They were forced to curse their God, to accuse themselves and one another of vile actions, and their wives of adultery and prostitution. I never met a prisoner who had escaped this kind of initiation, which lasted at least twelve hours and often much longer. Until it was over, any failure to obey an order, such as slapping another prisoner, or any help given a tortured prisoner was viewed as mutiny and swiftly punished by death.

The purpose of this massive initial abuse was to traumatize the prisoners and break their resistance; to change at least their behavior if not yet their personalities. This could be seen from the fact that tortures became less and less violent to the degree that prisoners stopped resisting and complied immediately with any SS order, even the most outrageous. . . .

It is hard to say just how much the process of personality change was speeded up by what prisoners experienced during the initiation. Most of them were soon totally exhausted; physically from abuse, loss of blood, thirst, etc.; psychologically from the need to control their anger and desperation before it could lead to a suicidal resistance. As a result they were only partly conscious of what happened. In general, they remembered details afterward and did not mind talking about them, but they did not like to talk about what they had thought or felt while being tortured. The few who volunteered information made vague statements that sounded like devious rationalizations to justify their having endured treatment so damaging to their self respect without trying to fight back. The few who did try to fight back could not tell about it; they were dead. . . .

. . . if I should try to sum up in one sentence what my main problem was during the whole time I spent in the camps, it would be: to protect my inner self in such a way that if, by any good fortune, I should regain liberty, I would be approximately the same person I was when deprived of liberty. So it seems that a split was soon forced upon me, the split between the inner self that might be able to retain its integrity, and the rest of the personality that would have to submit and adjust for survival.

Initial Adjustment

I have no doubt that I was able to endure the horrors of the transport and all that followed, because right from the beginning I became convinced that these dreadful and degrading experiences were somehow not happening to "me" as a subject, but only to "me" as an object. The prevalence of such an attitude was borne out by many statements of other prisoners, although none would go so far as to say definitely that it was clearly developed as early as the time of the transport. Usually they couched their feelings in more general terms such as, "The main problem is to remain alive and unchanged," without specifying what they meant by unchanged. From additional remarks it became apparent that what was to remain unchanged differed from person to person, but covered roughly that person's general attitudes and values. Unfortunately, staying alive and unchanged was very difficult, since every effort to assure remaining alive implied inner changes, while efforts to avoid change endangered survival.

All thoughts and feelings I had during the transport were extremely detached. It was as if I watched things happening in which I took part only vaguely. Later I learned that many prisoners developed this same feeling of detachment, as if what happened did not really matter to oneself. It was strongly mixed with a conviction that "This can't be true; such things just don't happen." Not only during the transport but for a long time to come, prisoners had to convince themselves that this was real and not just a nightmare. Some of them were never wholly successful. . . .

This attitude of denying "reality" to events so extreme as to threaten the prisoner's integration was a first step toward developing new mechanisms for surviving in the camp. By denying reality to overwhelming situations, they were somehow made bearable; but at the same time it constituted a major change in experiencing the world. Thus while the attitude was a necessary adjustment, it also implied personality change. The denial of reality was most obvious during extreme experiences that the prisoner could not have managed in any other way. . . .

It is also possible that prisoners resented minor abuses, in which they were dealt with as if they were silly children, more than extreme ones, because unconsciously they realized that the Gestapo was trying to reduce them to the status of children who have no rights and must obey blindly. Or it may have been that for severe punishment, the prisoner could expect to receive friendly support, which is some comfort. He could not reasonably expect it for being rapped on the knuckles with a ruler, or for a slap in the face. Moreover, if the suffering was great, he felt more like a man than a child, because children are not punished so brutally; or he may have felt a bit like a martyr suffering for a cause, and the martyr is supposed to accept his martyrdom, or at least to take it like a man. . . .

Besides traumatization, the Gestapo relied mainly on three other methods of destroying all personal autonomy. The first of these has just been touched on: that of forcing prisoners to adopt childlike be-

havior. The second was that of forcing them to give up individuality
and merge themselves into an amorphous mass. The third consisted
of destroying all capacity for self determination, all ability to predict
the future and thus to prepare for it.

THE PROCESS OF CHANGE

Childlike Behavior

To be filled with impotent rage is a situation frequent in childhood, but disastrous for one's mature integration. Therefore, the
prisoners' aggressions had to be dealt with somehow, and one of the
safest ways was to turn it against the self. This increased masochistic,
passive-dependent, and childlike attitudes which were "safe" because
they kept the prisoner out of conflict with the SS. But as a psychological mechanism inside the prisoner it coincided with SS efforts to
produce childlike inadequacy and dependency.

It has been mentioned that prisoners were often mistreated in ways
that a cruel and domineering father might use against helpless children. But just as even the cruelest parent threatens physical punishment much more often than he actually inflicts it, so childlike
feelings of helplessness were created much more effectively by the
constant threat of beatings than by actual torture. During a real beating one could, for example, take some pride in suffering manfully, in
not giving the foreman or guard the satisfaction of groveling before
him, etc. No such emotional protection was possible against the
mere threat.

While there were many days for many a prisoner when he went
unharmed, there was hardly an hour of the day when neither he nor
some of his friends were not being threatened with a lashing. The
vast majority of prisoners went through the camp without a public
flogging, but the screamed threat that they were going to get
twenty-five on the behind rang in their ears several times daily. To
have to accept and make one's peace with the fact that one was constantly under threat of such infantile punishment made it much
harder to retain one's self image as an adult than any actual beatings.

Threats like these, and also the curses thrown at prisoners by both
the SS and prisoner foremen were almost exclusively connected with
the anal sphere. "Shit" and "asshole" were so standard that it was

rare when a prisoner was addressed otherwise. It was as if every effort were being made to reduce prisoners to the level they were at before toilet training was achieved.

For example, they were forced to wet and soil themselves. All elimination was strictly regulated in the camp and was an important daily event, discussed in detail. At Buchenwald it was repeatedly forbidden to defecate during the entire work day. But even when exceptions were made a prisoner who needed to eliminate had to get permission from a guard and then report to him when he was finished in ways that shattered his self respect.

The formula he had to use was the same one required in all cases of asking for something of the guards, such as a letter from home, etc. It was a formula that emphasized both an absence of personal identity, and abject dependence; for a Jewish prisoner it would go: "Jewish prisoner number 34567 most obediently prays to be permitted to (whatever the request was)." Some decent guards would wave a condescending okay. But many made degrading remarks or asked questions that could only be answered in a self degrading way; others would keep the prisoner waiting for a while, as if debating if he had been abject enough, or if his need was really urgent. If permission to eliminate was granted, the prisoner, having relieved himself, had to report back using the same formula, much as an infant might report on having done his "duty." Here too it was as if the education to cleanliness were being repeated again. . . .

Another influence adding to regression into childhood behavior was the work prisoners were given to do. New prisoners in particular were given nonsensical tasks, such as carrying heavy rocks from one place to another, and after a while back to the place where they had picked them up. Or they were forced to dig holes in the ground with their bare hands although tools were available. They resented the senseless work, although it should have been immaterial to them whether their work was useful or not. They felt debased when they were forced to perform "childish" or stupid labor, and often preferred even harder work when it produced something that might be called useful. They felt even more debased when they were hitched like horses to heavy wagons and forced to gallop. By the same token, many prisoners hated singing rollicking songs by command of the SS more than being beaten by them. The less painful, the more nonsensical an activity was in itself, the more degrading it felt to have to perform it for the SS.

Frequently the SS assigned more meaningful tasks to old prisoners. This indicated that forcing nonsensical labor on the prisoners was a deliberate effort to speed their decline from self respecting adults to obedient children. There seems no doubt that the tasks they were given, as well as the mistreatment they had to endure, contributed to the disintegration of their self respect and made it impossible to see themselves and each other as fully adult persons any more.

Mass Behavior

The difference between certain practices at Dachau (organized in 1933) and Buchenwald (in 1937), reflects the growing depersonalization of all procedures during that period. At Dachau, for example, official punishment, as distinct from random abuse, was always directed at a particular individual. Beforehand he had a so-called hearing in the presence of a commissioned SS officer. According to Western legal standards these hearings were a farce, but compared to what later became standard procedure it showed great consideration for the individual because he was at least told what he was accused of and given a chance to refute the charges. If he knew what was good for him, he made no effort to defend himself. But he could add one or another detail and sometimes get off without punishment.

Before flogging, he was examined by the camp physician, another fairly empty procedure since the doctor rarely canceled the whipping, though he sometimes reduced the number of lashes. Even as late as 1939, prisoners at Dachau enjoyed some limited protection against too flagrant acts of injustice. When a guard shot or otherwise caused a prisoner's death he had to make a written report. That was all he had to do, but it was still something of a deterrent.

Such consideration of prisoners as individuals, though small enough, was out of the question at Buchenwald, which reflected a later phase of National Socialism. For example, prisoners who went insane—and there were quite a few of them—were no longer isolated, protected, or sent to mental institutions, but were ridiculed and chased about until they died.

But the greatest difference was that at Buchenwald it was nearly always the group that suffered, not the individual. At Dachau, a prisoner who tried to carry a small stone instead of a heavy one would have suffered for it; at Buchenwald the whole group including the foreman would have been punished.

It was almost impossible for prisoners not to cooperate with SS efforts to reduce them to passivity inside a deindividualized mass. Both the prisoner's self interest and SS pressure worked in the same direction. To remain independent implied dangers and many hardships; to comply with the SS seemed in the prisoner's own interest, because it automatically made life easier for him. Similar mechanisms were at work in the inhabitants of Germany outside the concentration camps, though not quite in such obvious form.

Whenever possible the prisoners were punished as a group so that the whole group suffered for and with the person who brought about the punishment. The Gestapo probably used this method because it was in line with its anti-individualistic philosophy and because they hoped that in this way the group would control the individual. It was in the group's interest to prevent anyone from endangering the group. As already noted, the fear of punishment was more frequent than the reality, which meant that the group asserted its power over the individual more often and more effectively than the SS. In many respects group pressure was practically permanent. Moreover, each prisoner was unusually dependent for survival on group cooperation. This added further to a situation where the group was constantly controlling the individual. . . .

The Fate of the Hero

. . . In some ways, heroism can be the highest assertion of individuality. It was therefore contrary to Gestapo ideology to allow a prisoner to gain prominence by heroic action. Since all prisoners were exposed to severe mistreatment, those who died because of it, though perhaps martyrs to political or religious convictions, were not considered heroes by other prisoners. Only those who suffered for their efforts to protect other prisoners were accepted as heroes.

The SS was usually successful in preventing martyrs or heroes from being created, through its consistent suppression of all individual action or, if this was not possible, by changing it into a group phenomenon. If a prisoner tried to protect others and it came to a guard's attention, the prisoner was usually killed. But if his action came to the knowledge of the camp administration, the whole group was always punished severely. In this way, the group came to resent its protector because he brought them suffering. The protector was also kept from rekindling respect for the individual, or from inspiring an appreciation of independence. Moreover, he could never become a hero or a leader (if he survived) or a martyr (if he died) around whom group resistance might have formed.

Here a further example may illustrate. It concerns a labor command at Buchenwald in which men carried bricks to a building site, a "safe" command for which wealthy prisoners paid heavily with food, money, and cigarettes. The load they carried was not too heavy, and there was little beating by the heavily bribed kapo.[2] Commands of unskilled labor carrying reasonable loads on regular trips (carrier columns) were often preferred by prisoners who were in any position to choose. They had many reasons, which have bearing on this example. Walking in twos or fours as these carriers did, made conversation possible; the return trip was made without a load so that half the time was spent in easy walking except when the SS was in sight and prisoners had to run. Moreover, each trip divided the endless day which was otherwise insufferably long and unbroken. . . .

One day, in October 1940, one such carrier column made up of Jewish prisoners[3] was "peacefully" returning after delivering its load. On the way they ran into the SS Sergeant Abraham who, as rumor had it, was particularly cruel to Jews because his fellow officers made jokes about his name. Noticing the group of prisoners walking without a load he ordered them to throw themselves down in the muddy road. He ordered them up and down again several times—a relatively harmless "sport."

In the column were two brothers from Vienna named Hamber. In throwing himself down, one of them lost his glasses which fell into a water-filled ditch beside the road. Using the correct formula, he asked the SS man's permission to leave the formation and recover his glasses. This was a request within reason, even for the camp situation, and was usually granted. But by asking permission to act outside the group he became conspicuous. He was no longer an anonymous member of a unit, but an individual.

[2] Prisoner foreman in charge of a labor command.
[3] The category a prisoner belonged to was plainly visible from insignia worn on his uniform.

Having gotten his permission, he dived into the waterfilled ditch looking for his glasses. He came up without them, and dived again. Then he was ready to give up. But now the SS man forced him to dive again and again. He had asked for permission to look for his glasses and he was told to keep diving until he found them. This was the SS man's revenge for having granted a personal request. When Hamber was utterly exhausted and resisted further diving, the SS man forced him down into the water again and again until he died— either by drowning or of heart failure.

What happened afterward is not entirely clear, since the available reports are somewhat contradictory. This, incidentally, is typical of the immediate distortion of all stories about camp happenings. Among other reasons was the fact that survival in the camp required not only that one be inconspicuous, but "unobservant" as well. The account as given here is based on three independent reports of the event which agree on the essentials as they happened, if not on the motives of the SS.

For reasons never quite verified, the camp commander felt that an investigation of Hamber's death had to be made—rumor had it because a German civilian witnessed the scene and reported it in disgust to some official. For whatever reason, the whole carrier group was brought before the commander of the camp that evening and asked to tell what they knew about the incident. Each of them stated he had seen nothing and could give no information, which was just what was expected of a prisoner, namely to see, hear, and say nothing of what took place in the camp. Only Hamber's brother felt obliged to do what he could to avenge his brother's killing. He stated that his brother died after being forced by the SS man to dive into the water beyond his endurance. When asked about witnesses, he stated that all prisoners of the command had seen the incident. With that the group was dismissed. It seemed to have been a routine interrogation with no consequences, such as often took place when a prisoner had been killed in front of civilian observers. The only difference was that this time a prisoner had claimed he could bear witness.

Later the same evening, Hamber was called to appear before the rapport leader.[4] By then he was in utter despair. It was clear that his courageous statement had not only endangered himself, but all his

---

[4] Senior SS officer, directly under the camp commander.

comrades in the labor group, including the kapo. They all feared the vengeance of the SS, but they also feared that their labor command might "explode," i.e., be dismissed and reformed with different prisoners. To lose a good command was disastrous. It was particularly disastrous for Jewish prisoners to whom most good commands were closed. Moreover, even if the command were to continue, it would be some time before it was a "good" one again, for it was now in the limelight and would be ridden by the SS. In addition, the kapo would certainly behave differently. However bribed, he would never forgive the fact that one of them had made his command conspicuous and thus endangered him as a kapo and a person.

Besides having lost a brother that day, Hamber now had to fear for his own life and for his labor command, and to face the reproaches of his comrades. These were the consequences for a prisoner who tried to behave as an individual and who put individual allegiance before personal safety and the safety of the group. Now Hamber realized the straits his emotional courage had led him to and was ready to recant. But in a hurried conference with his friends in the barracks, it was decided that he could not retract his original statement much as he now wished, because it would mean certain death for him as having falsely accused an SS man. It seemed better to stick to the truth.

When he presented himself for questioning, he was examined by the commander of the camp and other ranking SS officials. On his return to the barracks he reported that they had urged him to tell the truth, promising that nothing would happen to him if he did, but that he would suffer maximum punishment if he distorted it. He had therefore signed an affidavit giving a truthful account of what had happened.

It was late in the evening when he returned from this interview. In the middle of the same night he was taken out of his barracks and brought into the *Bunker* (the building for solitary confinement and special torture). It was ten days later before he was next seen there by chance. He did not then seem to be in bad shape, nor did he show signs of torture. But a few days later his corpse came into the morgue.

The official version was that he had hanged himself, but the towel he supposedly used, and which was brought in with the corpse, was far too short to strangulate a man. It was obvious he had been strangled in the *Bunker*. Nor was any of this unexpected. On the contrary, it was "quite in order." The SS always eliminated dangerous or inconvenient witnesses. The only unusual factor was that Hamber himself had brought about his death, and this was widely repeated as a warning to everyone to be even more careful not to see, hear, or talk.

Approximately eight days later, three prisoners of the command (all numbers had been taken down on the day of Hamber's killing) were ordered to appear for questioning. They never returned to the barracks, but three days later the first of them came into the morgue, followed by a second and third corpse. They had been killed by injection. A week later three more prisoners of the command were similarly "disposed" of. It took about three months before the command, and thus all possible witnesses, was eliminated. One can imagine the feelings of those who, after the second group was disposed of, knew their fate. Nevertheless, not one of them committed suicide.

Thus SS-imposed control by the group over the individual prisoner had its counterpart in the prisoner's self interest and made group control nearly inescapable. The treatment all prisoners suffered daily kept them explosive with justified rage. To give vent to it meant almost certain death. The group helped the individual to restrain himself.

SELF DETERMINATION

The Will to Live

The question arises as to why, in the concentration camp, although some prisoners survived and others got killed, such a sizeable percentage simply died. . . . The vast majority of the thousands of prisoners who died at Buchenwald each year died soon. They simply died of exhaustion, both physical and psychological, due to a loss of desire to live.

After one had learned how to live in the camps, the chances for survival increased greatly. Except for rare occasions, such as the Hamber episode, large scale executions of old prisoners were rare. While one was never without fear for one's life, the fact that several thousands of the prisoners liberated in 1945 had spent five and even ten years in the camps suggests that the death rate for old prisoners

was very different from what overall figures would suggest. . . .
On the other hand, the early death rate of new prisoners, particularly
during their first months in the camp, may have been as high as 15%
a month. This, of course, intensified the terror of new prisoners to an
unbearable pitch and explains why many of them soon deteriorated
into the deathlike state I will soon speak about. . . .

The Unpredictable Environment

What happened in the concentration camp suggests that under
conditions of extreme deprivation, the influence of the environment
over the individual can become total. Whether it does or not seems
to depend a great deal on impact and timing; on how sudden the impact, and how little (or how much) the individual is prepared for it
(because it is also destructive if someone has always expected something terrible to happen to him and it does). It depends even more on
how long the condition prevails, how well integrated the person is
whom it hits, and finally whether it remains unmitigated. Or to put
the last point differently: whether the conviction is given that no
matter what one does, no positive response can be drawn from the
environment through efforts of one's own.

This was so much so, that whether or not one survived may have
depended on one's ability to arrange to preserve some areas of independent action, to keep control of some important aspects of one's
life, despite an environment that seemed overwhelming and total. To
survive, not as a shadow of the SS but as a man, one had to find
some life experience that mattered, over which one was still in command.

This was taught me by a German political prisoner, a communist
worker who by then had been at Dachau for four years. I arrived
there in a sorry condition because of experiences on the transport. I
think that this man, by then an "old" prisoner, decided that, given
my condition, the chances of my surviving without help were slim.
So when he noticed that I could not swallow food because of physical pain and psychological revulsion, he spoke to me out of his rich
experience: "Listen you, make up your mind: do you want to live or
do you want to die? If you don't care, don't eat the stuff. But if you
want to live, there's only one way: make up your mind to eat whenever and whatever you can, never mind how disgusting. Whenever

you have a chance, defecate, so you'll be sure your body works. And whenever you have a minute, don't blabber, read by yourself, or flop down and sleep."

This advice, after a while, I made my own and none too soon for my survival. In my case, trying to find out what went on in the prisoners took the place of the activity he had had in mind when he suggested reading. Soon I became convinced of how sound his advice had been. But it took me years to fully grasp its psychological wisdom.

What was implied was the necessity, for survival, to carve out, against the greatest of odds, some areas of freedom of action and freedom of thought, however insignificant. The two freedoms, of activity and passivity, constitute our two most basic human attitudes, while intake and elimination, mental activity and rest, make up our most basic physiological activities. To have some small token experiences of being active and passive, each on one's own, and in mind as well as body—this, much more than the utility of any one such activity, was what enabled me and others like me to survive.[5]

By contrast, it was the senseless tasks, the lack of almost any time to oneself, the inability to plan ahead because of sudden changes in camp policies, that was so deeply destructive. By destroying man's ability to act on his own or to predict the outcome of his actions, they destroyed the feeling that his actions had any purpose, so many prisoners stopped acting. But when they stopped acting they soon stopped living. What seemed to make the critical difference was whether or not the environment—extreme as it was—permitted (or promised) some minimal choices, some leeway, some positive rewards, insignificant as they seem now, when viewed objectively against the tremendous deprivation.

That may be why the SS vacillated between extreme repression and the easing of tension: the torture of prisoners, but occasional punishment of particularly inhuman guards; sudden respect and reward from the SS for some random prisoner who insisted on his dignity; sudden days of rest, etc. Without these, for example, no identification with the SS could have taken place, to mention only

---

[5] Maybe I should explain why I call it a self-chosen act of freedom to force oneself to eat repellent food, etc. Given the initial decision—to stay alive—the forcing oneself to eat was self-imposed, not SS enforced, and unlike turning spy for survival it did not violate inner values or weaken self-respect. The patient who is critically ill likewise indicates an active desire to live when he swallows bitter medicine.

one outcome. Most prisoners who died, as opposed to those who got killed, were those who could no longer believe in, or take advantage of, those sudden remissions that happen in even the most extreme situations; in short those who had given up all will to live.

It was impressive to observe how skillfully the SS used this mechanism of destroying man's faith in his ability to predict the future. For want of evidence we cannot say if this was deliberate or unconscious but it worked with deadly effectiveness. If the SS wanted a group (Norwegians, political prisoners who were not Jewish, etc.) to adjust, survive, and serve in the camps, they would hold out the promise that their behavior had some influence on their fate. To those groups whom they wished to destroy (Eastern Jews, Poles, Ukrainians, etc.) they made it quite clear that no matter how. hard they worked or tried to please their masters, it would make no difference whatsoever.

Another means of destroying the prisoners' belief that they had some basis for hope, some influence over their fate, and therefore some reason for wanting to live, was to expose them to sudden radical changes in living conditions. At one camp, for example, a large group of Czech prisoners was utterly destroyed by giving them the promise that they were "honor" prisoners entitled to special privileges, letting them live in relative comfort without any work or hardship for a time, then suddenly throwing them into quarry work where labor conditions were worst and mortality highest, while at the same time reducing their food rations; then back again into good quarters and easy work, and after a few months back into the quarries with little food, etc. Soon they all died.

My own experience of three times being called up to be freed and each time being dressed in civilian clothes to be ready for release, is another example. Possibly it happened because I had provoked an SS official. The first time, nearly all other prisoners called up with me were released while I was sent back into the camp. The second time may have been chance, because quite a few besides myself were sent back, and rumor had it that the SS had run out of money and could not pay the sums due the prisoners for the trip home. In any case, when I was summoned the third time I refused to go and be put into civilian clothes because I was convinced it was just another effort of the SS official to break me. But this time the call was authentic.

The question is: why did I deliberately provoke an SS officer? I believe that in order not to collapse, I had to prove to myself that I had some power to influence my environment. I knew I could not do it positively, so I did it negatively. Nor was this reasoned out. I acted on the unconscious realization of what I needed most to survive.

The Penalty for Suicide

Since the main goal of the SS was to do away with independence of action and the ability to make personal decisions, even negative ways of achieving it were not neglected. The decision to remain alive or to die is probably a supreme example of self determination. Therefore the SS attitude toward suicide may be mentioned.

The stated principle was: the more prisoners to commit suicide, the better. But even there, the decision must not be the prisoner's. An SS man might provoke a prisoner to commit suicide by running against the electrically charged wire fence, and that was all right. But for those who took the initiative in killing themselves, the SS issued (in Dachau in 1933) a special order: prisoners who attempted suicide but did not succeed were to receive twenty-five lashes and prolonged solitary confinement. Supposedly this was to punish them for their failure to do away with themselves; but I am convinced it was much more to punish them for the act of self determination.

Also, since protecting life, either one's own or that of others, is a major act of self assertion, it too had to be inhibited. Therefore the same punishment was threatened to any prisoner who tried to prevent a suicide before it happened, or tried to bring back to life a prisoner who tried it. To my knowledge this punishment for attempted suicide or for helping a suicidal person was only once carried out; but it was not the punishment the SS was interested in, it was the threat of punishment and what that did to destroy self determination.

Muselmänner: The Walking Corpses

Prisoners who came to believe the repeated statements of the guards—that there was no hope for them, that they would never leave the camp except as a corpse—who came to feel that their environment was one over which they could exercise no influence whatsoever, these prisoners were, in a literal sense, walking corpses. In the camps they were called "moslems" (*Muselmänner*) because of what was erroneously viewed as a fatalistic surrender to the environment, as Mohammedans [Moslems] are supposed to blandly accept their fate.

But these people had not, like real Mohammedans, made an act of decision and submitted to fate out of free will. On the contrary, they were people who were so deprived of affect, self esteem, and every form of stimulation, so totally exhausted, both physically and emotionally, that they had given the environment total power over them. They did this when they gave up trying to exercise any further influence over their life or environment.

That is, as long as a prisoner fought in any way for survival, for some self assertion within and against the overpowering environment, he could not become a "moslem." Once his own life and the environment were viewed as totally beyond his ability to influence them, the only logical conclusion was to pay no attention to them whatsoever. Only then, all conscious awareness of stimuli coming from the outside was blocked out, and with it all response to anything but inner stimuli.

But even the moslems, being organisms, could not help reacting somehow to their environment, and this they did by depriving it of the power to influence them as subjects in any way whatsoever. To achieve this, they had to give up responding to it at all, and become objects, but with this they gave up being persons. These walking shadows all died very soon. Or to put it differently, after a certain point of extreme deprivation, the environment can only move around empty shells, as the camp routine did with these moslems; they behaved as if they were not thinking, not feeling, unable to act or respond, moved only by things outside themselves.

One might even speculate as to whether these organisms had by-passed the reflex arc that once extended from external or internal stimulus via frontal lobes to feeling and action. First they had given up all action as being utterly pointless; then feeling, because all feeling was merely painful or dangerous or both. Eventually this somehow extended backwards to blocking out the stimulation itself.

These things could be readily observed in the deterioration of moslems. It began when they stopped acting on their own. And that was the moment when other prisoners recognized what was happening and separated themselves from these now "marked" men, because any further association with them could lead only to one's own destruction. At this point such men still obeyed orders, but only blindly or automatically; no longer selectively or with inner reservation or any hatred at being so abused. They still looked about, or at least moved their eyes around. The looking stopped much later, though even then they still moved their bodies when ordered, but never did anything on their own any more. Typically, this stopping of action began when they no longer lifted their legs as they walked, but only shuffled them. When finally even the looking about on their own stopped, they soon died.

Don't Dare to Notice

That the process was not accidental may be seen from the ban on daring to notice anything. Compared with the all pervasive order not to be conspicuous (noticeable), the prisoners were less frequently told the commensurate "don't dare to notice." But to look and observe for oneself what went on in the camp—while absolutely necessary for survival—was even more dangerous than being noticed. Often this passive compliance—not to see or not to know—was not enough; in order to survive one had to actively pretend not to observe, not to know what the SS required one not to know.[6]

Among the worst mistakes a prisoner could make was to watch (to notice) another prisoner's mistreatment. There the SS seemed totally irrational, but only seemed so. For example, if an SS man was killing off a prisoner and other prisoners dared to look at what was going on in front of their eyes he would instantly go after them, too. But only seconds later the same SS would call the same prisoners' attention to what lay in store for anyone who dared to disobey, draw-

---

[6] Even trivial examples illustrate this: during some mistreatment on the transport my eyeglasses were broken. Since I can hardly see without them, I asked for permission, once I was at Dachau, to have new glasses sent to me from home. I had been warned in advance never to admit knowing of any mistreatment, including my own. So when asked why I needed glasses, I simply said that they got broken. When the SS officer heard this he began to deliver a beating and screamed, "*What* did you say happened?" I corrected myself, saying I had broken them accidentally. At this he immediately said, "Okay, just remember that for the future," and matter-of-factly sat down to give me written permission to receive glasses. His reaction, incidentally, was swift but by no means spontaneous; on the contrary, it was deliberate and purposeful. No sadist bent on satisfying his desires will instantly stop mistreatment on getting a correct formula reply. Only a person simply after a specific goal will behave in that way.

ing their attention to the killing as a warning example. This was no contradiction, it was simply an impressive lesson that said: you may notice only what we wish you to notice, but you invite death if you notice things on your own volition. The issue was again the same; the prisoner was not to have a will of his own.

Many examples showed that all this happened for a reason and a purpose. An SS man might seem to have gone berserk about what he viewed as some resistance or disobedience, and in this state beat up or even kill a prisoner. But in the midst of it he might call out a friendly "well done" to a passing work column who, having stumbled on the scene, would fall into a gallop, heads averted, so as to pass by as fast as possible without "noticing." Obviously their sudden break into running and their averted heads showed clearly that they had "noticed"; but that did not matter as long as they also showed so clearly that they had accepted the command not to know what they were not supposed to know.

This all important enforced behavior was equally apparent when the SS was provoking a prisoner to commit suicide. If the unfortunate succeeded, anyone watching it was immediately punished. But as soon as the punishment for having observed on one's own was over, the same SS might warn: "See what happened to that man? That's what'll happen to you!"

To know only what those in authority allow one to know is, more or less, all the infant can do. To be able to make one's own observations and to draw pertinent conclusions from them is where independent existence begins. To forbid oneself to make observations, and take only the observations of others in their stead, is relegating to nonuse one's own powers of reasoning, and the even more basic power of perception. Not observing where it counts most, not knowing where one wants so much to know, all this is most destructive to the functioning of one's personality. So is finding oneself in a situation where what once gave security (the power to observe correctly and to draw on one's own the right inferences) not only ceases to offer security, but actually endangers one's life. Deliberate nonuse of one's power of observation, as opposed to temporary inattention, which is different, leads to a withering away of this power.

To make matters worse, while to observe was dangerous, to react emotionally to what one saw was frankly suicidal. That is, a prisoner who noticed mistreatment was punished, but only mildly when compared to what happened if his feelings carried him away to the point of trying to give help. Knowing that such an emotional reaction was tantamount to suicide, and being unable at times not to react emotionally when observing what went on, left only one way out: not to observe, so as not to react. So both powers, those of observation and of reaction, had to be blocked out voluntarily as an act of preservation. But if one gives up observing, reacting, and taking action, one gives up living one's own life. And this is exactly what the SS wanted to happen.

Thus the truly extreme environment first blocks self-stimulated action (resisting or modifying the environment) and later also, response to any stimulus coming from the environment in terms of one's own personality (inner revulsion without overt action based on it). Finally, all this is replaced by no other than environment-imposed action without even an inner personal response to it. This last situation leads first to a blotting out of responses, later to a blotting out even of perception; except that death then follows.

Prisoners entered the moslem stage when emotion could no longer be evoked in them. For a time they fought for food, but after a few weeks even that stopped. Despite their hunger, even the food stimulus no longer reached their brain clearly enough to lead to action. Nobody and nothing could now influence these persons or their characters, because nothing from inside or outside was reaching them any more. Other prisoners often tried to be nice to them when they could, to give them food and so forth, but they could no longer respond to the emotional attitude that was behind someone's giving them food. So food they took, up to the point where they had reached the final stage of disintegration, but it no longer replenished them emotionally; it just entered an always empty stomach.

As long as they still asked for food, followed someone to get it, stretched out a hand for it and ate what was given eagerly, they could still, with great effort, have been returned to "normal" prisoner status, deteriorated as they were. In the next stage of disintegration, receiving food unexpectedly still led to a momentary lighting up of the face and a grateful hangdog look, though hardly any verbal response, but when they no longer reached out for it spontaneously, no longer responded with thanks, an effort to smile, or a look at the giver, they were nearly always beyond help. Later they took food, sometimes ate it, sometimes not, but no longer had a feeling response. In the last, just before the terminal stage, they no longer ate it.

The Last Human Freedom.

Even those prisoners who did not become moslems, who some-how managed to remain in control of some small aspect of their lives, eventually had to come to longer range terms with their new environment. The mere fact of survival meant that in the matter of Caesar's dues, it was no longer a question of whether to render them or not, nor even, with rare exceptions, of how much to render. But to survive as a man not a walking corpse, as a debased and degraded but still human being, one had first and foremost to remain informed and aware of what made up one's personal point of no return, the point beyond which one would never, under any circumstances, give in to the oppressor, even if it meant risking and losing one's life. It meant being aware that if one survived at the price of overreaching this point one would be holding on to a life that had lost all its mean-ing. It would mean surviving—not with a lowered self respect, but without any.

This point of no return was different from person to person, and changed for each person as time passed. At the beginning of their imprisonment, most inmates would have felt it beyond their point of no return to serve the SS as foreman or block chief, or to like wear-ing a uniform that made them look like the SS. Later, after years in the camp, such relatively external matters gave way to much more essential convictions which then became the core of their resistance. But those convictions one had to hold on to with utter tenacity. About them, one had to keep oneself informed at all times, because only then could they serve as the mainstay of a radically reduced but still present humanity. Much of the tenacity and relentlessness of po-litical prisoners in their factional warfare is thus explainable; for them, political loyalty to party was their point of no return.

Second in importance was keeping oneself informed of how one felt about complying when the ultimate decision as to where to stand firm was not called into question. While less radical, it was no less essential, because an awareness of one's attitude toward compliance was called for almost constantly. One had to comply with debasing and amoral commands if one wished to survive; but one had to remain cognizant that one's reason for complying was "to remain alive and unchanged as a person." Therefore, one had to decide, for any given action, whether it was truly necessary for one's safety or that of others, and whether committing it was good, neutral, or bad.

This keeping informed and aware of one's actions—though it could not alter the required act, save in extremities—this minimal distance from one's own behavior, and the freedom to feel differently about it depending on its character, this too was what permitted the prisoner to remain a human being. It was the giving up of all feelings, all inner reservations about one's actions, the letting go of a point at which one would hold fast no matter what, that changed prisoner into moslem.

Those prisoners who blocked out neither heart nor reason, neither feelings nor perception, but kept informed of their inner attitudes even when they could hardly ever afford to act on them, those prisoners survived and came to understand the conditions they lived under. They also came to realize what they had not perceived before; that they still retained the last, if not the greatest, of the human freedoms: to choose their own attitude in any given circumstance. Prisoners who understood this fully, came to know that this, and only this, formed the crucial difference between retaining one's humanity (and often life itself) and accepting death as a human being (or perhaps physical death): whether one retained the freedom to choose autonomously one's attitude to extreme conditions even when they seemed totally beyond one's ability to influence them.[7] . . .

[7] Kogon reports one of many incidents bearing this out: Once a command of Jewish prisoners was working alongside of some Polish Gentile prisoners. The supervising SS, spying two Jewish prisoners whom he thought to be slacking, ordered them to lie down in the ditch and called on a Polish prisoner, named Strzaska, to bury them alive. Strzaska, frozen in terror and anxiety, refused to obey. At this the SS seized a spade and beat the Pole, who nevertheless still refused to obey. Furiously, the SS now ordered the two Jews to get out of the ditch, Strzaska to get in, and the two Jews to bury *him*. In mortal anxiety, hoping to escape the fate themselves, they shoveled earth into the ditch and onto their fellow prisoner. When only Strzaska's head was barely visible the SS ordered them to stop, and unearth him. Once Strzaska was on his feet, the two Jews were ordered back into the ditch, and this time Strzaska obeyed the renewed command to bury them—possibly because they had not resisted burying him, or perhaps expecting that they too would be spared at the last minute. But this time there was no reprieve, and when the ditch was filled the SS stamped down the earth that still lay loosely over his victims. Five minutes later he called on two other prisoners to unearth them, but though they worked frantically, it was too late. One was already dead and the other dying, so the SS ordered them both taken to the crematorium.

2

Hannah Arendt

Eichmann in Jerusalem:
A Report on the Banality of Evil

Hannah Arendt (1906–1975), born and raised in Germany, was one of those creative European intellectuals who managed to flee their native lands in time to escape the Nazi grip. In the 1920s Arendt attended the University of Heidelberg, where, majoring in philosophy, she studied with such existentialists as Martin Heidegger and Karl Jaspers and, at age twenty-two, earned a doctorate with a dissertation on St. Augustine.

In 1933, with Hitler's rise to power, Arendt moved to Paris, where she worked for a relief organization that found homes in Palestine for orphaned Jewish children. Never ceasing to study and write, she immigrated to the United States in 1940 just before the fall of France; in 1950, she became a naturalized American citizen. Unable for several years to secure an academic position in her new country, Arendt worked as an editor and in various social agencies until the publication of her first major work, The Origins of Totalitarianism *(1951); this book analyzes Nazi and Communist forms of totalitarianism in terms of their roots in nineteenth-century imperialism and anti-Semitism. Other important volumes followed. Among them were* The Human Condition *(1958) and* Between Past and Future *(1961), both dealing with the general breakdown of the civilizing traditions of Western society;* On Revolution *(1963), which compares and contrasts the American and French revolutions; and* On Violence *(1970), which argues that destructive acts appear in the modern bureaucratic state as people are denied creative power. At the time of her death Arendt had completed two volumes of a three-volume philosophical work called* The Life of the Mind; *it was published posthumously in 1978.*

After the publication of The Origins of Totalitarianism, *Arendt was much in demand at American universities. She became the first woman to be appointed a full professor at Princeton University and also taught, for various periods, at California, Chicago, Columbia, Northwestern, and Cornell universities. Her last academic post was as University Professor of Political Philosophy at the New School for Social Research, in New York City.*

Arendt's Eichmann in Jerusalem: A Report on the Banality of Evil *(1963), the source of the following selection, is a book based upon the author's personal observation of the trial of Adolf Eichmann, the notorious Nazi war criminal executed in 1962 for his role in Hitler's "final solution" for the Jewish people. Upon its publication,* Eichmann in Jerusalem *generated widespread critical antagonism, much of it focusing on two of the book's unusual theses: (1) Eichmann was not a demoniacal anti-Semitic monster but rather a normal "banal" mediocrity, content to function as a cog in a totalitarian system and (2) the victims—especially the leaders of the Jewish communities in Nazi-occupied Europe—willingly cooperated in the destruction of their own communities and themselves. In a sense, Arendt expands upon Bettelheim's view (expressed in the preceding selection) regarding the behavior-conditioning nature of totalitarian societies and their elimination of personal autonomy. But while Bettelheim's* The Informed Heart *deals mainly with concentration camp inmates, the following excerpt—based on the Eichmann trial record—analyzes the psyche of a "typical" administrator in the society outside the camps.*

Throughout the trial, Eichmann tried to clarify, mostly without success, this second point in his plea of "not guilty in the sense of the indictment." The indictment implied not only that he had acted on purpose, which he did not deny, but out of base motives and in full knowledge of the criminal nature of his deeds. As for the base motives, he was perfectly sure that he was not what he called an *innerer Schweinehund,* a dirty bastard in the depths of his heart; and as for his conscience, he remembered perfectly well that he would have had a bad conscience only if he had not done what he had been ordered to do—to ship millions of men, women, and children to their death with great zeal and the most meticulous care. This, admittedly, was hard to take. Half a dozen psychiatrists had certified him as "normal"—"More normal, at any rate, than I am after having examined him," one of them was said to have exclaimed, while another had found that his whole psychological outlook, his attitude toward his wife and children, mother and father, brothers, sisters, and friends, was "not only normal but most desirable"—and finally the minister who had paid regular visits to him in prison after the Supreme Court had finished hearing his appeal reassured everybody by declaring Eichmann to be "a man with very positive ideas." Behind the comedy of the soul experts lay the hard fact that his was obviously no case of moral let alone legal insanity. . . . Worse, his was obviously also no case of insane hatred of Jews, of fanatical anti-Semitism or indoctrination of any kind. He "personally" never had anything whatever against Jews; on the contrary, he had plenty of "private reasons" for not being a Jew hater. . . .

Alas, nobody believed him. The prosecutor did not believe him, because that was not his job. Counsel for the defense paid no attention because he, unlike Eichmann, was, to all appearances, not interested in questions of conscience. And the judges did not believe him, because they were too good, and perhaps also too conscious of the very foundations of their profession, to admit that an average, "normal" person, neither feeble-minded nor indoctrinated nor cynical, could be perfectly incapable of telling right from wrong. They preferred to conclude from occasional lies that he was a liar—and missed the greatest moral and even legal challenge of the whole case. Their case rested on the assumption that the defendant, like all "normal persons," must have been aware of the criminal nature of his acts, and Eichmann was indeed normal insofar as he was "no exception within the Nazi regime." However, under the conditions of the Third Reich only "exceptions" could be expected to react "normally." This simple truth of the matter created a dilemma for the judges which they could neither resolve nor escape.

He was born on March 19, 1906, in Solingen, a German town in the Rhineland famous for its knives, scissors, and surgical instruments. Fifty-four years later, indulging in his favorite pastime of writing his memoirs, he described this memorable event as follows: "Today, fifteen years and a day after May 8, 1945, I begin to lead my thoughts back to that nineteenth of March of the year 1906, when at five o'clock in the morning I entered life on earth in the aspect of a human being." . . . According to his religious beliefs, which had not changed since the Nazi period (in Jerusalem Eichmann declared himself to be a *Gottgläubiger,* the Nazi term for those who had broken with Christianity, and he refused to take his oath on the Bible), this event was to be ascribed to "a higher Bearer of Meaning," an entity somehow identical with the "movement of the universe," to which human life, in itself devoid of "higher meaning," is subject. (The terminology is quite suggestive. To call God a *Höheren Sinnesträger* meant linguistically to give him some place in the military hierarchy, since the Nazis had changed the military "recipient of orders," the *Befehlsempfänger,* into a "bearer of orders," a *Befehlsträger,* indicating, as in the ancient "bearer of ill tidings," the burden of responsibility and of importance that weighed supposedly upon those who had to execute orders. Moreover, Eichmann, like everyone connected with the Final Solution, was officially a "bearer of secrets," a *Geheimnisträger,* as well, which as far as self-importance went certainly was nothing to sneeze at.) But Eichmann, not very much interested in metaphysics, remained singularly silent on any more intimate relationship between the Bearer of Meaning and the bearer of orders, and proceeded to a consideration of the other possible cause of his existence, his parents: "They would hardly have been so overjoyed at the arrival of their first-born had they been able to watch how in the hour of my birth the Norn of misfortune, to spite the Norn of good fortune, was already spinning threads of grief and sorrow into my life. But a kind, impenetrable veil kept my parents from seeing into the future."

The misfortune started soon enough; it started in school. Eichmann's father, first an accountant for the Tramways and Electricity Company in Solingen and after 1913 an official of the same corporation in Austria, in Linz, had five children, four sons and a daughter, of whom only Adolf, the eldest, it seems, was unable to finish high school, or even to graduate from the vocational school for engineering into which he was then put. Throughout his life, Eichmann deceived people about his early "misfortunes" by hiding behind the more honorable financial misfortunes of his father. In Israel, however, during his first sessions with Captain Avner Less, the police examiner who was to spend approximately 35 days with him and who produced 3,564 typewritten pages from 76 recorder tapes, he was in an ebullient mood, full of enthusiasm about this unique opportunity "to pour forth everything . . . I know" and, by the same token, to advance to the rank of the most cooperative defendant ever. (His enthusiasm was soon dampened, though never quite extinguished, when he was confronted with concrete questions based on irrefutable documents.) The best proof of his initial boundless confidence, obviously wasted on Captain Less (who said to Harry Mulisch: "I was Mr. Eichmann's father confessor"), was that for the first time in his life he admitted his early disasters, although he must have been aware of the fact that he thus contradicted himself on several important entries in all his official Nazi records.

Well, the disasters were ordinary: since he "had not exactly been the most hard-working" pupil—or, one may add, the most gifted— his father had taken him first from high school and then from vocational school, long before graduation. Hence, the profession that appears on all his official documents: construction engineer, had about as much connection with reality as the statement that his birthplace was Palestine and that he was fluent in Hebrew and Yiddish—another outright lie Eichmann had loved to tell both to his S.S. comrades and to his Jewish victims. It was in the same vein that he had always pretended he had been dismissed from his job as salesman for the Vacuum Oil Company in Austria because of membership in the National Socialist Party. The version he confided to Captain Less was less dramatic, though probably not the truth either: he had been fired because it was a time of unemployment, when unmarried employees were the first to lose their jobs. (This explanation, which at first seems plausible, is not very satisfactory, because he lost his job in the spring of 1933, when he had been engaged for two full years to Veronika, or Vera, Liebl, who later became his wife. Why had he not married her before, when he still had a good job? He finally married in March, 1935, probably because bachelors in the S.S., as in the Vacuum Oil Company, were never sure of their jobs and could not be promoted.) Clearly, bragging had always been one of his cardinal vices.

While young Eichmann was doing poorly in school, his father left the Tramway and Electricity Company and went into business for himself. He bought a small mining enterprise and put his unpromising youngster to work in it as an ordinary mining laborer, but only until he found him a job in the sales department of the Oberösterreichischen Elektrobau Company, where Eichmann remained for over two years. He was now about twenty-two years old and without any prospects for a career; the only thing he had learned, perhaps, was how to sell. What then happened was what he himself called his first break, of which, again, we have two rather different versions. In a handwritten biographical record he submitted in 1939 to win a promotion in the S.S., he described it as follows: "I worked during the years of 1925 to 1927 as a salesman for the Austrian Elektrobau Company. I left this position of my own free will, as the Vacuum Oil Company of Vienna offered me the representation for Upper Austria." The key word here is "offered," since, according to the story he told Captain Less in Israel, nobody had offered him anything. His own mother had died when he was ten years old, and his father had married again. A cousin of his stepmother—a man he called "uncle"—who was president of the Austrian Automobile Club and was married to the daughter of a Jewish businessman in Czechoslovakia, had used his connection with the general director of the Austrian Vacuum Oil Company, a Jewish Mr. Weiss, to obtain for his unfortunate relation a job as traveling salesman. Eichmann was properly grateful; the Jews in his family were among his "private reasons" for not hating Jews. Even in 1943 or 1944, when the Final Solution was in full swing, he had not forgotten: "The daughter of this marriage, half-Jewish according to the Nuremberg Laws, . . . came to see me in order to obtain my permission for her emigration into Switzerland. Of course, I granted this request, and the same uncle came also to see me to ask me to intervene for some Viennese Jewish couple. I mention this only to show that I myself had no hatred for Jews, for my whole education through my mother and my father had been strictly Christian; my mother, because of her Jewish relatives, held different opinions from those current in S.S. circles."

He went to considerable lengths to prove his point: he had never harbored any ill feelings against his victims, and, what is more, he had never made a secret of that fact. "I explained this to Dr. Löwenherz [head of the Jewish Community in Vienna] as I explained it to Dr. Kastner [vice-president of the Zionist Organization in Budapest]; I think I told it to everybody, each of my men knew it, they all heard it from me sometime. Even in elementary school, I had a classmate with whom I spent my free time, and he came to our house; a family in Linz by the name of Sebba. The last time we met we walked together through the streets of Linz, I already with the Party emblem of the N.S.D.A.P. [the Nazi Party] in my buttonhole, and he did not think anything of it." Had Eichmann been a bit less prim or the police examination (which refrained from cross-examination, presumably to remain assured of his cooperation) less discreet, his "lack of prejudice" might have shown itself in still another aspect. It seems that in Vienna, where he was so extraordinarily successful in arranging the "forced emigration" of Jews, he had a Jewish mistress, an "old flame" from Linz. *Rassenschande,* sexual intercourse with Jews, was probably the greatest crime a member of the S.S. could commit, and though during the war the raping of Jewish girls became a favorite pastime at the front, it was by no means common for a Higher S.S. officer to have an affair with a Jewish woman. Thus, Eichmann's repeated violent denunciations of Julius Streicher, the insane and obscene editor of *Der Stürmer,* and of his pornographic anti-Semitism, were perhaps personally motivated, and the expression of more than the routine contempt an "enlightened" S.S. man was supposed to show toward the vulgar passions of lesser Party luminaries.

The five and a half years with the Vacuum Oil Company must have been among the happier ones in Eichmann's life. He made a good living during a time of severe unemployment, and he was still living with his parents, except when he was out on the road. The date when this idyll came to an end—Pentecost, 1933—was among the few he always remembered. Actually, things had taken a turn for the worse somewhat earlier. At the end of 1932, he was unexpectedly transferred from Linz to Salzburg, very much against his inclinations: "I lost all joy in my work, I no longer liked to sell, to make calls." From such sudden losses of *Arbeitsfreude* Eichmann was to suffer throughout his life. The worst of them occurred when he was told of the Führer's order for the "physical extermination of the Jews," in which he was to play such an important role. This, too, came unexpectedly; he himself had "never thought of . . . such a solution through violence," and he described his reaction in the same words: "I now lost everything, all joy in my work, all initiative, all interest; I was, so to speak, blown out." A similar blowing out must have happened in 1932 in Salzburg, and from his own account it is clear that he cannot have been very surprised when he was fired, though one need not believe his saying that he had been "very happy" about his dismissal.

For whatever reasons, the year 1932 marked a turning point of his life. It was in April of this year that he joined the National Socialist Party and entered the S.S., upon an invitation of Ernst Kaltenbrunner, a young lawyer in Linz who later became chief of the Head Office for Reich Security (the *Reichssicherheitshauptamt* or R.S.H.A., as I shall call it henceforth), in one of whose six main departments—Bureau IV, under the command of Heinrich Müller—Eichmann was eventually employed as head of section B-4. In court, Eichmann gave the impression of a typical member of the lower middle classes, and this impression was more than borne out by every sentence he spoke or wrote while in prison. But this was misleading; he was rather the *déclassé* son of a solid middle-class family, and it was indicative of his comedown in social status that while his father was a good friend of Kaltenbrunner's father, who was also a Linz lawyer, the relationship of the two sons was rather cool: Eichmann was unmistakably treated by Kaltenbrunner as his social inferior. Before Eichmann entered the Party and the S.S., he had proved that he was a joiner, and May 8, 1945, the official date of Germany's defeat, was significant for him mainly because it then dawned upon him that thenceforward he would have to live without being a member of something or other. "I sensed I would have to live a leaderless and difficult individual life, I would receive no directives from anybody, no orders and commands would any longer be issued to me, no pertinent ordinances would be there to consult—in brief, a life never known before lay before me." When he was a child, his parents, uninterested in politics, had enrolled him in the Young Men's Christian Association, from which he later went into the German youth movement, the *Wandervogel*. During his four unsuccessful years in high school, he had joined the *Jungfrontkämpferverband,* the youth section of the German-Austrian organization of war veterans, which, though violently pro-German and anti-republican, was tolerated by the Austrian government. When Kaltenbrunner suggested that he enter the S.S., he was just on the point of becoming a member of an altogether different outfit, the Freemasons' Lodge Schlaraffia, "an association of businessmen, physicians, actors, civil servants, etc., who came together to cultivate merriment and gaiety. . . . Each member had to give a lecture from time to time whose tenor was to be humor, refined humor." Kaltenbrunner explained to Eichmann that he would have to give up this merry society because as a Nazi he could not be a Freemason—a word that at the time was unknown to him. The choice between the S.S. and Schlaraffia (the name derives from *Schlaraffenland,* the gluttons' Cloud-Cuckoo Land of German fairy tales) might have been hard to make, but he was "kicked out" of Schlaraffia anyhow; he had committed a sin that even now, as he told the story in the Israeli prison, made him blush with shame: "Contrary to my upbringing, I had tried, though I was the youngest, to invite my companions to a glass of wine."

A leaf in the whirlwind of time, he was blown from Schlaraffia, the Never-Never Land of tables set by magic and roast chickens that flew into your mouth—or, more accurately, from the company of respectable philistines with degrees and assured careers and "refined humor," whose worst vice was probably an irrepressible desire for practical jokes—into the marching columns of the Thousand-Year Reich, which lasted exactly twelve years and three months. At any rate, he did not enter the Party out of conviction, nor was he ever convinced by it—whenever he was asked to give his reasons, he repeated the same embarrassed clichés about the Treaty of Versailles and unemployment; rather, as he pointed out in court, "it was like being swallowed up by the Party against all expectations and without previous decision. It happened so quickly and suddenly." He had no time and less desire to be properly informed, he did not even know the Party program, he never read *Mein Kampf*. Kaltenbrunner had said to him: Why not join the S.S.? And he had replied, Why not? That was how it had happened, and that was about all there was to it.

Of course, that was not all there was to it. What Eichmann failed to tell the presiding judge in cross-examination was that he had been an ambitious young man who was fed up with his job as traveling salesman even before the Vacuum Oil Company was fed up with him. From a humdrum life without significance and consequence the wind had blown him into History, as he understood it, namely, into a Movement that always kept moving and in which somebody like him—already a failure in the eyes of his social class, of his family, and hence in his own eyes as well—could start from scratch and still make a career. And if he did not always like what he had to do (for example, dispatching people to their death by the trainload instead of forcing them to emigrate), if he guessed, rather early, that the whole business would come to a bad end, with Germany losing the war, if all his most cherished plans came to nothing (the evacuation of European Jewry to Madagascar, the establishment of a Jewish territory in the Nisko region of Poland, the experiment with carefully built defense installations around his Berlin office to repel Russian tanks), and if, to his greatest "grief and sorrow," he never advanced beyond the grade of S.S. *Obersturmbannführer* (a rank equivalent to lieutenant colonel)—in short, if, with the exception of the year in Vienna, his life was beset with frustrations, he never forgot what the alternative would have been. Not only in Argentina, leading the unhappy existence of a refugee, but also in the courtroom in Jerusalem, with his life as good as forfeited, he might still have preferred—if anybody had asked him—to be hanged as *Obersturmbannführer a.D.* [Lieutenant Colonel in retirement] rather than living out his life quietly and normally as a traveling salesman for the Vacuum Oil Company.

• • •

[In January 1942 Reinhardt Heydrich, Chief of Security and Intelligence for the Gestapo (secret police), called a conference of Undersecretaries of the German government ministries and the Civil Service. The purpose of the meeting was to coordinate all efforts toward the implementation of the Final Solution, the Nazi plan for the total destruction of the Jewish people. *Ed.*]

• • •

It was a very important occasion for Eichmann, who had never before mingled socially with so many "high personages"; he was by far the lowest in rank and social position of those present. He had sent out the invitations and had prepared some statistical material (full of incredible errors) for Heydrich's introductory speech—eleven million Jews had to be killed, an undertaking of some magnitude— and later he was to prepare the minutes. In short, he acted as secretary of the meeting. This was why he was permitted, after the dignitaries had left, to sit down near the fireplace with his chief Müller and Heydrich, "and that was the first time I saw Heydrich smoke and drink." They did not "talk shop, but enjoyed some rest after long hours of work," being greatly satisfied and, especially Heydrich, in very high spirits.

There was another reason that made the day of this conference unforgettable for Eichmann. Although he had been doing his best right along to help with the Final Solution, he had still harbored some doubts about "such a bloody solution through violence," and these doubts had now been dispelled. "Here now, during this conference, the most prominent people had spoken, the Popes of the Third Reich." Now he could see with his own eyes and hear with his own ears that not only Hitler, not only Heydrich or the "sphinx" Müller, not just the S.S. or the Party, but the élite of the good old Civil

Service were vying and fighting with each other for the honor of taking the lead in these "bloody" matters. "At that moment, I sensed a kind of Pontius Pilate feeling, for I felt free of all guilt." *Who was he to judge?* Who was he "to have [his] own thoughts in this matter"? Well, he was neither the first nor the last to be ruined by modesty.

• • •

Eichmann, in contrast to other elements in the Nazi movement, had always been overawed by "good society," and the politeness he often showed to German-speaking Jewish functionaries was to a large extent the result of his recognition that he was dealing with people who were socially his superiors. He was not at all, as one witness called him, a *"Landsknechtnatur,"* a mercenary, who wanted to escape to regions where there aren't no Ten Commandments an' a man can raise a thirst. What he fervently believed in up to the end was success, the chief standard of "good society" as he knew it. Typical was his last word on the subject of Hitler—whom he and his comrade Sassen[1] had agreed to "shirr out" of their story; Hitler, he said, "may have been wrong all down the line, but one thing is beyond dispute: the man was able to work his way up from lance corporal in the German Army to Führer of a people of almost eighty million. . . . His success alone proved to me that I should subordinate myself to this man." His conscience was indeed set at rest when he saw the zeal and eagerness with which "good society" everywhere reacted as he did. He did not need to "close his ears to the voice of conscience," as the judgment has it, not because he had none, but because his conscience spoke with a "respectable voice," with the voice of respectable society around him.

• • •

So Eichmann's opportunities for feeling like Pontius Pilate were many, and as the months and the years went by, he lost the need to feel anything at all. This was the way things were, this was the new law of the land, based on the Führer's order; whatever he did he did, as far as he could see, as a law-abiding citizen. He did his *duty,* as he told the police and the court over and over again; he not only obeyed

---

[1] Wilem Sassen, a journalist and former member of the S.S.—who, like Adolf Eichmann, was a fugitive from justice—interviewed Eichmann in 1955 in Argentina. After Eichmann was caught there in 1960 by Israeli agents, parts of the interview were published in American and German magazines.

orders, he also obeyed the *law.* Eichmann had a muddled inkling that this could be an important distinction, but neither the defense nor the judges ever took him up on it. The well-worn coins of "superior orders" versus "acts of state" were handed back and forth; they had governed the whole discussion of these matters during the Nuremberg Trials,[2] for no other reason than that they gave the illusion that the altogether unprecedented could be judged according to precedents and the standards that went with them. Eichmann, with his rather modest mental gifts, was certainly the last man in the courtroom to be expected to challenge these notions and to strike out on his own. Since, in addition to performing what he conceived to be the duties of a law-abiding citizen, he had also acted upon orders— always so careful to be "covered"—he became completely muddled, and ended by stressing alternately the virtues and the vices of blind obedience, or the "obedience of corpses," *Kadavergehorsam,* as he himself called it.

The first indication of Eichmann's vague notion that there was more involved in this whole business than the question of the soldier's carrying out orders that are clearly criminal in nature and intent appeared during the police examination, when he suddenly declared with great emphasis that he had lived his whole life according to Kant's moral precepts, and especially according to a Kantian definition of duty. This was outrageous, on the face of it, and also incomprehensible, since Kant's moral philosophy is so closely bound up with man's faculty of judgment, which rules out blind obedience. The examining officer did not press the point, but Judge Raveh, either out of curiosity or out of indignation at Eichmann's having dared to invoke Kant's name in connection with his crimes, decided to question the accused. And, to the surprise of everybody, Eichmann came up with an approximately correct definition of the categorical imperative: "I meant by my remark about Kant that the principle of my will must always be such that it can become the principle of general laws" (which is not the case with theft or murder, for instance, because the thief or the murderer cannot conceivably wish to live under a legal system that would give others the right to rob or murder him). Upon further questioning, he added that he had read Kant's *Critique of Practical Reason.* He then proceeded to explain

[2] After the defeat of Germany in the Second World War, the victorious nations brought some of the major Nazi war criminals to trial at Nuremberg, Germany.

that from the moment he was charged with carrying out the Final Solution he had ceased to live according to Kantian principles, that he had known it, and that he had consoled himself with the thought that he no longer "was master of his own deeds," that he was unable "to change anything." What he failed to point out in court was that in this "period of crimes legalized by the state," as he himself now called it, he had not simply dismissed the Kantian formula as no longer applicable, he had distorted it to read: Act as if the principle of your actions were the same as that of the legislator or of the law of the land—or, in Hans Frank's[3] formulation of "the categorical imperative in the Third Reich," which Eichmann might have known: "Act in such a way that the Führer, if he knew your action, would approve it" (*Die Technik des Staates,* 1942, pp. 15–16). Kant, to be sure, had never intended to say anything of the sort; on the contrary, to him every man was a legislator the moment he started to act: by using his "practical reason" man found the principles that could and should be the principles of law. But it is true that Eichmann's unconscious distortion agrees with what he himself called the version of Kant "for the household use of the little man." In this household use, all that is left of Kant's spirit is the demand that a man do more than obey the law, that he go beyond the mere call of obedience and identify his own will with the principle behind the law—the source from which the law sprang. In Kant's philosophy, that source was practical reason; in Eichmann's household use of him, it was the will of the Führer. Much of the horribly painstaking thoroughness in the execution of the Final Solution—a thoroughness that usually strikes the observer as typically German, or else as characteristic of the perfect bureaucrat—can be traced to the odd notion, indeed very common in Germany, that to be law-abiding means not merely to obey the laws but to act as though one were the legislator of the laws that one obeys. Hence the conviction that nothing less than going beyond the call of duty will do.

Whatever Kant's role in the formation of "the little man's" mentality in Germany may have been, there is not the slightest doubt that in one respect Eichmann did indeed follow Kant's precepts: a law was a law, there could be no exceptions. In Jerusalem, he admit-

---

[3] Hans Frank, tried and hanged at Nuremberg, had been Governor General of Poland during the German occupation.

ted only two such exceptions during the time when "eighty million Germans" had each had "his decent Jew": he had helped a half-Jewish cousin, and a Jewish couple in Vienna for whom his uncle had intervened. This inconsistency still made him feel somewhat uncomfortable, and when he was questioned about it during cross-examination, he became openly apologetic: he had "confessed his sins" to his superiors. This uncompromising attitude toward the performance of his murderous duties damned him in the eyes of the judges more than anything else, which was comprehensible, but in his own eyes it was precisely what justified him, as it had once silenced whatever conscience he might have had left. No exceptions—this was the proof that he had always acted against his "inclinations," whether they were sentimental or inspired by interest, that he had always done his "duty." . . .

In Jerusalem, confronted with documentary proof of his extraordinary loyalty to Hitler and the Führer's order, Eichmann tried a number of times to explain that during the Third Reich "the Führer's words had the force of law" (*Führerworte haben Gesetzeskraft*), which meant, among other things, that if the order came directly from Hitler it did not have to be in writing. He tried to explain that this was why he had never asked for a written order from Hitler (no such document relating to the Final Solution has ever been found; probably it never existed), but had demanded to see a written order from Himmler.[4] To be sure, this was a fantastic state of affairs, and whole libraries of very "learned" juridical comment have been written, all demonstrating that the Führer's *words,* his oral pronouncements, were the basic law of the land. Within this "legal" framework, every order contrary in letter or spirit to a word spoken by Hitler was, by definition, unlawful. Eichmann's position, therefore, showed a most unpleasant resemblance to that of the often-cited soldier who, acting in a normal legal framework, refuses to carry out orders that run counter to his ordinary experience of lawfulness and hence can be recognized by him as criminal. The extensive literature on the subject usually supports its case with the common equivocal meaning of the word "law," which in this context means sometimes the law of the land—that is, posited, positive

[4]Heinrich Himmler was the director of all the German police forces during the Nazi regime; he was captured in 1945 but committed suicide before he could be brought to trial.

law—and sometimes the law that supposedly speaks in all men's hearts with an identical voice. Practically speaking, however, orders to be disobeyed must be "manifestly unlawful" and unlawfulness must "fly like a black flag above [them] as a warning reading: 'Prohibited!' "—as the judgment pointed out. And in a criminal regime this "black flag" with its "warning sign" flies as "manifestly" above what normally is a lawful order—for instance, not to kill innocent people just because they happen to be Jews—as it flies above a criminal order under normal circumstances. To fall back on an unequivocal voice of conscience—or, in the even vaguer language of the jurists, on a "general sentiment of humanity" (Oppenheim-Lauterpacht in *International Law,* 1952)—not only begs the question, it signifies a deliberate refusal to take notice of the central moral, legal, and political phenomena of our century.

To be sure, it was not merely Eichmann's conviction that Himmler was now giving "criminal" orders [to stop the murders and destroy the evidence as German defeat approached] that determined his actions. But the personal element undoubtedly involved was not fanaticism, it was his genuine, "boundless and immoderate admiration for Hitler" (as one of the defense witnesses called it)—for the man who had made it "from lance corporal to Chancellor of the Reich." It would be idle to try to figure out which was stronger in him, his admiration for Hitler or his determination to remain a law-abiding citizen of the Third Reich when Germany was already in ruins. Both motives came into play once more during the last days of the war, when he was in Berlin and saw with violent indignation how everybody around him was sensibly enough getting himself fixed up with forged papers before the arrival of the Russians or the Americans. A few weeks later, Eichmann, too, began to travel under an assumed name, but by then Hitler was dead, and the "law of the land" was no longer in existence, and he, as he pointed out, was no longer bound by his oath. For the oath taken by the members of the S.S. differed from the military oath sworn by the soldiers in that it bound them only to Hitler, not to Germany.

The case of the conscience of Adolf Eichmann, which is admittedly complicated but is by no means unique, is scarcely comparable to the case of the German generals, one of whom, when asked at Nuremberg, "How was it possible that all you honorable generals could continue to serve a murderer with such unquestioning loyalty?," replied that it was "not the task of a soldier to act as judge over his supreme commander. Let history do that or God in heaven." (Thus General Alfred Jodl, hanged at Nuremberg.) Eichmann, much less intelligent and without any education to speak of, at least dimly realized that it was not an order but a law which had turned them all into criminals. The distinction between an order and the Führer's word was that the latter's validity was not limited in time and space, which is the outstanding characteristic of the former. This is also the true reason why the Führer's order for the Final Solution was followed by a huge shower of regulations and directives, all drafted by expert lawyers and legal advisers, not by mere administrators; this order, in contrast to ordinary orders, was treated as a law. Needless to add, the resulting legal paraphernalia, far from being a mere symptom of German pedantry or thoroughness, served most effectively to give the whole business its outward appearance of legality.

And just as the law in civilized countries assumes that the voice of conscience tells everybody "Thou shalt not kill," even though man's natural desires and inclinations may at times be murderous, so the law of Hitler's land demanded that the voice of conscience tell everybody: "Thou shalt kill," although the organizers of the massacres knew full well that murder is against the normal desires and inclinations of most people. Evil in the Third Reich had lost the quality by which most people recognize it—the quality of temptation. Many Germans and many Nazis, probably an overwhelming majority of them, must have been tempted *not* to murder, *not* to rob, *not* to let their neighbors go off to their doom (for that the Jews were transported to their doom they knew, of course, even though many of them may not have known the gruesome details), and not to become accomplices in all these crimes by benefiting from them. But, God knows, they had learned how to resist temptation.

* * *

The trouble with Eichmann was precisely that so many were like him, and that the many were neither perverted nor sadistic, that they were, and still are, terribly and terrifyingly normal. From the viewpoint of our legal institutions and of our moral standards of judgment, this normality was much more terrifying than all the atrocities put together, for it implied—as had been said at Nuremberg over and over again by the defendants and their counsels—that this new type of criminal, who is in actual fact *hostis generis humani,*[5] commits his crimes under circumstances that make it well-nigh impossible for him to know or to feel that he is doing wrong. . . .

[5]Latin: an enemy of the human race.

3

Mao Tse-tung
Quotations

❋

China, the country with the world's largest population, amounting to about one out of every five living humans, was, by 1949, officially a communist nation—the "People's Republic." The individual whose personal example and teachings would dominate the masses of China in the succeeding decades was Mao Tse-tung (1893–1976).★

Unlike the typical communist revolutionary leaders in Europe, Mao was born into a peasant family. Despite his father's objections he managed to acquire a literary education, encountering in his studies classics of Chinese literature that would later influence his uniquely nationalist view of communist theory. As a student in 1911 he was caught in the turmoil surrounding the downfall of the last Chinese imperial dynasty; and, by 1919, he had left the scholar's life and become a political organizer among the peasants in his home district. Eventually he worked with peasants throughout China, organizing them as an armed force and indoctrinating them in Marxism.

Among the epic events of Mao's revolutionary career was the Long March (1934–35), in which the outnumbered communist forces, fighting much of the way, marched six thousand miles from the south of China through the hinterlands to sanctuary in the rugged northwest. During China's struggle against the invading Japanese (1931–45), Mao's forces at times achieved an uneasy alliance with the "counter-revolutionary" Nationalists led by Chiang Kai-shek. The defeat of the Japanese, however, signalled the resumption of the inevitable domestic conflict. By 1949 the Nationalists, notwithstanding American military aid, had retreated from the Chinese mainland to the island of Taiwan. The communists were thus in control, and Mao exerted unchallenged authority from his position as "Chairman" of the Communist Party.

★A variant spelling of Mao's name is Mao Zedong.

The communism promoted by Mao varied from earlier Marxism-Leninism in that it used the peasantry as the base of the revolution rather than the urban proletariat—a nearly non-existent group in China. Furthermore, it incorporated many traditional attitudes of the peasantry into the party line and thereby adapted international communism to the mentality and cultural traditions of the Chinese people. This adaptation is apparent in the following selections from Quotations from Chairman Mao Tse-Tung, the "little red book" that has been committed to memory by millions of Chinese as the unifying "bible" of their secular faith.

Notable for its simplicity of expression, and considered by Mao to be a mass teaching device, the book is generally orthodox in its Marxism. There is in its passages an overwhelming sense of class-consciousness and the naturalness of conflict—both intellectual and physical—with assurance of the ultimate destruction of all "reactionary" forces. (This dialectical conflict might be compared to the traditional Chinese theory, absorbed by the young Mao, of Yin and Yang, the two great alternating principles of the universe.) Thus, for example, the passage "letting a hundred flowers blossom and a hundred schools of thought contend" may at first seem inconsistent with such earlier passages as "all culture, all literature and art . . . are geared to definite political lines." Much of Mao's thought must also be seen as part of his reaction against Soviet dominance in the communist world. The "hundred flowers" speech of 1957, for example, was delivered after the revelations of Stalin's tyranny in Russia and helped to justify an independent course for Chinese communism. Although in the years since his death the image of Mao in China has changed and he is no longer the object of near-religious veneration, it is clear that his example remains the foremost personal force of the Chinese revolution.

I. THE COMMUNIST PARTY

If there is to be revolution, there must be a revolutionary party. Without a revolutionary party, without a party built on the Marxist-Leninist revolutionary theory and in the Marxist-Leninist revolutionary style, it is impossible to lead the working class and the broad masses of the people in defeating imperialism and its running dogs.

(November 1948)

A well-disciplined Party armed with the theory of Marxism-Leninism, using the method of self-criticism and linked with the masses of the people; an army under the leadership of such a Party; a united front of all revolutionary classes and all revolutionary groups under the leadership of such a Party—these are the three main weapons with which we have defeated the enemy.

(June 30, 1949)

At no time and in no circumstances should a Communist place his personal interests first; he should subordinate them to the interests of the nation and of the masses. Hence, selfishness, slacking, corruption, seeking the limelight, and so on, are most contemptible, while selflessness, working with all one's energy, whole-hearted devotion to public duty, and quiet hard work will command respect.

(October 1938)

We Communists are like seeds and the people are like the soil. Wherever we go, we must unite with the people, take root and blossom among them.

(October 17, 1945)

II. CLASSES AND CLASS STRUGGLE

Classes struggle, some classes triumph, others are eliminated. Such is history, such is the history of civilization for thousands of years. To interpret history from this viewpoint is historical materialism; standing in opposition to this viewpoint is historical idealism.[1]

(August 14, 1949)

In class society everyone lives as a member of a particular class, and every kind of thinking, without exception, is stamped with the brand of a class.

(July 1937)

A revolution is not a dinner party, or writing an essay, or painting a picture, or doing embroidery; it cannot be so refined, so leisurely and gentle, so temperate, kind, courteous, restrained and mag-

---

[1] The philosophical concept that ideas, rather than material forces, are the shaping elements of history.

nanimous. A revolution is an insurrection, an act of violence by which one class overthrows another.

(March 1927)

III. SOCIALISM AND COMMUNISM

The socialist system will eventually replace the capitalist system; this is an objective law independent of man's will. However much the reactionaries try to hold back the wheel of history, sooner or later revolution will take place and will inevitably triumph.

(November 6, 1957)

Socialist revolution aims at liberating the productive forces. The change-over from individual to socialist, collective ownership in agriculture and handicrafts and from capitalist to socialist ownership in private industry and commerce is bound to bring about a tremendous liberation of the productive forces. Thus the social conditions are being created for a tremendous expansion of industrial and agricultural production.

(January 25, 1956)

We are now carrying out a revolution not only in the social system, the change from private to public ownership, but also in technology, the change from handicraft to large-scale modern machine production, and the two revolutions are interconnected. In agriculture, with conditions as they are in our country, co-operation must precede the use of big machinery (in capitalist countries agriculture develops in a capitalist way). Therefore we must on no account regard industry and agriculture, socialist industrialization and the socialist transformation of agriculture as two separate and isolated things, and on no account must we emphasize the one and play down the other.

(July 31, 1955)

Apart from their other characteristics, the outstanding thing about China's 600 million people is that they are "poor and blank." This may seem a bad thing, but in reality it is a good thing. Poverty gives rise to the desire for change, the desire for action, and the desire for revolution. On a blank sheet of paper free from any mark, the freshest and most beautiful characters can be written, the freshest and most beautiful pictures can be painted.

(April 15, 1958)

"Don't you want to abolish state power?" Yes, we do, but not right now; we cannot do it yet. Why? Because imperialism still exists, because domestic reaction still exists, because classes still exist in our country. Our present task is to strengthen the people's state apparatus—mainly the people's army, the people's police and the people's courts—in order to consolidate national defence and protect the people's interests.

(June 30, 1949)

Our state is a people's democratic dictatorship led by the working class and based on the worker-peasant alliance. What is this dictatorship for? Its first function is to suppress the reactionary classes and elements and those exploiters in our country who resist the socialist revolution, to suppress those who try to wreck our socialist construction, or in other words, to resolve the internal contradictions between ourselves and the enemy. For instance, to arrest, try and sentence certain counter-revolutionaries, and to deprive landlords and bureaucrat-capitalists of their right to vote and their freedom of speech for a specified period of time—all this comes within the scope of our dictatorship. To maintain public order and safeguard the interests of the people, it is likewise necessary to exercise dictatorship over embezzlers, swindlers, arsonists, murderers, criminal gangs and other scoundrels who seriously disrupt public order. The second function of this dictatorship is to protect our country from subversion and possible aggression by external enemies. In that event, it is the task of this dictatorship to resolve the external contradiction between ourselves and the enemy. The aim of this dictatorship is to protect all our people so that they can devote themselves to peaceful labour and build China into a socialist country with a modern industry, agriculture, science and culture.

(February 27, 1957)

IV. THE CORRECT HANDLING OF
CONTRADICTIONS AMONG THE PEOPLE

Qualitatively different contradictions can only be resolved by qualitatively different methods. For instance, the contradiction between the proletariat and the bourgeoisie is resolved by the method of socialist revolution; the contradiction between the great masses of the people and the feudal system is resolved by the method of democratic revolution; the contradiction between the colonies and imperialism is resolved by the method of national revolutionary war; the contradiction between the working class and the peasant class in socialist society is resolved by the method of collectivization and mechanization in agriculture; contradiction within the Communist Party is resolved by the method of criticism and self-criticism; the contradiction between society and nature is resolved by the method of developing the productive forces. . . . The principle of using different methods to resolve different contradictions is one which Marxist-Leninists must strictly observe.

(August 1937)

V. WAR AND PEACE

War is the highest form of struggle for resolving contradictions, when they have developed to a certain stage, between classes, nations, states, or political groups, and it has existed ever since the emergence of private property and of classes.

(December 1936)

"War is the continuation of politics." In this sense war is politics and war itself is a political action; since ancient times there has never been a war that did not have a political character. . . .

But war has its own particular characteristics and in this sense it cannot be equated with politics in general. "War is the continuation of politics by other . . . means."[2] When politics develops to a certain stage beyond which it cannot proceed by the usual means, war breaks out to sweep the obstacles from the way. . . . When the obstacle is removed and our political aim attained, the war will stop.

[2] A famous quotation from the German military theorist Karl von Clausewitz (1780–1831).

But if the obstacle is not completely swept away, the war will have to continue till the aim is fully accomplished. . . . It can therefore be said that politics is war without bloodshed, while war is politics with bloodshed.

(May 1938)

History shows that wars are divided into two kinds, just and unjust. All wars that are progressive are just, and all wars that impede progress are unjust. We Communists oppose all unjust wars that impede progress, but we do not oppose progressive, just wars. Not only do we Communists not oppose just wars, we actively participate in them. As for unjust wars, World War I is an instance in which both sides fought for imperialist interests; therefore the Communists of the whole world firmly opposed that war. The way to oppose a war of this kind is to do everything possible to prevent it before it breaks out and, once it breaks out, to oppose war with war, to oppose unjust war with just war, whenever possible.

(May 1938)

Revolutions and revolutionary wars are inevitable in class society, and without them, it is impossible to accomplish any leap in social development and to overthrow the reactionary ruling classes and, therefore, impossible for the people to win political power.

(August 1937)

Revolutionary war is an antitoxin which not only eliminates the enemy's poison but also purges us of our own filth. Every just, revolutionary war is endowed with tremendous power and can transform many things or clear the way for their transformation.

(May 1938)

Every Communist must grasp the truth, "Political power grows out of the barrel of a gun."

(November 6, 1938)

We are advocates of the abolition of war; we do not want war, but war can only be abolished through war, and in order to get rid of the gun it is necessary to take up the gun.

(November 6, 1938)

War, this monster of mutual slaughter among men, will be finally eliminated by the progress of human society, and in the not too distant future too. But there is only one way to eliminate it and that is to oppose war with war, to oppose counter-revolutionary war with revolutionary war, to oppose national counter-revolutionary war with national revolutionary war, and to oppose counter-revolutionary class war with revolutionary class war. . . . When human society advances to the point where classes and states are eliminated, there will be no more wars, counter-revolutionary or revolutionary, unjust or just; that will be the era of perpetual peace for mankind. Our study of the laws of revolutionary war springs from the desire to eliminate all wars; herein lies the distinction between us Communists and all the exploiting classes.

(December 1936)

VI. IMPERIALISM AND ALL REACTIONARIES ARE PAPER TIGERS

All reactionaries are paper tigers. In appearance, the reactionaries are terrifying, but in reality they are not so powerful. From a long-term point of view, it is not the reactionaries but the people who are really powerful.

(August 1946)

Just as there is not a single thing in the world without a dual nature (this is the law of the unity of opposites), so imperialism and all reactionaries have a dual nature—they are real tigers and paper tigers at the same time. In past history, before they won state power and for some time afterwards, the slave-owning class, the feudal landlord class and the bourgeoisie were vigorous, revolutionary and progressive; they were real tigers. But with the lapse of time, because their opposites—the slave class, the peasant class and the proletariat—grew in strength step by step, struggled against them more and more fiercely, these ruling classes changed step by step into the reverse, changed into reactionaries, changed into backward people, changed into paper tigers. And eventually they were overthrown, or will be overthrown, by the people. The reactionary, backward, decaying classes retained this dual nature even in their last life-and-death struggles against the people. On the one hand, they were real tigers; they devoured people, devoured people by the millions and tens of millions. The cause of the people's struggle went through a period of difficulties and hardships, and along the path there were many twists and turns. To destroy the rule of imperialism, feudalism and bureaucrat-capitalism in China took the Chinese people more than a hundred years and cost them tens of millions of lives before the victory in 1949. Look! Were these not living tigers, iron tigers, real tigers? But in the end they changed into paper tigers, dead tigers, bean-curd tigers. These are historical facts. Have people not seen or heard about these facts? There have indeed been thousands and tens of thousands of them! Thousands and tens of thousands! Hence, imperialism and all reactionaries, looked at in essence, from a long-term point of view, from a strategic point of view, must be seen for what they are—paper tigers. On this we should build our strategic thinking. On the other hand, they are also living tigers, iron tigers, real tigers which can devour people. On this we should build our tactical thinking.

(December 1, 1958)

I have said that all the reputedly powerful reactionaries are merely paper tigers. The reason is that they are divorced from the people. Look! Was not Hitler a paper tiger? Was Hitler not overthrown? I also said that the tsar of Russia, the emperor of China and Japanese imperialism were all paper tigers. As we know, they were all overthrown. U.S. imperialism has not yet been overthrown and it has the atom bomb. I believe it also will be overthrown. It, too, is a paper tiger.

(November 18, 1957)

IX. THE PEOPLE'S ARMY

Without a people's army the people have nothing.

(April 24, 1945)

This army is powerful because all its members have a conscious discipline; they have come together and they fight not for the private interests of a few individuals or a narrow clique, but for the interests of the broad masses and of the whole nation. The sole purpose of this army is to stand firmly with the Chinese people and to serve them whole-heartedly.

(April 24, 1945)

Our principle is that the Party commands the gun, and the gun must never be allowed to command the Party.

(November 6, 1938)

XI. THE MASS LINE

The people, and the people alone, are the motive force in the making of world history.

(April 24, 1945)

The masses are the real heroes, while we ourselves are often childish and ignorant, and without this understanding it is impossible to acquire even the most rudimentary knowledge.

(March/April 1941)

XII. THE ATOM BOMB

The atom bomb is a paper tiger which the U.S. reactionaries use to scare people. It looks terrible, but in fact it isn't. Of course, the atom bomb is a weapon of mass slaughter, but the outcome of a war is decided by the people, not by one or two new types of weapon.

(August 1946)

XVI. EDUCATION

Our educational policy must enable everyone who receives an education to develop morally, intellectually and physically and become a worker with both socialist consciousness and culture.

(February 27, 1957)

XXXI. WOMEN

A man in China is usually subjected to the domination of three systems of authority [political authority, clan authority and religious authority]. . . . As for women, in addition to being dominated by these three systems of authority, they are also dominated by the men (the authority of the husband). These four authorities—political, clan, religious and masculine—are the embodiment of the whole feudal-patriarchal ideology and system, and are the four thick ropes binding the Chinese people, particularly the peasants. How the peasants have overthrown the political authority of the landlords in the countryside has been described above. The political authority of the landlords is the backbone of all the other systems of authority. With that overturned, the clan authority, the religious authority and the authority of the husband all begin to totter. . . . As to the authority of the husband, this has always been weaker among the poor peasants because, out of economic necessity, their womenfolk have to do more manual labour than the women of the richer classes and therefore have more say and greater power of decision in family matters. With the increasing bankruptcy of the rural economy in recent years, the basis for men's domination over women has already been undermined. With the rise of the peasant movement, the women in many places have now begun to organize rural women's associations; the opportunity has come for them to lift up their heads, and the authority of the husband is getting shakier every day. In a word, the whole feudal-patriarchal ideology and system is tottering with the growth of the peasants' power.

(March 1927)

Enable every woman who can work to take her place on the labour front, under the principle of equal pay for equal work. This should be done as quickly as possible.

(1955)

XXXII. CULTURE AND ART

In the world today all culture, all literature and art belong to definite classes and are geared to definite political lines. There is in fact no such thing as art for art's sake, art that stands above classes, art that is detached from or independent of politics. Proletarian literature and art are part of the whole proletarian revolutionary cause; they are, as Lenin said, cogs and wheels in the whole revolutionary machine.

(May 1942)

Revolutionary culture is a powerful revolutionary weapon for the broad masses of the people. It prepares the ground ideologically before the revolution comes and is an important, indeed essential, fighting front in the general revolutionary front during the revolution.

(January 1940)

All our literature and art are for the masses of the people, and in the first place for the workers, peasants and soldiers; they are created for the workers, peasants and soldiers and are for their use.

(May 1942)

Our literary and art workers must accomplish this task and shift their stand; they must gradually move their feet over to the side of the workers, peasants and soldiers, to the side of the proletariat, through the process of going into their very midst and into the thick of practical struggles and through the process of studying Marxism and society. Only in this way can we have a literature and art that are truly for the workers, peasants and soldiers, a truly proletarian literature and art.

(May 1942)

Letting a hundred flowers blossom and a hundred schools of thought contend is the policy for promoting the progress of the arts and the sciences and a flourishing socialist culture in our land. Different forms and styles in art should develop freely and different schools in science should contend freely. We think that it is harmful to the growth of art and science if administrative measures are used to impose one particular style of art or school of thought and to ban another. Questions of right and wrong in the arts and sciences should be settled through free discussion in artistic and scientific circles and through practical work in these fields. They should not be settled in summary fashion.

(February 27, 1957)

An army without culture is a dull-witted army, and a dull-witted army cannot defeat the enemy.

(October 30, 1944)

XXXIII. STUDY

Now, there are two different attitudes towards learning from others. One is the dogmatic attitude of transplanting everything, whether or not it is suited to our conditions. This is no good. The other attitude is to use our heads and learn those things which suit our conditions, that is, to absorb whatever experience is useful to us. That is the attitude we should adopt.

(February 27, 1957)

The theory of Marx, Engels, Lenin and Stalin is universally applicable. We should regard it not as a dogma, but as a guide to action. Studying it is not merely a matter of learning terms and phrases but of learning Marxism-Leninism as the science of revolution. It is not just a matter of understanding the general laws derived by Marx, Engels, Lenin and Stalin from their extensive study of real life and revolutionary experience, but of studying their standpoint and method in examining and solving problems.

(October 1938)

In order to have a real grasp of Marxism, one must learn it not only from books, but mainly through class struggle, through practical work and close contact with the masses of workers and peasants. When in addition to reading some Marxist books our intellectuals have gained some understanding through close contact with the masses of workers and peasants and through their own practical work, we will all be speaking the same language, not only the common language of patriotism and the common language of the socialist system, but probably even the common language of the communist world outlook. If that happens, all of us will certainly work much better.

(March 12, 1957)

4

Herbert Marcuse
Liberation from the Affluent Society

❊

Among the principal intellectual heroes of the international student revolutionary movement in the 1960s was Herbert Marcuse (1898–1979), who, born in Berlin, Germany, earned his doctorate in philosophy at the University of Freiburg in 1922. His postdoctoral studies led him into the disciplines of sociology and psychoanalysis.

Having fled Europe in 1933 during Hitler's rise to power, Marcuse settled in the United States and became a member of Columbia University's Institute for Social Research. He became an American citizen in 1940 and, during and after the Second World War, served the military forces as an intelligence analyst. His career after 1950 included posts at various universities, notably Columbia, Harvard, Brandeis, and California–San Diego.

The first of the major works by Marcuse is Reason and Revolution *(1941), an attempt to demonstrate that Hegel's rationalism does not justify totalitarian society but points, rather, to revolutionary possibilities. In a later work,* Eros and Civilization *(1955), Marcuse pursues his twin themes of rationality and sexuality and disputes Freud's thesis that human sexual drives must be repressed in order to sustain a civilized society. Rational application of technology, he argues, could free individuals from deadening labors and allow for a healthy gratification of instinctual desires.*

One-Dimensional Man *(1964), Marcuse's most popular book, applies the ideas of* Eros and Civilization *to contemporary American society. All critical thought, it suggests, tends to be absorbed into a "one-dimensional" ideology based on materialistic mass values; the affluence of modern Ameri-*

Herbert Marcuse, "Liberation from the Affluent Society." From *To Free A Generation,* ed. David Cooper, Macmillan, 1969. Copyright © 1968 by The Institute of Phenomenological Studies, London, England, and reprinted with their permission. [Pp. 175–92.]

cans has dulled their sensitivities, and even their sexuality is subject to profit-seeking manipulation. In An Essay on Liberation *(1969), Marcuse proposes a radically Utopian alternative to the "global domination of corporate capitalism."*

In the late 1960s, during the great controversy over the war in Vietnam, such ideas gave rise to much antagonism. Some portrayed Marcuse as an "apostle of chaos" and condemned him for seemingly extolling emotion over restraint and reason. During his professorship at San Diego, critics outside the university demanded his dismissal, and threats against his life led to his departure from the community. At the same time Marcuse's works were enthusiastically echoed by student revolutionaries, "hippies," and the "New Left." The general thrust of these works was to adapt the theories of Hegel, Marx, and Freud—with an infusion of hedonism—to the liberating technological possibilities of today's culture. These possibilities, Marcuse believed, have not been properly pursued in either the East or the West. Instead, workers in the industrialized nations live in "exhausting, stupefying, inhuman slavery"—a veiled and subtle form of totalitarianism. Bribed by mass consumer goods, people are "systematically moronized" by the media, which preach a repressive ethic aimed at preserving existing economic inequities.

"Liberation from the Affluent Society" is a speech given by Marcuse at a conference held in England in 1967. In it he speaks of the need for "liberation" from the ills of advanced industrial societies, in which people are so manipulated that they are not aware of their own enslavement. He calls upon the intelligentsia to "pierce the ideological and material veil" in order to lead the masses into a Utopian socialism—a system qualitatively different from any now existing.

I am very happy to see so many flowers here and that is why I want to remind you that flowers, by themselves, have no power whatsoever, other than the power of men and women who protect them and take care of them against aggression and destruction.

As a hopeless philosopher for whom philosophy has become inseparable from politics, I am afraid I have to give here today a rather philosophical speech, and I must ask your indulgence. We are dealing with the dialectics of liberation (actually a redundant phrase, because I believe that all dialectic is liberation) and not only liberation in an intellectual sense, but liberation involving the mind and the body, liberation involving entire human existence. Think of Plato: the liberation from the existence in the cave. Think of Hegel: liberation in the sense of progress and freedom on the historical scale. Think of Marx. Now in what sense is all dialectic liberation? It is liberation from the repressive, from a bad, a false system—be it an organic system, be it a social system, be it a mental or intellectual system: liberation by forces developing within such a system. That is a decisive point. And liberation by virtue of the contradiction generated by the system, precisely because it is a bad, a false system.

I am intentionally using here moral, philosophical terms, values: 'bad', 'false'. For without an objectively justifiable goal of a better, a free human existence, all liberation must remain meaningless—at best, progress in servitude. I believe that in Marx too socialism *ought* to be. This 'ought' belongs to the very essence of scientific socialism. It *ought* to be; it is, we may almost say, a biological, sociological and political necessity. It is a biological necessity in as much as a socialist society, according to Marx, would conform with the very *logos* of life, with the essential possibilities of a human existence, not only mentally, not only intellectually, but also organically.

Now as to today and our own situation. I think we are faced with a novel situation in history, because today we have to be liberated from a relatively well-functioning, rich, powerful society. I am speaking here about liberation from the affluent society, that is to say, the advanced industrial societies. The problem we are facing is the need for liberation not from a poor society, not from a disintegrating society, not even in most cases from a terroristic society, but from a society which develops to a great extent the material and even cultural needs of man—a society which, to use a slogan, delivers the goods to an ever larger part of the population. And that implies, we are facing liberation from a society where liberation is apparently without a mass basis. We know very well the social mechanisms of manipulation, indoctrination, repression which are responsible for this lack of a mass basis, for the integration of the majority of the oppositional forces into the established social system. But I must emphasize again that this is not merely an ideological integration; that it is not merely a social integration; that it takes place precisely on the strong and rich basis which enables the society to develop and satisfy material and cultural needs better than before.

But knowledge of the mechanisms of manipulation or repression, which go down into the very unconscious of man, is not the whole story. I believe that we (and I will use 'we' throughout my talk) have been too hesitant, that we have been too ashamed, understandably ashamed, to insist on the integral, radical features of a socialist society, its qualitative difference from all the established societies: the qualitative difference by virtue of which socialism is indeed the negation of the established systems, no matter how productive, no matter how powerful they are or they may appear. In other words—and this is one of the many points where I disagree with Paul Goodman—our fault was not that we have been too immodest, but that we have been too modest. We have, as it were, repressed a great deal of what we should have said and what we should have emphasized.

If today these integral features, these truly radical features which make a socialist society a definite negation of the existing societies, if this qualitative difference today appears as Utopian, as idealistic, as metaphysical, this is precisely the form in which these radical features must appear if they are really to be a definite negation of the established society: if socialism is indeed the rupture of history, the radical break, the leap into the realm of freedom—a total rupture.

Let us give one illustration of how this awareness, or half-awareness, of the need for such a total rupture was present in some of the great social struggles of our period. Walter Benjamin quotes reports that during the Paris Commune,[1] in all corners of the city of Paris there were people shooting at the clocks on the towers of the churches, palaces and so on, thereby consciously or half-consciously expressing the need that somehow time has to be arrested; that at least the prevailing, the established time continuum has to be arrested, and that a new time has to begin—a very strong emphasis on the qualitative difference and on the totality of the rupture between the new society and the old.

In this sense, I should like to discuss here with you the repressed prerequisites of qualitative change. I say intentionally 'of qualitative change', not 'of revolution', because we know of too many revolutions through which the continuum of repression has been sustained, revolutions which have replaced one system of domination by an-

---

[1] In 1871, after the humiliating defeat of France by the Germans in the Franco-Prussian War, patriotic radicals in Paris refused to accept the terms of surrender. They established an insurrectionary regime known as the Commune of Paris, in defiance of the conservative national government; the Commune was eventually put down, with great slaughter, by the French army.

other. We must become aware of the essentially new features which distinguish a free society as a definite negation of the established societies, and we must begin formulating these features, no matter how metaphysical, no matter how Utopian, I would even say no matter how ridiculous we may appear to the normal people in all camps, on the right as well as on the left.

What is the dialectic of liberation with which we here are concerned? It is the construction of a free society, a construction which depends in the first place on the prevalence of the vital need for abolishing the established systems of servitude; and secondly, and this is decisive, it depends on the vital commitment, the striving, conscious as well as sub- and un-conscious, for the qualitatively different values of a free human existence. Without the emergence of such new needs and satisfactions, the needs and satisfactions of free men, all change in the social institutions, no matter how great, would only replace one system of servitude by another system of servitude. Nor can the emergence—and I should like to emphasize this—nor can the emergence of such new needs and satisfactions be envisaged as a mere by-product, the mere result, of changed social institutions. We have seen this, it is a fact of experience. The development of the new institutions must already be carried out and carried through by men with the new needs. That, by the way, is the basic idea underlying Marx's own concept of the proletariat as the historical agent of revolution. He saw the industrial proletariat as the historical agent of revolution, not only because it was the basic class in the material process of production, not only because it was at that time the majority of the population, but also because this class was 'free' from the repressive and aggressive competitive needs of capitalist society and therefore, at least potentially, the carrier of essentially new needs, goals and satisfactions.

We can formulate this dialectic of liberation also in a more brutal way, as a vicious circle. The transition from voluntary servitude (as it exists to a great extent in the affluent society) to freedom presupposes the abolition of the institutions and mechanism of repression. And the abolition of the institutions and mechanisms of repression already presupposes liberation from servitude, prevalence of the need for liberation. As to needs, I think we have to distinguish between the need for changing intolerable conditions of existence, and the need for changing the society as a whole. The two are by no means identical, they are by no means in harmony. *If* the need is for changing intolerable conditions of existence, with at least a reasonable chance that this can be achieved within the established society, with the growth and progress of the established society, then this is merely quantitative change. Qualitative change is a change of the very system as a whole.

I would like to point out that the distinction between quantitative and qualitative change is not identical with the distinction between reform and revolution. Quantitative change can mean and can lead to revolution. Only the conjunction, I suggest, of these two is revolution in the essential sense of the leap from pre-history into the history of man. In other words, the problem with which we are faced is the point where quantity can turn into quality, where the quantitative change in the conditions and institutions can become a qualitative change affecting all human existence.

Today the two potential factors of revolution which I have just mentioned are disjointed. The first is most prevalent in the underdeveloped countries, where quantitative change—that is to say, the creation of human living conditions—is in itself qualitative change, but is not yet freedom. The second potential factor of revolution, the prerequisites of liberation, are potentially there in the advanced industrial countries, but are contained and perverted by the capitalist organization of society.

I think we are faced with a situation in which this advanced capitalist society has reached a point where quantitative change can technically be turned into qualitative change, into authentic liberation. And it is precisely against this truly fatal possibility that the affluent society, advanced capitalism, is mobilized and organized on all fronts, at home as well as abroad.

Before I go on, let me give a brief definition of what I mean by an affluent society. A model, of course, is American society today, although even in the U.S. it is more a tendency, not yet entirely translated into reality. In the first place, it is a capitalist society. It seems to be necessary to remind ourselves of this because there are some people, even on the left, who believe that American society is no longer a class society. I can assure you that it is a class society. It is a capitalist society with a high concentration of economic and political power; with an enlarged and enlarging sector of automation and coordination of production, distribution and communication; with private ownership in the means of production, which however depends increasingly on ever more active and wide intervention by the government. It is a society in which, as I mentioned, the material as well as cultural needs of the underlying population are satisfied on a scale larger than ever before—but they are satisfied in line with the requirements and interests of the apparatus and of the powers which control the apparatus. And it is a society growing on the condition of accelerating waste, planned obsolescence and destruction, while the substratum of the population continues to live in poverty and misery.

I believe that these factors are internally interrelated, that they constitute the syndrome of late capitalism: namely, the apparently inseparable unity—inseparable for the system—of productivity and destruction, of satisfaction of needs and repression, of liberty within a system of servitude—that is to say, the subjugation of man to the apparatus, and the inseparable unity of rational and irrational. We can say that the rationality of the society lies in its very insanity, and that the insanity of the society is rational to the degree to which it is efficient, to the degree to which it delivers the goods.

Now the question we must raise is: why do we need liberation from such a society if it is capable—perhaps in the distant future, but apparently capable—of conquering poverty to a greater degree than ever before, of reducing the toil of labour and the time of labour, and of raising the standard of living? If the price for all goods delivered, the price for this comfortable servitude, for all these achievements, is exacted from people far away from the metropolis and far away from its affluence? If the affluent society itself hardly notices what it is doing, how it is spreading terror and enslavement, how it is fighting liberation in all corners of the globe?

We know the traditional weakness of emotional, moral and humanitarian arguments in the face of such technological achievement, in the face of the irrational rationality of such a power. These arguments do not seem to carry any weight against the brute facts—we might say brutal facts—of the society and its productivity. And yet, it is only the insistence on the real possibilities of a free society, which is blocked by the affluent society—it is only this insistence in practice as well as in theory, in demonstration as well as in discussion, which still stands in the way of the complete degradation of man to an object, or rather subject/object, of total administration. It is only this insistence which still stands in the way of the progressive brutalization and moronization of man. For—and I should like to emphasize this—the capitalist Welfare State is a Warfare State. It must have an Enemy, with a capital E, a total Enemy; because the perpetuation of servitude, the perpetuation of the miserable struggle for existence in the very face of the new possibilities of freedom, activates and intensifies in this society a primary aggressiveness to a degree, I think, hitherto unknown in history. And this primary aggressiveness must be mobilized in socially useful ways, lest it explode the system itself. Therefore the need for an Enemy, who must be there, and who must be created if he does not exist. Fortunately, I dare say, the Enemy does exist. But his image and his power must, in this society, be inflated beyond all proportions in order to be able to mobilize this aggressiveness of the affluent society in socially useful ways.

The result is a mutilated, crippled and frustrated human existence: a human existence that is violently defending its own servitude.

We can sum up the fatal situation with which we are confronted. Radical social change is objectively necessary, in the dual sense that it is the only chance to save the possibilities of human freedom and, furthermore, in the sense that the technical and material resources for the realization of freedom are available. But while this objective need is demonstrably there, the subjective need for such a change does not prevail. It does not prevail precisely among those parts of the population that are traditionally considered the agents of historical change. The subjective need is repressed, again on a dual ground: firstly, by virtue of the actual satisfaction of needs, and secondly, by a massive scientific manipulation and administration of needs—that is, by a systematic social control not only of the consciousness, but also of the unconscious of man. This control has been made possible by the very achievements of the greatest liberating sciences of our time, in psychology, mainly psychoanalysis and psychiatry. That they could become and have become at the same time powerful instruments of suppression, one of the most effective engines of suppression, is again one of the terrible aspects of the dialectic of liberation.

This divergence between the objective and the subjective need changes completely, I suggest, the basis, the prospects and the strategy of liberation. This situation presupposes the emergence of new needs, qualitatively different and even opposed to the prevailing aggressive and repressive needs: the emergence of a new type of man, with a vital, biological drive for liberation, and with a consciousness capable of breaking through the material as well as ideological veil of the affluent society. In other words, liberation seems to be predicated upon the opening and the activation of a depth dimension of human existence, this side of and underneath the traditional material base: not an idealistic dimension, over and above the material base, but a dimension even more material than the material base, a dimension underneath the material base. I will illustrate presently what I mean.

The emphasis on this new dimension does not mean replacing politics by psychology, but rather the other way around. It means finally taking account of the fact that society has invaded even the deepest roots of individual existence, even the unconscious of man. *We* must get at the roots of society in the individuals themselves, the individuals who, because of social engineering, constantly reproduce the continuum of repression even through the great revolution.

This change is, I suggest, not an ideological change. It is dictated by the actual development of an industrial society, which has introduced factors which our theory could formerly correctly neglect. It is dictated by the actual development of industrial society, by the tremendous growth of its material and technical productivity, which has surpassed and rendered obsolete the traditional goals and preconditions of liberation.

Here we are faced with the question: is liberation from the affluent society identical with the transition from capitalism to socialism? The answer I suggest is: It is not identical, if socialism is defined merely as the planned development of the productive forces, and the rationalization of resources (although this remains a precondition for all liberation). It is identical with the transition from capitalism to socialism, if socialism is defined in its most Utopian terms: namely, among others, the abolition of labour, the termination of the struggle for existence—that is to say, life as an end in itself and no longer as a means to an end—and the liberation of human sensibility and sensitivity, not as a private factor, but as a force for transformation of human existence and of its environment. To give sensitivity and sensibility their own right is, I think, one of the basic goals of integral socialism. These are the qualitatively different features of a free society. They presuppose, as you may already have seen, a total trans-valuation of values, a new anthropology. They presuppose a type of man who rejects the performance principles governing the established societies; a type of man who has rid himself of the aggressiveness and brutality that are inherent in the organization of established society, and in their hypocritical, puritan morality; a type of man who is biologically incapable of fighting wars and creating suffering; a type of man who has a good conscience of joy and pleasure, and who works, collectively and individually, for a social and natural environment in which such an existence becomes possible.

The dialectic of liberation, as turned from quantity into quality, thus involves, I repeat, a break in the continuum of repression which reaches into the depth dimension of the organism itself. Or, we may say that today qualitative change, liberation, involves organic, instinctual, biological changes at the same time as political and social changes.

The new needs and satisfactions have a very material basis, as I have indicated. They are not thought out but are the logical derivation from the technical, material and intellectual possibilities of advanced, industrial society. They are inherent in, and the expression of, the productivity of advanced industrial society, which has long since made obsolete all kinds of inner-worldly asceticism, the entire work discipline on which Judaeo-Christian morality has been based.

Why is this society surpassing and negating this type of man, the traditional type of man, and the forms of his existence, as well as the morality to which it owes much of its origins and foundations? This new, unheard-of and not anticipated productivity allows the concept of a technology of liberation. Here I can only briefly indicate what I have in mind: such amazing and indeed apparently Utopian tendencies as the convergence of technique and art, the convergence of work and play, the convergence of the realm of necessity and the realm of freedom. How? No longer subjected to the dictates of capitalist profitability and of efficiency, no longer to the dictates of scarcity, which today are perpetuated by the capitalist organization of society, socially necessary labour, material production, would and could become (we see the tendency already) increasingly scientific. Technical experimentation, science and technology would and could become a play with the hitherto hidden—methodically hidden and blocked—potentialities of men and things, of society and nature.

This means one of the oldest dreams of all radical theory and practice. It means that the creative imagination, and not only the rationality of the performance principle, would become a productive force applied to the transformation of the social and natural universe. It would mean the emergence of a form of reality which is the work and the medium of the developing sensibility and sensitivity of man.

And now I throw in the terrible concept: it would mean an 'aesthetic' reality—society as a work of art. This is the most Utopian, the most radical possibility of liberation today.

What does this mean, in concrete terms? I said, we are not concerned here with private sensitivity and sensibility, but with sensitivity and sensibility, creative imagination and play, becoming forces of transformation. As such they would guide, for example, the total reconstruction of our cities and of the countryside; the restoration of nature after the elimination of the violence and destruction of capitalist industrialization; the creation of internal and external space for privacy, individual autonomy, tranquillity; the elimination of noise, of captive audiences, of enforced togetherness, of pollution, of ugliness. These are not—and I cannot emphasize this strongly enough— snobbish and romantic demands. Biologists today have emphasized that these are organic needs for the human organism, and that their arrest, their perversion and destruction by capitalist society, actually mutilates the human organism, not only in a figurative way but in a very real and literal sense.

I believe that it is only in such a universe that man can be truly free, and truly human relationships between free beings can be established. I believe that the idea of such a universe guided also Marx's concept of socialism, and that these aesthetic needs and goals must from the beginning be present in the reconstruction of society, and not only at the end or in the far future. Otherwise, the needs and satisfactions which reproduce a repressive society would be carried over into the new society. Repressive men would carry over their repression into the new society.

Now, at this farthest point, the question is: how can we possibly envisage the emergence of such qualitatively different needs and goals as organic, biological needs and goals and not as superimposed values? How can we envisage the emergence of these needs and satisfactions within and against the established society—that is to say, prior to liberation? That was the dialectic with which I started, that in a very definite sense we have to be free from in order to create a free society.

Needless to say, the dissolution of the existing system is the precondition for such qualitative change. And the more efficiently the repressive apparatus of the affluent societies operates, the less likely is a gradual transition from servitude to freedom. The fact that today we cannot identify any specific class or any specific group as a revolutionary force, this fact is no excuse for not using any and every possibility and method to arrest the engines of repression in the individual. The diffusion of potential opposition among the entire underlying population corresponds precisely to the total character of our advanced capitalist society. The internal contradictions of the system are as grave as ever before and likely to be aggravated by the violent expansion of capitalist imperialism. Not only the most general contradictions between the tremendous social wealth on the one hand, and the destructive, aggressive and wasteful use of this wealth on the other; but far more concrete contradictions such as the necessity for the system to automate, the continued reduction of the human base in physical labour-power in the material reproduction of society and thereby the tendency towards the draining of the sources of surplus profit. Finally, there is the threat of technological unemployment which even the most affluent society may no longer be capable of compensating by the creation of ever more parasitic and unproductive labour: all these contradictions exist. In reaction to them suppression, manipulation and integration are likely to increase.

But fulfilment is there, the ground can and must be prepared. The multilated consciousness and the mutilated instincts must be broken. The sensitivity and the awareness of the new transcending, antagonistic values—they are there. And they are there, they are here, precisely among the still non-integrated social groups and among those who, by virtue of their privileged position, can pierce the ideological and material veil of mass communication and indoctrination—namely, the intelligentsia.

We all know the fatal prejudice, practically from the beginning, in the Labour Movement against the intelligentsia as catalyst of historical change. It is time to ask whether this prejudice against the intellectuals, and the inferiority complex of the intellectuals resulting from it, was not an essential factor in the development of the capitalist as well as the socialist societies: in the development and weakening of the opposition. The intellectuals usually went out to organize the others, to organize in the communities. They certainly did not use the potentiality they had to organize themselves, to organize among themselves not only on a regional, not only on a national, but on an international level. That is, in my view, today one of the most urgent tasks. Can we say that the intelligentsia is the agent of historical change? Can we say that the intelligentsia today is a revolutionary class? The answer I would give is: No, we cannot say that. But we can say, and I think we must say, that the intelligentsia has a decisive preparatory function, not more; and I suggest that this is plenty. By itself it is not and cannot be a revolutionary class, but it can become the catalyst, and it has a preparatory function—certainly not for the first time, that is in fact the way all revolution starts—but more, perhaps, today than ever before. Because—and for this too we have a very material and very concrete basis—it is from this group that the holders of decisive positions in the productive process will be recruited, in the future even more than hitherto. I refer to what we may call the increasingly scientific character of the material process of production, by virtue of which the role of the intelligentsia changes. It is the group from which the decisive holders of decisive positions will be recruited: scientists, researchers, technicians, engineers, even psychologists—because psychology will continue to be a socially necessary instrument, either of servitude or of liberation.

This class, this intelligentsia, has been called the new working class. I believe this term is at best premature. They are—and this we should not forget—today the pet beneficiaries of the established system. But they are also at the very source of the glaring contradictions between the liberating capacity of science and its repressive and enslaving use. To activate the repressed and manipulated contradiction, to make it operate as a catalyst of change, that is one of the main tasks of the opposition today. It remains and must remain a political task.

Education is our job, but education in a new sense. Being theory as well as practice, political practice, education today is more than discussion, more than teaching and learning and writing. Unless and until it goes beyond the classroom, until and unless it goes beyond the college, the school, the university, it will remain powerless. Education today must involve the mind *and* the body, reason *and* imagination, the intellectual *and* the instinctual needs, because our entire existence has become the subject/object of politics, of social engineering. I emphasize, it is not a question of making the schools and universities, of making the educational system political. The educational system is political already. I need only remind you of the incredible degree to which (I am speaking of the U.S.) universities are involved in huge research grants (the nature of which you know in many cases) by the government and the various quasi-governmental agencies.

The educational system *is* political, so it is not we who want to politicize the educational system. What we want is a counter-policy against the established policy. And in this sense we must meet this society on its own ground of total mobilization. We must confront indoctrination in servitude with indoctrination in freedom. We must each of us generate in ourselves, and try to generate in others, the instinctual need for a life without fear, without brutality, and without stupidity. And we must see that we can generate the instinctual and intellectual revulsion against the values of an affluence which spreads aggressiveness and suppression throughout the world.

Before I conclude I would like to say my bit about the Hippies.[2] It seems to me a serious phenomenon. If we are talking of the emergence of an instinctual revulsion against the values of the affluent society, I think here is a place where we should look for it. It seems to me that the Hippies, like any non-conformist movement on the left, are split. That there are two parts, or parties, or tendencies. Much of it is mere masquerade and clownery on the private level, and therefore indeed, as Gerassi suggested, completely harmless, very nice and charming in many cases, but that is all there is to it. But that is not the whole story. There is in the Hippies, and especially in such tendencies in the Hippies as the Diggers and the Provos,[3] an inherent political element—perhaps even more so in the U.S. than here. It is the appearance indeed of new instinctual needs and values. This experience is there. There is a new sensibility against efficient and insane reasonableness. There is the refusal to play the rules of a rigid game, a game which one knows is rigid from the beginning, and the revolt against the compulsive cleanliness of puritan morality and the aggression bred by this puritan morality as we see it today in Vietnam[4] among other things.

At least this part of the Hippies, in which sexual, moral and political rebellion are somehow united, is indeed a non-aggressive form of life: a demonstration of an aggressive non-aggressiveness which achieves, at least potentially, the demonstration of qualitatively different values, a transvaluation of values.

---

[2] A large unorganized number of people (mostly young) who, during the 1960s, rejected established institutions, values, and life-styles. Many wore unconventional clothing, often ornamented with flowers and beads, and some used psychedelic drugs.

[3] Radically egalitarian but non-violent groups of the late 1960s that often participated in a sort of "politics of the absurd."

[4] The United States' massive military operations in Vietnam, resulting in large losses of lives and equipment, continued from 1965 to 1973.

All education today is therapy: therapy in the sense of liberating man by all available means from a society in which, sooner or later, he is going to be transformed into a brute, even if he doesn't notice it any more. Education in this sense is therapy, and all therapy today is political theory and practice. What kind of political practice? That depends entirely on the situation. It is hardly imaginable that we should discuss this here in detail. I will only remind you of the various possibilities of demonstrations, of finding out flexible modes of demonstration which can cope with the use of institutionalized violence, of boycott, many other things—anything goes which is such that it indeed has a reasonable chance of strengthening the forces of the opposition.

We can prepare for it as educators, as students. Again I say, our role is limited. We are no mass movement. I do not believe that in the near future we will see such a mass movement.

I want to add one word about the so-called Third World.[5] I have not spoken of the Third World because my topic was strictly liberation from the affluent society. I agree entirely with Paul Sweezy, that without putting the affluent society in the framework of the Third World it is not understandable. I also believe that here and now our emphasis must be on the advanced industrial societies—not forgetting to do whatever we can and in whatever way we can to support, theoretically and practically, the struggle for liberation in the neo-colonial countries which, if again they are not the final force of liberation, at least contribute their share—and it is a considerable share—to the potential weakening and disintegration of the imperialist world system.

Our role as intellectuals is a limited role. On no account should we succumb to any illusions. But even worse than this is to succumb to the wide-spread defeatism which we witness. The preparatory role today is an indispensable role. I believe I am not being too optimistic—I have not in general the reputation of being too optimistic—when I say that we can already see the signs, not only that *They* are getting frightened and worried but that there are far more concrete, far more tangible manifestations of the essential weakness of the system. Therefore, let us continue with whatever we can—no illusions, but even more, no defeatism.

---

[5] For the most part, the countries of Asia and Africa that gained their independence from the great industrial powers in the twentieth century.

5

Aleksandr Solzhenitsyn

The Gulag Archipelago

❖

Russia's Bolshevik Revolution of 1917, and the ensuing Communist regime, seemed to many progressive thinkers of the time the beginning of a promising new era of liberated human equality. As the consequences of that revolution became apparent, however, expectation, for many individuals, was replaced by disillusionment. Today the most insistent voice expressing distress with the practice of communism in the Soviet Union—and with Marxism in general—is that of Aleksandr Solzhenitsyn (1918–   ). This Russian writer's criticism includes not only Marxism and the Enlightenment but reaches back in history to the Scientific Revolution, Renaissance humanism, and the rise of materialism.

Solzhenitsyn was raised, by his mother, in the city of Rostov, near the mouth of the Don River; his father had been killed at the German front during the First World War. Although he graduated from the local university with honors in mathematics and physics, Solzhenitsyn burned with "the desire to write . . . from a very early age, at nine or ten . . . to be not just a writer in general but a Russian *writer." Even while he pursued his scientific studies, he was enrolled in a correspondence course offered by the Moscow Institute of Philosophy, Literature, and History. The Second World War interrupted his formal literary studies, however. Commissioned as an artillery officer, Solzhenitsyn fought with distinction for nearly three years*

From *The Gulag Archipelago, 1918–1956: An Experiment in Literary Investigation* by Aleksandr I. Solzhenitsyn. Translated by Thomas P. Whitney. I–II copyright © 1973 by Aleksandr I. Solzhenitsyn. English translation copyright © 1973, 1974 by Harper & Row Publishers, Inc. III–IV copyright © 1974 by Aleksandr I. Solzhenitsyn. English language translation copyright © 1975 by Harper & Row Publishers, Inc. Reprinted by permission of Harper & Row Publishers, Inc. [I–II: Pp. 134–43, 24–26, 60–67, 129–31, 168, 173–75, 177–78, 591–92; III–IV: 209–11, 65–66, 309–10, 369–74, 466–67, 623–27.]

as the Germans were battered out of Russia. In February 1945, when his unit was already fighting within Germany, he was arrested by the Soviet government: in letters to an old friend he had included some veiled criticisms of Stalin, the Soviet leader and commander-in-chief. It was after this arrest that Solzhenitsyn's true education began.

Sentenced in 1945 to eight years in a labor camp, Solzhenitsyn served the full term. During these years he worked as common laborer, bricklayer, and foundry worker in Siberia and, for about half of the term, as a mathematician in a prison near Moscow—a prison for people with training in the sciences. The years in the Siberian labor camp provided the data for his first novel, One Day in the Life of Ivan Denisovich *(1963), the only book by Solzhenitsyn allowed official publication in the Soviet Union. The novel describes the constant struggle for survival in the day of a simple peasant inmate whose only "crime" was that he had been taken prisoner by the Germans during the war. This stark and frank picture of the Stalinist prison camps brought the author immediate international attention. The prison for those with scientific training provided the setting for Solzhenitsyn's* The First Circle *(1968), a novel about prisoners required to devise machinery for purposes they find morally abominable. The First Circle, the realm of these inmates, is bearable only when contrasted with the lower depths inhabited by such tormented creatures as Ivan Denisovich.*

Upon completion of his prison term, in 1953, Solzhenitsyn was sent into "eternal exile" in a remote part of the country. There he was hospitalized and treated for cancer of the stomach, from which he had suffered while in prison. This hospital experience was later fictionalized in The Cancer Ward *(1968), a novel that explores the reactions of a group of men under treatment for the deadly disease. The central figure, a man much like Solzhenitsyn, comes into conflict with another patient, a greedy materialist who holds some petty position in the Communist Party. The sickness throughout the ward serves as an allegory for the sickness of Russia and of modern humanity.*

In 1957, during the liberalizing "thaw" that followed Stalin's death, Solzhenitsyn's case was reviewed by the Soviet judiciary, which declared that the original charges had no substance. Freed from his exile, Solzhenitsyn returned to western Russia where, until the publication of One Day, *he taught high-school physics and mathematics.*

While experiencing mounting harassment within the Soviet Union, Solzhenitsyn was awarded the Nobel Prize for Literature (1970); he did not attend the presentation ceremony in Sweden, however, for fear of being denied re-entry to the Soviet Union. In 1974, after being threatened with renewed imprisonment (for alleged activities against the state), he was forcibly exiled from his homeland. He and his family eventually settled in the United States, where he resumed the writing of a sequence of novels that begins with August, 1914 *(1972). The series is intended to illuminate the history of Russia through the years of the First World War and the Bolshevik Revolution. In the vast scope of its characters and events the work may well be compared with Tolstoy's* War and Peace.

The following selection by Solzhenitsyn is from a work of a different sort, The Gulag Archipelago *(1973–78). It is Solzhenitsyn's comprehensive account of Soviet prisons as an integral part of systematic repression. (The sources for his "experiment in literary investigation" were mainly the "reports, memoirs, and letters" of hundreds of prison "witnesses." The "Gulag" of the title is a Russian acronym for Chief Administration of Corrective Labor Camps; these camps stretch, island-like, across the expanse of the Soviet Union.) In an ironic manner worthy of his great nineteenth-century predecessor Dostoevsky, the ex-Army officer tells of his own interrogation and sentencing for an act that would have been regarded as permissible behavior in most Western countries; he also describes in detail the Soviet prisons, their diverse inmates, and guards. Above all, he shows the conflict between materialistic and religious styles of life and illuminates the spiritual growth possible amidst the daily confrontations in the camps. The richly documented three volumes of* Gulag *are nothing less than an attempt—in the Biblical prophetic tradition—to call the Russian people to an accounting for all the crimes done in their name, and thus to begin purging the nation of its sins.*

THE INTERROGATION

Although we were front-line officers, Nikolai V. and I, who were involved in the same case, got ourselves into prison through a piece of childish stupidity. He and I corresponded during the war, between two sectors of the front; and though we knew perfectly well that wartime censorship of correspondence was in effect, we indulged in fairly outspoken expressions of our political outrage and in derogatory comments about the Wisest of the Wise, whom we labeled with the transparently obvious nickname of Pakhan or *Ringleader of the Thieves*.[1] (When, later on, I reported our *case* in various prisons, our naïveté aroused only laughter and astonishment. Other prisoners told me that two more such stupid jackasses couldn't exist. And I became convinced of it myself. Then suddenly, one day, reading some documents on the case of Aleksandr Ulyanov, Lenin's[2] elder brother, I learned that he and his confederates got caught in exactly the same way—a careless exchange of letters. And that was the only reason Alexander III didn't die on March 1, 1887.)

The office of my interrogator, I. I. Yezepov, was high-ceilinged, spacious and bright, with an enormous window. (The Rossiya Insurance Company had not been built with torture in mind.) And, putting to use its seventeen feet of height, a full-length, vertical, thirteen-foot portrait of that powerful Sovereign hung there, toward whom I, grain of sand that I was, had expressed my hatred. Sometimes the interrogator stood in front of the portrait and declaimed dramatically: "We are ready to lay down our lives for him! We are ready to lie down in the path of oncoming tanks for his sake!" Face to face with the altarlike grandeur of that portrait, my mumbling about some kind of purified Leninism seemed pitiful, and I myself seemed a blasphemous slanderer deserving only death.

The contents of our letters provided more than enough, in keeping with the standards of those times, to sentence us both. Therefore my interrogator did not have to invent anything. He merely tried to cast his noose around everyone I had ever written to or received a letter from. I had expressed myself vehemently in letters to friends my own age and had been almost reckless in spelling out seditious ideas, but my friends for some reason had continued to correspond with me! And some suspicious phrases could be found in their replies to my letters. And then Yezepov, like Porfiri Petrovich,[3] demanded that I explain it all in a coherent way: if we had expressed ourselves in such a fashion in letters that we knew were subject to censorship,

---

[1] The nickname refers to Iosif V. Stalin (1879–1953), who was the Soviet political leader during Solzhenitsyn's wartime service. Beginning in 1924, Stalin gradually eliminated political rivals in a series of purges, culminating in a series of great show trials, 1936–38.

[2] Vladimir I. Lenin (1870–1924), Communist revolutionary and first leader of the Soviet state. His elder brother was executed for his part in an unsuccessful plot to assassinate Tsar Alexander III.

[3] A police investigator who relentlessly pursues the main character in Dostoevsky's great novel *Crime and Punishment* (1866).

Array

what could we have said to each other face to face? I could not convince him that all my fire-eating talk was confined to my letters. And at that point, with muddled mind, I had to undertake to weave something credible about my meetings with my friends—meetings referred to in my letters. What I said had to jibe with the letters, in such a way as to be on the very edge of political matters and yet not fall under that Criminal Code. Moreover, these explanations had to pour forth quickly, all in one breath, so as to convince this veteran interrogator of my naïveté, my humility, my total honesty. The main thing was not to provoke my lazy interrogator to any interest in looking through that accursed load of stuff I had brought in my accursed suitcase—including many notebooks of my "War Diary," written in hard, light pencil in a needle-thin handwriting, with some of the notes already partially washed out. These diaries constituted my claim to becoming a writer. I had not believed in the capacities of our amazing memory, and throughout the war years I had tried to write down everything I saw. That would have been only half a catastrophe: I also wrote down everything I *heard* from other people. But opinions and stories which were so natural in front-line areas seemed to be treasonable here in the rear and reeked of raw imprisonment for my front-line comrades. So to prevent that interrogator from going to work on my "War Diary" and mining from it a whole case against a free front-line tribe, I repented just as much as I had to and pretended to see the light and reject my political mistakes. I became utterly exhausted from this balancing on a razor's edge, until I recognized that no one was being hauled in for a confrontation with me and distinguished the clear signs that the interrogation was drawing to an end . . . until, in the fourth month, all the notebooks of my "War Diary" were cast into the hellish maw of the Lubyanka[4] furnace, where they burst into flame—the red pyre of one more novel which had perished in Russia—and flew out of the highest chimney in black butterflies of soot.

We used to walk in the shadow of that chimney, our exercise yard a boxlike concrete enclosure on the roof of the Big Lubyanka, six floors up. The walls rose around us to approximately three times a man's height. With our own ears we could hear Moscow—automobile horns honking back and forth. But all we could see was

[4] A secret police headquarters and prison in central Moscow. Before the 1917 revolution the building housed the Rossiya (Russia) Insurance Company.

that chimney, the guard posted in a seventh-floor tower, and that segment of God's heaven whose unhappy fate it was to float over the Lubyanka.

Oh, that soot! It kept falling on and on in that first postwar May. So much of it fell during each of our walks that we decided the Lubyanka must be burning countless years of files. My doomed diary was only one momentary plume of that soot. I recalled a frosty sunny morning in March when I was sitting in the interrogator's office. He was asking his customary crude questions and writing down my answers, distorting my words as he did so. The sun played in the melting latticework of the frost on the wide window, through which at times I felt very much like jumping, so as to flash through Moscow at least in death and smash onto the sidewalk five floors below, just as, in my childhood, my unknown predecessor had jumped from House 33 in Rostov-on-the-Don. In the gaps where the frost had melted, the rooftops of Moscow could be seen, rooftop after rooftop, and above them merry little puffs of smoke. But I was staring not in that direction but at a mound of piled-up manuscripts—someone else's—covering the entire center of the floor in this half-empty room, thirty-six square yards in area, manuscripts which had been dumped there a little while before and had not yet been examined. In notebooks, in file folders, in homemade binders, in tied and untied bundles, and simply in loose pages. The manuscripts lay there like the burial mound of some interred human spirit, its conical top rearing higher than the interrogator's desk, almost blocking me from his view. And brotherly pity ached in me for the labor of that unknown person who had been arrested the previous night, these spoils from the search of his premises having been dumped that very morning on the parquet floor of the torture chamber, at the feet of that thirteen-foot Stalin. I sat there and I wondered: Whose extraordinary life had they brought in for torment, for dismemberment, and then for burning?

Oh, how many ideas and works had perished in that building—a whole lost culture? Oh, soot, soot, from the Lubyanka chimneys! And the most hurtful thing of all was that our descendants would consider our generation more stupid, less gifted, less vocal than in actual fact it was.

One needs to have only two points in order to draw a straight line between them.

In 1920, as Ehrenburg[5] recalls, the Cheka[6] addressed him as follows:

"*You* prove to us that you are *not* Wrangel's agent."[7]

And in 1950, one of the leading colonels of the MGB,[8] Foma Fomich Zheleznov, said to his prisoners: "We are not going to sweat to prove the prisoner's guilt to him. Let *him* prove to *us* that he did *not* have hostile intent."

And along this cannibalistically artless straight line lie the recollections of countless millions.

What a speed-up and simplification of criminal investigation previously unknown to mankind! The *Organs* altogether freed themselves of the burden of obtaining proof! Trembling and pale, the rabbit who had been caught, deprived of the right to write anyone, phone anyone, bring anything with him from freedom, deprived too of sleep, food, paper, pencils, and even buttons, seated on a bare stool in the corner of an office, had to try to find out for *himself* and display to that loafer of an interrogator *proof* that he did *not* have hostile *intentions*. If he could not discover such proof (and where would he find it?), by that very failure he provided the interrogation with *approximate* proof of his guilt!

I knew of a case in which a certain old man who had been a prisoner in Germany[9] managed nonetheless, sitting there on his bare stool and gesturing with his cold fingers, to prove to his monster of an interrogator that he did *not* betray his Motherland and even that he did *not* have any such intention! It was a scandal! And what happened? Did they free him? Of course not—after all, he told me about this in Butyrki[10] and not on Tverskoi Boulevard in the middle of Moscow. At that point a second interrogator joined the first and they spent a quiet evening reminiscing with the old man. Then the two interrogators signed witnesses' affidavits stating that in the course of the evening the hungry, sleepy old man had engaged in anti-Soviet propaganda! Things were said innocently—but they weren't listened

---

[5] Ilya G. Ehrenburg (1891–1967), a Soviet writer and journalist who was the author of memoirs of the Stalin era.

[6] Original name of the Soviet secret police (1917–22).

[7] Pyotr N. Wrangel (1878–1928), a tsarist military commander; he led anti-Communist forces in the South during the civil war that followed the 1917 revolution.

[8] The initials for the Soviet secret police (1946–53).

[9] Russians who had been captured by the Germans, especially those imprisoned in Germany, were generally regarded by Stalin as spies and/or traitors.

[10] A large prison in Moscow, named after a local district.

to innocently. The old man was then turned over to a third interrogator, who quashed the treason indictment and neatly nailed him with that very same *tenner* [11] for Anti-Soviet Agitation during his interrogation.

Given that interrogations had ceased to be an attempt to get at the truth, for the interrogators in difficult cases they became a mere exercise of their duties as executioners and in easy cases simply a pastime and a basis for receiving a salary.

And easy cases always existed, even in the notorious year 1937. For example, Borodko was accused of having visited his parents in Poland sixteen years before without having a passport for foreign travel. (His papa and mama lived all of ten versts—six miles—away, but the diplomats had signed away that part of Byelorussia to Poland, and in 1921 people had not yet gotten used to that fact and went back and forth as they pleased.) The interrogation took just half an hour. Question: Did you go there? Answer: I did. Question: How? Answer: Horseback, of course. Conclusion: Take ten years for KRD. [12]

But that sort of pace smells of the Stakhanovite [13] movement, a movement which found no disciples among the bluecaps. According to the Code of Criminal Procedure every interrogation was supposed to take two months. And if it presented difficulties, one was allowed to ask the prosecutor for several continuations of a month apiece (which, of course, the prosecutors never refused). Thus it would have been stupid to risk one's health, not to take advantage of these postponements, and, speaking in factory terms, to raise one's work norms. Having worked with voice and fist in the initial assault week of every interrogation, and thereby expended one's will and *character* (as per Vyshinsky), [14] the interrogators had a vital interest in dragging out the remainder of every case as long as possible. That way more old, subdued cases were on hand and fewer new ones. It was considered just indecent to complete a political interrogation in two months.

[11] A sentence of ten years in prison.
[12] Counter-Revolutionary Activity.
[13] Aleksei Stakhanov was a miner who, in one night-shift in 1935, allegedly dug 102 tons of coal. He was hailed as a "hero of Soviet labor," and all other workers were urged to follow his example of speedy work.
[14] Andrei Vyshinsky (1883–1954), a lawyer and diplomat, was the chief state prosecutor in the "show trials" (1936–38), trials—with the outcomes predetermined—that were staged for propaganda purposes.

The state system itself suffered from its own lack of trust and from its rigidity. These interrogators were selected personnel, but they weren't trusted either. In all probability they, too, were required to check in on arriving and check out on leaving, and the prisoners were, of course, checked in and out when called for questioning. What else could the interrogators do to keep the bookkeepers' accounts straight? They would summon one of their defendants, sit him down in a corner, ask him some terrifying question—and then forget about him while they themselves sat for a long time reading the paper, writing an outline for a political indoctrination course or personal letters, or went off to visit one another, leaving guards to act as watchdogs in their place. Peacefully batting the breeze on the sofa with a colleague who had just dropped in, the interrogator would come to himself once in a while, look threateningly at the accused, and say:

"Now there's a rat! There's a real rat for you! Well, that's all right, we'll not be stingy about his *nine grams!*" [i.e., a bullet]

My interrogator also made frequent use of the telephone. For example, he used to phone home and tell his wife—with his sparkling eyes directed at me—that he was going to be working all night long so she mustn't expect him before morning. (My heart, of course, fell. That meant he would be working *me* over all night long!) But then he would immediately dial the phone number of his mistress and, in purring tones, make a date with her for the night. (So: I would be able to get some sleep! I felt relieved.)

Thus it was that the faultless system was moderated only by the shortcomings of those who carried it out.

Certain of the more curious interrogators used to enjoy using "empty" interrogations to broaden their knowledge of life. They might ask the accused prisoner about the front (about those very German tanks beneath which they never quite managed to find the time to throw themselves). Or perhaps about the customs of European countries and lands across the sea which the prisoner had visited: about the stores and the merchandise sold in them, and particularly about procedures in foreign whorehouses and about all kinds of adventures with women.

The Code of Criminal Procedure provided that the prosecutor was to review continuously the course of every interrogation to ensure its being conducted correctly. But no one in our time ever saw him face to face until the so-called "questioning by the prosecutor," which meant the interrogation was nearing its end. I, too, was taken to such a "questioning." Lieutenant Colonel Kotov, a calm, well-nourished, impersonal blond man, who was neither nasty nor nice but essentially a cipher, sat behind his desk and, yawning, examined for the first time the file on my case. He spent fifteen minutes acquainting himself with it while I watched. (Since this "questioning" was quite unavoidable and since it was also recorded, there would have been no sense at all in his studying the file at some earlier, unrecorded time and then having had to remember details of the case for a certain number of hours.) Finally, he raised his indifferent eyes to stare at the wall and asked lazily what I wanted to add to my testimony.

He was required by law to ask what complaints I had about the conduct of the interrogation and whether coercion had been used or any violations of my legal rights had occurred. But it had been a long time since prosecutors asked such questions. And what if they had? After all, the existence of that entire Ministry building with its thousands of rooms, and of all five thousand of the Ministry's other interrogation buildings, railroad cars, caves, and dugouts scattered throughout the Soviet Union, was based on violations of legal rights. And it certainly wasn't up to Lieutenant Colonel Kotov and me to reverse that whole process.

Anyway, all the prosecutors of any rank at all held their positions with the approval of that very same State Security which . . . they were supposed to check up on.

His own wilted state, his lack of combativeness, and his fatigue from all those endless stupid cases were somehow transmitted to me. So I didn't raise questions of truth with him. I requested only that one too obvious stupidity be corrected: two of us had been indicted in the same case, but our interrogations were conducted in different places—mine in Moscow and my friend's at the front. Therefore I was processed *singly,* yet charged under Section 11—in other words, as a *group,* an *organization.* As persuasively as possible, I requested him to cancel this additional charge under Section 11.

He leafed through the case for another five minutes, sighed, spread out his hands, and said:

"What's there to say? One person is a person and two persons are . . . people."

But one person and a half—is that an organization?

And he pushed the button for them to come and take me away.

0 8 4 7

BUSINESS REPLY CARD

FIRST CLASS   PERMIT NO. 250   LIVINGSTON, N.J.

POSTAGE WILL BE PAID BY ADDRESSEE

Newsweek

College Store Service Bureau
National Association of College Stores
528 East Lorain Street
Oberlin, Ohio 44074-9989

Soon after that, late one evening in late May, in that same office with a sculptured bronze clock on the marble mantel, my interrogator summoned me for a "206" procedure. This was, in accordance with the provisions of the Code of Criminal Procedure, the defendant's review of the case before his final signature. Not doubting for one moment that I would sign, the interrogator was already seated, writing the conclusion of the indictment.

I opened the cover of the thick file, and there, on the inside of the cover in printed text, I read an astonishing statement. It turned out that during the interrogation I had had the right to make written complaints against anything improper in its conduct, and that the interrogator was obliged to staple these complaints into my record! During the interrogation! Not at its end.

Alas, not one of the thousands with whom I was later imprisoned had been aware of this right.

I turned more pages. I saw photocopies of my own letters and a totally distorted interpretation of their meaning by unknown commentators. . . . I saw the hyperbolized lie in which Captain Yezepov had wrapped up my careful testimony. And, last but not least, I saw the idiocy whereby I, one individual, was accused as a "group"!

"I won't sign," I said, without much firmness. "You conducted the interrogation improperly."

"All right then, let's begin it all over again!" Maliciously he compressed his lips. "We'll send you off to the place where we keep the Polizei." [15]

He even stretched out his hand as though to take the file away from me. (At that point I held onto it.)

Somewhere outside the fifth-floor windows of the Lubyanka, the golden sunset sun glowed. Somewhere it was May. The office windows, like all the windows facing outward, were tightly closed and had not yet been unsealed after the winter—so that fresh air and the fragrance of things in bloom should not creep into those hidden rooms. The bronze clock on the mantel, from which the last rays of the sun had disappeared, quietly chimed.

Begin all over again? It seemed to me it would be easier to die than to begin all over again. Ahead of me loomed at least some kind of life. (If I had only known what kind!) And then what about that

---

[15] German: police; a designation for Russians who served as police under German occupation.

place where they kept the Polizei? And, in general, it was a bad idea to make him angry. It would influence the tone in which he phrased the conclusion of the indictment.

And so I signed. I signed it complete with Section 11, the significance of which I did not then know. They told me only that it would not add to my prison term. But because of that Section 11 I was later put into a hard-labor camp. Because of that Section 11 I was sent, even after "liberation," and without any additional sentence, into eternal exile.

Maybe it was all for the best. Without both those experiences, I would not have written this book.

My interrogator had used no methods on me other than sleeplessness, lies, and threats—all completely legal. Therefore, in the course of the "206" procedure, he didn't have to shove at me—as did interrogators who had made a mess of things and wanted to play safe—a document on nondisclosure for me to sign: that I, the undersigned, under pain of criminal penalty, swore never to tell anyone about the methods used in conducting my interrogation. (No one knows, incidentally, what article of the Code this comes under.)

In several of the provincial administrations of the NKVD [16] this measure was carried out in sequence: the typed statement on non-disclosure was shoved at a prisoner along with the verdict of the OSO. [17] And later a similar document was shoved at prisoners being released from camp, whereby they guaranteed never to disclose to anyone the state of affairs in camp.

And so? Our habit of obedience, our bent (or broken) backbone, did not suffer us either to reject this gangster method of burying loose ends or even to be enraged by it.

We have lost *the measure of freedom*. We have no means of determining where it begins and where it ends. We are an Asiatic people. On and on and on they go, taking from us those endless pledges of nondisclosure—everyone not too lazy to ask for them.

By now we are even unsure whether we have the right to talk about the events of our own lives.

• • •

[16] The initials for the Soviet secret police (1934–43).
[17] The initials designating a "special board," one of the three-man boards of the NKVD with powers to sentence "socially dangerous" persons without trial; the boards were not officially abolished until 1953.

THE HISTORY OF OUR SEWAGE DISPOSAL SYSTEM

When people today decry *the abuses of the cult*,[18] they keep getting hung up on those years which are stuck in our throats, '37 and '38. And memory begins to make it seem as though arrests were never made *before* or *after*, but only in those two years.

Although I have no statistics at hand, I am not afraid of erring when I say that the *wave* of 1937 and 1938 was neither the only one nor even the main one, but only one, perhaps, of the three biggest waves which strained the murky, stinking pipes of our prison sewers to bursting.

Before it came the wave of 1929 and 1930, the size of a good River Ob, which drove a mere fifteen million peasants, maybe even more, out into the taiga and the tundra.[19] But peasants are a silent people, without a literary voice, nor do they write complaints or memoirs. No interrogators sweated out the night with them, nor did they bother to draw up formal indictments—it was enough to have a decree from the village soviet. This wave poured forth, sank down into the permafrost, and even our most active minds recall hardly a thing about it. It is as if it had not even scarred the Russian conscience. And yet Stalin (and you and I as well) committed no crime more heinous than this.

And *after* it there was the wave of 1944 to 1946, the size of a good Yenisei, when they dumped whole *nations* down the sewer pipes, not to mention millions and millions of others who (because of us!) had been prisoners of war, or carried off to Germany and subsequently repatriated. (This was Stalin's method of cauterizing the wounds so that scar tissue would form more quickly, and thus the body politic as a whole would not have to rest up, catch its breath, regain its strength.) But in this wave, too, the people were of the simpler kind, and they wrote no memoirs.

But the wave of 1937 swept up and carried off to the Archipelago people of position, people with a Party past, yes, educated people, around whom were many who had been wounded and remained in

---

[18] The "cult of personality" in which Stalin held absolute power. This power was particularly demonstrated during the Great Purge (1936–38) by the show trials, the executions of thousands of leading Communists, and the forced relocation and hard labor of many others.

[19] A reference to the forced dispossession of resisting farmers during Stalin's land collectivization program.

the cities . . . and what a lot of them had pen in hand! And today they are all writing, speaking, remembering: "Nineteen thirty-seven!" A whole Volga of the people's grief!

But just say "Nineteen thirty-seven" to a Crimean Tatar, a Kalmyk, a Chechen,[20] and he'll shrug his shoulders. And what's 1937 to Leningrad when 1935 had come before it? And for the *second-termers* (i.e., *repeaters*), or people from the Baltic countries—weren't 1948 and 1949 harder on them? And if sticklers for style and geography should accuse me of having omitted some Russian rivers, and of not yet having named some of the waves, then just give me enough paper! There were enough waves to use up the names of all the rivers of Russia!

It is well known that any *organ* withers away if it is not used. Therefore, if we know that the Soviet Security organs, or *Organs* (and they christened themselves with this vile word), praised and exalted above all living things, have not died off even to the extent of one single tentacle, but, instead, have grown new ones and strengthened their muscles—it is easy to deduce that they have had *constant* exercise.

Through the sewer pipes the flow pulsed. Sometimes the pressure was higher than had been projected, sometimes lower. But the prison sewers were never empty. The blood, the sweat, and the urine into which we were pulped pulsed through them continuously. The history of this sewage system is the history of an endless swallow and flow; flood alternating with ebb and ebb again with flood; waves pouring in, some big, some small; brooks and rivulets flowing in from all sides; trickles oozing in through gutters; and then just plain individually scooped-up droplets.

The chronological list which follows, in which waves made up of millions of arrested persons are given equal attention with ordinary streamlets of unremarkable handfuls, is quite incomplete, meager, miserly, and limited by my own capacity to penetrate the past. What is really needed is a great deal of additional work by survivors familiar with the material.

● ● ●

Paradoxically enough, every act of the all-penetrating, eternally wakeful *Organs,* over a span of many years, was based solely on *one*

---

[20] Members of non-Russian ethnic groups within the Soviet Union.

article of the 140 articles of the nongeneral division of the Criminal Code of 1926. One can find more epithets in praise of this article than Turgenev once assembled to praise the Russian language, or Nekrasov[21] to praise Mother Russia: great, powerful, abundant, highly ramified, multiform, wide-sweeping 58, which summed up the world not so much through the exact terms of its sections as in their extended dialectical interpretation.

Who among us has not experienced its all-encompassing embrace? In all truth, there is no step, thought, action, or lack of action under the heavens which could not be punished by the heavy hand of Article 58.

The article itself could not be worded in such broad terms, but it proved possible to interpret it this broadly.

Article 58 was not in that division of the Code dealing with political crimes; and nowhere was it categorized as "political." No. It was included, with crimes against public order and organized gangsterism, in a division of "crimes against the state." Thus the Criminal Code starts off by refusing to recognize anyone under its jurisdiction as a political offender. All are simply criminals.

Article 58 consisted of fourteen sections.

In Section 1 we learn that any action (and, according to Article 6 of the Criminal Code, any absence of action) directed toward the weakening of state power was considered to be counterrevolutionary.

Broadly interpreted, this turned out to include the refusal of a prisoner in camp to work when in a state of starvation and exhaustion. This was a weakening of state power. And it was punished by execution. (The execution of *malingerers* during the war.)

From 1934 on, when we were given back the term *Motherland,* subsections were inserted on *treason to the Motherland* — 1a, 1b, 1c, 1d. According to these subsections, all actions directed against the military might of the U.S.S.R. were punishable by execution (1b), or by ten years' imprisonment (1a), but the lighter penalty was imposed only when mitigating circumstances were present and upon civilians only.

Broadly interpreted: when our soldiers were sentenced to only ten years for allowing themselves to be taken prisoner (action injurious to Soviet military might), this was humanitarian to the point

---

[21]Ivan Turgenev and Nikolai Nekrasov were nineteenth-century Russian writers.

of being illegal. According to the Stalinist code, they should all have been shot on their return home.

(Here is another example of broad interpretation. I remember well an encounter in the Butyrki in the summer of 1946. A certain Pole had been born in Lemberg when that city was part of the Austro-Hungarian Empire. Until World War II he lived in his native city, by then located in Poland; then he went to Austria, where he entered the service, and in 1945 he was arrested there by the Russians. Since by this time Austrian Lemberg had become Ukrainian Lvov, he received a *tenner* under Article 54-1a of the Ukrainian Criminal Code: i.e., for treason to his motherland, *the Ukraine!* [22] And at his interrogation the poor fellow couldn't prove that treason to the Ukraine had not been his purpose when he went to Vienna! And that's how he conned his way into becoming a traitor.)

One important additional broadening of the section on treason was its application "via Article 19 of the Criminal Code"—"via intent." In other words, no treason had taken place; but the interrogator envisioned an *intention* to betray—and that was enough to justify a full term, the same as for actual treason. True, Article 19 proposes that there be no penalty for intent, but only for *preparation,* but given a dialectical reading one can understand intention as preparation. And "preparation is punished in the same way [i.e., with the same penalty] as the crime itself" (Criminal Code). In general, "we draw no distinction between *intention* and the *crime* itself, and this is an instance of the *superiority* of Soviet legislation to bourgeois legislation."

Section 2 listed armed rebellion, seizure of power in the capital or in the provinces, especially for the purpose of severing any part of the U.S.S.R. through the use of force. For this the penalties ranged up to and included execution (as in *every* succeeding section).

This was expanded to mean something which could not be explicitly stated in the article itself but which revolutionary sense of justice could be counted on to suggest: it applied to every attempt of any national republic to act upon its right to leave the U.S.S.R. After all, the word "force" is not defined in terms of *whom* it applies to. Even when the entire population of a republic wants to secede, if Moscow is opposed, the attempted secession will be *forc-*

---

[22] One of the constituent republics of the Soviet Union.

ible. Thus, all Estonian, Latvian, Lithuanian, Ukrainian, and Tur-
kestan nationalists very easily received their *tens* and their
twenty-fives under this section.

Section 3 was "assisting in any way or by any means a foreign
state at war with the U.S.S.R."

This section made it possible to condemn *any* citizen who had
been in occupied territory—whether he had nailed on the heel of a
German soldier's shoe or sold him a bunch of radishes. And it
could be applied to any citizeness who had helped lift the fighting
spirit of an enemy soldier by dancing and spending the night with
him. Not everyone *was* actually sentenced under this section—
because of the huge numbers who had been in occupied territory.
But everyone who had been in occupied territory *could* have been
sentenced under it.

Section 4 spoke about (fantastic!) aid to the international bourgeoisie.

To whom, one wonders, could this possibly refer? And yet,
broadly interpreted, and with the help of a revolutionary conscience, it was easy to find categories: All émigrés who had left
the country before 1920, i.e., several years before the Code was
even written, and whom our armies came upon in Europe a
quarter-century later—in 1944 and 1945—received 58-4: ten years
or execution. What could they have been doing abroad other than
aiding the international bourgeoisie? . . . They were, in addition,
aided by all SR's,[23] all Mensheviks[24] (the section was drafted with
them in mind), and, subsequently, by the engineers of the State
Planning Commission and the Supreme Council of the Economy.
Section 5 was inciting a foreign state to declare war against the
U.S.S.R.

A chance was missed to apply this section against Stalin and his
diplomatic and military circle in 1940–1941. Their blindness and
insanity led to just that. Who if not they drove Russia into shameful, unheard-of defeats, incomparably worse than the defeats of
Tsarist Russia in 1904 or 1915? Defeats such as Russia had never
known since the thirteenth century.

---

[23] Members of the Socialist Revolutionary Party, an anti-tsarist political organization
that was eventually destroyed after Lenin's Bolsheviks came to power.

[24] Mensheviks (so-called after the Russian word for "minority") were those who, believing in a gradual approach to socialism, split from Lenin's majority Bolsheviks
within the Russian Social Democratic Party.

Section 6 was espionage.

This section was interpreted so broadly that if one were to count up all those sentenced under it one might conclude that during Stalin's time our people supported life not by agriculture or industry, but only by espionage on behalf of foreigners, and by living on subsidies from foreign intelligence services. Espionage was very convenient in its simplicity, comprehensible both to an undeveloped criminal and to a learned jurist, to a journalist and to public opinion.[25]

The breadth of interpretation of Section 6 lay further in the fact that people were sentenced not only for actual espionage but also for:

PSh—Suspicion of Espionage—or NSh—Unproven Espionage—for which they gave the whole works.

And even SVPSh—Contacts Leading to (!) Suspicion of Espionage.

In other words, let us say that an acquaintance of an acquaintance of your wife had a dress made by the same seamstress (who was, of course, an NKVD agent) used by the wife of a foreign diplomat.

These 58-6 PSh's and SVPSh's were sticky sections. They required the strict confinement and incessant supervision of those convicted (for, after all, an intelligence service might reach out its tentacles to its protégé even in a camp); also, such prisoners could be moved only under convoy—armed escort. In general, all the *lettered articles*—which were, in fact, not articles of the Code at all but frightening combinations of capital letters (and we shall encounter more of them in this chapter)—always contained a touch of the enigmatic, always remained incomprehensible, and it wasn't at all clear whether they were offshoots of Article 58 or independent and extremely dangerous. In many camps prisoners convicted under the provisions of these lettered articles were subjected to restrictions even more stringent than those of the ordinary 58's.

---

[25] And very likely spy mania was not merely the narrow-minded predilection of Stalin alone. It was very useful for everyone who possessed any privileges. It became the natural justification for increasingly widespread secrecy, the withholding of information, closed doors and security passes, fenced-off dachas and secret, restricted special shops. People had no way of penetrating the armor plate of spy mania and learning how the bureaucracy made its cozy arrangements, loafed, blundered, ate, and took its amusements. [Solzhenitsyn's note. *Ed.*]

Section 7 applied to subversion of industry, transport, trade, and the circulation of money.

In the thirties, extensive use was made of this section to catch masses of people—under the simplified and widely understood catchword *wrecking*. In reality, everything enumerated under Section 7 was very obviously and plainly being subverted daily. So didn't someone have to be guilty of it all? For centuries the people had built and created, always honorably, always honestly, even for serf-owners and nobles. Yet no one, from the days of Ryurik[26] on, had ever heard of *wrecking*. But now, when for the first time all the wealth had come to belong to the people, hundreds of thousands of the best sons of the people inexplicably rushed off to *wreck*. (Section 7 did not provide for wrecking in *agriculture,* but since it was impossible otherwise to explain rationally how and why the fields were choked with weeds, why harvests were falling off, why machines were breaking down, then dialectic sensitivity brought agriculture, too, under its sway.)

Section 8 covered terror (not that terror from above for which the Soviet Criminal Code was supposed to "provide a foundation and basis in legality," but terrorism from below).

Terror was construed in a very broad sense, not simply a matter of putting bombs under governors' carriages, but, for example, smashing in the face of a personal enemy if he was an activist in the Party, the Komsomol,[27] or the *police!* —that was already terror. The *murder* of an activist, especially, was always treated more seriously than the murder of an ordinary person (as in the Code of Hammurabi in the eighteenth century B.C.). If a husband killed his wife's lover, it was very fortunate for him if the victim turned out not to be a Party member; he would be sentenced under Article 136 as a common criminal, who was a "social ally" and didn't require an armed escort. But if the lover turned out to have been a Party member, the husband became an enemy of the people, with a 58-8 sentence.

An even more important extension of the concept was attained by interpreting Section 8 in terms of that same Article 19, i.e., intent in the sense of *preparation,* to include not only a direct threat against an activist uttered near a beer hall ("Just you wait!") but

---

[26] Legendary prince who founded the first Russian dynasty (ninth century).
[27] Russian acronym for Young Communist League.

also the quick-tempered retort of a peasant woman at the market ("Oh, drop dead!"). Both qualified as TN—Terrorist Intent—and provided a basis for applying the article in all its severity.

Section 9 concerned destruction or damage by explosion or arson (always with a counterrevolutionary purpose), for which the abbreviated term was "diversion"—in other words, sabotage.

The expansion of this section was based on the fact that the counterrevolutionary purpose could be discerned by the interrogator, who knew best what was going on in the criminal's mind. And every human error, failure, mistake at work or in the production process, remained unforgiven, and was therefore considered to be a case of "diversion."

But there was no section in Article 58 which was interpreted as broadly and with so ardent a revolutionary conscience as Section 10. Its definition was: "Propaganda or agitation, containing an appeal for the overthrow, subverting, or weakening of the Soviet power . . . and, equally, the dissemination or preparation or possession of literary materials of similar content." For this section in *peacetime* a minimum penalty only was set (not any less! not too light!); *no upper limit* was set for the maximum penalty.

Such was the fearlessness of the great Power when confronted by the *word* of a subject.

The famous extensions of this famous section were as follows: The scope of "agitation containing an appeal" was enlarged to include a face-to-face conversation between friends or even between husband and wife, or a private letter. The word "appeal" could mean personal advice. And we say "could mean" because, in fact, *it did*.

"Subverting and weakening" the government could include any idea which did not coincide with or rise to the level of intensity of the ideas expressed in the newspaper on any particular day. After all, anything which *does not strengthen* must *weaken*: Indeed, anything which does not completely fit in, coincide, *subverts!*

> And he who sings not with us today
> is against
> us!
> —MAYAKOVSKY[28]

----

[28] Vladimir Mayakovsky (1893–1930), a Russian poet and revolutionary; he committed suicide.

The term "preparation of literary materials" covered every letter, note, or private diary, even when only the original document existed.

Thus happily expanded, what *thought* was there, whether merely in the mind, spoken aloud, or jotted down, which was not covered by Section 10?

Section 11 was a special one; it had no independent content of its own, but provided for an aggravating factor in any of the preceding ones: if the action was undertaken by an organization or if the criminal joined an organization.

In actual practice, the section was so broadened that no organization whatever was required. I myself experienced the subtle application of this section. *Two* of us had secretly exchanged thoughts—*in other words* we were the beginnings of an organization, *in other words* an organization!

Section 12 concerned itself closely with the conscience of our citizens: it dealt with the *failure to make a denunciation* of any action of the types listed. And the penalty for the mortal sin of failure to make a denunciation *carried no maximum limit!*

This section was in itself such a fantastic extension of everything else that no further extension was needed. *He knew and he did not tell* became the equivalent of "He did it himself"!

Section 13, presumably long since out of date, had to do with service in the Tsarist secret police—the Okhrana.[29] (A subsequent form of analogous service was, on the contrary, considered patriotic.)

Section 14 stipulated the penalties for "conscious failure to carry out defined duties or intentionally careless execution of same." In brief this was called "sabotage" or "economic counter-revolution"—and the penalties, of course, included execution.

It was only the interrogator who, after consulting his revolutionary sense of justice, could separate what was intentional from what was unintentional. This section was applied to peasants who failed to come across with food deliveries. It was also applied to

[29]There are psychological bases for suspecting I. Stalin of having been liable under this section of Article 58 also. By no means all the documents relating to this type of service survived February, 1917, to become matters of public knowledge. V. F. Dzhunkovsky, a former tsarist police director, who died in the Kolyma, declared that the hasty burning of police archives in the first days of the February Revolution was a joint effort on the part of certain self-interested revolutionaries. [Solzhenitsyn's note. *Ed.*]

collective farmers who failed to work the required minimum number of "labor days"; to camp prisoners who failed to complete their work norms; and, in a peculiar ricochet, after the war it came to be applied to members of Russia's organized underworld of thieves, the blatnye or blatari, for escaping from camp. In other words, by an extension, a thief's flight from camp was interpreted as subversion of the camp system rather than as a dash to freedom.

Such was the last rib of the fan of Article 58—a fan whose spread encompassed all human existence.

Now that we have completed our review of this great Article of the Criminal Code, we are less likely to be astounded further on. Wherever the law is, crime can be found.

•   •   •

THE INTERROGATION [continued]

. . . The victims of the Bolsheviks[30] from 1918 to 1946 never conducted themselves so despicably as the leading Bolsheviks when the lightning struck them. If you study in detail the whole history of the arrests and trials of 1936 to 1938, the principal revulsion you feel is not against Stalin and his accomplices, but against the humiliatingly repulsive defendants—nausea at their spiritual baseness after their former pride and implacability.

So what is the answer? How can you stand your ground when you are weak and sensitive to pain, when people you love are still alive, when you are unprepared?

What do you need to make you stronger than the interrogator and the whole trap?

From the moment you go to prison you must put your cozy past firmly behind you. At the very threshold, you must say to yourself: "My life is over, a little early to be sure, but there's nothing to be done about it. I shall never return to freedom. I am condemned to die—now or a little later. But later on, in truth, it will be even

---

[30]Originally the revolutionary wing of the Russian Social Democratic Party in exile, the Bolsheviks (led by Lenin) came to power through the October revolution of 1917.

harder, and so the sooner the better. I no longer have any property whatsoever. For me those I love have died, and for them I have died. From today on, my body is useless and alien to me. Only my spirit and my conscience remain precious and important to me."

Confronted by such a prisoner, the interrogation will tremble.

Only the man who has renounced everything can win that victory.

But how can one turn one's body to stone?

Well, they managed to turn some individuals from the Berdyayev circle into puppets for a trial, but they didn't succeed with Berdyayev.[31] They wanted to drag him into an open trial; they arrested him twice; and (in 1922) he was subjected to a night interrogation by Dzerzhinsky[32] himself. Kamenev[33] was there too (which means that he, too, was not averse to using the Cheka in an ideological conflict). But Berdyayev did not humiliate himself. He did not beg or plead. He set forth firmly those religious and moral principles which had led him to refuse to accept the political authority established in Russia. And not only did they come to the conclusion that he would be useless for a trial, but they liberated him.

A human being has *a point of view!*

N. Stolyarova recalls an old woman who was her neighbor on the Butyrki bunks in 1937. They kept on interrogating her every night. Two years earlier, a former Metropolitan of the Orthodox Church, who had escaped from exile, had spent a night at her home on his way through Moscow. "But he wasn't the former Metropolitan, he was the Metropolitan! Truly, I was worthy of receiving him." "All right then. To whom did he go when he left Moscow?" "I know, but I won't tell you!" (The Metropolitan had escaped to Finland via an underground railroad of believers.) At first the interrogators took turns, and then they went after her in groups. They shook their fists in the little old woman's face, and she replied: "There is nothing you can do with me even if you cut me into pieces. After all, you are afraid of your bosses, and you are afraid of each other, and you are even afraid of killing me." (They would lose contact with the un-

[31] Nikolai Berdyayev (1874–1948), a philosopher and religious thinker who opposed atheism and materialism; he was expelled from Russia in 1922.
[32] Feliks Dzerzhinsky (1877–1926), first chief of the Soviet secret police (Cheka-GPU-OGPU).
[33] Lev Kamenev (1883–1936), a prominent Bolshevik leader; he was executed in 1936 after a show trial.

derground railroad.) "But I am not afraid of anything. I would be glad to be judged by God right this minute."

There were such people in 1937 too, people who did not return to their cell for their bundles of belongings, who chose death, who *signed* nothing denouncing anyone.

• • •

THE BLUECAPS[34]

So let the reader who expects this book to be a political exposé slam its covers shut right now.

If only it were all so simple! If only there were evil people somewhere insidiously committing evil deeds, and it were necessary only to separate them from the rest of us and destroy them. But the line dividing good and evil cuts through the heart of every human being. And who is willing to destroy a piece of his own heart?

During the life of any heart this line keeps changing place; sometimes it is squeezed one way by exuberant evil and sometimes it shifts to allow enough space for good to flourish. One and the same human being is, at various ages, under various circumstances, a totally different human being. At times he is close to being a devil, at times to sainthood. But his name doesn't change, and to that name we ascribe the whole lot, good and evil.

Socrates taught us: *Know thyself!*

Confronted by the pit into which we are about to toss those who have done us harm, we halt, stricken dumb: it is after all only because of the way things worked out that they were the executioners and we weren't.

• • •

. . . To do evil a human being must first of all believe that what he's doing is good, or else that it's a well-considered act in conformity with natural law. Fortunately, it is in the nature of the human being to seek a *justification* for his actions.

Macbeth's[35] self-justifications were feeble—and his conscience

---

[34] The members of the security police; the service caps they wore were blue.

[35] In Shakespeare's *Macbeth* (1606), the title-character, driven by ambition and his wife's urging, murders his king—and then continues to murder to protect his new royal position. Eventually, a psychologically broken man, he is killed in battle.

devoured him. Yes, even Iago[36] was a little lamb too. The imagination and the spiritual strength of Shakespeare's evildoers stopped short at a dozen corpses. Because they had no *ideology*.

Ideology—that is what gives evildoing its long-sought justification and gives the evildoer the necessary steadfastness and determination. That is the social theory which helps to make his acts seem good instead of bad in his own and others' eyes, so that he won't hear reproaches and curses but will receive praise and honors. That was how the agents of the Inquisition[37] fortified their wills: by invoking Christianity; the conquerors of foreign lands, by extolling the grandeur of their Motherland; the colonizers, by civilization; the Nazis, by race;[38] and the Jacobins[39] (early and late), by equality, brotherhood, and the happiness of future generations.

Thanks to *ideology*, the twentieth century was fated to experience evildoing on a scale calculated in the millions. This cannot be denied, nor passed over, nor suppressed. How, then, do we dare insist that evildoers do not exist? And who was it that destroyed these millions? Without evildoers there would have been no Archipelago.

There was a rumor going the rounds between 1918 and 1920 that the Petrograd Cheka, headed by Uritsky, and the Odessa Cheka, headed by Deich, did not shoot all those condemned to death but fed some of them alive to the animals in the city zoos. I do not know whether this is truth or calumny, or, if there were any such cases, how many there were. But I wouldn't set out to look for proof, either. Following the practice of the bluecaps, I would propose that they prove to us that this was impossible. How else could they get food for the zoos in those famine years? Take it away from the working class? Those enemies were going to die anyway, so why couldn't their deaths support the zoo economy of the Republic and thereby assist our march into the future? Wasn't it *expedient*?

That is the precise line the Shakespearean evildoer could not cross. But the evildoer with ideology does cross it, and his eyes remain dry and clear.

[36] The manipulative, murderous villain in Shakespeare's *Othello* (1604).

[37] An agency of the Roman Catholic Church that attempted to eliminate all forms of "heresy," often by brutal means; it was especially active in Spain from the fifteenth century to the nineteenth.

[38] The Nazi Party was the only official political party of the German nation during the years 1933 to 1945. It advanced a racist philosophy that advocated the elimination or subordination of all other races to the "master race."

[39] Members of a radical political organization, active mainly from 1789 to 1794, that promoted the Reign of Terror during the French Revolution.

Physics is aware of phenomena which occur only at *threshold* magnitudes, which do not exist at all until a certain *threshold* encoded by and known to nature has been crossed. No matter how intense a yellow light you shine on a lithium sample, it will not emit electrons. But as soon as a weak bluish light begins to glow, it does emit them. (The threshold of the photoelectric effect has been crossed.) You can cool oxygen to 100 degrees below zero Centigrade and exert as much pressure as you want; it does not yield, but remains a gas. But as soon as minus 183 degrees is reached, it liquefies and begins to flow.

Evidently evildoing also has a threshold magnitude. Yes, a human being hesitates and bobs back and forth between good and evil all his life. He slips, falls back, clambers up, repents, things begin to darken again. But just so long as the threshold of evildoing is not crossed, the possibility of returning remains, and he himself is still within reach of our hope. But when, through the density of evil actions, the result either of their own extreme degree or of the absoluteness of his power, he suddenly crosses that threshold, he has left humanity behind, and without, perhaps, the possibility of return. . . .

We have to condemn publicly the very *idea* that some people have the right to repress others. In keeping silent about evil, in burying it so deep within us that no sign of it appears on the surface, we are *implanting* it, and it will rise up a thousandfold in the future. When we neither punish nor reproach evildoers, we are not simply protecting their trivial old age, we are thereby ripping the foundations of justice from beneath new generations. It is for this reason, and not because of the "weakness of indoctrinational work," that they are growing up "indifferent." Young people are acquiring the conviction that foul deeds are never punished on earth, that they always bring prosperity.

It is going to be uncomfortable, horrible, to live in such a country!

• • •

. . . What about the main thing in life, all its riddles? If you want, I'll spell it out for you right now. Do not pursue what is illusory—property and position: all that is gained at the expense of your nerves decade after decade, and is confiscated in one fell night. Live with a steady superiority over life—don't be afraid of misfortune, and do not yearn after happiness; it is, after all, all the same: the bitter doesn't last forever, and the sweet never fills the cup to overflowing.

It is enough if you don't freeze in the cold and if thirst and hunger don't claw at your insides. If your back isn't broken, if your feet can walk, if both arms can bend, if both eyes see, and if both ears hear, then whom should you envy? And why? Our envy of others devours us most of all. Rub your eyes and purify your heart—and prize above all else in the world those who love you and who wish you well. Do not hurt them or scold them, and never part from any of them in anger; after all, you simply do not know: it might be your last act before your arrest, and that will be how you are imprinted in their memory!

· · ·

THE WAY OF LIFE AND CUSTOMS OF THE NATIVES

It has been known for centuries that Hunger . . . rules the world! (And all your Progressive Doctrine is, incidentally, built on Hunger, on the thesis that hungry people will inevitably revolt against the well-fed.) Hunger rules every hungry human being, unless he has himself consciously decided to die. Hunger, which forces an honest person to reach out and steal ("When the belly rumbles, conscience flees"). Hunger, which compels the most unselfish person to look with envy into someone else's bowl, and to try painfully to estimate what weight of ration his neighbor is receiving. Hunger, which darkens the brain and refuses to allow it to be distracted by anything else at all, or to think about anything else at all, or to speak about anything else at all except food, food, and food. Hunger, from which it is impossible to escape even in dreams—dreams are about food, and insomnia is over food. And soon—just insomnia. Hunger, after which one cannot even eat up; the man has by then turned into a one-way pipe and everything emerges from him in exactly the same state in which it was swallowed.

And this, too, the Russian cinema screen must see: how the last-leggers, jealously watching their competitors out of the corners of their eyes, stand duty at the kitchen porch waiting for them to bring out the slops in the dishwater. How they throw themselves on it, and fight with one another, seeking a fish head, a bone, vegetable parings. And how one last-legger dies, killed in that scrimmage. And how immediately afterward they wash off this waste and boil it and eat it. (And inquisitive cameramen can continue with their shooting and show us how, in 1947 in Dolinka, Bessarabian peasant women who had been brought in from *freedom* hurled themselves with that very same intent on slops which the last-leggers had *already checked over*.) The screen will show bags of bones which are still joined together lying under blankets at the hospital, dying almost without movement—and then being carried out. And on the whole . . . how simply a human being dies: he was speaking—and he fell silent; he was walking along the road—and he fell down. "Shudder and it's over." How (in camp at Unzha and Nuksha) the fat-faced, socially friendly work assigner jerks a zek[40] by the legs to get him out to line-up—and he turns out to be dead, and the corpse falls on its head on the floor. "Croaked, the scum!" And he gaily gives him a kick for good measure. (At those camps during the war there was no doctor's aide, not even an orderly, and as a result there were no sick, and anyone who pretended to be sick was taken out to the woods in his comrades' arms, and they also took a board and rope along so they could drag the corpse back the more easily. At work they laid the sick person down next to the bonfire, and it was to the interest of both the zeks and the convoy to have him die the sooner.)

What the screen cannot catch will be described to us in slow, meticulous prose, which will distinguish between the nuances of the various paths to death, which are sometimes called scurvy, sometimes pellagra, sometimes alimentary dystrophy. For instance, if there is blood on your bread after you have taken a bite—that is scurvy. From then on your teeth begin to fall out, your gums rot, ulcers appear on your legs, your flesh will begin to fall off in whole chunks, and you will begin to smell like a corpse. Your bloated legs collapse. They refuse to take such cases into the hospital, and they crawl on all fours around the camp compound. But if your face grows dark and your skin begins to peel and your entire organism is racked by diarrhea, this is pellagra. It is necessary to halt the diarrhea somehow—so they take three spoons of chalk a day, and they say that in this case if you can get and eat a lot of herring the food will begin to hold. But where are you going to get herring? The man grows weaker, weaker, and the bigger he is, the faster it goes. He has already become so weak that he cannot climb to the top bunks, he cannot step across a log in his path; he has to lift his leg with his two hands or else crawl on all fours. The diarrhea takes out of a man

---

[40]Russian prison slang for *prisoner*.

both strength and all interest—in other people, in life, in himself. He grows deaf and stupid, and he loses all capacity to weep, even when he is being dragged along the ground behind a sledge. He is no longer afraid of death; he is wrapped in a submissive, rosy glow. He has crossed all boundaries and has forgotten the name of his wife, of his children, and finally his own name too. Sometimes the entire body of a man dying of starvation is covered with blue-black pimples like peas, with pus-filled heads smaller than a pinhead—his face, arms, legs, his trunk, even his scrotum. It is so painful he cannot be touched. The tiny boils come to a head and burst and a thick wormlike string of pus is forced out of them. The man is rotting alive.

If black astonished head lice are crawling on the face of your neighbor on the bunks, it is a sure sign of death.

Fie! What naturalism. Why keep talking about all that?

And that is why they usually say today, those who did not themselves suffer, who were themselves the executioners, or who have washed their hands of it, or who put on an innocent expression: Why remember all that? Why rake over old wounds? (*Their* wounds!!)

Lev Tolstoi[41] had an answer for that—to Biryukov[42]: "What do you mean, why remember? If I have had a terrible illness, and I have succeeded in recovering from it and been cleansed of it, I will always remember gladly. The only time I will refuse to remember is when I am still ill and have got worse, and when I wish to deceive myself. If we remember the old and look it straight in the face, then our new and present violence will also disclose itself."

• • •

THE ARCHIPELAGO RISES FROM THE SEA

However, here is what it was like. In the summer of 1930 they brought to Solovki[43] several dozen religious sectarians who rejected

[41] Tolstoi (1828–1910), a great Russian novelist, dramatist, and philosopher—the author of such enormously successful works as *War and Peace*. In his later years he rejected all worldly values in order to live a simple, pacifistic, saintly life that rejected the organized church and state.

[42] Pavel Biryukov (1860–1931), a biographer and disciple of Tolstoi.

[43] A colloquial reference to the Solovetsky Islands, a group of islands in the White Sea that were the site of several monasteries; these were used as a place of exile for rebellious priests in the Middle Ages and as a forced-labor camp after the 1917 revolution.

anything that came from anti-Christ: they refused to accept any documents, including passports, and they refused to sign for anything or to handle any money. At their head was a gray-bearded old man of eighty, blind and bearing a long staff. Every enlightened person could clearly see that these sectarians could never ever enter into socialism, because that required having a great deal to do with papers—and that therefore the best thing for them to do was to die. And so they sent them off to Maly Zayatsky Island, the smallest in the entire Solovetsky archipelago—sandy, unforested desert, containing a summer hut of the former monk-fishermen. And they expressed willingness to give them two months' rations, the condition being that *each one* of the sectarians would have to sign for them on the invoice. Of course they refused. At this point the indefatigable Anna Skripnikova intervened; notwithstanding her own youth and the youth of the Soviet government, she had already been arrested for the fourth time. She dashed back and forth between the accounting office, the work assigners, and the chief of the camp himself, who was engaged in putting into effect the humanitarian regimen. She first besought compassion for them, and after that she begged to be sent to the Zayatsky Islands with the sectarians as their clerk, undertaking the obligation of issuing food to them each day and conducting all the bookkeeping formalities for them. And it would appear that this didn't conflict in any respect with the camp system. And the chiefs refused. "But they feed insane people without asking for signatures on receipts!" Anna cried. Zarin only burst out laughing. And a woman work assigner replied: "Maybe those are Moscow's orders—we don't really know. . . ." (Of course, they were instructions from Moscow—for who else would have taken the responsibility?) And so they were *sent off without food.* Two months later (exactly two months because they were then to be asked to sign for their food for the next two months) they sailed over to Maly Zayatsky and found only corpses which had been picked by the birds. Everyone was there. No one had escaped.

So who now is going to seek out those guilty? In the sixties of our great century?

• • •

IN PLACE OF POLITICALS

And not only socialists were now politicals. The politicals were splashed in tubfuls into the fifteen-million-criminal ocean, and they were invisible and inaudible to us. They were mute. They were muter than all the rest. Their image was the fish.

The fish, symbol of the early Christians. And the Christians were their principal contingent. Clumsy, semiliterate, unable to deliver speeches from the rostrum or compose an underground proclamation (which their faith made unnecessary anyway), they went off to camp to face tortures and death—only so as not to renounce their faith! They knew very well *for what* they were serving time, and they were unwavering in their convictions! They were the only ones, perhaps, to whom the camp philosophy and even the camp language did not stick. And were these not politicals? Well, you'd certainly not call them riffraff.

And women among them were particularly numerous. The Tao[44] says: When faith collapses, that is when the true believers appear. Because of our enlightened scoffing at Orthodox priests, the squalling of the Komsomol members on Easter night, and the whistles of the thieves at the transit prisons, we overlooked the fact that the sinful Orthodox Church had nonetheless nurtured daughters worthy of the first centuries of Christianity—sisters of those thrown to the lions in the arenas.

There was a multitude of Christians: prisoner transports and graveyards, prisoner transports and graveyards. Who will count those millions? They died unknown, casting only in their immediate vicinity a light like a candle. They were the best of Russia's Christians. The worst had all . . . trembled, recanted, and gone into hiding.

Is this not *more?* Was there ever a time when Tsarist Russia had known that many politicals? Tsarist Russia could not even count them in tens of thousands.

• • •

[44] The ultimate principle of the universe in the Chinese mystical philosophy of Taoism.

KNOCK, KNOCK, KNOCK . . .

. . . The skill of the security officer consisted in immediately picking the right master key. In one of the Siberian camps, a native of one of the Baltic countries, U., who knew Russian well (which was why the choice fell on him), was summoned "to the chief." And there in the chief's office sat an unfamiliar captain with an aquiline nose and the hypnotic gaze of a cobra. "Shut the door tight!" he warned very gravely, as if enemies were about to burst in, without lowering his burning eyes, which stared at U. from beneath shaggy brows—and inside U. everything wilted, something burned and suffocated him. Before summoning U., of course, the captain had gathered all the information available about him, and without even having seen him had determined that keys 1, 2, 3, and 4 would all be of no avail, that here only the last and strongest key could be used, but he kept staring for several minutes into U.'s unclouded, defenseless eyes, checking him out with his own eyes and at the same time depriving him of his will power, and already invisibly raising above him that which would immediately descend upon him.

The security chief took time for only the briefest introduction, speaking not in the tone of an abstract political catechism, but tensely, as if something were about to explode today or tomorrow right there in their own camp. "Do you know the world is divided into two camps, and one will be defeated, and we know very well which it will be? Do you know which? So that's how it is: if you want to survive, you must break away from the doomed capitalist shore and swim across to the new shore. Are you familiar with Latsis'[45] *To the New Shore?*" And he added a few more such phrases, and did not for a moment lower his hot threatening gaze, and having finally confirmed in his own mind the number of the key, he then asked with alarmed seriousness: "And *what about your family?*" And one by one, without ceremony, he reeled off all their names! And he knew the ages of the children too! That meant he had already familiarized himself with the family—that was very serious! "You understand, of course," he pronounced hypnotically, "that you and your family are

[45]Vilis Latsis (1904–66), a Latvian Communist novelist, served as premier of Soviet Latvia from 1940 to 1959. The prisoner was probably a Latvian. Thus, the security officer was intimating how the prisoner's countryman had cooperated with Soviet power.

a single whole. If you make a mistake and perish, your family will immediately perish too. We do not permit *the families of traitors* [his voice grew more meaningful] to go on living in the healthy Soviet environment. So make your choice between the two worlds! Between life and death! I am offering you an opportunity to pledge to assist the Security Section! In case you refuse, your entire family will be immediately imprisoned in camp! In our hands we have full power [how right he was!] and we are not accustomed to backtrack on our decisions. [Once again he was right!] Since we have chosen you, you *will* work with us!''

All this was loosed suddenly on U.'s head. He was not prepared for it. He would never have thought of it. He had considered that only scoundrels became informers. But that they might approach him? A blow—direct, without waste motion, without the cushion of time—and the captain was waiting for his answer, and was about to explode right then, and then everything would explode! And U. took thought: What is there that is really impossible for them? When have they ever spared anyone's family? They didn't hesitate to liquidate the "kulak"[46] families right down to tiny children, and they even wrote about it proudly in the newspaper. U. had also seen the work of the Organs in 1940 and 1941 in the Baltic States, and had gone to the prison yards to look at the pile of executed prisoners during the Soviet retreat. And in 1944 he had heard the Baltic broadcasts from Leningrad. Like the captain's gaze at this moment, they had been full of threats and had breathed revenge. They promised reprisals against *all,* against every last person who had aided the enemy.

And so what was there to compel them to show mercy now? To ask for it was useless. It was necessary to choose. (But here is what U., himself a victim of the myth of the Organs, did not yet realize: That machine possessed no such magnificent coordination and interlinked responsiveness as would ensure that when he refused today to become an informer in a Siberian camp his family would be hauled off to Siberia in a week's time. And there was one more thing he didn't realize either. No matter how poor his opinion of the Organs, they were even worse than he thought: the hour would soon strike when all these families, all these hundreds of thousands of

---

[46] The comparatively wealthy peasants who owned their own land before the October revolution of 1917.

families, would troop off into common exile, where they would perish, without any reference to how the fathers were behaving in camp.)

Fear for himself would not have shaken him. But U. pictured his wife and daughter in camp conditions—in these same barracks where lechery wasn't even curtained off, where there was no defense whatever for any woman under sixty. And . . . he shuddered. The correct key had been picked. None other would have opened the door, but this one did.

But he still dragged things out a bit: "I have to think it over." "All right, think it over for three days, but don't talk it over with even a single person. *You will be shot for disclosure!"* (And U. goes to get advice from a fellow national—the very same, in fact, against whom he is being told to write his first denunciation, and, in fact, they edit it together. For this friend admits it is impossible to risk his family.)

On his second visit to the captain, U. signs the devil's receipt, and receives his assignment and his contact; he is not to go to the office any more; he is to conduct all his business through the unconvoyed trusty Frol Ryabinin.

This is an important constituent of the work of the camp security chief: These "residents" are scattered throughout the camp. Frol Ryabinin is the most vociferous of all "among the people," a prankster. Frol Ryabinin is a popular personality. Frol Ryabinin has some sort of under-the-counter work or other, and a separate cabin of his own, and always has money. With the security chief's help he has got into the depths and currents of camp life, and he hovers in them, comfortably at home. Such "residents" as he are the cables on which the whole network hangs.

Frol Ryabinin instructs U. that he must transmit his reports in a dark nook. ("In *our* work the main thing is conspiracy.") He summons him to his private quarters: "The captain is dissatisfied with your report. You have to write so that there's *material* against a person. I'm going to teach you how."

And this stinking snoot teaches the wan, depressed intellectual U. how to write filth against people! But U.'s downcast look leads Ryabinin to his own conclusion: it is necessary to liven this ninny up, to heat him up a little! And he says to him in a friendly way: "Listen, your life is a hard one. You sometimes want to buy something to add to your bread ration. The captain wants to help you. Here, take this!" And he takes a fifty-ruble bill from his billfold.

(And this is the captain's! And that is how free of auditors *they* are, and maybe they are the only ones in the whole country!) And he shoves it at U.

And suddenly, at the sight of this pale-green toad which has been pushed into his hands, all the spells cast by the cobra captain, all the hypnosis, all the constraint, even all the fear for his family—all that has taken place, its entire meaning, is objectified in this loathsome bill with its greenish phlegm, these commonplace Judas silver pieces. And without even stopping to think what will happen to his family, with the natural gesture of warding off filth, U. pushes away the fifty-ruble bill, and the uncomprehending Ryabinin shoves it at him again, and U. throws it on the floor and gets up, already relieved, already *free* both of the moral teachings of Ryabinin and of his signature given to the captain, free of those paper conditions in the face of the great duty of a human being! He leaves without asking permission! He walks through the camp compound on legs light as air: "I'm free! I'm free!"

Well, not entirely so. A stupid security chief would have kept on hauling him in. But the cobra captain understood that the stupid Ryabinin had spoiled the threading, had used the wrong key. And the pincers no longer sought out U. in that camp, and Ryabinin would pass him without greeting. U. calmed down and was glad. And at this point they began to send the 58's off to the Special Camps, and he was sent to Steplag. And he thought that this prisoner transport would break the chain all the more.

But not at all! A notation evidently remained in his file. At his new place U. was summoned to a colonel: "They tell me you agreed to work with us but that you *do not deserve our trust.* Perhaps they didn't explain it to you clearly."

However, this colonel inspired no fear in U. And, in addition, U.'s family, like the families of many of the inhabitants of the Baltic States, had been resettled in Siberia by this time. There was no doubt about it: he had to get them off his back. But what pretext could he use?

The colonel turned him over to a lieutenant for the latter to work him over. And this lieutenant jumped up and down and threatened and promised while U. kept trying to find a way of forcefully and decisively turning them down.

Though he was an enlightened and irreligious person, U. discovered that the only defense against them was to hide behind Christ.

This was not very honest, but it was a sure thing. He lied: "I must tell you frankly that I had a Christian upbringing, and therefore it is quite impossible for me to work with you!"

And that ended it! And all the lieutenant's chatter, which had by then lasted many hours, simply stopped! The lieutenant understood he had drawn a bad number. "We need you like a dog needs five legs," he exclaimed petulantly. "Give me a written refusal." (Once again "written"!) "And write just that, explaining about your damned god!"

Apparently they have to close the case of every informer with a separate piece of paper, just as they open it with one. The reference to Christ satisfied the lieutenant completely: none of the security officers would accuse him subsequently of failing to use every effort he could.

And does the impartial reader not find that they flee from Christ like devils from the sign of the cross, from the bells calling to matins?

And that is why our Soviet regime can never come to terms with Christianity!

• • •

THE KIDS

Zoya Leshcheva managed to outdo her whole family. And here is how. Her father, her mother, her grandfather, her grandmother, and her elder adolescent brothers had all been scattered to distant camps because of their faith in God. But Zoya was a mere ten years old. They took her to an orphanage in Ivanovo Province. And there she declared she would never remove the cross from around her neck, the cross which her mother had hung there when she said farewell. And she tied the knot of the cord tighter so they would not be able to remove it when she was asleep. The struggle went on and on for a long time. Zoya became enraged: "You can strangle me and then take it off a corpse!" Then she was sent to an orphanage *for retarded children* — because she would not submit to their training. And in that orphanage were the dregs, a category of kids worse than anything described in this chapter. The struggle for the cross went on and on. Zoya stood her ground. Even here she refused to learn to steal or to curse. "A mother as sacred as mine must never have a daughter who is a criminal. I would rather be a political, like my whole family."

And she became a political! And the more her instructors and the radio praised Stalin, the more clearly she saw in him the culprit responsible for all their misfortunes. And, refusing to give in to the criminals, she now began to win them over to her views! In the courtyard stood one of those mass-produced plaster statues of Stalin. And mocking and indecent graffiti began to appear on it. (Kids love sport! The important thing is to point them in the right direction.) The administration kept repainting the statue, kept watch over it, and reported the situation to the MGB. And the graffiti kept on appearing, and the kids kept on laughing. Finally one morning they found that the statue's head had been knocked off and turned upside down, and inside it were feces.

This was a terrorist act! The MGB came. And began, in accordance with all their rules, their interrogations and threats: "Turn over the gang of terrorists to us, otherwise *we are going to shoot the lot of you* for terrorism!" (And there would have been nothing remarkable if they had: so what, 150 children shot! If He Himself had known about it, he would himself have given the order.)

It's not known whether the kids would have stood up to them or given in, but Zoya Leshcheva declared: "I did it all myself! What else is the head of that papa good for?"

And she was tried. And she was sentenced *to the supreme measure,* no joke. But because of the intolerable humanitarianism of the 1950 law on the restoration of capital punishment the execution of a four-teen-year-old was forbidden. And therefore they gave her a "ten-ner"(it's surprising it wasn't twenty-five). Up to the age of eighteen she was in ordinary camps, and from the age of eighteen on she was in Special Camps. For her directness and her language she got a second camp sentence and, it seems, a third one as well.

Zoya's parents had already been freed and her brothers too, but Zoya languished on in camp.

Long live our tolerance of religion!
Long live our children, the masters of Communism!
And let any country speak up that can say it has loved its children as we have ours!

• • •

OR CORRUPTION?

Shalamov[47] says: Everyone imprisoned in camp was spiritually impoverished. But whenever I recall or encounter a former zek, I find a real personality.

Elsewhere Shalamov himself writes that he wouldn't betray other zeks! He wouldn't become a brigadier and compel others to work.

Why is that, Varlam Tikhonovich? Why is it that out of a clear sky it appears that you would refuse to become either a stoolie or a brigadier—if it is the case that no one in camp can avoid or sidestep that slippery slope of corruption? Given the fact that truth and falsehood . . . are kin sisters? Does it mean that you did nonetheless grasp at some branch sticking out? Does it mean that you found a footing on some stone—and did not slide down any further? And maybe, despite everything, anger is not really the most long-lived feeling there is? Do you not refute your own concept with your character and verses?

And how is it that genuine religious believers survived in camp (as we mentioned more than once)? In the course of this book we have already mentioned their self-confident procession through the Archipelago—a sort of silent religious procession with invisible candles. How some among them were mowed down by machine guns and those next in line continued their march. A steadfastness unheard of in the twentieth century! And it was not in the least for show, and there weren't any declamations. Take some Aunt Dusya Chmil, a round-faced, calm, and quite illiterate old woman. The convoy guards called out to her: "Chmil! What is your article?"

And she gently, good-naturedly replied: "Why are you asking, my boy? It's all written down there. I can't remember them all." (She had a bouquet of sections under Article 58.)

"Your term!"

Auntie Dusya sighed. She wasn't giving such contradictory answers in order to annoy the convoy. In her own simplehearted way she pondered this question: Her term? Did they really think it was given to human beings to know their terms?

"What term! . . . Till God forgives my sins—till then I'll be serving time."

---

[47]Varlam Tikhonovich Shalamov (1907–   ), a Soviet writer who spent seventeen years in the prison camps.

"You are a silly, you! A silly!" The convoy guards laughed. "Fifteen years you've got, and you'll serve them all, and maybe some more besides."

But after two and a half years of her term had passed, even though she had sent no petitions—all of a sudden a piece of paper came: release!

How could one not envy those people? Were circumstances more favorable for them? By no means! It is a well-known fact that the "nuns" were kept only with prostitutes and thieves at penalty camps. And yet who was there among the religious believers whose soul was corrupted? They died—most certainly, but . . . they were not corrupted.

And how can one explain that certain unstable people found faith right there in camp, that they were strengthened by it, and that they survived uncorrupted?

And many more, scattered about and unnoticed, came to their allotted turning point and made no mistake in their choice. Those who managed to see that things were not only bad for them, but even worse, even harder, for their neighbors.

And all those who, under the threat of a penalty zone and a new term of imprisonment, refused to become stoolies?

How, in general, can one explain Grigory Ivanovich Grigoryev, a soil scientist? A scientist who volunteered for the People's Volunteer Corps in 1941—and the rest of the story is a familiar one. Taken prisoner near Vyazma, he spent his whole captivity in a German camp. And the subsequent story is also familiar. When he returned, he was arrested by us and given a tenner. I came to know him in winter, engaged in general work in Ekibastuz. His forthrightness gleamed from his big quiet eyes, some sort of unwavering forthrightness. This man was never able to bow in spirit. And he didn't bow in camp either, even though he worked only two of his ten years in his own field of specialization, and didn't receive food parcels from home for nearly the whole term. He was subjected on all sides to the camp philosophy, to the camp corruption of soul, but he was incapable of adopting it. In the Kemerovo camps (Antibess) the security chief kept trying to recruit him as a stoolie. Grigoryev replied to him quite honestly and candidly: "I find it quite *repulsive* to talk to you. You will find many willing without me." "You bastard, you'll crawl on all fours." "I would be better off hanging myself on the first branch." And so he was sent off to a penalty situation. He stood it for half a year. And he made *mistakes* which were even more unforgivable: When he was sent on an agricultural work party, he refused (as a soil scientist) to accept the post of brigadier offered him. He hoed and scythed with enthusiasm. And even more stupidly: in Ekibastuz at the stone quarry he refused to be a work checker—only because he would have had to pad the work sheets for the sloggers, for which, later on, when they caught up with it, the eternally drunk free foreman would have to pay the penalty. (But would he?) And so he went to break rocks! His honesty was so monstrously unnatural that when he went out to process potatoes with the vegetable storeroom brigade, he did not steal any, though everyone else did. When he was in a good post, in the privileged repair-shop brigade at the pumping-station equipment, he left simply because he refused to wash the socks of the free bachelor construction supervisor, Treivish. (His fellow brigade members tried to persuade him: Come on now, isn't it all the same, the kind of work you do? But no, it turned out it was not at all the same to him!) How many times did he select the worst and hardest lot, just so as not to have to offend against conscience—and he didn't, not in the least, and I am a witness. And even more: because of the astounding influence on his body of his bright and spotless human spirit (though no one today believes in any such influence, no one understands it) the organism of Grigory Ivanovich, who was no longer young (close to fifty), grew stronger in camp; his earlier rheumatism of the joints disappeared completely, and he became particularly healthy after the typhus from which he recovered: in winter he went out in cotton sacks, making holes in them for his head and his arms—and he did not catch cold!

So wouldn't it be more correct to say that no camp can corrupt those who have a stable nucleus, who do not accept that pitiful ideology which holds that "human beings are created for happiness," an ideology which is done in by the first blow of the work assigner's cudgel?

Those people became corrupted in camp who before camp had not been enriched by any morality at all or by any spiritual upbringing. (This is not at all a theoretical matter—since during our glorious half-century millions of them grew up.)

Those people became corrupted in camp who had already been corrupted out in freedom or who were ready for it. Because people are corrupted in freedom too, sometimes even more effectively than in camp.

The convoy officer who ordered that Moiseyevaite[48] be tied to a post in order to be mocked—had he not been corrupted more profoundly than the camp inmates who spat on her?

And for that matter did every one of the brigade members spit on her? Perhaps only two from each brigade did. In fact, that is probably what happened.

Tatyana Falike writes: "Observation of people convinced me that no man could become a scoundrel in camp if he had not been one before."

If a person went swiftly bad in camp, what it might mean was that he had not just gone bad, but that that inner foulness which had not previously been needed had disclosed itself.

M. A. Voichenko has his opinion: "In camp, existence did not determine consciousness, but just the opposite: consciousness and steadfast faith in the human essence decided whether you became an animal or remained a human being."

A drastic, sweeping declaration! . . . But he was not the only one who thought so. The artist Ivashev-Musatov passionately argued exactly the same thing.

Yes, camp corruption was a mass phenomenon. But not only because the camps were awful, but because in addition we Soviet people stepped upon the soil of the Archipelago spiritually disarmed—long since prepared to be corrupted, already tinged by it out in freedom, and we strained our ears to hear from the old camp veterans "how to live in camp."

But we ought to have known how to live (and how to die) without any camp.

And perhaps, Varlam Tikhonovich Shalamov, as a general rule friendship between people does arise in need and misfortune, even in extreme misfortune too—but not between such withered and nasty people as we were, given our decades of upbringing?

If corruption was so inevitable, then why did Olga Lvovna Sliozberg not abandon her freezing friend on the forest trail, but stay behind for nearly certain death together with her—and save her? Wasn't that an extreme of misfortune?

And if corruption was so inevitable, then where did Vasily Mefodyevich Yakovenko spring from? He served out two terms, had only

---

[48] A prisoner. The names mentioned in subsequent paragraphs are likewise those of prisoners or former prisoners.

just been released, was living as a free employee in Vorkuta, and was just beginning to crawl around without an escort and acquire his first tiny nest. It was 1949. In Vorkuta they began to rearrest former zeks and give them new sentences. An arrest psychosis! There was panic among the free employees! How could they hold on to their freedom? How could they be less noticeable? But Y. D. Grodzensky, a friend of Yakovenko from the same Vorkuta camp, was arrested. During the interrogation he was losing strength and was close to death. There was no one to bring him food parcels. And Yakovenko fearlessly brought him food parcels! If you want to, you dogs, rake me in too!

Why was *this man* not corrupted!

And do not *all* those who survived remember one or another person who reached out a hand to him in camp and saved him at a difficult moment?

Yes, the camps were calculated and intended to corrupt. But this didn't mean that they succeeded in crushing *everyone*.

Just as in nature the process of oxidation never occurs without an accompanying reduction (one substance oxidizes while at the same time another reduces), so in camp, too (and everywhere in life), there is no corruption without ascent. They exist alongside one another. . . .

II
Technology

6

C. P. Snow

The Two Cultures

The increasing difficulty in communicating ideas and feelings between those educated in the traditional literary culture and those trained in the new scientific attitudes is a special concern of C(harles) P(ercy) Snow (1905–). Born to a poor English family in the industrial city of Leicester, Snow desired a career as a writer but decided early on that he could more likely make his way in the world as a scientist. By winning a series of scholarships he eventually earned degrees in chemistry and physics from Leicester University and a doctorate in physics from Cambridge University (1930). He remained associated with Cambridge for the next twenty years as Fellow of Christ's College.

With the outbreak of the Second World War, Snow became director of technical personnel for the Ministry of Labor. At the end of the war he was appointed a Civil Service Commissioner with the special task of selecting scientists for government projects; he also held the post of physicist-director of the English Electric Company (1947–64). Snow at last fulfilled his literary ambition by combining his scientific training, administrative experience, and knowledge of social classes in the creation of a series of eleven novels called Strangers and Brothers (1939–), his most noted literary work. Snow's credibility is strongest in the novels when he depicts academic politics and the moral dilemmas of scientists and other "new men" who pace the "corridors of power." Some critics, however, have held his characters to be essentially sterile, moving with scientific precision like mechanical men. In any event, the public service and literary works of C. P. Snow have been recognized of-

ficially by the British government: knighthood was conferred upon him in 1957 and he was made a lord (Baron of Leicester) in 1964.

In the following selection Lord Snow defines and deplores the hostility between the scientific and literary "cultures." The book from which the selection is taken, The Two Cultures: And a Second Look *(1963), is an expanded version of a lecture given by Snow in 1959 and called "The Two Cultures and the Scientific Revolution." The sometimes defensive tone of the later version, as shown in the excerpt, reflects the savage personal attack made upon Snow by F. R. Leavis, of Cambridge University, after Snow's original lecture. Leavis had attempted to demolish Snow's reputation as a novelist, repudiating what he considered to be Snow's "anti-human" views of science.*

In both versions of The Two Cultures *the second theme employed by Snow is the widening gap between the rich nations and the poor ones, which can be remedied, he believes, by a worldwide diffusion of the scientific revolution. The "decision-makers" of all countries, therefore, must be capable of evaluating scientific advice—which, as in the two-culture conflict over the advisability of utilizing nuclear power, is often difficult. Snow ends his piece with a plea for intellectually unified education in which "our better minds . . . are not ignorant of imaginative experience, both in the arts and in science" and will, therefore, be in a position to abolish "the remediable suffering of most of their fellow humans."*

In our society (that is, advanced western society) we have lost even the pretence of a common culture. Persons educated with the greatest intensity we know can no longer communicate with each other on the plane of their major intellectual concern. This is serious for our creative, intellectual and, above all, our normal life. It is leading us to interpret the past wrongly, to misjudge the present, and to deny our hopes of the future. It is making it difficult or impossible for us to take good action.

I gave the most pointed example of this lack of communication in the shape of two groups of people, representing what I have christened "the two cultures." One of these contained the scientists, whose weight, achievement and influence did not need stressing. The other contained the literary intellectuals. I did not mean that literary intellectuals act as the main decision-makers of the western world. I meant that literary intellectuals represent, vocalise, and to some extent shape and predict the mood of the non-scientific culture: they do not make the decisions, but their words seep into the minds of those who do. Between these two groups—the scientists and the literary intellectuals—there is little communication and, instead of fellow-feeling, something like hostility.

This was intended as a description of, or a very crude first approximation to, our existing state of affairs. That it was a state of affairs I passionately disliked, I thought was made fairly clear. . . .

To finish this précis. There is, of course, no complete solution. In the conditions of our age, or any age which we can foresee, Renaissance man is not possible. But we can do something. The chief means open to us is education—education mainly in primary and secondary schools, but also in colleges and universities. There is no excuse for letting another generation be as vastly ignorant, or as devoid of understanding and sympathy, as we are ourselves.

From the beginning, the phrase "the two cultures" evoked some protests. The word "culture" or "cultures" has been objected to: so, with much more substance, has the number two. (No one, I think, has yet complained about the definite article.)

I must have a word about these verbal points before I come to the more wide-reaching arguments. The term "culture" in my title has two meanings, both of which are precisely applicable to the theme. First, "culture" has the sense of the dictionary definition, "intellectual development, development of the mind." For many years this definition has carried overtones, often of a deep and ambiguous sort. It happens that few of us can help searching for a refined use of the word: if anyone asks, What is culture? Who is cultured? the needle points, by an extraordinary coincidence, in the direction of ourselves.

But that, though a pleasing example of human frailty, doesn't matter: what does matter is that any refined definition, from Coleridge[1] onwards, applies at least as well (and also as imperfectly) to the development a scientist achieves *in the course of his professional vocation* as to the "traditional" mental development or any of its offshoots. Coleridge said "cultivation" where we should say "cul-

---

[1] Samuel Taylor Coleridge (1772–1834), an English poet, philosopher, and critic.

ture"—and qualified it as "the harmonious development of those qualities and faculties which characterise our humanity." Well, none of us manages that; in plain truth, either of our cultures, whether literary or scientific, only deserves the name of subculture. *"Qualities and faculties which characterise our humanity."* Curiosity about the natural world, the use of symbolic systems of thought, are two of the most precious and the most specifically human of all human qualities. The traditional methods of mental development left them to be starved. So, in reverse, does scientific education starve our verbal faculties—the language of symbols is given splendid play, the language of words is not. On both sides we underestimate the spread of a human being's gifts.

But, if we are to use "culture" in its refined sense at all, it is only lack of imagination, or possibly blank ignorance, which could deny it to scientists. There is no excuse for such ignorance. A whole body of literature has been built up over a generation, written, incidentally, in some of the most beautiful prose of our time, to demonstrate the intellectual, aesthetic and moral values inherent in the pursuit of science (compare A. N. Whitehead's *Science and the Modern World,* G. H. Hardy's *A Mathematician's Apology,* J. Bronowski's *Science and Human Values*). There are valuable insights scattered all over American and English writing of the last decade—Needham, Toulmin, Price, Piel, Newman, are only a few of the names that come to mind.

In the most lively of all contributions to this subject, a Third Programme feature[2] not yet published, Bronowski deliberately avoided the word "culture" for either side and chose as his title "Dialogue between Two World Systems." For myself, I believe the word is still appropriate and carries its proper meaning to sensible persons. But, while sticking to that word, I want to repeat what was intended to be my main message, but which has somehow got overlaid: that neither the scientific system of mental development, nor the traditional, is adequate for our potentialities, for the work we have in front of us, for the world in which we ought to begin to live.

The word "culture" has a second and technical meaning, which I pointed out explicitly in the original lecture. It is used by anthropologists to denote a group of persons living in the same environment, linked by common habits, common assumptions, a common way of

---

[2] A radio lecture series of the British Broadcasting Corporation.

life. Thus one talks of a Neanderthal culture, a La Tène culture, a Trobriand Island culture: the term, which is a very useful one, has been applied to groups within our own societies. For me this was a very strong additional reason for selecting the word; it isn't often one gets a word which can be used in two senses, both of which one explicitly intends. For scientists on the one side, literary intellectuals on the other, do in fact exist as cultures within the anthropological scope. There are, as I said before, common attitudes, common standards and patterns of behaviour, common approaches and assumptions. This does not mean that a person within a culture loses his individuality and free will. It does mean that, without knowing it, we are more than we think children of our time, place and training. Let me take two trivial and non-controversial examples. The overwhelming majority of the scientific culture (that is, the group of scientists observed through anthropological eyes) would feel certain, without needing to cogitate or examine their souls, that research was the primary function of a university. This attitude is automatic, it is part of their culture: but it would not be the attitude of such a proportion in the literary culture. On the other hand, the overwhelming majority of the literary culture would feel just as certain that not the slightest censorship of the printed word is, in any circumstances, permissible. This position doesn't have to be reached by individual thought: again it is part of the culture. It is such an unquestioned part, in fact, that the literary intellectuals have got their way more absolutely than, thirty years ago, would have seemed conceivable. . . . So the phrase "the two cultures" still seems appropriate for the purpose I had in mind. I now think, however, that I should have stressed more heavily that I was speaking as an Englishman, from experience drawn mainly from English society. I did in fact say this, and I said also that this cultural divide seems at its sharpest in England. I now realise that I did not emphasise it enough.

In the United States, for example, the divide is nothing like so unbridgeable. There are pockets of the literary culture, influenced by the similar culture in England, which are as extreme in resisting communication and in ceasing to communicate: but that isn't generally true over the literary culture as a whole, much less over the entire intellectual society. And, just because the divide is not so deep, just because the situation is not accepted as a fact of life, far more active steps are being taken to improve it. This is an interesting example of one of the laws of social change: change doesn't happen when things are at their worst, but when they are looking up. So it is at Yale and Princeton and Michigan and California, that scientists of world standing are talking to nonspecialised classes: at M.I.T. and Cal. Tech. where students of the sciences are receiving a serious humane education. In the last few years, all over the country, a visitor cannot help being astonished by the resilience and inventiveness of American higher education—ruefully so, if he happens to be an Englishman.

• • •

Major scientific breakthroughs, and in particular those as closely connected to human flesh and bone as this one in molecular biology, or even more, another which we may expect in the nature of the higher nervous system, are bound to touch both our hopes and our resignations. That is: ever since men began to think introspectively about themselves, they have made guesses, and sometimes had profound intuitions, about those parts of their own nature which seemed to be predestined. It is possible that within a generation some of these guesses will have been tested against exact knowledge. No one can predict what such an intellectual revolution will mean: but I believe that one of the consequences will be to make us feel not less but more responsible towards our brother men.

It was for this reason among others that, in the original lecture, I drew a distinction between the individual condition and the social condition. In doing so, I stressed the solitariness, the ultimate tragedy, at the core of each individual life; and this has worried a good many who found the rest of the statement acceptable. It is very hard, of course, to subdue the obsessions of one's own temperament; this specific note creeps into a good deal of what I have written, as Alfred Kazin[3] has shrewdly pointed out: it is not an accident that my novel sequence is called *Strangers and Brothers*. Nevertheless, this distinction, however it is drawn, is imperative, unless we are going to sink into the facile social pessimism of our time, unless we are going to settle into our own egocentric chill.

So I will try to make the statement without much emphasis of my own. We should most of us agree, I think, that in the individual life of each of us there is much that, in the long run, one cannot do anything about. Death is a fact—one's own death, the deaths of those

[3] An American literary critic (1915–   ).

one loves. There is much that makes one suffer which is irremediable: one struggles against it all the way, but there is an irremediable residue left. These are facts: they will remain facts as long as man remains man. This is part of the individual condition: call it tragic, comic, absurd, or, like some of the best and bravest of people, shrug it off.

But it isn't all. One looks outside oneself to other lives, to which one is bound by love, affection, loyalty, obligation: each of those lives has the same irremediable components as one's own; but there are also components that one can help, or that can give one help. It is in this tiny extension of the personality, it is in this seizing on the possibilities of hope, that we become more fully human: it is a way to improve the quality of one's life: it is, for oneself, the beginning of the social condition.

Finally, one can try to understand the condition of lives, not close to one's own, which one cannot know face to face. Each of these lives—that is, the lives of one's fellow human beings—again has limits of irremediability like one's own. Each of them has needs, some of which can be met: the totality of all is the social condition.

We cannot know as much as we should about the social condition all over the world. But we can know, we do know, two most important things. First we can meet the harsh facts of the flesh, on the level where all of us are, or should be, one. We know that the vast majority, perhaps two-thirds, of our fellow men are living in the immediate presence of illness and premature death; their expectation of life is half of ours, most are under-nourished, many are near to starving, many starve. Each of these lives is afflicted by suffering, different from that which is intrinsic in the individual condition. But this suffering is unnecessary and can be lifted. This is the second important thing which we know—or, if we don't know it, there is no excuse or absolution for us.

We cannot avoid the realisation that applied science has made it possible to remove unnecessary suffering from a billion individual human lives—to remove suffering of a kind, which, in our own privileged society, we have largely forgotten, suffering so elementary that it is not genteel to mention it. For example, we *know* how to heal many of the sick: to prevent children dying in infancy and mothers in childbirth: to produce enough food to alleviate hunger: to throw up a minimum of shelter: to ensure that there aren't so many births that our other efforts are in vain. All this we *know* how to do.

It does not require one additional scientific discovery, though new scientific discoveries must help us. It depends on the spread of the scientific revolution all over the world. There is no other way. For most human beings, this is the point of hope. It will certainly happen. It may take longer than the poor will peacefully accept. How long it takes, and the fashion in which it is done, will be a reflex of the quality of our lives, especially of the lives of those of us born lucky: as most in the western world were born. When it is achieved, then our consciences will be a little cleaner; and those coming after us will at least be able to think that the elemental needs of others aren't a daily reproach to any sentient person, that for the first time some genuine dignity has come upon us all.

Man doesn't live by bread alone—yes, that has been said often enough in the course of these discussions. It has been said occasionally with a lack of imagination, a provincialism, that makes the mind boggle: for it is not a remark that one of us in the western world can casually address to most Asians, to most of our fellow human beings, in the world as it now exists. But we can, we should, say it to ourselves. For we know how, once the elemental needs are satisfied, we do not find it easy to do something worthy and satisfying with our lives. Probably it will never be easy. Conceivably men in the future, if they are as lucky as we are now, will struggle with our existential discontents, or new ones of their own. They may, like some of us, try—through sex or drink or drugs—to intensify the sensational life. Or they may try to improve the quality of their lives, through an extension of their responsibilities, a deepening of the affections and the spirit, in a fashion which, though we can aim at it for ourselves and our own societies, we can only dimly perceive.

But, though our perception may be dim, it isn't dim enough to obscure one truth: that one mustn't despise the elemental needs, when one has been granted them and others have not. To do so is not to display one's superior spirituality. It is simply to be inhuman, or more exactly anti-human.

Here, in fact, was what I intended to be the centre of the whole argument. Before I wrote the lecture I thought of calling it "The Rich and the Poor," and I rather wish that I hadn't changed my mind.

The scientific revolution is the only method by which most people can gain the primal things (years of life, freedom from hunger, survival for children)—the primal things which we take for granted and which have in reality come to us through having had our own scientific revolution not so long ago. Most people want these primal things. Most people, wherever they are being given a chance, are rushing into the scientific revolution.

To misunderstand this position is to misunderstand both the present and the future. It simmers beneath the surface of world politics. Though the form of politics may look the same, its content is being altered as the scientific revolution pours in. We have not been as quick as we should to draw the right consequences, very largely because of the division of the cultures. It has been hard for politicians and administrators to grasp the practical truth of what scientists were telling them. But now it is beginning to be accepted. It is often accepted most easily by men of affairs, whatever their political sympathies, engineers, or priests, or doctors, all those who have a strong comradely physical sympathy for other humans. If others can get the primal things—yes, that is beyond argument; that is simply good.

Curiously enough, there are many who would call themselves liberals and yet who are antipathetic to this change. Almost as though sleepwalking they drift into an attitude which, to the poor of the world, is a denial of all human hope. This attitude, which misinterprets both the present and the future, seems to be connected with a similar misinterpretation of the past. It is on this point that representatives of the putative third culture have been speaking with trenchancy.

The argument is about the first wave of the scientific revolution, the transformation which we call the industrial revolution, and it is occupied with questions about what, in the most elementary human terms, life was like in pre-industrial as compared with industrial society. We can gain some insights, of course, from the present world, which is a vast sociological laboratory in which one can observe all kinds of society from the neolithic to the advanced industrial. We are also now accumulating substantial evidence of our own past.

When I made some remarks about the industrial revolution, I had imagined that the findings of recent research in social history were better known. Otherwise I should have documented what I said: but that seemed like documenting a platitude. Did anyone think that, in the primal terms in which I have just been discussing the poor countries of the present world, our ancestors' condition was so very different? Or that the industrial revolution had not brought us in three or four generations to a state entirely new in the harsh, unrecorded continuity of poor men's lives? I couldn't believe it. I knew, of course, the force of nostalgia, myth, and plain snobbery. In all families, at all times, there are stories of blessed existences, just before one's childhood: there were in my own. Myth—I ought to have remembered what Malinowski[4] taught us, that people believe their myths as fact. I certainly ought to have remembered that, when anyone is asked what he would have been in a previous incarnation, he nominates—if he is modest—something like a Jacobean cleric or an eighteenth-century squire. He wouldn't have been any such thing. The overwhelming probability is that he would have been a peasant. If we want to talk about our ancestors, that is whence we came.

I was at fault, I suppose, in not trying to be more persuasive against these kinds of resistance. Anyway, there is no need for me to say much more. There are plenty of scholars professionally concerned with pre-industrial social history. Now we know something of the elemental facts of the lives and deaths of peasants and agricultural labourers in seventeenth- and eighteenth-century England and France. They are not comfortable facts. J. H. Plumb, in one of his attacks on the teaching of a pretty-pretty past, has written: "No one in his senses would choose to have been born in a previous age unless he could be certain that he would have been born into a prosperous family, that he would have enjoyed extremely good health, and that he could have accepted stoically the death of the majority of his children."

● ● ●

This leads me to the major theme of what I set out to say. Let me try again to make myself clear. It is dangerous to have two cultures which can't or don't communicate. In a time when science is determining much of our destiny, that is, whether we live or die, it is dangerous in the most practical terms. Scientists can give bad advice and decision-makers can't know whether it is good or bad. On the other hand, scientists in a divided culture provide a knowledge of some potentialities which is theirs alone. All this makes the political

[4] Bronislaw Malinowski (1884–1942), a Polish-American anthropologist.

process more complex, and in some ways more dangerous, than we should be prepared to tolerate for long, either for the purposes of avoiding disasters, or for fulfilling—what is waiting as a challenge to our conscience and goodwill—a definable social hope.

At present we are making do in our half-educated fashion, struggling to hear messages, obviously of great importance, as though listening to a foreign language in which one only knows a few words. Sometimes, and perhaps often, the logic of applied science is modifying or shaping the political process itself. This has happened over nuclear tests, where we have been lucky enough to see, what hasn't been common in our time, a triumph for human sense.[5] The triumph might have come sooner, if the logic of applied science had been as much at educated persons' disposal as the logic of language. But still, let's not minimise our triumphs. The worst doesn't always happen, as a friend said to me in the summer of 1940.[6] I am beginning to believe that we shall escape or circumvent the greater dangers with which science has confronted us. If I wrote the lecture again now, there would still be anxiety in it, but less dread.

Escaping the dangers of applied science is one thing. Doing the simple and manifest good which applied science has put in our power is another, more difficult, more demanding of human qualities, and in the long run far more enriching to us all. It will need energy, self-knowledge, new skills. It will need new perceptions into both closed and open politics.

In the original lecture, as now, I was isolating only one small corner of the situation: I was talking primarily to educators and those being educated, about something which we all understand and which is within our grasp. Changes in education will not, by themselves, solve our problems: but without those changes we shan't even realise what the problems are.

Changes in education are not going to produce miracles. The division of our culture is making us more obtuse than we need be: we can repair communications to some extent: but, as I have said before, we are not going to turn out men and women who understand as

---

[5] A reference to the international agreement on the cessation of nuclear explosions in the atmosphere (1962).

[6] The worst German air raids against England during the Second World War occurred in the summer of 1940, when most of Europe had been subdued and only the English still resisted Hitler's armies.

much of our world as Piero della Francesca[7] did of his, or Pascal,[8] or Goethe.[9] With good fortune, however, we can educate a large proportion of our better minds so that they are not ignorant of imaginative experience, both in the arts and in science, nor ignorant either of the endowments of applied science, of the remediable suffering of most of their fellow humans, and of the responsibilities which, once they are seen, cannot be denied.

[7] An Italian Renaissance painter and mathematician (*ca.* 1420–92).
[8] Blaise Pascal (1623–62), a French mathematician, physicist, theologian, and man of letters.
[9] Johann Wolfgang von Goethe (1749–1832), a German poet, dramatist, novelist, politician, and scientist; considered by some to be "the last of the great universal geniuses."

7

Jacques Ellul

The Technological Society

Since the industrial revolution of the late eighteenth century, there has been a constantly accelerating tendency to achieve planned results through standard-ized means with maximum efficiency. Jacques Ellul (1912–), a French sociologist, uses the term technique *to define this tendency. He means not only the growth of material technology but also the dehumanizing philosophical and psychological attitudes that accompany it. Technique is "the totality of methods rationally arrived at and having absolute efficiency . . . in every field of human activity." Ellul's writings illuminate what he considers the essential tragedy of a civilization increasingly dominated by technique.*

Born in Bordeaux, Ellul studied at the universities of Bordeaux and Paris, earning degrees in history, sociology, and law. When the Second World War began, he was Director of Studies at the University of Stras-bourg, in eastern France. After his dismissal from that post by a French gov-ernment collaborating with the German occupation, he joined the underground forces resisting the Germans. Following the war, Ellul turned from a promising political career to devote himself to teaching and writing; in 1947 he began a long association with the University of Bordeaux as Profes-sor of History and Sociology of Institutions.

The many books written by Ellul fall into two general categories: social philosophy and theology. (Since his conversion at age twenty-two, he has been an active member of the Protestant Reformed Church of France, serving at times as a member of its national council.) In the United States he is best

known for his trilogy on contemporary Western civilization: The Technological Society *(1964),* Propaganda *(1965), and* The Political Illusion
(1967).

In the following first excerpt from The Technological Society, *Ellul
describes "the tendencies of our human techniques to create the mass man."
He then cites the use of advertising as an example of the techniques that intentionally create "psychological collectivism." (A hint of his Christian convictions can be seen in his observation that advertising is effective because
"there are no spiritual values to form and inform life.") Ellul's philosophical
insights may be compared to the comments of economist John Kenneth Galbraith—see the next selection—on the subordination of the individual to the
goals of the "technostructure."*

*In the second excerpt offered in the following selection Ellul looks at the
probable future, in which "a world-wide totalitarian dictatorship . . . will
allow technique its full scope." It is clear that in* The Technological Society *he is primarily concerned about the prospects of individual freedom in a
context ever more hostile to its achievement.*

HUMAN TECHNIQUES

• • •

Mass Man

Modern society is moving toward a mass society, but the human
being is still not fully adapted to this new form.

The purpose of human techniques is to defend man, and the first
line of defense is that he be able to live. If these techniques strengthen
him in his nineteenth-century individualism (itself no ideal state of
affairs), they only aggravate the split between the material structures
of society, the social institutions, and the forces of production, on
the one hand, and man's personal tendencies, on the other. This
presupposes that technique can in fact defend man's individuality.
But such a disruption is technically impossible because it would entail insupportable disorders for man. Human techniques must therefore act to adapt man to the mass. Moreover, these techniques
remain at variance with the other material techniques on which they

depend. They must contribute to making man a mass man and help put an end to what has hitherto been considered the normal type of humanity. The type that will emerge and the type that will disappear will be the subjects of a forthcoming work. For the moment, it suffices to establish concretely the tendencies of our human techniques to create the mass man.

Material techniques usually result in a collective social form by means of a process which is largely involuntary. But it is sometimes voluntary; the technician, in agreement with the technical data, may consider a collectivity a higher social form. Involuntary and voluntary action are both to be observed, for example, in the sphere of psychological collectivization. I have indicated . . . the means by which this involuntary and, in a way, automatic adaptation appears. I shall refer to one other striking phenomenon of involuntary psychological collectivization: advertising.

The primary purpose of advertising technique is the creation of a certain way of life. And here it is much less important to convince the individual rationally than to implant in him a certain conception of life. The object offered for sale by the advertiser is naturally indispensable to the realization of this way of life. Now, objects advertised are all the result of the same technical progress and are all of identical type from a cultural point of view. Therefore, advertisements seeking to prove that these objects are indispensable refer to the same conception of the world, man, progress, ideals—in short, life. Once again we are confronted by a technical phenomenon completely indifferent to all local and accidental differences. Indeed, American, Soviet, and Nazi advertisements are in inspiration closely akin; they express the same conception of life, despite all superficial differences of doctrine. The Soviet Union, after having for a period violently rejected the technical system of advertising publicity, has more recently found it indispensable.

Advertising, which is founded on massive psychological research that must be effective, can "put across" the technical way of life. Any man who buys a given object participates in this way of life and, by falling prey to the compulsive power of advertising, enters involuntarily and unconsciously into its psychological framework.

One of the great designs of advertising is to create needs; but this is possible only if these needs correspond to an ideal of life that man accepts. The way of life offered by advertising is all the more compelling in that it corresponds to certain easy and simple tendencies of man and refers to a world in which there are no spiritual values to form and inform life. When men feel and respond to the needs advertising creates, they are adhering to its ideal of life. This explains the extremely rapid development, for example, of hygiene and cocktails. No one, before the advent of advertising, felt the need to be clean for cleanliness' sake. It is clear that the models used in advertising (Elsie the Cow, for instance) represent an ideal type, and they are convincing in proportion to their ideality. The human tendencies upon which advertising like this is based may be strikingly simple-minded, but they nonetheless represent pretty much the level of our modern life. Advertising offers us the ideal we have always wanted (and that ideal is certainly not a heroic way of life).

Advertising goes about its task of creating a psychological collectivism by mobilizing certain human tendencies in order to introduce the individual into the world of technique. Advertising also carries these tendencies to the ideal, absolute limit. It accomplishes this by playing down all other human tendencies. Every man is concerned, for example, about his bodily health—but show him Superman and it becomes his destiny to be Superman. In addition, advertising offers man the means for realizing material desires which hitherto had the tiresome propensity of not being realized. In these three ways, psychological collectivism is brought into being.

Advertising must affect all people; or at least an overwhelming majority. Its goal is to persuade the masses to buy. It is therefore necessary to base advertising on general psychological laws, which must then be unilaterally developed by it. The inevitable consequence is the creation of the mass man. As advertising of the most varied products is concentrated, a new type of human being, precise and generalized, emerges. We can get a general impression of this new human type by studying America, where human beings tend clearly to become identified with the ideal of advertising. In America advertising enjoys universal popular adherence, and the American way of life is fashioned by it.

In addition to the involuntary, psychological activity which leads to the creation of the mass man, there are certain conscious means which can be used to attain the same end. We must not misunderstand the qualification *conscious* in this connection. The degree of choice is very small; the process is effectively conditioned by material techniques and the beliefs they engender. However, this consciously concerted action is geared to psychological collectivization and, unlike advertising techniques, exerts a direct effect. It has a twofold basis and a twofold orientation, and centers about the notions of group integration and unanimity. . . .

Up to now, in discussing human techniques we have considered only man's need for adaptation with a view to his happiness or, at least, his equilibrium. This plays a role here too. For example, it can be shown that in our society the individual experiences tranquility only in a consciously gregarious state. This involves not only the undeniable "strength in unity" and "forgetfulness of one's lot in the crowd," but also the conscious recognition of the need to apply adequate remedies to social dangers. In our culture, the person who is not consciously adapted to his group cannot put up adequate resistance. Lewin's studies of anti-Semitism, for example, indicate that the Zionist groups with their collective psychology were able to withstand persecution much more readily than were the unorganized Jews who had retained an individualistic mentality.

It cannot be denied that this kind of conscious psychological adaptation, which gives the individual a chance to survive and even be happy, can produce beneficial effects. Though he loses much personal responsibility, he gains as compensation a spirit of co-operation and a certain self-respect in his relations with other members of the group. These are eminently collectivist virtues, but they are not negligible, and they assure the individual a certain human dignity in the collectivity of mass men.

While I have insisted on the "humanistic" tendencies of human techniques and, starting from the premise that man must be adapted to be happy, have tried to demonstrate the necessity of these techniques and their interrelation with all other techniques, my attitude has been resolutely optimistic. I have presupposed that technical practices and the intentions of the technicians were subordinated to a concern with human good. And when I traced the background of the human techniques, I proceeded from the most favorable position, that of integral humanism, which, it is claimed, is their foundation.

But there are more compelling realities. The tendency toward psychological collectivization does not have man's welfare as its end. It is designed just as well for his exploitation. In today's world, psychological collectivization is the *sine qua non*[1] of technical action.

---

[1] Indispensable condition; literally, without which not (Latin).

Munson says: "By building the morale of the troops, we are trying to increase their yield, to substitute enthusiastic self-discipline for forced obedience, to stimulate their will and their attention—in short, we are pursuing success." There he gives us the key to this kind of psychological action: the yield is greater when man acts from consent, rather than constraint. The problem then is to get the individual's consent artificially through depth psychology, since he will not give it of his own free will. But the decision to give consent must appear to be spontaneous. Anyone who prates about furnishing man an ideal or a faith to live by is helping to bring about technique's ascendency, however much he talks about "good will." The "ideal" becomes so through the agency of purely technical means whose purpose is to enable men to support an insupportable situation created within the framework of technical culture. This attitude is not the antithesis of the humanistic attitude; the two are interwoven and it is completely artificial to try to separate them.

Human activity in the technical milieu must correspond to this milieu and also must be collective. It must belong to the order of the conditioned reflex. Complete human discipline must respond to technical necessity. And as the technical milieu concerns all men, no mere handful of them but the totality of society is to be conditioned in this way. The reflex must be a collective one. As Munson says: "In peacetime, morale building aims at creating among the troops the state of mental *receptivity* which makes them susceptible to *every psychological excitation* of wartime." And this "receptivity" must also be installed in every other human group in the technical culture, and especially in the masses of the workers.

Psychological conditioning presupposes collectivity, for masses of men are more receptive to suggestion than individuals, and, as we have seen, suggestion is one of the most important weapons in the psychological arsenal. At the same time, the masses are intolerant and think everything must be black or white. This results from the moral categories imposed by technique and is possible only if the masses are of a single mind and if countercurrents are not permitted to form.

The conditions for psychological efficiency are, first, group integration and, second, group unanimity. (This should not be taken to mean that on a larger scale there may not be a certain diversity.) I am speaking of a determinate group (for example, a political party, the army, an industrial plant) which has a definite technical function to fulfill. The purpose of psychological methods is to neutralize or eliminate aberrant individuals and tendencies to fractionation. Simultaneously, the tendency to collectivization is reinforced in order to "immunize" the environment against any possible virus of disagreement.

When psychological techniques, in close co-operation with material techniques, have at last succeeded in creating unity, all possible diversity will have disappeared and the human race will have become a bloc of complete and irrational solidarity.

• • •

A LOOK AT THE FUTURE

. . . the human race is beginning confusedly to understand at last that it is living in a new and unfamiliar universe. The new order was meant to be a buffer between man and nature. Unfortunately, it has evolved autonomously in such a way that man has lost all contact with his natural framework and has to do only with the organized technical intermediary which sustains relations both with the world of life and with the world of brute matter. Enclosed within his artificial creation, man finds that there is "no exit"; that he cannot pierce the shell of technology to find again the ancient milieu to which he was adapted for hundreds of thousands of years.

The new milieu has its own specific laws which are not the laws of organic or inorganic matter. Man is still ignorant of these laws. It nevertheless begins to appear with crushing finality that a new necessity is taking over from the old. It is easy to boast of victory over ancient oppression, but what if victory has been gained at the price of an even greater subjection to the forces of the artificial necessity of the technical society which has come to dominate our lives?

In our cities there is no more day or night or heat or cold. But there is overpopulation, thraldom to press and television, total absence of purpose. All men are constrained by means external to them to ends equally external. The further the technical mechanism develops which allows us to escape natural necessity, the more we are subjected to artificial technical necessities. . . . The artificial necessity of technique is not less harsh and implacable for being much less obviously menacing than natural necessity. When the Communists claim that they place the development of the technical society in a historical framework that automatically leads to freedom through the medium of the dialectical process; when Humanists such as Bergson, or Catholics such as Mounier, assert that man must regain control over the technical "means" by an additional quantity of soul, all of them alike show both their ignorance of the technical phenomenon and an impenitent idealism that unfortunately bears no relation to truth or reality.

Alongside these parades of mere verbalisms, there has been a real effort, on the part of the technicians themselves, to control the future of technical evolution. The principle here is the old one we have so often encountered: "A technical problem demands a technical solution." At present, there are two kinds of new techniques which the technicians propose as solutions.

The first solution hinges on the creation of new technical instruments able to mediate between man and his new technical milieu. Robert Jungk, for example, in connection with the fact that man is not completely adaptable to the demands of the technical age, writes that "it is impossible to create interstellar man out of the existing prime matter; auxiliary technical instruments and apparatus must compensate for his insufficiencies." The best and most striking example of such subsidiary instruments is furnished by the complex of so-called "thinking machines," which certainly belong to a very different category of techniques than those that have been applied up to now. But the whole ensemble of means designed to permit human mastery of what were means and have now become milieu are techniques of the second degree, and nothing more. Pierre de Latil, in his *La Pensée artificielle* [*Artificial Thought*], gives an excellent characterization of some of these machines of the second degree:

"In the machine, the notion of finality makes its appearance, a notion sometimes attributed in living beings to some intelligence inherent in the species, innate to life itself. Finality is artificially built into the machine and regulates it, an effect requiring that some factor be modified or reinforced so that the effect itself does not disturb the equilibrium . . . Errors are corrected without human analysis, or knowledge, without even being suspected. The error itself corrects the error. A deviation from the prescribed track itself enables the automatic pilot to rectify the deviation . . . For the machine, as for animals, error is fruitful; it conditions the correct path."

The second solution revolves about the effort to discover (or rediscover) a new end for human society in the technical age. The aims of technology, which were clear enough a century and a half ago, have gradually disappeared from view. Humanity seems to have forgotten the wherefore of all its travail, as though its goals had been translated into an abstraction or had become implicit; or as though its ends rested in an unforeseeable future of undetermined date, as in the case of Communist society. Everything today seems to happen as though ends disappear, as a result of the magnitude of the very means at our disposal.

Comprehending that the proliferation of means brings about the disappearance of the ends, we have become preoccupied with redis-covering a purpose or a goal. Some optimists of good will assert that they have rediscovered a Humanism to which the technical move-ment is subordinated. The orientation of this Humanism may be Communist or non-Communist, but it hardly makes any difference. In both cases it is merely a pious hope with no chance whatsoever of influencing technical evolution. The further we advance, the more the purpose of our techniques fades out of sight. Even things which not long ago seemed to be immediate objectives—rising living stan-dards, hygiene, comfort—no longer seem to have that character, possibly because man finds the endless adaptation to new circum-stances disagreeable. In many cases, indeed, a higher technique obliges him to sacrifice comfort and hygienic amenities to the evolv-ing technology which possesses a monopoly of the instruments neces-sary to satisfy them. Extreme examples are furnished by the scientists isolated at Los Alamos in the middle of the desert because of the danger of their experiments; or by the would-be astronauts who are forced to live in the discomfort of experimental camps in the manner so graphically described by Jungk.

But the optimistic technician is not a man to lose heart. If ends and goals are required, he will find them in a finality which can be im-posed on technical evolution precisely because this finality can be technically established and calculated. It seems clear that there must be some common measure between the means and the ends subordi-nated to it. The required solution, then, must be a technical inquiry into ends, and this alone can bring about a systematization of ends and means. The problem becomes that of analyzing individual and social requirements technically, of establishing, numerically and me-chanistically, the constancy of human needs. It follows that a com-plete knowledge of ends is requisite for mastery of means. But, as Jacques Aventur has demonstrated, such knowledge can only be technical knowledge. Alas, the panacea of merely theoretical human-ism is as vain as any other.[2]

"Man, in his biological reality, must remain the sole possible refer-ence point for classifying needs," writes Aventur. Aventur's dictum must be extended to include man's psychology and sociology, since these have also been reduced to mathematical calculation. Technol-ogy cannot put up with intuitions and "literature." It must necessar-ily don mathematical vestments. Everything in human life that does not lend itself to mathematical treatment must be excluded—because it is not a possible end for technique—and left to the sphere of dreams.

Who is too blind to see that a profound mutation is being advo-cated here? A new dismembering and a complete reconstitution of the human being so that he can at last become the objective (and also the total object) of techniques. Excluding all but the mathematical el-ement, he is indeed a fit end for the means he has constructed. He is also completely despoiled of everything that traditionally constituted his essence. Man becomes a pure appearance, a kaleidoscope of exter-nal shapes, an abstraction in a milieu that is frighteningly concrete—an abstraction armed with all the sovereign signs of Jupiter the Thunderer.

A Look at the Year 2000

In 1960 the weekly *l'Express* of Paris published a series of extracts from texts by American and Russian scientists concerning society in the year 2000. As long as such visions were purely a literary concern of science-fiction writers and sensational journalists, it was possible to smile at them.[3] Now we have like works from Nobel Prize win-ners, members of the Academy of Sciences of Moscow, and other scientific notables whose qualifications are beyond dispute. The vi-sions of these gentlemen put science fiction in the shade. By the year

---

[2] It must be clear that the ends sought cannot be determined by moral science. The dubiousness of ethical judgments, and the differences between systems, make moral science unfit for establishing these ends. But, above all, its subjectivity is a fatal blemish. It depends essentially on the refinement of the individual moral conscience. An average morality is ceaselessly confronted with excessive demands with which it cannot comply. Technical modalities cannot tolerate subjectivity. [Ellul's note. *Ed.*]

[3] Some excellent works, such as Robert Jungk's *Le Futur a déjà commencé* [*The Future Has Already Begun*], were included in this classification. [Ellul's note. *Ed.*]

2000, voyages to the moon will be commonplace; so will inhabited artificial satellites. All food will be completely synthetic. The world's population will have increased fourfold but will have been stabilized. Sea water and ordinary rocks will yield all the necessary metals. Disease, as well as famine, will have been eliminated; and there will be universal hygienic inspection and control. The problems of energy production will have been completely resolved. Serious scientists, it must be repeated, are the source of these predictions, which hitherto were found only in philosophic utopias.

The most remarkable predictions concern the transformation of educational methods and the problem of human reproduction. Knowledge will be accumulated in "electronic banks" and transmitted directly to the human nervous system by means of coded electronic messages. There will no longer be any need of reading or learning mountains of useless information; everything will be received and registered according to the needs of the moment. There will be no need of attention or effort. What is needed will pass directly from the machine to the brain without going through consciousness.

In the domain of genetics, natural reproduction will be forbidden. A stable population will be necessary, and it will consist of the highest human types. Artificial insemination will be employed. This, according to Muller, will "permit the introduction into a carrier uterus of an ovum fertilized *in vitro*,[4] ovum and sperm . . . having been taken from persons representing the masculine ideal and the feminine ideal, respectively. The reproductive cells in question will preferably be those of persons dead long enough that a true perspective of their lives and works, free of all personal prejudice, can be seen. Such cells will be taken from cell banks and will represent the most precious genetic heritage of humanity . . . The method will have to be applied universally. If the people of a single country were to apply it intelligently and intensively . . . they would quickly attain a practically invincible level of superiority . . ." Here is a future Huxley[5] never dreamed of.

Perhaps, instead of marveling or being shocked, we ought to reflect a little. A question no one ever asks when confronted with the scientific wonders of the future concerns the interim period. Con-

[4] Latin: literally, in glass (test tube).
[5] Aldous Huxley (1894–1963), an English writer, is the author of the famous Utopian novel *Brave New World*. (See selection 10.)

sider, for example, the problems of automation, which will become acute in a very short time. How, socially, politically, morally, and humanly, shall we contrive to get there? How are the prodigious economic problems, for example, of unemployment, to be solved? And, in Muller's more distant utopia, how shall we force humanity to refrain from begetting children naturally? How shall we force them to submit to constant and rigorous hygienic controls? How shall man be persuaded to accept a radical transformation of his traditional modes of nutrition? How and where shall we relocate a billion and a half persons who today make their livings from agriculture and who, in the promised ultrarapid conversion of the next forty years, will become completely useless as cultivators of the soil? How shall we distribute such numbers of people equably over the surface of the earth, particularly if the promised fourfold increase in population materializes? How will we handle the control and occupation of outer space in order to provide a stable *modus vivendi?* [6] How shall national boundaries be made to disappear? (One of the last two would be a necessity.) There are many other "hows," but they are conveniently left unformulated. When we reflect on the serious although relatively minor problems that were provoked by the industrial exploitation of coal and electricity, when we reflect that after a hundred and fifty years these problems are still not satisfactorily resolved, we are entitled to ask whether there are any solutions to the infinitely more complex "hows" of the next forty years. In fact, there is one and only one means to their solution, a world-wide totalitarian dictatorship which will allow technique its full scope and at the same time resolve the concomitant difficulties. It is not difficult to understand why the scientists and worshippers of technology prefer not to dwell on this solution, but rather to leap nimbly across the dull and uninteresting intermediary period and land squarely in the golden age. We might indeed ask ourselves if we will succeed in getting through the transition period at all, or if the blood and the suffering required are not perhaps too high a price to pay for this golden age.

If we take a hard, unromantic look at the golden age itself, we are struck with the incredible naïveté of these scientists. They say, for example, that they will be able to shape and reshape at will human emotions, desires, and thoughts and arrive scientifically at certain ef-

[6]Latin: way of living.

ficient, pre-established collective decisions. They claim they will be in a position to develop certain collective desires, to constitute certain homogeneous social units out of aggregates of individuals, to forbid men to raise their children, and even to persuade them to renounce having any. At the same time, they speak of assuring the triumph of freedom and of the necessity of avoiding dictatorship at any price.[7] They seem incapable of grasping the contradiction involved, or of understanding that what they are proposing, even after the intermediary period, is in fact the harshest of dictatorships. In comparison, Hitler's was a trifling affair. That it is to be a dictatorship of test tubes rather than of hobnailed boots will not make it any less a dictatorship.

When our savants characterize their golden age in any but scientific terms, they emit a quantity of down-at-the-heel platitudes that would gladden the heart of the pettiest politician. Let's take a few samples. "To render human nature nobler, more beautiful, and more harmonious." What on earth can this mean? What criteria, what content, do they propose? Not many, I fear, would be able to reply. "To assure the triumph of peace, liberty, and reason." Fine words with no substance behind them. "To eliminate cultural lag." What culture? And would the culture they have in mind be able to subsist in this harsh social organization? "To conquer outer space." For what purpose? The conquest of space seems to be an end in itself, which dispenses with any need for reflection.

We are forced to conclude that our scientists are incapable of any but the emptiest platitudes when they stray from their specialties. It makes one think back on the collection of mediocrities accumulated by Einstein[8] when he spoke of God, the state, peace, and the meaning of life. It is clear that Einstein, extraordinary mathematical genius that he was, was no Pascal;[9] he knew nothing of political or human reality, or, in fact, anything at all outside his mathematical reach. The banality of Einstein's remarks in matters outside his specialty is as astonishing as his genius within it. It seems as though the special-

[7] The material here and below is cited from actual texts. [Ellul's note. *Ed.*]
[8] Albert Einstein (1879–1955), a German-born theoretical physicist, was the originator of relativity theory, one of the basic conceptions of twentieth-century physics. He was awarded the Nobel Prize in 1921.
[9] Blaise Pascal (1623–62), a French mathematician, physicist, theologian, and man of letters.

ized application of all one's faculties in a particular area inhibits the consideration of things in general. Even J. Robert Oppenheimer,[10] who seems receptive to a general culture, is not outside this judgment. His political and social declarations, for example, scarcely go beyond the level of those of the man in the street. And the opinions of the scientists quoted by *l'Express* are not even on the level of Einstein or Oppenheimer. Their pomposities, in fact, do not rise to the level of the average. They are vague generalities inherited from the nineteenth century, and the fact that they represent the furthest limits of thought of our scientific worthies must be symptomatic of arrested development or of a mental block. Particularly disquieting is the gap between the enormous power they wield and their critical ability, which must be estimated as null. To wield power well entails a certain faculty of criticism, discrimination, judgment, and option. It is impossible to have confidence in men who apparently lack these faculties. Yet it is apparently our fate to be facing a "golden age" in the power of sorcerers who are totally blind to the meaning of the human adventure. When they speak of preserving the seed of outstanding men, whom, pray, do they mean to be the judges. It is clear, alas, that they propose to sit in judgment themselves. It is hardly likely that they will deem a Rimbaud[11] or a Nietzsche[12] worthy of posterity. When they announce that they will conserve the genetic mutations which appear to them most favorable, and that they propose to modify the very germ cells in order to produce such and such traits; and when we consider the mediocrity of the scientists themselves outside the confines of their specialties, we can only shudder at the thought of what they will esteem most "favorable."

None of our wise men ever pose the question of the end of all their marvels. The "wherefore" is resolutely passed by. The response which would occur to our contemporaries is: for the sake of happiness. Unfortunately, there is no longer any question of that. One of our best-known specialists in diseases of the nervous system writes: "We will be able to modify man's emotions, desires and thoughts, as

[10] J. Robert Oppenheimer (1904–67), an American theoretical physicist; during the Second World War, he directed the laboratory at Los Alamos, New Mexico, which produced the first atomic bomb.
[11] Arthur Rimbaud (1854–91), a French symbolist poet who was violently amoral in his writings and in his life.
[12] Friedrich Nietzsche (1844–1900), a German philosopher, denounced conventional society and championed the doctrine of human perfectibility through the forceful self-assertion of the "superman."

we have already done in a rudimentary way with tranquilizers." It will be possible, says our specialist, to produce a conviction or an impression of happiness without any real basis for it. Our man of the golden age, therefore, will be capable of "happiness" amid the worst privations. Why, then, promise us extraordinary comforts, hygiene, knowledge, and nourishment if, by simply manipulating our nervous systems, we can be happy without them? The last meager motive we could possibly ascribe to the technical adventure thus vanishes into thin air through the very existence of technique itself.

But what good is it to pose questions of motives? of Why? All that must be the work of some miserable intellectual who balks at technical progress. The attitude of the scientists, at any rate, is clear. Technique exists because it is technique. The golden age will be because it will be. Any other answer is superfluous.

8

John Kenneth Galbraith
The New Industrial State

In the Western world's modern industrial societies, the role of the economic analyst and planner has become magnified. Perhaps the best-known and most influential economist of the present era—at least for the general reader—is John Kenneth Galbraith (1908–). Born in Canada, Galbraith earned a bachelor's degree at the University of Toronto in 1931 and a doctorate at the University of California, Berkeley, in 1934. In the same year he began his long and distinguished teaching career at Harvard University. During the Second World War he left teaching to serve the United States government; first as deputy administrator of the Office of Price Administration, later as a director of the U. S. Strategic Bombing Survey, which estimated the effects of Allied air attacks upon the German and Japanese economies. Immediately after peace was declared he directed a study of the postwar economic recovery of western Europe.

In the 1960s Galbraith again interrupted his teaching at Harvard to serve as President John Kennedy's ambassador to India (1961–63) and later as an advisor to President Lyndon Johnson. In his role as prominent "liberal" thinker and activist, he served also for a time as chairman of a like-minded national group, the Americans for Democratic Action.

The author of more than thirty books, Galbraith has written in a wide range of literary forms—from technical economic text to travel memoir, from political essay to popular novel. He has, however, consistently concerned himself with one major issue: the relationship of individual freedom to the sources of economic power.

In American Capitalism (*1952*) *he describes the modern concentration of power in large industrial corporations but also puts forward a theory of "countervailing" power, in the struggle among large buyers, large sellers, and labor unions. His later book,* The Affluent Society (*1958*), *urges a shift in national expenditure from the private to the public sector—for example, to public health and education. The book also laments the prevailing emphasis on production of consumer goods, for which mass advertising creates an artificial demand.*

In The New Industrial State (*1967*), *the source of the following selection, Galbraith expands the glimpses offered in* The Affluent Society *into a general picture of the "world of great corporations." The individual, he asserts, is "increasingly subordinate to the goals of the producing organization." Ultimately, these goals are determined by the industrial bureaucracy, the "technostructure." This is true, he states further, in all industrial societies, whether capitalist or socialist. Bureaucratic planning has replaced the ebb and flow of the marketplace, and the corporation tends "to become part of the administrative complex of the state." The industrial system as a whole, therefore, diminishes individual liberty. Galbraith raises the hope, however, that the managerial elite, while directing the system to serve the goal of increased productivity and consumption, will be willing to subordinate this goal to higher moral, aesthetic, and intellectual purposes.*

A SUMMARY

The principal topography of the industrial system is now in view. Most will think it a formidable sight. Few will minimize the complexity of its probable social effect; the only man who must surely be wrong about the industrial system is the one who essays a simple judgment upon it.

The system produces goods and renders services in vast and increasing volume. There are many poor people left in the industrial countries, and notably in the United States. The fact that they are not the central theme of this treatise should not be taken as proof either of ignorance of their existence or indifference to their fate. But the poor, by any applicable tests, are outside the industrial system. They are those who have not been drawn into its service or who cannot qualify. And not only has the industrial system—its boundaries as here defined are to be kept in mind—eliminated poverty for those who have been drawn into its embrace but it has also greatly reduced the burden of manual toil. Only those who have never experienced hard and tedious labor, long continued, can be wholly indifferent to its elimination.

Once it was imagined that the economic system provided man with the artifacts by which he has anciently surrounded himself in response to his original and sovereign desires. This source of economic motivation is still celebrated in the formal liturgy of the system. But, as we have sufficiently seen, the system, if it accommodates to man's wants, also and increasingly accommodates men to its needs. And it must. This latter accommodation is no trivial exercise in salesmanship. It is deeply organic. High technology and heavy capital use cannot be subordinate to the ebb and flow of market demand. They require planning; it is the essence of planning that public behavior be made predictable—that it be subject to control.

And from this control flow further important consequences. It insures that men and increasing numbers of women will work with undiminished effort however great their supply of goods. And it helps insure that the society will measure its accomplishment by its annual increase in production. Nothing would be more discomfiting for economic discipline than were men to establish goals for themselves and on reaching them say, "I've got what I need. That is all for this week." Not by accident is such behavior thought irresponsible and feckless. It would mean that increased output would no longer have high social urgency. Enough would be enough. The achievement of the society could then no longer be measured by the annual increase in Gross National Product. And if increased production ceased to be of prime importance, the needs of the industrial system would no longer be accorded automatic priority. The required readjustment in social attitudes would be appalling.

The management to which we are subject is not onerous. It works not on the body but on the mind. It first wins acquiescence or belief; action is in response to this mental conditioning and thus devoid of any sense of compulsion. It is not that we are required to have a newly configured automobile or a novel reverse-action laxative; it is because we believe that we must have them. It is open to anyone who can resist belief to contract out of this control. But we are no less managed because we are not physically compelled. On the contrary, though this is poorly understood, physical compulsion would have a far lower order of efficiency.

2

The industrial system has brought its supply of capital, and in substantial measure also its labor supply, within its control, and thus within the ambit of its planning. And it has extended its influence deeply into the state. Those policies of the state that are vital for the industrial system—regulation of aggregate demand, maintenance of the large public (if preferably technical) sector on which this regulation depends, underwriting of advanced technology and provision of an increasing volume of trained and educated manpower—are believed to be of the highest social urgency. This belief accords with the needs of the system. And the influence of the technostructure of the mature firm extends to shaping the demand for its particular product or range of products. Individual members of the technostructure identify themselves with the design, development and production of items purchased by the government as the technostructure identifies itself with the social goal (say) of an effective national defense. And the members of the technostructure adapt design, development or need for items procured by the government to what accords with their own goals. These goals reflect, inevitably, the needs of the technostructure and of its planning.

Paralleling these changes, partly as a result and partly as a cause, has been a profound shift in the locus of economic and political power. The financier and the union leader are dwindling influences in the society. They are honored more for their past eminence than for their present power. The technostructure exercises less direct political power than did the antecedent entrepreneur. But that is because it has far more influence as an arm and extension of the public bureaucracy and in its influence on the larger climate of belief. The scientific, technical, organizational and planning needs of the technostructure have brought into being a large educational and scientific estate. And, while the commitment of the culture, under the tutelage of the industrial system, to a single-minded preoccupation with the production of goods is strong, it is not complete. Rising income also nurtures a further artistic and intellectual community outside of the industrial system.

3

Such in briefest sketch are the principal results of this pilgrimage. Two questions inevitably follow: Where does it take us? How should it be guided?

Neither question is, in fact, as important as those already considered, and, one hopes, resolved. Agreeable as it is to know where one is proceeding, it is far more important to know where one has arrived. And while there will always be resistance to accepting what has come to exist—a resistance nurtured by nostalgia, vested interest in painfully acquired error which is thus understandably precious, and the omnipresent need to sustain belief in what is convenient as distinct from what is real—one has, where the present is concerned, appellate rights in two great courts, namely, the internal consistency of the ideas and their coherence with what can be seen. It will perhaps be agreed that these tests have rendered good service here. I venture to think that most readers will find themselves reassured thereby. When one turns to the future, these guides are lost. There are wise and foolish predictions but the difference between them is not so clear.

There are also difficulties in talking, at the same time, about what will happen and what should happen. Marx[1] must on occasion have wondered, if revolution were inevitable, as he proclaimed, why it required the passionate and unrelenting advocacy which he accorded it. Should baleful tendencies be predicted when one hopes that popular understanding will bring the reaction that reverses them? No one who believes in ideas and their advocacy can ever persuade himself that they are uninfluential. Nor are they. And those who deal in ideas, if they are wise, will welcome attack. Only a peaceful passage should dismay them for it proves that the ideas do not affect anyone very much. I have hopes that popular understanding will reverse some of the less agreeable tendencies of the industrial system and in-

---

[1] Karl Marx (1818–83), a German-born political philosopher and economist, was the main author of *The Communist Manifesto* and *Das Kapital,* the major originating texts of modern socialist theory.

validate, therewith, the predictions that proceed from these tendencies. And I am not without hope for the controversy that attests the importance of such change.

4

There is another reason why, whatever the inconvenience, the future must be faced. Although those who presume to loftier, scientific attitudes regularly deplore it, the Anglo-American tradition in economic discourse is strongly normative. The test of whether a diagnostician is to be taken seriously or not is his response to the question: "Well, what would *you* do?" I have been primarily concerned to tell what the industrial system is like. But to do this and no more would be to persuade most people that the description was not terribly useful.

Moreover, some problems of no small importance have been suggested by the preceding discussion. There is, for example, the prime role of technology in the industrial system and its peculiar association with weapons of unimaginable ferocity and destructiveness. How are we to be saved from these? There is also the question of the individual in this system—a system that requires, both in production and consumption, that individuality be suppressed. Given our commitment to the sovereignty and sanctity of the person, by what means, if at all, is human personality to be saved? Obviously there are dimensions of life, those of art for example, which the industrial system does not serve. One is led to inquire whether education remains education when it is chained too tightly to the wheel of the industrial system. And there is the relation of the industrial system to intellectual expression and political pluralism. This requires a special word.

5

For most of man's history, as philosophers of such diverse views as Marx and Alfred Marshall[2] have agreed, political interest and conflict have originated in economic interest and economic conflict. And so it has been in the United States. Our politics have been the ex-

[2]Marshall (1842–1924), an English economist, was a founder of "neoclassical economics," which asserted the value of a free-enterprise system.

pression, in various conflicts and coalitions, of debtor and creditor interests, domestic and export interests, urban and rural interests, consumer and producer interests and, notably and classically, of the interests of the capitalist entrepreneur and the industrial working class.

To a remarkable extent, as we have seen, the industrial system absorbs these class interests. It does so partly by minimizing the reality of conflict and partly by exploiting the resulting malleability of attitude to win control of belief. The goals of the industrial system, in this process, become the goals of all who are associated with it and thus, by slight extension, the goals of the society itself.

In the past, criticism and introspection concerning the economic system and its goals have been both allowed and induced by the conflict in economic interest and the resulting political division. The capitalist entrepreneur or the labor leader has rarely been a source of penetrating criticism of himself or his own goals. But, with his spokesmen, sympathizers, captive scholars and sycophants he has been a good deal less restrained in discussing those with whom he has been economically at war. And much scholarship has also flourished in the interstices of this conflict. When its conclusions were unfavorable to one side they had the implicit protection of the other.

The question arises whether the industrial system, in absorbing economic conflict, ends all examination of social goals. Do its techniques of control—its management of market behavior and its identification with and adaptation of social goals—serve also to minimize social introspection? In brief, is the industrial system monolithic by nature? And also very bland? To what extent does a society draw strength from pluralism of economic interests which, in turn, sustains pluralism of political discussion and social thought?

An interesting and widely remarked political phenomenon of recent years has been an ill-defined discontent, especially among students and intellectuals, with the accepted and approved modalities of social thought. These, whether espoused by professed liberals or conservatives, are held to be the views of "The Establishment." Not inappropriately, the rejection extends not only to the economic, social and political views of the Establishment but also to its clothing, conventional housing and even to the soap, depilatory apparatus and other goods, the production of which is the sanctioned measure of success. All these are eschewed by the dissidents in a highly visible manner. Is this the natural line of dissent in a society in which the previous lines of conflict have been subsumed?

• • •

THE FUTURE OF THE INDUSTRIAL SYSTEM

In the latter part of the last century and the early decades of this, no subject was more discussed than the future of capitalism. Economists, men of unspecific wisdom, Chautauqua[3] lecturers, editorial writers, knowledgeable ecclesiastics and socialists contributed their personal revelation. It was taken largely for granted that the economic system was in a state of development and in time would transform itself into something hopefully better but certainly different. Socialists drew strength from the belief that theirs was the plausible next stage in a natural process of change.

The future of the industrial system, by contrast, is not discussed. The prospect for agriculture is subject to debate—it is assumed to be in course of change. So are the chances for survival for the small entrepreneur or the private medical practitioner. But General Motors, General Electric and U.S. Steel are an ultimate achievement. One does not wonder where one is going if one is already there.

Yet to suppose that the industrial system is a terminal phenomenon is, *per se*,[4] implausible. It is itself the product, in the last seventy years, of a vast and autonomous transformation. During this time the scale of the individual corporation has grown enormously. The entrepreneurial corporation has declined. The technostructure has developed, removed itself from control by the stockholders and acquired its own internal sources of capital. There has been a large change in its relations with the workers and a yet larger one in its relations with the state. It would be strange were such a manifestation of social dynamics to be now at an end. So to suggest is to deny one of the philosophical tenets of the system itself, one that is solemnly articulated on all occasions of business ritual—conventions, stockholders' meetings, board meetings, executive committee

---

[3] A popular American educational institution which, in the nineteenth and early twentieth centuries, provided a series of traveling lectures, concerts, and plays.

[4] Latin: in or by itself.

meetings, management development conferences, budget conferences, product review meetings, senior officer retreats and dealer relations workshops. It is that change is the law of economic life.

The future of the industrial system is not discussed partly because of the power it exercises over belief. It has succeeded, tacitly, in excluding the notion that it is a transitory, which would be to say that it is a somehow imperfect, phenomenon. More important, perhaps, to consider the future would be to fix attention on where it has already arrived. Among the least enchanting words in the business lexicon are planning, government control, state underwriting and socialism. To consider the likelihood of these in the future would be to bring home the appalling extent to which they are already a fact. And it would not be ignored that these grievous things have arrived, at a minimum with the acquiescence and, at a maximum, on the demand, of the system itself.

2

Such reflection on the future would also emphasize the convergent tendencies of industrial societies, however different their popular or ideological billing; the convergence being to a roughly similar design for organization and planning. A word in review may be worthwhile. Convergence begins with modern large-scale production, with heavy requirements of capital, sophisticated technology and, as a prime consequence, elaborate organization. These require control of prices and, so far as possible, of what is bought at those prices. This is to say that planning must replace the market. In the Soviet-type economies, the control of prices is a function of the state. The management of demand (eased by the knowledge that their people will mostly want what Americans and Western Europeans already have) is partly by according preference to the alert and early-rising who are first to the store; partly, as in the case of houseroom, by direct allocation to the recipient; and partly, as in the case of automobiles, by making patience (as well as political position or need) a test of eligibility. With us this management is accomplished less formally by the corporations, their advertising agencies, salesmen, dealers and retailers. But these, obviously, are differences in method rather than purpose. Large-scale industrialism requires, in both cases, that the market and consumer sovereignty be extensively superseded.

Large-scale organization also requires autonomy. The intrusion of an external and uninformed will is damaging. In the non-Soviet systems this means excluding the nonparticipating capitalist from effective power. But the same imperative operates in the socialist economy. There the business firm seeks to minimize or exclude control by the official bureaucracy. To gain autonomy for the enterprise is what, in substantial measure, the modern Communist theoretician calls reform. Nothing in our time is more interesting than that the erstwhile capitalist corporation and the erstwhile Communist firm should, under the imperatives of organization, come together as oligarchies of their own members. Ideology is not the relevant force. Large and complex organizations can use diverse knowledge and talent and thus function effectively only if under their own authority. This, it must be stressed once more, is not autonomy that subordinates a firm to the market. It is autonomy that allows the firm authority over its planning.

The industrial system has no inherent capacity for regulating total demand—for insuring a supply of purchasing power sufficient to acquire what it produces. So it relies on the state for this. At full employment there is no mechanism for holding prices and wages stable. This stabilization too is a function of the state. The Soviet-type systems also make a careful calculation of the income that is being provided in relation to the value of the goods available for purchase. Stabilization of wages and prices in general is, of course, a natural consequence of fixing individual prices and wage rates.

Finally, the industrial system must rely on the state for trained and educated manpower, now the decisive factor of production. So it also is under socialist industrialism. The flight of the first Sputnik precipitated a great and fashionable concern in the United States over the state of scientific and technical education. Many argued that the Soviet system, with its higher priority for state functions, among which education is prominent, had a natural advantage in this regard.

Thus convergence between the two ostensibly different industrial systems occurs at all fundamental points. This is an exceedingly fortunate thing. In time, and perhaps in less time than may be imagined, it will dispose of the notion of inevitable conflict based on irreconcilable difference. This will not be soon agreed. Marx did not foresee the convergence and he is accorded, with suitable interpretation, the remarkable, even supernatural, power of foreseeing all. Those on the other side who speak for the unbridgeable gulf that divides the free world from the Communist world and free enterprise from Communism are protected by an equally ecclesiastical faith that whatever the evolution of free enterprise may be, it cannot conceivably come to resemble socialism. But these positions can survive the evidence only for a time. Only the most committed ideologist or the most fervent propagandist can stand firm against the feeling that an increasing number of people regard him as obsolete. Vanity is a great force for intellectual modernization.

To recognize that industrial systems are convergent in their development will, one imagines, help toward agreement on the common dangers in the weapons competition, on ending it or shifting it to more benign areas. Perhaps nothing casts more light on the future of the industrial system than this, for it implies, in contrast with the present images, that it could have a future.

3

Given the deep dependence of the industrial system on the state and the nature of its motivational relationship to the state, i.e., its identification with public goals and the adaptation of these to its needs, the industrial system will not long be regarded as something apart from government. Rather it will increasingly be seen as part of a much larger complex which embraces both the industrial system and the state. Private enterprise was anciently so characterized because it was subordinate to the market and those in command derived their power from ownership of private property. The modern corporation is no longer subordinate to the market; those who run it no longer depend on property ownership for their authority. They must have autonomy within a framework of goals. But this allows them to work easily in association with the bureaucracy and, indeed, to perform for the bureaucracy tasks that it cannot do, or cannot do as well, for itself. In consequence, so we have seen, for tasks of technical sophistication, there is a close fusion of the industrial system with the state. Members of the technostructure work closely with their public counterparts not only in the development and manufacture of products but in advising them of their needs. Were it not so celebrated in ideology, it would long since have been agreed that the line that now divides public from so-called private organization in military procurement, space exploration and atomic energy is so indistinct as to be nearly imperceptible. Men move easily across the line. On retirement, admirals and generals, as well as high civil servants, go more or less automatically to the more closely associated industries. One highly experienced observer has called these firms the "semi-nationalized" branch of the economy. It has been noted, "the Market mechanism, [is replaced by] . . . the administrative mechanism. For the profit share of private entrepreneurs, it substitutes the fixed fee, a payment in lieu of profits foregone. And for the independent private business unit, it substitutes the integrated hierarchical structure of an organization composed of an agency . . . and its contractors."[5]

The foregoing refers to firms which sell most of their output to the government—Lockheed, General Dynamics, Grumman. But firms which have a smaller proportion of sales to the government are more dependent on it for the regulation of aggregate demand and equally for the underwriting of especially expensive or risky technology and the supply of trained and educated manpower.

So comprehensive a relationship cannot be denied or ignored indefinitely. Increasingly it will be recognized that the mature corporation, as it develops, becomes part of the larger administrative complex associated with the state. In time the line between the two will disappear. Men will look back in amusement at the pretense that once caused people to refer to General Dynamics and North American Aviation and A. T. & T. as *private* business.

Though this recognition will not be universally welcomed, it will be healthy. There is always a presumption in social matters in favor of reality as opposed to myth. The autonomy of the technostructure is, to repeat yet again, a functional necessity of the industrial system. But the goals this autonomy serves allow some range of choice. If the mature corporation is recognized to be part of the penumbra of the state, it will be more strongly in the service of social goals. It cannot plead its inherently private character or its subordination to the market as cover for the pursuit of different goals of particular interest to itself. The public agency has an unquestioned tendency to pursue goals that reflect its own interest and convenience and to

[5] A quotation from Richard Tybout, *Government Contracting in Atomic Energy* (1956), p. 175.

adapt social objective thereto. But it cannot plead this as a superior right. There may well be danger in this association of public and economic power. But it is less if it is recognized.

Other changes can be imagined. As the public character of the mature corporation comes to be recognized, attention will doubtless focus on the position of the stockholder in this corporation. This is anomalous. He is a passive and functionless figure, remarkable only in his capacity to share, without effort or even without appreciable risk, in the gains from the growth by which the technostructure measures its success. No grant of feudal privilege has ever equaled, for effortless return, that of the grandparent who bought and endowed his descendants with a thousand shares of General Motors, General Electric or I.B.M. The beneficiaries of this foresight have become and remain rich by no exercise of effort or intelligence beyond the decision to do nothing, embracing as it did the decision not to sell. But these matters need not be pursued here. Questions of equity and social justice as between the fortuitously rich have their own special expertise.

4

Most of the individual developments which are leading, if the harshest term may be employed, to the socialization of the mature corporation will be conceded, even by men of the most conservative disposition. The control by the mature corporation over its prices, its influence on consumer behavior, the euthanasia of stockholder power, the regulation by the state of aggregate demand, the effort to stabilize prices and wages, the role of publicly supported research and development, the role of military, space and related procurement, the influence of the firm on these government activities and the modern role of education are, more or less, accepted facts of life.

What is avoided is reflection on the consequences of putting them all together, of seeing them as a system. But it cannot be supposed that the principal beams and buttresses of the industrial system have all been changed and that the structure remains as before. If the parts have changed, so then has the whole. If this associates the mature corporation inextricably with the state, the fact cannot be exorcised by a simple refusal to add.

It will be urged, of course, that the industrial system is not the whole economy. Apart from the world of General Motors, Standard Oil, Ford, General Electric, U.S. Steel, Chrysler, Texaco, Gulf, Western Electric and Du Pont is that of the independent retailer, the farmer, the shoe repairman, the bookmaker, narcotics peddler, pizza merchant and that of the car and dog laundry. Here prices are not controlled. Here the consumer is sovereign. Here pecuniary motivation is unimpaired. Here technology is simple and there is no research or development to make it otherwise. Here there are no government contracts; independence from the state is a reality. None of these entrepreneurs patrol the precincts of the Massachusetts Institute of Technology in search of talent. The existence of all this I concede. And this part of the economic system is not insignificant. It is not, however, the part of the economy with which this book has been concerned. It has been concerned with the world of the large corporation. This too is important; and it is more deeply characteristic of the modern industrial scene than the dog laundry or the small manufacturer with a large idea. One should always cherish his critics and protect them where possible from error. The tendency of the mature corporation in the industrial system to become part of the administrative complex of the state ought not to be refuted by appeal to contrary tendencies outside the industrial system.

Some who dislike the notion that the industrial system merges into the state in its development will be tempted to assault not the tendency but those who adumbrate it. This, it must be urged, is not in keeping with contemporary ethics and manners. Once the bearers of bad tidings were hanged, disemboweled or made subject to some other equally sanguinary mistreatment. Now such reaction is regarded as lacking in delicacy. A doctor can inform even the most petulant client that he has terminal cancer without fear of adverse physical consequences. The aide who must advise a politician that a new poll shows him to be held in all but universal distaste need exercise only decent tact. Those who find unappealing the present intelligence are urged to exercise similar restraint.

They should also be aware of the causes. It is part of the vanity of modern man that he can decide the character of his economic system. His area of decision is, in fact, exceedingly small. He could, conceivably, decide whether or not he wishes to have a high level of industrialization. Thereafter the imperatives of organization, technology and planning operate similarly, and we have seen to a broadly similar result, on all societies. Given the decision to have modern industry, much of what happens is inevitable and the same.

5

The two questions most asked about an economic system are whether it serves man's physical needs and whether it is consistent with his liberty. There is little doubt as to the ability of the industrial system to serve man's needs. As we have seen, it is able to manage them only because it serves them abundantly. It requires a mechanism for making men want what it provides. But this mechanism would not work—wants would not be subject to manipulation— had not these wants been dulled by sufficiency.

The prospects for liberty involve far more interesting questions. It has always been imagined, especially by conservatives, that to associate all, or a large part, of economic activity with the state is to endanger freedom. The individual and his preferences, in one way or another, will be sacrificed to the needs and conveniences of the apparatus created ostensibly to serve him. As the industrial system evolves into a penumbra[6] of the state, the question of its relation to liberty thus arises in urgent form. In recent years, in the Soviet-type economies, there has been an ill-concealed conflict between the state and the intellectuals. In essence, this has been a conflict between those for whom the needs of the government, including above all its needs as economic planner and producer of goods, are pre-eminent and those who assert the high but inconvenient claims of uninhibited intellectual and artistic expression. Is this a warning?

The instinct which warns of dangers in this association of economic and public power is sound. It comes close to being the subject of this book. But conservatives have looked in the wrong direction for the danger. They have feared that the state might reach out and destroy the vigorous, money-making entrepreneur. They have not noticed that, all the while, the successors to the entrepreneur were uniting themselves ever more closely with the state and rejoicing in the result. They were also, and with enthusiasm, accepting abridgement of their freedom. Part of this is implicit in the subordination of

[6] Extension.

individual personality to the needs of organization. Some of it is in the exact pattern of the classical business expectation. The president of Republic Aviation is not much more likely in public to speak critically, or even candidly, of the Air Force than is the head of a Soviet *combinat* [7] of the ministry to which he reports. No modern head of the Ford Motor Company will ever react with the same pristine vigor to the presumed foolishness of Washington as did its founder. No head of Montgomery Ward will ever again breathe defiance of a President as did Sewell Avery.[8] Manners may be involved. But it would also be conceded that "too much is at stake."

The problem, however, is not the freedom of the businessman. Business orators have spoken much about freedom in the past. But it can be laid down as a rule that those who speak most of liberty are least inclined to use it. The high executive who speaks fulsomely of personal freedom carefully submits his speeches on the subject for review and elimination of controversial words, phrases and ideas, as befits a good organization man. The general who tells his troops, and the world, that they are in the forefront of the fight for freedom is a man who has always submitted happily to army discipline. The pillar of the foreign policy establishment who adverts most feelingly to the values of the free world is the man who extravagantly admires the orthodoxy of his own views.

The danger to liberty lies in the subordination of belief to the needs of the industrial system. In this the state and the industrial system will be partners. This threat has already been assessed, as also the means for minimizing it.

6

If we continue to believe that the goals of the industrial system—the expansion of output, the companion increase in consumption, technological advance, the public images that sustain it—are coordinate with life, then all of our lives will be in the service of these goals. What is consistent with these ends we shall have or be allowed; all else will be off limits. Our wants will be managed in accordance with the needs of the industrial system; the policies of the state will

[7] A state economic organization.
[8] Avery was the chief executive officer of Montgomery Ward who, during a labor dispute in the 1930s, defied a legal order issued by President Franklin D. Roosevelt.

be subject to similar influence; education will be adapted to industrial need; the disciplines required by the industrial system will be the conventional morality of the community. All other goals will be made to seem precious, unimportant or antisocial. We will be bound to the ends of the industrial system. The state will add its moral, and perhaps some of its legal, power to their enforcement. What will eventuate, on the whole, will be the benign servitude of the household retainer who is taught to love her mistress and see her interests as her own, and not the compelled servitude of the field hand. But it will not be freedom.

If, on the other hand, the industrial system is only a part, and relatively a diminishing part, of life, there is much less occasion for concern. Aesthetic goals will have pride of place; those who serve them will not be subject to the goals of the industrial system; the industrial system itself will be subordinate to the claims of these dimensions of life. Intellectual preparation will be for its own sake and not for the better service to the industrial system. Men will not be entrapped by the belief that apart from the goals of the industrial system—apart from the production of goods and income by progressively more advanced technical methods—there is nothing important in life.

The foregoing being so, we may, over time, come to see the industrial system in fitting light as an essentially technical arrangement for providing convenient goods and services in adequate volume. Those who rise through its bureaucracy will so see themselves. And the public consequences will be in keeping, for if economic goals are the only goals of the society it is natural that the industrial system should dominate the state and the state should serve its ends. If other goals are strongly asserted, the industrial system will fall into its place as a detached and autonomous arm of the state, but responsive to the larger purposes of the society.

We have seen wherein the chance for salvation lies. The industrial system, in contrast with its economic antecedents, is intellectually demanding. It brings into existence, to serve its intellectual and scientific needs, the community that, hopefully, will reject its monopoly of social purpose.

9

B. F. Skinner
Beyond Freedom and Dignity

✺

Behaviorism, a leading school of modern psychology, explains human behavior as physical responses to environmentally based stimuli and holds that the scientific method of studying behavior is the only way to understand human nature. B(urrhus) F(rederic) Skinner (1904–   ) is the most notable American exponent of the behavioral doctrine.

Born in Pennsylvania, Skinner received a bachelor's degree in English literature in 1926 from Hamilton College in Clinton, New York. After an unsuccessful period as a writer of fiction, he became interested in the behavioral theories of the Russian physiologist Ivan Pavlov and the American psychologist John Watson. He then undertook graduate work in experimental psychology at Harvard University, earning a doctorate in 1931. After teaching at Minnesota and Indiana universities, Skinner returned to Harvard in 1947 and remained on the faculty there until his retirement in 1975.

During the Second World War his interests in behavior led Skinner to the directorship of a secret government project aimed at training pigeons to pilot explosive missiles, such as bombs and torpedoes, by pecking at the center of target images. Such pecking by a pigeon placed in the nose of a missile would generate electrical impulses that would, in turn, control the missile's guidance system. Although the training was successful, the pecking pilots were never used in combat.

After the war, Skinner turned his inventiveness to more pacific pursuits. Seeking an optimum crib for his own infant, he devised the Air-Crib, a glass-sided, atmospherically controlled baby-tender. Later he developed the

Skinner box, a mechanism for observing and measuring changes in animal behavior; it is now used primarily by pharmaceutical researchers studying the effects of drugs on laboratory animals.

In the late 1950s, Skinner developed the concept of programmed instruction. *As proposed by Skinner, this instructional method includes the devising of a series of minute steps through which the learner is led to acquire complex forms of behavior or knowledge; such steps are presented to the learner by means of a "teaching machine." The deviser of the machine's "program" is seeking to control behavior. The learner—whether beast or human—is led through the program by the techniques of reinforcement, or reward. For humans using a teaching machine, the reinforcement at each step is the achievement of a correct answer. Food is often used in the training of other species. When Skinner trained pigeons to play ping-pong, for example, their reward was a grain of corn for every correct move.*

The major works written by Skinner—including a Utopian novel, Walden Two *(1948)—all tend to advance his behavioral thesis.* Beyond Freedom and Dignity *(1971), from which the following selection is taken, provoked especially bitter criticism among those who saw its views as destructive of traditional human values. In it, Skinner approves, as necessary for human survival, those same manipulative techniques that Ellul and Galbraith warn against. To adopt Skinner's "science of behavior" is to abandon the old notions of individual autonomy and free will. These concepts—like freedom and dignity—are "pre-scientific" ideas that Skinner believes are no longer appropriate to the human condition.*

Two features of autonomous man are particularly troublesome. In the traditional view, a person is free. He is autonomous in the sense that his behavior is uncaused. He can therefore be held responsible for what he does and justly punished if he offends. That view, together with its associated practices, must be re-examined when a scientific analysis reveals unsuspected controlling relations between behavior and environment. A certain amount of external control can be tolerated. Theologians have accepted the fact that man must be predestined to do what an omniscient God knows he will do, and the Greek dramatist took inexorable fate as his favorite theme. Soothsayers and astrologers often claim to predict what men will do, and they have always been in demand. Biographers and historians have searched for "influences" in the lives of individuals and peoples. Folk wisdom and the insights of essayists like Montaigne and Bacon imply some kind of predictability in human conduct, and the statistical and actuarial evidences of the social sciences point in the same direction.

Autonomous man survives in the face of all this because he is the happy exception. Theologians have reconciled predestination with free will, and the Greek audience, moved by the portrayal of an inescapable destiny, walked out of the theater free men. The course of history has been turned by the death of a leader or a storm at sea, as a life has been changed by a teacher or a love affair, but these things do not happen to everyone, and they do not affect everyone in the same way. Some historians have made a virtue of the unpredictability of history. Actuarial evidence is easily ignored; we read that hundreds of people will be killed in traffic accidents on a holiday weekend and take to the road as if personally exempt. Very little behavioral science raises "the specter of predictable man." On the contrary, many anthropologists, sociologists, and psychologists have used their expert knowledge to prove that man is free, purposeful, and responsible. Freud[1] was a determinist—on faith, if not on the evidence—but many Freudians have no hesitation in assuring their patients that they are free to choose among different courses of action and are in the long run the architects of their own destinies.

This escape route is slowly closed as new evidences of the predictability of human behavior are discovered. Personal exemption from a complete determinism is revoked as a scientific analysis progresses, particularly in accounting for the behavior of the individual. Joseph Wood Krutch has acknowledged the actuarial facts while insisting on personal freedom: "We can predict with a considerable degree of accuracy how many people will go to the seashore on a day when the temperature reaches a certain point, even how many will jump off a bridge . . . although I am not, nor are you, compelled to do either." But he can scarcely mean that those who go to the seashore do not go for good reason, or that circumstances in the life of a suicide do not have some bearing on the fact that he jumps off a bridge. The distinction is tenable only so long as a word like "compel" suggests a

---

[1] Sigmund Freud (1856–1939), an Austrian physician, was the founder of the therapeutic technique of psychoanalysis, which reveals the instinctual drives that dominate human behavior.

particularly conspicuous and forcible mode of control. A scientific analysis naturally moves in the direction of clarifying all kinds of controlling relations.

By questioning the control exercised by autonomous man and demonstrating the control exercised by the environment, a science of behavior also seems to question dignity or worth. A person is responsible for his behavior, not only in the sense that he may be justly blamed or punished when he behaves badly, but also in the sense that he is to be given credit and admired for his achievements. A scientific analysis shifts the credit as well as the blame to the environment, and traditional practices can then no longer be justified. These are sweeping changes, and those who are committed to traditional theories and practices naturally resist them.

There is a third source of trouble. As the emphasis shifts to the environment, the individual seems to be exposed to a new kind of danger. Who is to construct the controlling environment and to what end? Autonomous man presumably controls himself in accordance with a built-in set of values: he works for what he finds good. But what will the putative controller find good, and will it be good for those he controls? Answers to questions of this sort are said, of course, to call for value judgments.

Freedom, dignity, and value are major issues, and unfortunately they become more crucial as the power of a technology of behavior becomes more nearly commensurate with the problems to be solved. The very change which has brought some hope of a solution is responsible for a growing opposition to the kind of solution proposed. This conflict is itself a problem in human behavior and may be approached as such. A science of behavior is by no means as far advanced as physics or biology, but it has an advantage in that it may throw some light on its own difficulties. Science *is* human behavior, and so is the opposition to science. What has happened in man's struggle for freedom and dignity, and what problems arise when scientific knowledge begins to be relevant in that struggle? Answers to these questions may help to clear the way for the technology we so badly need. . . .

Almost all our major problems involve human behavior, and they cannot be solved by physical and biological technology alone. What is needed is a technology of behavior, but we have been slow to develop the science from which such a technology might be drawn. One difficulty is that almost all of what is called behavioral science continues to trace behavior to states of mind, feelings, traits of character, human nature, and so on. Physics and biology once followed similar practices and advanced only when they discarded them. The behavioral sciences have been slow to change partly because the explanatory entities often seem to be directly observed and partly because other kinds of explanations have been hard to find. The environment is obviously important, but its role has remained obscure. It does not push or pull, it *selects,* and this function is difficult to discover and analyze. The role of natural selection in evolution was formulated only a little more than a hundred years ago, and the selective role of the environment in shaping and maintaining the behavior of the individual is only beginning to be recognized and studied. As the interaction between organism and environment has come to be understood, however, effects once assigned to states of mind, feelings, and traits are beginning to be traced to accessible conditions, and a technology of behavior may therefore become available. It will not solve our problems, however, until it replaces traditional prescientific views, and these are strongly entrenched. Freedom and dignity illustrate the difficulty. They are the possessions of the autonomous man of traditional theory, and they are essential to practices in which a person is held responsible for his conduct and given credit for his achievements. A scientific analysis shifts both the responsibility and the achievement to the environment. It also raises questions concerning "values." Who will use a technology and to what ends? Until these issues are resolved, a technology of behavior will continue to be rejected, and with it possibly the only way to solve our problems.

· · ·

The evidence for a crude environmentalism is clear enough. People are extraordinarily different in different places, and possibly just because of the places. The nomad on horseback in Outer Mongolia and the astronaut in outer space are different people, but, as far as we know, if they had been exchanged at birth, they would have taken each other's place. (The expression "change places" shows how closely we identify a person's behavior with the environment in which it occurs.) But we need to know a great deal more before that fact becomes useful. What is it about the environment that produces a Hottentot?[2] And what would need to be changed to produce an English conservative instead?

Both the enthusiasm of the environmentalist and his usually ignominious failure are illustrated by Owen's utopian experiment at New Harmony.[3] A long history of environmental reform—in education, penology, industry, and family life, not to mention government and religion—has shown the same pattern. Environments are constructed on the model of environments in which good behavior has been observed, but the behavior fails to appear. Two hundred years of this kind of environmentalism has very little to show for itself, and for a simple reason. We must know how the environment works before we can change it to change behavior. A mere shift in emphasis from man to environment means very little.

Let us consider some examples in which the environment takes over the function and role of autonomous man. The first, often said to involve human nature, is *aggression*. Men often act in such a way that they harm others, and they often seem to be reinforced by signs of damage to others. The ethologists have emphasized contingencies of survival which would contribute these features to the genetic endowment of the species, but the contingencies of reinforcement in the lifetime of the individual are also significant, since anyone who acts aggressively to harm others is likely to be reinforced in other ways— for example, by taking possession of goods. The contingencies explain the behavior quite apart from any state or feeling of aggression or any initiating act by autonomous man.

Another example involving a so-called "trait of character" is *industry*. Some people are industrious in the sense that they work energetically for long periods of time, while others are lazy and idle in the sense that they do not. "Industry" and "laziness" are among thousands of so-called "traits." The behavior they refer to can be explained in other ways. Some of it may be attributed to genetic idiosyncrasies (and subject to change only through genetic measures), and the rest to environmental contingencies, which are much more important than is usually realized. Regardless of any normal

[2] A people native to southern Africa.
[3] Robert Owen (1771–1858) was a British industrialist, socialist, and philanthropist. Utilizing his environmentalist ideas, he established a "co-operative" community at New Harmony, Indiana, in 1825.

genetic endowment, an organism will range between vigorous activity and complete quiescence depending upon the schedules on which it has been reinforced. The explanation shifts from a trait of character to an environmental history of reinforcement.

A third example, a "cognitive" activity, is *attention*. A person responds only to a small part of the stimuli impinging upon him. The traditional view is that he himself determines which stimuli are to be effective by "paying attention" to them. Some kind of inner gatekeeper is said to allow some stimuli to enter and to keep all others out. A sudden or strong stimulus may break through and "attract" attention, but the person himself seems otherwise to be in control. An analysis of the environmental circumstances reverses the relation. The kinds of stimuli which break through by "attracting attention" do so because they have been associated in the evolutionary history of the species or the personal history of the individual with important—e.g., dangerous—things. Less forceful stimuli attract attention only to the extent that they have figured in contingencies of reinforcement. We can arrange contingencies which ensure that an organism—even such a "simple" organism as a pigeon—will attend to one object and not to another, or to one property of an object, such as its color, and not to another, such as its shape. The inner gatekeeper is replaced by the contingencies to which the organism has been exposed and which select the stimuli to which it reacts.

In the traditional view a person perceives the world around him and acts upon it to make it known to him. In a sense he reaches out and grasps it. He "takes it in" and possesses it. He "knows" it in the Biblical sense in which a man knows a woman. It has even been argued that the world would not exist if no one perceived it. The action is exactly reversed in an environmental analysis. There would, of course, be no perception if there were no world to be perceived, but an existing world would not be perceived if there were no appropriate contingencies. We say that a baby perceives his mother's face and knows it. Our evidence is that the baby responds in one way to his mother's face and in other ways to other faces or other things. He makes this distinction not through some mental act of perception but because of prior contingencies. Some of these may be contingencies of survival. Physical features of a species are particularly stable parts of the environment in which a species evolves. (That is why courtship and sex and relations between parent and offspring are given such a prominent place by ethologists.) The face and facial expressions of the human mother have been associated with security, warmth, food, and other important things, during both the evolution of the species and the life of the child.

We learn to perceive in the sense that we learn to respond to things in particular ways because of the contingencies of which they are a part. We may perceive the sun, for example, simply because it is an extremely powerful stimulus, but it has been a permanent part of the environment of the species throughout its evolution and more specific behavior with respect to it could have been selected by contingencies of survival (as it has been in many other species). The sun also figures in many current contingencies of reinforcement: we move into or out of sunlight depending on the temperature; we wait for the sun to rise or set to take practical action; we talk about the sun and its effects; and we eventually study the sun with the instruments and methods of science. Our perception of the sun depends on what we do with respect to it. Whatever we do, and hence however we perceive it, the fact remains that it is the environment which acts upon the perceiving person, not the perceiving person who acts upon the environment.

The perceiving and knowing which arise from verbal contingencies are even more obviously products of the environment. We react to an object in many practical ways because of its color; thus, we pick and eat red apples of a particular variety but not green. It is clear that we can "tell the difference" between red and green, but something more is involved when we say that we *know* that one apple is red and the other green. It is tempting to say that knowing is a cognitive process altogether divorced from action, but the contingencies provide a more useful distinction. When someone asks about the color of an object which he cannot see, and we tell him that it is red, *we* do nothing about the object in any other way. It is the person who has questioned us and heard our answer who makes a practical response which depends on color. Only under verbal contingencies can a speaker respond to an isolated property to which a nonverbal response cannot be made. A response made to the property of an object without responding to the object in any other way is called *abstract*. Abstract thinking is the product of a particular kind of environment, not of a cognitive faculty.

As listeners we acquire a kind of knowledge from the verbal behavior of others which may be extremely valuable in permitting us to avoid direct exposure to contingencies. We learn from the experience of others by responding to what they say about contingencies. When we are warned against doing something or are advised to do something, there may be no point in speaking of knowledge, but when we learn more durable kinds of warnings and advice in the form of maxims or rules, we may be said to have a special kind of knowledge about the contingencies to which they apply. The laws of science are descriptions of contingencies of reinforcement, and one who knows a scientific law may behave effectively without being exposed to the contingencies it describes. (He will, of course, have very different feelings about the contingencies, depending on whether he is following a rule or has been directly exposed to them. Scientific knowledge is "cold," but the behavior to which it gives rise is as effective as the "warm" knowledge which comes from personal experience.) . . .

It is in the nature of an experimental analysis of human behavior that it should strip away the functions previously assigned to autonomous man and transfer them one by one to the controlling environment. The analysis leaves less and less for autonomous man to do. But what about man himself? Is there not something about a person which is more than a living body? Unless something called a self survives, how can we speak of self-knowledge or self-control? To whom is the injunction "Know thyself" addressed?

It is an important part of the contingencies to which a young child is exposed that his own body is the only part of his environment which remains the same (*idem*) from moment to moment and day to day. We say that he discovers his *identity* as he learns to distinguish between his body and the rest of the world. He does this long before the community teaches him to call things by name and to distinguish "me" from "it" or "you."

A self is a repertoire of behavior appropriate to a given set of contingencies. A substantial part of the conditions to which a person is exposed may play a dominant role, and under other conditions a person may report, "I'm not myself today," or, "I couldn't have done what you said I did, because that's not like me." The identity conferred upon a self arises from the contingencies responsible for the behavior. Two or more repertoires generated by different sets of contingencies compose two or more selves. A person possesses one repertoire appropriate to his life with his friends and another appropriate to his life with his family, and a friend may find him a very different person if he sees him with his family or his family if they see him with his friends. The problem of identity arises when situations are intermingled, as when a person finds himself with both his family and his friends at the same time.

Self-knowledge and self-control imply two selves in this sense. The self-knower is almost always a product of social contingencies, but the self that is known may come from other sources. The controlling self (the conscience or superego) is of social origin, but the controlled self is more likely to be the product of genetic susceptibilities to reinforcement (the id,[4] or the Old Adam). The controlling self generally represents the interests of others, the controlled self the interests of the individual.

The picture which emerges from a scientific analysis is not of a body with a person inside, but of a body which *is* a person in the sense that it displays a complex repertoire of behavior. The picture is, of course, unfamiliar. The man thus portrayed is a stranger, and from the traditional point of view he may not seem to be a man at all. "For at least one hundred years," said Joseph Wood Krutch, "we have been prejudiced in every theory, including economic determinism, mechanistic behaviorism, and relativism, that reduces the stature of man until he ceases to be man at all in any sense that the humanists of an earlier generation would recognize." Matson has argued that "the empirical behavioral scientist . . . denies, if only by implication, that a unique being, called Man, exists." "What is now under attack," said Maslow, "is the 'being' of man." C. S. Lewis put it quite bluntly: Man is being abolished.

There is clearly some difficulty in identifying the man to whom these expressions refer. Lewis cannot have meant the human species, for not only is it not being abolished, it is filling the earth. (As a result it may eventually abolish itself through disease, famine, pollution, or a nuclear holocaust, but that is not what Lewis meant.) Nor are individual men growing less effective or productive. We are told that what is threatened is "man *qua* man," or "man in his humanity," or "man as Thou not It," or "man as a person not a thing." These are not very helpful expressions, but they supply a clue. What is being abolished is autonomous man—the inner man, the homun-

---

[4] In Freudian psychoanalysis, the unconscious part of the psyche that is the source of instinctual energies.

culus, the possessing demon, the man defended by the literatures of freedom and dignity.

His abolition has long been overdue. Autonomous man is a device used to explain what we cannot explain in any other way. He has been constructed from our ignorance, and as our understanding increases, the very stuff of which he is composed vanishes. Science does not dehumanize man, it de-homunculizes him, and it must do so if it is to prevent the abolition of the human species. To man *qua* man we readily say good riddance. Only by dispossessing him can we turn to the real causes of human behavior. Only then can we turn from the inferred to the observed, from the miraculous to the natural, from the inaccessible to the manipulable.

It is often said that in doing so we must treat the man who survives as a mere animal. "Animal" is a pejorative term, but only because "man" has been made spuriously honorific. Krutch has argued that whereas the traditional view supports Hamlet's exclamation, "How like a god!," Pavlov, the behavioral scientist, emphasized "How like a dog!" But that was a step forward. A god is the archetypal pattern of an explanatory fiction, of a miracle-working mind, of the metaphysical. Man is much more than a dog, but like a dog he is within range of a scientific analysis.

It is true that much of the experimental analysis of behavior has been concerned with lower organisms. Genetic differences are minimized by using special strains; environmental histories can be controlled, perhaps from birth; strict regimens can be maintained during long experiments; and very little of this is possible with human subjects. Moreover, in working with lower animals the scientist is less likely to put his own responses to the experimental conditions among his data, or to design contingencies with an eye to their effect on him rather than on the experimental organism he is studying. No one is disturbed when physiologists study respiration, reproduction, nutrition, or endocrine systems in animals; they do so to take advantage of very great similarities. Comparable similarities in behavior are being discovered. There is, of course, always the danger that methods designed for the study of lower animals will emphasize only those characteristics which they have in common with men, but we cannot discover what is "essentially" human until we have investigated nonhuman subjects. Traditional theories of autonomous man have exaggerated species differences. Some of the complex contingencies of reinforcement now under investigation generate behavior in lower organisms which, if the subjects were human, would traditionally be said to involve higher mental processes.

Man is not made into a machine by analyzing his behavior in mechanical terms. Early theories of behavior, as we have seen, represented man as a push-pull automaton, close to the nineteenth-century notion of a machine, but progress has been made. Man is a machine in the sense that he is a complex system behaving in lawful ways, but the complexity is extraordinary. His capacity to adjust to contingencies of reinforcement will perhaps be eventually simulated by machines, but this has not yet been done, and the living system thus simulated will remain unique in other ways.

Nor is man made into a machine by inducing him to use machines. Some machines call for behavior which is repetitious and monotonous, and we escape from them when we can, but others enormously extend our effectiveness in dealing with the world around us. A person may respond to very small things with the help of an electron microscope and to very large things with radiotelescopes, and in doing so he may seem quite inhuman to those who use only their unaided senses. A person may act upon the environment with the delicate precision of a micromanipulator or with the range and power of a space rocket, and his behavior may seem inhuman to those who rely only on muscular contractions. (It has been argued that the apparatus used in the operant laboratory misrepresents natural behavior because it introduces an external source of power, but men use external sources when they fly kites, sail boats, or shoot bows and arrows. They would have to abandon all but a small fraction of their achievements if they used only the power of their muscles.) People record their behavior in books and other media, and the use they make of the records may seem quite inhuman to those who can use only what they remember. People describe complex contingencies in the form of rules, and rules for manipulating rules, and they introduce them into electronic systems which "think" with a speed that seems quite inhuman to the unaided thinker. Human beings do all this with machines, and they would be less than human if they did not. What we now regard as machine-like behavior was, in fact, much commoner before the invention of these devices. The slave in the cotton field, the bookkeeper on his high stool, the student being drilled by a teacher—these were the machine-like men.

Machines replace people when they do what people have done,

and the social consequences may be serious. As technology advances, machines will take over more and more of the functions of men, but only up to a point. We build machines which reduce some of the aversive features of our environment (grueling labor, for example) and which produce more positive reinforcers. We build them precisely because they do so. We have no reason to build machines to be reinforced by these consequences, and to do so would be to deprive ourselves of reinforcement. If the machines man makes eventually make him wholly expendable, it will be by accident, not design.

An important role of autonomous man has been to give human behavior direction, and it is often said that in dispossessing an inner agent we leave man himself without a purpose. As one writer has put it, "Since a scientific psychology must regard human behavior objectively, as determined by necessary laws, it must represent human behavior as unintentional." But "necessary laws" would have this effect only if they referred exclusively to antecedent conditions. Intention and purpose refer to selective consequences, the effects of which can be formulated in "necessary laws." Has life, in all the forms in which it exists on the surface of the earth, a purpose, and is this evidence of intentional design? The primate hand evolved *in order that* things might be more successfully manipulated, but its purpose is to be found not in a prior design but rather in the process of selection. Similarly, in operant conditioning the purpose of a skilled movement of the hand is to be found in the consequences which follow it. A pianist neither acquires nor executes the behavior of playing a scale smoothly because of a prior intention of doing so. Smoothly played scales are reinforcing for many reasons, and they select skilled movements. In neither the evolution of the human hand nor in the acquired use of the hand is any prior intention or purpose at issue.

The argument for purpose seems to be strengthened by moving back into the darker recesses of mutation. Jacques Barzun has argued that Darwin[5] and Marx[6] both neglected not only human purpose but the creative purpose responsible for the variations upon which

[5] Charles Darwin (1809–82), an English naturalist who developed a theory of biological evolution based on natural selection.
[6] Karl Marx (1818–83), a German-born political philosopher, was the major originator of the modern socialist theory that human history is determined by the conflict of impersonal economic forces.

natural selection plays. It may prove to be the case, as some geneticists have argued, that mutations are not entirely random, but nonrandomness is not necessarily the proof of a creative mind. Mutations will not be random when geneticists explicitly design them in order that an organism will meet specific conditions of selection more successfully, and geneticists will then seem to be playing the role of the creative Mind in pre-evolutionary theory, but the purpose they display will have to be sought in their culture, in the social environment which has induced them to make genetic changes appropriate to contingencies of survival.

There is a difference between biological and individual purpose in that the latter can be felt. No one could have felt the purpose in the development of the human hand, whereas a person can in a sense feel the purpose with which he plays a smooth scale. But he does not play a smooth scale *because* he feels the purpose of doing so; what he feels is a by-product of his behavior in relation to its consequences. The relation of the human hand to the contingencies of survival under which it evolved is, of course, out of reach of personal observation; the relation of the behavior to contingencies of reinforcement which have generated it is not.

A scientific analysis of behavior dispossesses autonomous man and turns the control he has been said to exert over to the environment. The individual may then seem particularly vulnerable. He is henceforth to be controlled by the world around him, and in large part by other men. Is he not then simply a victim? Certainly men have been victims, as they have been victimizers, but the word is too strong. It implies despoliation, which is by no means an essential consequence of interpersonal control. But even under benevolent control is the individual not at best a spectator who may watch what happens but is helpless to do anything about it? Is he not "at a dead end in his long struggle to control his own destiny"?

It is only autonomous man who has reached a dead end. Man himself may be controlled by his environment, but it is an environment which is almost wholly of his own making. The physical environment of most people is largely man-made. The surfaces a person walks on, the walls which shelter him, the clothing he wears, many of the foods he eats, the tools he uses, the vehicles he moves about in, most of the things he listens to and looks at are human products. The social environment is obviously man-made—it generates the language a person speaks, the customs he follows, and the behavior he exhibits with respect to the ethical, religious, governmental, economic, educational, and psychotherapeutic institutions which control him. The evolution of a culture is in fact a kind of gigantic exercise in self-control. As the individual controls himself by manipulating the world in which he lives, so the human species has constructed an environment in which its members behave in a highly effective way. Mistakes have been made, and we have no assurance that the environment man has constructed will continue to provide gains which outstrip the losses, but man as we know him, for better or for worse, is what man has made of man.

This will not satisfy those who cry "Victim!" C. S. Lewis protested: ". . . the power of man to make himself what he pleases . . . means . . . the power of some men to make other men what they please." This is inevitable in the nature of cultural evolution. The controlling *self* must be distinguished from the controlled self, even when they are both inside the same skin, and when control is exercised through the design of an external environment, the selves are, with minor exceptions, distinct. The person who unintentionally or intentionally introduces a new cultural practice is only one among possibly billions who will be affected by it. If this does not seem like an act of self-control, it is only because we have misunderstood the nature of self-control in the individual.

When a person changes his physical or social environment "intentionally"—that is, in order to change human behavior, possibly including his own—he plays two roles: one as a controller, as the designer of a controlling culture, and another as the controlled, as the product of a culture. There is nothing inconsistent about this; it follows from the nature of the evolution of a culture, with or without intentional design.

The human species has probably not undergone much genetic change in recorded time. We have only to go back a thousand generations to reach the artists of the caves of Lascaux.[7] Features which bear directly on survival (such as resistance to disease) change substantially in a thousand generations, but the child of one of the Lascaux artists transplanted to the world of today might be almost indistinguishable from a modern child. It is possible that he would

---

[7]The ceilings and walls of these caves in central France bear paintings (mainly of animals) that were done by hunter-artists of nearly fifteen thousand years ago.

learn more slowly than his modern counterpart, that he could maintain only a smaller repertoire without confusion, or that he would forget more quickly; we cannot be sure. But we can be sure that a twentieth-century child transplanted to the civilization of Lascaux would not be very different from the children he met there, for we have seen what happens when a modern child is raised in an impoverished environment.

Man has greatly changed himself as a person in the same period of time by changing the world in which he lives. Something of the order of a hundred generations will cover the development of modern religious practices, and something of the same order of magnitude modern government and law. Perhaps no more than twenty generations will account for modern industrial practices, and possibly no more than four or five for education and psychotherapy. The physical and biological technologies which have increased man's sensitivity to the world around him and his power to change that world have taken no more than four or five generations.

Man has "controlled his own destiny," if that expression means anything at all. The man that man has made is the product of the culture man has devised. He has emerged from two quite different processes of evolution: the biological evolution responsible for the human species and the cultural evolution carried out by that species. Both of these processes of evolution may now accelerate because they are both subject to intentional design. Men have already changed their genetic endowment by breeding selectively and by changing contingencies of survival, and they may now begin to introduce mutations directly related to survival. For a long time men have introduced new practices which serve as cultural mutations, and they have changed the conditions under which practices are selected. They may now begin to do both with a clearer eye to the consequences.

Man will presumably continue to change, but we cannot say in what direction. No one could have predicted the evolution of the human species at any point in its early history, and the direction of intentional genetic design will depend upon the evolution of a culture which is itself unpredictable for similar reasons. "The limits of perfection of the human species," said Étienne Cabet in *Voyage en Icarie,* "are as yet unknown." But, of course, there are no limits. The human species will never reach a final state of perfection before it is exterminated—"some say in fire, some in ice," and some in radiation.

The individual occupies a place in a culture not unlike his place in the species, and in early evolutionary theory that place was hotly debated. Was the species simply a type of individual, and if so, in what sense could it evolve? Darwin himself declared species "to be purely subjective inventions of the taxonomist." A species has no existence except as a collection of individuals, nor has a family, tribe, race, nation, or class. A culture has no existence apart from the behavior of the individuals who maintain its practices. It is always an individual who behaves, who acts upon the environment and is changed by the consequences of his action, and who maintains the social contingencies which *are* a culture. The individual is the carrier of both his species and his culture. Cultural practices, like genetic traits, are transmitted from individual to individual. A new practice, like a new genetic trait, appears first in an individual and tends to be transmitted if it contributes to his survival as an individual.

Yet, the individual is at best a locus in which many lines of development come together in a unique set. His individuality is unquestioned. Every cell in his body is a unique genetic product, as unique as that classic mark of individuality, the fingerprint. And even within the most regimented culture every personal history is unique. No intentional culture can destroy that uniqueness, and, as we have seen, any effort to do so would be bad design. But the individual nevertheless remains merely a stage in a process which began long before he came into existence and will long outlast him. He has no ultimate responsibility for a species trait or a cultural practice, even though it was he who underwent the mutation or introduced the practice which became part of the species or culture. Even if Lamarck had been right in supposing that the individual could change his genetic structure through personal effort, we should have to point to the environmental circumstances responsible for the effort, as we shall have to do when geneticists begin to change the human endowment. And when an individual engages in the intentional design of a cultural practice, we must turn to the culture which induces him to do so and supplies the art or science he uses.

One of the great problems of individualism, seldom recognized as such, is death—the inescapable fate of the individual, the final assault on freedom and dignity. Death is one of those remote events which are brought to bear on behavior only with the aid of cultural practices. What we see is the death of others, as in Pascal's famous metaphor: "Imagine a number of men in chains, all under sentence of death, some of whom are each day butchered in the sight of the others; those remaining see their own condition in that of their fellows, and looking at each other with grief and despair await their turn. This is an image of the human condition." Some religions have made death more important by picturing a future existence in heaven or hell, but the individualist has a special reason to fear death, engineered not by a religion but by the literatures of freedom and dignity. It is the prospect of personal annihilation. The individualist can find no solace in reflecting upon any contribution which will survive him. He has refused to act for the good of others and is therefore not reinforced by the fact that others whom he has helped will outlive him. He has refused to be concerned for the survival of his culture and is not reinforced by the fact that the culture will long survive him. In the defense of his own freedom and dignity he has denied the contributions of the past and must therefore relinquish all claim upon the future.

• • •

Science has probably never demanded a more sweeping change in a traditional way of thinking about a subject, nor has there ever been a more important subject. In the traditional picture a person perceives the world around him, selects features to be perceived, discriminates among them, judges them good or bad, changes them to make them better (or, if he is careless, worse), and may be held responsible for his action and justly rewarded or punished for its consequences. In the scientific picture a person is a member of a species shaped by evolutionary contingencies of survival, displaying behavioral processes which bring him under the control of the environment in which he lives, and largely under the control of a social environment which he and millions of others like him have constructed and maintained during the evolution of a culture. The direction of the controlling relation is reversed: a person does not act upon the world, the world acts upon him.

It is difficult to accept such a change simply on intellectual grounds and nearly impossible to accept its implications. The reaction of the traditionalist is usually described in terms of feelings. One of these, to which the Freudians have appealed in explaining the resistance to psychoanalysis, is wounded vanity. Freud himself expounded, as Ernest Jones has said, "the three heavy blows which narcissism or self-love of mankind had suffered at the hands of science. The first was cosmological and was dealt by Copernicus;[8] the second was biological and was dealt by Darwin; the third was psychological and was dealt by Freud." (The blow was suffered by the belief that something at the center of man knows all that goes on within him and that an instrument called will power exercises command and control over the rest of one's personality.) But what are the signs or symptoms of wounded vanity, and how shall we explain them? What people *do* about such a scientific picture of man is call it wrong, demeaning, and dangerous, argue against it, and attack those who propose or defend it. They do so not out of wounded vanity but because the scientific formulation has destroyed accustomed reinforcers. If a person can no longer take credit or be admired for what he does, then he seems to suffer a loss of dignity or worth, and behavior previously reinforced by credit or admiration will undergo extinction. Extinction often leads to aggressive attack.

Another effect of the scientific picture has been described as a loss of faith or "nerve," as a sense of doubt or powerlessness, or as discouragement, depression, or despondency. A person is said to feel that he can do nothing about his own destiny. But what he feels is a weakening of old responses which are no longer reinforced. People are indeed "powerless" when long-established verbal repertoires prove useless. For example, one historian has complained that if the deeds of men are "to be dismissed as simply the product of material and psychological conditioning," there is nothing to write about; "change must be at least partially the result of conscious mental activity."

Another effect is a kind of nostalgia. Old repertoires break through, as similarities between present and past are seized upon and exaggerated. Old days are called the good old days, when the inherent dignity of man and the importance of spiritual values were recognized. Such fragments of outmoded behavior tend to be "wistful"—that is, they have the character of increasingly unsuccessful behavior.

---

[8] Nicolaus Copernicus (1473–1543), a Polish astronomer, was the first modern scientist to state that the sun—not the earth—is the center of the solar system.

These reactions to a scientific conception of man are certainly unfortunate. They immobilize men of good will, and anyone concerned with the future of his culture will do what he can to correct them. No theory changes what it is a theory about. Nothing is changed because we look at it, talk about it, or analyze it in a new way. Keats drank confusion to Newton for analyzing the rainbow, but the rainbow remained as beautiful as ever and became for many even more beautiful. Man has not changed because we look at him, talk about him, and analyze him scientifically. His achievements in science, government, religion, art, and literature remain as they have always been, to be admired as one admires a storm at sea or autumn foliage or a mountain peak, quite apart from their origins and untouched by a scientific analysis. What does change is our chance of doing something about the subject of a theory. Newton's analysis of the light in a rainbow was a step in the direction of the laser.

The traditional conception of man is flattering; it confers reinforcing privileges. It is therefore easily defended and can be changed only with difficulty. It was designed to build up the individual as an instrument of countercontrol, and it did so effectively but in such a way as to limit progress. We have seen how the literatures of freedom and dignity, with their concern for autonomous man, have perpetuated the use of punishment and condoned the use of only weak nonpunitive techniques, and it is not difficult to demonstrate a connection between the unlimited right of the individual to pursue happiness and the catastrophes threatened by unchecked breeding, the unrestrained affluence which exhausts resources and pollutes the environment, and the imminence of nuclear war.

Physical and biological technologies have alleviated pestilence and famine and many painful, dangerous, and exhausting features of daily life, and behavioral technology can begin to alleviate other kinds of ills. In the analysis of human behavior it is just possible that we are slightly beyond Newton's position in the analysis of light, for we are beginning to make technological applications. There are wonderful possibilities—and all the more wonderful because traditional approaches have been so ineffective. It is hard to imagine a world in which people live together without quarreling, maintain themselves by producing the food, shelter, and clothing they need, enjoy themselves and contribute to the enjoyment of others in art, music, literature, and games, consume only a reasonable part of the resources of the world and add as little as possible to its pollution, bear no more

children than can be raised decently, continue to explore the world
around them and discover better ways of dealing with it, and come
to know themselves accurately and, therefore, manage themselves effectively. Yet all this is possible, and even the slightest sign of progress should bring a kind of change which in traditional terms would
be said to assuage wounded vanity, offset a sense of hopelessness or
nostalgia, correct the impression that "we neither can nor need to do
anything for ourselves," and promote a "sense of freedom and dignity" by building "a sense of confidence and worth." In other
words, it should abundantly reinforce those who have been induced
by their culture to work for its survival. . . .

10

Aldous Huxley
Brave New World

Scientific methods of studying and, ultimately, manipulating human behavior have grimly dehumanizing possibilities. An early warning of these oppressive prospects was given by Aldous Huxley (1894–1963), an English writer and social critic. In several of his works, Huxley predicted the tragic consequences of a "free" individual's conflict with a totalitarian society able to employ scientific techniques in human conditioning, techniques similar to those that B. F. Skinner and other behaviorists would find socially necessary.

A member of one of England's most intellectually distinguished families, Huxley once intended to be a doctor; however, while in school he contracted an eye disease that left him nearly blind for several years. Thus denied a medical career, he turned toward literature, typing out a first novel even though unable to read it. Eventually, one eye recovered enough to allow him to read with the aid of a magnifying glass; he was soon able to enroll at Oxford University and, in 1915, obtained a degree in English literature. In later years Huxley was to call his eye trouble "the most important single event" in his life, for the lack of sight forced him to live mainly on his "own inner resources."

After leaving Oxford, Huxley made his living as a writer and editor, traveling throughout Europe, India, and Central America. In 1937 he settled permanently in southern California where techniques for training his eyes were particularly advanced. To him, the method of eye training he followed there demonstrated "the possibility of becoming the master of one's circumstances instead of their slave." Free of severe physical handicap, Huxley declared that "It is with the problem of personal, psychological freedom that I now find myself predominantly concerned." In his later years he became very interested in mysticism as a means of liberating oneself from the bondage of the ego and also experimented with the drug mescalin for that purpose. (See selection 40.)

In the novel Brave New World (1932) Huxley dramatically depicts the dangers of external controls over the individual. The following excerpt from the opening chapters of the book shows the principles of standardized assembly-line production applied to human breeding in the year A.F. (after Ford) 632. Physiological differentiations are given to embryos by chemical means; all individuals are trained to fulfill and accept their respective specialized roles. In the interest of avoiding violence and providing personal happiness (pleasure), the members of each social class are conditioned to "like their unescapable social destiny." Daily doses of soma, a tranquilizing "happy pill," dissolve any feelings of boredom or unpleasantness. The plot develops out of the intellectual and moral conflicts between certain individuals and the society. Despite the incessant conditioning in the "brave new world," a few nonconforming individuals attempt to survive with "freedom and dignity."

An essay by Huxley published in 1958, "Brave New World Revisited," considers the quickening pace toward "total organization" in the two decades following publication of the novel. Observing this pace, Huxley changes his projection regarding the arrival of "dystopia" from six centuries away to "just around the next corner."

CHAPTER ONE

A squat grey building of only thirty-four stories. Over the main entrance the words, CENTRAL LONDON HATCHERY AND CONDITIONING CENTRE, and, in a shield, the World State's motto, COMMUNITY, IDENTITY, STABILITY.

The enormous room on the ground floor faced towards the north. Cold for all the summer beyond the panes, for all the tropical heat of the room itself, a harsh thin light glared through the windows, hungrily seeking some draped lay figure, some pallid shape of academic goose-flesh, but finding only the glass and nickel and bleakly shining porcelain of a laboratory. Wintriness responded to wintriness. The overalls of the workers were white, their hands gloved with a pale corpse-coloured rubber. The light was frozen, dead, a ghost. Only from the yellow barrels of the microscopes did it borrow a certain rich and living substance, lying along the polished tubes like butter, streak after luscious streak in long recession down the work tables.

"And this," said the Director opening the door, "is the Fertilizing Room."

Bent over their instruments, three hundred Fertilizers were plunged, as the Director of Hatcheries and Conditioning entered the room, in the scarcely breathing silence, the absent-minded, soliloquizing hum or whistle, of absorbed concentration. A troop of newly arrived students, very young, pink and callow, followed nervously, rather abjectly, at the Director's heels. Each of them carried a notebook, in which, whenever the great man spoke, he desperately scribbled. Straight from the horse's mouth. It was a rare privilege. The D.H.C. for Central London always made a point of personally conducting his new students round the various departments.

"Just to give you a general idea," he would explain to them. For of course some sort of general idea they must have, if they were to do their work intelligently—though as little of one, if they were to be good and happy members of society, as possible. For particulars, as every one knows, make for virtue and happiness; generalities are intellectually necessary evils. Not philosophers but fret-sawyers[1] and stamp collectors compose the backbone of society.

"To-morrow," he would add, smiling at them with a slightly menacing geniality, "you'll be settling down to serious work. You won't have time for generalities. Meanwhile . . ."

Meanwhile, it was a privilege. Straight from the horse's mouth into the notebook. The boys scribbled like mad.

Tall and rather thin but upright, the Director advanced into the room. He had a long chin and big, rather prominent teeth, just covered, when he was not talking, by his full, floridly curved lips. Old, young? Thirty? Fifty? Fifty-five? It was hard to say. And anyhow the question didn't arise; in this year of stability, A.F. 632, it didn't occur to you to ask it.

"I shall begin at the beginning," said the D.H.C. and the more zealous students recorded his intention in their notebooks: *Begin at*

---

[1] People who carve elaborate decorative patterns (frets).

the beginning. "These," he waved his hand, "are the incubators." And opening an insulated door he showed them racks upon racks of numbered test-tubes. "The week's supply of ova. Kept," he explained, "at blood heat; whereas the male gametes," and here he opened another door, "they have to be kept at thirty-five instead of thirty-seven. Full blood heat sterilizes." Rams wrapped in theremogene beget no lambs.

Still leaning against the incubators he gave them, while the pencils scurried illegibly across the pages, a brief description of the modern fertilizing process; spoke first, of course, of its surgical introduction—"the operation undergone voluntarily for the good of Society, not to mention the fact that it carries a bonus amounting to six months' salary"; continued with some account of the technique for preserving the excised ovary alive and actively developing; passed on to a consideration of optimum temperature, salinity, viscosity; referred to the liquor in which the detached and ripened eggs were kept; and, leading his charges to the work tables, actually showed them how this liquor was drawn off from the test-tubes; how it was let out drop by drop onto the specially warmed slides of the microscopes; how the eggs which it contained were inspected for abnormalities, counted and transferred to a porous receptacle; how (and he now took them to watch the operation) this receptacle was immersed in a warm bouillon containing free-swimming spermatozoa—at a minimum concentration of one hundred thousand per cubic centrimetre, he insisted; and how, after ten minutes, the container was lifted out of the liquor and its contents re-examined; how, if any of the eggs remained unfertilized, it was again immersed, and, if necessary, yet again; how the fertilized ova went back to the incubators; where the Alphas and Betas remained until definitely bottled; while the Gammas, Deltas and Epsilons were brought out again, after only thirty-six hours, to undergo Bokanovsky's Process.

"Bokanovsky's Process," repeated the Director, and the students underlined the words in their little notebooks.

One egg, one embryo, one adult—normality. But a bokanovskified egg will bud, will proliferate, will divide. From eight to ninety-six buds, and every bud will grow into a perfectly formed embryo, and every embryo into a full-sized adult. Making ninety-six human beings grow where only one grew before. Progress.

"Essentially," the D.H.C. concluded, "bokanovskification consists of a series of arrests of development. We check the normal growth and, paradoxically enough, the egg responds by budding."

Responds by budding. The pencils were busy.

He pointed. On a very slowly moving band a rack-full of test-tubes was entering a large metal box, another rack-full was emerging. Machinery faintly purred. It took eight minutes for the tubes to go through, he told them. Eight minutes of hard X-rays being about as much as an egg can stand. A few died; of the rest, the least susceptible divided into two; most put out four buds; some eight; all were returned to the incubators, where the buds began to develop; then, after two days, were suddenly chilled, chilled and checked. Two, four, eight, the buds in their turn budded; and having budded were dosed almost to death with alcohol; consequently burgeoned again and having budded—bud out of bud out of bud—were thereafter—further arrest being generally fatal—left to develop in peace. By which time the original egg was in a fair way to becoming anything from eight to ninety-six embryos—a prodigious improvement, you will agree, on nature. Identical twins—but not in piddling twos and threes as in the old viviparous days, when an egg would sometimes accidentally divide; actually by dozens, by scores at a time.

"Scores," the Director repeated and flung out his arms, as though he were distributing largesse. "Scores."

But one of the students was fool enough to ask where the advantage lay.

"My good boy!" The Director wheeled sharply round on him. "Can't you see? Can't you *see?*" He raised a hand; his expression was solemn. "Bokanovsky's Process is one of the major instruments of social stability!"

Major instruments of social stability.

Standard men and women; in uniform batches. The whole of a small factory staffed with the products of a single bokanovskified egg.

"Ninety-six identical twins working ninety-six identical machines!" The voice was almost tremulous with enthusiasm. "You really know where you are. For the first time in history." He quoted the planetary motto. "Community, Identity, Stability." Grand words. "If we could bokanovskify indefinitely the whole problem would be solved."

Solved by standard Gammas, unvarying Deltas, uniform Epsilons.

Millions of identical twins. The principle of mass production at last applied to biology.

"But, alas," the Director shook his head, "we *can't* bokanovskify indefinitely."

Ninety-six seemed to be the limit; seventy-two a good average. From the same ovary and with gametes of the same male to manufacture as many batches of identical twins as possible—that was the best (sadly a second best) that they could do. And even that was difficult.

"For in nature it takes thirty years for two hundred eggs to reach maturity. But our business is to stabilize the population at this moment, here and now. Dribbling out twins over a quarter of a century—what would be the use of that?"

Obviously, no use at all. But Podsnap's Technique had immensely accelerated the process of ripening. They could make sure of at least a hundred and fifty mature eggs within two years. Fertilize and bokanovskify—in other words, multiply by seventy-two—and you get an average of nearly eleven thousand brothers and sisters in a hundred and fifty batches of identical twins, all within two years of the same age.

"And in exceptional cases we can make one ovary yield us over fifteen thousand adult individuals."

Beckoning to a fair-haired, ruddy young man who happened to be passing at the moment, "Mr. Foster," he called. The ruddy young man approached. "Can you tell us the record for a single ovary, Mr. Foster?"

"Sixteen thousand and twelve in this Centre," Mr. Foster replied without hesitation. He spoke very quickly, had a vivacious blue eye, and took an evident pleasure in quoting figures. "Sixteen thousand and twelve; in one hundred and eighty-nine batches of identicals. But of course they've done much better," he rattled on, "in some of the tropical Centres. Singapore has often produced over sixteen thousand five hundred; and Mombasa has actually touched the seventeen thousand mark. But then they have unfair advantages. You should see the way a negro ovary responds to pituitary! It's quite astonishing, when you're used to working with European material. Still," he added, with a laugh (but the light of combat was in his eyes and the lift of his chin was challenging), "still, we mean to beat them if we can. I'm working on a wonderful Delta-Minus ovary at this moment. Only just eighteen months old. Over twelve thousand seven hundred children already, either decanted or in embryo. And still going strong. We'll beat them yet."

"That's the spirit I like!" cried the Director, and clapped Mr. Foster on the shoulder. "Come along with us and give these boys the benefit of your expert knowledge."

Mr. Foster smiled modestly. "With pleasure." They went.

In the Bottling Room all was harmonious bustle and ordered activity. Flaps of fresh sow's peritoneum ready cut to the proper size came shooting up in little lifts from the Organ Store in the sub-basement. Whizz and then, click! the lift-hatches flew open; the bottle-liner had only to reach out a hand, take the flap, insert, smooth-down, and before the lined bottle had had time to travel out of reach along the endless band, whizz, click! another flap of peritoneum had shot up from the depths, ready to be slipped into yet another bottle, the next of that slow interminable procession on the band.

Next to the Liners stood the Matriculators. The procession advanced; one by one the eggs were transferred from their test-tubes to the larger containers; deftly the peritoneal lining was slit, the morula dropped into place, the saline solution poured in . . . and already the bottle had passed, and it was the turn of the labellers. Heredity, date of fertilization, membership of Bokanovsky Group—details were transferred from test-tube to bottle. No longer anonymous, but named, identified, the procession marched slowly on; on through an opening in the wall, slowly on into the Social Predestination Room.

"Eighty-eight cubic metres of card-index," said Mr. Foster with relish, as they entered.

"Containing *all* the relevant information," added the Director.

"Brought up to date every morning."

"And co-ordinated every afternoon."

"On the basis of which they make their calculations."

"So many individuals, of such and such quality," said Mr. Foster.

"Distributed in such and such quantities."

"The optimum Decanting Rate at any given moment."

"Unforeseen wastages promptly made good."

"Promptly," repeated Mr. Foster. "If you knew the amount of overtime I had to put in after the last Japanese earthquake!" He laughed good-humouredly and shook his head.

"The Predestinators send in their figures to the Fertilizers."

"Who give them the embryos they ask for."

"And the bottles come in here to be predestinated in detail."

"After which they are sent down to the Embryo Store."

"Where we now proceed ourselves."

And opening a door Mr. Foster led the way down a staircase into the basement.

The temperature was still tropical. They descended into a thickening twilight. Two doors and a passage with a double turn insured the cellar against any possible infiltration of the day.

"Embryos are like photograph film," said Mr. Foster waggishly, as he pushed open the second door. "They can only stand red light."

And in effect the sultry darkness into which the students now followed him was visible and crimson, like the darkness of closed eyes on a summer's afternoon. The bulging flanks of row on receding row and tier above tier of bottles glinted with innumerable rubies, and among the rubies moved the dim red spectres of men and women with purple eyes and all the symptoms of lupus. The hum and rattle of machinery faintly stirred the air.

"Give them a few figures, Mr. Foster," said the Director, who was tired of talking.

Mr. Foster was only too happy to give them a few figures.

Two hundred and twenty metres long, two hundred wide, ten high. He pointed upwards. Like chickens drinking, the students lifted their eyes towards the distant ceiling.

Three tiers of racks: ground floor level, first gallery, second gallery.

The spidery steel-work of gallery above gallery faded away in all directions into the dark. Near them three red ghosts were busily unloading demijohns from a moving staircase.

The escalator from the Social Predestination Room.

Each bottle could be placed on one of fifteen racks, each rack, though you couldn't see it, was a conveyor travelling at the rate of thirty-three and a third centimetres an hour. Two hundred and sixty-seven days at eight metres a day. Two thousand one hundred and thirty-six metres in all. One circuit of the cellar at ground level, one on the first gallery, half on the second, and on the two hundred and sixty-seventh morning, daylight in the Decanting Room. Independent existence—so called.

"But in the interval," Mr. Foster concluded, "we've managed to do a lot to them. Oh, a very great deal." His laugh was knowing and triumphant.

"That's the spirit I like," said the Director once more. "Let's walk round. You tell them everything, Mr. Foster."

Mr. Foster duly told them.

Told them of the growing embryo on its bed of peritoneum. Made them taste the rich blood surrogate on which it fed. Explained why it had to be stimulated with placentin and thyroxin. Told them of the *corpus luteum* extract. Showed them the jets through which at every twelfth metre from zero to 2040 it was automatically injected. Spoke of those gradually increasing doses of pituitary administered during the final ninety-six metres of their course. Described the artificial maternal circulation installed on every bottle at Metre 112; showed them the reservoir of blood-surrogate, the centrifugal pump that kept the liquid moving over the placenta and drove it through the synthetic lung and waste-product filter. Referred to the embryo's troublesome tendency to anæmia, to the massive doses of hog's stomach extract and foetal foal's liver with which, in consequence, it had to be supplied.

Showed them the simple mechanism by means of which, during the last two metres out of every eight, all the embryos were simultaneously shaken into familiarity with movement. Hinted at the gravity of the so-called "trauma of decanting," and enumerated the precautions taken to minimize, by a suitable training of the bottled embryo, that dangerous shock. Told them of the tests for sex carried out in the neighbourhood of metre 200. Explained the system of labelling—a T for the males, a circle for the females and for those who were destined to become freemartins a question mark, black on a white ground.

"For of course," said Mr. Foster, "in the vast majority of cases, fertility is merely a nuisance. One fertile ovary in twelve hundred— that would really be quite sufficient for our purposes. But we want to have a good choice. And of course one must always leave an enormous margin of safety. So we allow as many as thirty per cent. of the female embryos to develop normally. The others get a dose of male sex-hormone every twenty-four metres for the rest of the course. Result: they're decanted as freemartins—structurally quite normal (except," he had to admit, "that they *do* have just the slightest tendency to grow beards), but sterile. Guranteed sterile. Which brings us at last," continued Mr. Foster, "out of the realm of mere slavish imitation of nature into the much more interesting world of human invention."

He rubbed his hands. For of course, they didn't content themselves with merely hatching out embryos: any cow could do that.

"We also predestine and condition. We decant our babies as socialized human beings, as Alphas or Epsilons, as future sewage workers or future . . ." He was going to say "future World controllers," but correcting himself, said "future Directors of Hatcheries," instead.

The D.H.C. acknowledged the compliment with a smile.

They were passing Metre 320 on rack 11. A young Beta-Minus mechanic was busy with screwdriver and spanner on the blood-surrogate pump of a passing bottle. The hum of the electric motor deepened by fractions of a tone as he turned the nuts. Down, down . . . A final twist, a glance at the revolution counter, and he was done. He moved two paces down the line and began the same process on the next pump.

"Reducing the number of revolutions per minute," Mr. Foster explained. "The surrogate goes round slower; therefore passes through the lung at longer intervals; therefore gives the embryo less oxygen. Nothing like oxygen-shortage for keeping an embryo below par." Again he rubbed his hands.

"But why do you want to keep the embryo below par?" asked an ingenuous student.

"Ass!" said the Director, breaking a long silence. "Hasn't it occurred to you that an Epsilon embryo must have an Epsilon environment as well as an Epsilon heredity?"

It evidently hadn't occurred to him. He was covered with confusion.

"The lower the caste," said Mr. Foster, "the shorter the oxygen." The first organ affected was the brain. After that the skeleton. At seventy per cent. of normal oxygen you got dwarfs. At less than seventy eyeless monsters.

"Who are no use at all," concluded Mr. Foster.

Whereas (his voice became confidential and eager), if they could discover a technique for shortening the period of maturation what a triumph, what a benefaction to Society!

"Consider the horse."

They considered it.

Mature at six; the elephant at ten. While at thirteen a man is not yet sexually mature; and is only full-grown at twenty. Hence, of course, that fruit of delayed development, the human intelligence.

"But in Epsilons," said Mr. Foster very justly, "we don't need human intelligence."

Didn't need and didn't get it. But though the Epsilon mind was mature at ten, the Epsilon body was not fit to work till eighteen. Long years of superfluous and wasted immaturity. If the physical development could be speeded up till it was as quick, say, as a cow's, what an enormous saving to the Community!

"Enormous!" murmured the students. Mr. Foster's enthusiasm was infectious.

He became rather technical; spoke of the abnormal endocrine coordination which made men grow so slowly; postulated a germinal mutation to account for it. Could the effects of this germinal mutation be undone? Could the individual Epsilon embryo be made a revert, by a suitable technique, to the normality of dogs and cows? That was the problem. And it was all but solved.

Pilkington, at Mombasa, had produced individuals who were sexually mature at four and full-grown at six and a half. A scientific triumph. But socially useless. Six-year-old men and women were too stupid to do even Epsilon work. And the process was an all-or-nothing one; either you failed to modify at all, or else you modified the whole way. They were still trying to find the ideal compromise between adults of twenty and adults of six. So far without success. Mr. Foster sighed and shook his head.

Their wanderings through the crimson twilight had brought them to the neighbourhood of Metre 170 on Rack 9. From this point onwards Rack 9 was enclosed and the bottles performed the remainder of their journey in a kind of tunnel, interrupted here and there by openings two or three metres wide.

"Heat conditioning," said Mr. Foster.

Hot tunnels alternated with cool tunnels. Coolness was wedded to discomfort in the form of hard X-rays. By the time they were decanted the embryos had a horror of cold. They were predestined to emigrate to the tropics, to be miners and acetate silk spinners and steel workers. Later on their minds would be made to endorse the judgment of their bodies. "We condition them to thrive on heat," concluded Mr. Foster. "Our colleagues upstairs will teach them to love it."

"And that," put in the Director sententiously, "that is the secret of happiness and virtue—liking what you've *got* to do. All conditioning aims at that: making people like their unescapable social destiny."

In a gap between two tunnels, a nurse was delicately probing with a long fine syringe into the gelatinous contents of a passing bottle. The students and their guides stood watching her for a few moments in silence.

"Well, Lenina," said Mr. Foster, when at last she withdrew the syringe and straightened herself up.

The girl turned with a start. One could see that, for all the lupus and the purple eyes, she was uncommonly pretty.

"Henry!" Her smile flashed redly at him—a row of coral teeth.

"Charming, charming," murmured the Director and, giving her two or three little pats, received in exchange a rather deferential smile for himself.

"What are you giving them?" asked Mr. Foster, making his tone very professional.

"Oh, the usual typhoid and sleeping sickness."

"Tropical workers start being inoculated at Metre 150," Mr. Foster explained to the students. "The embryos still have gills. We immunize the fish against the future man's diseases." Then, turning back to Lenina, "Ten to five on the roof this afternoon," he said, "as usual."

"Charming," said the Director once more, and, with a final pat, moved away after the others.

On Rack 10 rows of next generation's chemical workers were being trained in the toleration of lead, caustic soda, tar, chlorine. The first of a batch of two hundred and fifty embryonic rocket-plane engineers was just passing the eleven hundred metre mark on Rack 3. A special mechanism kept their containers in constant rotation. "To improve their sense of balance," Mr. Foster explained. "Doing repairs on the outside of a rocket in mid-air is a ticklish job. We slacken off the circulation when they're right way up, so that they're half starved, and double the flow of surrogate when they're upside down. They learn to associate topsy-turvydom with well-being; in fact, they're only truly happy when they're standing on their heads.

"And now," Mr. Foster went on, "I'd like to show you some very interesting conditioning for Alpha Plus Intellectuals. We have a big batch of them on Rack 5. First Gallery level," he called to two boys who had started to go down to the ground floor.

"They're round about Metre 900," he explained. "You can't really do any useful intellectual conditioning till the foetuses have lost their tails. Follow me."

But the Director had looked at his watch. "Ten to three," he said. "No time for the intellectual embryos, I'm afraid. We must go up to the Nurseries before the children have finished their afternoon sleep."

Mr. Foster was disappointed. "At least one glance at the Decanting Room," he pleaded.

"Very well then." The Director smiled indulgently. "Just one glance."

CHAPTER TWO

Mr. Foster was left in the Decanting Room. The D.H.C. and his students stepped into the nearest lift and were carried up to the fifth floor.

INFANT NURSERIES. NEO-PAVLOVIAN CONDITIONING ROOMS, announced the notice board.

The Director opened a door. They were in a large bare room, very bright and sunny; for the whole of the southern wall was a single window. Half a dozen nurses, trousered and jacketed in the regulation white viscose-linen uniform, their hair aseptically hidden under white caps, were engaged in setting out bowls of roses in a long row across the floor. Big bowls, packed tight with blossom. Thousands of petals, ripe-blown and silkily smooth, like the cheeks of innumerable little cherubs, but of cherubs, in that bright light, not exclusively pink and Aryan, but also luminously Chinese, also Mexican, also apopletic with too much blowing of celestial trumpets, also pale as death, pale with the posthumous whiteness of marble.

The nurses stiffened to attention as the D.H.C. came in.

"Set out the books," he said curtly.

In silence the nurses obeyed his command. Between the rose bowls the books were duly set out—a row of nursery quartos opened invitingly each at some gaily coloured image of beast or fish or bird.

"Now bring in the children."

They hurried out of the room and returned in a minute or two, each pushing a kind of tall dumb-waiter laden, on all its four wire-

netted shelves, with eight-month-old babies, all exactly alike (a Bokanovsky Group, it was evident) and all (since their caste was Delta)
dressed in khaki.

"Put them down on the floor."

The infants were unloaded.

"Now turn them so that they can see the flowers and books."

Turned, the babies at once fell silent, then began to crawl towards
those clusters of sleek colours, those shapes so gay and brilliant on
the white pages. As they approached, the sun came out of a momentary eclipse behind a cloud. The roses flamed up as though with a
sudden passion from within; a new and profound significance
seemed to suffuse the shining pages of the books. From the ranks of
the crawling babies came little squeals of excitement, gurgles and
twitterings of pleasure.

The Director rubbed his hands. "Excellent!" he said. "It might almost have been done on purpose."

The swiftest crawlers were already at their goal. Small hands
reached out uncertainly, touched, grasped, unpetaling the transfig-
ured roses, crumpling the illuminated pages of the books. The Director waited until all were happily busy. Then, "Watch carefully," he
said. And, lifting his hand, he gave the signal.

The Head Nurse, who was standing by a switchboard at the other
end of the room, pressed down a little lever.

There was a violent explosion. Shriller and ever shriller, a siren
shrieked. Alarm bells maddeningly sounded.

The children started, screamed; their faces were distorted with terror.

"And now," the Director shouted (for the noise was deafening),
"now we proceed to rub in the lesson with a mild electric shock."

He waved his hand again, and the Head Nurse pressed a second
lever. The screaming of the babies suddenly changed its tone. There
was something desperate, almost insane, about the sharp spasmodic
yelps to which they now gave utterance. Their little bodies twitched
and stiffened; their limbs moved jerkily as if to the tug of unseen
wires.

"We can electrify that whole strip of floor," bawled the Director
in explanation. "But that's enough," he signalled to the nurse.

The explosions ceased, the bells stopped ringing, the shriek of the
siren died down from tone to tone into silence. The stiffly twitching
bodies relaxed, and what had become the sob and yelp of infant

maniacs broadened out once more into a normal howl of ordinary terror.

"Offer them the flowers and the books again."

The nurses obeyed; but at the approach of the roses, at the mere sight of those gaily-coloured images of pussy and cock-a-doodle-doo and baa-baa black sheep, the infants shrank away in horror; the volume of their howling suddenly increased.

"Observe," said the Director triumphantly, "observe."

Books and loud noises, flowers and electric shocks—already in the infant mind these couples were compromisingly linked; and after two hundred repetitions of the same or a similar lesson would be wedded indissolubly. What man has joined, nature is powerless to put asunder.

"They'll grow up with what the psychologists used to call an 'instinctive' hatred of books and flowers. Reflexes unalterably conditioned. They'll be safe from books and botany all their lives." The Director turned to his nurses. "Take them away again."

Still yelling, the khaki babies were loaded on to their dumbwaiters and wheeled out, leaving behind them the smell of sour milk and a most welcome silence.

One of the students held up his hand; and though he could see quite well why you couldn't have lower-caste people wasting the Community's time over books, and that there was always the risk of their reading something which might undesirably decondition one of their reflexes, yet . . . well, he couldn't understand about the flowers. Why go to the trouble of making it psychologically impossible for Deltas to like flowers?

Patiently the D.H.C. explained. If the children were made to scream at the sight of a rose, that was on grounds of high economic policy. Not so very long ago (a century or thereabouts), Gammas, Deltas, even Epsilons, had been conditioned to like flowers— flowers in particular and wild nature in general. The idea was to make them want to be going out into the country at every available opportunity, and so compel them to consume transport.

"And didn't they consume transport?" asked the student.

"Quite a lot," the D.H.C. replied. "But nothing else."

Primroses and landscapes, he pointed out, have one grave defect: they are gratuitous. A love of nature keeps no factories busy. It was decided to abolish the love of nature, at any rate among the lower classes; to abolish the love of nature, but *not* the tendency to consume transport. For of course it was essential that they should keep on going to the country, even though they hated it. The problem was to find an economically sounder reason for consuming transport than a mere affection for primroses and landscapes. It was duly found.

"We condition the masses to hate the country," concluded the Director. "But simultaneously we condition them to love all country sports. At the same time, we see to it that all country sports shall entail the use of elaborate apparatus. So that they consume manufactured articles as well as transport. Hence those electric shocks."

"I see," said the student, and was silent, lost in admiration.

There was a silence; then, clearing his throat, "Once upon a time," the Director began, "while our Ford was still on earth, there was a little boy called Reuben Rabinovitch. Reuben was the child of Polish-speaking parents." The Director interrupted himself. "You know what Polish is, I suppose?"

"A dead language."

"Like French and German," added another student, officiously showing off his learning.

"And 'parent'?" questioned the D.H.C.

There was an uneasy silence. Several of the boys blushed. They had not yet learned to draw the significant but often very fine distinction between smut and pure science. One, at last, had the courage to raise a hand.

"Human beings used to be . . ." he hesitated; the blood rushed to his cheeks. "Well, they used to be viviparous."

"Quite right." The Director nodded approvingly.

"And when the babies were decanted . . ."

" 'Born'," came the correction.

"Well, then they were the parents—I mean, not the babies, of course; the other ones." The poor boy was overwhelmed with confusion.

"In brief," the Director summed up, "the parents were the father and the mother." The smut that was really science fell with a crash into the boys' eye-avoiding silence. "Mother," he repeated loudly rubbing in the science; and, leaning back in his chair, "These," he said gravely, "are unpleasant facts; I know it. But then most historical facts *are* unpleasant."

He returned to Little Reuben—to Little Reuben, in whose room, one evening, by an oversight, his father and mother (crash, crash!) happened to leave the radio turned on.

("For you must remember that in those days of gross viviparous reproduction, children were always brought up by their parents and not in State Conditioning Centres.")

While the child was asleep, a broadcast programme from London suddenly started to come through; and the next morning, to the astonishment of his crash and crash (the more daring of the boys ventured to grin at one another), Little Reuben woke up repeating word for word a long lecture by that curious old writer ("one of the very few whose works have been permitted to come down to us"), George Bernard Shaw, who was speaking, according to a well-authenticated tradition, about his own genius. To Little Reuben's wink and snigger, this lecture was, of course, perfectly incomprehensible and, imagining that their child had suddenly gone mad, they sent for a doctor. He, fortunately, understood English, recognized the discourse as that which Shaw had broadcasted the previous evening, realized the significance of what had happened, and sent a letter to the medical press about it.

"The principle of sleep-teaching, or hypnopædia, had been discovered." The D.H.C. made an impressive pause.

The principle had been discovered; but many, many years were to elapse before that principle was usefully applied.

"The case of Little Reuben occurred only twenty-three years after Our Ford's first T-Model was put on the market." (Here the Director made a sign of the T on his stomach and all the students reverently followed suit.) "And yet . . ."

Furiously the students scribbled. *"Hypnopædia, first used officially in A.F. 214. Why not before? Two reasons. (a) . . ."*

"These early experimenters," the D.H.C. was saying, "were on the wrong track. They thought that hypnopædia could be made an instrument of intellectual education . . ."

(A small boy asleep on his right side, the right arm stuck out, the right hand hanging limp over the edge of the bed. Through a round grating in the side of a box a voice speaks softly.

"The Nile is the longest river in Africa and the second in length of all the rivers of the globe. Although falling short of the length of the Mississippi-Missouri, the Nile is at the head of all rivers as regards

the length of its basin, which extends through 35 degrees of latitude
. . ."

At breakfast the next morning, "Tommy," some one says, "do
you know which is the longest river in Africa?" A shaking of the
head. "But don't you remember something that begins: The Nile is
the . . ."

"The-Nile-is-the-longest-river-in-Africa-and-the-second-in-
length-of-all-the-rivers-of-the-globe . . ." The words come rushing
out. "Although-falling-short-of . . ."

"Well now, which is the longest river in Africa?"

The eyes are blank. "I don't know."

"But the Nile, Tommy."

"The-Nile-is-the-longest-river-in-Africa-and-second . . ."

"Then which river is the longest Tommy?"

Tommy bursts into tears. "I don't know," he howls.)

That howl, the Director made it plain, discouraged the earliest in-
vestigators. The experiments were abandoned. No further attempt
was made to teach children the length of the Nile in their sleep.
Quite rightly. You can't learn a science unless you know what it's all
about.

"Whereas, if they'd only started on *moral* education," said the
Director, leading the way towards the door. The students followed
him, desperately scribbling as they walked and all the way up in the
lift. "Moral education, which ought never, in any circumstances, to
be rational."

"Silence, silence," whispered a loud speaker as they stepped out at
the fourteenth floor, and "Silence, silence," the trumpet mouths in-
defatigably repeated at intervals down every corridor. The students
and even the Director himself rose automatically to the tips of their
toes. They were Alphas, of course; but even Alphas have been well
conditioned. "Silence, silence." All the air of the fourteenth floor
was sibilant with the categorical imperative.

Fifty yards of tiptoeing brought them to a door which the Director
cautiously opened. They stepped over the threshold into the twilight
of a shuttered dormitory. Eighty cots stood in a row against the
wall. There was a sound of light regular breathing and a continuous
murmur, as of very faint voices remotely whispering.

A nurse rose as they entered and came to attention before the
Director.

"What's the lesson this afternoon?" he asked.

"We had Elementary Sex for the first forty minutes," she answered. "But now it's switched over to Elementary Class Consciousness."

The Director walked slowly down the long line of cots. Rosy and relaxed with sleep, eighty little boys and girls lay softly breathing. There was a whisper under every pillow. The D.H.C. halted and, bending over one of the little beds, listened attentively.

"Elementary Class Consciousness, did you say? Let's have it repeated a little louder by the trumpet."

At the end of the room a loud speaker projected from the wall. The Director walked up to it and pressed a switch.

". . . all wear green," said a soft but very distinct voice, beginning in the middle of a sentence, "and Delta children wear khaki. Oh no, I don't want to play with Delta children. And Epsilons are still worse. They're too stupid to be able to read or write. Besides they wear black, which is such a beastly colour. I'm *so* glad I'm a Beta."

There was a pause; then the voice began again.

"Alpha children wear grey. They work much harder than we do, because they're so frightfully clever. I'm really awfully glad I'm a Beta, because I don't work so hard. And then we are much better than the Gammas and Deltas. Gammas are stupid. They all wear green, and Delta children wear khaki. Oh no, I *don't* want to play with Delta children. And Epsilons are still worse. They're too stupid to be able . . ."

The Director pushed back the switch. The voice was silent. Only its thin ghost continued to mutter from beneath the eighty pillows.

"They'll have that repeated forty or fifty times more before they wake; then again on Thursday, and again on Saturday. A hundred and twenty times three times a week for thirty months. After which they go on to a more advanced lesson."

Roses and electric shocks, the khaki of Deltas and a whiff of asafœtida—wedded indissolubly before the child can speak. But wordless conditioning is crude and wholesale; cannot bring home the finer distinctions, cannot inculcate the more complex courses of behaviour. For that there must be words, but words without reason. In brief, hypnopædia.

"The greatest moralizing and socializing force of all time."

The students took it down in their little books. Straight from the horse's mouth.

Once more the Director touched the switch.

". . . so frightfully clever," the soft, insinuating, indefatigable voice was saying. "I'm really awfully glad I'm a Beta, because . . ."

Not so much like drops of water, though water, it is true, can wear holes in the hardest granite; rather, drops of liquid sealing-wax, drops that adhere, incrust, incorporate themselves with what they fall on, till finally the rock is all one scarlet blob.

"Till at last the child's mind *is* these suggestions, and the sum of the suggestions *is* the child's mind. And not the child's mind only. The adult's mind too—all his life long. The mind that judges and desires and decides—made up of these suggestions. But all these suggestions are *our* suggestions!" The Director almost shouted in his triumph. "Suggestions from the State." He banged the nearest table. "It therefore follows . . ."

A noise made him turn around.

"Oh, Ford!" he said in another tone, "I've gone and woken the children."

11

C. Wright Mills
The Higher Immorality

*As a result of the massive destruction of life and property in Europe during
two world wars, the United States by 1950 had become the leader of the
Western nations and held an unprecedented position of world power. An in-
cisive analyst and critic of this new power was C. Wright Mills
(1916–1962). Born in Waco, Texas, Mills earned degrees in philosophy
and sociology from the University of Texas and, in 1941, a doctorate in sociology and anthropology from the University of Wisconsin. Thereafter he
taught sociology at the University of Maryland and, from 1945 until his
death, at Columbia University.*

*Evident in the many works by Mills is his belief that there exists in
American society a concentration of power wielded by a small elite group. In
his book* The Power Elite *(1956), he describes this group as an interlocking
triumvirate of those who "rule the big corporations . . . , run the machinery of the state, and . . . direct the military establishment." The following selection is a reprinting of the final chapter of* The Power Elite. *In
it Mills attacks the "higher immorality" of that dominating triumvirate
which has divorced power from knowledge, substituted "personality" for
depth of character, and selected for leadership mediocre men who thrive in a
condition of "organized irresponsibility."*

The higher immorality can neither be narrowed to the political
sphere nor understood as primarily a matter of corrupt men in fun-

damentally sound institutions. Political corruption is one aspect of a more general immorality; the level of moral sensibility that now prevails is not merely a matter of corrupt men. The higher immorality is a systematic feature of the American elite; its general acceptance is an essential feature of the mass society.

Of course, there may be corrupt men in sound institutions, but when institutions are corrupting many of the men who live and work in them are necessarily corrupted. In the corporate era, economic relations become impersonal—and the executive feels less personal responsibility. Within the corporate worlds of business, war-making and politics, the private conscience is attenuated—and the higher immorality is institutionalized. It is not merely a question of a corrupt administration in corporation, army, or state; it is a feature of the corporate rich, as a capitalist stratum, deeply intertwined with the politics of the military state.

From this point of view, the most important question, for instance, about the campaign funds of ambitious young politicians is not whether the politicians are morally insensitive, but whether or not any young man in American politics, who has come so far and so fast, could very well have done so today without possessing or acquiring a somewhat blunted moral sensibility. Many of the problems of "white-collar crime" and of relaxed public morality, of high-priced vice and of fading personal integrity, are problems of *structural* immorality. They are not merely the problem of the small character twisted by the bad milieu. And many people are at least vaguely aware that this is so. As news of higher immoralities breaks, they often say, "Well, another one got caught today," thereby implying that the cases disclosed are not odd events involving occasional characters but symptoms of a widespread condition. There is good probative evidence that they are right. But what is the underlying condition of which all these instances are symptoms?

1

The moral uneasiness of our time results from the fact that older values and codes of uprightness no longer grip the men and women of the corporate era, nor have they been replaced by new values and codes which would lend moral meaning and sanction to the corporate routines they must now follow. It is not that the mass public has explicitly rejected received codes; it is rather that to many of the members these codes have become hollow. No moral terms of acceptance are available, but neither are any moral terms of rejection. As individuals they are morally defenseless; as groups, they are politically indifferent. It is this generalized lack of commitment that is meant when it is said that "the public" is morally confused.

But, of course, not only "the public" is morally confused in this way. "The tragedy of official Washington," James Reston[1] has commented, "is that it is confounded at every turn by the hangover of old political habits and outworn institutions but is no longer nourished by the ancient faith on which it was founded. It clings to the bad things and casts away the permanent. It professes belief but does not believe. It knows the old words but has forgotten the melody. It is engaged in an ideological war without being able to define its own ideology. It condemns the materialism of an atheistic enemy, but glorifies its own materialism."

In economic and political institutions the corporate rich now wield enormous power, but they have never had to win the moral consent of those over whom they hold this power. Every such naked interest, every new, unsanctioned power of corporation, farm bloc, labor union, and governmental agency that has risen in the past two generations has been clothed with morally loaded slogans. For what is *not* done in the name of the public interest? As these slogans wear out, new ones are industriously made up, also to be banalized in due course. And all the while, recurrent economic and military crises spread fears, hesitations, and anxieties which give new urgency to the busy search for moral justifications and decorous excuses.

"Crisis" is a bankrupted term, because so many men in high places have evoked it in order to cover up their extraordinary policies and deeds; as a matter of fact, it is precisely the absence of crises that is a cardinal feature of the higher immorality. For genuine crises involve situations in which men at large are presented with genuine alternatives, the moral meanings of which are clearly opened to public debate. The higher immorality, the general weakening of older values and the organization of irresponsibility have not involved any public crises; on the contrary, they have been matters of a creeping indifference and a silent hollowing out.

The images that generally prevail of the higher circles are the

---

[1] An American (Scottish-born) newspaper columnist (1909–   ).

images of the elite seen as celebrities. In discussing the professional celebrities, I noted that the instituted elites of power do not monopolize the bright focus of national acclaim. They share it nationally with the frivolous or the sultry creatures of the world of celebrity, which thus serves as a dazzling blind of their true power. In the sense that the volume of publicity and acclaim is mainly and continuously upon those professional celebrities, it is not upon the power elite. So the social visibility of that elite is lowered by the status distraction, or rather public vision of them is through the celebrity who amuses and entertains—or disgusts, as the case may be.

The absence of any firm moral order of belief makes men in the mass all the more open to the manipulation and distraction of the world of the celebrities. In due course, such a "turnover" of appeals and codes and values as they are subjected to leads them to distrust and cynicism, to a sort of Machiavellianism-for-the-little-man. Thus they vicariously enjoy the prerogatives of the corporate rich, the nocturnal antics of the celebrity, and the sad-happy life of the very rich.

But with all this, there is still one old American value that has not markedly declined: the value of money and of the things money can buy—these, even in inflated times, seem as solid and enduring as stainless steel. "I've been rich and I've been poor," Sophie Tucker has said, "and believe me, rich is best." As many other values are weakened, the question for Americans becomes not "Is there anything that money, used with intelligence, will not buy?" but, "How many of the things that money will *not* buy are valued and desired more than what money *will* buy?" Money is the one unambiguous criterion of success, and such success is still the sovereign American value.

Whenever the standards of the moneyed life prevail, the man with money, no matter how he got it, will eventually be respected. A million dollars, it is said, covers a multitude of sins. It is not only that men want money; it is that their very standards are pecuniary. In a society in which the money-maker has had no serious rival for repute and honor, the word "practical" comes to mean useful for private gain, and "common sense," the sense to get ahead financially. The pursuit of the moneyed life is the commanding value, in relation to which the influence of other values has declined, so men easily become morally ruthless in the pursuit of easy money and fast estate-building.

A great deal of American corruption—although not all of it—is simply a part of the old effort to get rich and then to become richer. But today the context in which the old drive must operate has changed. When both economic and political institutions were small and scattered—as in the simpler models of classical economics and Jeffersonian democracy—no man had it in his power to bestow or to receive great favors. But when political institutions and economic opportunities are at once concentrated and linked, then public office can be used for private gain.

Governmental agencies contain no more of the higher immorality than do business corporations. Political men can grant financial favors only when there are economic men ready and willing to take them. And economic men can seek political favors only when there are political agents who can bestow such favors. The publicity spotlight, of course, shines brighter upon the transactions of the men in government, for which there is good reason. Expectations being higher, publics are more easily disappointed by public officials. Businessmen are supposed to be out for themselves, and if they successfully skate on legally thin ice, Americans generally honor them for having gotten away with it. But in a civilization so thoroughly business-penetrated as America, the rules of business are carried over into government—especially when so many businessmen have gone into government. How many executives would really fight for a law requiring a careful and public accounting of all executive contracts and "expense accounts"? High income taxes have resulted in a network of collusion between big firm and higher employee. There are many ingenious ways to cheat the spirit of the tax laws, as we have seen, and the standards of consumption of many high-priced men are determined more by complicated expense accounts than by simple take-home pay. Like prohibition, the laws of income taxes and the regulations of wartime exist without the support of firm business convention. It is merely illegal to cheat them, but it is smart to get away with it. Laws without supporting moral conventions invite crime, but much more importantly, they spur the growth of an expedient, amoral attitude.

A society that is in its higher circles and on its middle levels widely believed to be a network of smart rackets does not produce men with an inner moral sense; a society that is merely expedient does not produce men of conscience. A society that narrows the meaning of "success" to the big money and in its terms condemns failure as the

chief vice, raising money to the plane of absolute value, will produce
the sharp operator and the shady deal. Blessed are the cynical, for
only they have what it takes to succeed.

2

In the corporate world, in the political directorate, and increasingly
in the ascendant military, the heads of the big hierarchies and power
machines are seen not only as men who have succeeded, but as wield-
ers of the patronage of success. They interpret and they apply to
individuals the criteria of success. Those immediately below them
are usually members of their clique, of their clientele, sound men as
they themselves are sound. But the hierarchies are intricately related
to one another, and inside each clique are some whose loyalties are to
other cliques. There are personal loyalties as well as official ones,
personal as well as impersonal criteria for advancement. As we trace
the career of the individual member of various higher circles, we are
also tracing the history of his loyalties, for the first and overshadow-
ing fact about the higher circles, from the standpoint of what it takes
to succeed within them, is that they are based upon self-co-optation.[2]
The second fact about these hierarchies of success is that they do not
form one monolithic structure; they are a complex set of variously
related and often antagonistic cliques. The third fact we must recognize is that, in any such world, younger men who would succeed
attempt to relate themselves to those in charge of their selection as
successes.

Accordingly, the American literature of practical aspiration—which carries the great fetish of success—has undergone a significant shift in its advice about "what it takes to succeed." The
sober, personal virtues of will power and honesty, of high-mind-
edness and the constitutional inability to say "yes" to The Easy
Road of women, tobacco, and wine—this later nineteenth-century
image has given way to "the most important single factor, the effective personality," which "commands attention by charm," and "ra-
diates self-confidence." In this "new way of life," one must smile
often and be a good listener, talk in terms of the other man's interests

[2] The tendency, according to Mills, of those already in the "higher circles" of power
to select (co-opt) for advancement into those circles only those who reflect their
own career values.

and make the other feel important—and one must do all this sincerely. Personal relations, in short, have become part of "public relations," a sacrifice of selfhood on a personality market, to the sole end of individual success in the corporate way of life. Being justified by superior merit and hard work, but being founded on co-optation by a clique, often on quite other grounds, the elite careerist must continually persuade others and himself as well that he is the opposite of what he actually is.

It is the proud claim of the higher circles in America that their members are entirely self-made. That is their self-image and their well-publicized myth. Popular proof of this is based on anecdotes; its scholarly proof is supposed to rest upon statistical rituals whereby it is shown that varying proportions of the men at the top are sons of men of lower rank. We have already seen the proportions of given elite circles composed of the men who have risen. But what is more important than the proportions of the sons of wage workers among these higher circles is the criteria of admission to them, and the question of who applies these criteria. We cannot from upward mobility infer higher merit. Even if the rough figures that now generally hold were reversed, and 90 per cent of the elite were sons of wage workers—but the criteria of co-optation by the elite remained what they now are—we could not from that mobility necessarily infer merit. Only if the criteria of the top positions were meritorious, and only if they were self-applied, as in a purely entrepreneurial manner, could we smuggle merit into such statistics—from any statistics—of mobility. The idea that the self-made man is somehow "good" and that the family-made man is not good makes moral sense only when the career is independent, when one is on one's own as an entrepreneur. It would also make sense in a strict bureaucracy where examinations control advancement. It makes little sense in the system of corporate co-optation.

There is, in psychological fact, no such thing as a self-made man. No man makes himself, least of all the members of the American elite. In a world of corporate hierarchies, men are selected by those above them in the hierarchy in accordance with whatever criteria they use. In connection with the corporations of America, we have seen the current criteria. Men shape themselves to fit them, and are thus made by the criteria, the social premiums that prevail. If there is no such thing as a self-made man, there is such a thing as a self-used man, and there are many such men among the American elite.

Under such conditions of success, there is no virtue in starting out poor and becoming rich. Only where the ways of becoming rich are such as to require virtue or to lead to virtue does personal enrichment imply virtue. In a system of co-optation from above, whether you began rich or poor seems less relevant in revealing what kind of man you are when you have arrived than in revealing the principles of those in charge of selecting the ones who succeed.

All this is sensed by enough people below the higher circles to lead to cynical views of the lack of connection between merit and mobility, between virtue and success. It is a sense of the immorality of accomplishment, and it is revealed in the prevalence of such views as: "it's all just another racket," and "it's not what you know but who you know." Considerable numbers of people now accept the immorality of accomplishment as a going fact.

Some observers are led by their sense of the immorality of accomplishment to the ideology, obliquely set forth by academic social science, of human relations in industry; still others to the solace of mind provided by the newer literature of resignation, of peace of mind, which in some quietened circles replaces the old literature of frenzied aspiration, of how to get ahead. But, regardless of the particular style of reaction, the sense of the immorality of accomplishment often feeds into that level of public sensibility which we have called the higher immorality. The old self-made man's is a tarnished image, and no other image of success has taken its once bright place. Success itself, as the American model of excellence, declines as it becomes one more feature of the higher immorality.

3

Moral distrust of the American elite—as well as the fact of organized irresponsibility—rests upon the higher immorality, but also upon vague feelings about the higher ignorance. Once upon a time in the United States, men of affairs were also men of sensibility: to a considerable extent the elite of power and the elite of culture coincided, and where they did not coincide they often overlapped as circles. Within the compass of a knowledgeable and effective public, knowledge and power were in effective touch; and more than that, this public decided much that was decided.

"Nothing is more revealing," James Reston has written, "than to read the debate in the House of Representatives in the Eighteen Thirties on Greece's fight with Turkey for independence and the Greek-Turkish debate in the Congress in 1947. The first is dignified and eloquent, the argument marching from principle through illustration to conclusion; the second is a dreary garble of debating points, full of irrelevancies and bad history." George Washington in 1783 relaxed with Voltaire's "letters" and Locke's "On Human Understanding"; Eisenhower read cowboy tales and detective stories. For such men as now typically arrive in higher political, economic and military circles, the briefing and the memorandum seem to have pretty well replaced not only the serious book, but the newspaper as well. Given the immorality of accomplishment, this is perhaps as it must be, but what is somewhat disconcerting about it is that they are below the level on which they might feel a little bit ashamed of the uncultivated style of their relaxation and of their mental fare, and that no self-cultivated public is in a position by its reactions to educate them to such uneasiness.

By the middle of the twentieth century, the American elite have become an entirely different breed of men from those who could on any reasonable grounds be considered a cultural elite, or even for that matter cultivated men of sensibility. Knowledge and power are not truly united inside the ruling circles; and when men of knowledge do come to a point of contact with the circles of powerful men, they come not as peers but as hired men. The elite of power, wealth, and celebrity do not have even a passing acquaintance with the elite of culture, knowledge and sensibility; they are not in touch with them—although the ostentatious fringes of the two worlds sometimes overlap in the world of the celebrity.

Most men are encouraged to assume that, in general, the most powerful and the wealthiest are also the most knowledgeable or, as they might say, "the smartest." Such ideas are propped up by many little slogans about those who "teach because they can't *do*," and about "if you're so smart, why aren't you rich?" But all that such wisecracks mean is that those who use them assume that power and wealth are sovereign values for all men and especially for men "who are smart." They assume also that knowledge always pays off in

such ways, or surely ought to, and that the test of genuine knowledge is just such pay-offs. The powerful and the wealthy *must* be the
men of most knowledge, otherwise how could they be where they
are? But to say that those who succeed to power must be "smart," is
to say that power *is* knowledge. To say that those who succeed to
wealth must be smart, is to say that wealth *is* knowledge.

The prevalence of such assumptions does reveal something that is
true: that ordinary men, even today, are prone to explain and to justify power and wealth in terms of knowledge or ability. Such assumptions also reveal something of what has happened to the kind of
experience that knowledge has come to be. Knowledge is no longer
widely felt as an ideal; it is seen as an instrument. In a society of
power and wealth, knowledge is valued as an instrument of power
and wealth, and also, of course, as an ornament in conversation.

What knowledge does to a man (in clarifying what he is, and setting him free)—that is the personal ideal of knowledge. What
knowledge does to a civilization (in revealing its human meaning,
and setting it free)—that is the social ideal of knowledge. But today,
the personal *and* the social ideals of knowledge have coincided in
what knowledge does *for* the smart guy—it gets him ahead; and for
the wise nation—it lends cultural prestige, sanctifying power with
authority.

Knowledge seldom lends power to the man of knowledge. But the
supposed, and secret, knowledge of some men-on-the-make, and
their very free use thereof, has consequence for other men who have
not the power of defense. Knowledge, of course, is neither good nor
bad, nor is its use good or bad. "Bad men increase in knowledge as
fast as good men," John Adams wrote, "and science, arts, taste,
sense and letters, are employed for the purpose of injustice as well as
for virtue." That was in 1790; today we have good reason to know
that it is so.

The problem of knowledge and power is, and always has been, the
problem of the relations of men of knowledge with men of power.
Suppose we were to select the one hundred most powerful men,
from all fields of power, in America today and line them up. And
then, suppose we selected the one hundred most knowledgeable
men, from all fields of social knowledge, and lined them up. How
many men would be in *both* our line-ups? Of course our selection
would depend upon what we mean by power and what we mean by

knowledge—especially what we mean by knowledge. But, if we mean what the words seem to mean, surely we would find few if any men in America today who were in both groups, and surely we could find many more at the time the nation was founded than we could find today. For, in the eighteenth century, even in this colonial outpost, men of power pursued learning, and men of learning were often in positions of power. In these respects we have, I believe, suffered grievous decline.

There is little union in the same persons of knowledge and power; but persons of power do surround themselves with men of some knowledge, or at least with men who are experienced in shrewd dealings. The man of knowledge has not become a philosopher king; but he has often become a consultant, and moreover a consultant to a man who is neither king-like nor philosophical. It is, of course, true that the chairman of the pulp writers section of the Authors' League helped a leading senator "polish up the speeches he delivered in the 1952 senatorial campaign." But it is not natural in the course of their careers for men of knowledge to meet with those of power. The links between university and government are weak, and when they do occur, the man of knowledge appears as an "expert" which usually means as a hired technician. Like most others in this society, the man of knowledge is himself dependent for his livelihood upon the job, which nowadays is a prime sanction of thought control. Where getting ahead requires the good opinions of more powerful others, their judgments become prime objects of concern. Accordingly, in so far as intellectuals serve power directly—in a job hierarchy—they often do so unfreely.

The democratic man assumes the existence of a public, and in his rhetoric asserts that this public is the very seat of sovereignty. Two things are needed in a democracy: articulate and knowledgeable publics, and political leaders who if not men of reason are at least reasonably responsible to such knowledgeable publics as exist. Only where publics and leaders are responsive and responsible, are human affairs in democratic order, and only when knowledge has public relevance is this order possible. Only when mind has an autonomous basis, independent of power, but powerfully related to it, can mind exert its force in the shaping of human affairs. This is democratically possible only when there exists a free and knowledgeable public, to which men of knowledge may address themselves, and to which men of power are truly responsible. Such a public and such men—either of power or of knowledge—do not now prevail, and accordingly, knowledge does not now have democratic relevance in America.

The characteristic member of the higher circles today is an intellectual mediocrity, sometimes a conscientious one, but still a mediocrity. His intelligence is revealed only by his occasional realization that he is not up to the decisions he sometimes feels called upon to confront. But usually he keeps such feelings private, his public utterances being pious and sentimental, grim and brave, cheerful and empty in their universal generality. He is open only to abbreviated and vulgarized, predigested and slanted ideas. He is a commander of the age of the phone call, the memo, and the briefing.

By the mindlessness and mediocrity of men of affairs, I do not, of course, mean that these men are not sometimes intelligent—although that is by no means automatically the case. It is not, however, primarily a matter of the distribution of "intelligence"—as if intelligence were a homogeneous something of which there may be more or less. It is rather a matter of the type of intelligence, of the quality of mind that is selected and formed. It is a matter of the evaluation of substantive rationality as the chief value in a man's life and character and conduct. That evaluation is what is lacking in the American power elite. In its place there are "weight" and "judgment" which count for much more in their celebrated success than any subtlety of mind or force of intellect.

All around and just below the weighty man of affairs are his technical lieutenants of power who have been assigned the role of knowledge and even of speech: his public relations men, his ghost, his administrative assistants, his secretaries. And do not forget The Committees. With the increased means of decision, there is a crisis of understanding among the political directorate of the United States, and accordingly, there is often a commanding indecision.

The lack of knowledge as an experience among the elite ties in with the malign ascendancy of the expert, not only as fact but as legitimation. When questioned recently about a criticism of defense policies made by the leader of the opposition party, the Secretary of Defense replied, "Do you think he is an expert in the matter?" When pressed further by reporters he asserted that the "military chiefs think it is sound, and I think it is sound," and later, when asked about specific cases, added: "In some cases, all you can do is ask the Lord." With such a large role so arrogantly given to God and to experts, what room is there for political leadership? Much less for public debate of what is after all every bit as much a political and a moral as a military issue. But then, from before Pearl Harbor,[3] the trend has been the abdication of debate and the collapse of opposition under the easy slogan of bi-partisanship.

Beyond the lack of intellectual cultivation by political personnel and advisory circle, the absence of publicly relevant mind has come to mean that powerful decisions and important policies are not made in such a way as to be justified or attacked; in short, debated in any intellectual form. Moreover, the attempt to so justify them is often not even made. Public relations displace reasoned argument; manipulation and undebated decisions of power replace democratic authority. More and more, since the nineteenth century, as administration has replaced politics, the decisions of importance do not carry even the panoply of reasonable discussion, but are made by God, by experts, and by men like Mr. Wilson.[4]

More and more the area of the official secret expands, as well as the area of the secret listening in on those who might divulge in public what the public, not being composed of experts with Q clearance,[5] is not to know. The entire sequence of decisions concerning the production and the use of atomic weaponry has been made without any genuine public debate, and the facts needed to engage in that debate intelligently have been officially hidden, distorted, and even lied about. As the decisions become more fateful, not only for Americans but literally for mankind, the sources of information are closed up, and the relevant facts needed for decision (even the decisions made!) are, as politically convenient "official secrets," withheld from the heavily laden channels of information.

In those channels, meanwhile, political rhetoric seems to slide lower and lower down the scale of cultivation and sensibility. The height of such mindless communications to masses, or what are thought to be masses, is probably the demagogic assumption that suspicion and accusation, if repeated often enough, somehow equal

[3] That is, even before the attack by Japanese naval air forces against the American naval base at Pearl Harbor, in Hawaii—December 7, 1941—and the subsequent entry of the United States into the Second World War.

[4] Charles Wilson (1890–1961), Secretary of Defense during President Dwight D. Eisenhower's first administration (1953–57).

[5] A government security classification that allowed those possessing it to have access to "secret" information.

proof of guilt—just as repeated claims about toothpaste or brands of cigarettes are assumed to equal facts. The greatest kind of propaganda with which America is beset, the greatest at least in terms of volume and loudness, is commercial propaganda for soap and cigarettes and automobiles; it is to such things, or rather to Their Names, that this society most frequently sings its loudest praises. What is important about this is that by implication and omission, by emphasis and sometimes by flat statement, this astounding volume of propaganda for commodities is often untruthful and misleading; and is addressed more often to the belly or to the groin than to the head or to the heart. Public communications from those who make powerful decisions, or who would have us vote them into such decision-making places, more and more take on those qualities of mindlessness and myth which commercial propaganda and advertising have come to exemplify.

In America today, men of affairs are not so much dogmatic as they are mindless. Dogma has usually meant some more or less elaborated justification of ideas and values, and thus has had some features (however inflexible and closed) of mind, of intellect, of reason. Nowadays what we are up against is precisely the absence of mind of any sort as a public force; what we are up against is a disinterest in and a fear of knowledge that might have liberating public relevance. What this makes possible are decisions having no rational justifications which the intellect could confront and engage in debate.

It is not the barbarous irrationality of dour political primitives that is the American danger; it is the respected judgments of Secretaries of State, the earnest platitudes of Presidents, the fearful self-righteousness of sincere young American politicians from sunny California. These men have replaced mind with platitude, and the dogmas by which they are legitimated are so widely accepted that no counter-balance of mind prevails against them. Such men as these are crackpot realists: in the name of realism they have constructed a paranoid reality all their own; in the name of practicality they have projected a utopian image of capitalism. They have replaced the responsible interpretation of events with the disguise of events by a maze of public relations; respect for public debate with unshrewd notions of psychological warfare; intellectual ability with agility of the sound, mediocre judgment; the capacity to elaborate alternatives and gauge their consequences with the executive stance.

4

Despite—perhaps because of—the ostracism of mind from public affairs, the immorality of accomplishment, and the general prevalence of organized irresponsibility, the men of the higher circles benefit from the total power of the institutional domains over which they rule. For the power of these institutions, actual or potential, is ascribed to them as the ostensible decision-makers. Their positions and their activities, and even their persons, are hallowed by these ascriptions; and, around all the high places of power, there is a penumbra[6] of prestige in which the political directorate, the corporate rich, the admirals and generals are bathed. The elite of a society, however modest its individual member, embodies the prestige of the society's power. Moreover, few individuals in positions of such authority can long resist the temptation to base their self-images, at least in part, upon the sounding board of the collectivity which they head. Acting as the representative of his nation, his corporation, his army, in due course, he comes to consider himself and what he says and believes as expressive of the historically accumulated glory of the great institutions with which he comes to identify himself. When he speaks in the name of his country or its cause, its past glory also echoes in his ears.

Status, no longer rooted primarily in local communities, follows the big hierarchies, which are on a national scale. Status follows the big money, even if it has a touch of the gangster about it. Status follows power, even if it be without background. Below, in the mass society, old moral and traditional barriers to status break down and Americans look for standards of excellence among the circles above them, in terms of which to model themselves and judge their self-esteem. Yet nowadays, it seems easier for Americans to recognize such representative men in the past than in the present. Whether this is due to a real historical difference or merely to the political ease and expediency of hindsight is very difficult to tell. At any rate it is a fact that in the political assignments of prestige there is little disparagement of Washington, Jefferson, and Lincoln, but much disagreement about current figures. Representative men seem more easily recognizable after they have died; contemporary political leaders are

[6]Surrounding atmosphere.

merely politicians; they may be big or little, but they are not great, and increasingly they are seen in terms of the higher immorality.

Now again status follows power, and older types of exemplary figures have been replaced by the fraternity of the successful—the professional executives who have become the political elite, who are now the *official* representative men. It remains to be seen whether they will become representative men in the images and aspirations of the mass public, or whether they will endure any longer than the displaced liberals of the 'thirties. Their images are controversial, deeply involved in the immorality of accomplishment and the higher immorality in general. Increasingly, literate Americans feel that there is something synthetic about them. Their style and the conditions under which they become "big" lend themselves too readily to the suspicion of the build-up; the shadows of the ghost writer and the make-up man loom too large; the slickness of the fabrication is too apparent.

We should, of course, bear in mind that men of the higher circles may or may not seek to impose themselves as representative upon the underlying population, and that relevant public sectors of the population may or may not accept their images. An elite may try to impose its claims upon the mass public, but this public may not cash them in. On the contrary, it may be indifferent or even debunk their values, caricature their image, laugh at their claim to be representative men.

In his discussion of models of national character, Walter Bagehot[7] does not go into such possibilities; but it is clear that for our contemporaries we must consider them, since precisely this reaction has led to a sometimes frenzied and always expensive practice of what is known as "public relations." Those who have both power and status are perhaps best off when they do not actively have to seek acclaim. The truly proud old families will not seek it; the professional celebrities are specialists in seeking it actively. Increasingly, the political, economic, and military elite—as we have seen—compete with the celebrities and seek to borrow their status. Perhaps those who have unprecedented power without the aura of status, will always seek it, even if uneasily, among those who have publicity without power.

For the mass public, there is the status distraction of the celebrity,

[7] A British philosopher and political theorist (1826–77).

as well as the economic distraction of war prosperity; for the liberal intellectual, who does look to the political arena, there is the political distraction of the sovereign localities and of the middle levels of power, which sustain the illusion that America is still a self-balancing society. If the mass media focus on the professional celebrities, the liberal intellectuals, especially the academic social scientists among them, focus upon the noisy middle levels. Professional celebrities and middle-level politicians are the most visible figures of the system; in fact, together they tend to monopolize the communicated or public scene that is visible to the members of the mass society, and thus to obscure and to distract attention from the power elite.

The higher circles in America today contain, on the one hand, the laughing, erotic, dazzling glamour of the professional celebrity, and, on the other, the prestige aura of power, of authority, of might and wealth. These two pinnacles are not unrelated. The power elite is not so noticeable as the celebrities, and often does not want to be; the "power" of the professional celebrity is the power of distraction. America as a national public is indeed possessed of a strange set of idols. The professionals, in the main, are either glossy little animals or frivolous clowns; the men of power, in the main, rarely seem to be models of representative men.

Such moral uneasiness as prevails among the American elite themselves is accordingly quite understandable. Its existence is amply confirmed by the more serious among those who have come to feel that they represent America abroad. There, the double-faced character of the American celebrity is reflected both by the types of Americans who travel to play or to work, and in the images many literate and articulate Europeans hold of "Americans." Public honor in America tends now to be either frivolous or grim; either altogether trivial or portentous of a greatly tightened-up system of prestige.

The American elite is not composed of representative men whose conduct and character constitute models for American imitation and aspiration. There is no set of men with whom members of the mass public can rightfully and gladly identify. In this fundamental sense, America is indeed without leaders. Yet such is the nature of the mass public's morally cynical and politically unspecified distrust that it is readily drained off without real political effect. That this is so, after the men and events of the last thirty years, is further proof of the extreme difficulty of finding and of using in America today the political means of sanity for morally sane objectives.

America—a conservative country without any conservative ideology—appears now before the world a naked and arbitrary power, as, in the name of realism, its men of decision enforce their often crackpot definitions upon world reality. The second-rate mind is in command of the ponderously spoken platitude. In the liberal rhetoric, vagueness, and in the conservative mood, irrationality, are raised to principle. Public relations and the official secret, the trivializing campaign and the terrible fact clumsily accomplished, are replacing the reasoned debate of political ideas in the privately incorporated economy, the military ascendancy, and the political vacuum of modern America.

The men of the higher circles are not representative men; their high position is not a result of moral virtue; their fabulous success is not firmly connected with meritorious ability. Those who sit in the seats of the high and the mighty are selected and formed by the means of power, the sources of wealth, the mechanics of celebrity, which prevail in their society. They are not men selected and formed by a civil service that is linked with the world of knowledge and sensibility. They are not men shaped by nationally responsible parties that debate openly and clearly the issues this nation now so unintelligently confronts. They are not men held in responsible check by a plurality of voluntary associations which connect debating publics with the pinnacles of decision. Commanders of power unequaled in human history, they have succeeded within the American system of organized irresponsibility.

12

Lewis Mumford

The City in History

❉

*Among the alarming trends in the social organization of the United States is
the continuing deterioration within the core of its large cities. Many of
today's centers function poorly, are inhabited by large numbers of the unem-
ployed and dispossessed, and are, for many residents, physically and psychologically hazardous. The most eloquent and prolific critic of the failures in
planning and administering American cities has been Lewis Mumford
(1895–   ).*

*Born and raised in the New York City area, Mumford studied at various
colleges in the region but never received a degree. Instead, he became a self-
taught student of the city itself, using its superb libraries, museums, and theaters as the basis for his personal curriculum. In later years his youthful wanderings through the city would be reflected in his essays on architecture for* The
New Yorker *magazine. Because of his outstanding popular and scholarly
contributions to urban theory, Mumford, though having earned no academic
degree, was appointed to professorships at such distinguished universities as
Dartmouth, Stanford, Pennsylvania, and M.I.T.*

The first lengthy work by Mumford, The Story of Utopia *(1922), foreshadowed the direction of most of his subsequent writings on urban living.
By the 1930s he was advocating the girdling of cities with parklike "green
belts" and the constructing of new cities built to the pedestrian's scale, with
an "organic" relationship among the various urban functions. After the Second World War, he worried about the destruction of American cities through
massive "urban renewal," encroaching highway systems, and nuclear war.*

The City in History *(1961), from which the following selection is*

From *The City in History,* © 1961, by Lewis Mumford. Reprinted from chapters 16
and 17 by permission of Harcourt Brace Jovanovich, Inc.

taken, is a book in which Mumford summarizes much of his prior theorizing, thereby creating a most searching general inquiry into the human prospect. He begins with a detailed historical essay on the nature, origin, and development of cities, from the earliest villages to the contemporary metropolis, then proceeds to document what he considers to be unnecessary evils of modern urban life. Mumford observes, for example, that the exodus from central city to suburbs has resulted in a class-segregated "low-grade uniform environment." In his view, this "purposeless expansion" of the new metropolis—useful only to the land speculator—has resulted in a dehumanizing, mechanically oriented mass society dominated by technology. Mumford contends, however, that there is still hope for the urban situation. He believes that an "organic" solution—a solution geared to people, not machines—is still possible.

SUBURBIA—AND BEYOND

The Historic Suburb

All through history, those who owned or rented land outside the city's walls valued having a place in the country, even if they did not actively perform agricultural labor: a cabin, a cottage, a vine-shaded shelter, built for temporary retreat if not for permanent occupancy. Early city dwellers did not wait for rapid transportation to take advantage of this rural surcease. As long as the city remained relatively compact and self-contained, it was possible to keep a balance between rural and urban occupations, yes, and between rural and urban pleasures: eating, drinking, dancing, athletic sports, love-making, every manner of relaxation had a special aura of festivity in a verdant, sunlit landscape. One of the chief penalties for continued urban growth was that it put this pleasurable setting at such a distance and confined it more and more to the ruling classes. . . .

The early appearance of the suburb points to another, even more important, fact: the life-maintaining agencies, gardening and farming, recreation and games, health sanatoria and retreats belong to the surrounding countryside, even when the functions they fostered spring from the town's needs or deficiencies. By the eighteenth century, it is true, the romantic movement had produced a new rationale for the suburban exodus, and the increasingly smoky and overcrowded town provided a new incentive. But it would be an error to regard suburbanism as a mere derivative of this ideology, for it had older, deeper roots. What needs to be accounted for is not the cult of nature that became popular in the eighteenth century, affecting everything from medicine to education, from architecture to cookery, but rather the obstinacy with which people had often clung for centuries to a crowded, depleted, denatured, and constricted environment, whose chief solace for misery was the company of equally miserable people. . . .

The ultimate outcome of the suburb's alienation from the city became visible only in the twentieth century, with the extension of the democratic ideal through the instrumentalities of manifolding and mass production. In the mass movement into suburban areas a new kind of community was produced, which caricatured both the historic city and the archetypal suburban refuge: a multitude of uniform, unidentifiable houses, lined up inflexibly, at uniform distances, on uniform roads, in a treeless communal waste, inhabited by people of the same class, the same income, the same age group, witnessing the same television performances, eating the same tasteless prefabricated foods, from the same freezers, conforming in every outward and inward respect to a common mold, manufactured in the central metropolis. Thus the ultimate effect of the suburban escape in our time is, ironically, a low-grade uniform environment from which escape is impossible. What has happened to the suburban exodus in the United States now threatens, through the same mechanical instrumentalities, to take place, at an equally accelerating rate, everywhere else—unless the most vigorous countermeasures are taken.

•   •   •

The Suburban Way of Life

•   •   •

By the very nature of the retreat, the suburb could be identified by a number of related social characteristics. And first, it was a segregated community, set apart from the city, not merely by space but by class stratification: a sort of green ghetto dedicated to the elite. That smug Victorian phrase, "We keep ourselves to ourselves," expresses the spirit of the suburb, in contrast to the city; for the city, by its nature, is a multi-form non-segregated environment. Little groups may indeed form social islands within a city, as the various tribes tended to do in the early cities of Islam, or again as people from a Greek or a Polish village might form temporary nests together in the same block in Chicago or New York. But the metropolis was a mixture of people who came from different places, practiced different occupations, encountered other personalities, meeting and mingling, co-operating and clashing, the rich with the poor, the proud with the humble.

Except where the suburb enclosed an original small town core, it tended to remain a one-class community, with just a sufficient fringe of tradesmen and servants to keep it going—the latter often condemned to use the central metropolis as their dormitory. Segregation, in practice, means compulsory association, or at least cohabitation; for if there are any choices, they lie outside the immediate community. Hence the great residual freedom of the suburbanite is that of locomotion. For esthetic and intellectual stimulus, the suburb remains dependent upon the big city: the theater, the opera, the orchestra, the art gallery, the university, the museum are no longer part of the daily environment. The problem of reestablishing connections, on a regional rather than a metropolitan basis, is one of the main problems of city planning in our time.

Not merely did the suburb keep the busier, dirtier, more productive enterprises at a distance, it likewise pushed away the creative activities of the city. Here life ceased to be a drama, full of unexpected challenges and tensions and dilemmas: it became a bland ritual of competitive spending. "Half your trouble," Rudyard Kipling wrote to William James in 1896, "is the curse of America—sheer, hopeless, well-ordered boredom; and that is going some day to be the curse of the world." Kipling put his finger, at that early date, upon the weakness of the suburban way of life.

Thus the genuine biological benefits of the suburb were undermined by its psychological and social defects: above all, the irreality of its retreat. In the town poor men demonstrated: beggars held out their hands in the street: disease spread quickly from poor quarters to the residences of the comfortable, via the delivery boy, the washerwoman, the seamstress, or other necessary menials: the eye, if not carefully averted, would, on a five-minute walk in any direction, behold a slum, or at least a slum child, ragged and grimy.

Even in the heyday of Coketown,[1] sensitive and intelligent souls could not remain long in such an environment without banding together to do something about it: they would exhort and agitate, hold meetings and form parades, draw up petitions and besiege legislators, extract money from the rich and dispense aid to the poor, founding soup kitchens and model tenements, passing housing legislation and acquiring land for parks, establishing hospitals and health centers, libraries and universities, in which the whole community played a part and benefitted.

In the suburb one might live and die without marring the image of an innocent world, except when some shadow of its evil fell over a column in the newspaper. Thus the suburb served as an asylum for the preservation of illusion. Here domesticity could flourish, forgetful of the exploitation on which so much of it was based. Here individuality could prosper, oblivious of the pervasive regimentation beyond. This was not merely a child-centered environment: it was based on a childish view of the world, in which reality was sacrificed to the pleasure principle.

As an attempt to recover what was missing in the city, the suburban exodus could be amply justified, for it was concerned with primary human needs. But there was another side: the temptation to retreat from unpleasant realities, to shirk public duties, and to find the whole meaning of life in the most elemental social group, the family, or even in the still more isolated and self-centered individual. What was properly a beginning was treated as an end.

• • •

Railroad Line, Greenbelt, Motor Sprawl

• • •

What has happened to the suburb is now a matter of historic record. As soon as the motor car became common, the pedestrian scale of the suburb disappeared, and with it most of its individuality and charm. The suburb ceased to be a neighborhood unit: it became a diffused low-density mass, enveloped by the conurbation and then further enveloping it. The suburb needed its very smallness, as it needed its rural background, to achieve its own kind of semi-rural

[1] A general name used by Mumford for the coal-burning factory towns spawned by the Industrial Revolution.

perfection. Once that limit was overpassed, the suburb ceased to be a refuge from the city and became part of the inescapable metropolis, "la ville tentaculaire," whose distant outlying open spaces and public parks were themselves further manifestations of the crowded city. This fact that will not cease to be true even if jet transportation brings an area twelve hundred miles away as near as one sixty miles distant today. For when one conquers space one also increases the populations to whom that distant space is accessible. The prospective net gain is considerably less than zero.

As long as the railroad stop and walking distances controlled suburban growth, the suburb had a form. The very concentration of shops and parking facilities around the railroad station in the better suburbs even promoted a new kind of market area, more concentrated than the linear market along an avenue. This was a spontaneous prototype of the suburban shopping center, whose easy facilities for parking gave it advantages over more central urban establishments, once the private motor car became the chief mode of transportation. But the motor car had done something more than remove the early limits and destroy the pedestrian scale. It either doubled the number of cars needed per family, or it turned the suburban housewife into a full time chauffeur.

These duties became even more imperative because the advent of the motor car was accompanied by the deliberate dismantling of the electric (rail) transportation system. In the more urbanized parts of America, electric transportation, often on its own private right of way, like the steam railroad, achieved far higher rates of speed than the present motor bus. Far from supplementing public rail transportation, the private motor car became largely a clumsy substitute for it. Instead of maintaining a complex transportation system, offering alternative choices of route and speed to fit the occasion, the new suburban sprawl has become abjectly dependent upon a single form, the private motor car, whose extension has devoured the one commodity the suburb could rightly boast: space. Instead of buildings set in a park, we now have buildings set in a parking lot.

Whilst the suburb served only a favored minority it neither spoiled the countryside nor threatened the city. But now that the drift to the outer ring has become a mass movement, it tends to destroy the value of both environments without producing anything but a dreary substitute, devoid of form and even more devoid of the original suburban values. We are faced by a curious paradox: the new subur-

ban form has now produced an anti-urban pattern. With the destruction of walking distances has gone the destruction of walking as a
normal means of human circulation: the motor car has made it unsafe
and the extension of the suburb has made it impossible. . . .

What an effective network requires is the largest number of alternative modes of transportation, at varying speeds and volumes, for
different functions and purposes. The fastest way to move a hundred
thousand people within a limited urban area, say a half mile radius, is
on foot: the slowest way of moving them would be to put them all
into motor cars. The entire daytime population of historic Boston
could assemble by foot on Boston Common, probably in less than
an hour if the streets were clear of motor traffic. If they were transported by motor car, they would take many hours, and unless they
abandoned their unparkable vehicles would never reach their destination.

Our highway engineers and our municipal authorities, hypnotized
by the popularity of the private motor car, feeling an obligation to
help General Motors to flourish, even if General Chaos results, have
been in an open conspiracy to dismantle all the varied forms of transportation necessary to a good system, and have reduced our facilities
to the private motor car (for pleasure, convenience, or trucking) and
the airplane. They have even duplicated railroad routes and repeated
all the errors of the early railroad engineers, while piling up in the
terminal cities a population the private motor car cannot handle
unless the city itself is wrecked to permit movement and storage of
automobiles.

If technical experts and administrators had known their business,
they would have taken special measures to safeguard more efficient
methods of mass transportation, in order to maintain both the city's
existence and the least time-wasting use of other forms of transportation. To have a complete urban structure capable of functioning
fully, it is necessary to find appropriate channels for every form of
transportation: it is the deliberate articulation of the pedestrian, the
mass transit system, the street, the avenue, the expressway, and the
airfield that alone can care for the needs of a modern community.
Nothing less will do.

By favoring the truck over the railroad for long-distance traffic,
we have replaced a safe and efficient service by a more dangerous and
inefficient one. If we want to improve our highway system, we
should be zealous to keep as large a part of goods haulage as possible

on the rails. Not the least reason for saving the passenger and freight railroad service and mass transportation is to ensure free movement by private vehicles on highways. Similarly, if the expressways that we have built around our cities are to function as such, mass transit must be improved and widened, not permitted to go out of existence.

The only effective cure for urban congestion is to so relate industrial and business zones to residential areas that a large part of their personnel can either walk or cycle to work, or use a public bus, or take a railroad train. By pushing all forms of traffic onto high speed motor ways, we burden them with a load guaranteed to slow down peak traffic to a crawl; and if we try to correct this by multiplying motor ways, we only add to the total urban wreckage by flinging the parts of the city ever farther away in a formless mass of thinly spread semi-urban tissue. The spatial dissociation of functions in suburbia results in an extreme specialization of the individual parts: segregated residence areas without local shops: segregated shopping centers without industries: segregated industrial plants without eating facilities unless provided by the management. In escaping the complex co-operations of the city Suburbia recovers the original vices of over-specialization and rigid control.

Good urban planning must provide a place for the motor car: that goes without saying. But this does not in the least mean that the motor car must be permitted to penetrate every part of the city and stay there, even though it disrupts all other activities. Neither does it mean that the auto shall dictate the whole scheme of living; nor yet does it mean that its manufacturers should be permitted to flout the requirements of the city by designing ever broader and longer vehicles. Quite the contrary, the time has come to discriminate between two functions of the motor car—urban movement and countrywide movement. For the latter, a big car with plenty of room to house a family and hold their baggage is admirable. In the city, however, such cars should be encouraged to stay on the outskirts, and be heavily taxed for the privilege of parking within it; while special favors should be given to the design and distribution of small cars, electric powered, for ordinary intra-urban movement, to supplement rather than replace mass transportation. Moderate speed, quiet, ease and compactness of parking—these are the characteristics of a town car.

It is an absurdly impoverished technology that has only one answer to the problem of transportation; and it is a poor form of city planning that permits that answer to dominate its entire scheme of existence.

Mass Suburbia as Anti-city

Under the present dispensation we have sold our urban birthright for a sorry mess of motor cars. As poor a bargain as Esau's pottage.[2] Future generations will perhaps wonder at our willingness, indeed our eagerness, to sacrifice the education of our children, the care of the ill and the aged, the development of the arts, to say nothing of ready access to nature, for the lopsided system of mono-transportation, going through low density areas at sixty miles an hour, but reduced in high density areas to a bare six. But our descendants will perhaps understand our curious willingness to expend billions of dollars to shoot a sacrificial victim into planetary orbit, if they realize that our cities are being destroyed for the same superstitious religious ritual: the worship of speed and empty space. Lacking sufficient municipal budgets to deal adequately with all of life's requirements that can be concentrated in the city, we have settled for a single function, transportation, or rather for a single part of an adequate transportation system, locomotion by private motor car.

By allowing mass transportation to deteriorate and by building expressways out of the city and parking garages within, in order to encourage the maximum use of the private car, our highway engineers and city planners have helped to destroy the living tissue of the city and to limit the possibilities of creating a larger urban organism on a regional scale. Mass transportation for short distances, under a mile, should rely mainly upon the pedestrian. By discouraging and eliminating the pedestrian, by failing to extend and to perfect mass transportation, our municipal officials and highway engineers have created a situation that calls for extremely low residential densities. Here again the monopoly of private space not merely reduces the social facilities of the city but sacrifices public open space to private.

The absurd belief that space and rapid locomotion are the chief ingredients of a good life has been fostered by the agents of mass suburbia. That habit of low density building is the residual bequest

[2] A reference to an Old Testament story. Esau, being very hungry, exchanged his paternal inheritance for a bowl of his brother Jacob's soup (Genesis 25:27–34).

of the original romantic movement, and by now it is one of the chief obstacles to reassembling the parts of the city and uniting them in a new pattern that shall offer much richer resources for living than either the congested and disordered central metropolis or the outlying areas reached by its expressways. The *reductio ad absurdum* of this myth is, notoriously, Los Angeles. Here the suburban standards of open space, with free standing houses, often as few as five houses to the acre, has been maintained: likewise the private motor car, as the major means of transportation has supplanted what was only a generation or so ago an extremely efficient system of public transportation.

Los Angeles has now become an undifferentiated mass of houses, walled off into sectors by many-laned expressways, with ramps and viaducts that create special bottlenecks of their own. These expressways move but a small fraction of the traffic per hour once carried by public transportation, at a much lower rate of speed, in an environment befouled by smog, itself produced by the lethal exhausts of the technologically backward motor cars. More than a third of the Los Angeles area is consumed by these grotesque transportation facilities; *two-thirds* of central Los Angeles are occupied by streets, freeways, parking facilities, garages. This is space-eating with a vengeance. The last stage of the process already beckons truly progressive minds—to evict the remaining inhabitants and turn the entire area over to automatically propelled vehicles, completely emancipated from any rational human purpose.

Even in cities as spacious as Washington, it is only the original central area that has a residential density of ten or more families per acre: on the spreading outskirts, under ten is the rule, and a fast moving tide is putting an ever larger tract under a density of settlement less than five per acre. This is ruinous both to urban living and to leisured recreation; for the attempt to service the distant areas with expressways will not merely sterilize more and more of the land, but will scatter social facilities that should be concentrated in new cities, organized so as to diffuse and amplify the central facilities.

The conclusion should be plain. Any attempt to create an adequate transportation system without creating in advance sufficient reserves of public land, without laying down a desirable density for balanced urban occupation *higher than the present suburban level,* without providing for a regional network largely independent of the bigger trunk line highways, will degrade the landscape without bringing any permanent benefits to its new inhabitants.

To keep the advantages first incorporated in the romantic suburb, we must acclimate them to the building of cities. To keep the advantages first discovered in the closed city, we must create a more porous pattern, richer in both social and esthetic variety. Residential densities of about one hundred people per net acre, exclusive of streets and sidewalks, will provide usable private gardens and encourage small public inner parks for meeting and relaxing. This can be achieved without erecting the sterile, space-mangling high-rise slabs that now grimly parade, in both Europe and America, as the ultimate contribution of "modern" architecture. If we are concerned with human values, we can no longer afford either sprawling Suburbia or the congested Metropolis: still less can we afford a congested Suburbia, whose visual openness depends upon the cellular isolation and regimentation of its component families in mass structures.

Families in Space

As it has worked out under the impact of the present religion and myth of the machine, mass Suburbia has done away with most of the freedoms and delights that the original disciples of Rousseau[3] sought to find through their exodus from the city. Instead of centering attention on the child in the garden, we now have the image of "Families in Space." For the wider the scattering of the population, the greater the isolation of the individual household, and the more effort it takes to do privately, even with the aid of many machines and automatic devices, what used to be done in company often with conversation, song, and the enjoyment of the physical presence of others.

The town housewife, who half a century ago knew her butcher, her grocer, her dairyman, her various other local tradesmen, as individual persons, with histories and biographies that impinged on her own, in a daily interchange, now has the benefit of a single weekly expedition to an impersonal supermarket, where only by accident is she likely to encounter a neighbor. If she is well-to-do, she is sur-

[3] Jean Jacques Rousseau (1712–78), a French (Swiss-born) philosopher and writer. One of the forerunners of the romantic movement, he rejected civilization and asserted the moral superiority of the "return to nature."

rounded with electric or electronic devices that take the place of flesh and blood companions: her real companions, her friends, her mentors, her lovers, her fillers-up of unlived life, are shadows on the television screen, or even less embodied voices. She may answer them, but she cannot make herself heard: as it has worked out, this is a one-way system. The greater the area of expansion, the greater the dependence upon a distant supply center and remote control.

On the fringe of mass Suburbia, even the advantages of the primary neighborhood group disappear. The cost of this detachment in space from other men is out of all proportion to its supposed benefits. The end product is an encapsulated life, spent more and more either in a motor car or within the cabin of darkness before a television set: soon, with a little more automation of traffic, mostly in a motor car, travelling even greater distances, under remote control, so that the one-time driver may occupy himself with a television set, having lost even the freedom of the steering wheel. Every part of this life, indeed, will come through official channels and be under supervision. Untouched by human hand at one end: untouched by human spirit at the other. Those who accept this existence might as well be encased in a rocket hurtling through space, so narrow are their choices, so limited and deficient their permitted responses. Here indeed we find "The Lonely Crowd." [4]

The organizers of the ancient city had something to learn from the new rulers of our society. The former massed their subjects within a walled enclosure, under the surveillance of armed guardians within the smaller citadel, the better to keep them under control. That method is now obsolete. With the present means of long-distance mass communication, sprawling isolation has proved an even more effective method of keeping a population under control. With direct contact and face-to-face association inhibited as far as possible, all knowledge and direction can be monopolized by central agents and conveyed through guarded channels, too costly to be utilized by small groups or private individuals. To exercise free speech in such a scattered, dissociated community one must "buy time" on the air or "buy space" in the newspaper. Each member of Suburbia becomes imprisoned by the very separation that he has prized: he is fed through a narrow opening: a telephone line, a radio band, a televi-

---

[4] *The Lonely Crowd: A Study of the Changing American Character* (1950) is a critical view of contemporary mass society written by David Riesman (1909–), an American sociologist.

sion circuit. This is not, it goes without saying, the result of a conscious conspiracy by a cunning minority: it is an organic by-product of an economy that sacrifices human development to mechanical processing.

In a well-organized community, all these technological improvements might admirably widen the scope of social life: in the disorganized communities of today, they narrow the effective range of the person. Under such conditions, nothing can happen spontaneously or autonomously—not without a great deal of mechanical assistance. Does this not explain in some degree the passiveness and docility that has crept into our existence? In the recent Caracas revolution that deposed a brutal dictatorship in Venezuela, the starting signal, I have been told by an eye-witness, was the honking of motor car horns. That honking, growing louder, coming nearer, converging from every quarter of the city upon the palace, struck terror into the hearts of the rulers. That, too, was an urban phenomenon. Suburbia offers poor facilities for meeting, conversation, collective debate, and common action—it favors silent conformity, not rebellion or counter-attack. So Suburbia has become the favored home of a new kind of absolutism: invisible but all-powerful.

I might be uneasy about the validity of this analysis had not the prescient de Tocqueville[5] anticipated it long ago, in "Democracy in America." He sought to "trace the novel features under which despotism may appear in the world." "The first thing that strikes observation," he says, "is an uncountable number of men, all equal and alike, incessantly endeavoring to produce the petty and paltry pleasures with which they glut their lives. Each of them living apart, is a stranger to the fate of all the rest—his children and his private friends constitute to him the whole of mankind; as for the rest of his fellow-citizens, he is close to them, but he sees them not; he touches them, but he feels them not; he exists but in himself and for himself alone; and if his kindred still remain to him, he may be said at any rate to have lost his country."

De Tocqueville was describing in anticipation the temper and habit of life in Suburbia, a habit that has worked back into the city and made even democratic nations submit, with hardly a murmur, to every manner of totalitarian compulsion and corruption. What this

---

[5] Alexis de Tocqueville (1805–59), an enlightened French aristocrat. His *Democracy in America* (1835, 1840) is a thorough survey of American society during the Age of Jackson.

great political philosopher foresaw with his inner eye, less gifted observers can now see with their outer eye. This is the last stage in the breakup of the city. The expansion of our technology only quickens the pace of this change. What is left, if no counter-movement takes place, will not be worth saving. For when the container changes as rapidly as its contents nothing can in fact be saved.

• • •

THE MYTH OF MEGALOPOLIS

• • •

The Removal of Limits

Let us now view the situation of the metropolis in more general terms: what some have called the urban explosion is in fact a symptom of a more general state—the removal of quantitative limits. This marks the change from an organic system to a mechanical system, from purposeful growth to purposeless expansion.

Until the nineteenth century the limitations of both local and regional transportation placed a natural restriction upon the growth of cities. Even the biggest centers, Rome, Babylon, Alexandria, Antioch, were forced to respect that limit. But by the middle of the nineteenth century the tendency toward metropolitan monopoly was supplemented with a new factor brought in by the effective utilization of coal and iron and the extension of the railroad: in terms of purely physical requirements the area of settlement coincided with the coal beds, the ore beds, the railroad network. Patrick Geddes, early in the present century, pointed out the significance of the new population maps, which graphically disclosed a general thickening and spreading of the urban mass: he showed that entire provinces and counties were becoming urbanized, and he proposed to differentiate such diffused formations by a name that would distinguish them from the historic city: the "conurbation."

Meanwhile the original forces that created the conurbation were supplemented by the electric power grid, the electric railway, and still later by the motor car and the motor road: so that a movement that was at first confined largely to the area accessible to the railroad now is taking place everywhere. Whereas the first extension of the factory system produced a multitude of new cities and greatly augmented the population of existing centers, the present diffusion of the area of settlement has largely halted this growth and has enormously increased the production of relatively undifferentiated urban tissue, without any relation either to an internally coherent nucleus or an external boundary of any sort.

The result threatens to be a universal conurbation. Those who ignored Geddes's original definition half a century ago have recently re-discovered the phenomenon itself, and treated it as if it were an entirely new development. Some have even misapplied to the conurbation the inappropriate term Megalopolis, though it represents, in fact, the precise opposite of the tendency that brought the original city of this name into existence. The overgrown historic city was still, residually, an entity: the conurbation is a nonentity, and becomes more patently so as it spreads.

What this removal of limits means can perhaps best be grasped by referring to the extension of historic centers. When Rome was surrounded by the Aurelian Wall in A.D. 274, it covered a little more than five square miles. The present area of London is 130 times as great as this; while it is roughly 650 times as big as the area of medieval London, which was 677 acres. The conurbation of New York is even more widespread: it covers something like 2,514 square miles. If no human purposes supervene to halt the blotting out of the countryside and to establish limits for the growth and colonization of cities, the whole coastal strip from Maine to Florida might coalesce into an almost undifferentiated conurbation. But to call this mass a "regional city" or to hold that it represents the new scale of settlement to which modern man must adapt his institutions and his personal needs is to mask the realities of the human situation and allow seemingly automatic forces to become a substitute for human purposes.

These vast urban masses are comparable to a routed and disorganized army, which has lost its leaders, scattered its battalions and companies, torn off its insignia, and is fleeing in every direction. "Sauve qui peut."[6] The first step toward handling this situation, besides establishment of an over-all command, is to re-group in units that can be effectively handled. Until we understand the function of the smaller units and can bring them under discipline we cannot command and deploy the army as a whole over a larger area. The scale of distances has changed, and the "regional city" is a potential

---

[6] French: save (himself) who can; that is, every man for himself.

reality, indeed a vital necessity. But the condition for success in these endeavors lies in our abilities to recognize and to impose organic limitations. This means the replacement of the machine-oriented metropolitan economy by one directed toward the goods and goals of life.

Though the removal of limits is one of the chief feats of the metropolitan economy, this does not imply any abdication of power on the part of the chiefs in charge: for there is one countervailing condition to this removal, and that is the processing of all operations through the metropolis and its increasingly complicated mechanisms. The metropolis is in fact a processing center, in which a vast variety of goods, material and spiritual, is mechanically sorted and reduced to a limited number of standardized articles, uniformly packaged, and distributed through controlled channels to their destination, bearing the approved metropolitan label.

"Processing" has now become the chief form of metropolitan control; and the need for its constant application has brought into existence a whole range of inventions, mechanical and electronic, from cash registers to electronic computers, which handle every operation from book-keeping to university examinations. Interests and aptitudes that do not lend themselves to processing are automatically rejected. So complicated, so elaborate, so costly are the processing mechanisms that they cannot be employed except on a mass scale: hence they eliminate all activities of a fitful, inconsecutive, or humanly subtle nature—just as "yes" or "no" answers eliminate those more delicate and accurate discriminations that often lie at one point or another in between the spuriously "correct" answer. That which is local, small, personal, autonomous, must be suppressed. Increasingly, he who controls the processing mechanism controls the lives and destinies of those who must consume its products, and who on metropolitan terms cannot seek any others. For processing and packaging do not end on the production line: they finally make over the human personality.

In short the monopoly of power and knowledge that was first established in the citadel has come back, in a highly magnified form, in the final stages of metropolitan culture. In the end every aspect of life must be brought under control: controlled weather, controlled movement, controlled association, controlled production, controlled prices, controlled fantasy, controlled ideas. But the only purpose of control, apart from the profit, power, and prestige of the controllers, is to accelerate the process of mechanical control itself.

The priests of this regime are easy to identify: the whole system, in its final stages, rests on the proliferation of secret, and thus controllable, knowledge; and the very division of labor that makes specialized scientific research possible also restricts the number of people capable of putting the fragments together. But where are the new gods? The nuclear reactor is the seat of their power: radio transmission and rocket flight their angelic means of communication and transportation: but beyond these minor agents of divinity the Control Room itself, with its Cybernetic Deity,[7] giving His lightning-like decisions and His infallible answers: omniscience and omnipotence, triumphantly mated by science. Faced with this electronic monopoly of man's highest powers, the human can come back only at the most primitive level. Sigmund Freud[8] detected the beginnings of creative art in the infant's pride over his bowel movements. We can now detect its ultimate manifestation in paintings and sculpture whose contents betray a similar pride and a similar degree of autonomy—and a similar product.

One of the ancient prerogatives of the gods was to create man out of their flesh, like Atum,[9] or in their own image, like Yahweh.[10] When the accredited scientific priesthood go a little farther with their present activities, the new life-size homunculus [artificial man] will be processed, too: one can already see anticipatory models in our art galleries. He will look remarkably like a man accoutered in a "space-suit": outwardly a huge scaly insect. But the face inside will be incapable of expression, as incapable as that of a corpse. And who will know the difference?

Sprawling Giantism

· · ·

The image of modern industrialism that Charlie Chaplin[11] carried over from the past into "Modern Times" is just the opposite of

[7] Cybernetics is the comparative study of the controlling systems in the human body and of mechanical and electrical systems that incorporate similar controls; hence, Mumford's "Cybernetic Deity" would be essentially the computer viewed as God.
[8] An Austrian physician who became the founder of psychoanalysis (1856–1939).
[9] A primeval Egyptian god (often spelled "Atmu").
[10] Ancient form of the Hebrew name for God.
[11] Great comic actor of the early cinema (1889–1977): his film *Modern Times* is a classic satire of the demands placed upon workers by the organization and machinery of the factory system.

megalopolitan reality. He pictured the worker as an old-fashioned drudge, chained to the machine, mechanically fed while he continued to operate it. That image belongs to Coketown. The new worker, in the metropolis, has been progressively released from the productive process: the grinding, impoverished toil that made the nineteenth-century factory so hideous has been lifted by social services and security, by mechanical aids and by complete automation. Work is no longer so brutal in the light industries: but automation has made it even more boring. The energy and application that once went into the productive process must now be addressed to consumption.

By a thousand cunning attachments and controls, visible and subliminal, the workers in an expanding economy are tied to a consumption mechanism: they are assured of a livelihood provided they devour without undue selectivity all that is offered by the machine— and demand nothing that is not produced by the machine. The whole organization of the metropolitan community is designed to kill spontaneity and self-direction. You stop on the red light and go on the green. You see what you are supposed to see, think what you are supposed to think: your personal contributions, like your income and security taxes, are deductible at source. To choose, to select, to discriminate, to exercise prudence or continence or forethought, to carry self-control to the point of abstinence, to have standards other than those of the market, and to set limits other than those of immediate consumption—these are impious heresies that would challenge the whole megalopolitan myth and deflate its economy. In such a "free" society Henry Thoreau[12] must rank as a greater public enemy than Karl Marx.[13]

The metropolis, in its final stage of development, becomes a collective contrivance for making this irrational system work, and for giving those who are in reality its victims the illusion of power, wealth, and felicity, of standing at the very pinnacle of human achievement. But in actual fact their lives are constantly in peril, their wealth is tasteless and ephemeral, their leisure is sensationally monotonous, and their pathetic felicity is tainted by constant, well-justified anticipations of violence and sudden death. Increasingly they find themselves "strangers and afraid," in a world they never

---

[12] An American essayist, poet, and naturalist (1817–62) who developed in his life and writings a doctrine of self-sufficiency and simplicity.
[13] A major originator of communist theory (1818–83).

made:[14] a world ever less responsive to direct human command, ever more empty of human meaning.

The Shadows of Success

To believe, therefore, that human culture has reached a marvellous final culmination in the modern metropolis one must avert one's eyes from the grim details of the daily routine. And that is precisely what the metropolitan denizen schools himself to do: he lives, not in the real world, but in a shadow world projected around him at every moment by means of paper and celluloid and adroitly manipulated lights: a world in which he is insulated by glass, cellophane, pliofilm from the mortifications of living. In short, a world of professional illusionists and their credulous victims.

The swish and crackle of paper is the underlying sound of the metropolis. What is visible and real in this world is only what has been transferred to paper or has been even further etherialized on a microfilm or a tape recorder. The essential daily gossip of the metropolis is no longer that of people meeting face to face at a cross-roads, at the dinner table, in the marketplace: a few dozen people writing in the newspapers, a dozen or so more broadcasting over radio and television, provide the daily interpretation of movements and happenings with slick professional adroitness. Thus even the most spontaneous human activities come under professional surveillance and centralized control. The spread of manifolding devices of every sort gives to the most ephemeral and mediocre products of the mind a temporary durability they do not deserve: whole books are printed to justify the loose evacuations of the tape recorder. . . .

This metropolitan world, then, is a world where flesh and blood are less real than paper and ink and celluloid. It is a world where the great masses of people, unable to achieve a more full-bodied and satisfying means of living, take life vicariously, as readers, spectators, listeners, passive observers. Living thus, year in and year out, at second hand, remote from the nature that is outside them, and no less remote from the nature that is within, it is no wonder that they

---

[14] From "The Laws of God, The Laws of Man" (1922) by the English poet and classical scholar A. E. Housman (1859–1936):

> I, a stranger and afraid
> In a world I never made.

turn more and more of the functions of life, even thought itself, to the machines that their inventors have created. In this disordered environment only machines retain some of the attributes of life, while human beings are progressively reduced to a bundle of reflexes, without self-starting impulses or autonomous goals: "behaviorist man." [15]

• • •

Destiny of Megalopolis

In following the growth of megalopolitan culture to its conclusion we reach a whole series of terminal processes, and it would be simple-minded to believe that they have any prospect of continuing in existence indefinitely. A life that lacks any meaning, value, or purpose, except that of keeping the mechanism of breathing and ingestion going, is little better than life in an iron lung, which is only supportable because the patient still has hope of recovery and escape.

The metropolitan regime now threatens to reach its climax in a meaningless war, one of total extermination, whose only purpose would be to relieve the anxieties and fears produced by the citadels' wholesale commitment to weapons of annihilation and extermination. Thus absolute power has become in fact absolute nihilism. Scientific and technological over-elaboration, unmodified by human values and aims, has committed countries like the United States and Russia to collective mechanisms of destruction so rigid that they cannot be modified or brought under control without being completely dismantled. Even instinctual animal intelligence remains inoperative in this system: the commitment to the machine overthrows all the safeguards to life, including the ancient law of self-preservation. For the sake of rapid locomotion, we in the United States kill some 40,000 people outright every year and fatally maim hundreds of thousands of others. For the sake of wielding absolute nuclear power our leaders are brazenly prepared to sacrifice from fifty to seventy-five million of their own citizens on the first day of an all-out nuclear war, and mutilate, or even possibly in the end eliminate the human race. The illusionist phrase to cover these psychotic plans is "national security," or even, more absurdly, "national survival."

[15] For a contrasting opinion of the value of "behaviorist man," see selection 9, from B. F. Skinner's *Beyond Freedom and Dignity*.

Now, in every organism, the anabolic and the catabolic processes, the creative and the destructive, are constantly at work. Life and growth depend, not on the absence of negative conditions, but on a sufficient degree of equilibrium, and a sufficient surplus of constructive energy to permit continued repair, to absorb novelties, to regulate quantities, and to establish give-and-take relations with all the other organisms and communities needed to maintain balance. The negative factors in metropolitan existence might have provided the conditions for a higher development if the very terms of expansion had not given them the upper hand and tended to make their domination permanent, in ever more destructive processes. . . .

Remarkably, the wholesale rehabilitation of the cities of Europe [after World War II] at a higher level than they had achieved in the past, took place in less than a dozen years. That almost superhuman mobilization of energies demonstrated that urban reconstruction and renewal on a far greater scale might be accomplished, within a single generation, provided the economy was directly oriented to human needs, and that the major part of the national income was not diverted to the studious consumptive dissipations and planned destructions demanded by the expanding metropolitan economy: above all, by ceaseless preparations for collective genocide and suicide.

Unfortunately, as soon as the economy recovered and returned to the pursuit of its original ends, all its irrational features likewise came back: to keep going, an ever larger part of its energies must be dissipated in pyramid-building. Nowhere have the irrationalities of the current metropolitan myth been more fully exposed than in the development of so-called "absolute" weapons for limitless nuclear, bacterial, and chemical genocide. The building up of these weapons among the "Nuclear Powers" has given the "death-wish" the status of a fixed national policy, and made a universal extermination camp the ideal terminus of this whole civilization.

Even if the nations take timely measures to eliminate the stock of such weapons, it will be long before the vicious moral effects of this policy are dissipated: adult delinquency, on the scale not merely contemplated but actually prepared for in detail, requires therapeutic counter-measures that may take a full century to show any positive effect. This is the last and worst bequest of the citadel (read "Pentagon" and "Kremlin") to the culture of cities.

In a few short years our civilization has reached the point that

Henry Adams,[16] with uncanny prescience, foresaw more than half a century ago. "At the present rate of progression, since 1600," he wrote, "it will not need another century or half a century to tip thought upside down. Law, in that case would disappear as theory or a priori principle and give place to force. Morality would become police. Explosives would reach cosmic violence. Disintegration would overcome integration." Every part of this prophecy has already been fulfilled; and it is useless to speculate about the future of cities until we have reckoned with the forces of annihilation and extermination that now, almost automatically, and at an ever-accelerating rate, are working to bring about a more general breakdown.

Metropolitan civilization thus embodies and carries to its conclusion the radical contradiction we found already embedded in the life course of the city from the moment of its foundation: a contradiction that comes out of the dual origin of the city, and the perpetual ambivalence of its goals. From the village, the city derives its nature as a mothering and life-promoting environment, stable and secure, rooted in man's reciprocal relations with other organisms and communities. From the village, too, it derives the ways and values of an ungraded democracy in which each member plays his appropriate role at each stage in the life cycle.

On the other hand, the city owed its existence, and even more its enlargement, to concentrated attempts at mastering other men and dominating, with collective force, the whole environment. Thus the city became a power-trapping utility, designed by royal agents gathering the dispersed energies of little communities into a mighty reservoir, collectively regulating their accumulation and flow, and directing them into new channels—now favoring the smaller units by beneficently re-molding the landscape, but eventually hurling its energies outward in destructive assaults against other cities. Release and enslavement, freedom and compulsion, have been present from the beginning in urban culture.

Out of this inner tension some of the creative expressions of urban life have come forth: yet only in scattered and occasional instances do we discover political power well distributed in small communities, as in seventeenth-century Holland or Switzerland, or the ideals of life

[16] Henry Brooks Adams (1838–1918), an American historian, developed as the central thesis of his later writings the contrast between the integrating unity of the Middle Ages and the disintegrating multiplicity of the twentieth century.

constantly regulating the eccentric manifestations of power. Our present civilization is a gigantic motor car moving along a one-way road at an ever-accelerating speed. Unfortunately as now constructed the car lacks both steering wheel and brakes, and the only form of control the driver exercises consists in making the car go faster, though in his fascination with the machine itself and his commitment to achieving the highest speed possible, he has quite forgotten the purpose of the journey. This state of helpless submission to the economic and technological mechanisms modern man has created is curiously disguised as progress, freedom, and the mastery of man over nature. As a result, every permission has become a morbid compulsion. Modern man has mastered every creature above the level of the viruses and bacteria—except himself.

Never before has the "citadel" exercised such atrocious power over the rest of the human race. Over the greater part of history, the village and the countryside remained a constant reservoir of fresh life, constrained indeed by the ancestral patterns of behavior that had helped make man human, but with a sense of both human limitations and human possibilities. No matter what the errors and aberrations of the rulers of the city, they were still correctible. Even if whole urban populations were destroyed, more than nine-tenths of the human race still remained outside the circle of destruction. Today this factor of safety has gone: the metropolitan explosion has carried both the ideological and the chemical poisons of the metropolis to every part of the earth; and the final damage may be irretrievable.

These terminal possibilities did not, I repeat, first become visible with the use of nuclear weapons: they were plain to alert and able minds, like Burckhardt in the eighteen-sixties, and like Henry Adams at the beginning of the present century.

Adams' contemporary, Henry James,[17] put the human situation in an image that curiously holds today: that of the Happy Family and the Infernal Machine. "The machine so rooted as to defy removal, and the family still so indifferent, while it carries on the family business of buying and selling, of chattering and dancing, to the danger of being blown up." The machine James referred to was the political machine of Philadelphia, then the classic embodiment of corruption and criminality; but only a too-guileless observer can fail to see that it applies to other demoralized mechanisms in our expanding metro-

---

[17] An American novelist (1843–1916).

politan civilization. Once-local manifestations of criminality and irrationality now threaten our whole planet, smugly disguised as sound
business enterprise, technological progress, communist efficiency, or
democratic statesmanship. No wonder the popular existentialists,
mirroring our time, equate "reality" with the "absurd." A large portion of the painting and sculpture of the past generation symbolically
anticipates the catastrophic end products of this death-oriented culture: total dismemberment and dehumanization in a lifeless, feature-
less void. Some of the best of this art, like Henry Moore's archaic
pinheaded figures,[18] foretells a new beginning at a level so primitive
that the mind has hardly yet begun to operate.

Now, if the total picture were as grim as that I have painted in the
present chapter, there would be no excuse for writing this book; or
rather, it would be just as irrational a contribution as the many other
irrationalities and futilities I have touched on. If I have duly emphasized the disintegrations of the metropolitan stage, it has been for but
one reason: only those who are aware of them will be capable of
directing our collective energies into more constructive processes. It
was not the diehard Romans of the fifth century A.D., still boasting
of Rome's achievements and looking forward to another thousand
years of them, who understood what the situation required: on the
contrary, it was those who rejected the Roman premises and set their
lives on a new foundation who built up a new civilization that in the
end surpassed Rome's best achievements, even in engineering and
government.

And so today: those who work within the metropolitan myth,
treating its cancerous tumors as normal manifestations of growth,
will continue to apply poultices, salves, advertising incantations,
public relations magic, and quack mechanical remedies until the patient dies before their own failing eyes. No small part of the urban
reform and correction that has gone on these last hundred years, and
not least this last generation—slum demolition, model housing, civic
architectural embellishment, suburban extension, "urban renewal"—
has only continued in superficially new forms the same purposeless
concentration and organic de-building that prompted the remedy.

Yet in the midst of all this disintegration fresh nodules of growth
have appeared and, even more significantly, a new pattern of life has

---

[18]Moore (1898–), leading British sculptor. See selection 39 for some of Moore's
comments on primitive art.

begun to emerge. This pattern necessarily is based on radically different premises from those of the ancient citadel builders or those of their modern counterparts, the rocket-constructors and nuclear exterminators. If we can distinguish the main outlines of this multi-dimensional, life-oriented economy we should also be able to describe the nature and the functions of the emerging city and the future pattern of human settlement. Above all, we should anticipate the next act in the human drama, provided mankind escapes the death-trap our blind commitment to a lopsided, power-oriented, anti-organic technology has set for it. . . .

13

Zbigniew Brzezinski

The Global Impact of the Technetronic Revolution

Zbigniew Brzezinski (1928–   ), a scholar and foreign policy adviser, is another of the great number displaced from their European homelands during the Second World War. Born in Warsaw, the son of a Polish diplomat, Brzezinski traveled with his parents to Montreal, Canada, in 1938, where his father served as Polish consul-general throughout the war. In 1945, when the Communists gained control of the Polish government and Brzezinski's father left Poland's diplomatic service, the family remained in Canada.

By 1950, Brzezinski had earned a bachelor's degree and a master's degree, in economics and political science, from Montreal's McGill University. He continued his studies at Harvard University and in 1953 received a doctorate in government studies. Having chosen to remain in the United States permanently, Brzezinski accepted a teaching post at Harvard and in 1958 became a naturalized American citizen. During his years as a member of the Harvard faculty, he published his doctoral thesis, The Permanent Purge: Politics in Soviet Totalitarianism.

In 1960 Brzezinski became associated with Columbia University, where he was soon named director of the newly formed Institute on Communist Affairs. From this forum he attracted considerable attention, eventually becoming a foreign policy adviser to President Kennedy and to President Johnson. During their administrations he supported the American military intervention in Vietnam as necessary for political stability in Asia. After the election of Jimmy Carter to the presidency in 1976, Brzezinski was appointed to the powerful post of national security adviser to the President.

Brzezinski's scholarship extends to fields beyond foreign affairs and communism. In the following selection from his seventh book, Between Two Ages: America's Role in the Technetronic Era *(1970), Brzezinski defines contemporary post-industrial society as "technetronic," since it is "shaped culturally, psychologically, socially, and economically by the impact of technology and electronics." As a result, he suggests, even the patterns of conceptual thought have changed. Where earlier industrial societies promoted the use of the printed page, which makes for static ideological systems, the technetronic society facilitates instant audio-visual communication, which makes for more changeable, non-systematic views of reality. The danger of "intellectual fragmentation" is, therefore, increased.*

Brzezinski believes that this new reality, based upon wide-ranging electronic communications, will not bring people together in the intimacy of that "global village" enthusiastically suggested by the communications theorist Marshall McLuhan. Rather, it will create a "global city" with all the fragmentation and tensions of urban life. In Brzezinski's view, the United States, the main disseminator of the technetronic revolution, is already building the global city—in its own changing image.

1. THE ONSET OF THE TECHNETRONIC AGE

The impact of science and technology on man and his society, especially in the more advanced countries of the world, is becoming the major source of contemporary change. Recent years have seen a proliferation of exciting and challenging literature on the future. In the United States, in Western Europe, and, to a lesser degree, in Japan and in the Soviet Union, a number of systematic, scholarly efforts have been made to project, predict, and grasp what the future holds for us.

The transformation that is now taking place, especially in America, is already creating a society increasingly unlike its industrial predecessor. The post-industrial society is becoming a "technetronic" society: a society that is shaped culturally, psychologically, socially, and economically by the impact of technology and electronics—particularly in the area of computers and communications. The industrial process is no longer the principal determinant of social change, altering the mores, the social structure, and the values of society. In the industrial society technical knowledge was applied primarily to one specific end: the acceleration and improvement of production techniques. Social consequences were a later by-product of this paramount concern. In the technetronic society scientific and technical knowledge, in addition to enhancing production capabilities, quickly spills over to affect almost all aspects of life directly. Accordingly, both the growing capacity for the instant calculation of the most complex interactions and the increasing availability of biochemical means of human control augment the potential scope of consciously chosen direction, and thereby also the pressures to direct, to choose, and to change.

Reliance on these new techniques of calculation and communication enhances the social importance of human intelligence and the immediate relevance of learning. The need to integrate social change is heightened by the increased ability to decipher the patterns of change; this in turn increases the significance of basic assumptions concerning the nature of man and the desirability of one or another form of social organization. Science thereby intensifies rather than diminishes the relevance of values, but it demands that they be cast in terms that go beyond the more crude ideologies of the industrial age. . . .

New Social Patterns

For Norbert Wiener,[1] "the locus of an earlier industrial revolution before the main industrial revolution" is to be found in the fifteenth-century research pertaining to navigation (the nautical compass), as well as in the development of gunpowder and printing. Today the functional equivalent of navigation is the thrust into space, which requires a rapid computing capacity beyond the means of the human brain; the equivalent of gunpowder is modern nuclear physics, and that of printing is television and long-range instant communications. The consequence of this new technetronic revolution is the progressive emergence of a society that increasingly differs from the industrial one in a variety of economic, political, and social aspects. The

[1] An American mathematician (1874–1964). He was also a pioneer in the development of cybernetics, the comparative study of the body's automatic control systems and of mechanical and electrical systems that incorporate similar controls.

following examples may be briefly cited to summarize some of the contrasts:

(1) In an industrial society the mode of production shifts from agriculture to industry, with the use of human and animal muscle supplanted by machine operation. In the technetronic society industrial employment yields to services, with automation and cybernetics replacing the operation of machines by individuals.

(2) Problems of employment and unemployment—to say nothing of the prior urbanization of the post-rural labor force—dominate the relationship between employers, labor, and the market in the industrial society, and the assurance of minimum welfare to the new industrial masses is a source of major concern. In the emerging new society questions relating to the obsolescence of skills, security, vacations, leisure, and profit sharing dominate the relationship, and the psychic well-being of millions of relatively secure but potentially aimless lower-middle-class blue-collar workers becomes a growing problem.

(3) Breaking down traditional barriers to education, and thus creating the basic point of departure for social advancement, is a major goal of social reformers in the industrial society. Education, available for limited and specific periods of time, is initially concerned with overcoming illiteracy and subsequently with technical training, based largely on written, sequential reasoning. In the technetronic society not only is education universal but advanced training is available to almost all who have the basic talents, and there is far greater emphasis on quality selection. The essential problem is to discover the most effective techniques for the rational exploitation of social talent. The latest communication and calculating techniques are employed in this task. The educational process becomes a lengthier one and is increasingly reliant on audio-visual aids. In addition, the flow of new knowledge necessitates more and more frequent refresher studies.

(4) In the industrial society social leadership shifts from the traditional rural-aristocratic to an urban-plutocratic elite. Newly acquired wealth is its foundation, and intense competition the outlet—as well as the stimulus—for its energy. In the technetronic society plutocratic pre-eminence is challenged by the political leadership, which is itself increasingly permeated by individuals possessing special skills and intellectual talents. Knowledge becomes a tool of power and the effective mobilization of talent an important way to acquire power.

(5) The university in an industrial society—in contrast to the situation in medieval times—is an aloof ivory tower, the repository of irrelevant, even if respected, wisdom, and for a brief time the fountainhead for budding members of the established social elite. In the technetronic society the university becomes an intensely involved "think tank," the source of much sustained political planning and social innovation.

(6) The turmoil inherent in the shift from a rigidly traditional rural society to an urban one engenders an inclination to seek total answers to social dilemmas, thus causing ideologies to thrive in the industrializing society. (The American exception to this rule was due to the absence of a feudal tradition, a point well developed by Louis Hartz.) In the industrial age literacy makes for static interrelated conceptual thinking, congenial to ideological systems. In the technetronic society audio-visual communications prompt more changeable, disparate views of reality, not compressible into formal systems, even as the requirements of science and the new computative techniques place a premium on mathematical logic and systematic reasoning. The resulting tension is felt most acutely by scientists, with the consequence that some seek to confine reason to science while expressing their emotions through politics. Moreover, the increasing ability to reduce social conflicts to quantifiable and measurable dimensions reinforces the trend toward a more pragmatic approach to social problems, while it simultaneously stimulates new concerns with preserving "humane" values.

(7) In the industrial society, as the hitherto passive masses become active there are intense political conflicts over such matters as disenfranchisement and the right to vote. The issue of political participation is a crucial one. In the technetronic age the question is increasingly one of ensuring real participation in decisions that seem too complex and too far removed from the average citizen. Political alienation becomes a problem. Similarly, the issue of political equality of the sexes gives way to a struggle for the sexual equality of women. In the industrial society woman—the operator of machines—ceases to be physically inferior to the male, a consideration of some importance in rural life, and begins to demand her political rights. In the emerging technetronic society automation threatens both males and females, intellectual talent is computable, the "pill" encourages sexual equality, and women begin to claim complete equality.

(8) The newly enfranchised masses are organized in the industrial society by trade unions and political parties and unified by relatively simple and somewhat ideological programs. Moreover, political attitudes are influenced by appeals to nationalist sentiments, communicated through the massive increase of newspapers employing, naturally, the readers' national language. In the technetronic society the trend seems to be toward aggregating the individual support of millions of unorganized citizens, who are easily within the reach of magnetic and attractive personalities, and effectively exploiting the latest communication techniques to manipulate emotions and control reason. Reliance on television—and hence the tendency to replace language with imagery, which is international rather than national, and to include war coverages or scenes of hunger in places as distant as, for example, India—creates a somewhat more cosmopolitan, though highly impressionistic, involvement in global affairs.

(9) Economic power in the early phase of industrialization tends to be personalized by either great entrepreneurs like Henry Ford or bureaucratic industrial officials like Kaganovich,[2] or Minc (in Stalinist Poland). The tendency toward depersonalization of economic power is stimulated in the next stage by the appearance of a highly complex interdependence between governmental institutions (including the military), scientific establishments, and industrial organizations. As economic power becomes inseparably linked with political power, it becomes more invisible and the sense of individual futility increases.

(10) In an industrial society the acquisition of goods and the accumulation of personal wealth become forms of social attainment for an unprecedentedly large number of people. In the technetronic society the adaptation of science to humane ends and a growing concern with the quality of life become both possible and increasingly a moral imperative for a large number of citizens, especially the young.

Eventually, these changes and many others, including some that more directly affect the personality and quality of the human being himself, will make the technetronic society as different from the industrial as the industrial was from the agrarian. And just as the shift from an agrarian economy and feudal politics toward an industrial society and political systems based on the individual's emotional

---

[2] Lazar Kaganovich (1893–?), a Soviet politician and close associate of Stalin, was, at various times, Russia's commissar for railways and for heavy industries.

identification with the nation-state gave rise to contemporary international politics, so the appearance of the technetronic society reflects the onset of a new relationship between man and his expanded global reality.

Social Explosion/Implosion

This new relationship is a tense one: man has still to define it conceptually and thereby render it comprehensible to himself. Our expanded global reality is simultaneously fragmenting and thrusting itself in upon us. The result of the coincident explosion and implosion is not only insecurity and tension but also an entirely novel perception of what many still call international affairs.

Life seems to lack cohesion as environment rapidly alters and human beings become increasingly manipulable and malleable. Everything seems more transitory and temporary: external reality more fluid than solid, the human being more synthetic than authentic. Even our senses perceive an entirely novel "reality"—one of our own making but nevertheless, in terms of our sensations, quite "real." More important, there is already widespread concern about the possibility of biological and chemical tampering with what has until now been considered the immutable essence of man. Human conduct, some argue, can be predetermined and subjected to deliberate control. Man is increasingly acquiring the capacity to determine the sex of his children, to affect through drugs the extent of their intelligence, and to modify and control their personalities. Speaking of a future at most only decades away, an experimenter in intelligence control asserted, "I foresee the time when we shall have the means and therefore, inevitably, the temptation to manipulate the behavior and intellectual functioning of all the people through environmental and biochemical manipulation of the brain."

Thus it is an open question whether technology and science will in fact increase the options open to the individual. Under the headline "Study Terms Technology a Boon to Individualism," *The New York Times* reported the preliminary conclusions of a Harvard project on the social significance of science. Its participants were quoted as concluding that "most Americans have a greater range of personal choice, wider experience and a more highly developed sense of self-worth than ever before." This may be so, but a judgment of this sort rests essentially on an intuitive—and comparative—insight into the present and past states of mind of Americans. In this connection a word of warning from an acute observer is highly relevant: "It behooves us to examine carefully the degree of validity, as measured by actual behavior, of the statement that a benefit of technology will be to increase the number of options and alternatives the individual can choose from. In principle, it could; in fact, the individual may use any number of psychological devices to avoid the discomfort of information overload, and thereby keep the range of alternatives to which he responds much narrower than that which technology in principle makes available to him." In other words, the real questions are how the individual will exploit the options, to what extent he will be intellectually and psychologically prepared to exploit them, and in what way society as a whole will create a favorable setting for taking advantage of these options. Their availability is not of itself proof of a greater sense of freedom or self-worth.

Instead of accepting himself as a spontaneous given, man in the most advanced societies may become more concerned with conscious self-analysis according to external, explicit criteria: What is my IQ? What are my aptitudes, personality traits, capabilities, attractions, and negative features? The "internal man"—spontaneously accepting his own spontaneity—will more and more be challenged by the "external man"—consciously seeking his self-conscious image; and the transition from one to the other may not be easy. It will also give rise to difficult problems in determining the legitimate scope of social control. The possibility of extensive chemical mind control, the danger of loss of individuality inherent in extensive transplantation, the feasibility of manipulating the genetic structure will call for the social definition of common criteria of use and restraint. As the previously cited writer put it ". . . while the chemical affects the individual, the person is significant to himself and to society in his *social* context—at work, at home, at play. The consequences are social consequences. In deciding how to deal with such alterers of the ego and of experience (and consequently alterers of the personality after the experience), and in deciding how to deal with the 'changed' human beings, we will have to face new questions such as 'Who am I?' 'When am I who?' 'Who are *they* in relation to me?' "

Moreover, man will increasingly be living in man-made and rapidly man-altered environments. By the end of this century approximately two-thirds of the people in the advanced countries will live in cities. Urban growth has so far been primarily the by-product of accidental economic convenience, of the magnetic attraction of population centers, and of the flight of many from rural poverty and exploitation. It has not been deliberately designed to improve the quality of life. The impact of "accidental" cities is already contributing to the depersonalization of individual life as the kinship structure contracts and enduring relations of friendship become more difficult to maintain. Julian Huxley was perhaps guilty of only slight exaggeration when he warned that "overcrowding in animals leads to distorted neurotic and downright pathological behavior. We can be sure that the same is true in principle of people. City life today is definitely leading to mass mental disease, to growing vandalism and possible eruptions of mass violence."

The problem of identity is likely to be complicated by a generation gap, intensified by the dissolution of traditional ties and values derived from extended family and enduring community relationships. The dialogue between the generations is becoming a dialogue of the deaf. It no longer operates within the conservative-liberal or nationalist-internationalist framework. The breakdown in communication between the generations—so vividly evident during the student revolts of 1968—was rooted in the irrelevance of the old symbols to many younger people. Debate implies the acceptance of a common frame of reference and language; since these were lacking, debate became increasingly impossible.

Though currently the clash is over values—with many of the young rejecting those of their elders, who in turn contend that the young have evaded the responsibility of articulating theirs—in the future the clash between generations will be also over expertise. Within a few years the rebels in the more advanced countries who today have the most visibility will be joined by a new generation making its claim to power in government and business: a generation trained to reason logically; as accustomed to exploiting electronic aids to human reasoning as we have been to using machines to increase our own mobility; expressing itself in a language that functionally relates to these aids; accepting as routine managerial processes current innovations such as planning-programming-budgeting systems (PPBS) and the appearance in high business echelons of "top computer executives." As the older elite defends what it considers not only its own vested interests but more basically its own way of life, the resulting clash could generate even more intense conceptual issues.

Global Absorption

But while our immediate reality is being fragmented, global reality increasingly absorbs the individual, involves him, and even occasionally overwhelms him. Communications are the obvious, already much discussed, immediate cause. The changes wrought by communications and computers make for an extraordinarily interwoven society whose members are in continuous and close audio-visual contact—constantly interacting, instantly sharing the most intense social experiences, and prompted to increased personal involvement in even the most distant problems. The new generation no longer defines the world exclusively on the basis of reading, either of ideologically structured analyses or of extensive descriptions; it also experiences and senses it vicariously through audio-visual communications. This form of communicating reality is growing more rapidly—especially in the advanced countries—than the traditional written medium, and it provides the principal source of news for the masses. . . . "By 1985 distance will be no excuse for delayed information from any part of the world to the powerful urban nerve centers that will mark the major concentrations of the people on earth." Global telephone dialing that in the more advanced states will include instant visual contact and a global television-satellite system that will enable some states to "invade" private homes in other countries will create unprecedented global intimacy.

The new reality, however, will not be that of a "global village." McLuhan's[3] striking analogy overlooks the personal stability, interpersonal intimacy, implicitly shared values, and traditions that were

[3] Marshall McLuhan (1911–   ), a Canadian cultural critic and communications theorist, happily predicted, in his influential book *The Gutenberg Galaxy* (1962), the coming of the "global village" through instantaneous electronic communication. His later works, such as *Understanding Media: The Extensions of Man* (1964) and *The Medium is the Massage* (1967), develop further implications of his perception that the electronic media have extended the human central nervous system beyond the individual's brain and body, thus re-creating the intimate, preliterate "village" mentality.

important ingredients of the primitive village. A more appropriate analogy is that of the "global city"—a nervous, agitated, tense, and fragmented web of interdependent relations. That interdependence, however, is better characterized by interaction than by intimacy. Instant communications are already creating something akin to a global nervous system. Occasional malfunctions of this nervous system—because of blackouts or breakdowns—will be all the more unsettling, precisely because the mutual confidence and reciprocally reinforcing stability that are characteristic of village intimacy will be absent from the process of that "nervous" interaction.

Man's intensified involvement in global affairs is reflected in, and doubtless shaped by, the changing character of what has until now been considered local news. Television has joined newspapers in expanding the immediate horizons of the viewer or reader to the point where "local" increasingly means "national," and global affairs compete for attention on an unprecedented scale. Physical and moral immunity to "foreign" events cannot be very effectively maintained under circumstances in which there are both a growing intellectual awareness of global interdependence and the electronic intrusion of global events into the home.

This condition also makes for a novel perception of foreign affairs. Even in the recent past one learned about international politics through the study of history and geography, as well as by reading newspapers. This contributed to a highly structured, even rigid, approach, in which it was convenient to categorize events or nations in somewhat ideological terms. Today, however, foreign affairs intrude upon a child or adolescent in the advanced countries in the form of disparate, sporadic, isolated—but involving—events: catastrophes and acts of violence both abroad and at home become intermeshed, and though they may elicit either positive or negative reactions, these are no longer in the neatly compartmentalized categories of "we" and "they." Television in particular contributes to a "blurred," much more impressionistic—and also involved—attitude toward world affairs. Anyone who teaches international politics senses a great change in the attitude of the young along these lines.

Such direct global intrusion and interaction, however, does not make for better "understanding" of our contemporary affairs. On the contrary, it can be argued that in some respects "understanding"—in the sense of possessing the subjective confidence that one can evaluate events on the basis of some organized principle—is today much more difficult for most people to attain. Instant but vicarious participation in events evokes uncertainty, especially as it becomes more and more apparent that established analytical categories no longer adequately encompass the new circumstances.

The science explosion—the most rapidly expanding aspect of our entire reality, growing more rapidly than population, industry, and cities—intensifies, rather than reduces, these feelings of insecurity. It is simply impossible for the average citizen and even for men of intellect to assimilate and meaningfully organize the flow of knowledge for themselves. In every scientific field complaints are mounting that the torrential outpouring of published reports, scientific papers, and scholarly articles and the proliferation of professional journals make it impossible for individuals to avoid becoming either narrow-gauged specialists or superficial generalists. The sharing of new common perspectives thus becomes more difficult as knowledge expands; in addition, traditional perspectives such as those provided by primitive myths or, more recently, by certain historically conditioned ideologies can no longer be sustained.

The threat of intellectual fragmentation, posed by the gap between the pace in the expansion of knowledge and the rate of its assimilation, raises a perplexing question concerning the prospects for mankind's intellectual unity. It has generally been assumed that the modern world, shaped increasingly by the industrial and urban revolutions, will become more homogeneous in its outlook. This may be so, but it could be the homogeneity of insecurity, of uncertainty, and of intellectual anarchy. The result, therefore, would not necessarily be a more stable environment.

2. THE AMBIVALENT DISSEMINATOR

The United States is the principal global disseminator of the technetronic revolution. It is American society that is currently having the greatest impact on all other societies, prompting a far-reaching cumulative transformation in their outlook and mores. At various stages in history different societies have served as a catalyst for change by stimulating imitation and adaptation in others. What in the remote past Athens and Rome were to the Mediterranean world, or China to much of Asia, France has more recently been to Europe. French letters, arts, and political ideas exercised a magnetic attraction, and the French Revolution was perhaps the single most powerful stimulant to the rise of populist nationalism during the nineteenth century.

In spite of its domestic tensions—indeed, in some respects because of them . . . —the United States is the innovative and creative society of today. It is also a major disruptive influence on the world scene. In fact communism, which many Americans see as the principal cause of unrest, primarily capitalizes on frustrations and aspirations, whose major source is the American impact on the rest of the world. The United States is the focus of global attention, emulation, envy, admiration, and animosity. No other society evokes feelings of such intensity; no other society's internal affairs—including America's racial and urban violence—are scrutinized with such attention; no other society's politics are followed with such avid interest—so much so that to many foreign nationals United States domestic politics have become an essential extension of their own; no other society so massively disseminates its own way of life and its values by means of movies, television, multimillion-copy foreign editions of its national magazines, or simply by its products; no other society is the object of such contradictory assessments. . . .

New Imperialism?

. . .

It is the novelty of America's relationship with the world—complex, intimate, and porous—that the more orthodox, especially Marxist, analyses of imperialism fail to encompass. To see that relationship merely as the expression of an imperial drive is to ignore the part played in it by the crucial dimension of the technological-scientific revolution. That revolution not only captivates the imagination of mankind (who can fail to be moved by the spectacle of man reaching the moon?) but inescapably compels imitation of the more advanced by the less advanced and stimulates the export of new techniques, methods, and organizational skills from the former to the latter. There is no doubt that this results in an asymmetrical relationship, but the content of that asymmetry must be examined before it is called imperialism. Like every society, America no doubt prefers to be more rather than less advanced; yet it is also striking that no other country has made so great an effort, governmentally and privately, through business and especially through foundations, to export its know-how, to make public its space findings, to promote new agricultural techniques, to improve educational facilities, to control population growth, to improve health care, and so on. All of this has imperial overtones, and yet it is misleading to label it as such.

Indeed, unable to understand fully what is happening in their own society, Americans find it difficult to comprehend the global impact that that society has had in its unique role as disseminator of the technetronic revolution. This impact is contradictory: it both promotes and undermines American interests as defined by American policymakers; it helps to advance the cause of cooperation on a larger scale even as it disrupts existing social or economic fabrics; it both lays the groundwork for well-being and stability and enhances the forces working for instability and revolution. Unlike traditional imperialistic powers, which relied heavily on the principle of *divide et impera*[4] (practiced with striking similarity by the British in India and more recently by the Russians in Eastern Europe), America has striven to promote regionalism both in Europe and in Latin America. Yet in so doing, it is helping to create larger entities that are more capable of resisting its influence and of competing with it economically. Implicitly and often explicitly modeled on the American pattern, modernization makes for potentially greater economic well-being, but in the process it disrupts existing institutions, undermines prevailing mores, and stimulates resentment that focuses directly on the source of change—America. The result is an acute tension between the kind of global stability and order that America subjectively seeks and the instability, impatience, and frustration that America unconsciously promotes. . . .

---

[4] Latin: divide and rule—a maxim of Niccolò Machiavelli (1469–1527), author of *The Prince,* the classic discourse on the gaining and maintaining of political power.

14

Theodosius Dobzhansky

Man and Natural Selection

As the twentieth century brought ever-growing specialization within modern science, there arose a need for unifying syntheses setting forth the human significance of the vast accumulations of data. Theodosius Dobzhansky (1900–1975), an authority on genetics and evolution, who spent decades investigating the workings of heredity in the fruit fly, was among the more articulate speculators on the philosophical and social implications of modern biological science.

Born in tsarist Russia, Theodosius Grigorievich Dobzhansky was reared and educated in Kiev, graduating from high school there in 1917, the year of the Bolshevik Revolution. An interest in genetics and evolution, which developed when he read Darwin's Origin of Species *at age fifteen, took Dobzhansky to the University of Kiev to study biology. After receiving a degree in 1921, he taught zoology for a few years at Kiev's Institute of Agriculture and, later, lectured on genetics at the University of Leningrad. Attracted by genetic research in the United States and disturbed by the growing influence of political ideology over scientific method in the Soviet Union, Dobzhansky left his homeland in 1927 and accepted a teaching position at Columbia University. Later, he followed Thomas Hunt Morgan, Nobel laureate in Physiology and Medicine, from Columbia to the California Institute of Technology. Dobzhansky remained on the faculty there until 1940, when he returned to Columbia to serve as director of the genetics laboratory. In 1962, Dobzhansky left Columbia again and, until 1971, continued his research at the Rockefeller Institute. He had become a naturalized American citizen in 1937.*

Among Dobzhansky's many scientific writings is Genetics and the Origin of Species *(1937), cited in the scientific community as "undoubtedly the single most influential book published on evolution since Darwin." Throughout his later career Dobzhansky concerned himself with the interdependence of biological heredity and cultural change. The human species, he asserted, is the result not only of organic adaptation or evolution, but of "superorganic" or cultural evolution as well. Of all the species, human beings alone decide to alter their environment to suit their desires and then find themselves obliged to adapt to their newly created environment. Thus, only humans can shape (in part) their own evolutionary destiny.*

In the 1961 lecture that is the source of the following selection, Dobzhansky raises some of the ethical questions involved in "genetic management" of the human species. Both organic and superorganic adaptive evolution, he maintains, must be directed "toward humanly desirable goals." In order to avoid the narrow functionalism so graphically imagined by Huxley in Brave New World, *Dobzhansky urges that human evolution be consciously directed by more traditional ethical precepts.*

MAN'S EVOLUTIONARY UNIQUENESS

By changing what he knows about the world, man changes the world he knows; and by changing the world in which he lives, he changes himself. Herein lies a danger and a hope; a danger because random changes of a biological nature are likely to produce deterioration rather than improvement; a hope because changes resulting from knowledge can also be directed by knowledge.

The human species *Homo sapiens,* mankind, is the unique and most successful product of biological evolution so far. This has sometimes been questioned, I suspect without too much conviction on the part of the doubters, perhaps only to mock man's pretensions or to challenge his values. But man *is* the most successful product of evolution, by any reasonable definition of biological success. Man began his career as a rare animal, living somewhere in the tropics or subtropics of the Old World, probably in Africa. From this obscure beginning, mankind multiplied to become one of the most numerous mammals, for there will soon be about three billion men living. Numbers may not be an unadulterated blessing, but they are one of the measures of biological success of a species. . . .

The evolutionary uniqueness of man lies in that the biological evolution in mankind has transcended itself. With man commences a new, superorganic, mode of evolution, which is the evolution of culture. Culture is a tremendously potent instrument for adaptation to the environment. A very large part of the evolutionary progress, both biologically and culturally, has come from adversity. Life faces environments which are more often niggardly than bountiful, more frequently inimical than benign. For life to endure, it must develop defenses and adaptations. Biological adaptation occurs through natural selection; new genes arise through mutation, sexual recombination creates new combinations of genes, and natural selection acts to multiply the successful genetic endowments and to reduce the frequencies of the unsuccessful ones. In man, and in man alone, adaptation may occur also through alteration of culture. Many species of mammals have become adapted to cold climates by growing warm fur; man alone has achieved the same end by donning a fur coat. Birds have mastered the air by becoming flying machines; man has conquered the air by building flying machines.

Biological and cultural evolutions of man are not independent; they are interdependent. The superorganic has an organic basis. Formation and maintenance of culture presuppose a human genotype. Even the most clever ape cannot learn human culture. Some writers have jumped to the conclusion that the genetic development of the human species was completed before culture appeared, and that the evolution of culture has replaced biological evolution. This is not true. The two evolutions go together, interacting and usually mutually reinforcing each other. There is feedback between genetics and culture. Culture is an adaptive mechanism supplemental to, but not incompatible with, biological adaptation. To be sure, adaptation by culture proved to be more efficacious and, before all else, more rapid than adaptation by genes. This is why the emergence of the genetic basis of culture was the master stroke of the biological evolution of the human species. The genetic basis of culture should be improved or at least maintained. It should not be allowed to deteriorate.

• • •

ARE CULTURE AND NATURAL SELECTION COMPATIBLE?

We have seen that several forms of natural selection operate in modern mankind. But they certainly do not operate as they did during the Stone Age or even as they did a century ago. Neither does natural selection operate always in the same way in wild and "natural" species, quite "unspoiled" by culture. This is inevitable. Natural selection depends on environments, and environments change. Human environments have changed a great deal in a century, not to speak of millennia.

The real problem is not whether natural selection in man is going on, but whether it is going on toward what we, humans, regard as betterment or deterioration. Natural selection tends to enhance the reproductive proficiency of the population in which it operates. Such proficiency is, however, not the only estimable quality with which we wish to see people endowed. And besides, a high reproductive fitness in one environment does not even insure the survival of the population or the species when the environment changes.

Normalizing selection is, as we have seen, not the only form of natural selection; the relaxation of some of its functions is, however, a cause for apprehension. Medicine, hygiene, civilized living save many lives which would otherwise be extinguished. This situation is here to stay; we would not want it to be otherwise, even if we could. Some of the lives thus saved will, however, engender lives that will stand in need of being saved in the generations to come. Can it be that we help the ailing, the lame, and the deformed only to make our descendants more ailing, more lame, and more deformed?

Suppose that we have learned how to save the lives of persons afflicted with a hereditary disease, such as retinoblastoma,[1] which previously was incurably fatal. In genetic terms, this means that the Darwinian fitness of the victims of the disease has increased, and that the normalizing selection against this disease is relaxed. What will be the consequence? The incidence of the disease in the population will increase from generation to generation. The increase is likely to be slow, generally no more than by one mutation rate per generation. It may take centuries or millennia to notice the difference for any one disease or malformation, but the average health and welfare of the

---

[1] A malignant tumor of the retina (inner lining of the eyeball).

population are liable to show adverse effects of relaxed selection much sooner.

The process of mutation injects into every generation a certain number of harmful genes in the gene pool of the population; the process of normalizing selection eliminates a certain number of these genes. With environment reasonably stable, the situation tends to reach a state of equilibrium. At equilibrium, the mutation and the elimination are equal. If mutation becomes more frequent (as it does in man because of exposure to high-energy radiations and perhaps to some chemicals), or if the elimination is lagging because of relaxation of normalizing selection, the incidence of harmful mutant genes in the population is bound to increase. And take note of this: If the classical theory of population structure were correct, all harmful mutations would be in a sense equivalent. For at equilibrium there is one elimination for every mutation, regardless of whether the mutation causes a lethal hereditary disease like retinoblastoma, or a malformation like achondroplasia,[2] or a relatively mild defect such as myopia.[3]

It would no doubt be desirable to eliminate from human populations all harmful mutant genes and to substitute for them favorable genes. But how is this end to be attained? A program of eugenics to achieve genetic health and eventual improvement of the human species has, in recent years, been urged with great eloquence, particularly by Muller, and many other authors: The fortunate few who happen to carry mostly "normal" or favorable genes should be better progenitors of the coming generations than are those who carry average, or heavier than average, genetic loads. Let us then take the semen of the superior males, and use it to produce numerous progeny by artificial insemination of women who will be happy to be mothers of children of the superior sires. Techniques will eventually be invented to obtain also the egg cells of superior females; indeed, the ovaries of human females are capable of producing numerous egg cells, most of which are at present wasted. It will then be possible to combine the finest egg cells with choicest sperms; the uteri of women who happen to be carriers of average or higher-than-average genetic loads will be good enough for the development of the genetically superior fetuses. But not even this would guarantee

[2] A failure in the development of cartilage, resulting in dwarfism.
[3] Nearsightedness.

the best possible genetic endowments in the progeny. Very distinguished parents sometimes produce commonplace, and even inferior, children. The distant vista envisaged by Muller is tissue culture of (diploid) body cells of the very best donors, and a technique to stimulate these cells to develop without fertilization (parthenogenetically), thus giving rise to numerous individuals [clones], all as similar to the donor and to each other as identical twins.

It may be doubted, however, whether modern genetics has progressed far enough to embark on a program as far-reaching as Muller suggests. Wright considers that the situation calls rather for research in what he describes neatly as "unfortunately the unpopular and scientifically somewhat unrewarding borderline fields of genetics and the social sciences." Although at equilibrium there may be one genetic elimination for every mutation, it is unrealistic to equate the human and social consequences of different mutations. The elimination of a lethal mutant which causes death of an embryo before implantation in the uterus is scarcely noticed by the mother or by anyone else. Suffering accompanies the elimination of a mutant, such as retinoblastoma, which kills an infant apparently normal at birth. Many mutants, such as hemophilia[4] or Huntington's chorea,[5] kill children, adolescents, or adults, cause misery to their victims, and disruption of the lives of their families. There is no way to measure precisely the amount of human anguish; yet one may surmise that the painful and slow death of the victims of so many hereditary diseases is torment greater than that involved in the elimination of a gene for achondroplasia owing to the failure of an achondroplastic dwarf to beget children.

Looked at from the angle of the costs to the society, the nonequivalence of different mutants is no less evident. Myopia may be inherited as a recessive trait. Increases of the frequency in populations of the gene for myopia are undesirable. Yet it may become more and more common in future generations. However, only a fanatic might advocate sterilization of the myopics or other radical measures to prevent the spread of this gene. One may hope that civilized societies can tolerate some more myopics; many of them are very useful citizens, and their defect can rather easily be corrected by a relatively inexpensive environmental change—wearing glasses. The effort

---

[4] A tendency to uncontrollable bleeding.
[5] An inherited nervous disorder that develops in adult life and ends in a deteriorated mental condition.

needed to eradicate or to reduce the frequency of myopia genetically would exceed that requisite to rectify their defect environmentally, by manufacturing more pairs of glasses.

Diabetes mellitus[6] is, given the present level of medicine, more difficult and expensive to correct than is myopia. Some diabetics may nevertheless be treated successfully by insulin therapy, helped to live to old age, and enabled to raise families as large as nondiabetics. The incidence of diabetes may therefore creep up slowly in the generations to come. Now, most people would probably agree that it is better to be free of diabetes than to have it under control, no matter how successfully, by insulin therapy or other means. The prospect is not a pleasant one to contemplate. Insulin injections may perhaps be almost as common in some remote future as taking aspirin tablets is at present.

TOWARD GUIDANCE OF HUMAN EVOLUTION

We are faced, then, with a dilemma—if we enable the weak and the deformed to live and to propagate their kind, we face the prospect of a genetic twilight; but if we let them die or suffer when we can save them we face the certainty of a moral twilight. How to escape this dilemma?

I can well understand the impatience which some of my readers may feel if I refuse to provide an unambiguous answer to so pressing a problem. Let me plead with you, however, that infatuation with oversimple answers to very complex and difficult problems is one of the earmarks of intellectual mediocrity. I am afraid that the problem of guidance of human evolution has no simple solution. At least I have not found one, nor has anybody else in my opinion. Each genetic condition will have to be considered on its own merits, and the solutions that may be adopted for different conditions will probably be different. Suppose that everybody agrees that the genes causing myopia, achondroplasia, diabetes, and retinoblastoma are undesirable. We shall nevertheless be forced to treat them differently. Some genetic defects will have to be put up with and managed environmentally; others will have to be treated genetically, by artificial selection, and the eugenic measures that may be needed can be ef-

---

[6] A constitutional disorder of carbohydrate metabolism.

fected without accepting any kind of biological Brave New World.[7]

Let us face this fact: Our lives depend on civilization and technology, and the lives of our descendants will be even more dependent on civilized environments. I can imagine a wise old ape-man who deplored the softness of his contemporaries who used stone knives to carve their meat instead of doing this with their teeth; or a solid conservative Peking man[8] viewing with alarm the newfangled habit of using fire to make oneself warm. I have yet to hear anyone seriously proposing that we give up the use of knives and fire now. Nor does anyone in his right mind urge that we let people die of smallpox or tuberculosis, in order that genetic resistance to these diseases be maintained. The remedy for our genetic dependence on technology and medicine is more, not less, technology and medicine. You may, if you wish, feel nostalgic for the good old days of our cave-dwelling ancestors; the point of no return was passed in the evolution of our species many millennia before anyone could know what was happening.

Of course, not all genetic defects can be corrected by tools or remedies or medicines. Even though new and better tools and medicines will, one may hope, be invented in the future, this will not make all genetic equipments equally desirable. It is a relatively simple matter to correct for lack of genetic resistance to smallpox by vaccination, or for myopia by suitable glasses. It is not so simple with many other genetic defects. Surgical removal of the eyes is called for in cases of retinoblastoma; this saves the lives of the victims, but leaves them blind. No remedies are known for countless other genetic defects. Human life is sacred; yet the social costs of some genetic variants are so great, and their social contributions are so small, that avoidance of their birth is ethically the most acceptable as well as the wisest solution. This does not necessarily call for enactment of Draconian eugenic laws; it is perhaps not over-optimistic to hope that spreading biological education and understanding may be a real help. Make persons whose progeny is likely to inherit a serious genetic defect aware of this fact; they may draw the conclusions themselves.

The strides accomplished by biochemical genetics in recent years have led some biologists to hope that methods will soon be discovered to induce specific changes in human genes of our choice. This

---

[7] A reference to the dehumanizing world portrayed in Aldous Huxley's futuristic novel *Brave New World* (1932)—see selection 10.

[8] An extinct form of human known from fossil remains.

would indeed be a radical solution of the problem of management of the evolution of our species and of other species as well. We would simply change the genes which we do not like, in ways conforming to our desires. Now, if the history of science has any lesson to teach us, it is the unwisdom of declaring certain goals to be unattainable. The cavalier way in which the progress of science often treats such predictions should instill due humility even in the most doctrinaire prophets. The best that can be said about the possibility of changing specific genes in man in accordance with our desires is that, although such an invention would be a great boon, it is not within reach yet. And it cannot be assumed to be achievable.

Let us also not exaggerate the urgency of the problem of the genetic management of the evolution of our species. Another problem, that of the runaway overpopulation of our planet, is far more immediate and critical. If mankind will prove unable to save itself from being choked by crowding it hardly needs to worry about its genetic quality. Although the problems of numbers and of quality are not one and the same, they may yet be closely connected in practice. As steps toward regulation of the size of population begin to be taken, and this surely cannot be postponed much longer, the genetic problem will inexorably obtrude itself. The questions, "how many people" and "what kind of people" will be solved together, if they will be solved at all.

Some people believe that all would be well with mankind if only natural selection were permitted to operate without obstruction by medicine and technology. Let us not forget, however, that countless biological species of the past have become extinct, although their evolution was directed by natural selection unadulterated by culture. What we want is not simply natural selection, but selection, natural and artificial, directed toward humanly desirable goals. What are these goals? This is the central problem of human ethics and of human evolution. Darwinian fitness is no guide here. If, in some human society, genetically duller people produce more progeny than the brighter ones, this simply means that, in the environment of that particular society, being a bit thick-headed increases the Darwinian fitness, and being too intelligent decreases it. Natural selection will act accordingly, and will not be any less "natural" on that account.

Human cultural evolution has resulted in the formation of a system of values, of *human* values. These are the values to which we wish human evolution to conform. These values are products of cultural evolution, conditioned of course by the biological evolution, yet not deducible from the latter. Where do we find a criterion by which these values are to be judged? I know of no better one than that proposed by the ancient Chinese sage: "Every system of moral laws must be based upon man's own consciousness, verified by the common experience of mankind, tested by due sanction of historical experience and found without error, applied to the operations and processes of nature in the physical universe and found to be without contradiction, laid before the gods without question or fear, and able to wait a hundred generations and have it confirmed without a doubt by a Sage of posterity."

III
Man
and
Nature

15

Barry Commoner

The Closing Circle

*Among the popular movements of the late twentieth century with strong po-
litical and social implications is the environmental movement. Although the
roots of environmentalism stretch back at least to the reactions of early nineteenth-century romantic poets against the Industrial Revolution, not until after
the Second World War did the quality of the environment become a widespread concern and ecological principles begin to influence political action. In
the 1960s and 70s Barry Commoner (1917–), a biologist, became one of
the most eloquent expositors of the need for human beings to restructure their
relationship to the natural environment and, thereby, to one another.*

*Commoner, a city boy fascinated by nature, was born in Brooklyn, New
York, and earned a bachelor's degree in biology from Columbia University
in 1937 and a master's degree and a doctorate in biology from Harvard University. After completing his education in 1941 he became an instructor of biology at Queens College, New York City, served in the Naval Air Force
during the Second World War, and was an associate editor of* Science Illustrated *magazine. Since 1947 he has been on the faculty of Washington University, St. Louis, Missouri, where, since 1965, he has been director of the
Center for the Biology of Natural Systems.*

*The author of several hundred technical papers, Commoner first placed his
views before the general public in his book* Science and Survival *(1966).
But it was the success of* The Closing Circle: Nature, Man and Technology *(1971)—from which the following selection is taken—that made
Commoner's basic thesis widely influential. It was not a new thesis, but the*

rigorous clarity of Commoner's scientific statements proved more persuasive in many quarters than the environmental romanticism of many writers.

Essentially, The Closing Circle *argues that neither population nor affluence in themselves have caused the "environmental crisis." The problem stems instead from postwar technologies that produce products that are not part of natural ecological cycles—for example, non-degradable detergents instead of soap, nylon instead of wool or cotton. The cause of this shift into wasteful technology, Commoner asserts, is the desire for short-term profits in private industry. Thus he feels that the environmental crisis is inextricably linked to the socio-economic-political system. The book ends with a plea to "close the circle," that is, to integrate future technology into an ecological cycle harmonious with nature, putting an end to the present linear course of technology. Either we use the earth's resources in a more rational way, Commoner warns, or we enter a "new barbarism" that will prove suicidal for civilization.*

History *does* repeat itself. In 1970 the environmental crisis burst upon a surprised world; four years later, still struggling to clean up the environment, we find ourselves in the grip of an equally unexpected energy crisis. And once more, as in the early days of the environmental crisis, confusion reigns. In rapid succession, theories about the reason for the energy crisis are shot from the publicity guns like puffed cereal, only to turn soggy when immersed in facts.

Oil companies blame environmentalist opposition for their failure to drill for still-plentiful domestic oil; but the fact is that since 1957—long before environmentalism—oil companies have steadily reduced domestic exploration in favor of more profitable areas abroad. Automobile manufacturers blame gasoline shortages on antipollution devices that have cut down gasoline mileage; but the fact is that before these devices were installed the wizards of Detroit had already managed to reduce the gasoline mileage of the average American passenger car more than 10 percent, compared to 1946, by building big, high-powered cars, and that environmentalists opposed the new exhaust devices because they fail to control the key pollutant that triggers the smog reaction—nitrogen oxides.

Much of this kind of confusion about the energy crisis could have been eliminated if the lessons of the environmental crisis had been learned. The basic reasons for environmental degradation in the United States and all other industrialized countries since World War II are drastic changes in the technology of agricultural and industrial production and transportation: we now wash our clothes in detergents instead of soap; we drink beer out of throwaway bottles instead of returnable ones; we use man-made nitrogen fertilizer to grow food, instead of manure or crop rotation; we wear clothes made of synthetic fibers instead of cotton or wool; we drive heavy cars with high-powered, high-compression engines instead of the lighter, low-powered low-compression prewar types; we travel in airplanes and private cars and ship our freight by truck instead of using the railroads for both.

All of these changes have worsened environmental degradation: when a washerful of detergent goes down the drain it causes much more pollution than the same amount of soap; a throwaway beer bottle delivers the same amount of beer as a returnable one, but at a much higher cost in pollution and trash, since the returnable bottle is used dozens of times before it is discarded; the heavy use of chemical nitrogen fertilizer pollutes rivers and lakes, while the older agricultural methods did not; synthetic fibers, unlike natural ones, are not biodegradable, so that when discarded they are either burned—causing air pollution—or clutter up the environment forever; the modern car pollutes the air with smog and lead, while the prewar car was smog-free and could run on unleaded gasoline; airlines and private cars produce much more air pollution per passenger mile, and trucks more pollution per ton mile, than the railroads.

In every one of these cases the new, more polluting technology is also more wasteful of energy than the one it has displaced. Detergents and synthetic fibers are made out of petroleum, while natural fibers and the fat needed for soap are produced, by plants, from carbon dioxide, water and solar energy, all freely available in the environment; it takes more energy to make a throwaway bottle than it does to wash a returnable one and use it again; the modern high compression engine delivers fewer miles to the gallon than the prewar engines; nitrogen fertilizer is made out of natural gas, an energy cost not incurred when manure or crop rotation is used; railroads use much less fuel per passenger mile than passenger cars or airplanes, and much less fuel per ton mile than trucks.

The record is clear: The same technological changes that have created the environmental crisis have reduced the efficiency with which we use fuel. No one who understands why detergents, synthetic fibers and plastics, throwaway bottles, fertilizer, high-powered automobiles and trucks pollute the environment need be surprised to discover that they also waste energy.

The reason why the new technologies that waste energy and pollute the environment have been introduced is one that every businessman will understand: they are more profitable than the technologies that they have displaced. . . . The new technologies are more profitable because they use cheap energy in place of expensive labor. However, for that very reason they are economically vulnerable to real or threatened disruptions in the energy supply and to an increase in its price. As a result, energy problems automatically become production problems: automobile assembly lines are halted by the lack of electric wire, in short supply because the plastic insulation is made of petroleum products, which have been rapidly rising in price (dealers are likely to hold goods back from the market if they expect to get a better price a little later); thousands of auto workers are laid off because the manufacturers did not anticipate that, faced with rising gasoline prices, their customers would prefer small fuel-efficient cars to big gasoline-gulping ones; food production is threatened because the price of propane has increased so much (under the pressure of intense demand for propane from plastics manufacturers) that farmers may be hard pressed to find propane when they need it to dry their grain crop. Because of the energy crisis, we may have to choose between food and plastic olive-stabbers.

In sum, what has been signalized by the environmental crisis, and demonstrated by the energy crisis, is that in adopting the new postwar production technologies the economic system has gained in short-term profitability, at the expense of a polluted environment and a productive system that is highly vulnerable to disruption.

The issues raised by the environmental and energy crises are too deep and pervasive to be solved by technical sleight-of-hand, clever tax schemes, or patchwork legislation. They call for a great national debate, to discover how the resources of the United States can best be used to serve long-term social need rather than short-term private profit.

THE ENVIRONMENTAL CRISIS

The environment has just been rediscovered by the people who live in it. In the United States the event was celebrated in April 1970, during Earth Week. It was a sudden, noisy awakening. School children cleaned up rubbish; college students organized huge demonstrations; determined citizens recaptured the streets from the automobile, at least for a day. Everyone seemed to be aroused to the environmental danger and eager to do something about it.

They were offered lots of advice. Almost every writer, almost every speaker, on the college campuses, in the streets and on television and radio broadcasts, was ready to fix the blame and pronounce a cure for the environmental crisis.

Some regarded the environmental issue as politically innocuous:

> Ecology has become the political substitute for the word "motherhood."—Jesse Unruh, Democratic Leader of the State of California Assembly

But the FBI took it more seriously:

> On April 22, 1970, representatives of the FBI observed about two hundred persons on the Playing Fields shortly after 1:30 p.m. They were joined a few minutes later by a contingent of George Washington University students who arrived chanting "Save Our Earth." . . . A sign was noted which read "God Is Not Dead; He Is Polluted on Earth." . . . Shortly after 8:00 p.m. Senator Edmund Muskie (D), Maine, arrived and gave a short anti-pollution speech. Senator Muskie was followed by journalist I. F. Stone, who spoke for twenty minutes on the themes of anti-pollution, anti-military, and anti-administration.—FBI report entered into Congressional Record by Senator Muskie on April 14, 1971

Some blamed pollution on the rising population:

> The pollution problem is a consequence of population. It did not much matter how a lonely American frontiersman disposed of his waste. . . . But as population became denser, the natural chemical and biological recycling processes became overloaded. . . . Freedom to breed will bring ruin to all.—Garrett Hardin, biologist

> The causal chain of the deterioration [of the environment] is easily followed to its source. Too many cars, too many factories, too much detergent, too much pesticide, multiplying contrails, inadequate sewage

treatment plants, too little water, too much carbon dioxide—all can be traced easily to *too many people.*—Paul R. Ehrlich, biologist

Some blamed affluence:

The affluent society has become an effluent society. The 6 percent of the world's population in the United States produces 70 percent or more of the world's solid wastes.—Walter S. Howard, biologist

And praised poverty:

Blessed be the starving blacks of Mississippi with their outdoor privies, for they are ecologically sound, and they shall inherit a nation.—Wayne H. Davis, biologist

But not without rebuttal from the poor:

You must not embark on programs to curb economic growth without placing a priority on maintaining income, so that the poorest people won't simply be further depressed in their condition but will have a share, and be able to live decently.—George Wiley, chemist and chairman, National Welfare Rights Organization

And encouragement from industry:

It is not industry *per se,* but the demands of the public. And the public's demands are increasing at a geometric rate, because of the increasing standard of living and the increasing growth of population. . . . If we can convince the national and local leaders in the environmental crusade of this basic logic, that population causes pollution, then we can help them focus their attention on the major aspect of the problem.—Sherman R. Knapp, chairman of the board, Northeast Utilities

Some blamed man's innate aggressiveness:

The first problem, then, is people. . . . The second problem, a most fundamental one, lies within us—our basic aggressions. . . . As Anthony Storr has said: "The sombre fact is that we are the cruelest and most ruthless species that has ever walked the earth."—William Roth, director, Pacific Life Assurance Company

While others blamed what man had learned:

People are afraid of their humanity because systematically they have been taught to become inhuman. . . . They have no understanding of what it is to love nature. And so our airs are being polluted, our rivers are being poisoned, and our land is being cut up.—Arturo Sandoval, student, Environmental Action

A minister blamed profits:

> Environmental rape is a fact of our national life only because it is more profitable than responsible stewardship of earth's limited resources. — Channing E. Phillips, Congregationalist minister

While a historian blamed religion:

> Christianity bears a huge burden of guilt. . . . We shall continue to have a worsening ecologic crisis until we reject the Christian axiom that nature has no reason for existence save to serve man. — Lynn White, historian

A politician blamed technology:

> A runaway technology, whose only law is profit, has for years poisoned our air, ravaged our soil, stripped our forests bare, and corrupted our water resources. — Vance Hartke, senator from Indiana

While an environmentalist blamed politicians:

> There is a peculiar paralysis in our political branches of government, which are primarily responsible for legislating and executing the policies environmentalists are urging. . . . Industries who profit by the rape of our environment see to it that legislators friendly to their attitudes are elected, and that bureaucrats of similar attitude are appointed. — Roderick A. Cameron, of the Environmental Defense Fund

Some blamed capitalism:

> Yes, it's official — the conspiracy against pollution. And we have a simple program — arrest Agnew and smash capitalism. We make only one exception to our pollution stand — everyone should light up a joint and get stoned. . . . We say to Agnew country that Earth Day is for the sons and daughters of the American Revolution who are going to tear this capitalism down and set us free. — Rennie Davis, a member of the "Chicago Seven"

While capitalists counterattacked:

> The point I am trying to make is that we are solving most of our problems . . . that conditions are getting better not worse . . . that American industry is spending over three billion dollars a year to clean up the environment and additional billions to develop products that will *keep* it clean . . . and that the real danger is *not* from the free-enterprise Establishment that has made ours the most prosperous, most powerful and most charitable nation on earth. No, the danger today resides in the Disaster Lobby — those crepe-hangers who, for personal gain or out of

sheer ignorance, are undermining the American system and threatening the lives and fortunes of the American people. Some people have let the gloom-mongers scare them beyond rational response with talk about atomic annihilation. . . . Since World War II over one *billion* human beings who worried about A-bombs and H-bombs died of other causes. They worried for nothing. — Thomas R. Shepard, Jr., publisher, *Look* Magazine

And one keen observer blamed everyone:

We have met the enemy and he is us. — Pogo[1]

Earth Week and the accompanying outburst of publicity, preaching, and prognostication surprised most people, including those of us who had worked for years to generate public recognition of the environmental crisis. What surprised me most were the numerous, confident explanations of the cause and cure of the crisis. For having spent some years in the effort simply to detect and describe the growing list of environmental problems — radioactive fallout, air and water pollution, the deterioration of the soil — and in tracing some of their links to social and political processes, the identification of a single cause and cure seemed a rather bold step. During Earth Week, I discovered that such reticence was far behind the times.

After the excitement of Earth Week, I tried to find some meaning in the welter of contradictory advice that it produced. It seemed to me that the confusion of Earth Week was a sign that the situation was so complex and ambiguous that people could read into it whatever conclusion their own beliefs — about human nature, economics, and politics — suggested. Like a Rorschach ink blot,[2] Earth Week mirrored personal convictions more than objective knowledge.

Earth Week convinced me of the urgency of a deeper public understanding of the origins of the environmental crisis and its possible cures. That is what this book is about. It is an effort to find out what the environmental crisis *means*.

Such an understanding must begin at the source of life itself: the earth's thin skin of air, water, and soil, and the radiant solar fire that bathes it. Here, several billion years ago, life appeared and was

[1] The philosophizing opossum who inhabits the Okefenokee Swamp in the popular American comic strip *Pogo,* created by Walt Kelly (1913–73).
[2] A series of ink-blot designs forms the basis of the Rorschach test, which is intended to reveal the underlying personality structure of an individual through the associations evoked by the blots.

nourished by the earth's substance. As it grew, life evolved, its old forms transforming the earth's skin and new ones adapting to these changes. Living things multiplied in number, variety, and habitat until they formed a global network, becoming deftly enmeshed in the surroundings they had themselves created. This is the *ecosphere,* the home that life has built for itself on the planet's outer surface.

Any living thing that hopes to live on the earth must fit into the ecosphere or perish. The environmental crisis is a sign that the finely sculptured fit between life and its surroundings has begun to corrode. As the links between one living thing and another, and between all of them and their surroundings, begin to break down, the dynamic interactions that sustain the whole have begun to falter and, in some places, stop.

Why, after millions of years of harmonious co-existence, have the relationships between living things and their earthly surroundings begun to collapse? Where did the fabric of the ecosphere begin to unravel? How far will the process go? How can we stop it and restore the broken links?

Understanding the ecosphere comes hard because, to the modern mind, it is a curiously foreign place. We have become accustomed to think of separate, singular events, each dependent upon a unique, singular cause. But in the ecosphere every effect is also a cause: an animal's waste becomes food for soil bacteria; what bacteria excrete nourishes plants; animals eat the plants. Such ecological cycles are hard to fit into human experience in the age of technology, where machine A always yields product B, and product B, once used, is cast away, having no further meaning for the machine, the product, or the user.

Here is the first great fault in the life of man in the ecosphere. We have broken out of the circle of life, converting its endless cycles into man-made, linear events: oil is taken from the ground, distilled into fuel, burned in an engine, converted thereby into noxious fumes, which are emitted into the air. At the end of the line is smog. Other man-made breaks in the ecosphere's cycles spew out toxic chemicals, sewage, heaps of rubbish—testimony to our power to tear the ecological fabric that has, for millions of years, sustained the planet's life.

Suddenly we have discovered what we should have known long before: that the ecosphere sustains people and everything that they do; that anything that fails to fit into the ecosphere is a threat to its finely balanced cycles; that wastes are not only unpleasant, not only toxic, but, more meaningfully, evidence that the ecosphere is being driven towards collapse.

If we are to survive, we must understand *why* this collapse now threatens. Here, the issues become far more complex than even the ecosphere. Our assaults on the ecosystem are so powerful, so numerous, so finely interconnected, that although the damage they do is clear, it is very difficult to discover how it was done. By which weapon? In whose hand? Are we driving the ecosphere to destruction simply by our growing numbers? By our greedy accumulation of wealth? Or are the machines which we have built to gain this wealth—the magnificent technology that now feeds us out of neat packages, that clothes us in man-made fibers, that surrounds us with new chemical creations—at fault?

This book is concerned with these questions. It begins with the ecosphere, the setting in which civilization has done its great—and terrible—deeds. Then it moves to a description of some of the damage we have done to the ecosphere—to the air, the water, the soil. However, by now such horror stories of environmental destruction are familiar, even tiresome. Much less clear is what we need to learn from them, and so I have chosen less to shed tears for our past mistakes than to try to understand them. Most of this book is an effort to discover which human acts have broken the circle of life, and why. I trace the environmental crisis from its overt manifestations in the ecosphere to the ecological stresses which they reflect, to the faults in productive technology—and in its scientific background—that generate these stresses, and finally to the economic, social, and political forces which have driven us down this self-destructive course. All this in the hope—and expectation—that once we understand the origins of the environmental crisis, we can begin to manage the huge undertaking of surviving it.

• • •

THE CLOSING CIRCLE

In this book I have been concerned with the links between the environmental crisis and the social systems of which it is a part. The book shows, I believe, that the logic of ecology sheds considerable light on many of the troubles which afflict the earth and its inhabitants. An understanding of the environmental crisis illuminates the need for social changes which contain, in their broader sweep, the solution of the environmental crisis as well.

But there is a sharp contrast between the logic of ecology and the state of the real world in which environmental problems are embedded. Despite the constant reference to palpable, everyday life experiences—foul air, polluted water, and rubbish heaps—there is an air of unreality about the environmental crisis. The complex chemistry of smog and fertilizers and their even more elaborate connections to economic, social, and political problems are concepts that deal with real features of modern life, but they remain *concepts*. What is real in our lives and, in contrast to the reasonable logic of ecology, chaotic and intractable, is the apparently hopeless inertia of the economic and political system; its fantastic agility in sliding away from the basic issues which logic reveals; the selfish maneuvering of those in power, and their willingness to use, often unwittingly, and sometimes cynically, even environmental deterioration as a step toward more political power; the frustration of the individual citizen confronted by this power and evasion; the confusion that we all feel in seeking a way out of the environmental morass. To bring environmental logic into contact with the real world we need to relate it to the over-all social, political, and economic forces that govern both our daily lives and the course of history.

We live in a time that is dominated by enormous technical power and extreme human need. The power is painfully self-evident in the megawattage of power plants, and in the megatonnage of nuclear bombs. The human need is evident in the sheer numbers of people now and soon to be living, in the deterioration of their habitat, the earth, and in the tragic world-wide epidemic of hunger and want. The gap between brute power and human need continues to grow, as the power fattens on the same faulty technology that intensifies the need.

Everywhere in the world there is evidence of a deep-seated failure in the effort to use the competence, the wealth, the power at human disposal for the maximum good of human beings. The environmental crisis is a major example of this failure. For we are in an environmental crisis because the means by which we use the ecosphere to produce wealth are destructive of the ecosphere itself. The present system of production is self-destructive; the present course of human civilization is suicidal.

The environmental crisis is somber evidence of an insidious fraud hidden in the vaunted productivity and wealth of modern, technology-based society. This wealth has been gained by rapid short-term exploitation of the environmental system, but it has blindly accumulated a debt to nature (in the form of environmental destruction in developed countries and of population pressure in developing ones)—a debt so large and so pervasive that in the next generation it may, if unpaid, wipe out most of the wealth it has gained us. In effect, the account books of modern society are drastically out of balance, so that, largely unconsciously, a huge fraud has been perpetrated on the people of the world. The rapidly worsening course of environmental pollution is a warning that the bubble is about to burst, that the demand to pay the global debt may find the world bankrupt.

This does *not* necessarily mean that, to survive the environmental crisis, the people of industrialized nations will need to give up their "affluent" way of life. For as shown earlier, this "affluence," as judged by conventional measures—such as GNP,[3] power consumption, and production of metals—is itself an illusion. To a considerable extent it reflects ecologically faulty, socially wasteful types of production rather than the actual welfare of individual human beings. Therefore, the needed productive reforms can be carried out without seriously reducing the present level of *useful* goods available to the individual; and, at the same time, by controlling pollution the quality of life can be improved significantly.

There are, however, certain luxuries which the environmental crisis, and the approaching bankruptcy that it signifies, will, I believe, force us to give up. These are the *political* luxuries which have so long been enjoyed by those who can benefit from them: the luxury of allowing the wealth of the nation to serve preferentially the interests of so few of its citizens; of failing fully to inform citizens of what they need to know in order to exercise their right of political governance; of condemning as anathema any suggestion which re-examines basic economic values; of burying the issues revealed by logic in a morass of self-serving propaganda.

To resolve the environmental crisis, we shall need to forego, at last, the luxury of tolerating poverty, racial discrimination, and war. In our unwitting march toward ecological suicide we have run out of

---

[3] Gross national product—the total monetary value of all goods and services produced in a country.

options. Now that the bill for the environmental debt has been presented, our options have become reduced to two: either the rational, social organization of the use and distribution of the earth's resources, or a new barbarism.

This iron logic has recently been made explicit by one of the most insistent proponents of population control, Garrett Hardin. Over recent years he has expounded on the "tragedy of the commons"— the view that the world ecosystem is like a common pasture where each individual, guided by a desire for personal gain, increases his herd until the pasture is ruined for all. Until recently, Hardin drew two rather general conclusions from this analogy: first, that "freedom in a commons brings ruin to all," and second, that the freedom which must be constrained if ruin is to be avoided is not the derivation of private gain from a social good (the commons), but rather "the freedom to breed."

Hardin's logic is clear, and follows the course outlined earlier: if we accept as unchangeable the present governance of a social good (the commons, or the ecosphere) by private need, then survival requires the immediate, drastic limitation of population. Very recently, Hardin has carried this course of reasoning to its logical conclusion; in an editorial in *Science,* he asserts:

> Every day we [i.e., Americans] are a smaller minority. We are increasing at only one per cent a year; the rest of the world increases twice as fast. By the year 2000, one person in twenty-four will be an American; in one hundred years only one in forty-six. . . . If the world is one great commons, in which all food is shared equally, then we are lost. Those who breed faster will replace the rest. . . . In the absence of breeding control a policy of "one mouth one meal" ultimately produces one totally miserable world. In a less than perfect world, the allocation of rights based on territory must be defended if a ruinous breeding race is to be avoided. It is unlikely that civilization and dignity can survive everywhere; but better in a few places than in none. Fortunate minorities must act as the trustees of a civilization that is threatened by uninformed good intentions.

Here, only faintly masked, is barbarism. It denies the equal right of all the human inhabitants of the earth to a humane life. It would condemn most of the people of the world to the material level of the barbarian, and the rest, the "fortunate minorities," to the moral level of the barbarian. Neither within Hardin's tiny enclaves of "civilization," nor in the larger world around them, would anything that we seek to preserve—the dignity and the humaneness of man, the grace of civilization—survive.

In the narrow options that are possible in a world gripped by environmental crisis, there is no apparent alternative between barbarism and the acceptance of the economic consequence of the ecological imperative—that the social, global nature of the ecosphere must determine a corresponding organization of the productive enterprises that depend on it.

One of the common responses to a recitation of the world's environmental ills is a deep pessimism, which is perhaps the natural aftermath to the shock of recognizing that the vaunted "progress" of modern civilization is only a thin cloak for global catastrophe. I am convinced, however, that once we pass beyond the mere awareness of impending disaster and begin to understand *why* we have come to the present predicament, and where the alternative paths ahead can lead, there is reason to find in the very depths of the environmental crisis itself a source of optimism.

There is, for example, cause for optimism in the very complexity of the issues generated by the environmental crisis; once the links between the separate parts of the problem are perceived, it becomes possible to see new means of solving the whole. Thus, confronted separately, the need of developing nations for new productive enterprises, and the need of industrialized countries to reorganize theirs along ecologically sound lines, may seem hopelessly difficult. However, when the link between the two—the ecological significance of the production of synthetic substitutes for natural products—is recognized, ways of solving both can be seen. In the same way, we despair over releasing the grip of the United States on so much of the world's resources until it becomes clear how much of this "affluence" stresses the environment rather than contributes to human welfare. Then the very magnitude of the present United States share of the world's resources is a source of hope—for its reduction through ecological reform can then have a large and favorable impact on the desperate needs of the developing nations.

I find another source of optimism in the very nature of the environmental crisis. It is not the product of man's *biological* capabilities, which could not change in time to save us, but of his *social* actions—which are subject to much more rapid change. Since the environmental crisis is the result of the social mismanagement of the world's resources, then it can be resolved and man can survive in a humane condition when the social organization of man is brought into harmony with the ecosphere.

Here we can learn a basic lesson from nature: that nothing can survive on the planet unless it is a cooperative part of a larger, global whole. Life itself learned that lesson on the primitive earth. For it will be recalled that the earth's first living things, like modern man, consumed their nutritive base as they grew, converting the geochemical store of organic matter into wastes which could no longer serve their needs. Life, as it first appeared on the earth, was embarked on a linear, self-destructive course.

What saved life from extinction was the invention, in the course of evolution, of a new life-form which reconverted the waste of the primitive organisms into fresh, organic matter. The first photosynthetic organisms transformed the rapacious, linear course of life into the earth's first great ecological cycle. By closing the circle, they achieved what no living organism, alone, can accomplish—survival.

Human beings have broken out of the circle of life, driven not by biological need, but by the social organization which they have devised to "conquer" nature: means of gaining wealth that are governed by requirements conflicting with those which govern nature. The end result is the environmental crisis, a crisis of survival. Once more, to survive, we must close the circle. We must learn how to restore to nature the wealth that we borrow from it.

In our progress-minded society, anyone who presumes to explain a serious problem is expected to offer to solve it as well. But none of us—singly or sitting in committee—can possibly blueprint a specific "plan" for resolving the environmental crisis. To pretend otherwise is only to evade the real meaning of the environmental crisis: that the world is being carried to the brink of ecological disaster not by a singular fault, which some clever scheme can correct, but by the phalanx of powerful economic, political, and social forces that constitute the march of history. Anyone who proposes to cure the environmental crisis undertakes thereby to change the course of history.

But this is a competence reserved to history itself, for sweeping social change can be designed only in the workshop of rational, informed, collective social action. That we must act is now clear. The question which we face is how.

16

Konrad Lorenz

On Aggression

In recent decades a "new biology" has developed which, in its Darwinian premises, stands in opposition to the behaviorist school. Konrad Lorenz (1903–) is considered the principal founder and developer of a branch of the new biology known as ethology: the comparative study of the behavior of animals in their natural environments. Since humans are also members of the animal kingdom, ethologists like Lorenz have felt justified in writing about human behavior in the light of their observations of other animals. For his contributions to the understanding of human instinctual behavior, Lorenz was awarded the Nobel Prize for Physiology in 1973. The behavior patterns of animals, ethologists assert, are the result of natural selection, not—as Skinner and the other behaviorists would have it—learned or conditioned responses to external stimuli.

Born and raised in Vienna, Austria, Lorenz was able to pursue his early interest in animals at his family's large summer estate on the Danube River, just a few miles north of the city. He was allowed as a child to bring home a vast array of "pets," including fish, water insects, small crustaceans, dogs, geese, and monkeys. At age ten Lorenz became aware of Darwin's theory of evolution, and it had an enduring effect on his thought, inspiring him to make the study of animals his lifework. In 1928, after specializing in comparative anatomy, he earned a medical degree from the University of Vienna; in 1933 he received a doctorate in zoology.

In 1937 Lorenz was appointed lecturer on comparative anatomy and animal psychology at the University of Vienna; in 1940 he became professor of psychology at the University of Königsberg, Germany. Drafted into the

Excerpted from *On Aggression* by Konrad Lorenz, copyright © 1963 by Dr. Borotha-Schoeler Verlag, Wien; copyright © 1966 by Konrad Lorenz. Translated by Marjorie Kerr Wilson. Reprinted by permission of Harcourt Brace Jovanovich, Inc. [Pp. 236–40, 269–74, 275, 276–78, 297–99.]

German army as a doctor in 1941, he was captured by the advancing Russians in 1944 and held in a prison camp for almost four years.

After his return from Russia, Lorenz once again assembled and studied groups of animals; he also began to express his observations to a large, non-scientific readership. Lorenz's King Solomon's Ring: New Light on Animal Ways (1952), a delightful children's book illustrated by the author, introduced ethology to the general public. In a similar work, Man Meets Dog (1955), he recounts the historical development of the relationship between humans and their canine (and feline) companions.

Statements by Lorenz about the similarities between the instinctual behavior of humans and that of other animals brought him into direct conflict with the behaviorists, especially after the publication of his best-selling volume On Aggression (1966). As the following selection shows, Lorenz defines aggression as behavior directed against members of the same species. Perhaps surprisingly, he finds most aggression beneficial: it tends to preserve the species through natural selection—the most "fit" individual getting the food, the mate, the space, and the best chance to reproduce. Among most animals, he points out, aggression seldom leads directly to the death of the losers; they are saved by instinctive patterns of flight or submission to rituals of dominance. Only humans have been frequent killers of their own species. Essential to an understanding of this historical pattern of homicide is the fact that humans learned to use weapons created by their own intelligence before they evolved sufficient instinctual inhibitions against killing their own kind.

Two key concepts in On Aggression that are based on Lorenz's early observations of crows and geese are imprinting and innate releasing mechanisms. Imprinting is that process whereby an animal, at some genetically determined time early in its life, becomes attached to and identifies with another animal, usually its mother. A releasing mechanism is an inherited behavior pattern, within an animal's nervous system, that responds to a triggering event. For example, the strong brooding instincts of hens and geese can be released only by the squeaking sounds of chicks and goslings.

In the following selection, as an example of the source of one form of aggression that can be either constructive or destructive for humanity, Lorenz describes militant enthusiasm, an enthusiasm for the object that has been imprinted on the human being, causing the individual to generate aggression toward anything that threatens the object. Clearly, this enthusiasm carries its own releasing mechanism. Lorenz hopes, however, that understanding of such instinctual drives will some day enable humanity to restrict them to positive goals. If the human species is to survive, culture and instinct must evolve in harmony.

ECCE HOMO![1]

Let us imagine that an absolutely unbiased investigator on another planet, perhaps on Mars, is examining human behavior on earth, with the aid of a telescope whose magnification is too small to enable him to discern individuals and follow their separate behavior, but large enough for him to observe occurrences such as migrations of peoples, wars, and similar great historical events. He would never gain the impression that human behavior was dictated by intelligence, still less by responsible morality. If we suppose our extraneous observer to be a being of pure reason, devoid of instincts himself and unaware of the way in which all instincts in general and aggression in particular can miscarry, he would be at a complete loss how to explain history at all. The ever-recurrent phenomena of history do not have reasonable causes. It is a mere commonplace to say that they are caused by what common parlance so aptly terms "human nature." Unreasoning and unreasonable human nature causes two nations to compete, though no economic necessity compels them to do so; it induces two political parties or religions with amazingly similar programs of salvation to fight each other bitterly, and it impels an Alexander or a Napoleon to sacrifice millions of lives in his attempt to unite the world under his scepter. We have been taught to regard some of the persons who have committed these and similar absurdities with respect, even as "great" men, we are wont to yield to the political wisdom of those in charge, and we are all so accustomed to these phenomena that most of us fail to realize how abjectly stupid and undesirable the historical mass behavior of humanity actually is.

Having realized this, however, we cannot escape the question why reasonable beings do behave so unreasonably. Undeniably, there must be superlatively strong factors which are able to overcome the commands of individual reason so completely and which are so ob-

[1] Latin: Behold the man! — the words with which Pilate presented Jesus, crowned with thorns, to his accusers.

viously impervious to experience and learning. As Hegel said, "What experience and history teach us is this—that people and governments never have learned anything from history, or acted on principles deduced from it."

All these amazing paradoxes, however, find an unconstrained explanation, falling into place like the pieces of a jigsaw puzzle, if one assumes that human behavior, and particularly human social behavior, far from being determined by reason and cultural tradition alone, is still subject to all the laws prevailing in all phylogenetically adapted instinctive behavior. Of these laws we possess a fair amount of knowledge from studying the instincts of animals. Indeed, if our extra-mundane observer were a knowledgeable ethologist, he would unavoidably draw the conclusion that man's social organization is very similar to that of rats, which, like humans, are social and peaceful beings within their clans, but veritable devils toward all fellow members of their species not belonging to their own community. If, furthermore, our Martian naturalist knew of the explosive rise in human populations, the ever-increasing destructiveness of weapons, and the division of mankind into a few political camps, he would not expect the future of humanity to be more rosy than that of several hostile clans of rats on a ship almost devoid of food. And this prognosis would even be optimistic, for in the case of rats, reproduction stops automatically when a certain state of overcrowding is reached while man as yet has no workable system for preventing the so-called population explosion. Furthermore, in the case of the rats it is likely that after the wholesale slaughter enough individuals would be left over to propagate the species. In the case of man, this would not be so certain after the use of the hydrogen bomb.

It is a curious paradox that the greatest gifts of man, the unique faculties of conceptual thought and verbal speech which have raised him to a level high above all other creatures and given him mastery over the globe, are not altogether blessings, or at least are blessings that have to be paid for very dearly indeed. All the great dangers threatening humanity with extinction are direct consequences of conceptual thought and verbal speech. They drove man out of the paradise in which he could follow his instincts with impunity and do or not do whatever he pleased. There is much truth in the parable of the tree of knowledge and its fruit, though I want to make an addition to it to make it fit into my own picture of Adam: that apple was thoroughly unripe! Knowledge springing from conceptual thought robbed man of the security provided by his well-adapted instincts long, long before it was sufficient to provide him with an equally safe adaptation. Man is, as Arnold Gehlen has so truly said, by nature a jeopardized creature.

Conceptual thought and speech changed all man's evolution by achieving something which is equivalent to the inheritance of acquired characters. We have forgotten that the verb "inherit" had a juridic connotation long before it acquired a biological one. When a man invents, let us say, bow and arrow, not only his progeny but his entire community will inherit the knowledge and the use of these tools and possess them just as surely as organs grown on the body. Nor is their loss any more likely than the rudimentation of an organ of equal survival value. Thus, within one or two generations a process of ecological adaptation can be achieved which, in normal phylogeny and without the interference of conceptual thought, would have taken a time of an altogether different, much greater order of magnitude. Small wonder, indeed, if the evolution of social instincts and, what is even more important, social inhibitions could not keep pace with the rapid development forced on human society by the growth of traditional culture, particularly material culture.

Obviously, instinctive behavior mechanisms failed to cope with the new circumstances which culture unavoidably produced even at its very dawn. There is evidence that the first inventors of pebble tools, the African Australopithecines, promptly used their new weapon to kill not only game, but fellow members of their species as well. Peking Man, the Prometheus who learned to preserve fire, used it to roast his brothers: beside the first traces of the regular use of fire lie the mutilated and roasted bones of Sinanthropus pekinensis himself.

One is tempted to believe that every gift bestowed on man by his power of conceptual thought has to be paid for with a dangerous evil as the direct consequence of it. Fortunately for us, this is not so. Besides the faculty of conceptual thought, another constituent characteristic of man played an important role in gaining a deeper understanding of his environment, and this is curiosity. Insatiable curiosity is the root of exploration and experimentation, and these activities, even in their most primitive form, imply a function akin to asking questions. Explorative experimentation is a sort of dialogue with surrounding nature. Asking a question and recording an answer leads to anticipating the latter, and, given conceptual thought, to the linking of cause and effect. From hence it is but a step to consciously foreseeing the consequences of one's actions. Thus, the same human faculties which supplied man with tools and with power dangerous to himself, also gave him the means to prevent their misuse: rational responsibility. . . .

Militant enthusiasm is particularly suited for the paradigmatic illustration of the manner in which a phylogenetically evolved pattern of behavior interacts with culturally ritualized social norms and rites, and in which, though absolutely indispensable to the function of the compound system, it is prone to miscarry most tragically if not strictly controlled by rational responsibility based on causal insight. The Greek word *enthousiasmos* implies that a person is possessed by a god; the German *Begeisterung* means that he is controlled by a spirit, a *Geist,* more or less holy.

In reality, militant enthusiasm is a specialized form of communal aggression, clearly distinct from and yet functionally related to the more primitive forms of petty individual aggression. Every man of normally strong emotions knows, from his own experience, the subjective phenomena that go hand in hand with the response of militant enthusiasm. A shiver runs down the back and, as more exact observation shows, along the outside of both arms. One soars elated, above all the ties of everyday life, one is ready to abandon all for the call of what, in the moment of this specific emotion, seems to be a sacred duty. All obstacles in its path become unimportant; the instinctive inhibitions against hurting or killing one's fellows lose, unfortunately, much of their power. Rational considerations, criticism, and all reasonable arguments against the behavior dictated by militant enthusiasm are silenced by an amazing reversal of all values, making them appear not only untenable but base and dishonorable. Men may enjoy the feeling of absolute righteousness even while they commit atrocities. Conceptual thought and moral responsibility are at their lowest ebb. As a Ukrainian proverb says: "When the banner is unfurled, all reason is in the trumpet."

The subjective experiences just described are correlated with the following, objectively demonstrable phenomena. The tone of the entire striated musculature is raised, the carriage is stiffened, the arms are raised from the sides and slightly rotated inward so that the elbows point outward. The head is proudly raised, the chin stuck out, and the facial muscles mime the "hero face," familiar from the films. On the back and along the outer surface of the arms the hair stands on end. This is the objectively observed aspect of the shiver!

Anybody who has ever seen the corresponding behavior of the male chimpanzee defending his band or family with self-sacrificing courage will doubt the purely spiritual character of human enthusiasm. The chimp, too, sticks out his chin, stiffens his body, and raises his elbows; his hair stands on end, producing a terrifying magnification of his body contours as seen from the front. The inward rotation of his arms obviously has the purpose of turning the longest-haired side outward to enhance the effect. The whole combination of body attitude and hair-raising constitutes a bluff. This is also seen when a cat humps its back, and is calculated to make the animal appear bigger and more dangerous than it really is. Our shiver, which in German poetry is called a *"heiliger Schauer,"* a "holy" shiver, turns out to be the vestige of a prehuman vegetative response of making a fur bristle which we no longer have.

To the humble seeker of biological truth there cannot be the slightest doubt that human militant enthusiasm evolved out of a communal defense response of our prehuman ancestors. The unthinking single-mindedness of the response must have been of high survival value even in a tribe of fully evolved human beings. It was necessary for the individual male to forget all his other allegiances in order to be able to dedicate himself, body and soul, to the cause of the communal battle. *"Was schert mich Weib, was schert mich Kind"* — "What do I care for wife or child," says the Napoleonic soldier in a famous poem by Heinrich Heine, and it is highly characteristic of the reaction that this poet, otherwise a caustic critic of emotional romanticism, was so unreservedly enraptured by his enthusiasm for the "great" conqueror as to find this supremely apt expression.

The object which militant enthusiasm tends to defend has changed with cultural development. Originally it was certainly the community of concrete, individually known members of a group, held together by the bond of personal love and friendship. With the growth of the social unit, the social norms and rites held in common by all its members became the main factor holding it together as an entity, and therewith they became automatically the symbol of the unit. By a process of true Pavlovian conditioning[2] plus a certain amount of irreversible imprinting these rather abstract values have in

---

[2] Ivan Pavlov (1849–1936), a Russian physiologist, discovered the "conditioned reflex" by experimenting with dogs.

every human culture been substituted for the primal, concrete object of the communal defense reaction.

This traditionally conditioned substitution of object has important consequences for the function of militant enthusiasm. On the one hand, the abstract nature of its object can give it a definitely inhuman aspect and make it positively dangerous—what do I care for wife or child; on the other hand it makes it possible to recruit militant enthusiasm in the service of really ethical values. Without the concentrated dedication of militant enthusiasm neither art, nor science, nor indeed any of the great endeavors of humanity would ever have come into being. Whether enthusiasm is made to serve these endeavors, or whether man's most powerfully motivating instinct makes him go to war in some abjectly silly cause, depends almost entirely on the conditioning and/or imprinting he has undergone during certain susceptible periods of his life. There is reasonable hope that our moral responsibility may gain control over the primeval drive, but our only hope of its ever doing so rests on the humble recognition of the fact that militant enthusiasm is an instinctive response with a phylogenetically determined releasing mechanism and that the only point at which intelligent and responsible supervision can get control is in the conditioning of the response to an object which proves to be a genuine value under the scrutiny of the categorical question.

Like the triumph ceremony of the greylag goose, militant enthusiasm in man is a true autonomous instinct: it has its own appetitive behavior, its own releasing mechanisms, and, like the sexual urge or any other strong instinct, it engenders a specific feeling of intense satisfaction. The strength of its seductive lure explains why intelligent men may behave as irrationally and immorally in their political as in their sexual lives. Like the triumph ceremony, it has an essential influence on the social structure of the species. Humanity is not enthusiastically combative because it is split into political parties, but it is divided into opposing camps because this is the adequate stimulus situation to arouse militant enthusiasm in a satisfying manner. "If ever a doctrine of universal salvation should gain ascendancy over the whole earth to the exclusion of all others," writes Erich von Holst, "it would at once divide into two strongly opposing factions (one's own true one and the other heretical one) and hostility and war would thrive as before, mankind being—unfortunately—what it is!"

The first prerequisite for rational control of an instinctive behavior pattern is the knowledge of the stimulus situation which releases it. Militant enthusiasm can be elicited with the predictability of a reflex when the following environmental situations arise. First of all, a social unit with which the subject identifies himself must appear to be threatened by some danger from outside. That which is threatened may be a concrete group of people, the family or a little community of close friends, or else it may be a larger social unit held together and symbolized by its own specific social norms and rites. As the latter assume the character of autonomous values, . . . they can, quite by themselves, represent the object in whose defense militant enthusiasm can be elicited. From all this it follows that this response can be brought into play in the service of extremely different objects, ranging from the sports club to the nation, or from the most obsolete mannerisms or ceremonials to the ideal of scientific truth or of the incorruptibility of justice.

A second key stimulus which contributes enormously to the releasing of intense militant enthusiasm is the presence of a hated enemy from whom the threat to the above "values" emanates. This enemy, too, can be of a concrete or of an abstract nature. It can be "the" Jews, Huns, Boches, tyrants, etc., or abstract concepts like world capitalism, Bolshevism, fascism, and any other kind of ism; it can be heresy, dogmatism, scientific fallacy, or what not. Just as in the case of the object to be defended, the enemy against whom to defend it is extremely variable, and demagogues are well versed in the dangerous art of producing supranormal dummies to release a very dangerous form of militant enthusiasm.

A third factor contributing to the environmental situation eliciting the response is an inspiring leader figure. Even the most emphatically antifascistic ideologies apparently cannot do without it, as the giant pictures of leaders displayed by all kinds of political parties prove clearly enough. Again the unselectivity of the phylogenetically programmed response allows for a wide variation in the conditioning to a leader figure. Napoleon, about whom so critical a man as Heinrich Heine became so enthusiastic, does not inspire me in the least; Charles Darwin[3] does.

A fourth, and perhaps the most important, prerequisite for the full eliciting of militant enthusiasm is the presence of many other indi-

---

[3] An English naturalist who was the originator of the theory of evolution by natural selection (1809–82).

viduals, all agitated by the same emotion. Their absolute number has a certain influence on the quality of the response. Smaller numbers at issue with a large majority tend to obstinate defense with the emotional value of "making a last stand," while very large numbers inspired by the same enthusiasm feel the urge to conquer the whole world in the name of their sacred cause. Here the laws of mass enthusiasm are strictly analogous to those of flock formation; . . . here, too, the excitation grows in proportion, perhaps even in geometrical progression, with the increasing number of individuals. This is exactly what makes militant mass enthusiasm so dangerous.

I have tried to describe, with as little emotional bias as possible, the human response of enthusiasm, its phylogenetic origin, its instinctive as well as its traditionally handed-down components and prerequisites. I hope I have made the reader realize, without actually saying so, what a jumble our philosophy of values is. What is a culture? A system of historically developed social norms and rites which are passed on from generation to generation because emotionally they are felt to be values. What is a value? Obviously, normal and healthy people are able to appreciate something as a high value for which to live and, if necessary, to die, for no other reason than that it was evolved in cultural ritualization and handed down to them by a revered elder. Is, then, a value only defined as the object on which our instinctive urge to preserve and defend traditional social norms has become fixated? Primarily and in the early stages of cultural development this indubitably was the case. The obvious advantages of loyal adherence to tradition must have exerted a considerable selection pressure. However, the greatest loyalty and obedience to culturally ritualized norms of behavior must not be mistaken for responsible morality. Even at their best, they are only functionally analogous to behavior controlled by rational responsibility. In this respect, they are no whit different from the instinctive patterns of social behavior. . . . Also they are just as prone to miscarry under circumstances for which they have not been "programmed" by the great constructor, natural selection.

In other words, the need to control, by wise rational responsibility, all our emotional allegiances to cultural values is as great as, if not greater than, the necessity to keep in check our other instincts. None of them can ever have such devastating effects as unbridled militant enthusiasm when it infects great masses and overrides all other considerations by its single-mindedness and its specious nobil-

ity. It is not enthusiasm in itself that is in any way noble, but humanity's great goals which it can be called upon to defend. That indeed is
the Janus[4] head of man: The only being capable of dedicating himself
to the very highest moral and ethical values requires for this purpose
a phylogenetically adapted mechanism of behavior whose animal
properties bring with them the danger that he will kill his brother,
convinced that he is doing so in the interests of these very same high
values. *Ecce homo!*

AVOWAL OF OPTIMISM

. . . I am really being far from presumptuous when I profess my
conviction that in the very near future not only scientists, but the
majority of tolerably intelligent people, will consider as an obvious
and banal truth all that has been said in this book about instincts in
general and intra-specific aggression[5] in particular, about phylogenetic and cultural ritualization, and about the factors that build up the
ever-increasing danger of human society's becoming completely disintegrated by the misfunctioning of social behavior patterns.

There is less hazard of my meeting with disbelief than of incurring
the reproach of banality when I now proceed to summarize the most
important inferences from what has been said in this book by formulating simple precepts for preventive measures against that danger. I
am aware that these measures must appear feeble and ineffective after
all I have said in the last chapter about the present situation of mankind. This, however, does not argue against the correctness of my
inferences. In medicine, too, all therapeutic measures appear slight
and ineffectual when compared with the amount of physiological and
pathological knowledge and insight which had to be gained before
any reasonable therapy at all could be planned. Science seldom effects
dramatic changes in the course of history, except, of course, in the
sense of destruction, for it is all too easy to misuse the power af-
forded by causal insight. To use the knowledge gained by scientific
research in a creative and beneficial fashion demands no less perspicac-

---

[4] Two-faced: Janus, the ancient Roman god of doorways and of beginnings, was
usually represented as having one head with two bearded faces, back to back, looking
in opposite directions.
[5] Aggression of individuals against members of their own species.

ity and meticulous application to detail than were necessary to gain it.

The first, the most obvious, and the most important precept is the old Τνῶθι σεαυτὸν, "Know thyself": we must deepen our insight into the causal concatenations governing our own behavior. The lines along which an applied science of human behavior will probably develop are just beginning to appear. One line is the objective, ethological investigation of all the possibilities of discharging aggression in its primal form on substitute objects, and we already know that there are better ones than to kick empty carbide tins. The second is the psychoanalytic study of so-called sublimation. We may anticipate that a deeper knowledge of this specifically human form of catharsis will do much toward the relief of undischarged aggressive drives. The third way of avoiding aggression, though an obvious one, is still worth mentioning: it is the promotion of personal acquaintance and, if possible, friendship between individual members of different ideologies or nations. The fourth and perhaps the most important measure to be taken immediately is the intelligent and responsible channeling of militant enthusiasm, in other words helping a younger generation which, on the one hand, is highly critical and even suspicious and, on the other, emotionally starved, to find genuine causes that are worth serving in the modern world. I shall now discuss all these precepts one by one.

Even at its present modest stage, our knowledge of the nature of aggression is sufficient to tell us what measures against its damaging effects have no hope of success whatever, and this in itself is of value. To anybody who is unaware of the essential spontaneity of instinctive drives and who is wont to think of behavior exclusively in terms of conditioned and unconditioned responses, it must seem a hopeful undertaking to diminish or even eliminate aggression by shielding mankind from all stimulus situations eliciting aggressive behavior. . . . Another unpromising attempt is to control aggression by putting a moral veto on it. The practical application of both these methods would be about as judicious as trying to counteract the increasing pressure in a continuously heated boiler by screwing down the safety valve more tightly.

A further, theoretically possible but in my opinion highly inadvisable measure would be to attempt to breed out the aggressive drive by eugenic planning. We know . . . that there is intra-specific aggression in the human reaction of enthusiasm and this, though dangerous, is nevertheless indispensable for the achievement of the highest human goals. We know . . . that aggression in very many animals and probably also in man is an essential component of personal friendship. Finally, in the chapter on the great parliament of instincts, we have learned how complex is the interaction of different drives. It would have quite unpredictable consequences if one of them—and one of the strongest—were to disappear entirely. We do not know how many important behavior patterns of man include aggression as a motivating factor, but I believe it occurs in a great many. What is certain is that, with the elimination of aggression, the *"aggredi"* in the original and widest sense, the tackling of a task or problem, the self-respect without which everything that a man does from morning till evening, from the morning shave to the sublimest artistic or scientific creations, would lose all impetus; everything associated with ambition, ranking order, and countless other equally indispensable behavior patterns would probably also disappear from human life. In the same way, a very important and specifically human faculty would probably disappear too: laughter.

The most promising means we can apply in our attempt to cope with the miscarrying of aggression—and that of other patterns of social behavior—are those which have proved their efficiency in the course of phylogenetic and cultural evolution.

$$\bullet \quad \bullet \quad \bullet$$

From the discussion of what I know I have gradually passed to the account of what I think probable and, finally, to a profession of what I believe. There is no law barring the scientist from doing so. I believe, in short, in the ultimate victory of truth. I know that this sounds rather pompous, but I honestly do think it is the most likely thing to happen. I might even say that I regard it as inevitable, provided the human species does not commit suicide in the near future, as well it may. Otherwise it is quite predictable that the simple truths concerning the biology of mankind and the laws governing its behavior will sooner or later become generally accepted public property, in the same way as the older scientific truths . . . have done; they, too, were at first unacceptable to an all too complacent humanity because they disturbed its exaggerated self-esteem. Is it too much to hope that the fear of imminent self-destruction may have a sobering effect and act as a monitor of self-knowledge?

I do not consider in any way as utopian the possibility of convey-ing a sufficient knowledge of the essential biological facts to any sen-sible human being. They are indeed much easier to understand than, for instance, integral calculus or the computing of compound inter-est. Moreover, biology is a fascinating study, provided it is taught intelligently enough to make the pupil realize that he himself, being a living being, is directly concerned with what he is being told. *"Tua res agitur."* [6] Expert teaching of biology is the one and only founda-tion on which really sound opinions about mankind and its relation to the universe can be built. Philosophical anthropology of a type neglecting biological fact has done its worst by imbuing humanity with that sort of pride which not only comes before, but causes, a fall. It is plain biology of Homo sapiens L. that ought to be consid-ered the "big science."

Sufficient knowledge of man and of his position in the universe would, as I have said, automatically determine the ideals for which we have to strive. Sufficient humor may make mankind blessedly in-tolerant of phony, fraudulent ideals. Humor and knowledge are the two great hopes of civilization. There is a third, more distant hope based on the possibilities of human evolution; it is to be hoped that the cultural factors just mentioned will exert a selection pressure in a desirable direction. Many characters of man which, from the Paleo-lithic to recent times, were accounted the highest virtues, today seem dangerous to thinking people and funny to people with a sense of humor. If it is true that, within a few hundred years, selection brought about a devastating hypertrophy of aggression in the Utes,[7] that most unhappy of all peoples, we may hope without exaggerated optimism that a new kind of selection may, in civilized peoples, reduce the aggressive drive to a tolerable measure without, however, disturbing its indispensable function.

The great constructors of evolution will solve the problems of po-litical strife and warfare, but they will not do so by entirely eliminat-ing aggression and its communal form of militant enthusiasm. This would not be in keeping with their proven methods. If, in a newly arising biological situation, a drive begins to become injurious, it is never atrophied and removed entirely, for this would mean dispens-ing with all its indispensable functions. Invariably, the problem is

[6] Latin: You are the thing under discussion.
[7] A North American Indian tribe.

solved by the evolution of a new inhibitory mechanism adapted to dealing specifically with the new situation and obviating the particular detrimental effects of the drive without otherwise interfering with its functions.

We know that, in the evolution of vertebrates, the bond of personal love and friendship was the epoch-making invention created by the great constructors when it became necessary for two or more individuals of an aggressive species to live peacefully together and to work for a common end. We know that human society is built on the foundation of this bond, but we have to recognize the fact that the bond has become too limited to encompass all that it should: it prevents aggression only between those who know each other and are friends, while obviously it is all active hostility between all men of all nations or ideologies that must be stopped. The obvious conclusion is that love and friendship should embrace all humanity, that we should love all our human brothers indiscriminately. This commandment is not new. Our reason is quite able to understand its necessity as our feeling is able to appreciate its beauty, but nevertheless, made as we are, we are unable to obey it. We can feel the full, warm emotion of friendship and love only for individuals, and the utmost exertion of will power cannot alter this fact. But the great constructors can, and I believe they will. I believe in the power of human reason, as I believe in the power of natural selection. I believe that reason can and will exert a selection pressure in the right direction. I believe that this, in the not too distant future, will endow our descendants with the faculty of fulfilling the greatest and most beautiful of all commandments.

17

Werner Heisenberg

The Role of Modern Physics in the Present Development of Human Thinking

In the first half of the twentieth century, discoveries in physics upset the basic assumptions about reality that had dominated scientific thought ever since the Renaissance. A key figure in the overthrow of established causal concepts of classical physics was Werner Heisenberg (1901–1976).

Born in Duisberg, Germany, Heisenberg was reared and educated in Munich, receiving his doctorate in theoretical physics from the University of Munich in 1923. Physics flourished in Germany in the pre-Nazi years, and Heisenberg had the good fortune to be directly inspired by many great minds, including Max Planck and Albert Einstein. After studying in Göttingen with Max Born, and in Copenhagen with the Nobel laureate Niels Bohr, Heisenberg returned to Germany in 1927 as professor of physics at the University of Leipzig. He remained in Germany during the Second World War, becoming the director of Berlin's Kaiser Wilhelm Institute for Physics. After the war he returned to Göttingen and became director of the Max Planck Institute for Physics and Astrophysics.

The seminal theories of Heisenberg, for which he was to receive the Nobel Prize at the youthful age of thirty-one, were conceived in the mid and late 1920s. His principle of "indeterminacy" or "uncertainty," announced in 1927, states that cause-and-effect relationships cannot be observed at the

From *Physics and Philosophy: The Revolution in Modern Science* by Werner Heisenberg. Volume Nineteen of the World Perspective Series, edited and planned by Ruth Nanda Anshen. Copyright © 1958 by Werner Heisenberg. Reprinted by permission of Harper & Row, Publishers, Inc. [Pp. 194–206.]

subatomic level; all that scientists can do is work out statistical probabilities for the behavior of subatomic particles in large numbers. Thus, as continued experiments have seemed to verify, the law of assured material causality must be replaced (or supplemented) at the subatomic level by the principle of "probability." Heisenberg thus proposes that more than one system is possible in the universe; no one law or principle governs all phenomena.

The implications of this anti-deterministic view of ultimate reality have been hotly contested. Some, for example, acceptingly cite indeterminacy in nature to "prove" free will in humans; others cite the same mathematics to "prove" that the world is chaotic and all things happen by chance. Einstein, on the other hand, disturbed at Heisenberg's destruction of "classical" physics, pungently commented that "God does not play at dice with the universe." Einstein and many others felt that physics would one day be able to establish a unifying principle of causal connection where previously only chance could be seen.

In the following selection, from the concluding chapter of Physics and Philosophy *(1958), Heisenberg traces the development of materialistic physical science from the Renaissance and shows how that science has been discredited. He asserts that as modern science penetrates into those areas of the world that base their doctrines on nineteenth-century deterministic philosophy (Hegel and Marx), the narrowness of those absolutistic dogmas will become clear. The openness of the new science's world view, Heisenberg hopes, will influence those societies toward greater tolerance.*

It has frequently been discussed among the historians whether the rise of natural science after the sixteenth century was in any way a natural consequence of earlier trends in human thinking. It may be argued that certain trends in Christian philosophy led to a very abstract concept of God, that they put God so far above the world that one began to consider the world without at the same time also seeing God in the world. The Cartesian[1] partition may be called a final step in this development. Or one may point out that all the theological

---

[1]René Descartes (1596–1650), a French mathematician and philosopher, established a system of mathematical exactness for determining philosophical truth. He separated his system from traditional Christian theology by concluding that its "revealed truths . . . are quite above our intelligence."

controversies of the sixteenth century produced a general discontent about problems that could not really be settled by reason and were exposed to the political struggles of the time; that this discontent favored interest in problems which were entirely separated from the theological disputes. Or one may simply refer to the enormous activity, the new spirit that had come into the European societies through the Renaissance. In any case during this period a new authority appeared which was completely independent of Christian religion or philosophy or of the Church, the authority of experience, of the empirical fact. One may trace this authority back into older philosophical trends, for instance, into the philosophy of Occam[2] and Duns Scotus,[3] but it became a vital force of human activity only from the sixteenth century onward. Galileo did not only *think* about the mechanical motions, the pendulum and the falling stone; he tried out by experiments, quantitatively, how these motions took place. This new activity was in its beginning certainly not meant as a deviation from the traditional Christian religion. On the contrary, one spoke of two kinds of revelation of God. The one was written in the Bible and the other was to be found in the book of nature. The Holy Scripture had been written by man and was therefore subject to error, while nature was the immediate expression of God's intentions.

However, the emphasis on experience was connected with a slow and gradual change in the aspect of reality. While in the Middle Ages what we nowadays call the symbolic meaning of a thing was in some way its primary reality, the aspect of reality changed toward what we can perceive with our senses. What we can see and touch became primarily real. And this new concept of reality could be connected with a new activity: we can experiment and see how things really are. It was easily seen that this new attitude meant the departure of the human mind into an immense field of new possibilities, and it can be well understood that the Church saw in the new movement the dangers rather than the hopes. The famous trial of Galileo in con-

---

[2] William of Occam (*ca*. 1280–1349), an English philosopher, set forth the doctrine of nominalism by stating that the real is always individual, not universal — he thereby assisted in the separation of philosophy from Christian theology.

[3] John Duns Scotus (*ca*. 1265–1308), a Scottish theologian and a teacher of William of Occam, argued *against* the dominant medieval philosophy that God's will is always rational and that, therefore, theoretical knowledge is superior to experience in matters of religion.

nection with his views on the Copernican system[4] marked the beginning of a struggle that went on for more than a century. In this controversy the representatives of natural science could argue that experience offers an undisputable truth, that it cannot be left to any human authority to decide about what really happens in nature, and that this decision is made by nature or in this sense by God. The representatives of the traditional religion, on the other hand, could argue that by paying too much attention to the material world, to what we perceive with our senses, we lose the connection with the essential values of human life, with just that part of reality which is beyond the material world. These two arguments do not meet, and therefore the problem could not be settled by any kind of agreement or decision.

In the meantime natural science proceeded to get a clearer and wider picture of the material world. In physics this picture was to be described by means of those concepts which we nowadays call the concepts of classical physics. The world consisted of things in space and time, the things consist of matter, and matter can produce and can be acted upon by forces. The events follow from the interplay between matter and forces; every event is the result and the cause of other events. At the same time the human attitude toward nature changed from a contemplative one to the pragmatic one. One was not so much interested in nature as it is; one rather asked what one could do with it. Therefore, natural science turned into technical science; every advancement of knowledge was connected with the question as to what practical use could be derived from it. This was true not only in physics; in chemistry and biology the attitude was essentially the same, and the success of the new methods in medicine or in agriculture contributed essentially to the propagation of the new tendencies.

In this way, finally, the nineteenth century developed an extremely rigid frame for natural science which formed not only science but also the general outlook of great masses of people. This frame was supported by the fundamental concepts of classical physics, space, time, matter and causality; the concept of reality applied to the things

[4] Nicolaus Copernicus (1473–1543), a Polish astronomer, was the first to demonstrate mathematically that the sun — not the earth — is the center of the solar system. Galileo Galilei (1564–1642), an astronomer and physicist, was tried by the Inquisition in 1633 because of his writings in support of the Copernican system.

or events that we could perceive by our senses or that could be observed by means of the refined tools that technical science had provided. Matter was the primary reality. The progress of science was pictured as a crusade of conquest into the material world. Utility was the watchword of the time.

On the other hand, this frame was so narrow and rigid that it was difficult to find a place in it for many concepts of our language that had always belonged to its very substance, for instance, the concepts of mind, of the human soul or of life. Mind could be introduced into the general picture only as a kind of mirror of the material world; and when one studied the properties of this mirror in the science of psychology, the scientists were always tempted—if I may carry the comparison further—to pay more attention to its mechanical than to its optical properties. Even there one tried to apply the concepts of classical physics, primarily that of causality. In the same way life was to be explained as a physical and chemical process, governed by natural laws, completely determined by causality. Darwin's concept of evolution provided ample evidence for this interpretation. It was especially difficult to find in this framework room for those parts of reality that had been the object of the traditional religion and seemed now more or less only imaginary. Therefore, in those European countries in which one was wont to follow the ideas up to their extreme consequences, an open hostility of science toward religion developed, and even in the other countries there was an increasing tendency toward indifference toward such questions; only the ethical values of the Christian religion were excepted from this trend, at least for the time being. Confidence in the scientific method and in rational thinking replaced all other safeguards of the human mind.

Coming back now to the contributions of modern physics, one may say that the most important change brought about by its results consists in the dissolution of this rigid frame of concepts of the nineteenth century. Of course many attempts had been made before to get away from this rigid frame which seemed obviously too narrow for an understanding of the essential parts of reality. But it had not been possible to see what could be wrong with the fundamental concepts like matter, space, time and causality that had been so extremely successful in the history of science. Only experimental research itself, carried out with all the refined equipment that technical science could offer, and its mathematical interpretation, provided the basis for a critical analysis—or, one may say, enforced the critical analysis—of these concepts, and finally resulted in the dissolution of the rigid frame.

This dissolution took place in two distinct stages. The first was the discovery, through the theory of relativity, that even such fundamental concepts as space and time could be changed and in fact must be changed on account of new experience. This change did not concern the somewhat vague concepts of space and time in natural language; but it did concern their precise formulation in the scientific language of Newtonian mechanics, which had erroneously been accepted as final. The second stage was the discussion of the concept of matter enforced by the experimental results concerning the atomic structure. The idea of the reality of matter had probably been the strongest part in that rigid frame of concepts of the nineteenth century, and this idea had at least to be modified in connection with the new experience. Again the concepts so far as they belonged to the natural language remained untouched. There was no difficulty in speaking about matter or about facts or about reality when one had to describe the atomic experiments and their results. But the scientific extrapolation of these concepts into the smallest parts of matter could not be done in the simple way suggested by classical physics, though it had erroneously determined the general outlook on the problem of matter.

These new results had first of all to be considered as a serious warning against the somewhat forced application of scientific concepts in domains where they did not belong. The application of the concepts of classical physics, e.g., in chemistry, had been a mistake. Therefore, one will nowadays be less inclined to assume that the concepts of physics, even those of quantum theory, can certainly be applied everywhere in biology or other sciences. We will, on the contrary, try to keep the doors open for the entrance of new concepts even in those parts of science where the older concepts have been very useful for the understanding of the phenomena. Especially at those points where the application of the older concepts seems somewhat forced or appears not quite adequate to the problem we will try to avoid any rash conclusions.

Furthermore, one of the most important features of the development and the analysis of modern physics is the experience that the concepts of natural language, vaguely defined as they are, seem to be more stable in the expansion of knowledge than the precise terms of scientific language, derived as an idealization from only limited groups of phenomena. This is in fact not surprising since the concepts of natural language are formed by the immediate connection with reality; they represent reality. It is true that they are not very well defined and may therefore also undergo changes in the course of the centuries, just as reality itself did, but they never lose the immediate connection with reality. On the other hand, the scientific concepts are idealizations; they are derived from experience obtained by refined experimental tools, and are precisely defined through axioms and definitions. Only through these precise definitions is it possible to connect the concepts with a mathematical scheme and to derive mathematically the infinite variety of possible phenomena in this field. But through this process of idealization and precise definition the immediate connection with reality is lost. The concepts still correspond very closely to reality in that part of nature which had been the object of the research. But the correspondence may be lost in other parts containing other groups of phenomena.

Keeping in mind the intrinsic stability of the concepts of natural language in the process of scientific development, one sees that—after the experience of modern physics—our attitude toward concepts like mind or the human soul or life or God will be different from that of the nineteenth century, because these concepts belong to the natural language and have therefore immediate connection with reality. It is true that we will also realize that these concepts are not well defined in the scientific sense and that their application may lead to various contradictions, for the time being we may have to take the concepts, unanalyzed as they are; but still we know that they touch reality. It may be useful in this connection to remember that even in the most precise part of science, in mathematics, we cannot avoid using concepts that involve contradictions. For instance, it is well known that the concept of infinity leads to contradictions that have been analyzed, but it would be practically impossible to construct the main parts of mathematics without this concept.

The general trend of human thinking in the nineteenth century had been toward an increasing confidence in the scientific method and in precise rational terms, and had led to a general skepticism with regard to those concepts of natural language which do not fit into the closed frame of scientific thought—for instance, those of religion. Modern physics has in many ways increased this skepticism; but it has at the same time turned it against the overestimation of precise specific concepts, against a too-optimistic view on progress in general, and finally against skepticism itself. The skepticism against precise scientific concepts does not mean that there should be a definite limitation for the application of rational thinking. On the contrary, one may say that the human ability to understand may be in a certain sense unlimited. But the existing scientific concepts cover always only a very limited part of reality, and the other part that has not yet been understood is infinite. Whenever we proceed from the known into the unknown we may hope to understand, but we may have to learn at the same time a new meaning of the word "understanding." We know that any understanding must be based finally upon the natural language because it is only there that we can be certain to touch reality, and hence we must be skeptical about any skepticism with regard to this natural language and its essential concepts. Therefore, we may use these concepts as they have been used at all times. In this way modern physics has perhaps opened the door to a wider outlook on the relation between the human mind and reality.

This modern science, then, penetrates in our time into other parts of the world where the cultural tradition has been entirely different from the European civilization. There the impact of this new activity in natural and technical science must make itself felt even more strongly than in Europe, since changes in the conditions of life that have taken two or three centuries in Europe will take place there within a few decades. One should expect that in many places this new activity must appear as a decline of the older culture, as a ruthless and barbarian attitude, that upsets the sensitive balance on which all human happiness rests. Such consequences cannot be avoided; they must be taken as one aspect of our time. But even there the openness of modern physics may help to some extent to reconcile the older traditions with the new trends of thought. For instance, the great scientific contribution in theoretical physics that has come from Japan since the last war may be an indication for a certain relationship between philosophical ideas in the tradition of the Far East and the philosophical substance of quantum theory. It may be easier to adapt oneself to the quantum-theoretical concept of reality when one has not gone through the naïve materialistic way of thinking that still prevailed in Europe in the first decades of this century.

Of course such remarks should not be misunderstood as an underestimation of the damage that may be done or has been done to old cultural traditions by the impact of technical progress. But since this whole development has for a long time passed far beyond any control by human forces, we have to accept it as one of the most essential features of our time and must try to connect it as much as possible with the human values that have been the aim of the older cultural and religious traditions. It may be allowed at this point to quote a story from the Hasidic religion:[5] There was an old rabbi, a priest famous for his wisdom, to whom all people came for advice. A man visited him in despair over all the changes that went on around him, deploring all the harm done by so-called technical progress. "Isn't all this technical nuisance completely worthless," he exclaimed "if one considers the real values of life?" "This may be so," the rabbi replied, "but if one has the right attitude one can learn from everything." "No," the visitor rejoined, "from such foolish things as railway or telephone or telegraph one can learn nothing whatsoever." But the rabbi answered, "You are wrong. From the railway you can learn that you may by being one instant late miss everything. From the telegraph you can learn that every word counts. And from the telephone you can learn that what we say here can be heard there." The visitor understood what the rabbi meant and went away.

Finally, modern science penetrates into those large areas of our present world in which new doctrines were established only a few decades ago as foundations for new and powerful societies. There modern science is confronted both with the content of the doctrines, which go back to European philosophical ideas of the nineteenth century (Hegel and Marx), and with the phenomenon of uncompromising belief. Since modern physics must play a great role in these countries because of its practical applicability, it can scarcely be avoided that the narrowness of the doctrines is felt by those who have really understood modern physics and its philosophical meaning. Therefore, at this point an interaction between science and the general trend of thought may take place. Of course the influence of science should not be overrated; but it might be that the openness of modern science could make it easier even for larger groups of people to see that the doctrines are possibly not so important for the society

[5] A Jewish mystical sect founded in Poland around 1750.

as had been assumed before. In this way the influence of modern science may favor an attitude of tolerance and thereby may prove valuable.

On the other hand, the phenomenon of uncompromising belief carries much more weight than some special philosophical notions of the nineteenth century. We cannot close our eyes to the fact that the great majority of the people can scarcely have any well-founded judgment concerning the correctness of certain important general ideas or doctrines. Therefore, the word "belief" can for this majority not mean "perceiving the truth of something" but can only be understood as "taking this as the basis for life." One can easily understand that this second kind of belief is much firmer, is much more fixed than the first one, that it can persist even against immediate contradicting experience and can therefore not be shaken by added scientific knowledge. The history of the past two decades has shown by many examples that this second kind of belief can sometimes be upheld to a point where it seems completely absurd, and that it then ends only with the death of the believer. Science and history can teach us that this kind of belief may become a great danger for those who share it. But such knowledge is of no avail, since one cannot see how it could be avoided, and therefore such belief has always belonged to the great forces in human history. From the scientific tradition of the nineteenth century one would of course be inclined to hope that all belief should be based on a rational analysis of every argument, on careful deliberation; and that this other kind of belief, in which some real or apparent truth is simply taken as the basis for life, should not exist. It is true that cautious deliberation based on purely rational arguments can save us from many errors and dangers, since it allows readjustment to new situations, and this may be a necessary condition for life. But remembering our experience in modern physics it is easy to see that there must always be a fundamental complementarity between deliberation and decision. In the practical decisions of life it will scarcely ever be possible to go through all the arguments in favor of or against one possible decision, and one will therefore always have to act on insufficient evidence. The decision finally takes place by pushing away all the arguments—both those that have been understood and others that might come up through further deliberation—and by cutting off all further pondering. The decision may be the result of deliberation, but it is at the same time complementary to deliberation; it excludes deliberation. Even the most important decisions in life must always contain this inevitable element of irrationality. The decision itself is necessary, since there must be something to rely upon, some principle to guide our actions. Without such a firm stand our own actions would lose all force. Therefore, it cannot be avoided that some real or apparent truth form the basis of life; and this fact should be acknowledged with regard to those groups of people whose basis is different from our own.

Coming now to a conclusion from all that has been said about modern science, one may perhaps state that modern physics is just one, but a very characteristic, part of a general historical process that tends toward a unification and a widening of our present world. This process would in itself lead to a diminution of those cultural and political tensions that create the great danger of our time. But it is accompanied by another process which acts in the opposite direction. The fact that great masses of people become conscious of this process of unification leads to an instigation of all forces in the existing cultural communities that try to ensure for their traditional values the largest possible role in the final state of unification. Thereby the tensions increase and the two competing processes are so closely linked with each other that every intensification of the unifying process— for instance, by means of new technical progress—intensifies also the struggle for influence in the final state, and thereby adds to the instability of the transient state. Modern physics plays perhaps only a small role in this dangerous process of unification. But it helps at two very decisive points to guide the development into a calmer kind of evolution. First, it shows that the use of arms in the process would be disastrous and, second, through its openness for all kinds of concepts it raises the hope that in the final state of unification many different cultural traditions may live together and may combine different human endeavors into a new kind of balance between thought and deed, between activity and meditation.

18

Gary Snyder

Smokey the Bear Sutra

A *radically romantic movement—containing elements of both anarchism and pacifism—began in the San Francisco area in the mid-1950s. This trend, originally known as the "beat" movement, was to have a noticeable influence on the temper of the times. Characterized by a search for higher human consciousness as well as by a general antagonism toward technology, capitalism, and established institutions, the "beats" were essentially anti-scientific in their outlook, contrasting sharply with such scientific ecologists as Barry Commoner. By the mid-1960s, in somewhat vulgarized form, the movement had become a part of popular culture. Gary Snyder (1930–   ) was one of the founding figures of this quest for a new consciousness.*

Born in San Francisco and raised in Portland, Oregon, Snyder graduated from Reed College in 1951, having earned a bachelor's degree in anthropology and literature. He later studied Oriental languages at the University of California, Berkeley. Snyder's many outdoor experiences—as farmer, seaman, logger, and Forest Service worker—would have an enduring influence on his life and poetry. The other major influences on his thinking include the years he spent in the Orient, especially in Japan, studying with the masters of Zen Buddhism.

Snyder's personal philosophy is a blend of Zen Buddhism (with radical political overtones), the lore of American Indians, and the mystique of the wilderness. In 1965 Snyder wrote the following exposition of his ideas and values: "America five hundred years ago was clouds of birds, miles of bison, endless forests and grass and clear water. Today it is the tired ground of the world's dominant culture. Only Americans and a few western Europeans have lived with industry and the modern mass so long—the Africans and Chinese are fascinated children. . . . As poet I hold the most archaic values on earth. They go back to the Neolithic: the fertility of the soil, the magic of animals, the power-vision in solitude, the terrifying initiation and rebirth, the love and ecstasy of the dance, the common work of the tribe. . . . I try to hold both history and the wilderness in mind, that my poems may approach the true measure of things and stand against the unbalance and ignorance of our times."

"Smokey the Bear Sutra," the following selection, was published anonymously (around 1969) by Snyder, who circulated the poem as an unsigned broadside with the stipulation that it "be reproduced free forever." The word sutra *is meant to suggest an instructional discourse of Buddha; it is one of several terms associated with East Indian philosophy that Snyder employs to achieve an exotic but universal effect. He chooses Smokey the Bear, a special species of American folk hero, to present his views on the relationship of humanity to the land in the technological age.*

Once in the Jurassic, about 150 million years ago,
the Great Sun Buddha in this corner of the Infinite
Void gave a great Discourse to all the assembled elements
and energies: to the standing beings, the walking beings,
the flying beings, and the sitting beings—even grasses,
to the number of thirteen billion, each one born from a
seed, were assembled there: a Discourse concerning
Enlightenment on the planet Earth.

"In some future time, there will be a continent called
America. It will have great centers of power called
such as Pyramid Lake, Walden Pond, Mt. Rainier, Big Sur,
Everglades, and so forth; and powerful nerves and channels
such as Columbia River, Mississippi River, and Grand Canyon.
The human race in that era will get into troubles all over
its head, and practically wreck everything in spite of
its own strong intelligent Buddha-nature."

"The twisting strata of the great mountains and the pulsings
of great volcanoes are my love burning deep in the earth.
My obstinate compassion is schist and basalt and
granite, to be mountains, to bring down the rain. In that

future American Era I shall enter a new form: to cure
the world of loveless knowledge that seeks with blind hunger;
and mindless rage eating food that will not fill it."

And he showed himself in his true form of

SMOKEY THE BEAR

A handsome smokey-colored brown bear standing on his
hind legs, showing that he is aroused and watchful.

Bearing in his right paw the Shovel that digs to the
truth beneath appearances; cuts the roots of useless attachments, and flings damp sand on the fires of greed and war;

His left paw in the Mudra[1] of Comradely Display—indicating
that all creatures have the full right to live to their limits
and that deer, rabbits, chipmunks, snakes, dandelions,
and lizards all grow in the realm of the Dharma;[2]

Wearing the blue work overalls symbolic of slaves and
laborers, the countless men oppressed by a civilization
that claims to save but only destroys;

Wearing the broad-brimmed hat of the West, symbolic of
the forces that guard the Wilderness, which is the Natural
State of the Dharma and the True Path of man on earth;
all true paths lead through mountains—

With a halo of smoke and flame behind, the forest fires
of the kali-yuga,[3] fires caused by the stupidity of those
who think things can be gained and lost whereas in truth all
is contained vast and free in the Blue Sky and Green Earth
of One Mind;

Round-bellied to show his kind nature and that the great
earth has food enough for everyone who loves her and trusts
her;

Trampling underfoot wasteful freeways and needless
suburbs; smashing the worms of capitalism and totalitarianism;

[1] A gesture of the hand with a specific meaning in yoga and in classical Indian dancing.
[2] In Hinduism and Buddhism, the basic principles of the universe.
[3] In Indian religious thinking, the last of the four ages through which the cycle of creation passes. It is the most evil and corrupt of the phases.

Indicating the Task: his followers, becoming free of cars,
houses, canned food, universities, and shoes, master the
Three Mysteries of their own Body, Speech, and Mind; and
fearlessly chop down the rotten trees and prune out the
sick lambs of this country America and then burn the leftover
trash.

Wrathful but Calm, Austere but Comic, Smokey the Bear will
Illuminate those who would help him; but for those who would
hinder or slander him,

HE WILL PUT THEM OUT.

Thus his great Mantra: [4]

Namah samanta vajranam chanda maharoshana
Sphataya hum traka ham mam

"I DEDICATE MYSELF TO THE UNIVERSAL DIAMOND
BE THIS RAGING FURY DESTROYED"

And he will protect those who love woods and rivers,
Gods and animals, hobos and madmen, prisoners and sick
people, musicians, playful women, and hopeful children;

And if anyone is threatened by advertising, air pollution,
or the police, they should chant SMOKEY THE BEAR'S
WAR SPELL;
DROWN THEIR BUTTS
CRUSH THEIR BUTTS
DROWN THEIR BUTTS
CRUSH THEIR BUTTS

And SMOKEY THE BEAR will surely appear to put the enemy out
with his vajra[5]-shovel.

Now those who recite this Sutra and then try to put it in
practice will accumulate merit as countless as the sands
of Arizona and Nevada,
Will help save the planet Earth from total oil slick,
Will enter the age of harmony of man and nature,
Will win the tender love and caresses of men, women, and
beasts

---

[4] In Hinduism and some branches of Buddhism, a mystical formula to be recited.
[5] Literally (in the ancient Indian Sanskrit), thunderbolt.

Will always have ripe blackberries to eat and a sunny spot
   under a pine tree to sit at,

AND IN THE END WILL WIN HIGHEST PERFECT
   ENLIGHTENMENT

      thus have we heard.

(may be reproduced free forever)

IV
The
Human
Malaise

19

Franz Kafka
Before the Law

Franz Kafka (1883–1924), a Czech who wrote in German, is one of the seminal literary influences of the twentieth century. Reviving parable and allegory as literary forms in his short stories and novels, Kafka wrote in a clinically precise, restrained style, often describing grotesque events. His simple sentences reveal complex layers of meaning and hint at multiple personal alienations: from his Czech national identity (as a cultural German), from his Jewish religious background, from his family (especially his dominating father), and from the possibility of a satisfying emotional life (Kafka was engaged to be married several times but always broke off the engagements).

*After earning a degree in law from the German University of Prague, Kafka secured a position in that city with the government's Workers' Accident Insurance Institute. This job gave him ample time for wide reading in several languages. He published his first story in 1913 and in the next ten years wrote all of his works that have survived. Kafka destroyed most of what he wrote and, aware of his fatal tuberculosis, ordered that all the manuscripts remaining at his death be destroyed by his lifetime friend Max Brod. Fortunately for modern literature, after great moral struggle, Brod decided instead to edit and publish his dead friend's writings. Thus, Kafka's three major novels—*The Trial, The Castle, Amerika*—were published posthumously. Brod also wrote the earliest biography of Kafka.*

The first significant work published by Kafka was the short novel The Metamorphosis *(1915), which begins with the following sentence: "As*

Gregor Samsa awoke one morning from uneasy dreams he found himself transformed in his bed into a gigantic insect.'' The bug apparently is an embodiment of Gregor's (Kafka's?) sense of dehumanized existence. Eventually, after maltreatment and isolation by embarrassed relatives, the dead, dry remains of the insect are swept out of the house by a servant.

The three novels by Kafka published after his death are similarly startling in their imagery. The Trial (1925) presents a man, one Joseph K., who is arrested, condemned, and executed for a crime that is never named nor ever understood by him. In The Castle (1926), a land surveyor ("K.") arrives at a town dominated by a castle for whose lord he is supposed to begin working. Staying at the town's inn, K. is never able to gain admittance to the castle, nor is he ever able to find out just what he is supposed to do there, or who the inhabitants really are. Amerika (1927), unfinished like the other posthumously published novels, tells of the hero's immigration to America, where, after many misfortunes and adventures, he joins a traveling theatrical company amid intimations of future wealth and happiness.

"Before the Law," the brief selection that follows, is contained in the ninth chapter of The Trial, but was published separately by Kafka in 1916. It is a parable told by a priest to the protagonist, Joseph K. Like Kafka's other writings, the story contains no single clear meaning; it is one of the many provocative ambiguities found in The Trial. A "man from the country" fails to gain admittance to the august "Law." This failure represents, perhaps, the man's inability to gain his life's goal. That goal might be earthly happiness (prevented by the bureaucracy of the legal system or by his own ineffectual nature), or heavenly salvation (prevented by his separation from God, through his own sense of original sin). Hence, Kafka may be suggesting that we are all equally helpless yet equally responsible.

Before the law stands a doorkeeper. To this doorkeeper there comes a man from the country and prays for admittance to the Law. But the doorkeeper says that he cannot grant admittance at the moment. The man thinks it over and then asks if he will be allowed in later. "It is possible," says the doorkeeper, "but not at the moment." Since the gate stands open, as usual, and the doorkeeper steps to one side, the man stoops to peer through the gateway into the interior. Observing that, the doorkeeper laughs and says: "If you are so drawn to it, just try to go in despite my veto. But take note: I am powerful. And I am only the least of the doorkeepers. From hall to hall there is one doorkeeper after another, each more powerful than the last. The third doorkeeper is already so terrible that even I cannot bear to look at him." These are difficulties the man from the country has not expected; the Law, he thinks, should surely be accessible at all times and to everyone, but as he now takes a closer look at the doorkeeper in his fur coat, with his big sharp nose and long, thin, black Tartar beard, he decides that it is better to wait until he gets permission to enter. The doorkeeper gives him a stool and lets him sit down at one side of the door. There he sits for days and years. He makes many attempts to be admitted, and wearies the doorkeeper by his importunity. The doorkeeper frequently has little interviews with him, asking him questions about his home and many other things, but the questions are put indifferently, as great lords put them, and always finish with the statement that he cannot be let in yet. The man, who has furnished himself with many things for his journey, sacrifices all he has, however valuable, to bribe the doorkeeper. The doorkeeper accepts everything, but always with the remark: "I am only taking it to keep you from thinking you have omitted anything." During these many years the man fixes his attention almost continuously on the doorkeeper. He forgets the other doorkeepers, and this first one seems to him the sole obstacle preventing access to the Law. He curses his bad luck, in his early years boldly and loudly; later, as he grows old, he only grumbles to himself. He becomes childish, and since in his yearlong contemplation of the doorkeeper he has come to know even the fleas in his fur collar, he begs the fleas as well to help him and to change the doorkeeper's mind. At length his eyesight begins to fail, and he does not know whether the world is really darker or whether his eyes are only deceiving him. Yet in his darkness he is now aware of a radiance that streams inextinguishably from the gateway of the Law. Now he has not very long to live. Before he dies, all his experiences in these long years gather themselves in his head to one point, a question he has not yet asked the doorkeeper. He waves him nearer, since he can no longer raise his stiffening body. The doorkeeper has to bend low toward him, for the difference in height between them has altered much to the man's disadvantage. "What do you want to know now?" asks the doorkeeper; "you are insatiable." "Everyone strives to reach the Law," says the man, "so how does it happen that for all these many years no one but myself has ever begged for admittance?" The doorkeeper recognizes that the man has reached his end, and, to let his failing senses catch the words, roars in his ear: "No one else could ever be admitted here, since this gate was made only for you. I am now going to shut it."

20

Albert Camus

The Guest

*The work of Albert Camus (1913–1960), according to his Nobel Prize cita-
tion (1957), "with clearsighted earnestness illuminates the problem of the
human conscience of our time." As a French boy growing up in a colonial
Algerian society and later as a fighter in the underground resistance to Nazi
occupation of France, Camus constantly witnessed the moral choices that
must be made in the face of terror. His experiences led him to develop a
humanist philosophy that rejects "any ideology that claims control over all of
human life."*

*Raised in desperately poor circumstances by his illiterate mother after his
father's death in the First World War, Camus found pleasure in the elements
of nature—the blazing Algerian sun and the cool Mediterranean Sea—
which were to become recurring images in his work. A superb student, he
won scholarships that took him from grade school through graduate studies in
philosophy at the University of Algiers; he was also an excellent athlete.
Unfortunately, his plans for university teaching were overturned by repeated
attacks of tuberculosis.*

*Unable to teach, Camus supported himself in Algeria with a series of odd
jobs, joined the Communist Party briefly (1934–35), and eventually found
permanent employment as a journalist, writing articles that documented the
injustice of the French administration toward the native Arab population.
After the outbreak of the Second World War, Camus moved to France,
where, during the Nazi occupation, he published the first books that brought
him significant recognition:* The Stranger *(1942), a short novel, and* The

Myth of Sisyphus (*1942*), *a collection of philosophical essays. Both works define the "absurd" opposition between the human desire for rationally just coherence and the essentially hostile, meaningless universe.*

By 1943 Camus was living in Paris and editing Combat, *a clandestine newspaper of the anti-Nazi movement. After the liberation, going beyond the moral blankness of the "absurd" position, he published* The Plague (*1947*), *a complex novel that illustrates the moral necessity of continuing rebellion against oppression. Set in the plague-infested Algerian city of Oran, the novel depicts human beings struggling, without transcendent religious faith, against disease-bearing rats, which represent the ever-present forces that bring human suffering and destruction.*

Camus had a noted falling-out with fellow writer and philosopher Jean-Paul Sartre in 1952 because of Sartre's support of the Communist Party — which Camus had come to believe supported present human misery and injustice for the sake of an ideologically pure future. He died eight years later in an automobile accident, while at the height of his creative powers.

"The Guest," the short story presented as the following selection, is taken from Exile and the Kingdom (*1957*), *the last book Camus published. Its central character, Daru, a schoolmaster in Algeria, has established a fragile "kingdom" of community with man and nature in the schoolhouse where he teaches children and distributes grain to famine-stricken families. Like Camus himself, Daru does not wish to be involved in a dehumanizing, narrow loyalty to either side in the morally ambiguous rebellion of the natives against the French. And like Camus, therefore, he ultimately finds himself alone, in a state of "exile."*

The schoolmaster was watching the two men climb toward him. One was on horseback, the other on foot. They had not yet tackled the abrupt rise leading to the schoolhouse built on the hillside. They were toiling onward, making slow progress in the snow, among the stones, on the vast expanse of the high, deserted plateau. From time to time the horse stumbled. Without hearing anything yet, he could see the breath issuing from the horse's nostrils. One of the men, at least, knew the region. They were following the trail although it had disappeared days ago under a layer of dirty white snow. The schoolmaster calculated that it would take them half an hour to get onto the hill. It was cold; he went back into the school to get a sweater.

He crossed the empty, frigid classroom. On the blackboard the four rivers of France, drawn with four different colored chalks, had been flowing toward their estuaries for the past three days. Snow had suddenly fallen in mid-October after eight months of drought without the transition of rain, and the twenty pupils, more or less, who lived in the villages scattered over the plateau had stopped coming. With fair weather they would return. Daru now heated only the single room that was his lodging, adjoining the classroom and giving also onto the plateau to the east. Like the class windows, his window looked to the south too. On that side the school was a few kilometers from the point where the plateau began to slope toward the south. In clear weather could be seen the purple mass of the mountain range where the gap opened onto the desert.

Somewhat warmed, Daru returned to the window from which he had first seen the two men. They were no longer visible. Hence they must have tackled the rise. The sky was not so dark, for the snow had stopped falling during the night. The morning had opened with a dirty light which had scarcely become brighter as the ceiling of clouds lifted. At two in the afternoon it seemed as if the day were merely beginning. But still this was better than those three days when the thick snow was falling amidst unbroken darkness with little gusts of wind that rattled the double door of the classroom. Then Daru had spent long hours in his room, leaving it only to go to the shed and feed the chickens or get some coal. Fortunately the delivery truck from Tadjid, the nearest village to the north, had brought his supplies two days before the blizzard. It would return in forty-eight hours.

Besides, he had enough to resist a siege, for the little room was cluttered with bags of wheat that the administration left as a stock to distribute to those of his pupils whose families had suffered from the drought. Actually they had all been victims because they were all poor. Every day Daru would distribute a ration to the children. They had missed it, he knew, during these bad days. Possibly one of the fathers or big brothers would come this afternoon and he could supply them with grain. It was just a matter of carrying them over to the next harvest. Now shiploads of wheat were arriving from France and the worst was over. But it would be hard to forget that poverty, that army of ragged ghosts wandering in the sunlight, the plateaus burned to a cinder month after month, the earth shriveled up little by little, literally scorched, every stone bursting into dust under one's foot. The sheep had died then by thousands and even a few men, here and there, sometimes without anyone's knowing.

In contrast with such poverty, he who lived almost like a monk in his remote schoolhouse, nonetheless satisfied with the little he had and with the rough life, had felt like a lord with his white-washed walls, his narrow couch, his unpainted shelves, his well, and his weekly provision of water and food. And suddenly this snow, without warning, without the foretaste of rain. This is the way the region was, cruel to live in, even without men—who didn't help matters either. But Daru had been born here. Everywhere else, he felt exiled.

He stepped out onto the terrace in front of the schoolhouse. The two men were now halfway up the slope. He recognized the horseman as Balducci, the old gendarme he had known for a long time. Balducci was holding on the end of a rope an Arab who was walking behind him with hands bound and head lowered. The gendarme waved a greeting to which Daru did not reply, lost as he was in contemplation of the Arab dressed in a faded blue jellaba,[1] his feet in sandals but covered with socks of heavy raw wool, his head surmounted by a narrow, short *chèche*.[2] They were approaching. Balducci was holding back his horse in order not to hurt the Arab, and the group was advancing slowly.

Within earshot, Balducci shouted: "One hour to do the three kilometers from El Ameur!" Daru did not answer. Short and square in his thick sweater, he watched them climb. Not once had the Arab raised his head. "Hello," said Daru when they got up onto the terrace. "Come in and warm up." Balducci painfully got down from his horse without letting go the rope. From under his bristling mustache he smiled at the schoolmaster. His little dark eyes, deep-set under a tanned forehead, and his mouth surrounded with wrinkles made him look attentive and studious. Daru took the bridle, led the horse to the shed, and came back to the two men, who were now waiting for him in the school. He led them into his room. "I am going to heat up the classroom," he said. "We'll be more comfortable there." When he entered the room again, Balducci was on the

[1] A loose woolen cloak usually having a hood.
[2] A long scarf worn as a turban; headdress.

couch. He had undone the rope tying him to the Arab, who had squatted near the stove. His hands still bound, the *chèche* pushed back on his head, he was looking toward the window. At first Daru noticed only his huge lips, fat, smooth, almost Negroid; yet his nose was straight, his eyes were dark and full of fever. The *chèche* revealed an obstinate forehead and, under the weathered skin now rather discolored by the cold, the whole face had a restless and rebellious look that struck Daru when the Arab, turning his face toward him, looked him straight in the eyes. "Go into the other room," said the schoolmaster, "and I'll make you some mint tea." "Thanks," Balducci said. "What a chore! How I long for retirement." And addressing his prisoner in Arabic: "Come on, you." The Arab got up and, slowly, holding his bound wrists in front of him, went into the classroom.

With the tea, Daru brought a chair. But Balducci was already enthroned on the nearest pupil's desk and the Arab had squatted against the teacher's platform facing the stove, which stood between the desk and the window. When he held out the glass of tea to the prisoner, Daru hesitated at the sight of his bound hands. "He might perhaps be untied." "Sure," said Balducci. "That was for the trip." He started to get to his feet. But Daru, setting the glass on the floor, had knelt beside the Arab. Without saying anything, the Arab watched him with his feverish eyes. Once his hands were free, he rubbed his swollen wrists against each other, took the glass of tea, and sucked up the burning liquid in swift little sips.

"Good," said Daru. "And where are you headed?"

Balducci withdrew his mustache from the tea. "Here, son."

"Odd pupils! And you're spending the night?"

"No. I'm going back to El Ameur. And you will deliver this fellow to Tinguit. He is expected at police headquarters."

Balducci was looking at Daru with a friendly little smile.

"What's this story?" asked the schoolmaster. "Are you pulling my leg?"

"No, son. Those are the orders."

"The orders? I'm not . . ." Daru hesitated, not wanting to hurt the old Corsican. "I mean, that's not my job."

"What! What's the meaning of that? In wartime people do all kinds of jobs."

"Then I'll wait for the declaration of war!"

Balducci nodded.

"O.K. But the orders exist and they concern you too. Things are brewing, it appears. There is talk of a forthcoming revolt. We are mobilized, in a way."

Daru still had his obstinate look.

"Listen, son," Balducci said. "I like you and you must understand. There's only a dozen of us at El Ameur to patrol throughout the whole territory of a small department and I must get back in a hurry. I was told to hand this guy over to you and return without delay. He couldn't be kept there. His village was beginning to stir; they wanted to take him back. You must take him to Tinguit tomorrow before the day is over. Twenty kilometers shouldn't faze a husky fellow like you. After that, all will be over. You'll come back to your pupils and your comfortable life."

Behind the wall the horse could be heard snorting and pawing the earth. Daru was looking out the window. Decidedly, the weather was clearing and the light was increasing over the snowy plateau. When all the snow was melted, the sun would take over again and once more would burn the fields of stone. For days, still, the unchanging sky would shed its dry light on the solitary expanse where nothing had any connection with man.

"After all," he said, turning around toward Balducci, "what did he do?" And, before the gendarme had opened his mouth, he asked: "Does he speak French?"

"No, not a word. We had been looking for him for a month, but they were hiding him. He killed his cousin."

"Is he against us?"

"I don't think so. But you can never be sure."

"Why did he kill?"

"A family squabble, I think. One owed the other grain, it seems. It's not at all clear. In short, he killed his cousin with a billhook. You know, like a sheep, *kreezk!*"

Balducci made the gesture of drawing a blade across his throat and the Arab, his attention attracted, watched him with a sort of anxiety. Daru felt a sudden wrath against the man, against all men with their rotten spite, their tireless hates, their blood lust.

But the kettle was singing on the stove. He served Balducci more tea, hesitated, then served the Arab again, who, a second time, drank avidly. His raised arms made the jellaba fall open and the schoolmaster saw his thin, muscular chest.

"Thanks, kid," Balducci said. "And now, I'm off."

He got up and went toward the Arab, taking a small rope from his pocket.

"What are you doing?" Daru asked dryly.

Balducci, disconcerted, showed him the rope.

"Don't bother."

The old gendarme hesitated. "It's up to you. Of course, you are armed?"

"I have my shotgun."

"Where?"

"In the trunk."

"You ought to have it near your bed."

"Why? I have nothing to fear."

"You're crazy, son. If there's an uprising, no one is safe, we're all in the same boat."

"I'll defend myself. I'll have time to see them coming."

Balducci began to laugh, then suddenly the mustache covered the white teeth.

"You'll have time? O.K. That's just what I was saying. You have always been a little cracked. That's why I like you, my son was like that."

At the same time he took out his revolver and put it on the desk.

"Keep it; I don't need two weapons from here to El Ameur."

The revolver shone against the black paint of the table. When the gendarme turned toward him, the schoolmaster caught the smell of leather and horseflesh.

"Listen, Balducci," Daru said suddenly, "every bit of this disgusts me, and first of all your fellow here. But I won't hand him over. Fight, yes, if I have to. But not that."

The old gendarme stood in front of him and looked at him severely.

"You're being a fool," he said slowly. "I don't like it either. You don't get used to putting a rope on a man even after years of it, and you're even ashamed—yes, ashamed. But you can't let them have their way."

"I won't hand him over," Daru said again.

"It's an order, son, and I repeat it."

"That's right. Repeat to them what I've said to you: I won't hand him over."

Balducci made a visible effort to reflect. He looked at the Arab and at Daru. At last he decided.

"No, I won't tell them anything. If you want to drop us, go ahead; I'll not denounce you. I have an order to deliver the prisoner and I'm doing so. And now you'll just sign this paper for me."

"There's no need. I'll not deny that you left him with me."

"Don't be mean with me. I know you'll tell the truth. You're from hereabouts and you are a man. But you must sign, that's the rule."

Daru opened his drawer, took out a little square bottle of purple ink, the red wooden penholder with the "sergeant-major" pen he used for making models of penmanship, and signed. The gendarme carefully folded the paper and put it into his wallet. Then he moved toward the door.

"I'll see you off," Daru said.

"No," said Balducci. "There's no use being polite. You insulted me."

He looked at the Arab, motionless in the same spot, sniffed peevishly, and turned away toward the door. "Good-by, son," he said. The door shut behind him. Balducci appeared suddenly outside the window and then disappeared. His footsteps were muffled by the snow. The horse stirred on the other side of the wall and several chickens fluttered in fright. A moment later Balducci reappeared outside the window leading the horse by the bridle. He walked toward the little rise without turning around and disappeared from sight with the horse following him. A big stone could be heard bouncing down. Daru walked back toward the prisoner, who, without stirring, never took his eyes off him. "Wait," the schoolmaster said in Arabic and went toward the bedroom. As he was going through the door, he had a second thought, went to the desk, took the revolver, and stuck it in his pocket. Then, without looking back, he went into his room.

For some time he lay on his couch watching the sky gradually close over, listening to the silence. It was this silence that had seemed painful to him during the first days here, after the war. He had requested a post in the little town at the base of the foothills separating the upper plateaus from the desert. There, rocky walls, green and black to the north, pink and lavender to the south, marked the frontier of eternal summer. He had been named to a post farther north, on the plateau itself. In the beginning, the solitude and the silence had been hard for him on these wastelands peopled only by stones. Occasionally, furrows suggested cultivation, but they had been dug

to uncover a certain kind of stone good for building. The only plow-
ing here was to harvest rocks. Elsewhere a thin layer of soil accumulated in the hollows would be scraped out to enrich paltry
village gardens. This is the way it was: bare rock covered three
quarters of the region. Towns sprang up, flourished, then disappeared; men came by, loved one another or fought bitterly, then
died. No one in this desert, neither he nor his guest, mattered. And
yet, outside this desert neither of them, Daru knew, could have really lived.

When he got up, no noise came from the classroom. He was
amazed at the unmixed joy he derived from the mere thought that
the Arab might have fled and that he would be alone with no decision to make. But the prisoner was there. He had merely stretched
out between the stove and the desk. With eyes open, he was staring
at the ceiling. In that position, his thick lips were particularly noticeable, giving him a pouting look. "Come," said Daru. The Arab
got up and followed him. In the bedroom, the schoolmaster pointed
to a chair near the table under the window. The Arab sat down
without taking his eyes off Daru.

"Are you hungry?"

"Yes," the prisoner said.

Daru set the table for two. He took flour and oil, shaped a cake in
a frying pan, and lighted the little stove that functioned on bottled
gas. While the cake was cooking, he went out to the shed to get
cheese, eggs, dates, and condensed milk. When the cake was done he
set it on the window sill to cool, heated some condensed milk diluted
with water, and beat up the eggs into an omelette. In one of his motions he knocked against the revolver stuck in his right pocket. He
set the bowl down, went into the classroom, and put the revolver in
his desk drawer. When he came back to the room, night was falling.
He put on the light and served the Arab. "Eat," he said. The Arab
took a piece of the cake, lifted it eagerly to his mouth, and stopped
short.

"And you?" he asked.

"After you. I'll eat too."

The thick lips opened slightly. The Arab hesitated, then bit into
the cake determinedly.

The meal over, the Arab looked at the schoolmaster. "Are you the
judge?"

"No, I'm simply keeping you until tomorrow."

"Why do you eat with me?"

"I'm hungry."

The Arab fell silent. Daru got up and went out. He brought back a folding bed from the shed, set it up between the table and the stove, perpendicular to his own bed. From a large suitcase which, upright in a corner, served as a shelf for papers, he took two blankets and arranged them on the camp bed. Then he stopped, felt useless, and sat down on his bed. There was nothing more to do or to get ready. He had to look at this man. He looked at him, therefore, trying to imagine his face bursting with rage. He couldn't do so. He could see nothing but the dark yet shining eyes and the animal mouth.

"Why did you kill him?" he asked in a voice whose hostile tone surprised him.

The Arab looked away.

"He ran away. I ran after him."

He raised his eyes to Daru again and they were full of a sort of woeful interrogation. "Now what will they do to me?"

"Are you afraid?"

He stiffened, turning his eyes away.

"Are you sorry?"

The Arab stared at him openmouthed. Obviously he did not understand. Daru's annoyance was growing. At the same time he felt awkward and self-conscious with his big body wedged between the two beds.

"Lie down there," he said impatiently. "That's your bed."

The Arab didn't move. He called to Daru:

"Tell me!"

The schoolmaster looked at him.

"Is the gendarme coming back tomorrow?"

"I don't know."

"Are you coming with us?"

"I don't know. Why?"

The prisoner got up and stretched out on top of the blankets, his feet toward the window. The light from the electric bulb shone straight into his eyes and he closed them at once.

"Why?" Daru repeated, standing beside the bed.

The Arab opened his eyes under the blinding light and looked at him, trying not to blink.

"Come with us," he said.

In the middle of the night, Daru was still not asleep. He had gone to bed after undressing completely; he generally slept naked. But when he suddenly realized that he had nothing on, he hesitated. He felt vulnerable and the temptation came to him to put his clothes back on. Then he shrugged his shoulders; after all, he wasn't a child and, if need be, he could break his adversary in two. From his bed he could observe him, lying on his back, still motionless with his eyes closed under the harsh light. When Daru turned out the light, the darkness seemed to coagulate all of a sudden. Little by little, the night came back to life in the window where the starless sky was stirring gently. The schoolmaster soon made out the body lying at his feet. The Arab still did not move, but his eyes seemed open. A faint wind was prowling around the schoolhouse. Perhaps it would drive away the clouds and the sun would reappear.

During the night the wind increased. The hens fluttered a little and then were silent. The Arab turned over on his side with his back to Daru, who thought he heard him moan. Then he listened for his guest's breathing, become heavier and more regular. He listened to that breath so close to him and mused without being able to go to sleep. In this room where he had been sleeping alone for a year, this presence bothered him. But it bothered him also by imposing on him a sort of brotherhood he knew well but refused to accept in the present circumstances. Men who share the same rooms, soldiers or prisoners, develop a strange alliance as if, having cast off their armor with their clothing, they fraternized every evening, over and above their differences, in the ancient community of dream and fatigue. But Daru shook himself; he didn't like such musings, and it was essential to sleep.

A little later, however, when the Arab stirred slightly, the schoolmaster was still not asleep. When the prisoner made a second move, he stiffened, on the alert. The Arab was lifting himself slowly on his arms with almost the motion of sleepwalker. Seated upright in bed, he waited motionless without turning his head toward Daru, as if he were listening attentively. Daru did not stir; it had just occurred to him that the revolver was still in the drawer of his desk. It was better to act at once. Yet he continued to observe the prisoner, who, with the same slithery motion, put his feet on the ground, waited again, then began to stand up slowly. Daru was about to call out to him when the Arab began to walk, in a quite natural but extraordinarily silent way. He was heading toward the door at the end of the room that opened into the shed. He lifted the latch with precaution and went out, pushing the door behind him but without shutting it. Daru had not stirred. "He is running away," he merely thought. "Good riddance!" Yet he listened attentively. The hens were not fluttering; the guest must be on the plateau. A faint sound of water reached him, and he didn't know what it was until the Arab again stood framed in the doorway, closed the door carefully, and came back to bed without a sound. Then Daru turned his back on him and fell asleep. Still later he seemed, from the depths of his sleep, to hear furtive steps around the schoolhouse. "I'm dreaming! I'm dreaming!" he repeated to himself. And he went on sleeping.

When he awoke, the sky was clear; the loose window let in a cold, pure air. The Arab was asleep, hunched up under the blankets now, his mouth open, utterly relaxed. But when Daru shook him, he started dreadfully, staring at Daru with wild eyes as if he had never seen him and such a frightened expression that the schoolmaster stepped back. "Don't be afraid. It's me. You must eat." The Arab nodded his head and said yes. Calm had returned to his face, but his expression was vacant and listless.

The coffee was ready. They drank it seated together on the folding bed as they munched their pieces of the cake. Then Daru led the Arab under the shed and showed him the faucet where he washed. He went back into the room, folded the blankets and the bed, made his own bed and put the room in order. Then he went through the classroom and out onto the terrace. The sun was already rising in the blue sky; a soft, bright light was bathing the deserted plateau. On the ridge the snow was melting in spots. The stones were about to reappear. Crouched on the edge of the plateau, the schoolmaster looked at the deserted expanse. He thought of Balducci. He had hurt him, for he had sent him off in a way as if he didn't want to be associated with him. He could still hear the gendarme's farewell and, without knowing why, he felt strangely empty and vulnerable. At that moment, from the other side of the schoolhouse, the prisoner coughed. Daru listened to him almost despite himself and then, furious, threw a pebble that whistled through the air before sinking into the snow. That man's stupid crime revolted him, but to hand him over was contrary to honor. Merely thinking of it made him smart with humiliation. And he cursed at one and the same time his own people who had sent him this Arab and the Arab too who had dared to kill and not managed to get away. Daru got up, walked in a circle on the terrace, waited motionless, and then went back into the schoolhouse.

The Arab, leaning over the cement floor of the shed, was washing his teeth with two fingers. Daru looked at him and said: "Come." He went back into the room ahead of the prisoner. He slipped a hunting-jacket on over his sweater and put on walking-shoes. Standing, he waited until the Arab had put on his *chèche* and sandals. They went into the classroom and the schoolmaster pointed to the exit, saying: "Go ahead." The fellow didn't budge. "I'm coming," said Daru. The Arab went out. Daru went back into the room and made a package of pieces of rusk, dates, and sugar. In the classroom, before going out, he hesitated a second in front of his desk, then crossed the threshold and locked the door. "That's the way," he said. He started toward the east, followed by the prisoner. But, a short distance from the schoolhouse, he thought he heard a slight sound behind them. He retraced his steps and examined the surroundings of the house; there was no one there. The Arab watched him without seeming to understand. "Come on," said Daru.

They walked for an hour and rested beside a sharp peak of limestone. The snow was melting faster and faster and the sun was drinking up the puddles at once, rapidly cleaning the plateau, which gradually dried and vibrated like the air itself. When they resumed walking, the ground rang under their feet. From time to time a bird rent the space in front of them with a joyful cry. Daru breathed in deeply the fresh morning light. He felt a sort of rapture before the vast familiar expanse, now almost entirely yellow under its dome of blue sky. They walked an hour more, descending toward the south. They reached a level height made up of crumbly rocks. From there on, the plateau sloped down, eastward, toward a low plain where there were a few spindly trees and, to the south, toward outcroppings of rock that gave the landscape a chaotic look.

Daru surveyed the two directions. There was nothing but the sky on the horizon. Not a man could be seen. He turned toward the Arab, who was looking at him blankly. Daru held out the package to him. "Take it," he said. "There are dates, bread, and sugar. You can hold out for two days. Here are a thousand francs too." The Arab took the package and the money but kept his full hands at chest level as if he didn't know what to do with what was being given him. "Now look," the schoolmaster said as he pointed in the direction of the east, "there's the way to Tinguit. You have a two-hour walk. At

Tinguit you'll find the administration and the police. They are expecting you." The Arab looked toward the east, still holding the package and the money against his chest. Daru took his elbow and turned him rather roughly toward the south. At the foot of the height on which they stood could be seen a faint path. "That's the trail across the plateau. In a day's walk from here you'll find pasturelands and the first nomads. They'll take you in and shelter you according to their law." The Arab had now turned toward Daru and a sort of panic was visible in his expression. "Listen," he said. Daru shook his head: "No, be quiet. Now I'm leaving you." He turned his back on him, took two long steps in the direction of the school, looked hesitantly at the motionless Arab, and started off again. For a few minutes he heard nothing but his own step resounding on the cold ground and did not turn his head. A moment later, however, he turned around. The Arab was still there on the edge of the hill, his arms hanging now, and he was looking at the schoolmaster. Daru felt something rise in his throat. But he swore with impatience, waved vaguely, and started off again. He had already gone some distance when he again stopped and looked. There was no longer anyone on the hill.

Daru hesitated. The sun was now rather high in the sky and was beginning to beat down on his head. The schoolmaster retraced his steps, at first somewhat uncertainly, then with decision. When he reached the little hill, he was bathed in sweat. He climbed it as fast as he could and stopped, out of breath, at the top. The rock fields to the south stood out sharply against the blue sky, but on the plain to the east a steamy heat was already rising. And in that slight haze, Daru, with heavy heart, made out the Arab walking slowly on the road to prison.

A little later, standing before the window of the classroom, the schoolmaster was watching the clear light bathing the whole surface of the plateau, but he hardly saw it. Behind him on the blackboard, among the winding French rivers, sprawled the clumsily chalked-up words he had just read: "You handed over our brother. You will pay for this." Daru looked at the sky, the plateau, and, beyond, the invisible lands stretching all the way to the sea. In this vast landscape he had loved so much, he was alone.

21

Samuel Beckett

Act Without Words

"The theatre of the absurd," a literary and stage phenomenon of the present century, has as its philosophical premise an acceptance of the absurdity of the human condition, as described in the early works of Albert Camus. ★ *It portrays human beings divorced from their own lives and assumes a purposeless and hostile universe devoid of God. To convey their perceptions of the senselessness of existence, playwrights associated with the theatre of the absurd abandoned the theatrical traditions of plot, character, and setting through which drama had always tried to make sense to its audience. Where Camus presents his philosophy of the absurd with clear and logical reasoning, the playwrights of the absurd present concrete but often non-rational verbal and visual images; some being consciously "anti-literary."*

Foremost among such playwrights is Samuel Beckett (1906–   ), who was born near Dublin, Ireland, on Friday the thirteenth (of April)—a birthday he regards as a symptom—into a comfortable Anglo-Irish Protestant family. In his youth he was an outstanding athlete and scholar and in 1927 received a bachelor's degree in French and Italian from Trinity College, Dublin. Leaving Ireland in 1928 he became an invited lecturer in English at the prestigious École Normale Superieure in Paris, where he came to know many of the other expatriates partaking of the city's stimulating artistic life. During these years in Paris, for example, Beckett helped the great Irish novelist James Joyce, then nearly blind, by setting down from dictation parts of Joyce's manuscript of Finnegans Wake. *Beckett returned to Trinity College in 1930 to lecture in French and earned a master's degree there;*

however, he soon resigned his promising faculty position because "he could not bear the absurdity of teaching to others what he did not know himself."

After five years spent mostly wandering in Europe, Beckett settled in Paris. In 1938 he published Murphy, *his first novel, a grotesque portrait of a man steadily dissolving his ties with humankind as he turns to contemplate the "closed system" of his own inner world. During the Second World War Beckett chose to remain in Paris, and, during the German occupation, fought for the French underground forces. After the Nazis captured his comrades, he escaped to the south where he worked as a farm laborer. With the liberation of France he served in an Irish Red Cross unit and was eventually decorated for his activities.*

After the war Beckett wrote a trilogy of novels that elaborate upon the themes of Murphy. *By this time he had adopted French as his language in composition, later translating each work into English. It was a play,* Waiting for Godot *(1954), that brought Beckett public recognition—and, often, hostility. The play shows two awkward, bickering tramps waiting on a bare stage for Godot. A boy enters to say that Godot is not coming that day but will come the next. All the two tramps can do is wait, knowing they have kept their appointment; the audience can only speculate as to the identity of the unexplained Godot, who, of course, never arrives: Is Godot God? Despite the painful obscurity of expression and the silences employed by Beckett, the weight of meaning in his works is always intense—a feat that helped to gain him the Nobel Prize for Literature in 1969. Having no taste for what he considers the absurdity of fame, he chose not to go to Stockholm to accept the prize.*

"Act Without Words I: A Mime for One Player" (1958), is reprinted here in its entirety. It is in the form of a series of stage directions and reflects Beckett's increasing movement toward silence in the years after Godot. *In an absurd world, speech becomes difficult as communication between humans seems ever more futile. The self-absorbed immobility into which Beckett's player is finally reduced represents the sort of peace that comes from renunciation of all desires (whose fulfillment is not possible) and a recognition that nothingness is the only reality.*

Desert. Dazzling light.
The man is flung backwards on stage from right wing. He falls, gets up immediately, dusts himself, turns aside, reflects.

Whistle from right wing.

He reflects, goes out right.

Immediately flung back on stage he falls, gets up immediately, dusts himself, turns aside, reflects.

Whistle from left wing.

He reflects, goes out left.

Immediately flung back on stage he falls, gets up immediately, dusts himself, turns aside, reflects.

Whistle from left wing.

He reflects, goes towards left wing, hesitates, thinks better of it, halts, turns aside, reflects.

A little tree descends from flies,* lands. It has a single bough some three yards from ground and at its summit a meagre tuft of palms casting at its foot a circle of shadow.

He continues to reflect.

Whistle from above.

He turns, sees tree, reflects, goes to it, sits down in its shadow, looks at his hands.

A pair of tailor's scissors descends from flies, comes to rest before tree, a yard from ground.

He continues to look at his hands.

Whistle from above.

He looks up, sees scissors, takes them and starts to trim his nails.

The palms close like a parasol, the shadow disappears.

He drops scissors, reflects.

A tiny carafe, to which is attached a huge label inscribed WATER, descends from flies, comes to rest some three yards from ground.

He continues to reflect.

Whistle from above.

He looks up, sees carafe, reflects, gets up, goes and stands under it, tries in vain to reach it, renounces, turns aside, reflects.

A big cube descends from flies, lands.

He continues to reflect.

Whistle from above.

He turns, sees cube, looks at it, at carafe, reflects, goes to cube, tests its stability, gets up on it, tries in vain to reach carafe, renounces, gets down, carries cube back to its place, turns aside, reflects.

* The space above the stage and out of sight of the audience.

A second smaller cube descends from flies, lands.

He continues to reflect.

Whistle from above.

He turns, sees second cube, looks at it, at carafe, goes to second cube, takes it up, carries it over and sets it down under carafe, tests its stability, gets up on it, tries in vain to reach carafe, renounces, gets down, takes up second cube to carry it back to its place, hesitates, thinks better of it, sets it down, goes to big cube, takes it up, carries it over and puts it on small one, tests their stability, gets up on them, the cubes collapse, he falls, gets up immediately, brushes himself, reflects.

He takes up small cube, puts it on big one, tests their stability, gets up on them and is about to reach carafe when it is pulled up a little way and comes to rest beyond his reach.

He gets down, reflects, carries cubes back to their place, one by one, turns aside, reflects.

A third still smaller cube descends from flies, lands.

He continues to reflect.

Whistle from above.

He turns, sees third cube, looks at it, reflects, turns aside, reflects.

The third cube is pulled up and disappears in flies.

Beside carafe a rope descends from flies, with knots to facilitate ascent.

He continues to reflect.

Whistle from above.

He turns, sees rope, reflects, goes to it, climbs up it and is about to reach carafe when rope is let out and deposits him back on ground.

He reflects, looks round for scissors, sees them, goes and picks them up, returns to rope and starts to cut it with scissors.

The rope is pulled up, lifts him off ground, he hangs on, succeeds in cutting rope, falls back on ground, drops scissors, falls, gets up again immediately, brushes himself, reflects.

The rope is pulled up quickly and disappears in flies.

With length of rope in his possession he makes a lasso with which he tries to lasso the carafe.

The carafe is pulled up quickly and disappears in flies.

He turns aside, reflects.

He goes with lasso in his hand to tree, looks at bough, turns and looks at cubes, looks again at bough, drops lasso, goes to cubes, takes up small one, carries it over and sets it down under bough, goes back for big one, takes it up and carries it over under bough, makes to put it on small one, hesitates, thinks better of it, sets it down, takes up small one and puts it on big one, tests their stability, turns aside and stoops to pick up lasso.

The bough folds down against trunk.

He straightens up with lasso in his hand, turns and sees what has happened.

He drops lasso, turns aside, reflects.

He carries back cubes to their place, one by one, goes back for lasso, carries it over to the cubes and lays it in a neat coil on small one.

He turns aside, reflects.

Whistle from right wing.

He reflects, goes out right.

Immediately flung back on stage he falls, gets up immediately, brushes himself, turns aside, reflects.

Whistle from left wing.

He does not move.

He looks at his hands, looks around for scissors, sees them, goes and picks them up, starts to trim his nails, stops, reflects, runs his finger along blade of scissors, goes and lays them on small cube, turns aside, opens his collar, frees his neck and fingers it.

The small cube is pulled up and disappears in flies, carrying away rope and scissors.

He turns to take scissors, sees what has happened.

He turns aside, reflects.

He goes and sits down on big cube.

The big cube is pulled from under him. He falls. The big cube is pulled up and disappears in flies.

He remains lying on his side, his face towards auditorium, staring before him.

The carafe descends from flies and comes to rest a few feet from his body.

He does not move.

Whistle from above.

He does not move.

The carafe descends further, dangles and plays about his face.

He does not move.

The carafe is pulled up and disappears in flies.

The bough returns to horizontal, the palms open, the shadow returns.

Whistle from above.

He does not move.

The tree is pulled up and disappears in flies.

He looks at his hands.

CURTAIN

22

Joseph Heller

Something Happened

❋

*The most popular novel of the early 1960s was a "novel of the absurd"
about the Second World War,* Catch–22 *(1961), by Joseph Heller
(1923–   ). Its anti-hero, a physically and emotionally exhausted Air
Force captain named Yossarian, tries desperately to get out of combat; but a
mysterious military principle, "Catch–22," always seems to prevent his release. For example, it turns out that a man is considered to be insane if he
continues to fly hazardous combat missions beyond a normal "tour of duty,"
but he must, nevertheless, put in a formal request to be relieved from such
missions. The act of making the request, however, indicates that the man is
sane and therefore ineligible to be relieved on account of insanity.*

    Heller's second novel, Something Happened *(1974), the source of the
following selection, shows Yossarian's middle-class generation a decade after
the war. The wild hilarity of the earlier book has been replaced by an overwhelming sense of boredom and inadequacy, a symptom of the spiritual
rootlessness of "nice people."*

    *Heller was born in Brooklyn, New York, and flew sixty combat missions
over Italy during the Second World War. As a veteran, he went to college at
government expense, earning a bachelor's degree in English from New York
University in 1948 and then a master's degree from Columbia University.
During 1949 and 1950 he attended Oxford University as a Fulbright
Scholar, and during the following two years was an instructor of freshman
composition at Pennsylvania State University. Leaving the campus environment, Heller worked for nine years, while writing* Catch–22, *as an adver-*

tising writer and promotion manager for various magazines, including Time. (*He has said that the office and personnel material in* Something Happened *is based on his experience at* Time.) *Since the success of his first novel he has taught creative writing at various universities, including Yale, Pennsylvania, and the City College of New York.*

In the selection from Something Happened *we see the pecking order of fear among minor executives and the general feeling of disillusionment in their personal lives. Also present is a sense of the madness beneath the bland business-like surface. The narrator is reminiscent of Beckett's silent player in "Act Without Words," * suggesting a similar reduction to spiritual inertia and erosion of a sense of selfhood.*

THE OFFICE IN WHICH I WORK

In the office in which I work there are five people of whom I am afraid. Each of these five people is afraid of four people (excluding overlaps), for a total of twenty, and each of these twenty people is afraid of six people, making a total of one hundred and twenty people who are feared by at least one person. Each of these one hundred and twenty people is afraid of the other one hundred and nineteen, and all of these one hundred and forty-five people are afraid of the twelve men at the top who helped found and build the company and now own and direct it.

All these twelve men are elderly now and drained by time and success of energy and ambition. Many have spent their whole lives here. They seem friendly, slow, and content when I come upon them in the halls (they seem dead) and are always courteous and mute when they ride with others in the public elevators. They no longer work hard. They hold meetings, make promotions, and allow their names to be used on announcements that are prepared and issued by somebody else. Nobody is sure anymore who really runs the company (not even the people who are credited with running it), but the company does run. Sometimes these twelve men at the top work for the government for a little while. They don't seem interested in doing

*See selection 21.

much more. Two of them know what I do and recognize me, because I have helped them in the past, and they have been kind enough to remember me, although not, I'm sure, by name. They inevitably smile when they see me and say: "How are you?" (I inevitably nod and respond: "Fine.") Since I have little contact with these twelve men at the top and see them seldom, I am not really afraid of them. But most of the people I am afraid of in the company are.

Just about everybody in the company is afraid of somebody else in the company, and I sometimes think I am a cowering boy back in the automobile casualty insurance company for which I used to work very long ago, sorting and filing automobile accident reports after Mrs. Yerger was placed in charge of the file room and kept threatening daily to fire us all. She was a positive, large woman of overbearing confidence and nasty amiability who never doubted the wisdom of her biases. A witty older girl named Virginia sat under a big Western Union clock in that office and traded dirty jokes with me ("My name's Virginia—Virgin for short, but not for long, ha ha."); she was peppy and direct, always laughing and teasing (with me, anyway), and I was too young and dumb then to see that she wasn't just joking. (Good God—she used to ask me to get a room for us somewhere, and I didn't even know how! She was extremely pretty, I think now, although I'm not sure I thought so then, but I did like her, and she got me hot. Her father had killed himself a few years before.) Much went on there in that company too that I didn't know about. (Virginia herself had told me that one of the married claims adjusters had taken her out in his car one night, turned insistent, and threatened to rape her or put her out near a cemetery, until she pretended to start to cry.) I was afraid to open doors in that company too, I remember, even when I had been sent for by one of the lawyers or adjusters to bring in an important file or a sandwich. I was never sure whether to knock or walk right in, to tap deferentially or rap loudly enough to be heard at once and command admission. Either way, I would often encounter expressions of annoyance and impatience (or feel I did. I had arrived too soon or arrived too late).

Mrs. Yerger bullied us all. In a little while, nearly all of the file clerks quit, a few of the older ones to go into the army or navy, the rest of us for better jobs. I left for a job that turned out to be worse. It took nerve to give notice I was quitting, and it always has. (I rehearsed my resignation speech for days, building up the courage to deliver it, and formulated earnest, self-righteous answers to accusing questions about my reasons for leaving that neither Mrs. Yerger nor anyone else even bothered to ask.) I have this thing about authority, about walking right up to it and looking it squarely in the eye, about speaking right out to it bravely and defiantly, even when I know I am right and safe. (I can never make myself believe I *am* safe.) I just don't trust it.

That was my first job after graduating (or being graduated *from*) high school. I was seventeen then—that "older," witty, flirting girl under the Western Union clock, Virginia, was only twenty-one (too young now by at least a year or two, even for me)—and in every job I've had since, I've always been afraid I was about to be fired. Actually, I have never been fired from a job; instead, I receive generous raises and rapid promotions, because I am usually very alert (at the beginning) and grasp things quickly. But this feeling of failure, this depressing sense of imminent catastrophe and public shame, persists even here, where I do good work steadily and try to make no enemies. It's just that I find it impossible to know exactly what is going on behind the closed doors of all the offices on all the floors occupied by all the people in this and all the other companies in the whole world who might say or do something, intentionally or circumstantially, that could bring me to ruin. I even torture myself at times with the ominous speculation that the CIA, FBI, or Internal Revenue Service has been investigating me surreptitiously for years and is about to close in and arrest me, for no other reason than that I have some secret liberal sympathies and usually vote Democratic.

I have a feeling that someone nearby is soon going to find out something about me that will mean the end, although I can't imagine what that something is.

In the normal course of a business day, I fear Green and Green fears me. I am afraid of Jack Green because my department is part of his department and Jack Green is my boss; Green is afraid of me because most of the work in my department is done for the Sales Department, which is more important than his department, and I am much closer to Andy Kagle and the other people in the Sales Department than he is.

Green distrusts me fitfully. He makes it clear to me every now and then that he wishes to see everything coming out of my department before it is shown to other departments. I know he does not really mean this: he is too busy with his own work to pay that much attention to all of mine, and I will bypass him on most of our assignments rather than take up his time and delay their delivery to people who have (or think they have) an immediate need for them. Most of the work we do in my department is, in the long run, trivial. But Green always grows alarmed when someone from another department praises something that has come from my department. He turns scarlet with rage and embarrassment if he has not seen or heard of it. (He is no less splenetic if he *has* seen it and fails to remember it.)

The men in the Sales Department like me (or pretend to). They don't like Green. He knows this. They complain about him to me and make uncomplimentary remarks, and he knows this too. He pretends he doesn't. He feigns indifference, since he doesn't really like the men in the Sales Department. I don't really like them, either (but I pretend I do). Generally, Green makes no effort to get along with the men in the Sales Department and is pointedly aloof and disdainful. He worries, though, about the enmity he creates there. Green worries painfully that someday soon the Corporate-Operations Department will take my department away from his department and give it to the Sales Department. Green has been worrying about this for eighteen years.

In my department, there are six people who are afraid of me, and one small secretary who is afraid of all of us. I have one other person working for me who is not afraid of anyone, not even me, and I would fire him quickly, but I'm afraid of him. . . .

The company is benevolent. The people, for the most part, are nice, and the atmosphere, for the most part, is convivial. The decor of the offices, particularly in the reception rooms and anterooms, is bright and colorful. There is lots of orange and lots of sea green. There are lots of office parties. We get all legal holidays off and take days off with pay whenever we need them. We have many three- and four-day weekends. (I can't face these long weekends anymore and don't know how I survive them. I may have to take up skiing.)

Every two weeks we are paid with machine-processed checks manufactured out of stiff paper (they are not thick enough to be called cardboard) that are patterned precisely with neat, rectangular holes and words of formal, official warning in small, block letters that the checks must not be spindled, torn, defaced, stapled, or mutilated in any other way. (They must only be cashed.) If not for these words, it would never occur to me to do anything else with my check but deposit it. Now, though, I am occasionally intrigued. What would happen, I speculate gloomily every two weeks or so as I tear open the blank, buff pay envelope and stare dully at the holes and numbers and words on my punched-card paycheck as though hoping disappointedly for some large, unrectifiable mistake in my favor, if I did spindle, fold, tear, deface, staple, and mutilate it? (It's my paycheck, isn't it? Or is it?) What would happen if, deliberately, calmly, with malice aforethought and obvious premeditation, I disobeyed?

I know what would happen: nothing. Nothing would happen. And the knowledge depresses me. Some girl downstairs I never saw before (probably with a bad skin also) would simply touch a few keys on some kind of steel key punch that would set things right again, and it would be as though I had not disobeyed at all. My act of rebellion would be absorbed like rain on an ocean and leave no trace. I would not cause a ripple.

I suppose it is just about impossible for someone like me to rebel anymore and produce any kind of lasting effect. I have lost the power to upset things that I had as a child; I can no longer change my environment or even disturb it seriously. They would simply fire and forget me as soon as I tried. They would file me away. That's what will happen to Martha the typist when she finally goes crazy. She'll be fired and forgotten. She'll be filed away. She'll be given sick pay, vacation pay, and severance pay. She'll be given money from the pension fund and money from the profit-sharing fund, and then all traces of her will be hidden safely out of sight inside some old green cabinet for dead records in another room on another floor or in a dusty warehouse somewhere that nobody visits more than once or twice a year and few people in the company even know exists; not unlike the old green cabinets of dead records in all those accident folders in the storage room on the floor below the main offices of the automobile casualty insurance company for which I used to work when I was just a kid. When she goes crazy, her case will be closed.

I had never imagined so many dead records as I saw in that storage room (and there were thousands and thousands of even deader records at the warehouse I had to go to once or twice a year when a question arose concerning a record that had been dead a really long time). I remember them accurately, I remember the garish look of the data in grotesquely blue ink on the outside of each folder: a number, a name, an address, a date, and an abbreviated indication of whether the accident involved damage to property only (PD) or damage to people (PI, for personal injury). Often, I would bring sandwiches from home (baloney, cooked chopped meat with lots of ketchup, or tuna fish or canned salmon and tomato) and eat them in the storage room downstairs on my lunch hour, and if I ate there alone, I would read the New York *Mirror* (a newspaper now also dead) and then try to entertain myself by going through some old accident folders picked from the file cabinets at random. I was searching for action, tragedy, the high drama of detective work and courtroom suspense, but it was no use. They were dead. None of the names or appraisals or medical statements or investigations or eyewitness reports brought anything back to life. (The *Mirror* was better, and even its up-to-the-minute true stories of family and national misfortunes read just like the comic strips.) What impressed me most was the sheer immensity of all those dead records, the abounding quantity of all those drab old sagging cardboard file cabinets rising like joined, ageless towers from the floor almost to the ceiling, that vast, unending sequence of unconnected accidents that had been happening to people and cars long before I came to work there, were happening then, and are happening still.

There was a girl in that company too who went crazy while I was there. She was filed away. And in the company I worked for before this one, there was a man, a middle-minor executive, who went crazy and jumped out of a hotel window and killed himself; he left a note saying he was sorry he was jumping out of the hotel window and killing himself, that he would have shot himself instead but didn't know how to obtain a gun or use one. He was picked up off the ground by the police (probably) and filed away.

I think that maybe in every company today there is always at least one person who is going crazy slowly.

The company is having another banner year. It continues to grow, and in many respects we are the leader in the field. According to our latest Annual Report, it is bigger and better this year than it was last year.

We have twenty-nine offices now, twelve in this country, two in

Canada, four in Latin America, and eleven overseas. We used to have one in Cuba, but that was lost. We average three suicides a year: two men, usually on the middle-executive level, kill themselves every twelve months, almost always by gunshot, and one girl, usually unmarried, separated, or divorced, who generally does the job with sleeping pills. Salaries are high, vacations are long.

People in the company like to live well and are unusually susceptible to nervous breakdowns. They have good tastes and enjoy high standards of living. We are well-educated and far above average in abilities and intelligence. Everybody spends. Nobody saves. Nervous breakdowns are more difficult to keep track of than suicides because they are harder to recognize and easier to hush up. (A suicide, after all, is a suicide: there's something final about it. It's the last thing a person does. But who knows with certainty when a person is breaking down?) But nervous breakdowns do occur regularly in all age and occupational groups and among all kinds of people— thin people and fat people, tall people and short people, good people and bad people. In the few years I have been in charge of my department, one girl and one man here have each been out for extended absences because they broke down. Both have been fixed and are now back working for me, and not many people outside my department know why they were gone. (One of them, the man, hasn't been fixed too well, I think, and will probably break down again soon. He is already turning into a problem again, with me and with everyone else he talks to. He talks too much.)

In an average year, four people I know about in the company will die of natural causes and two-and-a-half more (two men one year, three the next) will go on sick leave for ailments that will eventually turn out to be cancer. Approximately two people will be killed in accidents every year, one in an auto, the other by fire or drowning. Nobody in the company has yet been killed in an airplane crash, and this is highly mysterious to me, for we travel a lot by air to visit other offices or call on customers, prospects, and suppliers in other cities and countries. When regular, full-time employees do go on sick leave, they are usually paid their full salary for as long as the illness lasts (even though it may last a lifetime. Ha, ha), for the company excels in this matter of employee benefits. Everybody is divorced (not me, though). Everyone drinks and takes two hours or more for lunch. The men all flirt. The women all respond, except for a few who are very religious or very dull, or a few very young ones who are out in the world for the first time and don't understand yet how things are.

Most of us like working here, even though we are afraid, and do not long to leave for jobs with other companies. We make money and have fun. We read books and go to plays. And somehow the time passes.

This fiscal period, I am flirting with Jane. Jane is new in the Art Department and not quite sure whether I mean it or not. She is just a few years out of college, where she majored in fine arts, and still finds things in the city daring, sophisticated, and intellectual. She goes to the movies a lot. She has not, I think, slept with a married man yet.

Jane is assistant head of the Art Department in Green's department. There are only three people in the Art Department. She has, like the rest of us, much time in which to brood and fantasize and make personal phone calls and kid around with whoever in the company (me) wants to kid around with her. She has a tall, slim figure that's pretty good and a clogged duct in one eye that maks it dribble with tears. She wears loose lamb's-wool sweaters that hug the long points of her small breasts beautifully. (Often, my fingertips would love to hug and roll those same long points of her small breasts just as beautifully, but I know from practice that my desire would not remain with her breasts for long. They make a convenient starting place.) Her good figure, prominent nipples, and clogged tear duct give me easy openings for suggestive wisecracks that cover the same ground as those I used to exchange with that older girl Virginia under that big Western Union clock in the automobile casualty insurance company (the company is still in business after all these years, at the same place, and probably the clock too is still there, running, although the office building is now slated to come down), except that now I am the older, more experienced (and more jaded) one and can control and direct things pretty much the way I choose. I have the feeling now that I can do whatever I want to with Jane, especially on days when she's had two vodka martinis for lunch instead of one (I, personally, hate vodka martinis and mistrust the mettle of people who drink them) or three whiskey sours instead of two. I could, if I wished, take her out for *three* vodka martinis after work one day and then up to Red Parker's apartment nearby, and the rest, I'd bet, would be as easy as pie (and possibly no more thrilling). I can make Jane laugh whenever I want to, and this, I know, can be worth more than half the game if I ever decide I seriously do want to play, but *I'm* not sure either whether I mean it or not.

Probably, I should be ashamed of myself, because she's only a decent young girl of twenty-four. Possibly I should be proud of myself, because she is, after all, a decent and very attractive young girl of only twenty-four whom I can probably lay whenever I want to. (I have her scheduled vaguely somewhere ahead, probably in the weeks before the convention, when I will be using everybody in the Art Department a great deal.) I don't really know how I am supposed to feel. I do know that girls in their early twenties are easy and sweet. (Girls in their late twenties are easier but sad, and that isn't so sweet.) They are easy, I think, because they are sweet, and they are sweet, I think, because they are dumb.

On days when *I've* had two martinis for lunch, Jane's breasts and legs can drive me almost wild as she parks her slender ass against the wall of one of the narrow corridors in the back offices near the Art Department when I stop to kid with her. Jane smiles a lot and is very innocent (she thinks I'm a very nice man, for example), although she is not, of course, without some sex experience, about which she boasts laughingly when I taunt her with being a virgin and denies laughingly when I taunt her with being a whore. I make teasing, rather mechanical and juvenile jokes (I've made them all before to other girls and ladies in one variation or another) about her eye or sweater or the good or bad life I pretend she is leading as I lean down almost slavering toward the front of her skirt (I don't know how she can bear me in these disgusting moments—but she can) and gaze lecherously over the long stretch of her thighs underneath, even though I know already I would probably find her legs a little thin when I had her undressed and would probably describe her as a bit too skinny if I ever spoke about her afterward to anyone.

I think I really do like Jane a lot. She is cheerful, open, trusting, optimistic—and I don't meet many of *those* anymore. Till now, I've decided to do nothing with her except continue the lascivious banter between us that tickles and amuses and encourages us both. Maybe her face and her figure are a little too good. I used to like girls who were tall and heavy, and slightly coarse, and maybe I still do, but I seem to be doing most of my sleeping these days with girls who are slim and pretty and mostly young. My wife is tall and slim and used to be very pretty when she was young.

The people in the company who are most afraid of most people are the salesmen. They live and work under pressure that is extraordinary. (I would not be able to stand it.) When things are bad, they are worse for the salesmen; when things are good, they are not much better.

They are always on trial, always on the verge of failure, collectively and individually. They strain, even the most secure and self-assured of them, to look good on paper; and there is much paper for them to look good on. Each week, for example, a record of the sales results of the preceding week for each sales office and for the Sales Department as a whole for each division of the company is kept and compared to the sales results for the corresponding week of the year before; the figures are photocopied on the latest photocopying machines and distributed throughout the company to all the people and departments whose work is related to selling. In addition to this, the sales record for each sales office for each quarter of each year for each division of the company and for the company as a whole is tabulated and compared to the sales record for the corresponding quarter of the year before; along with this, cumulative quarterly sales totals are also kept, and all these quarterly sales totals are photocopied and distributed too. In addition to this, quarterly and cumulative sales totals are compared with quarterly and cumulative sales totals * (* estimated) of other companies in the same field, and these figures are photocopied and distributed too. The figures are tabulated in stacks and layers of parallel lines and columns for snap comparisons and judgments by anyone whose eyes fall upon them. The result of all this photocopying and distributing is that there is almost continuous public scrutiny and discussion throughout the company of how well or poorly the salesmen in each sales office of each division of the company are doing at any given time.

When salesmen are doing well, there is pressure upon them to begin doing better, for fear they may start doing worse. When they are doing poorly, they are doing terribly. When a salesman lands a large order or brings in an important new account, his elation is brief, for there is danger he might lose that large order or important new account to a salesman from a competing company (or from a competing division of this company, which shows how complex and orderly the company has become) the next time around. It might even be canceled before it is filled, in which case no one is certain if anything was gained or lost. So there is crisis and alarm even in their triumphs.

Nevertheless, the salesmen love their work and would not choose any other kind. They are a vigorous, fun-loving bunch when they are not suffering abdominal cramps or brooding miserably about the future; on the other hand, they often turn cranky without warning and complain and bicker a lot. Some sulk, some bully; some bully and then sulk. All of them drink heavily until they get hepatitis or heart attacks or are warned away from heavy drinking for some other reason, and all of them, sooner or later, begin to feel they are being picked on and blamed unfairly. Each of them can name at least one superior in the company who he feels has a grudge against him and is determined to wreck his career.

The salesmen work hard and earn big salaries, with large personal expense accounts that they squander generously on other people in and out of the company, including me. They own good houses in good communities and play good games of golf on good private golf courses. The company encourages this. The company, in fact, will pay for their country club membership and all charges they incur there, if the club they get into is a good one. The company seeks and rewards salesmen who make a good impression on the golf course.

Unmarried men are not wanted in the Sales Department, not even widowers, for the company has learned from experience that it is difficult and dangerous for unmarried salesmen to mix socially with prominent executives and their wives or participate with them in responsible civic affairs. (Too many of the wives of these prominent and very successful men are no more satisfied with their marital situation than are their husbands.) If a salesman's wife dies and he is not ready to remarry, he is usually moved into an administrative position after several months of mourning. Bachelors are never hired for the sales force, and salesmen who get divorced, or whose wives die, know they had better remarry or begin looking ahead toward a different job.

(Red Parker has been a widower too long and is getting into trouble for that and for his excessive drinking. He is having too good a time.)

Strangely enough, the salesmen, who are aggressive, egotistical, and individualistic by nature, react very well to the constant pressure and rigid supervision to which they are subjected. They are stimulated and motivated by discipline and direction. They thrive on explicit guidance toward clear objectives. (This may be one reason golf appeals to them.) For the most part, they are cheerful, confident, and gregarious when they are not irritable, anxious, and depressed. There must be something in the makeup of a man that enables him not only to *be* a salesman, but to *want* to be one. Ours actually *enjoy* selling, although there seem to be many among them who suffer from colitis, hernia, hemorrhoids, and chronic diarrhea (I have one hemorrhoid, and that one comes and goes as it pleases and is no bother to me at all, now that I've been to a doctor and made sure it isn't cancer), not to mention the frequent breakdowns from tension and overwork that occur in the Sales Department as well as in other departments, and the occasional suicide that pops up among the salesmen about once every two years.

The salesmen are proud of their position and of the status and importance they enjoy within the company, for the function of my department, and of most other departments, is to help the salesmen sell. The company exists to sell. That's the reason we were hired, and the reason we are paid.

The people in the company who are least afraid are the few in our small Market Research Department, who believe in nothing and are concerned with collecting, organizing, interpreting, and reorganizing statistical information about the public, the market, the country, and the world. For one thing, their salaries are small, and they know they will not have much trouble finding jobs paying just as little in other companies if they lose their jobs here. Their budget, too, is small, for they are no longer permitted to undertake large projects.

Most of the information we use now is obtained free from trade associations, the U.S. Census Bureau, the Department of Commerce, the U.S. Chamber of Commerce, the National Association of Manufacturers, and the Pentagon, and there is no way of knowing anymore whether the information on which we base our own information for distribution is true or false. But that doesn't seem to matter; all that does matter is that the information come from a reputable source. People in the Market Research Department are never held to blame for conditions they discover outside the company that place us at a competitive disadvantage. What is, is—and they are not expected to change reality but merely to find it if they can and suggest ingenious ways of disguising it. To a great extent, that is the nature of my own work, and all of us under Green work closely with the Sales Department and the Public Relations Department in converting whole truths into half truths and half truths into whole ones.

I am very good with these techniques of deception, although I am not always able anymore to deceive myself (if I were, I would not know that, would I? Ha, ha). In fact, I am continually astonished by people in the company who do fall victim to their own (our own) propaganda. There are so many now who actually believe that what we do is really important. This happens not only to salesmen, who repeat their various sales pitches aloud so often that they acquire the logic and authority of a mumbo-jumbo creed, but to the shrewd, capable executives in top management, who have access to all data and ought to know better. It happens to people on my own level and lower. It happens to just about everybody in the company who graduated from a good business school with honors: these are uniformly the most competent and conscientious people in the company, and also the most gullible and naïve. Every time we launch a new advertising campaign, for example, people inside the company are the first ones to be taken in by it. Every time we introduce a new product, or an old product with a different cover, color, and name that we present as new, people inside the company are the first to rush to buy it—even when it's no good.

When salesmen and company spokesmen begin believing their own arguments, the result is not always bad, for they develop an outlook of loyalty, zeal, and conviction that is often remarkably persuasive in itself. It produces that kind of dedication and fanaticism that makes good citizens and good employees. When it happens to a person in my own department, however, the result can be disastrous, for he begins relying too heavily on what he now thinks is the truth and loses his talent for devising good lies. He is no longer convincing. It's exactly what happened to Holloway, the man in my own department who broke down (and is probably going to break down again soon).

"But it's true, don't you see?" he would argue softly to the salesmen, the secretaries, and even to me, with a knowing and indulgent smile, as though what he was saying ought to have been as obvious to everyone as it was to him. "We *are* the best." (The point he missed is that it didn't matter whether it was true or not; what mattered was what people *thought* was true.)

He is beginning to smile and argue that way again and to spend more time talking to us than we want to spend listening to him. My own wish when he is buttonholing me or bending the ear of someone else in my department is that he would hurry up and have his nervous breakdown already, if he is going to have one anyway, and get it—and himself—out of the way. He is the only one who talks to Martha, our typist who is going crazy, and she is the only one who listens to him without restlessness and irritation. She listens to him with great intensity because she is paying no attention to him at all.

Everyone grew impatient with him. And he lost his power to understand (as he is losing this power again) why the salesmen, who would come to him for solid proof to support their exaggerations and misrepresentations, turned skeptical, began to avoid him, and refused to depend on him any longer or even take him to lunch. He actually expected them to get by with only the "truth."

It's a wise person, I guess, who knows he's dumb, and an honest person who knows he's a liar. And it's a dumb person, I guess, who's convinced he is wise, I conclude to myself (wisely), as we wise grown-ups here at the company go gliding in and out all day long, scaring each other at our desks and cubicles and water coolers and trying to evade the people who frighten us. We come to work, have lunch, and go home. We goose-step in and goose-step out, change our partners and wander all about, sashay around for a pat on the head, and promenade home till we all drop dead. Really, I ask myself every now and then, depending on how well or poorly things are going with Green at the office or at home with my wife, or with my retarded son, or with my other son, or my daughter, or the colored maid, or the nurse for my retarded son, is this *all* there is for me to do? Is this really the *most* I can get from the few years left in this one life of mine?

And the answer I get, of course, is always . . . *YES!*

* * *

MY WIFE IS UNHAPPY

My wife is unhappy. She is one of those married women who are very, very bored and lonely, and I don't know what I can make myself do about it (except get a divorce, and make her unhappier still. I was with a married woman not long ago who told me she felt so lonely at times she turned ice cold and was literally afraid she was freezing to death from inside, and I believe I know what she meant).

My wife is a good person, really, or used to be, and sometimes I'm sorry for her. She drinks now during the day and flirts, or tries to, at parties we go to in the evening, although she really doesn't know how. (She is very bad at flirting—poor thing.) She is not a joyful woman, except on special occasions, and usually when she is at least a little bit high on wine or whiskey. (We don't get along well.) She thinks she has gotten older, heavier, and less attractive than she used to be—and, of course, she is right. She thinks it matters to me, and there she is wrong. I don't think I mind. (If she knew I didn't mind, she'd probably be even more unhappy.) My wife is not bad looking; she's tall, dresses well, and has a good figure, and I'm often proud to have her with me. (She thinks I *never* want her with me.) She thinks I do not love her anymore, and she may be right about that, too.

"You were with Andy Kagle today," she says.

"How can you tell?"

"You're walking with a limp."

There is this wretched habit I have of acquiring the characteristics of other people. I acquire these characteristics indiscriminately, even from people I don't like. If I am with someone who talks loud and fast and assertively, I will begin talking loud and fast right along with him (but by no means always assertively). If I am with someone who drawls lazily and is from the South or West, I will drawl lazily too and begin speaking almost as though I were from the South or West, employing authentic regional idioms as though they were part of my own upbringing, and not of someone else's.

I do not do this voluntarily. It's a weakness, I know, a failure of character or morals, this subtle, sneaky, almost enslaving instinct to be like just about anyone I happen to find myself with. It happens not only in matters of speech, but with physical actions as well, in ways I walk or sit or tilt my head or place my arms or hands. (Often, I am struck with fear that someone I am with will think I am aping him deliberately in order to ridicule and insult him. I try my best to keep this tendency under control.) It operates unconsciously (subconsciously?), whether I am sober or intoxicated (generally, I am a happy, pleasant, humorous drunk), with a determination of its own, in spite of my vigilance and aversion, and usually I do not realize I have slipped into someone else's personality until I am already there. (My wife tells me that at movies now, particularly comedies, I mug and gesticulate right along with the people on the screen, and I cannot say she is wrong.)

If I am lunching or having cocktails after work with Johnny Brown (God's angry man, by nature and coincidence), I will swear and complain a lot and talk and feel tough and strong. If I am with Arthur Baron, I will speak slowly and softly and intelligently and feel gentle and astute and dignified and refined, not only for the time I am with him but for a while afterward; his nature will be my nature until I come up against the next person who has more powerful personality traits than any of my own, or a more formidable business or social position. (When I am with Green, though, I do not feel graceful and articulate; I feel clumsy and incompetent—until I am away from him, and then I am apt to begin searching about for glib epigrams to use in my conversations with somebody else.) I often wonder what my own true nature is.

Do I have one?

I always dress well. But no matter what I put on, I always have the disquieting sensation that I am copying somebody; I can always remind myself of somebody else I know who dresses much that same way. I often feel, therefore, that my clothes are not my own. (There are times, in fact, when I open one of my closet doors and am struck with astonishment by the clothes I find hanging inside. They are all mine, of course, but, for a moment, it's as though I had never seen many of them before.) And I sometimes feel that I would not spend so much time and money and energy chasing around after girls and other women if I were not so frequently in the company of other men who do, or talk as though they wanted to. I'm still not sure it's all that much fun (although I *am* sure it's an awful lot of trouble). And if I'm not sure by now, I know I never will be.

If I argue with someone who stammers badly, I am in serious trouble; for I have a slight stammer of my own at times and the conversation soon threatens to disintegrate hopelessly into bursts of meaningless syllables. I am in absolute dread of talking to people who stutter; I have a deathly fear I will want to stutter too, will be lost for life if I ever have to watch the mouth of someone who stutters for more than a sentence or two; when I am with a stutterer, I can, if I let myself, almost feel a delicious, tantalizing quiver take shape and grow in both my lips and strive to break free and go permanently out of control. I am not comfortable in the presence of homosexuals, and I suspect it may be for the same reason (I might be tempted to become like them). I steer clear of people with tics, squints, and facial twitches; these are additional characteristics I *don't* want to acquire. The problem is that I don't know who or what I really am.

If I am with people who are obscene, I am obscene.

Who am I? (I'll need three guesses.)

My daughter is not obscene, but her speech is dirty now when she talks to her friends and growing dirty also when she talks to us. (*I talk dirty too.*) She is trying to establish some position with us or provoke some reaction, but my wife and I don't know what or why. She wants to become a part too, I guess, of what she sees is her environment, and she is, I fear, already merging with, dissolving into, her surroundings right before my eyes. She wants to be like other people her age. I cannot stop her; I cannot save her. Something happened to her, too, although I don't know what or when. She is not yet sixteen, and I think she is already lost. Her uniqueness is fading. As a child, she seemed to us to be so different from all other children. She does not seem so different anymore.

Who is she?

It amuses me in a discouraging way to know I borrow adjectives, nouns, verbs, and short phrases from people I am with and frequently find myself trapped inside their smaller vocabularies like a hamster in a cage. Their language becomes my language. My own vocabulary fails me (if it is indeed mine), and I am at a loss to supply even perfectly familiar synonyms. Rather than grope for words of my own, I fasten upon their words and carry their phraseologies away with me for use in subsequent conversations (even though the dialogue I steal may not be first rate).

If I talk to a Negro (*spade,* if I've been talking to a honky who calls a spade a spade), I will, if I am not on guard, begin using not only his vernacular (militant hip or bucolic Uncle Tom), but his pronunciation. I do the same thing with Puerto Rican cabdrivers; if I talk to cabdrivers at all (I try not to; I can't stand the whining malevolence of New York cabdrivers, *except* for the Puerto Ricans), it will be on their level rather than mine. (I don't know what *my* level is, ha, ha.) And the same thing happens when I talk to boys and girls of high school and college age; I bridge the generation gap; I copy them: I employ their argot and display an identification with their tastes and outlooks that I do not always feel. I used to think I was doing it to be charming; now I know I have no choice. (Most of my daughter's friends, particularly her girl friends, like me and look up to me; she doesn't.)

If I'm with Andy Kagle, I will limp.

"You were with Andy Kagle today," my wife says.

We are in the kitchen.

I have indeed been with Andy Kagle; I stop walking with Andy Kagle's limp; and I consider prudently if I have not been talking to my wife in a Spanish accent as well, for the girls Kagle and I were with this time were both Cuban and unattractive. They were prostitutes. Nobody likes to call a prostitute a prostitute anymore (least of all me. They are *hookers, hustlers,* and *call girls*), but that's what they were. Prostitutes. And I have taken the high-minded vow again (even as I was zipping up my pants and getting back into my undershirt, which smelled already under the sleeves from the morning's output of perspiration) that from this day forward, I am simply *not* going to make love anymore to girls I don't like.

We have done better with our whores, Kagle and I, than we have done this afternoon, and we have also done worse. Mine was the better looking of the two (Kagle always wants me to take the better looking of the two), with bleached red hair and black roots. She was not well-educated; but her skin was smooth (no pimples, cysts, or sores), and her clothes were neat. Her nature was gentle, her manner tender. She wanted to save up enough money to open a beauty parlor. She was friendly and obliging (they aren't always), and wanted to please me.

"Do you like to be teased?" she asked me softly.

When Kagle cannot run away from his home and the office by going on a business trip (like the one to Denver he has just got back from), he likes to run away to New York whores in dark hotels or walk-up efficiency apartments with thin walls. He asks me to accompany him. I always refuse. "Oh, come on," he says. And I always go.

I don't enjoy it. (Although I definitely do enjoy my sessions with one of those extraordinary, two-hundred-dollar call girls that are sent my way as a gift every now and then by one of the suppliers I buy from. I tell Kagle about these; all he does is smile. I don't believe he wants a pretty girl in a lovely apartment. I think he wants a whore.) I feel unclean. (I am inevitably repelled by the odor of my undershirt when I put it back on, even though it is my own odor and usually slight. On days when I don't wear an undershirt, the smell is there in my shirt, faint but unmistakable, even if I've used a deodorant. The smell is me—I?—and I guess I can't get away from myself for very long.) I know there is something unholy, something corrupt and definitely passé, about grown men, successful executives like Kagle and me, going cold sober to ordinary whores in our own home town. They aren't pretty or necessary, and they aren't much fun. I don't think Kagle enjoys it, either; we have never gone back to the same girls (although we *have* gone back to the same sleazy hotels).

Kagle always pays and charges it to the company as a legitimate business expense. (One of the things I do enjoy is the idea of fucking the company at the same time.) I pay for the taxi sometimes and buy the bottle of whiskey he likes to bring along. Once I'm there I'm all right (I fit right in); but once I finish, I want to be gone. Generally, I'm ready to leave before he is and depart alone. Kagle hates to go home (even more than I do). If things are going smoothly for him (they don't always, because of his bad leg), I leave him there with his whiskey and his whore. I never really want to go with him at all. He asks. And I do.

I began biting my fingernails pretty much that same way, because someone asked me to. (Lord knows, it wasn't *my* idea. I didn't even know people did such things. And I don't think I was inventive enough to come upon the habit on my own.) I was in the second half of my first year in elementary school, seven years old and already fatherless. (I don't remember much about my father. I did not grieve for him when he died; I acted as though he had not gone, which meant I had to act as though he had not been. I didn't miss him, since I didn't remember him, and I've never thought about him much. Till times like now.) All of my friends in the first grade (I had many friends in the first grade; I have always worked hard to be popular and I have always succeeded) began to bite their fingernails the same week, for no better purpose than to exasperate the teacher (Miss Lamb; in the second grade, it was Mrs. Wolf. I have an uncanny memory for names and similar petty details) and their parents and older sisters. (It originated as a childhood conspiracy.)

"C'mon, bite your nails," they told me.

So I did. I began biting my nails. In a little while, they all stopped. But I didn't. (They grew up and went away, leaving their bad habit with me.) I didn't even try (I know now that I didn't try to stop because I didn't want to and because I understood even then that I would not be able to). And for all these years since, I have been nibbling and gnawing away aggressively, swinishly, and vengefully at my own fingertips, obtaining an enormous satisfaction from these small assaults. (It's not so much a habit, of course, as a compulsion, vicious, uncouth, and frequently painful, but I like it. And I don't think, at this stage, that I would want to live without it, and nobody has been able to tell me why.) And I know now that I will continue chewing away at my fingernails and my surrounding flesh until I die (or until I have all my teeth pulled and am no longer able to. Ha, ha).

·   ·   ·

I'm sorry my wife drinks now in the afternoon, and perhaps takes a drink or two in the morning as well. I try not to say anything to her about it. That would be humiliating, and I would not want her to fear I was going to start bullying her about that, too. Usually, she will use some offhand way of informing me she's had a little something to drink that afternoon; she met her sister, or the wife of somebody, for lunch or fabric-shopping and had a cocktail or double scotch before coming home, or, as she did just now, she has been cooking with wine. Sometimes she will want to tell me but wait too long and won't, and I will have the feeling then that she is trembling inside herself, wondering if I have noticed and will criticize. (My wife is afraid of me; I don't particularly want her that way, but it makes things easier.) At times I pity her.

She has never been drunk in the daytime (she does get drunk at parties and have a good time—although never at any of our own. My wife is a superior hostess), and neither of the children has ever remarked about her drinking at home during the day, so it may be that she has not let them notice. But I remember that she never used to drink at all; I remember that she never used to flirt. (She never used to swear.) And she is still religious; she goes to church most Sundays and tries to make the rest of us go too. (None of us want to. Once in a while we will, when I decide it's a small enough way of paying her a favor we owe. She isn't quite sure about the minister we have now, and neither am I.)

My wife is also starting to learn how to use dirty words (in much the same self-conscious way other women take up painting at an advanced age or enroll in adult education courses in psychology, art history, or Jean Paul Sartre). She is not much good at that, either. Her *hell*'s and *damn*'s carry too much emphasis, although her *Oh shit*'s have the ring of authority by now. She is not as convincing as the rest of the men and women in our several social groups in the jaded indifference we affect toward obscenity. My fifteen-year-old daughter is already much better than my wife with dirty words. My daughter uses dirty language with us liberally in order to impress us with her intelligence; often, she uses it directly *at* us (especially at my wife), probing to see how far she will be allowed to go. (She's *not* allowed to go far by me.) And my boy, I can tell, is working up the courage to experiment at home with a dirty word or two. (He isn't sure what the word *fuck* means, although he knows it's dirty. He was under the impression *fuck* was the word for sexual intercourse, until I told him it usually wasn't).

It is painful for me to recall how my wife was, to know the kind of person she used to be and would have liked to remain, and to see what is happening to her now, as it is painful for me to witness the deterioration of any human being who has ever been dear (or even near) to me, even of chance acquaintances, or total strangers. (A spastic can affect me profoundly, and a person with some other kind of facial or leg paralysis can immobilize me with repugnance. I want to look away. I resent blind people when I see them on the street, grow angry with them for being blind and in danger on the street, and glance about desperately for somebody else to step alongside them before I have to and guide them safely across the intersection or around the unexpected sidewalk obstruction that throws them abruptly into such pathetic confusion. I will not let myself cope with such human distress; I refuse to accept such reality; I dump it all right down into my unconscious and sit on it as hard as I can. Let it all come out in bad dreams if it has to. I forget them anyway as soon as I wake up.) Martha the typist, that young, plain girl in our office who has bad skin and is going crazy, is a total stranger to me and was already well on her way toward going crazy when she was sent upstairs to us by Personnel (to finish going crazy); I am not responsible; I do not know her; I do not know her mother in Iowa who has married again and will not take her back, or her father (if she still has a father), or anyone else among the many people in this world who should be close to her; yet, if I let it, it could break my heart that she is going crazy. I say nothing to her about how I feel (or could feel). But I always speak kindly to her. My manner is undiscerning. I try not to let her see I care anything at all about what is happening to her (she might turn to me for help, if she knew I knew), and I try not to let myself care. I try not to let her see I know. (She might not know it yet herself.) It would probably be upsetting for her to learn that everyone around her knew she was going crazy.

So I am silent with Martha, and I am silent with my wife, out of the same coarse mixture of sympathy and self-interest, about her drinking and flirting and dirty words, as I was silent also with my mother when she had the first of her brain strokes, and am silent also with everyone else I know in whom I begin to perceive the first signs of irreversible physical decay and approaching infirmity and death. (I write these people off rapidly. They become dead records in my filing system long before they are even gone, at the first indications that they have begun to go.) I say nothing to anybody about anything bad once I see it's already too late for anyone to help. I said nothing to my mother about her brain stroke, even though I was with her when it happened and was the one who finally had to make the telephone call for the doctor. I did not want her to know she was having a brain stroke; and when she did know, I didn't want her to know I knew.

I pretended not to notice when her tongue began rattling suddenly against the roof of her mouth during one of my weekly visits to the apartment in which she lived alone. The same splintered syllable, the same glottal stutter, kept coming out. I masked my surprise and hid my concern. She broke off, that first time, with a puzzled, almost whimsical look, smiled faintly in apology, and tried again to complete what she had started to say. The same thing happened. It happened the next time she tried. And the next. And the time after that, her attempt was not wholehearted; she seemed to know in advance it was futile, that it was too late. She felt all right otherwise. But she nodded when I suggested we get a doctor; and as I telephoned, the poor old woman sat down and surrendered weakly with a mortified, misty-eyed, bewildered shrug. (She was frightened. And she was ashamed.)

The doctor explained patiently afterward that it was probably not a clot but only a spasm (there was no such things as strokes, he said; there were only hemorrhages, clots, and spasms) in a very small blood vessel in her brain. (Had the affected blood vessel been a larger one, she would have suffered paralysis too on one side and perhaps loss of memory.) But she never spoke again for as long as she lived, although she continued, forgetfully, to try (out of habit, I suppose, rather than from any expectations of success) until the second in her series of spasms (or strokes), and then stopped trying. I would visit her in the nursing home (where she hated to be); I would do all the talking and she would listen and motion for the things she wanted or rise from her chair or bed (until she could no longer stand up, either) and go for them herself. Occasionally, she would jot a request on a scrap of paper. I never mentioned her stroke to her or referred to any of the other growing disabilities that appeared and crept over her remorselessly (arthritis, particularly, and a pervasive physical and mental indolence that blended finally into morbid apathy) as I sat by her bedside during my visits and talked to her about pleasant matters, soon running out of things to say about me, my wife, my children, and my job that I thought might make her feel good. She never knew that Derek had been born with serious brain damage, although she did know he had been born. I always told her he was fine. (I always told her everybody was fine.) We didn't know it either about Derek until he was a few years old, and by then it was too late: we'd already had him; he had already happened. (I wish I were rid of him now, although I don't dare come right out and say so. I suspect all of us in the family feel this way. Except, possibly, my boy, who may reason that if we did get rid of Derek, we could get rid of him, too, and is already concerned that we secretly intend to. My boy watches and absorbs everything having to do with us and Derek, as though waiting to see how we finally dispose of him, which is something, he senses, that sooner or later we will probably have to do.)

My conversation to my mother, like my visits, was of no use to her. I pretended, by not speaking of it, for my sake as well as for hers (for my sake *more* than for hers) that she was not seriously ill and in a nursing home she hated, that she was not crippled and growing older and more crippled daily. I did not want her to know, as she did know (and I knew she knew), as she knew before I did, that she was dying, slowly, in stages, her organs failing and her faculties withering one by one. I brought her food (which, toward the end, when her mind was gone almost entirely and she could barely recollect who I was for more than a minute or two, she would seize with her shriveled fingers and devour ravenously right from the wrapping paper like some famished, caged, wizened, white-haired animal—my mother). I pretended she was perfect and said nothing to her about her condition until she finally died. I was no use to her (except to bring her food), as I am no help now to our typist who is going insane right before my eyes, and am no help either to my wife with her drinking and her flirting and her other rather awkward efforts to be vital and gay. (I have visions these days when I am lying alone in strange beds in hotels or motels, trying to put myself to sleep, of being assailed by filthy hordes of stinging fleas or bedbugs against which I am utterly inept because I am too squeamish to endure them and have no other place to go.) *I don't want my wife ever to find out she drinks too much at parties and sometimes behaves very badly with other people and makes an extremely poor impression when she thinks she is making a very good one!* If she did (if she ever had even an inkling of how clumsy and overbearing she sometimes becomes), the knowledge would crush her (she would be destroyed), and she is already dejected enough.

At home during the day, she drinks only wine; in the evening, before or after dinner, she might drink scotch if I do. Many evenings we will not drink at all. She doesn't really like the taste of whiskey (although she is starting to enjoy the taste of martinis and to welcome that numbing-enlivening effect they mercifully produce so quickly) and doesn't know how to mix cocktails. At parties now, she will drink whatever's handed her as soon as we walk in and try to get a little high as quickly as she can. Then she will stick to that same drink for the rest of the evening. If things have been fairly comfortable between us that day and she is feeling secure, she will have a loud, jolly, friendly good time, with me and everyone else, until she gets drunk (if she does), and sometimes dizzy and sick, and no real harm will be done, although she used to be a quiet, modest girl, somewhat shy and refined, almost demure, always tactful and well-mannered.

If things are not so good, if she is not happy that day with me, my daughter, or herself, she will flirt belligerently. She will usually frighten away the man (or men) she flirts with (they almost never hang around long enough to flirt back) because she doesn't know how; her approach is threatening, her invitation to seduction a challenging attack, and there may be something of a scene if I don't step in quickly enough. It will always be with some man she knows and feels thoroughly safe with (she doesn't really want to flirt at all, I suppose) and usually one who appears to be enjoying himself and bothering no one. (Perhaps he seems smug.) It is saddening for me to watch her; I do not want other people to dislike her.

She will challenge the man openly, sometimes right in the presence of his wife, with a bald and suggestive remark or enticement, sliding her hand heavily up his shoulder blade if he is standing or squeezing the inside of his thigh if he is seated; and then, as though he had already rejected her, turn taunting, vengeful, and contemptuous before he can respond at all. As neatly and promptly as I can, before much damage is done, I will move in to rescue her, to guide her away smoothly with a quip and a smile. I never rebuke her (although I am often furious and ashamed); I humor her, praise her, flatter. I want her to feel pleased with herself. (I don't know why.)

"You're just jealous," she will accuse defiantly, when I have led her away.

"Damned right, I am," I reply with a forced laugh, and sometimes I will put my hands on her intimately to help persuade her I am.

"You'd better be," she'll gloat triumphantly.

We have had better times together, my wife and I, than we are having now; but I do not think we will have them again.

23

Yeats, Frost, Auden, Jarrell, Larkin, Ginsberg
Twentieth-Century Poetry

Poets have endured an especially difficult trial in the twentieth century. Often feeling themselves irrelevant to this technological age, they have expressed nostalgia for a simpler past and rage toward the present. This sense of alienation has frequently given rise to complex experiments in poetic form that have in common a rejection of tradition. Contemporary poetry has, thus, often been deliberately obscure in meaning, some poets rejecting the possibility of an understanding mass audience. The last few decades, however, seem to have brought a new audience for poetry in America, growing partly out of the folk-song revival of the 1960s. Of the poets presented in the following selection, only two—Yeats and Frost—are clearly of world stature. The intention here is not to present the period's most celebrated poets but to show how modern poets, using a variety of subjects and formal structures, have tended to reflect a general mood of alienation.

William Butler Yeats (1865–1939)—an Irish poet, playwright, mystic, and nationalist—was awarded the Nobel Prize for Literature in 1923. In the autobiographical poem "The Circus Animals' Desertion" (1939), the old poet looks back on his early works and enumerates their themes. He realizes that it was the "dream" itself, the poetic images, that obsessed him, not the realities to which those images supposedly referred. Now old and without new themes, he feels that he must leave all lofty pretensions and return to the source of all images—the fertile corruption of the human heart.

Robert Frost (1874–1963) has probably been the most beloved American poet of recent decades, his skillful public readings—including an appearance at the inauguration of President John Kennedy (1961)—having given him unusual exposure to large audiences. Dealing primarily with the farming people of rural New England, Frost's poems avoid the easily sentimental;

they hint instead at the dark places within the soul. (Madness and suicide had claimed members of Frost's immediate family.) In "Directive" (1947) we see the yearning for that earlier time when men were "whole . . . beyond confusion."

W. H. Auden (1907–1973) was an Oxford-educated Englishman who, in 1946, became an American citizen. In his last years he was elected Professor of Poetry at Oxford and took up residence at his old college. During the 1930s he was regarded as the leading Marxist, anti-fascist poet in England; by the 1950s his poems were losing their radical political tone and were beginning to express a Christian point of view. He was primarily an ironically intellectual—rather than an emotional—poet. In "The Shield of Achilles" (1955) we see the world as it is depicted on heroic Achilles' shield by Hephaestos, the craftsman of the Olympian gods. Hephaestos has just made new armor for Achilles because of the tearful pleading of Thetis, Achilles' mother. According to Homer's Iliad, *Achilles, the deadliest fighter in the Greek war against Troy, had loaned his original armor to his dearest friend, Patroclus; after brutally killing Patroclus, the Trojans seized the armor. Now, in order to seek revenge, Achilles must have new armor— including, of course, the spectacularly decorated shield. Homer describes the shield as depicting the entire natural universe as well as the varied conditions of humankind; he includes scenes of both bountiful peace and destructive war. Auden's modern view of Achilles' shield, however, suggests only the cruelty of force, the depressing reality behind the heroic expectations. These aspects Auden shows through the eyes of Thetis—the "she" of the poem.*

Randall Jarrell (1914–1965)—an American poet, novelist, critic, and teacher—was born in Nashville, Tennessee, and earned degrees in English at Vanderbilt University. After a few years as a teacher at Kenyon College, in Ohio, he enlisted in the Army Air Corps and served in its ranks during the Second World War. "The Death of the Ball Turret Gunner" (1945) is one of many poems based on Jarrell's wartime experiences. The gunner it describes is killed, while curled like a foetus in his womb-shaped ball turret, and thus is seemingly born into his own death. From 1947 until 1965 Jarrell was a much-admired teacher at the Women's College of the University of North Carolina.

Philip Larkin (1922–   )—an Oxford-educated poet, novelist, critic, and writer on jazz—has earned his living mainly as a librarian at various English universities. He is regarded by many critics as the finest English poet of his uncommitted generation. Larkin's general tone is one of quiet disillusionment with the great ideas, accompanied by a gentle pleasure in the small and real things of life. His poetry is an even-tempered reaction against all forms of excess—whether the excessive romantic rhetoric of poets like Dylan Thomas, the excessive intellectual pretentiousness of poets like T. S. Eliot and Ezra Pound, or the excessive political commitment of poets like W. H. Auden. Typically, the three poems by Larkin reprinted here all carry a general sense of the cultural and spiritual decay present in the modern world. In "Church Going" (1955) we see an agnostic's reluctant respect for what the Christian churches had done toward giving unified meaning to the critical moments in human life: birth, marriage, and death. In "Wants" (1955) Larkin shares his belief that, despite all the available conveniences and social rituals, people are really ill at ease in the daily life of the modern world and desire separation from it. In "MCMXIV," published in 1964, Larkin describes long lines of Englishmen waiting to enlist at the beginning of the First World War (1914); he notes that never again shall we see the innocence that existed before that great slaughter changed history and, therefore, humanity.

Allen Ginsberg (1926–   )—an American poet, "prophet," and public figure—was born in Newark, New Jersey, and raised in the nearby industrial city of Paterson. His father was a high-school teacher and poet, his mother an idealistic radical whose mental health declined into madness. (She is the subject of "Kaddish," Ginsberg's most moving poem.) Ginsberg graduated from Columbia University in 1948 and in the early 1950s drifted to San Francisco where he and his friends (including Gary Snyder) became catalysts of the Beat movement, a protest against hypocritical puritanism and respectability. It was out of this milieu that "Howl" (1956) was written, originally intended only for private recitation among the Beats. The prosecution and eventual acquittal of the publisher on a charge of obscenity brought "Howl" immense publicity and sales. Beyond such considerations, it is noteworthy as a prophetic vision of the physical, mental, and spiritual destruction of part of a generation of young Americans. All seventy-eight lines in the first part of "Howl" are a single tidal sentence wherein Ginsberg catalogues the ways in which a hostile civilization has "destroyed by madness" the "best minds" of his generation. In recent years, Ginsberg has renounced the use of drugs, so much a part of "Howl," and advocated the use of yoga and meditation, which he learned in his travels to the Orient. A frequent guest speaker, he has become a benign, paternal figure on many American campuses, seeking to bring peace of mind to the present generation.

WILLIAM BUTLER YEATS

The Circus Animals' Desertion

I

I sought a theme and sought for it in vain,
I sought it daily for six weeks or so.
Maybe at last, being but a broken man,
I must be satisfied with my heart, although
Winter and summer till old age began
My circus animals were all on show,
Those stilted boys, that burnished chariot,
Lion and woman and the Lord knows what.[1]

II

What can I but enumerate old themes?
First that sea-rider Oisin led by the nose
Through three enchanted islands,[2] allegorical dreams,
Vain gaiety, vain battle, vain repose,
Themes of the embittered heart, or so it seems,
That might adorn old songs or courtly shows;
But what cared I that set him on to ride,
I, starved for the bosom of his faery bride?[3]

And then a counter-truth filled out its play,
The Countess Cathleen[4] was the name I gave it;
She, pity-crazed, had given her soul away,
But masterful Heaven had intervened to save it.

---

[1] Yeats alludes to the ancient Irish heroes and legends described in his early poetry. Also, he may be referring more generally to the intense imagery of poetry, now leaving him, as fascinating and unreal as the world of a circus.

[2] In Yeats's long allegorical poem "The Wanderings of Oisin" (1889) the hero is led by a fairy, Niamh, to the Islands of Delight, of Many Fears, and of Forgetfulness.

[3] Niamh; also probably a reference to the beautiful Irish actress-revolutionary, Maud Gonne, who rejected Yeats's love.

[4] A play (1892) in which the Countess (modeled on Yeats's view of Maud Gonne) sells her immortal soul to save the souls of the Irish people.

I thought my dear must her own soul destroy,
So did fanaticism and hate enslave it,
And this brought forth a dream and soon enough
This dream itself had all my thought and love.

And when the Fool and Blind Man stole the bread
Cuchulain fought the ungovernable sea; [5]
Heart-mysteries there, and yet when all is said
It was the dream itself enchanted me:
Character isolated by a deed
To engross the present and dominate memory.
Players and painted stage took all my love,
And not those things that they were emblems of.

III

Those masterful images because complete
Grew in pure mind, but out of what began?
A mound of refuse or the sweepings of a street,
Old kettles, old bottles, and a broken can,
Old iron, old bones, old rags, that raving slut
Who keeps the till. Now that my ladder's gone,
I must lie down where all the ladders start,
In the foul rag-and-bone shop of the heart.

ROBERT FROST

Directive

Back out of all this now too much for us,
Back in a time made simple by the loss
Of detail, burned, dissolved, and broken off

[5] An allusion to another early play, *On Baile's Strand* (1904), in which Cuchulain, maddened by the discovery that he has unwittingly killed his own son, rushes out to fight the waves; as all the people run to the shore to watch Cuchulain, the Fool and the Blind Man steal the bread from their ovens. Yeats may be implying his own ungovernable anguish when Maud Gonne married another.

Like graveyard marble sculpture in the weather,
There is a house that is no more a house
Upon a farm that is no more a farm
And in a town that is no more a town.
The road there, if you'll let a guide direct you
Who only has at heart your getting lost,
May seem as if it should have been a quarry—
Great monolithic knees the former town
Long since gave up pretense of keeping covered.
And there's a story in a book about it:
Besides the wear of iron wagon wheels
The ledges show lines ruled southeast-northwest,
The chisel work of an enormous Glacier
That braced his feet against the Arctic Pole.
You must not mind a certain coolness from him
Still said to haunt this side of Panther Mountain.
Nor need you mind the serial ordeal
Of being watched from forty cellar holes
As if by eye pairs out of forty firkins.
As for the woods' excitement over you
That sends light rustle rushes to their leaves,
Charge that to upstart inexperience.
Where were they all not twenty years ago?
They think too much of having shaded out
A few old pecker-fretted apple trees.
Make yourself up a cheering song of how
Someone's road home from work this once was,
Who may be just ahead of you on foot
Or creaking with a buggy load of grain.
The height of the adventure is the height
Of country where two village cultures faded
Into each other. Both of them are lost.
And if you're lost enough to find yourself
By now, pull in your ladder road behind you
And put a sign up CLOSED to all but me.
Then make yourself at home. The only field
Now left's no bigger than a harness gall.
First there's the children's house of make-believe,
Some shattered dishes underneath a pine,
The playthings in the playhouse of the children.

Weep for what little things could make them glad.
Then for the house that is no more a house,
But only a belilaced cellar hole,
Now slowly closing like a dent in dough.
This was no playhouse but a house in earnest.
Your destination and your destiny's
A brook that was the water of the house,
Cold as a spring as yet so near its source,
Too lofty and original to rage.
(We know the valley streams that when aroused
Will leave their tatters hung on barb and thorn.)
I have kept hidden in the instep arch
Of an old cedar at the waterside
A broken drinking goblet like the Grail[6]
Under a spell so the wrong ones can't find it,
So can't get saved, as Saint Mark says they mustn't.[7]
(I stole the goblet from the children's playhouse.)
Here are your waters and your watering place.
Drink and be whole again beyond confusion.

W. H. AUDEN

The Shield of Achilles

She looked over his shoulder
    For vines and olive trees,
Marble well-governed cities
    And ships upon untamed seas,
But there on the shining metal
    His hands had put instead
An artificial wilderness
    And a sky like lead.

[6] The Holy Grail — in medieval legend, the cup used by Jesus at the Last Supper; it became the object of many quests in Arthurian romance.

[7] An allusion to the Gospel of Mark 4: 11–12, in which Jesus says to his disciples: "To you has been given the secret of the kingdom of God, but for those outside everything is in parables; so that they may hear but not understand; lest they should turn again, and be forgiven."

A plain without a feature, bare and brown,
  No blade of grass, no sign of neighbourhood,
Nothing to eat and nowhere to sit down,
  Yet, congregated on its blankness, stood
  An unintelligible multitude.
A million eyes, a million boots in line,
Without expression, waiting for a sign.

Out of the air a voice without a face
  Proved by statistics that some cause was just
In tones as dry and level as the place:
  No one was cheered and nothing was discussed;
  Column by column in a cloud of dust
They marched away enduring a belief
Whose logic brought them, somewhere else, to grief.

        She looked over his shoulder
          For ritual pieties,
        White flower-garlanded heifers,
          Libation and sacrifice,
        But there on the shining metal
          Where the altar should have been,
        She saw by his flickering forge-light
          Quite another scene.

Barbed wire enclosed an arbitrary spot
  Where bored officials lounged (one cracked a joke)
And sentries sweated for the day was hot:
  A crowd of ordinary decent folk
  Watched from without and neither moved nor spoke
As three pale figures were led forth and bound
To three posts driven upright in the ground.

The mass and majesty of this world, all
  That carries weight and always weighs the same
Lay in the hands of others; they were small
  And could not hope for help and no help came:
  What their foes liked to do was done, their shame
Was all the worst could wish; they lost their pride
And died as men before their bodies died.

        She looked over his shoulder
          For athletes at their games,

> Men and women in a dance
>   Moving their sweet limbs
> Quick, quick, to music,
>   But there on the shining shield
> His hands had set no dancing-floor
>   But a weed-choked field.

A ragged urchin, aimless and alone,
   Loitered about that vacancy, a bird
Flew up to safety from his well-aimed stone:
   That girls are raped, that two boys knife a third,
   Were axioms to him, who'd never heard
Of any world where promises were kept,
Or one could weep because another wept.

> The thin-lipped armourer,
>   Hephaestos hobbled away,
> Thetis of the shining breasts
>   Cried out in dismay
> At what the god had wrought
>   To please her son, the strong
> Iron-hearted man-slaying Achilles
> Who would not live long.

RANDALL JARRELL

The Death of the Ball Turret Gunner[8]

From my mother's sleep I fell into the State,
And I hunched in its belly till my wet fur froze.
Six miles from earth, loosed from its dream of life,
I woke to black flak and the nightmare fighters.
When I died they washed me out of the turret with a hose.

[8] A ball turret was a plexiglass sphere set into the belly of a B-17 or B-24, and inhabited by two .50 caliber machine-guns and one man, a short small man. When this gunner tracked with his machine-guns a fighter attacking his bomber from below, he revolved with the turret; hunched upside-down in his little sphere, he looked like the foetus in the womb. The fighters which attacked him were armed with cannon firing explosive shells. The hose was a steam hose. [Jarrell's note. *Ed.*]

PHILIP LARKIN

Church Going

Once I am sure there's nothing going on
I step inside, letting the door thud shut.
Another church: matting, seats, and stone,
And little books; sprawlings of flowers, cut
For Sunday, brownish now; some brass and stuff
Up at the holy end; the small neat organ;
And a tense, musty, unignorable silence,
Brewed God knows how long. Hatless, I take off
My cycle-clips in awkward reverence,

Move forward, run my hand around the font.
From where I stand, the roof looks almost new—
Cleaned, or restored? Someone would know: I don't.
Mounting the lectern, I peruse a few
Hectoring large-scale verses, and pronounce
'Here endeth' much more loudly than I'd meant.
The echoes snigger briefly. Back at the door
I sign the book, donate an Irish sixpence,
Reflect the place was not worth stopping for.

Yet stop I did: in fact I often do,
And always end much at a loss like this,
Wondering what to look for; wondering, too,
When churches fall completely out of use
What we shall turn them into, if we shall keep
A few cathedrals chronically on show,
Their parchment, plate and pyx[9] in locked cases,
And let the rest rent-free to rain and sheep.
Shall we avoid them as unlucky places?

Or, after dark, will dubious women come
To make their children touch a particular stone;
Pick simples[10] for a cancer; or on some

[9] The box, often made of gold or silver, in which communion wafers are kept.
[10] Medicinal herbs.

Philip Larkin, "Church Going" and "Wants," are reprinted from *The Less Deceived* by Philip Larkin. Copyright © 1955 by the Marvell Press. Reprinted by permission of The Marvell Press. [Pp. 28–29, 22.]

Advised night see walking a dead one?
Power of some sort or other will go on
In games, in riddles, seemingly at random;
But superstition, like belief, must die,
And what remains when disbelief has gone?
Grass, weedy pavement, brambles, buttress, sky,

A shape less recognisable each week,
A purpose more obscure. I wonder who
Will be the last, the very last, to seek
This place for what it was; one of the crew
That tap and jot and know what rood-lofts were?
Some ruin-bibber, randy for antique,
Or Christmas-addict, counting on a whiff
Of gown-and-bands and organ-pipes and myrrh?
Or will he be my representative,

Bored, uninformed, knowing the ghostly silt
Dispersed, yet tending to this cross of ground
Through suburb scrub because it held unspilt
So long and equably what since is found
Only in separation—marriage, and birth,
And death, and thoughts of these—for whom was built
This special shell? For, though I've no idea
What this accoutred frowsty barn is worth,
It pleases me to stand in silence here;

A serious house on serious earth it is,
In whose blent air all our compulsions meet,
Are recognised, and robed as destinies.
And that much never can be obsolete,
Since someone will forever be surprising
A hunger in himself to be more serious,
And gravitating with it to this ground,
Which, he once heard, was proper to grow wise in,
If only that so many dead lie round.

Wants

Beyond all this, the wish to be alone:
However the sky grows dark with invitation-cards
However we follow the printed directions of sex
However the family is photographed under the flagstaff—
Beyond all this, the wish to be alone.

Beneath it all, desire of oblivion runs:
Despite the artful tensions of the calendar,
The life insurance, the tabled fertility rites,
The costly aversion of the eyes from death—
Beneath it all, desire of oblivion runs.

MCMXIV

Those long uneven lines
Standing as patiently
As if they were stretched outside
The Oval or Villa Park,[11]
The crowns of hats, the sun
On moustached archaic faces
Grinning as if it were all
An August Bank Holiday lark;

And the shut shops, the bleached
Established names on the sunblinds,
The farthings and sovereigns,[12]
And dark-clothed children at play
Called after kings and queens,
The tin advertisements
For cocoa and twist,[13] and the pubs
Wide open all day;

And the countryside not caring:
The place-names all hazed over

[11] Sports stadiums.
[12] English coins no longer in use.
[13] A thick roll of tobacco used, after shredding, by pipe-smokers.
Philip Larkin, "MCMXIV." Reprinted by permission of Faber and Faber Ltd from *The Whitsun Weddings* by Philip Larkin. Copyright © 1964 by Philip Larkin. [P. 28.]

With flowering grasses, and fields
Shadowing Domesday lines [14]
Under wheat's restless silence;
The differently-dressed servants
With tiny rooms in huge houses,
The dust behind limousines;

Never such innocence,
Never before or since,
As changed itself to past
Without a word—the men
Leaving the gardens tidy,
The thousands of marriages
Lasting a little while longer:
Never such innocence again.

ALLEN GINSBERG

Howl [15]

for
Carl Solomon [16]

I

I saw the best minds of my generation destroyed by madness, starving hysterical naked,
dragging themselves through the negro streets at dawn looking for
an angry fix,
angelheaded hipsters burning for the ancient heavenly connection to
the starry dynamo in the machinery of night,
who poverty and tatters and hollow-eyed and high sat up smoking in

---

[14] The survey of all the lands of England, ordered by William the Conqueror in 1086.
[15] This excerpt is part one of the three-part poem. (Part two was written during a
vision induced by ingesting peyote.)
[16] Ginsberg's friend, whose partly-true account of life as a mental patient is recounted
in "Howl," mainly in part three.

From Allen Ginsberg, *Howl and Other Poems.* Copyright © 1956, 1959 by Allen Ginsberg. Reprinted by permission of City Lights Books. [Pp. 9–16.]

the supernatural darkness of cold-water flats floating across the tops of cities contemplating jazz,

who bared their brains to Heaven under the El[17] and saw Mohammedan angels staggering on tenement roofs illuminated,

who passed through universities with radiant cool eyes hallucinating
Arkansas and Blake-light tragedy[18] among the scholars of war,

who were expelled from the academies for crazy & publishing obscene odes on the windows of the skull,[19]

who cowered in unshaven rooms in underwear, burning their money
in wastebaskets and listening to the Terror through the wall,

who got busted in their pubic beards returning through Laredo with
a belt of marijuana for New York,

who ate fire in paint hotels or drank turpentine in Paradise Alley,
death, or purgatoried their torsos night after night

with dreams, with drugs, with waking nightmares, alcohol and cock
and endless balls,

incomparable blind streets of shuddering cloud and lightning in the
mind leaping toward poles of Canada & Paterson, illuminating
all the motionless world of Time between,

Peyote solidities of halls, backyard green tree cemetery dawns, wine
drunkenness over the rooftops, storefront boroughs of teahead
joyride neon blinking traffic light, sun and moon and tree vibrations in the roaring winter dusks of Brooklyn, ashcan rantings
and kind king light of mind,

who chained themselves to subways for the endless ride from Battery to holy Bronx on benzedrine until the noise of wheels and
children brought them down shuddering mouth-wracked and
battered bleak of brain all drained of brilliance in the drear light
of Zoo,[20]

who sank all night in submarine light of Bickford's[21] floated out and
sat through the stale beer afternoon in desolate Fugazzi's,[22] listening to the crack of doom on the hydrogen jukebox,

---

[17] The elevated railway in New York City.
[18] Ginsberg had an auditory mystical experience in 1948 in which he heard William
Blake (1757–1827), the English poet, reciting from Blake's poems.
[19] Ginsberg was suspended twice from college: in 1945 for scrawling obscenities on his
dormitory window to provoke the cleaning woman into cleaning it, and in 1948
when he volunteered for psychiatric treatment.
[20] The Bronx Zoo.
[21] A cafeteria open twenty-four hours a day.
[22] A bar near bohemian Greenwich Village.

who talked continuously seventy hours from park to pad to bar to
Bellevue[23] to museum to the Brooklyn Bridge,

a lost battalion of platonic conversationalists jumping down the
stoops off fire escapes off windowsills off Empire State out of
the moon,

yacketayakking screaming vomiting whispering facts and memories
and anecdotes and eyeball kicks and shocks of hospitals and jails
and wars,

whole intellects disgorged in total recall for seven days and nights
with brilliant eyes, meat for the Synagogue cast on the pavement,

who vanished into nowhere Zen New Jersey leaving a trail of ambiguous picture postcards of Atlantic City Hall,

suffering Eastern sweats and Tangerian bone-grindings and mi-
graines of China under junk-withdrawal in Newark's bleak furnished room,

who wandered around and around at midnight in the railroad yard
wondering where to go, and went, leaving no broken hearts,

who lit cigarettes in boxcars boxcars boxcars racketing through
snow toward lonesome farms in grandfather night,

who studied Plotinus Poe St. John of the Cross[24] telepathy and bop
kaballa[25] because the cosmos instinctively vibrated at their feet
in Kansas,

who loned it through the streets of Idaho seeking visionary indian
angels who were visionary indian angels,

who thought they were only mad when Baltimore gleamed in supernatural ecstasy,

who jumped in limousines with the Chinaman of Oklahoma on the
impulse of winter midnight streetlight smalltown rain,

who lounged hungry and lonesome through Houston seeking jazz or
sex or soup, and followed the brilliant Spaniard to converse
about America and Eternity, a hopeless task, and so took ship to
Africa,

who disappeared into the volcanoes of Mexico leaving behind noth-

---

[23] A public hospital in New York, part of which serves as a receiving center for the
mentally disturbed.

[24] Ginsberg had studied these writers in college; he treasured them for their mystical
insights.

[25] "Bop" is a style of modern jazz. The kaballa is a mystical Hebraic system of interpreting the holy scripture; it asserts the supremacy of spirit over body.

ing but the shadow of dungarees and the lava and ash of poetry
scattered in fireplace Chicago,

who reappeared on the West Coast investigating the F.B.I. in beards
and shorts with big pacifist eyes sexy in their dark skin passing
out incomprehensible leaflets,

who burned cigarette holes in their arms protesting the narcotic tobacco haze of Capitalism,

who distributed Supercommunist pamphlets in Union Square weeping and undressing while the sirens of Los Alamos wailed them
down, and wailed down Wall, and the Staten Island ferry also
wailed,[26]

who broke down crying in white gymnasiums naked and trembling
before the machinery of other skeletons,

who bit detectives in the neck and shrieked with delight in policecars
for committing no crime but their own wild cooking pederasty
and intoxication,

who howled on their knees in the subway and were dragged off the
roof waving genitals and manuscripts,

who let themselves be fucked in the ass by saintly motorcyclists, and
screamed with joy,

who blew and were blown by those human seraphim, the sailors,
caresses of Atlantic and Caribbean love,

who balled in the morning in the evenings in rosegardens and the
grass of public parks and cemeteries scattering their semen freely
to whomever come who may,

who hiccupped endlessly trying to giggle but sound up with a sob
behind a partition in a Turkish Bath when the blonde & naked
angel came to pierce them with a sword,

who lost their loveboys to the three old shrews of fate the one eyed
shrew of the heterosexual dollar the one eyed shrew that winks
out of the womb and the one eyed shrew that does nothing but
sit on her ass and snip the intellectual golden threads of the
craftsman's loom,

who copulated ecstatic and insatiate with a bottle of beer a sweetheart a package of cigarettes a candle and fell off the bed, and

[26] Union Square, New York City, a traditional center for radical demonstrations; Los
Alamos, New Mexico, site of the atomic bomb's development; Wall Street, New
York City, the financial center of the United States, or perhaps a reference to the
Wailing Wall in Jerusalem; the Staten Island Ferry connects that borough to lower
Manhattan near the financial district.

continued along the floor and down the hall and ended fainting
on the wall with a vision of ultimate cunt and come eluding the
last gyzym of consciousness,

who sweetened the snatches of a million girls trembling in the sunset, and were red eyed in the morning but prepared to sweeten
the snatch of the sunrise, flashing buttocks under barns and
naked in the lake,

who went out whoring through Colorado in myriad stolen night-
cars, N.C.,[27] secret hero of these poems, cocksman and Adonis
of Denver—joy to the memory of his innumerable lays of girls
in empty lots & diner backyards, moviehouses' rickety rows, on
mountaintops in caves or with gaunt waitresses in familiar road-
side lonely petticoat upliftings & especially secret gas-station
solipsisms of johns, & hometown alleys too,

who faded out in vast sordid movies, were shifted in dreams, woke
on a sudden Manhattan, and picked themselves up out of base-
ments hungover with heartless Tokay and horrors of Third Avenue iron dreams & stumbled to unemployment offices,

who walked all night with their shoes full of blood on the snowbank
docks waiting for a door in the East River to open to a room full
of steamheat and opium,

who created great suicidal dramas on the apartment cliff-banks of the
Hudson under the wartime blue floodlight of the moon & their
heads shall be crowned with laurel in oblivion,

who ate the lamb stew of the imagination or digested the crab at the
muddy bottom of the rivers of Bowery,[28]

who wept at the romance of the streets with their pushcarts full of
onions and bad music,

who sat in boxes breathing in the darkness under the bridge, and
rose up to build harpsichords in their lofts,

who coughed on the sixth floor of Harlem crowned with flame
under the tubercular sky surrounded by orange crates of theology,

who scribbled all night rocking and rolling over lofty incantations
which in the yellow morning were stanzas of gibberish,

who cooked rotten animals lung heart feet tail borsht & tortillas
dreaming of the pure vegetable kingdom,

[27] Neal Cassady, Ginsberg's friend and the inspiration for characters in a number of
novels by Beat writers.
[28] The street in New York notorious for its numbers of derelicts.

who plunged themselves under meat trucks looking for an egg,

who threw their watches off the roof to cast their ballot for Eternity outside of Time, & alarm clocks fell on their heads every day for the next decade,

who cut their wrists three times successively unsuccessfully, gave up and were forced to open antique stores where they thought they were growing old and cried,

who were burned alive in their innocent flannel suits on Madison Avenue[29] amid blasts of leaden verse & the tanked-up clatter of the iron regiments of fashion & the nitroglycerine shrieks of the fairies of advertising & the mustard gas of sinister intelligent editors, or were run down by the drunken taxicabs of Absolute Reality,

who jumped off the Brooklyn Bridge this actually happened and walked away unknown and forgotten into the ghostly daze of Chinatown soup alleyways & firetrucks, not even one free beer,

who sang out of their windows in despair, fell out of the subway window, jumped in the filthy Passaic,[30] leaped on negroes, cried all over the street, danced on broken wineglasses barefoot smashed phonograph records of nostalgic European 1930's German jazz finished the whiskey and threw up groaning into the bloody toilet, moans in their ears and the blast of colossal steamwhistles,

who barreled down the highways of the past journeying to each other's hotrod-Golgotha[31] jail-solitude watch or Birmingham jazz incarnation,

who drove crosscountry seventytwo hours to find out if I had a vision or you had a vision or he had a vision to find out Eternity,

who journeyed to Denver, who died in Denver, who came back to Denver & waited in vain, who watched over Denver & brooded & loned in Denver and finally went away to find out the Time, & now Denver is lonesome for her heroes,

who fell on their knees in hopeless cathedrals praying for each other's salvation and light and breasts, until the soul illuminated its hair for a second,

who crashed through their minds in jail waiting for impossible crim-

[29] The location of New York's biggest advertising agencies.
[30] The river that flows past Paterson, New Jersey.
[31] The hill where Jesus was crucified.

inals with golden heads and the charm of reality in their hearts
who sang sweet blues to Alcatraz,

who retired to Mexico to cultivate a habit, or Rocky Mount to
tender Buddha or Tangiers to boys or Southern Pacific to the
black locomotive or Harvard to Narcissus to Woodlawn[32] to
the daisychain or grave,

who demanded sanity trials accusing the radio of hypnotism & were
left with their insanity & their hands & a hung jury,

who threw potato salad at CCNY lecturers on Dadaism[33] and subsequently presented themselves on the granite steps of the mad-
house with shaven heads and harlequin speech of suicide,
demanding instantaneous lobotomy,

and who were given instead the concrete void of insulin metrasol
electricity hydrotherapy psychotherapy occupational therapy
pingpong & amnesia,

who in humorless protest overturned only one symbolic pingpong
table, resting briefly in catatonia,

returning years later truly bald except for a wig of blood, and tears
and fingers, to the visible madman doom of the wards of the
madtowns of the East,

Pilgrim State's Rockland's and Greystone's[34] foetid halls, bickering
with the echoes of the soul, rocking and rolling in the midnight
solitude-bench dolmen-realms of love, dream of life a nightmare, bodies turned to stone as heavy as the moon,

with mother finally ✶✶✶✶✶✶,[35] and the last fantastic book flung out
of the tenement window, and the last door closed at 4 AM and
the last telephone slammed at the wall in reply and the last furnished room emptied down to the last piece of mental furniture,
a yellow paper rose twisted on a wire hanger in the closet, and
even that imaginary, nothing but a hopeful little bit of halluci-
nation—

ah, Carl, while you are not safe I am not safe, and now you're really
in the total animal soup of time—

and who therefore ran through the icy streets obsessed with a sudden

---

[32] A cemetery in the borough of the Bronx, New York City.

[33] An artistic movement based on accident and absurdity; CCNY is the City College
of New York.

[34] Mental hospitals in New York and New Jersey. Carl Solomon was a patient at
Pilgrim State and Rockland, Ginsberg's mother at Greystone.

[35] Naomi Ginsberg was permanently hospitalized for severe paranoia shortly after her
son graduated from Columbia; she died in 1956 not long after "Howl" was written.

flash of the alchemy of the use of the ellipse the catalog the
meter & the vibrating plane,
who dreamt and made incarnate gaps in Time & Space through
images juxtaposed, and trapped the archangel of the soul between 2 visual images and joined the elemental verbs and set the
noun and dash of consciousness together jumping with sensation
of Pater Omnipotens Aeterna Deus [36]
to recreate the syntax and measure of poor human prose and stand
before you speechless and intelligent and shaking with shame,
rejected yet confessing out the soul to conform to the rhythm of
thought in his naked and endless head,
the madman bum and angel beat in Time, unknown, yet putting
down here what might be left to say in time come after death,
and rose reincarnate in the ghostly clothes of jazz in the goldhorn
shadow of the band and blew the suffering of America's naked
mind for love into an eli eli lamma lamma sabacthani [37] saxophone cry that shivered the cities down to the last radio
with the absolute heart of the poem of life butchered out of their
own bodies good to eat a thousand years.

[36] Latin: All-powerful Father, Eternal God. Paul Cezanne (1839–1906), the French
Post-Impressionist painter, used this phrase to describe the sensations he received
from observing and reinventing the appearances of the natural world.
[37] Hebrew: "My God, my God, why have you forsaken me?" — the last words of
Jesus on the cross (Matthew 27:46).

V
The
Religious
Quest

24

Sigmund Freud

The Future of an Illusion

Sigmund Freud (1856–1939), perhaps more than any other individual, has helped bring about an understanding of the irrational forces that operate within all human beings. As a physician in Vienna, Austria, Freud became interested in treating patients whose ailments seemed to be psychologically—rather than physically—caused. He developed a technique of "free association," in which patients dredged up repressed memories that had been keeping them from functioning as whole persons. In the early years of the technique, Freud employed hypnotism to assist the patient's memory. Later, he discarded hypnotism, having discovered that it was the patient's narration itself that induced the therapeutic effect.

On the basis largely of personal observations derived from his extensive practice, Freud constructed general theories of the human mind and its disabling neuroses. The author of numerous influential volumes—such as The Interpretation of Dreams *(1900),* Totem and Taboo *(1913), and* The Ego and the Id *(1923)—Freud is considered the founder of the modern discipline of psychoanalysis. Although his work exposed the primary forces in human behavior as being unconsciously instinctual—for example, sex and aggression—he never lost faith in the powers of reason. The scientific method, Freud believed, would gain for humanity both self-understanding and self-control.*

It was probably the firm adherence to reason that turned Freud's attention to the "problem" of religion. Since the major religions rest primarily upon faith rather than reasoned inquiry, Freud feared that those systems of belief

Reprinted from *The Future of an Illusion* by Sigmund Freud. Translated and edited from the German by James Strachey. With the permission of W. W. Norton & Company, Inc. Copyright © 1961 by James Strachey. [Pp. 29–31, 38, 49.]

could not prove ultimately successful as guides to human behavior. Yet he was impressed (and perplexed) by the continuing appeal and power of religion in a scientific age. In The Future of an Illusion *(1928), the source of the following selection, Freud attempts to solve the riddle, at least for himself. He concludes that belief in God is an* illusion, *a form of infantile wish-fulfillment that a genuinely scientific "education to reality" would render unnecessary. For Freud, continued dependence on the supposed authority of God is a barrier to development of a genuinely mature humanistic ethic.*

. . . in past times religious ideas, in spite of their incontrovertible lack of authentication, have exercised the strongest possible influence on mankind. This is a fresh psychological problem. We must ask where the inner force of those doctrines lies and to what it is that they owe their efficacy, independent as it is of recognition by reason.

I think we have prepared the way sufficiently for an answer to both these questions. It will be found if we turn our attention to the psychical origin of religious ideas. These, which are given out as teachings, are not precipitates of experience or end-results of thinking: they are illusions, fulfilments of the oldest, strongest and most urgent wishes of mankind. The secret of their strength lies in the strength of those wishes. As we already know, the terrifying impression of helplessness in childhood aroused the need for protection—for protection through love—which was provided by the father; and the recognition that this helplessness lasts throughout life made it necessary to cling to the existence of a father, but this time a more powerful one. Thus the benevolent rule of a divine Providence allays our fear of the dangers of life; the establishment of a moral world-order ensures the fulfilment of the demands of justice, which have so often remained unfulfilled in human civilization; and the prolongation of earthly existence in a future life provides the local and temporal framework in which these wish-fulfilments shall take place. Answers to the riddles that tempt the curiosity of man, such as how the universe began or what the relation is between body and mind, are developed in conformity with the underlying assumptions of this system. It is an enormous relief to the individual psyche if the conflicts of its childhood arising from the father-complex—conflicts which it has never wholly overcome—are removed from it and brought to a solution which is universally accepted.

When I say that these things are all illusions, I must define the meaning of the word. An illusion is not the same thing as an error; nor is it necessarily an error. Aristotle's belief that vermin are developed out of dung (a belief to which ignorant people still cling) was an error; so was the belief of a former generation of doctors that *tabes dorsalis* [1] is the result of sexual excess. It would be incorrect to call these errors illusions. On the other hand, it was an illusion of Columbus's that he had discovered a new sea-route to the Indies. The part played by his wish in this error is very clear. One may describe as an illusion the assertion made by certain nationalists [2] that the Indo-Germanic race is the only one capable of civilization; or the belief, which was only destroyed by psycho-analysis, that chidren are creatures without sexuality. What is characteristic of illusions is that they are derived from human wishes. In this respect they come near to psychiatric delusions. But they differ from them, too, apart from the more complicated structure of delusions. In the case of delusions, we emphasize as essential their being in contradiction with reality. Illusions need not necessarily be false—that is to say, unrealizable or in contradiction to reality. For instance, a middle-class girl may have the illusion that a prince will come and marry her. This is possible; and a few such cases have occurred. That the Messiah will come and found a golden age is much less likely. Whether one classifies this belief as an illusion or as something analogous to a delusion will depend on one's personal attitude. Examples of illusions which have proved true are not easy to find, but the illusion of the alchemists that all metals can be turned into gold might be one of them. The wish to have a great deal of gold, as much gold as possible, has, it is true, been a good deal damped by our present-day knowledge of the determinants of wealth, but chemistry no longer regards the transmutation of metals into gold as impossible. Thus we call a belief an illusion when a wish-fulfilment is a prominent factor in its motivation, and in doing so we disregard its relations to reality, just as the illusion itself sets no store by verification.

Having thus taken our bearings, let us return once more to the

---

[1] A syphillitic disorder of the nervous system.

[2] By the spring of 1927, when Freud began to write this essay, the racist doctrines of the Nazi party were being widely distributed in Germany.

question of religious doctrines. We can now repeat that all of them are illusions and insusceptible of proof. No one can be compelled to think them true, to believe in them. Some of them are so improbable, so incompatible with everything we have laboriously discovered about the reality of the world, that we may compare them—if we pay proper regard to the psychological differences—to delusions. Of the reality value of most of them we cannot judge; just as they cannot be proved, so they cannot be refuted. We still know too little to make a critical approach to them. The riddles of the universe reveal themselves only slowly to our investigation; there are many questions to which science to-day can give no answer. But scientific work is the only road which can lead us to a knowledge of reality outside ourselves.

• • •

Let us consider the unmistakable situation as it is to-day. We have heard the admission that religion no longer has the same influence on people that it used to. (We are here concerned with European Christian civilization.) And this is not because its promises have grown less but because people find them less credible. Let us admit that the reason—though perhaps not the only reason—for this change is the increase of the scientific spirit in the higher strata of human society. Criticism has whittled away the evidential value of religious documents, natural science has shown up the errors in them, and comparative research has been struck by the fatal resemblance between the religious ideas which we revere and the mental products of primitive peoples and times.

The scientific spirit brings about a particular attitude towards worldly matters; before religious matters it pauses for a little, hesitates, and finally there too crosses the threshold. In this process there is no stopping; the greater the number of men to whom the treasures of knowledge become accessible, the more widespread is the falling-away from religious belief—at first only from its obsolete and objectionable trappings, but later from its fundamental postulates as well. . . .

Thus I must contradict you when you go on to argue that men are completely unable to do without the consolation of the religious illusion, that without it they could not bear the troubles of life and the cruelties of reality. That is true, certainly, of the men into whom you have instilled the sweet—or bitter-sweet—poison from childhood onwards. But what of the other men, who have been sensibly brought up? Perhaps those who do not suffer from the neurosis will need no intoxicant to deaden it. They will, it is true, find themselves in a difficult situation. They will have to admit to themselves the full extent of their helplessness and their insignificance in the machinery of the universe; they can no longer be the centre of creation, no longer the object of tender care on the part of a beneficent Providence. They will be in the same position as a child who has left the parental house where he was so warm and comfortable. But surely infantilism is destined to be surmounted. Men cannot remain children for ever; they must in the end go out into "hostile life." We may call this *"education to reality."* Need I confess to you that the sole purpose of my book is to point out the necessity for this forward step? . . .

25

Carl G. Jung
The Collective Unconscious

In modern psychiatry, significant dissent has been provoked by Freud's rationalistic materialism, which reduces religious experiences to infantile wish-fulfillments. Among the respected voices opposing Freud on religion is that of Carl Gustav Jung (1875–1961), a Swiss physician who founded modern "analytical" psychology. Jung believed that a religious outlook is necessary to an individual's psychic development. Religious images and beliefs, in his view, are essential responses to universal psychological urges.

Jung received a medical degree from the University of Basel in 1900 and began his professional career in Zurich—first at a psychiatric clinic, then at an asylum. During his internship he developed a new system of psychological testing, "the association method," in which he demonstrated that patients' illogical responses to stimulus words were caused by associations withheld from consciousness because of their unpleasant content. He coined the now standard term "complexes" for those groups of ideas in the unconscious region of the patient's psyche that have a disturbing influence. Years later, he was to develop his classification of personality types: extroverted (outward-looking) and introverted (inward-looking).

When Jung read Freud's Interpretation of Dreams *in 1903, he was attracted by the fact that Freud also recognized the significance of unconscious factors. The two men soon met, and their ensuing friendship and close collaboration lasted until 1912. Jung finally ended the association because he could not accept Freud's insistence on the exclusively sexual basis of mental disor-*

The Collected Works of C. G. Jung, trans. R. F. C. Hull, Bollingen Series XX. Vol. 8: *The Structure and Dynamics of the Psyche,* copyright © 1960, 1969 by Princeton University Press; Vol. 9, I, *The Archetypes and the Collective Unconscious,* copyright © 1959, 1969 by Princeton University Press. Excerpts reprinted by permission. [From Vol. 9, Part I: pp. 3–8, 43–44, 48–53; Vol. 8: 365–68, 371–73, 375–76, 381.]

ders. Also, contrary to Freud, Jung had come to believe that the unconscious is not solely personal—that region of the psyche into which disturbing thoughts and instinctual urges are repressed, sometimes emerging to cause mental illness—but also collective—the source of creative and destructive forces that may become conscious through dreams and fantasies. These forces may also be evoked by myths, fairy tales, and superstitions. Thus, among his major contributions after the break with Freud was Jung's concept of the "collective unconscious," that is, a universal psychological inheritance spanning the evolution of the species.

Another major Jungian contribution is the concept of "archetypes," contents of the collective unconscious that take the form of images recognized on a conscious level. "Earth mother" and "wise old man," for example, are archetypal images repeated in many myths, fantasies, and dreams at widely separated historical periods. According to Jung, genuine religious experience is characterized by the rising of certain psychic archetypes from the collective unconscious into the individual consciousness, like islands rising from a vast uncharted sea. These archetypal experiences cannot be neglected, Jung believed, without disturbing the individual's psychic balance.

Jung traveled among primitive peoples to study these archetypal patterns. He also visited the Orient where he examined the religious symbols (archetypes) of Buddhism, Hinduism, and Confucianism. He came to the conclusion that both primitive and Eastern peoples have experience of humankind's inner unconscious world, which has been neglected by Western civilization in its one-sided development toward rationalized technology. Jung searched for ways in which Western culture might compensate for its psychic narrowness.

The numerous and lengthy publications by Jung—dealing with issues in psychiatry, religion, and the history of culture—were intended mainly for psychiatric analysts and for scholars. Some, however, were written for the general reader. Among these are Modern Man in Search of a Soul (1933), an overview of modern religious dilemmas; Essays on Contemporary Events (1947), a study of psychological aspects of the Second World War, including the psychology of mass movements; and Memories, Dreams, Reflections (1963), a posthumously published autobiography. Reprinted in the following selection are excerpts from three essays published by Jung between 1931 and 1954; they elaborate his concepts of archetypes and the collective unconscious and their relationships to religion.

ARCHETYPES OF THE COLLECTIVE UNCONSCIOUS

The hypothesis of a collective unconscious belongs to the class of ideas that people at first find strange but soon come to possess and use as familiar conceptions. This has been the case with the concept of the unconscious in general. After the philosophical idea of the unconscious, in the form presented chiefly by Carus and von Hartmann, had gone down under the overwhelming wave of materialism and empiricism, leaving hardly a ripple behind it, it gradually reappeared in the scientific domain of medical psychology.

At first the concept of the unconscious was limited to denoting the state of repressed or forgotten contents. Even with Freud, who makes the unconscious—at least metaphorically—take the stage as the acting subject, it is really nothing but the gathering place of forgotten and repressed contents, and has a functional significance thanks only to these. For Freud, accordingly, the unconscious is of an exclusively personal nature,[1] although he was aware of its archaic and mythological thought-forms.

A more or less superficial layer of the unconscious is undoubtedly personal. I call it the *personal unconscious*. But this personal unconscious rests upon a deeper layer, which does not derive from personal experience and is not a personal acquisition but is inborn. This deeper layer I call the *collective unconscious*. I have chosen the term "collective" because this part of the unconscious is not individual but universal; in contrast to the personal psyche, it has contents and modes of behavior that are more or less the same everywhere and in all individuals. It is, in other words, identical in all men and thus constitutes a common psychic substrate of a suprapersonal nature which is present in every one of us.

Psychic existence can be recognized only by the presence of contents that are *capable of consciousness*. We can therefore speak of an unconscious only in so far as we are able to demonstrate its contents. The contents of the personal unconscious are chiefly the *feeling-toned complexes,* as they are called; they constitute the personal and private side of psychic life. The contents of the collective unconscious, on the other hand, are known as *archetypes*. . . .

---

[1] In his later works Freud differentiated the basic view mentioned here. He called the instinctual psyche the "id," and his "super-ego" denotes the collective consciousness, of which the individual is partly conscious and partly unconscious (because it is repressed). [Jung's note. *Ed.*]

. . . so far as the collective unconscious contents are concerned we are dealing with archaic or—I would say—primordial types, that is, with universal images that have existed since the remotest times. The term "représentations collectives," used by Lévy-Bruhl to denote the symbolic figures in the primitive view of the world, could easily be applied to unconscious contents as well, since it means practically the same thing. Primitive tribal lore is concerned with archetypes that have been modified in a special way. They are no longer contents of the unconscious, but have already been changed into conscious formulae taught according to tradition, generally in the form of esoteric teaching. This last is a typical means of expression for the transmission of collective contents originally derived from the unconscious.

Another well-known expression of the archetypes is myth and fairytale. But here too we are dealing with forms that have received a specific stamp and have been handed down through long periods of time. The term "archetype" thus applies only indirectly to the "représentations collectives," since it designates only those psychic contents which have not yet been submitted to conscious elaboration and are therefore an immediate datum of psychic experience. In this sense there is a considerable difference between the archetype and the historical formula that has evolved. Especially on the higher levels of esoteric teaching the archetypes appear in a form that reveals quite unmistakably the critical and evaluating influence of conscious elaboration. Their immediate manifestation, as we encounter it in dreams and visions, is much more individual, less understandable, and more naïve than in myths, for example. The archetype is essentially an unconscious content that is altered by becoming conscious and by being perceived, and it takes its colour from the individual consciousness in which it happens to appear.

What the word "archetype" means in the nominal sense is clear enough, then, from its relations with myth, esoteric teaching, and fairytale. But if we try to establish what an archetype is *psychologically,* the matter becomes more complicated. So far mythologists have always helped themselves out with solar, lunar, meteorological, vegetal, and other ideas of the kind. The fact that myths are first and foremost psychic phenomena that reveal the nature of the soul is something they have absolutely refused to see until now. Primitive man is not much interested in objective explanations of the obvious, but he has an imperative need—or rather, his unconscious psyche has an irresistible urge—to assimilate all outer sense experiences to inner, psychic events. It is not enough for the primitive to see the sun rise and set; this external observation must at the same time be a psychic happening: the sun in its course must represent the fate of a god or hero who, in the last analysis, dwells nowhere except in the soul of man. All the mythologized processes of nature, such as summer and winter, the phases of the moon, the rainy seasons, and so forth, are in no sense allegories of these objective occurrences; rather thay are symbolic expressions of the inner, unconscious drama of the psyche which becomes accessible to man's consciousness by way of projection—that is, mirrored in the events of nature. The projection is so fundamental that it has taken several thousand years of civilization to detach it in some measure from its outer object. . . .

Primitive man impresses us so strongly with his subjectivity that we should really have guessed long ago that myths refer to something psychic. His knowledge of nature is essentially the language and outer dress of an unconscious psychic process. But the very fact that this process is unconscious gives us the reason why man has thought of everything except the psyche in his attempts to explain myths. He simply didn't know that the psyche contains all the images that have ever given rise to myths, and that our unconscious is an acting and suffering subject with an inner drama which primitive man rediscovers, by means of analogy, in the processes of nature both great and small. . . .

Tribal lore is always sacred and dangerous. All esoteric teachings seek to apprehend the unseen happenings in the psyche, and all claim supreme authority for themselves. What is true of primitive lore is true in even higher degree of the ruling world religions. They contain a revealed knowledge that was originally hidden, and they set forth the secrets of the soul in glorious images. Their temples and their sacred writings proclaim in image and word the doctrine hallowed from of old, making it accessible to every believing heart, every sensitive vision, every farthest range of thought. Indeed, we are compelled to say that the more beautiful, the more sublime, the more comprehensive the image that has evolved and been handed down by tradition, the further removed it is from individual experience. We can just feel our way into it and sense something of it, but the original experience has been lost.

Why is psychology the youngest of the empirical sciences? Why have we not long since discovered the unconscious and raised up its treasure-house of eternal images? Simply because we had a religious formula for everything psychic—and one that is far more beautiful and comprehensive than immediate experience. Though the Christian view of the world has paled for many people, the symbolic treasure-rooms of the East are still full of marvels that can nourish for a long time to come the passion for show and new clothes. What is more, these images—be they Christian or Buddhist or what you will—are lovely, mysterious, richly intuitive. Naturally, the more familiar we are with them the more does constant usage polish them smooth, so that what remains is only banal superficiality and meaningless paradox. The mystery of the Virgin Birth, or the homoousia[2] of the Son with the Father, or the Trinity which is nevertheless not a triad—these no longer lend wings to any philosophical fancy. They have stiffened into mere objects of belief. So it is not surprising if the religious need, the believing mind, and the philosophical speculations of the educated European are attracted by the symbols of the East—those grandiose conceptions of divinity in India and the abysms of Taoist philosophy in China—just as once before the heart and mind of the men of antiquity were gripped by Christian ideas. There are many Europeans who began by surrendering completely to the influence of the Christian symbol until they landed themselves in a Kierkegaardian neurosis, or whose relation to God, owing to the progressive impoverishment of symbolism, developed into an unbearably sophisticated I-You relationship—only to fall victims in their turn to the magic and novelty of Eastern symbols. This surrender is not necessarily a defeat; rather it proves the receptiveness and vitality of the religious sense. We can observe much the same thing in the educated Oriental, who not infrequently feels drawn to the Christian symbol or to the science that is so unsuited to the Oriental mind, and even develops an enviable understanding of them. That people should succumb to these eternal images is entirely normal, in fact it is what these images are for. They are meant to attract, to convince, to fascinate, and to overpower. They are created out of the primal stuff of revelation and reflect the ever-unique experience of divinity. That is why they always give man a premonition of the divine while at the same time safeguarding him from immediate experience of it. Thanks to the labours of the human spirit over the centuries, these images have become embedded in a comprehensive

[2] Greek: sameness.

system of thought that ascribes an order to the world, and are at the same time represented by a mighty, far-spread, and venerable institution called the Church. . . .

THE CONCEPT OF THE COLLECTIVE UNCONSCIOUS

My thesis, then, is as follows: In addition to our immediate consciousness, which is of a thoroughly personal nature and which we believe to be the only empirical psyche (even if we tack on the personal unconscious as an appendix), there exists a second psychic system of a collective, universal, and impersonal nature which is identical in all individuals. This collective unconscious does not develop individually but is inherited. It consists of pre-existent forms, the archetypes, which can only become conscious secondarily and which give definite form to certain psychic contents.

The Psychological Meaning of the Collective Unconscious

Medical psychology, growing as it did out of professional practice, insists on the *personal* nature of the psyche. By this I mean the views of Freud and Adler.[3] It is a *psychology of the person,* and its aetiological or causal factors are regarded almost wholly as personal in nature. Nonetheless, even this psychology is based on certain general biological factors, for instance on the sexual instinct or on the urge for self-assertion, which are by no means merely personal peculiarities. It is forced to do this because it lays claim to being an explanatory science. Neither of these views would deny the existence of *a priori* instincts common to man and animals alike, or that they have a significant influence on personal psychology. Yet instincts are impersonal, universally distributed, hereditary factors of a dynamic or motivating character, which very often fail so completely to reach consciousness that modern psychotherapy is faced with the task of helping the patient to become conscious of them. Moreover, the in-

[3] Alfred Adler (1870–1937), an Austrian psychiatrist. Like Jung, Adler was an early follower of Freud who broke away mainly because of Freud's insistence that the sexual drive is the primary psychic force; Adler believed that the primary force in humans is the urge for self-assertion.

stincts are not vague and indefinite by nature, but are specifically formed motive forces which, long before there is any consciousness, and in spite of any degree of consciousness later on, pursue their inherent goals. Consequently they form very close analogies to the archetypes, so close, in fact, that there is good reason for supposing that the archetypes are the unconscious images of the instincts themselves, in other words, that they are *patterns of instinctual behaviour*.

The hypothesis of the collective unconscious is, therefore, no more daring than to assume there are instincts. One admits readily that human activity is influenced to a high degree by instincts, quite apart from the rational motivations of the conscious mind. So if the assertion is made that our imagination, perception, and thinking are likewise influenced by inborn and universally present formal elements, it seems to me that a normally functioning intelligence can discover in this idea just as much or just as little mysticism as in the theory of instincts. Although this reproach of mysticism has frequently been levelled at my concept, I must emphasize yet again that the concept of the collective unconscious is neither a speculative nor a philosophical but an empirical matter. The question is simply this: are there or are there not unconscious, universal forms of this kind? If they exist, then there is a region of the psyche which one can call the collective unconscious. It is true that the diagnosis of the collective unconscious is not always an easy task. It is not sufficient to point out the often obviously archetypal nature of unconscious products, for these can just as well be derived from acquisitions through language and education. . . .

. . . There is no lunacy people under the domination of an archetype will not fall a prey to. If thirty years ago anyone had dared to predict that our psychological development was tending towards a revival of the medieval persecutions of the Jews,[4] that Europe would again tremble before the Roman fasces[5] and the tramp of legions, that people would once more give the Roman salute, as two thousand years ago, and that instead of the Christian Cross an archaic swastika[6] would lure onward millions of warriors ready for death—

[4] Adolf Hitler's Nazi Party, which had anti-Semitism as its official policy, came to power in Germany in 1933. This section of the excerpts from Jung's works is from a lecture first delivered in London in 1936.
[5] Benito Mussolini's Fascist Party came to power in Italy in 1922. The Party's name came from the Roman *fasces,* a bundle of rods containing an ax with the blade projecting, carried in front of Roman magistrates as an emblem of official power.
[6] The official Nazi emblem.

why, that man would have been hooted at as a mystical fool. And today? Surprising as it may seem, all this absurdity is a horrible reality. Private life, private aetiologies, and private neuroses have become almost a fiction in the world of today. The man of the past who lived in a world of archaic "représentations collectives" has risen again into very visible and painfully real life, and this not only in a few unbalanced individuals but in many millions of people.

There are as many archetypes as there are typical situations in life. Endless repetition has engraved these experiences into our psychic constitution, not in the form of images filled with content, but at first only as *forms without content,* representing merely the possibility of a certain type of perception and action. When a situation occurs which corresponds to a given archetype, that archetype becomes activated and a compulsiveness appears, which, like an instinctual drive, gains its way against all reason and will, or else produces a conflict of pathological dimensions, that is to say, a neurosis.

Method of Proof

We must now turn to the question of how the existence of archetypes can be proved. Since archetypes are supposed to produce certain psychic forms, we must discuss how and where one can get hold of the material demonstrating these forms. The main source, then, is *dreams,* which have the advantage of being involuntary, spontaneous products of the unconscious psyche and are therefore pure products of nature not falsified by any conscious purpose. By questioning the individual one can ascertain which of the motifs appearing in the dream are known to him. From those which are unknown to him we must naturally exclude all motifs which *might* be known to him, as for instance—to revert to the case of Leonardo[7]—the vulture symbol. We are not sure whether Leonardo took this symbol from Horapollo[8] or not, although it would have been perfectly possible for an

---

[7] Leonardo da Vinci (1452–1519), an Italian Renaissance artist. Jung's reference to "the vulture symbol" in the case of Leonardo is actually based on a mistake by Freud. Leonardo, in his notebooks, mentioned a fantasy of having been visited in his cradle by a kite (a small hawk). Freud and others, however, mistranslated Leonardo's Italian into the German word for "vulture." Freud then proceeded to base a part of his psychoanalytical study of Leonardo on the specific "vulture" fantasy.

[8] Usually Horapollon (Horus Apollo); a fourth-century Greek grammarian who lived in Egypt, he is the supposed author of the *Hieroglyphica,* a work that deals with the

educated person of that time, because in those days artists were distinguished for their wide knowledge of the humanities. Therefore, although the bird motif is an archetype par excellence, its existence in Leonardo's fantasy would still prove nothing. Consequently, we must look for motifs which could not possibly be known to the dreamer and yet behave functionally in his dream in such a manner as to coincide with the functioning of the archetype known from historical sources.

Another source for the material we need is to be found in "active imagination." By this I mean a sequence of fantasies produced by deliberate concentration. I have found that the existence of unrealized, unconscious fantasies increases the frequency and intensity of dreams, and that when these fantasies are made conscious the dreams change their character and become weaker and less frequent. From this I have drawn the conclusion that dreams often contain fantasies which "want" to become conscious. The sources of dreams are often repressed instincts which have a natural tendency to influence the conscious mind. In cases of this sort, the patient is simply given the task of contemplating any one fragment of fantasy that seems significant to him—a chance idea, perhaps, or something he has become conscious of in a dream—until its context becomes visible, that is to say, the relevant associative material in which it is embedded. It is not a question of the "free association" recommended by Freud for the purpose of dream-analysis, but of elaborating the fantasy by observing the further fantasy material that adds itself to the fragment in a natural manner.

This is not the place to enter upon a technical discussion of the method. Suffice it to say that the resultant sequence of fantasies relieves the unconscious and produces material rich in archetypal images and associations. Obviously, this is a method that can only be used in certain carefully selected cases. The method is not entirely without danger, because it may carry the patient too far away from reality. A warning against thoughtless application is therefore in place.

Finally, very interesting sources of archetypal material are to be found in the delusions of paranoiacs, the fantasies observed in trance-states, and the dreams of early childhood, from the third to the fifth

---

meanings of ancient Egyptian picture-writings (one of the many depicted objects being a vulture).

year. Such material is available in profusion, but it is valueless unless one can adduce convincing mythological parallels. It does not, of course, suffice simply to connect a dream about a snake with the mythological occurrence of snakes, for who is to guarantee that the functional meaning of the snake in the dream is the same as in the mythological setting? In order to draw a valid parallel, it is necessary to know the functional meaning of the individual symbol, and then to find out whether the apparently parallel mythological symbol has a similar context and therefore the same functional meaning. . . .

An Example

. . .

About 1906 I came across a very curious delusion in a paranoid schizophrenic who had been interned for many years. The patient had suffered since his youth and was incurable. He had been educated at a State school and been employed as a clerk in an office. He had no special gifts, and I myself knew nothing of mythology or archaeology in those days, so the situation was not in any way suspect. One day I found the patient standing at the window, wagging his head and blinking into the sun. He told me to do the same, for then I would see something very interesting. When I asked him what he saw, he was astonished that I could see nothing, and said: "Surely you see the sun's penis—when I move my head to and fro, it moves too, and that is where the wind comes from." Naturally I did not understand this strange idea in the least, but I made a note of it. Then about four years later, during my mythological studies, I came upon a book by the late Albrecht Dieterich, the well-known philologist, which threw light on this fantasy. The work, published in 1910, deals with a Greek papyrus in the Bibliothèque Nationale, Paris. Dieterich believed he had discovered a Mithraic[9] ritual in one part of the text. The text is undoubtedly a religious prescription for carrying out certain incantations in which Mithras is named. It comes from the Alexandrian school of mysticism and shows affinities with certain passages in the Leiden papyri and the *Corpus Hermeticum*. In Dieterich's text we read the following directions:

[9]Pertaining to an ancient Oriental mystery cult for men that flourished in the late Roman Empire. Its members worshipped Mithras, a Persian god of the sun, light, and truth.

Draw breath from the rays, draw in three times as strongly as you can and you will feel yourself raised up and walking towards the height, and you will seem to be in the middle of the aerial region. . . . The path of the visible gods will appear through the disc of the sun, who is God my father. Likewise the so-called tube, the origin of the ministering wind. For you will see hanging down from the disc of the sun something that looks like a tube. And towards the regions westward it is as though there were an infinite east wind. But if the other wind should prevail towards the regions of the east, you will in like manner see the vision veering in that direction.

It is obviously the author's intention to enable the reader to experience the vision which he had, or which at least he believes in. The reader is to be initiated into the inner religious experience either of the author, or—what seems more likely—of one of those mystic communities of which Philo Judaeus [10] gives contemporary accounts. The fire- or sun-god here invoked is a figure which has close historical parallels, for instance with the Christ-figure of the Apocalypse. [11] It is therefore a "representation collective," as are also the ritual actions described, such as the imitating of animal noises, etc. The vision is embedded in a religious context of a distinctly ecstatic nature and describes a kind of initiation into mystic experience of the Deity.

Our patient was about ten years older than I. In his megalomania, he thought he was God and Christ in one person. His attitude towards me was patronizing; he liked me probably because I was the only person with any sympathy for his abstruse ideas. His delusions were mainly religious, and when he invited me to blink into the sun like he did and waggle my head he obviously wanted to let me share his vision. He played the role of the mystic sage and I was the neophyte. He felt he was the sun-god himself, creating the wind by wagging his head to and fro. The ritual transformation into the Deity is attested by Apuleius [12] in the Isis mysteries, [13] and moreover in the form of a Helios [14] apotheosis. The meaning of the "minister-

---

[10] A Greek-Jewish theologian and philosopher who lived in Alexandria, Egypt (*ca.* 30 B.C.–*ca.* 45 A.D.).

[11] The book of Revelation—the imagistic, prophetic final book of the New Testament.

[12] A second-century Roman philosopher and novelist.

[13] Secret cults that promised immortality of the soul to believers.

[14] Sun.

ing wind" is probably the same as the procreative pneuma,[15] which streams from the sun-god into the soul and fructifies it. The association of sun and wind frequently occurs in ancient symbolism.

It must now be shown that this is not a purely chance coincidence of two isolated cases. We must therefore show that the idea of a wind-tube connected with God or the sun exists independently of these two testimonies and that it occurs at other times and in other places. Now there are, as a matter of fact, medieval paintings that depict the fructification of Mary with a tube or hose-pipe coming down from the throne of God and passing into her body, and we can see the dove or the Christ-child flying down it. The dove represents the fructifying agent, the wind of the Holy Ghost.

Now it is quite out of the question that the patient could have had any knowledge whatever of a Greek papyrus published four years later, and it is in the highest degree unlikely that his vision had anything to do with the rare medieval representations of the Conception, even if through some incredibly improbable chance he had ever seen a copy of such a painting. The patient was certified in his early twenties. He had never travelled. And there is no such picture in the public art gallery in Zurich, his native town.

I mention this case not in order to prove that the vision is an archetype but only to show you my method of procedure in the simplest possible form. If we had only such cases, the task of investigation would be relatively easy, but in reality the proof is much more complicated. First of all, certain symbols have to be isolated clearly enough to be recognizable as typical phenomena, not just matters of chance. This is done by examining a series of dreams, say a few hundred, for typical figures, and by observing their development in the series. The same method can be applied to the products of active imagination. In this way it is possible to establish certain continuities or modulations of one and the same figure. You can select any figure which gives the impression of being an archetype by its behaviour in the series of dreams or visions. If the material at one's disposal has been well observed and is sufficiently ample, one can discover interesting facts about the variations undergone by a single type. Not only the type itself but its variants too can be substantiated by evidence from comparative mythology and ethnology. . . .

---

[15]The vital spirit, or soul.

ANALYTICAL PSYCHOLOGY AND *WELTANSCHAUUNG* [16]

. . .

Let us confine ourselves for the moment to the conclusions to be drawn from Freud's psychoanalysis. In Freudian theory, man appears as a creature of instinct who, in various ways, comes into conflict with the law, with moral precepts, and with his own insights, and who is consequently compelled to repress certain instincts either wholly or in part. The aim of the method is to bring these instinctual contents to consciousness and make repression unnecessary by conscious correction. The menace entailed by their liberation is countered by the explanation that they are nothing but infantile wish-fantasies, which can still be suppressed, though in a wiser way. It is also assumed that they can be "sublimated," to use the technical term, by which is meant a sort of bending of them to a suitable form of adaptation. But if anyone believes this can be done at will he is sadly mistaken—only absolute necessity can effectively inhibit a natural instinct. When there is no need and no inexorable necessity, the "sublimation" is merely a self-deception, a new and somewhat more subtle form of repression.

Does this theory and this conception of man contain anything valuable for our *Weltanschauung?* I hardly think so. It is the well-known rationalistic materialism of the late nineteenth century, which is the guiding principle of the interpretive psychology underlying Freud's psychoanalysis. From it can come no other picture of the world, and therefore no other attitude to the world. . . .

Psychoanalysis has removed the veil from facts that were known only to a few, and has even made an effort to deal with them. But has it any new attitude to them? Has the deep impression produced lasting and fruitful results? Has it altered our picture of the world and thus added to our *Weltanschauung?* The *Weltanschauung* of psychoanalysis is a rationalistic materialism, the *Weltanschauung* of an essentially practical science—and this view we feel to be inadequate. When we trace a poem of Goethe's to his mother-complex, when we seek to explain Napoleon as a case of masculine protest, or St. Francis as a case of sexual repression, a sense of profound dissatisfaction comes over us. The explanation is insufficient and does not do justice to the reality and meaning of things. What becomes of beauty, greatness,

---

[16] German: a concept of the universe and of man's relationship to it.

and holiness? These are vital realities without which human existence would be superlatively stupid. What is the right answer to the problem of terrible sufferings and conflicts? The true answer should strike a chord that at least reminds us of the magnitude of the suffering. But the merely reasonable, practical attitude of the rationalist, however desirable it may be in other respects, ignores the real meaning of suffering. It is simply set aside and explained away as irrelevant. It was a great noise about nothing. Much may fall into this category, but not everything.

The mistake, as I have said, lies in the circumstance that psychoanalysis has a scientific but purely rationalistic conception of the unconscious. When we speak of instincts we imagine that we are talking about something known, but in reality we are talking about something unknown. As a matter of fact, all we know is that effects come to us from the dark sphere of the psyche which somehow or other must be assimilated into consciousness if devastating disturbances of other functions are to be avoided. It is quite impossible to say offhand what the nature of these effects is, whether they originate in sexuality, the power instinct, or some other instinct. They have as many meanings and facets as the unconscious itself.

I have already pointed out that although the unconscious is a receptacle for everything that is forgotten, past, and repressed, it is also the sphere in which all subliminal processes take place. It contains sense-perceptions that are still too weak to reach consciousness, and, furthermore, is the matrix out of which the whole psychic future grows. Thus, just as a person can repress a disquieting wish and thereby cause its energy to contaminate other functions, so he can shut out a new idea that is alien to him so that its energy flows off into other functions and disturbs them. I have seen many cases where abnormal sexual fantasies disappeared, suddenly and completely, the moment a new idea or content became conscious, or when a migraine suddenly vanished when the patient became aware of an unconscious poem. Just as sexuality can express itself inappropriately in fantasies, so creative fantasy can express itself inappropriately in sexuality. . . .

If the human mind came into the world as a complete *tabula rasa* [17] these problems would not exist, for there would then be nothing in the mind that it had not acquired or that had not been implanted in

[17] Latin: clean slate; a mind not yet affected by experience.

it. But there are many things in the human psyche that were never acquired by the individual, for the human mind is not born a *tabula rasa,* nor is every man provided with a wholly new and unique brain. He is born with a brain that is the result of development in an endlessly long chain of ancestors. This brain is produced in each embryo in all its differentiated perfection, and when it starts functioning it will unfailingly produce the same results that have been produced innumerable times before in the ancestral line. The whole anatomy of man is an inherited system identical with the ancestral constitution, which will unfailingly function in the same way as before. Consequently, the possibility that anything new and essentially different will be produced becomes increasingly small. All those factors, therefore, which were essential to our near and remote ancestors will also be essential to us, since they are embedded in the inherited organic system. They are even necessities which make themselves felt as needs.

Do not fear that I shall speak to you of inherited ideas. Far from it. The autonomous contents of the unconscious, or, as I have called them, dominants, are not inherited ideas but inherited possibilities, not to say compelling necessities, for reproducing the images and ideas by which these dominants have always been expressed. Of course every region of the earth and every epoch has its own distinctive language, and this can be endlessly varied. It matters little if the mythological hero conquers now a dragon, now a fish or some other monster; the fundamental motif remains the same, and that is the common property of mankind, not the ephemeral formulations of different regions and epochs.

Thus man is born with a complicated psychic disposition that is anything but a *tabula rasa.* Even the boldest fantasies have their limits determined by our psychic inheritance, and through the veil of even the wildest fantasy we can still glimpse the dominants that were inherent in the human mind from the very beginning. It seems very remarkable to us when we discover that insane people develop fantasies that can be found in almost identical form among primitives. But it would be remarkable if it were otherwise.

I have called the sphere of our psychic heritage the collective unconscious. The contents of consciousness are all acquired individually. If the human psyche consisted simply and solely of consciousness, there would be nothing psychic that had not arisen in the course of the individual's life. In that case we would seek in vain for any prior conditions or influences behind a simple parental complex. With the reduction to father and mother the last word would be said, for they are the figures that first influenced the conscious psyche to the exclusion of all else. But actually the contents of consciousness did not come into existence simply through the influence of the environment; they were also influenced and arranged by our psychic inheritance, the collective unconscious. Naturally the image of the individual mother is impressive, but its peculiar impressiveness is due to the fact that it is blended with an unconscious aptitude or inborn image which is the result of the symbiotic relationship of mother and child that has existed from eternity. Where the individual mother fails in this or that respect, a loss is felt, and this amounts to a demand of the collective mother-image for fulfilment. An instinct has been balked, so to speak. This very often gives rise to neurotic disturbances, or at any rate to peculiarities of character. If the collective unconscious did not exist, everything could be achieved by education; one could reduce a human being to a psychic machine with impunity, or transform him into an ideal. But strict limits are set to any such enterprise, because the dominants of the unconscious make almost irresistible demands for fulfilment. . . .

If, in this lecture, I have helped you to recognize that the powers which men have always projected into space as gods, and worshipped with sacrifices, are still alive and active in our own unconscious psyche, I shall be content. This recognition should suffice to show that the manifold religious practices and beliefs which, from the earliest times, have played such an enormous role in history cannot be traced back to the whimsical fancies and opinions of individuals, but owe their existence far more to the influence of unconscious powers which we cannot neglect without disturbing the psychic balance. The example I gave of the mother-complex is naturally only one among many. The archetype of the mother is a single instance that could be supplemented by a number of other archetypes. This multiplicity of unconscious dominants helps to explain the diversity of religious ideas.

All these factors are still active in our psyche; only the expression and evaluation of them have been superseded, not their actual existence and effectiveness. The fact that we can now understand them as psychic quantities is a new formulation, a new expression, which may enable us to discover a new way of relating to the powers of the unconscious. I believe this possibility to be of immense significance, because the collective unconscious is in no sense an obscure corner of the mind, but the mighty deposit of ancestral experience accumulated over millions of years, the echo of prehistoric happenings to which each century adds an infinitesimally small amount of variation and differentiation. Because the collective unconscious is, in the last analysis, a deposit of world-processes embedded in the structure of the brain and the sympathetic nervous system, it constitutes in its totality a sort of timeless and eternal world-image which counterbalances our conscious, momentary picture of the world. It means nothing less than another world, a mirror-world if you will. But, unlike a mirror-image, the unconscious image possesses an energy peculiar to itself, independent of consciousness. By virtue of this energy it can produce powerful effects which do not appear on the surface but influence us all the more powerfully from within. These influences remain invisible to anyone who fails to subject his momentary picture of the world to adequate criticism, and who therefore remains hidden from himself. That the world has an inside as well as an outside, that it is not only outwardly visible but acts upon us in a timeless present, from the deepest and apparently most subjective recesses of the psyche—this I hold to be an insight which, even though it be ancient wisdom, deserves to be evaluated as a new factor in building a *Weltanschauung.* . . .

Hemmed round by rationalistic walls, we are cut off from the eternity of nature. Analytical psychology seeks to break through these walls by digging up again the fantasy-images of the unconscious which our rationalism has rejected. These images lie beyond the walls; they are part of the nature *in us,* which apparently lies buried in our past and against which we have barricaded ourselves behind the walls of reason. Analytical psychology tries to resolve the resultant conflict not by going "back to Nature" with Rousseau,[18] but by holding on to the level of reason we have successfully reached, and by enriching consciousness with a knowledge of man's psychic foundations. . . .

[18] Jean Jacques Rousseau (1712–78), a French (Swiss-born) philosopher, who was one of the first exponents of romanticism. Rousseau rejected civilization, which he blamed for the corruption of mankind, and asserted that the "good" life was one in harmony with unspoiled nature.

26

Elie Wiesel

The Death of God

In the years since the Second World War, "the death of God" has been a significant theological expression. For some, the "atheist" mood it suggests grew out of the inability of traditional religions to explain "God's silence" in the face of the Nazis' deliberate abuse and slaughter of millions of civilians. Among the most memorable eyewitness accounts of the Nazi death camps is the one by Elie Wiesel (1928–   ).

Born and raised in the town of Sighet in the Transylvanian highlands—an area that had been controlled alternately by Hungary and Romania—Wiesel, at age fifteen, was sent with his family to the concentration camp in Auschwitz, Poland. It was the spring of 1944, and all the Jews of Transylvania were being shipped out of that area as part of the German racial policy. His mother and youngest sister were selected for extermination on the night they arrived at Auschwitz. His father was killed, before Elie's eyes, in early 1945, soon after the father and son were marched to the concentration camp at Buchenwald, Germany.

Liberated by the advancing American army two months after his father's death, Wiesel refused repatriation to eastern Europe at the end of the war. Now stateless, he was denied immigration to Palestine, his first choice, which was still under the authority of the British government. Eventually he moved to Paris where, from 1948 to 1951, he studied philosophy, while earning his living as a choir director and teacher of the Bible.

During his sojourn in Paris, Wiesel took a brief assignment from a French newspaper to report on Israel's war of independence; later, he became chief

*foreign correspondent for a Tel Aviv daily. In 1956, while in New York on
a reporting mission for his newspaper, he was struck by a taxicab. During
his ensuing period of confinement in a New York hospital, he decided to
apply for American citizenship, which was granted to him in 1963. While
continuing his journalistic and literary careers, Wiesel has also been a professor, from 1973 to 1976, at the City University of New York and since then
at Boston University.*

*The ambition to become a "serious" writer has been with Wiesel since his
agony in the concentration camps. As a survivor he feels profoundly the need
"to bear witness, to testify" to their horrors. The selection that follows is from
his first book,* Night *(1960), which recounts his experiences in the camps—
the death of his father, and the death of his own faith in God. Having witnessed dehumanizing suffering and death, Wiesel accuses and rejects God for
His "silence."*

*Wiesel's many other writings also deal largely with the themes of Jewish
remembrance, survival, and identity in a world that permitted Auschwitz.
Among these works are* Dawn *(1961), a novel in which a death-camp survivor, now a member of a Jewish terrorist group in British-controlled Palestine, is given the ironically grim task of executing a British officer; and* The
Gates of the Forest *(1966), a complex novel of a Transylvanian Jew, sole
survivor of his village, who portrays Judas in a passion play, joins a par-
tisan group to fight the Germans, and eventually settles in the United States
where—like the author—he comes to a passionate reaffirmation of his own
identity, his relationship to other people and to God.*

*Wiesel, apart from his novels, has often concerned himself with the ongo-
ing plight of his co-religionists in other lands. In* The Jews of Silence
*(1966), for example, he recounts his 1965 journey to the Soviet Union and
speaks out against the silence of Western Jews regarding the oppression of
Soviet Jews. In recent years Wiesel has also written about happier aspects of
his tradition, as in* Souls on Fire *(1972), which retells tales of the mystical
Hasidic Jews.*

One day, the electric power station at Buna was blown up. The
Gestapo,[1] summoned to the spot, suspected sabotage. They found a

---

[1] The secret police of the Nazi regime.

trail. It eventually led to the Dutch Oberkapo.[2] And there, after a search, they found an important stock of arms.

The Oberkapo was arrested immediately. He was tortured for a period of weeks, but in vain. He would not give a single name. He was transferred to Auschwitz. We never heard of him again.

But his little servant had been left behind in the camp in prison. Also put to torture, he too would not speak. Then the SS[3] sentenced him to death, with two other prisoners who had been discovered with arms.

One day when we came back from work, we saw three gallows rearing up in the assembly place, three black crows. Roll call. SS all round us, machine guns trained: the traditional ceremony. Three victims in chains—and one of them, the little servant, the sad-eyed angel.

The SS seemed more preoccupied, more disturbed than usual. To hang a young boy in front of thousands of spectators was no light matter. The head of the camp read the verdict. All eyes were on the child. He was lividly pale, almost calm, biting his lips. The gallows threw its shadow over him.

This time the Lagerkapo[4] refused to act as executioner. Three SS replaced him.

The three victims mounted together onto the chairs.

The three necks were placed at the same moment within the nooses.

"Long live liberty!" cried the two adults.

But the child was silent.

"Where is God? Where is He?" someone behind me asked.

At a sign from the head of the camp, the three chairs tipped over.

Total silence throughout the camp. On the horizon, the sun was setting.

"Bare your heads!" yelled the head of the camp. His voice was raucous. We were weeping.

"Cover your heads!"

Then the march past began. The two adults were no longer alive. Their tongues hung swollen, blue-tinged. But the third rope was still moving; being so light, the child was still alive. . . .

[2] Head prisoner foreman (selected by the Nazis from among the prisoners).
[3] A special police force; one of its functions was to operate the camps.
[4] Prisoner foreman of the warehouse.

For more than half an hour he stayed there, struggling between life and death, dying in slow agony under our eyes. And we had to look him full in the face. He was still alive when I passed in front of him. His tongue was still red, his eyes were not yet glazed.

Behind me, I heard the same man asking:

"Where is God now?"

And I heard a voice within me answer him:

"Where is He? Here He is—He is hanging here on this gallows. . . ."

That night the soup tasted of corpses.

The summer was coming to an end. The Jewish year was nearly over.

On the eve of Rosh Hashanah, the last day of that accursed year, the whole camp was electric with the tension which was in all our hearts. In spite of everything, this day was different from any other. The last day of the year. The word "last" rang very strangely. What if it were indeed the last day?

They gave us our evening meal, a very thick soup, but no one touched it. We wanted to wait until after prayers. At the place of assembly, surrounded by the electrified barbed wire, thousands of silent Jews gathered, their faces stricken.

Night was falling. Other prisoners continued to crowd in, from every block, able suddenly to conquer time and space and submit both to their will.

"What are You, my God," I thought angrily, "compared to this afflicted crowd, proclaiming to You their faith, their anger, their revolt? What does Your greatness mean, Lord of the Universe, in the face of all this weakness, this decomposition, and this decay? Why do You still trouble their sick minds, their crippled bodies?"

Ten thousand men had come to attend the solemn service, heads of the blocks, Kapos, functionaries of death.

"Bless the Eternal. . . ."

The voice of the officiant had just made itself heard. I thought at first it was the wind.

"Blessed be the Name of the Eternal!"

Thousands of voices repeated the benediction; thousands of men prostrated themselves like trees before a tempest.

"Blessed be the Name of the Eternal!"

Why, but why should I bless Him? In every fiber I rebelled. Because He had had thousands of children burned in His pits? Because He kept six crematories working night and day, on Sundays and feast days? Because in His great might He had created Auschwitz, Birkenau, Buna, and so many factories of death? How could I say to Him: "Blessed art Thou, Eternal, Master of the Universe, Who chose us from among the races to be tortured day and night, to see our fathers, our mothers, our brothers, end in the crematory? Praised be Thy Holy Name, Thou Who hast chosen us to be butchered on Thine altar?"

I heard the voice of the officiant rising up, powerful yet at the same time broken, amid the tears, the sobs, the sighs of the whole congregation:

"All the earth and the Universe are God's!"

He kept stopping every moment, as though he did not have the strength to find the meaning beneath the words. The melody choked in his throat.

And I, mystic that I had been, I thought:

"Yes, man is very strong, greater than God. When You were deceived by Adam and Eve, You drove them out of Paradise. When Noah's generation displeased You, You brought down the Flood. When Sodom no longer found favor in Your eyes, You made the sky rain down fire and sulphur. But these men here, whom You have betrayed, whom You have allowed to be tortured, butchered, gassed, burned, what do they do? They pray before You! They praise Your name!"

"All creation bears witness to the Greatness of God!"

Once, New Year's Day had dominated my life. I knew that my sins grieved the Eternal; I implored his forgiveness. Once, I had believed profoundly that upon one solitary deed of mine, one solitary prayer, depended the salvation of the world.

This day I had ceased to plead. I was no longer capable of lamentation. On the contrary, I felt very strong. I was the accuser, God the accused. My eyes were open and I was alone—terribly alone in a world without God and without man. Without love or mercy. I had ceased to be anything but ashes, yet I felt myself to be stronger than the Almighty, to whom my life had been tied for so long. I stood amid that praying congregation, observing it like a stranger.

The service ended with the Kaddish.[5] Everyone recited the Kaddish over his parents, over his children, over his brothers, and over himself.

We stayed for a long time at the assembly place. No one dared to drag himself away from this mirage. Then it was time to go to bed and slowly the prisoners made their way over to their blocks. I heard people wishing one another a Happy New Year!

I ran off to look for my father. And at the same time I was afraid of having to wish him a Happy New Year when I no longer believed in it.

He was standing near the wall, bowed down, his shoulders sagging as though beneath a heavy burden. I went up to him, took his hand and kissed it. A tear fell upon it. Whose was that tear? Mine? His? I said nothing. Nor did he. We had never understood one another so clearly.

The sound of the bell jolted us back to reality. We must go to bed. We came back from far away. I raised my eyes to look at my father's face leaning over mine, to try to discover a smile or something resembling one upon the aged, dried-up countenance. Nothing. Not the shadow of an expression. Beaten.

Yom Kippur. The Day of Atonement.

Should we fast? The question was hotly debated. To fast would mean a surer, swifter death. We fasted here the whole year round. The whole year was Yom Kippur. But others said that we should fast simply because it was dangerous to do so. We should show God that even here, in this enclosed hell, we were capable of singing His praises.

I did not fast, mainly to please my father, who had forbidden me to do so. But further, there was no longer any reason why I should fast. I no longer accepted God's silence. As I swallowed my bowl of soup, I saw in the gesture an act of rebellion and protest against Him.

And I nibbled my crust of bread.

In the depths of my heart, I felt a great void. . . .

---

[5] A prayer of the Jewish liturgy that is recited at the end of a religious service and is also used as a mourner's prayer for those who have died.

27

John A. T. Robinson

Can a Truly Contemporary Person
Not Be an Atheist?

*Many moods and meanings are conveyed by the expression "the death of
God." It is not only the agonized cry of war survivors, such as Elie
Wiesel,* but an expression used by some prominent theologians seeking to
reconcile religion with the ways of contemporary secular society. One such
expositor of the "death" of the traditional God is the Anglican bishop John
Arthur Thomas Robinson (1919–   ).*

  *Born in Canterbury, England, his father a clergyman on the staff of Eng-
land's greatest cathedral, Robinson felt naturally drawn to the Anglican
ministry. He studied theology at Cambridge University and, after receiving
a doctorate in 1946, was soon ordained a priest in the Church of England.
Returning to Cambridge in 1951, Robinson lectured there in religious studies
until 1959; during these years he also spent time in the United States as a
visiting professor at Harvard University and at Union Theological Seminary, in Virginia. In 1959 he left his scholarly pursuits at Cambridge, for a
time, to accept the post of Assistant Bishop of Woolwich, serving in an
industrial area of southeast London. In recent years he has managed to combine his episcopal duties with further writing and lecturing in theology.*

  *Of Robinson's nearly twenty published books, the best known among the
general public is* Honest To God *(1963). Within a year of its publication,
it had sold almost a million copies, the largest sale in history for a new book
of erudite theology. In* Honest to God *Robinson follows the lead of other*

*See selection 26.

From *The New Reformation?* by John A. T. Robinson. Published in the USA 1965, by
the Westminster Press, Philadelphia. © SCM Press, Ltd., London, 1965. Used by
permission. [Pp. 106–22.]

"radical" theologians in attempting to sweep away the "mythology" that has been a barrier to faith for many persons in modern secular society. He argues that the traditional picture of God in man's image "up there" is ludicrous in the space age. However, he does not deny the existence of God, but rather states that the ultimate reality at the root of each person's life is God. It is God's will that we mature enough to understand that morality should no longer be an external code divinely enforced through fear, but rather a personal code maintained through deep love. That is, God should now be basic to all one's life, not relegated to that part of life controlled by an institutional church.

The following selection presents the full text of a lecture given by Robinson in November 1964 at the opening of an exhibition on atheism held at the University of Frankfurt in West Germany. The bishop's invitation to speak there was probably due to the belief, based on a misreading of Honest To God, *that he is an atheist. The standard atheist assertion that the God "hypothesis" is not justifiable—intellectually, psychologically, or morally—does appear to be endorsed at one level in this lecture by Robinson. The God he rejects, however, fits only the concept of the "absentee controller"; the God he welcomes is the one who—like the suffering Jesus on the cross—enters into and embraces the secular world.*

A bishop lecturing on atheism still strikes people, in England at any rate, as incongruous—though since I have freely been called "the atheist bishop" (as well as plenty of other things!) many will simply assume that I have now reached my proper level. Indeed, I have discovered at least one virtue in what I believe to be the unhappy German title of *Honest to God, Gott ist Anders* (God is Different). A friend of mine found that he was able to take as many copies as he liked to East Germany—they thought it was atheistic propaganda!

In fact I want to treat the question of atheism as a very serious one for those of us who would call ourselves Christians. So I have deliberately posed it, for myself as well as for you, in the form: "Can a truly contemporary person *not* be an atheist?" For I believe there is an important sense in which a person who is fully a man of our times *must*—or, at any rate, *may*—be an atheist before he can be a Christian. That is to say, there is so much in the atheist's case which is true that for many people today the only Christian faith which can be valid *for them* is one that takes over *post mortem dei,* after the death of God as "God" has traditionally been understood. I put this strongly—and can afford to put it strongly—as I shall insist equally strongly on the faith. But it is a faith which I suspect for increasing numbers of our contemporaries will only be possible through, and out the other side of, the atheist critique. The Christian should therefore take atheism seriously, not only so that he may be able to "answer" it, but so that he himself may still be able to be a believer in the mid-twentieth century.

With this in mind, I would ask you to expose yourselves to the three thrusts of modern atheism. These are not so much three types of atheism—each is present, in varying degree, in any representative type—so much as three motives which have impelled men, particularly over the past hundred years, to question the God of their upbringing and ours. They may be represented by three summary statements: 1. God is intellectually superfluous; 2. God is emotionally dispensable; 3. God is morally intolerable. Let us consider each of them in turn.

1. GOD IS INTELLECTUALLY SUPERFLUOUS

"I have no need of that hypothesis": so Laplace, the great astronomer, replied to Napoleon, when asked where God fitted into his system. Within the terms of an astronomical system, he was clearly correct. To bring in God to fill the gaps in our science or to deal with life at the point at which things get beyond human explanation or control is intellectual laziness or practical superstition. And yet, ever since the scientific and technological revolution which created our modern world, the defense of Christianity has in fact been bound up with staving off the advance of secularization, whose effect is precisely to close the gaps in the circle of explanation and control. Bonhoeffer[1] put it accurately enough in the well-known passage in his *Letters:*

---

[1]Dietrich Bonhoeffer (1906–45), a German pastor executed for his involvement as a courier in the July 1944 conspiracy of German generals who attempted to assassinate Hitler. Bonhoeffer's *Letters and Papers from Prison* (1953) was the primary stimulus that set Robinson to writing *Honest to God.*

Man has learned to cope with all questions of importance without recourse to God as a working hypothesis. In questions concerning science, art, and even ethics, this has become an understood thing which one scarcely dares to tilt at any more. But for the last hundred years or so it has become increasingly true of religious questions also: it is becoming evident that everything gets along without "God," and just as well as before. As in the scientific field, so in human affairs generally, what we call "God" is being more and more edged out of life, losing more and more ground. . . .

Christian apologetic has taken the most varying forms of opposition to this self-assurance. Efforts are made to prove to a world thus come of age that it cannot live without the tutelage of "God." Even though there has been a surrender on all secular problems, there still remain the so-called ultimate questions—death, guilt—on which only "God" can furnish an answer, and which are the reason why God and the Church and the pastor are needed. . . . But what if one day they no longer exist as such, if they too can be answered without "God"?

One has only to raise this question to recognize the threat that most churchmen instinctively feel and the vested interest which we still have in the "God of the gaps." Indeed, when we hear it from the atheist, we take it as the attack for which it is clearly intended. Here, for instance, is Sir Julian Huxley:[2]

The god hypothesis is no longer of any pragmatic value for the interpretation or comprehension of nature, and indeed often stands in the way of better and truer interpretation. . . .

It will soon be as impossible for an intelligent, educated man or woman to believe in a god as it is now to believe that the earth is flat, that flies can be spontaneously generated, that disease is a divine punishment, or that death is always due to witchcraft.

God is an *x* in the equation whom we cannot get on without, a cause, controller or designer whom we are bound to posit or allow room for—this hypothesis seems to men today more and more superfluous. There is nothing indeed that *disproves* it. It is simply, in the words of Anthony Flew, the linguistic philosopher, being "killed

---

[2] Elder brother to Aldous Huxley and a distinguished biologist (1887–1975). His appointment as Director-General of UNESCO caused some uproar because of his atheism. Huxley's most noteworthy writings deal with the relationship of science to human society and especially to religion. (The other modern authors quoted by Robinson are mainly theologians.)

by inches"; it is dying "the death of a thousand qualifications." And he vividly illustrates how this happens in the parable from which Paul van Buren starts his *Secular Meaning of the Gospel:*

> Once upon a time two explorers came upon a clearing in the jungle. In the clearing were growing many flowers and many weeds. One explorer says, "Some gardener must tend this plot." The other disagrees. "There is no gardener." So they pitch their tents and set a watch. No gardener is ever seen. "But perhaps he is an invisible gardener." So they set up a barbed-wire fence. They electrify it. They patrol it with bloodhounds. . . . But no shrieks ever suggest that some intruder has received a shock. No movement of the wire ever betrays an invisible climber. The bloodhounds never give cry. Yet still the Believer is not convinced. "But there is a gardener, invisible, intangible, insensible to electric shocks, a gardener who has no scent and makes no sound, a gardener who comes secretly to look after the garden which he loves." At last the Skeptic despairs, "But what is left of your original assertion? Just how does what you call an invisible, intangible, eternally elusive gardener differ from an imaginary gardener or even from no gardener at all?"

And what is true at the level of explanation is equally true at the level of control. Neither to account for sickness nor to deal with it does it occur to men today to bring in "God." Or if it does occur to them, it is when they have reached the end of their tether and "turn to prayer." But this simply confirms the judgment of Werner Pelz that "When we use the word 'God' we are talking about something which no longer connects with anything in most people's life, except with whatever happens to be left over when all the vital connections have been made." Most of us today are practical atheists. The "god-hypothesis" is as irrelevant for running an economy or coping with the population explosion as it was for Laplace's system. As a factor you must take into account in the practical business of living, God is "out"—and no amount of religious manipulation can force him back in. He is peripheral, redundant, incredible—and therefore *as God* displaced: in Julian Huxley's words, "not a ruler, but the last fading smile of a cosmic Cheshire Cat."

I am very far from saying this is the whole truth or that all the atheist's arguments on this front, or any other, are valid (many of them reflect a very superficial or crudely tendentious understanding even of the traditional theology). What I am urging is that we allow ourselves to feel the full force of this attack rather than spend our time looking for yet another hole in the wire fence.

2. GOD IS EMOTIONALLY DISPENSABLE

The reference earlier to Bonhoeffer's theme of man come of age shows the close connection. Man is discovering that he no longer *needs* God or religion. He finds he can stand on his own feet without having to refer constantly to Daddy in the background or to run to Mummy's apron strings.

According to this line of attack religion is a prop or a sop. It is not merely something incredible and superfluous: it is a dangerous illusion which can prevent men facing reality and shouldering responsibility. This lies at the heart of the Freudian critique of religion as the universal neurosis or the Marxist attack on it as "the opium of the people." God and the gods are the projection of men's fears, insecurities and longings. They act as a debilitating crutch which men must have the courage to discard if they are to grow up and shake off the sense of helplessness which religion both induces and sanctions.

The call of atheism here is to man to cut the strings, to move out of the shadow of the Father figure, to cease treating God as a peg, or a refuge, or a compensation for miseries which he should be fighting. Secularization means that man must accept responsibility for his own destiny, neither trying to blame it on the gods nor expecting some providence to relieve him of it or see him through.

Again I believe we must recognize the essential truth of this attack. Whatever as Christians we may wish to add or come back with, we should not be caught trying to defend this God or save him from death by artificial respiration. This was the strength of Bonhoeffer's courageous acceptance of the edging out of the "God of religion": unless a man is prepared to be "forsaken" by that God, he cannot find what Jesus is showing us on the Cross. But are we prepared to let that God go? In varying degrees we all *need* religion, and nowhere more than here is the thrust of atheism seen as a threat. The tearing down of the traditional structure in which "the good Lord provides" and surrounds the whole of life with the protective comfort of the womb is viewed as an act of sacrilege which must be withstood, if not for our own sake, at any rate for the sake of the weaker brethren to whose pastoral care we hasten. Or, as an alternative line of defense, we seek to dismiss those who try, as someone has put it, to "destroy my grandmother's religion with my grandfather's science." But if we are honest, our "grandmother's religion" probably plays a much larger role in our conscious and unconscious life than we care to admit.

Consider, for instance, the quite central belief in Providence. The trust that in and through and despite everything there meets one a love, stronger than death, from which nothing can separate us is fundamental to the Christian confidence. But I am sure there are some forms of belief in providence which merely pander to emotional immaturity. And these are the forms which secretly retain God in the gaps of our ignorance or fears, or which see him as a celestial manipulator rearranging, interrupting, or taking over from, the forces which would otherwise be at work. And when these forces are those of human responsibility their "providential overruling" can quickly lead to the debilitation, the superstition, and even the fatalism, of which the atheists accuse the religious.

Each time I go to London Airport I am met by a large notice, greeting me with the assurance: "BOAC takes good care of you." What are we to make of this declaration of secular providence? If it fails, whom are we to blame—BOAC or God? When first I flew, I used to indulge in additional "cover" for those tense thirty seconds of takeoff as one waits to see whether the plane will make it and leave the ground. Did my prayer in the gap—when somehow a little supernatural "lift" would always be welcome—do credit to my trust in God? I think not. I suspect that this is where a Christian *ought* to be a practical atheist—and trust the pilot. If this is the sort of God he believes in—and logically he should only believe in him if he is a God who *does* take over—then the protest of the atheist is valid. Men need to be weaned, however painfully, from refusal to accept the burden of responsibility. A God who relieves them of this requires killing.

This clamor for the death of a God who keeps men languid and dispossessed, associated with Feuerbach before Marx, Engels and Freud developed it in their different ways, leads directly into the even more strident protest which expresses itself in the third statement.

3. GOD IS MORALLY INTOLERABLE

This reverses Voltaire's dictum that "If God did not exist, we should have to invent him." It says rather, "If God did exist, we should have to abolish him." This is the tradition that derives again from Feuerbach, and runs through Bakunin, Proudhon and Nietzsche to Camus and Sartre. It represents the real quick of twentieth-century atheism, in contrast with its dying nerves—if one may dare to thus speak of Marxism, as I think one can, as somewhat dated. It is what Jacques Maritain has called "positive atheism." It centers in the determination that God must *die* if man is to *live*. It is not content with accepting the negative absence of God and carrying on as though everything remained the same. It is concerned positively in living in "a world without God"—creating the justice and the meaning and the freedom which God, the great bloodsucker, has drained away.

But we should be careful not to state it in too emotive language. It would be easy to discredit this whole protest as the titanism of a Nietzsche or the outburst of a few intellectuals. But if this was once true, it is certainly true no longer. Camus spoke for an entire emerging generation. There is a dispassionate quality about modern atheism, of a piece with our whole urban-secular civilization. It is not vindictive or despairing, and it is noticeably losing its overtones of an anti-religion. A speaker can deliberately ask to be introduced on the television, as happened in my presence, as an "atheist" rather than an "agnostic" without any sense of defiance. And this I believe is a healthy development. For in "the secular city" constructive debate will only become possible if atheism, like Christianity, can discover what it means to be "religionless," and the various competing "ologies" and "isms" are "desacralized."

This is not in the least to suggest that this particular form of atheism, above all, should lapse into indifferentism. It has a moral nerve which must not be cut, if it is to continue to purge and purify. For it draws its strength from the seriousness with which it takes the problem of evil. A God who "causes" or "allows" the suffering of a single child is morally intolerable. So the debate ranges, back and forth, in some of the great dialogues of modern literature—in Dostoevsky's *Brothers Karamazov,* in Camus's *The Plague* and, most recently, in Peter de Vries's *The Blood of the Lamb* (describing the agony of a father watching his girl die of leukemia). But, of course, this is no intellectuals' debate. It is the root of atheism in most ordinary people, and today it is openly asserted even by the young. Here, for instance, is a girl of nineteen interviewed in the *Daily Mirror:*

> "Do you believe in God?"
> "No. I used to, but not now. I don't see how there can be a benevolent God. There are too many tragedies—personal and in the world. . . . RELIGION IS DISGUSTING."

Religion is disgusting. God does not solve the problem of suffering: he only magnifies it. To push off evil onto God simply makes him into a Devil—and in any case represents a cowardly evasion. Men must carry the can and refuse the temptation to dissociation or transference.

I believe that this is a profoundly moral response, and one that must be taken with the utmost seriousness. Any glib notion of a God who "causes" cancer or "sends" the streptococcus *is* a blasphemy. Most traditional theodicy, so far from justifying the ways of God to man, has the effect of strengthening atheism. "Whatever your sickness is," the priest is instructed to say in the seventeenth-century Anglican Book of Common Prayer, "know certainly that it is God's visitation." Who could speak like that today? Atheism has done its purifying work. For there is nothing that provokes our generation to doubt or blasphemy more than the idea of a Being who sends such events into the lives of individuals. One of the liberating effects of secularization is that *this* idea of divine causation has at any rate been discredited. People rightly look for natural rather than supernatural causes. *But they still assume that Christians teach otherwise*—and their God is dismissed with them with indignation and disgust.

AFTER THE DEATH OF GOD

Can a truly contemporary person *not* be an atheist? It is a very real question. Not all people will feel the force of each of these thrusts. Their God may survive any or indeed all of them. I would certainly not want to suggest that a contemporary Christian *must* go through the mill of first being an atheist. But I firmly believe that he *may,* and that increasingly many will.

But *post mortem dei,* what? Is, in fact, faith possible out the other side? I believe that it is, and that not merely despite the death of God but even because of it. For this, after all, is no new situation for the people of God. The faith of Abraham, the father of faith, was born, as St. Paul reminds us, out of "contemplating his own body, now as good as dead, and the deadness of Sarah's womb."[3] The faith of Job was possible to him only after all that he trusted in had first been removed. Even Jesus himself had to go through the process of the death of God—of the One who allowed it all to happen, "with a million angels watching, and they never move a wing." But, above all, Christianity itself was "born in the grave" (some of you may know the remarkable little sermon of that title in Tillich's *Shaking of the Foundations*): it could only come into being at all *post mortem dei*. And for each one of us in some degree the Resurrection can only happen after the death of God. Though it looks as if everything is taken away—even the body of the Lord—yet this is not the destruction of Christianity but its liberation.

For—with all metaphysical security shattered, with even the word "God" of doubtful currency, with no theodicy of our own that we can establish—we find that we still cannot get shot of God: after his death he is disturbingly alive. No one that I know has wrestled through this problem more compellingly in our day than William Hamilton of Colgate Rochester Divinity School, New York. His *New Essence of Christianity* seeks in an age of theological "reduction" to lay claim to those few things that are certain, and in a chapter called "Belief in a Time of the Death of God" he writes:

> In one sense God seems to have withdrawn from the world and its sufferings, and this leads us to accuse him of either irrelevance or cruelty. But in another sense, he is experienced as a pressure and a wounding from which we would love to be free. For many of us who call ourselves Christians, therefore, believing in the time of the "death of God" means that he is there when we do not want him, in ways we do not want him, and he is not there when we do want him.

Is not the situation of many of us today that we feel we *must* be atheists, and yet we *cannot* be atheists? God as we have been led to posit him *is* intellectually superfluous, *is* emotionally dispensable, *is* morally intolerable—and yet, in grace and demand, he *will not* let us go. The hound of heaven still dogs us, the "beyond in our midst"

---

[3] Romans 4:17–25. [Robinson's note. *Ed.*]

still encounters us, when all the images, all the projections, even all the words for God have been broken.

Can a truly contemporary person *not* be an atheist? In one sense, he can hardly fail to be. There is no going back to the pre-secular view of the world, where God is always "there" to be brought in, run to, or blamed. Yet, in another sense, he may find that he *cannot* be an atheist, however much he would like to be. For on the Emmaus[4] road, on the way back from the tomb, the risen Christ comes up with him and he knows himself constrained.

What then, in the last analysis, remains the difference between the atheist and the one who cannot finally rest in that name? In *Honest to God* I wrote:

> So conditioned for us is the word "God" by association with a Being out there [with all, in other words, that the anti-theist finds superfluous, dispensable or intolerable] that Tillich warns us . . . "You must forget everything traditional you have learned about God, perhaps even that word itself." Indeed, the line between those who believe in God and those who do not bears little relation to their profession of the existence or non-existence of such a Being. It is a question, rather, of their openness to the holy, the sacred, in the unfathomable depths of even the most secular relationship. As Martin Buber puts it of the person who professedly denies God, "When he, too, who abhors the name, and believes himself to be godless, gives his whole being to addressing the Thou of his life, as a Thou that cannot be limited by another, he addresses God."

There, I suggest, lies the clue to the real difference. Let me use a familiar analogy. In dealing with other people it is possible for us to treat them simply as things—to use them, control them, manipulate them. This is what John Macmurray calls the *instrumental* relationship. Or, if for no other reason than that we soon discover they are not wholly amenable to such treatment, we can relate ourselves to them in what he calls the *functional* relationship, of cooperation with them. This is the most common relation we have with others, in which we treat them often as means to an end but never merely as means. But, thirdly, we can give ourselves to them in pure *personal* relationship, responding to them in love and trust for their own

---

[4] The village where Jesus appeared to two of his disciples after his crucifixion (Luke 24:13–35).

sakes. And ultimately it is only in this relationship that we can know them—and we ourselves be known—*as persons.*

To transfer this analogy to the universe, to life as a whole, we can respond to it in a purely instrumental, scientific relationship—at the level of its mathematical regularities. We can regard reality as ultimately nothing more than a collocation of atoms, and we can even try to run history as a piece of social engineering. But there are few purely mechanistic materialists today. Much more common are those whose ultimate frame of reference is a functional one—humanists, whether dialectical, evolutionary or idealistic. And the atheist is the man who in his attitude to life stops there—for whom nothing finally is absolute or unconditional, for whom all is a means (though not merely a means).

The man who finds himself compelled to acknowledge the reality of *God,* whatever he may call him or however he may image him, is the man who, through the mathematical regularities and through the functional values, is met by the same grace and the same claim that he recognizes in the I-Thou relation with another person. It may come to him through nature, through the claims of artistic integrity or scientific truth, through the engagements of social justice or of personal communion. Yet always it comes with an overmastering givenness and demand such as no other thing or person has the power to convey or the right to require. Like the child Samuel in the Temple, confusing the call of God with the voice of Eli, he may think at first that it can simply be identified with or contained within the finite relationship by which it is mediated. He may not be able to tell what to make of it, he may find it profoundly disturbing, but he knows it in the end to be inescapable and unconditional. In this relationship, too, he discovers himself known and judged and accepted for what ultimately he is. He finds in it for himself the way, the truth and the life. And if he is a Christian, he recognizes and acknowledges this grace and claim supremely in the person of Jesus Christ, the definition at one and the same time of a genuinely human existence and of this intangible, ineffable reality of "God." He agrees, passionately, with the atheist that such a reality cannot be *used* or *needed.* A God like that *is* superfluous, dispensable, intolerable. In fact it is *no* God. And then, when that God is dead, the Lord appears.

The Lord appears—not as one who is needed, nor as one who intrudes, forcing men's freedom or curtailing their responsibility, but as one who "makes as though he would go further."[5] Like the disciples on the road to Emmaus, we find ourselves faced with the bewildering double adjustment of learning at one and the same time to live in a world without God and in a world with God. It is a new situation, a post-resurrection world, in which the old *is* dead. There is no question of introducing that God again by the back door or of returning to the *status quo ante*.[6] Yet, despite the irreversibility of that change, there is the constraint of the other reality with which to come to terms. How, then, does it stand in relation to three thrusts we examined before?

In the first place, God remains intellectually superfluous, in the sense that he does not need to be "brought in." There is no "place" for him in the system—or for that matter on its edge. The ring has been closed in which before an opening was left for God. Secularization must be gladly accepted—and no attempt made to find another hole in the fence or to reinstate him outside it.

There is a parallel here, to return to our previous analogy, with attempts to "locate" the element of the distinctively personal—the free, spiritual reality of "I" and "Thou"—in our description of human behavior. Clearly this does not depend on establishing gaps in the chemistry or the psychology. Efforts to secure a place for freedom and the spirit in that way are foredoomed. Nor is there any more hope in representing it as external to a closed system, which a free spirit, depicted as a sort of supernatural self, controls and directs from the outside—though such a model has been a common presupposition both in psychology and theology. To know a man as a person is not to posit another invisible factor between or beyond the regularities which the scientist investigates. It is to respond to a total reality which engages one in, through and under the regularities, which in no way denies them and yet is related to them like another dimension.

Similarly with God. As a factor introduced to make the system work he is redundant. In that sense it is possible to answer every question without God—even the ones that before were thought to admit only of a religious solution. And at the level of control things get along for good or for ill, just as well without him. It is not necessary to bring him in.

[5] Luke 24:28 [Robinson's note. *Ed.*]
[6] Latin: condition existing before.

But in another sense it is not possible to leave him out—any more than it is possible to run an economy or cope with the population explosion without in the last analysis treating persons as persons, without reckoning with the dimension of the "Thou." God is a reality of life whom one cannot ultimately evade. Huxley, quite legitimately, may not need him as a hypothesis, nor Flew be able to trap him in his mesh. Like the scientist or philosopher who looks in vain for the "Thou" in the person he is analyzing without addressing, the searcher for God finds himself in the position of Job:

> Behold, I go forward, but he is not there;
> and backward, but I cannot perceive him;
> on the left hand I seek him, but I cannot behold him;
> I turn to the right hand, but I cannot see him.

But then he adds, aware of the presence by which all the while he is being explored:

> But he knows the way that I take.

The one who is superfluous as a hypothesis becomes all too present as a subject in encounter.

Then, secondly, God continues to be emotionally dispensable. The returning Lord does not come as compensation for the gap left by the God of the gaps. There is no solace to restore the old relationships. The crutches are broken, and it remains "good for you that I go away."[7] Nothing relieves of responsibility those who have to live by the Spirit.

Yet man come of age is still called to be a son. It is a mark of our religious immaturity that the "Father" image inextricably suggests emotional dependence, if not domination. The son never seems to grow up. Yet in fact the New Testament "sonship" is a figure for freedom and stands precisely for man who has passed out of his minority and come of age.[8] The Christian faith, so far from seeking to keep men in strings, calls them to maturity, not the maturity of the adolescent revolting *against* a father, but of the "full-grown man" entering into the responsible freedom of the son and heir.

There is nothing in the God of the New Testament—nor indeed in the God who said to the prophet, "Son of man, stand upon your

---

[7] John 16:7. [Robinson's note. *Ed.*]
[8] See especially John 8:31–8 and Galatians 4:1–7. [Robinson's note. *Ed.*]

feet and I will speak with you"[9]—which would keep men languid or dispossessed. The call is to bear and to share the terrible freedom of love. And faith in the fatherly reality to which sonship is the response is not a belief in anything that undercuts this. Speaking of a mature trust in providence, Tillich writes:

> The man who believes in providence does not believe that a special divine activity will alter the conditions of finitude and estrangement. He believes, and asserts with the courage of faith, that no situation whatsoever can frustrate the fulfillment of his ultimate destiny, that nothing can separate him from the love of God which is in Jesus Christ.

And again:

> Providence means that there is a creative and saving possibility implied in every situation, which cannot be destroyed by any event.

The prayer that is immature is the prayer that cannot trust this, but resorts to reliance on physical or mental interference. True prayer is not for additional "cover" that, if the worst comes to the worst, the controls may be taken over by celestial manipulation. True prayer is prayer for the pilot, and by the pilot, that his responsibility may be heightened, not diminished, by trusting the love his life exists to serve and from which not even "the worst" can separate it.

This brings us, lastly, to the third charge, that God is morally intolerable. Again, it is a charge that stands. A Being who "sends" the worst into the lives of individuals or who stands aside to "permit" it is a God who must die. But that is precisely what the Christian faith proclaims happened at Calvary. The God who could have sent "twelve legions of angels" and did not is exposed as the God who failed even his Son. The obituary read by the atheist is valid, even if sometimes shrill.

Nothing in the Christian faith implies the rehabilitation of that God. Yet the Christian, as he looks back on the Cross from the other side of the Resurrection, sees not a world without God at its borders but a world with God at its center. What it means to believe in love as the final reality is to be discerned not in the absentee controller who allows the suffering but in the crucified transfiguring figure who bears it. The New Testament "answer" to the problem of evil is given not majestically out of the whirlwind but agonizingly out of

---

[9] Ezekiel 2:1. [Robinson's note. *Ed.*]

the darkness. As Bonhoeffer saw, in that situation "only a suffering God can help." The God of the Christian faith, who alone can be "our" God, can ultimately be revealed and responded to only as love which *takes* responsibility for evil—transformingly and victoriously.

For men to adjust to life in a world with that as its central reality is no intellectual exercise: it is, in Bonhoeffer's words again, to "range themselves with God in his suffering." That is the test he saw distinguishing Christians from unbelievers. And even among professed unbelievers there may at the point of dereliction, where the choice of our ultimate allegiance stands forth most starkly, be many who find that they cannot rail.

"For Christians, heathens alike he hangeth dead." Such is the reality Bonhoeffer recognized as the common presupposition of our age—replacing what he called "the religious premise." Atheists and Christians start there together. And on their walk from the tomb, sharing the disenchantment of other more facile hopes, the dialogue can begin.

28

Harvey Cox

The Feast of Fools

The radical theology of "the death of God" movement has been useful for its focus on religion's obligation to embrace the secular world. Even some of its proponents, however, suggest that, in its desire to improve the human condition, the new theology tends to ignore the importance of festivity and fantasy. One such critic is Harvey Cox (1929–   ), a prominent American theologian.

Cox, born and raised in towns around Philadelphia, received a bachelor's degree in history from the University of Pennsylvania in 1951 and then attended the Yale University Divinity School. After graduating from Yale in 1955 he went to Ohio to become director of religious activities at Oberlin College. In 1956 he was ordained a minister of the American Baptist Church, and soon left Oberlin for a succession of positions in the overseas ministry. By 1963 he had also achieved a doctorate in history and the philosophy of religion from Harvard University, followed by a teaching position at Andover Newton Theological School, in Massachusetts. Since 1965 he has been a member of the faculty at the Harvard University Divinity School.

Cox's best-known book is The Secular City (1965), an analysis of contemporary urban society and Christianity's relationship to it. Cox, seeming to place himself with the radical "death of God" theologians, celebrated the emergence of the new secular city and urged Christians to participate in it. Since the church can no longer control culture and politics, Cox asserted that Christians should welcome that change as "an authentic consequence of biblical faith" and should develop an appropriately secularized system of belief. He wrote that "if theology is to survive and make any sense to the contempo-

Reprinted by permission of the author and the publishers from *The Feast of Fools: A Theological Essay on Festivity and Fantasy*, by Harvey Cox, Cambridge, Mass.: Harvard University Press, Copyright © 1969 by Harvey Cox. [Pp. 3–18, 161–62.]

rary world, it must neither cling to a metaphysical world-view, nor collapse into a mystical mode. It must push on into the living lexicon of the urban-secular man." (Cox had validated his own secular "living lexicon" by going to jail in 1963 for his participation in a civil-rights campaign.)

At the end of the 1960s Cox turned from the social activism of The Secular City *to a renewed sense of the value of religious celebration and liturgy.* The Feast of Fools: A Theological Essay on Festivity and Fantasy *(1969) "criticizes the catastrophic decline of festivity and fantasy in a civilization that has enthroned production, performance, growth, competition and instrumental values." Christ the clown, an early Christian representation, is an appropriate image for us to revive, since "only by learning to laugh at the hopelessness around us can we touch the hem of hope." Cox believes that in order for humankind to survive, both physically and spiritually, we must reach toward a sense of* world *community, analogous to the sense of community felt by medieval Christians through their periodic religious festivals. He also believes that medieval people placed a higher value on imagination than do most contemporary people. For example, he asks, would the non-conformist St. Francis find a place in our world? We need both rationality and fantasy, Cox concludes, in order to realize the high potential of our emotional and spiritual being.*

OVERTURE

During the medieval era there flourished in parts of Europe a holiday known as the Feast of Fools. On that colorful occasion, usually celebrated about January first, even ordinarily pious priests and serious townsfolk donned bawdy masks, sang outrageous ditties, and generally kept the whole world awake with revelry and satire. Minor clerics painted their faces, strutted about in the robes of their superiors, and mocked the stately rituals of church and court. Sometimes a Lord of Misrule, a Mock King, or a Boy Bishop was elected to preside over the events. In some places the Boy Bishop even celebrated a parody mass. During the Feast of Fools, no custom or convention was immune to ridicule and even the highest personages of the realm could expect to be lampooned.

The Feast of Fools was never popular with the higher-ups. It was constantly condemned and criticized. But despite the efforts of fidgety ecclesiastics and an outright condemnation by the Council of Basel in 1431, the Feast of Fools survived until the sixteenth century. Then in the age of Reformation and Counter-Reformation it gradually died out. Its faint shade still persists in the pranks and revelry of Halloween and New Year's Eve.

Chroniclers of Western history seldom lament the passing of the Feast of Fools. There are reasons why they do not. Often it did degenerate into debauchery and lewd buffoonery. Still, its death was a loss. The Feast of Fools had demonstrated that a culture could periodically make sport of its most sacred royal and religious practices. It could imagine, at least once in a while, a wholly different kind of world—one where the last was first, accepted values were inverted, fools became kings, and choirboys were prelates. The demise of the Feast of Fools signaled a significant change in the Western cultural mood: an enfeeblement of our civilization's capacity for festivity and fantasy. Its demise showed that people were beginning to see their social roles and sacred conventions through eyes that could not permit such strident satire, that they no longer had the time or the heart for such trenchant social parody.

Why did the Feast of Fools disappear? The question is part of a much larger one that scholars have debated for years. Are the religious patterns of postmedieval Europe the cause or the effect of the new social and economic practices that culminated in capitalism and the industrial revolution? Why did the virtues of sobriety, thrift, industry, and ambition gain such prominence at the expense of other values? Why did mirth, play, and festivity come in for such scathing criticism during the Protestant era?

I do not wish to join in that debate here. This is not a historical treatise and I recall the Feast of Fools only as a symbol of the subject of this book. It is important to notice however that festivity and fantasy do play a less central role among us now than they did in the days of holy fools, mystical visionaries, and a calendar full of festivals. And we are the poorer for it.

There are those who would claim that we still have festivity and fantasy, but that they take a different form. We celebrate at office parties, football games, and cocktail gatherings. Our fantasies glitter in the celluloid world of the cinema and on the pages of *Playboy*. Science fiction still conjures up fanciful worlds. Perhaps. But my contention in this book is that whatever forms of festivity and fantasy remain to us are shrunken and insulated. Our celebrations do not relate us, as they once did, to the parade of cosmic history or to the great stories of man's spiritual quest. Our fantasies tend to be cautious, eccentric, and secretive. When they do occasionally soar, they are appreciated only by an elite. Our feasting is sporadic or obsessive, our fantasies predictable and politically impotent. Neither provides the inspiration for genuine social transformation.

At least all of this has been true until quite recently. Now, however, we are witnessing a rebirth of the spirit of festivity and fantasy. Though we have no annual Feast of Fools, the life affirmation and playful irreverence once incarnated in that day are bubbling up again in our time. As expected, the bishops and the bosses are not happy about it, but it is happening anyway. This incipient renaissance of fantasy and festivity is a good sign. It shows that our period may be rediscovering the value of two components of culture both of which were once seen in the Feast of Fools. The first is the feast or festival itself: important because it puts work in its place. It suggests that work, however rewarding, is not the highest end of life but must contribute to personal human fulfillment. We need stated times for nonwork to remind us that not even an astronomical gross national product and total employment can bring a people salvation. On feast days we stop working and enjoy those traditional gestures and moments of human conviviality without which life would not be human. Festivity, like play, contemplation, and making love, is an end in itself. It is not instrumental.

The other important cultural component of the Feast of Fools is fantasy and social criticism. Unmasking the pretence of the powerful always makes their power seem less irresistible. That is why tyrants tremble before fools and dictators ban political cabarets. Though a stated occasion for political persiflage can be exploited by the powerful to trivialize criticism, it need not be. From the oppressor's point of view satire can always get out of hand or give people ideas, so it is better not to have it at all.

The Feast of Fools thus had an implicitly radical dimension. It exposed the arbitrary quality of social rank and enabled people to see that things need not always be as they are. Maybe that is why it made the power-wielders uncomfortable and eventually had to go. The divine right of kings, papal infallibility, and the modern totalitarian state all flowered after the Feast of Fools disappeared.

Today in the late twentieth century we need the spirit represented by the Feast of Fools. In a success- and money-oriented society, we need a rebirth of patently unproductive festivity and expressive celebration. In an age that has quarantined parody and separated politics from imagination we need more social fantasy. We need for our time and in our own cultural idiom a rediscovery of what was right and good about the Feast of Fools. We need a renaissance of the spirit, and there are signs that it is coming.

INTRODUCTION

> I know nothing, except what everyone knows—
> if there when Grace dances, I should dance.
> —W. H. Auden, "Whitsunday in Kirchstetten"

Mankind has paid a frightful price for the present opulence of Western industrial society. Part of the price is exacted daily from the poor nations of the world whose fields and forests garnish our tables while we push their people further into poverty. Part is paid by the plundered poor who dwell within the gates of the rich nations without sharing in the plenty. But part of the price has been paid by affluent Western man himself. While gaining the whole world he has been losing his own soul. He has purchased prosperity at the cost of a staggering impoverishment of the vital elements of his life. These elements are *festivity*—the capacity for genuine revelry and joyous celebration, and *fantasy*—the faculty for envisioning radically alternative life situations.

Festivity and fantasy are not only worthwhile in themselves, they are absolutely vital to human life. They enable man to relate himself to the past and the future in ways that seem impossible for animals. The *festival,* the special time when ordinary chores are set aside while man celebrates some event, affirms the sheer goodness of what is, or observes the memory of a god or hero, is a distinctly human activity. It arises from man's peculiar power to incorporate into his own life the joys of other people and the experience of previous generations. Porpoises and chimpanzees may play. Only man celebrates. Festivity is a human form of play through which man appropriates an extended area of life, including the past, into his own experience.

Fantasy is also uniquely human. A hungry lion may dream about a zebra dinner but only man can mentally invent wholly new ways of living his life as an individual and as a species. If festivity enables man to enlarge his experience by reliving events of the past, fantasy is a form of play that extends the frontiers of the future.

Festivity, of course, does not focus solely on the past any more than fantasy reaches only toward the future. We also sometimes celebrate *coming* events, and our minds often re-create bygone experiences. But despite this obvious overlap, festivity is more closely related to memory, and fantasy is more akin to hope. Together they help make man a creature who sees himself with an origin and a destiny, not just as an ephemeral bubble.

Both our enjoyment of festivity and our capacity for fantasy have deteriorated in modern times. We still celebrate but our feasts and parties often lack real verve or feeling. Take for example a typical American New Year's Eve. It is a celebration, but there is something undeniably vacuous and frenetic about it. People seem anxiously, even obsessively determined to have a good time. Not to have a date for New Year's Eve is the ultimate adolescent tragedy. Even adults usually hate to spend the evening alone. On New Year's Eve we bring out the champagne and hurl paper streamers. But under the surface of Dionysiac carousing we feel something is missing. The next day we often wonder why we bothered.

Our mixed feelings about New Year's Eve reveal two things about us. First, we are still essentially festive and ritual creatures. Second, our contemporary feasts and rites are in a dismal state. The reason New Year's Eve is important is that it so vividly energizes both memory and hope. As hoping and remembering creatures, we rightly sense something of unusual symbolic significance about that peculiar magical time when the old year disappears forever and the new one begins. We personify the occasion with a bearded old man and a pink baby. We take a cup of kindness for the past (for "old acquaintance"), we kiss, we toast the future. The New Year's Eve party demonstrates the vestigial survival of forgotten feasts and rituals.

But the vaguely desperate air lurking behind the noisemakers and funny hats is also significant. We dimly sense on New Year's Eve and sometimes on other occasions a whole world of empyrean ecstasy and fantastic hope, a world with which we seem to have lost touch. Our sentimentality and wistfulness arise from the fact that we have so few festivals left, and the ones we have are so stunted in their ritual and celebrative power.

Still, we are not wholly lost, and the fact that we still do ring out the old and ring in the new reminds us that celebration, however weakened, is not yet dead.

While festivity languishes, our fantasy life has also become anemic. Once effulgent, it now ekes out a sparse and timid existence. Our night dreams are quickly forgotten. Our daydreams are stealthy, clandestine, and unshared. Unable to conjure up fantasy images on our own, we have given over the field to mass production. Walt Disney and his imitators have populated it with virtuous mice and friendly skunks. Low-grade cinema and formula-TV producers have added banal symbols and predictable situations. But the enfeeblement of fantasy cannot be blamed on the mass media. It is the symptom of a much larger cultural debility. Indeed, the sportive inventiveness of today's best filmmakers proves both that it is not the technology which is at fault and that human fantasy still survives in a dreary, fact-ridden world.

What are the reasons for the long, slow decay of festivity and fantasy in the West? The sources of our sickness are complex. During the epoch of industrialization we grew more sober and industrious, less playful and imaginative. Work schedules squeezed festivity to a minimum. The habits formed are still so much with us that we use our new technologically provided leisure either to "moonlight," or to plan sober consultations on the "problem of leisure," or to wonder why we are not enjoying our "free time" the way we should.

The age of science and technology has also been hard on fantasy. We have J. R. R. Tolkien's hobbits [1] and the visions of science fiction. But our fact-obsessed era has taught us to be cautious: always check impulsive visions against the hard data. Secularism erodes the religious metaphors within which fantasy can roam. Scientific method directs our attention away from the realm of fantasy and toward the manageable and the feasible. True, we are now discovering that science without hunches or visions gets nowhere, but we still live in a culture where fantasy is tolerated, not encouraged. Part of the blame belongs to secularism. There was a time when visionaries were canonized, and mystics were admired. Now they are stud-

---

[1] Amiable elvish creatures who inhabit "Middle Earth" in Tolkien's fantasy-novel *The Hobbit* (1937) and in his epic trilogy *The Lord of the Rings* (1954–55).

ied, smiled at, perhaps even committed. All in all, fantasy is viewed with distrust in our time.

But why should we care if festivity and fantasy now play a smaller role in human life? Why not simply turn the world over to sobriety and rational calculation? Is anything significant lost? I believe that it is.

In the first place, the disappearance of festivity and fantasy simply makes life duller. They should be nurtured for their own sake. Further, man's very survival as a species has been placed in grave jeopardy by our repression of the human celebrative and imaginative faculties. I must also argue from theological premises that man will grasp his divine origin and destiny only if he regains the capacity for festive revelry and the ability to fantasize. Let me state these three theses as clearly as possible.

(1) Man is by his very nature a creature who not only works and thinks but who sings, dances, prays, tells stories, and celebrates. He is *homo festivus*. Notice the universal character of festivity in human life. No culture is without it. African pygmies and Australian primitives frolic in honor of the equinox. Hindus revel at Holi. Moslems feast after the long fast of Ramadan. In some societies the principal festival comes at harvest or when the moon reaches a particular position. In others the anniversary of some event in the life of a cultural or religious hero supplies the cause for jubilation. There are important differences, as we shall mention later, between the cultures that stress cosmic or seasonal festivals and those that emphasize historical holidays, but all provide an occasion for singing old songs, saluting heroes, and reaffirming new and old aspirations. When festivity disappears from a culture something universally human is endangered.

Man is also *homo fantasia,* the visionary dreamer and mythmaker. If no culture is without some form of celebration, there is certainly none that lacks its share of wild and improbable stories. Fairies, goblins, giants, and elves—or their equivalent—inhabit the imagination of every race. Also, in most societies, one can find legends of a golden age in the past and, in some, stories of a wondrous age to come. Students of prehistoric man have often said more about man's tools than about his tales. Perhaps this derives from our present obsessive interest in technology. Perhaps it is because clubs and knives remain to be found, although myths disappear. Still, both were there very early and it was just as much his propensity to dream and fan-

446   Harvey Cox

tasize as it was his augers and axes that first set man apart from the beasts.

Man is *homo festivus* and *homo fantasia*. No other creature we know of relives the legends of his forefathers, blows out candles on a birthday cake, or dresses up and pretends he is someone else.

But in recent centuries something has happened that has undercut man's capacity for festivity and fantasy. In Western civilization we have placed an enormous emphasis on man as worker (Luther[2] and Marx[3]) and man as thinker (Aquinas[4] and Descartes[5]). Man's celebrative and imaginative faculties have atrophied. This worker-thinker emphasis, enforced by industrialization, ratified by philosophy, and sanctified by Christianity, helped to produce the monumental achievements of Western science and industrial technology. Now, however, we can begin to see that our productivity has exacted a price. Not only have we gotten it at the expense of millions of other people in the poor nations, not only have we ruined countless rivers and lakes and poisoned our atmosphere, we have also terribly damaged the inner experience of Western man. We have pressed him so hard toward useful work and rational calculation he has all but forgotten the joy of ecstatic celebration, antic play, and free imagination. His shrunken psyche is just as much a victim of industrialization as were the bent bodies of those luckless children who were once confined to English factories from dawn to dusk.

Man is essentially festive and fanciful. To become fully human, Western industrial man, and his non-Western brothers insofar as they are touched by the same debilitation, must learn again to dance and to dream.

(2) The survival of mankind as a species has also been placed in jeopardy by the repression of festivity and fantasy. This is because man inhabits a world of constant change, and in such a world both festival and fantasy are indispensable for survival. If he is to survive man must be both innovative and adaptive. He must draw from the richest wealth of experience available to him and must never be bound to existing formulas for solving problems. Festivity, by

[2] Martin Luther (1483–1546), a German theologian and leader of the Protestant Reformation.
[3] Karl Marx (1818–83), a German political philosopher and a major originator of communist doctrine.
[4] St. Thomas Aquinas (*ca.* 1225–74), a medieval Christian theologian.
[5] René Descartes (1596–1650), a French philosopher and mathematician.

breaking routine and opening man to the past, enlarges his experience and reduces his provincialism. Fantasy opens doors that merely empirical calculation ignores. It widens the possibilities for innovation. Together, festivity and fantasy enable man to experience his present in a richer, more joyful, and more creative way. Without them he may go the way of the diplodocus and the tyrannosaurus.

Psychiatrists remind us that the loss of a sense of time is a symptom of personal deterioration. Cut a man off from his memories or his visions and he sinks to a depressed state. The same is true for a civilization. So long as it can absorb what has happened to it and move confidently toward what is yet to come its vitality persists. But when a civilization becomes alienated from its past and cynical about its future, as Rome once did, its spiritual energy flags. It stumbles and declines.

Much has been written in recent years about man as a "historical" being, a spirit who perceives himself in time. These analyses have contributed much to our understanding of man. What they often overlook, however, is that our capacity to relate ourselves to time requires more than merely intellectual competence. Well-tabulated chronicles and sober planning alone do not keep us alive to time. We recall the past not only by recording it but by reliving it, by making present again its fears and delectations. We anticipate the future not only by preparing for it but by conjuring up and creating it. Our links to yesterday and tomorrow depend also on the aesthetic, emotional, and symbolic aspects of human life—on saga, play, and celebration. Without festivity and fantasy man would not really be a historical being at all.

In our present world it is also crucial for the rich Western nations to recover something of their capacity for sympathetic imagination and noninstrumental *joie de vivre* [6] if they are to keep in touch with the so-called "underdeveloped world." Otherwise, the rich Western nations will become increasingly static and provincial or they will try to inflict their worship of work on the rest of the world. Unable to put themselves in someone else's shoes, they will grow more insensitive to the enclaves of poverty in their midst and the continents of hunger around them. Without relearning a measure of festivity on their own they will not be able to appreciate the gusto of Africa and Latin America. Deprived of joy they will become more hateful and

---

[6] French: joy of living.

suspicious toward "others." Without fantasy not even the radicals of the affluent world can identify with oppressed peoples in their battles for independence and national dignity. Without social imagination no one will be able to think up fundamentally new ways to relate to the rest of the world. Unless the industrialized world recovers its sense of festivity and fantasy, it will die or be destroyed.

(3) Our loss of the capacity for festivity and fantasy also has profound religious significance. The religious man is one who grasps his own life within a larger historical and cosmic setting. He sees himself as part of a greater whole, a longer story in which he plays a part. Song, ritual, and vision link a man to this story. They help him place himself somewhere between Eden and the Kingdom of God; they give him a past and a future. But without real festive occasions and without the nurture of fantasy man's spirit as well as his psyche shrinks. He becomes something less than man, a gnat with neither origin nor destiny.

This may account in part for the malaise and tedium of our time. Celebration requires a set of common memories and collective hopes. It requires, in short, what is usually thought of as a religion. For centuries Christianity provided our civilization with both the feast days that kept its history alive, and with the images of the future that sustained its expectations. Stories of Adam, Noah, and Abraham rooted us in the recesses of our prehistory. The saints supplied images of human perfection. The Kingdom of God and the New Jerusalem with their visions of peace and social fulfillment kept us hopeful about the future. At Christmas and Easter, and to some extent during the other holy days, the figure of Jesus somehow enlivened both our primal memories and our wildest hopes. The last of the prophets of Israel, Jesus was also seen as the first citizen of an epoch still to be fulfilled. Thus did Western man, richly supplied with cultural memories and vivid aspirations, once celebrate his place in history and in the cosmos.

Today, however, something seems to be wrong. Our feast days have lost their vitality. Christmas is now largely a family reunion, Easter a spring style show, and on Thanksgiving there is no one to thank. The potency has drained from the religious symbols that once kept us in touch with our forebears. The images that fired our hopes for the future have lost their glow. We often see the past as a cage from which we must escape, and the future as a dull elongation of what we now have. Without a past that is somehow truly our own, and devoid of a really engaging vision of the future, Western man today either frets in a dreary present with no exit or spends himself in the frenzied pursuit of goals that turn to ashes in his grasp.

The blame for this state of affairs is usually placed on the thinkers and seers of Christianity themselves. Challenged by modern science, industrialization, pluralism, and secularization, they have not yet accomplished the badly needed intellectual reformation of the faith. This is true as far as it goes. But there is another side to the story too. Christianity has often adjusted too quickly to the categories of modernity. It has speeded industrialization by emphasizing man as the soberly responsible worker and husbandman. It has nourished science by stressing the order of creation and the gift of reason. In fact, without Protestant ethics and medieval scholasticism, our scientific civilization might never have developed. Christianity has recognized that man is the worker and toolmaker, the reasoner and thinker. But in doing all this, it has often failed to give sufficient attention to vital dimensions of the human reality, some of which are more clearly seen by other religious traditions. Consequently Western Christian culture, though we rightly speak of it as "highly developed" in some senses, is woefully underdeveloped in others. It has produced too many pedestrian personalities whose capacity for vision and ecstasy is sadly crippled. It has resulted in a deformed man whose sense of a mysterious origin and cosmic destiny has nearly disappeared. A race that has lost touch with past and future through the debilitation of ritual, revelry, and visionary aspirations will soon shrink to a tribe of automatons. Machines, as we know, can be astonishingly efficient. But there are some things they cannot do. Among other things they cannot really play, pretend, or prevaricate. They cannot frolic or fantasize. These activities are somehow uniquely human and if they vanish man loses essential reminders of his singularity.

It is important to emphasize that among other things man in his very essence is *homo festivus* and *homo fantasia*. Celebrating and imagining are integral parts of his humanity. But Western industrial man in the past few centuries has begun to lose his capacity for festivity and fantasy, and this loss is calamitous for three reasons: (1) it deforms man by depriving him of an essential ingredient in human existence, (2) it endangers his very survival as a species by rendering him provincial and less adaptive, and (3) it robs him of a crucial means of sensing his important place in fulfilling the destiny of the cosmos. The loss is personal, social, and religious.

The picture, however, is not quite as bleak as I have painted it so far. Despite the long-term erosion, it is also true that, in very recent years, industrial man has begun to rediscover the festive and the fanciful dimensions of life. A centuries-long process may be reversing itself. Our recent increased exposure both to non-Western cultures and to those sectors of our own civilization that have escaped complete integration into the industrialization process have made us aware that we are missing something. Technologically produced leisure has forced us to ask ourselves some hard questions about our traditional worship of work. Young people in industrial societies everywhere are demonstrating that expressive play and artistic creation belong in the center of life, not at its far periphery. A theatre of the body replete with mime, dance, and acrobatics is upstaging our inherited theatre of the mind. Street festivals, once disappearing as fast as the whooping crane, are coming back. Psychiatrists and educators are beginning to reject their traditional roles as the punishers of fantasy. Some are even searching for ways to encourage it. The awakened interest of white people in the black experience has enhanced our appreciation for a more festive and feeling-oriented approach to life. We call it "soul." Films, novels, and plays explore the world of dreams and even some philosophers are rediscovering the significance of fantasy. Even in the churches, dance, color, movement, and new kinds of music dramatize the recovery of celebration. In short we may be witnessing the overture to a sweeping cultural renaissance, a revolution of human sensibilities in which the faculties we have starved and repressed during the centuries of industrialization will be nourished and appreciated again.

But it could turn out differently. What we take as the evidence of a cultural rebirth in our midst may be a deceptive flush on the cheek of a dying age. Or, an equally grim prospect, the hesitant beginnings of a festive resurrection in our time could be smashed or spoiled. Still worse, the present rebirth of spontaneous celebration and unfettered imagining could veer off into destructive excess or vacuous frivolity.

Which of these things will happen? We do not know. In fact the fate of our embryonic cultural revolution is still open and undecided.

What will happen to it is largely up to us. . . . I do not labor under the delusion that theology can either spark or stave off a cultural revolution in our time. It may play a role in the eventual outcome but its role will probably be a minor one. Nevertheless, theology has a deep stake in the outcome of our crisis not just because it is committed to man but also because the crisis is in part a religious one. If twentieth-century man finally succumbs and does lose the last remnants of his faculties for festivity and fantasy, the result will be disastrous. The heart of the religious view of man and the cosmos, especially in its Christian version, will be torn out. Correspondingly, if the battle for man's humanity is to be won at all, a religious vision will have to play an important role in that victory.

• • •

CODA[7]

The Feast of Fools flourished during a period when people had a well-developed capacity for festivity and fantasy. We need to develop that capacity again today. We cannot and should not try to resuscitate the jesters and gargoyles of the Middle Ages. But neither need we exclude medieval man entirely from our consciousness. We can benefit from the experience of that time to enrich and vitalize our own, just as we can learn from other historical epochs and other civilizations.

What the medieval period had was a kind of festivity which related men to history and bound them to each other in a single community. Neither national holidays nor periodic but empty "long weekends" had yet appeared to divide and trivialize human celebration. Today we need a rebirth of festivity that will make us part of a larger history than they knew and will link us to an immensely expanded world community. Our survival as a species may depend in part on whether such authentically worldwide festivals, with their symbols of a single global community, emerge among us.

The Middle Ages also displayed a capacity for fantasy that, although it became more constricted during the industrial centuries, may now be staging a comeback. Medieval man, for all his limitations, placed a higher value on imagination than we do. He could make believe more easily. His saints and holy people did things we

[7]Conclusion.

would not permit. Would St. Francis and St. Theresa escape incarceration, at least for purposes of observation, in the modern world?
We need fantasy today. Can we make a more secure place for it in
our cognitively[8] overdeveloped schools? Can we mold a universal
symbolism within which we can both fantasize and still communicate? Can we become less doctrinaire about what constitutes
"mental health" and encourage a much more generous range of life
styles? A rebirth of fantasy need not result in the death of rational
thought. Both belong in any healthy culture.

Will we make it? Will we move into this world of revitalized celebration and creative imagination? Or will we destroy ourselves with
nuclear bombs or man-made plagues? Or will we survive as a precar-
ious planet where a small affluent elite perches fearfully on the top of
three continents of hungry peons? Or will we all end up in a subhu-
man world of efficiently lobotomized robots?

The world symbolized by the Feast of Fools is neither *Walden Two*
nor *1984*.[9] It is much more heterogeneous, messier, more sensuous,
more variegated, more venturesome, more playful. It is a world for
which a fiesta or even a love-in is a better symbol than a computer or
a rocket. Technology need not be the enemy of the spirit in the modern world. But it should be a means to man's human fulfillment, not
the symbol or goal of that fulfillment itself.

When we honestly ask ourselves whether we can have such a life-
affirming world, we must move beyond mere optimism or pessimism, for the empirical evidence is either mixed or unfavorable.
But we can hope. Hope in the religious sense rests in part on nonem-
pirical grounds. Christian hope suggests that man is destined for a
City. It is not just any city, however. If we take the Gospel images as
well as the symbols of the book of Revelation into consideration, it is
not only a City where injustice is abolished and there is no more crying. It is a city in which a delightful wedding feast is in progress,
where the laughter rings out, the dance has just begun, and the best
wine is still to be served.

[8] Related to the acquisition of factual knowledge.

[9] *Walden Two*, published in 1948, is a utopian novel of a scientifically controlled society, written by the behavioristic psychologist B. F. Skinner (see selection 9); *1984* is a
dystopian novel by George Orwell, published in 1949, which tells how the behavioristic techniques of a totalitarian society crush the individual's spirit.

29

Pope John XXIII

Pacem in Terris

✸

The most influential figure in twentieth-century Roman Catholicism is a man who reigned as pope for less than five years, from 1958 to 1963. The Catholic Church has never been quite the same since Pope John XXIII convoked an ecumenical council for the purpose of adapting the Church to contemporary secular life.

Pope John was born Angelo Giuseppe Roncalli (1881–1963) into a family of tenant farmers living near Bergamo, in northern Italy. At age twelve, following his elementary education, Roncalli left home to begin preparing for the priesthood at a local seminary; he spent his vacations with his family, however, and remained close to them all his life. He did well enough at the seminary to be sent to Rome for further theological studies. In 1904, after an interruption of a year for compulsory military training, he was ordained a priest. Eventually, continuing his studies in Rome, he earned a doctorate in the law of the Catholic Church.

Assigned to his home seminary at Bergamo as professor of theology, Roncalli also served as secretary to the local bishop, a member of the Italian nobility who was known as the most vigorous and progressive bishop in Italy. Here, the young priest gained much experience among the working class and the poor. In 1914, with the outbreak of the First World War, Roncalli enlisted in the army as a medical aide; later he became a military chaplain.

Because of his skill in personal relations, Roncalli was assigned to the papal diplomatic service, and in 1925 was appointed the papal representative in Bulgaria. In keeping with the tradition of that post, he was made an arch-

Pope John XXIII, "Pacem in Terris." From *The Encyclicals and Other Messages of John XXIII.* Copyright © 1964 by TPS Press. Excerpts reprinted by permission. [Pp. 327, 355–57, 361–63, 364–65, 368–69, 370–71, 372–73.]

bishop before he left Rome. Having gained experience in the delicate minority position of a Roman Catholic representative in an Eastern Orthodox nation, he was called upon in 1934 to be the pope's representative in Greece (also Eastern Orthodox) and Turkey (Muslim). Stationed in neutral Turkey during the Second World War, he was able to assist many Jewish refugees in their flight from German-occupied central Europe.

After the liberation of France in late 1944, Pope Pius XII named Roncalli his representative to that torn country. The head of the Catholic hierarchy in France and many of the French bishops had collaborated with the occupying German forces; Roncalli's job was to heal the hatreds that had developed among French Catholics during the occupation and resistance. So skillfully did he reconcile the various hostile interests that in 1953 Pius XII named him a cardinal of the Church and patriarch of Venice. Having assumed his career to be complete, Roncalli was astonished when, on the death of Pius XII, in 1958, he was elected pope by the College of Cardinals as a "compromise candidate." The new pope took the name John XXIII. He was seventy-six, and it was assumed that because of his advanced years he would be merely a "caretaker pope" and thus acceptable to the various factions within the Catholic hierarchy. Instead, he became one of the most influential popes in history by generating basic changes both within the Church and beyond.

The major change in the Church was to be a turn toward the contemporary world. In 1959 Pope John summoned an ecumenical council (a meeting of the Roman Catholic bishops from all of Christendom) for the purpose of "aggiornamento," that is, "a bringing up to date." Known as the Second Vatican Council, it was the first since 1870 and only the twenty-first such meeting in the Church's two thousand-year history. Pope John believed that the Council could make a new start toward Christian unity only by acknowledging the Roman Catholic share of responsibility for the division of Christianity. He cordially invited Eastern Orthodox, Anglican, and Protestant religious leaders to send official observers to the Council, and he also deleted from the Good Friday liturgy certain words offensive to Jews. Although he did not live to see the conclusion of Vatican II, Pope John's efforts toward modernization and reconciliation were to become an irrepressible movement within the Roman Catholic Church.

Pacem in Terris (Peace on Earth), 1963, the source of the following selection, was the first papal encyclical ever addressed to "all men of good will," regardless of their religious or non-religious affiliations. In it, Pope John supported mutual disarmament and the banning of nuclear weapons; he also expressed his hope that the United Nations would become an effective *instrument for the preservation of peace among nations and the attainment of natural rights among individuals. By suggesting that peaceful coexistence between communist and non-communist societies was essential for the survival of humanity, Pope John redirected much of the energy of the Church away from militant anti-Communism and toward the universal encouragement of "truth, justice, charity and freedom."*

Peace on earth—which man throughout the ages has so longed for and sought after—can never be established, never guaranteed, except by the diligent observance of the divinely established order.

• • •

Causes of the Arms Race

109. . . . We are deeply distressed to see the enormous stocks of armaments that have been, and continue to be, manufactured in the economically more developed countries. This policy is involving a vast outlay of intellectual and material resources, with the result that the people of these countries are saddled with a great burden, while other countries lack the help they need for their economic and social development.

110. There is a common belief that under modern conditions peace cannot be assured except on the basis of an equal balance of armaments and that this factor is the probable cause of this stock-piling of armaments. Thus, if one country increases its military strength, others are immediately roused by a competitive spirit to augment their own supply of armaments. And if one country is equipped with atomic weapons, others consider themselves justified in producing such weapons themselves, equal in destructive force.

111. Consequently people are living in the grip of constant fear. They are afraid that at any moment the impending storm may break upon them with horrific violence. And they have good reasons for their fear, for there is certainly no lack of such weapons. While it is difficult to believe that anyone would dare to assume responsibility for initiating the appalling slaughter and destruction that war would bring in its wake, there is no denying that the conflagration could be

started by some chance and unforeseen circumstance. Moreover, even though the monstrous power of modern weapons does indeed act as a deterrent, there is reason to fear that the very testing of nuclear devices for war purposes can, if continued, lead to serious danger for various forms of life on earth.

Need for Disarmament

112.   Hence justice, right reason, and the recognition of man's dignity cry out insistently for a cessation to the arms race. The stockpiles of armaments which have been built up in various countries must be reduced all round and simultaneously by the parties concerned. Nuclear weapons must be banned. A general agreement must be reached on a suitable disarmament program, with an effective system of mutual control. In the words of Pope Pius XII: [1] "The calamity of a world war, with the economic and social ruin and the moral excesses and dissolution that accompany it, must not on any account be permitted to engulf the human race for a third time."

113.   Everyone, however, must realize that, unless this process of disarmament be thoroughgoing and complete, and reach men's very souls, it is impossible to stop the arms race, or to reduce armaments, or—and this is the main thing—ultimately to abolish them entirely. Everyone must sincerely co-operate in the effort to banish fear and the anxious expectation of war from men's minds. But this requires that the fundamental principle upon which peace is based in today's world be replaced by an altogether different one, namely, the realization that true and lasting peace among nations cannot consist in the possession of an equal supply of armaments but only in mutual trust. And We are confident that this can be achieved, for it is a thing which not only is dictated by common sense, but is in itself most desirable and most fruitful of good.

Three Motives

114.   Here, then, we have an objective dictated first of all by reason. There is general agreement—or at least there should be—

---

[1] The reign of Pius XII (Eugenio Pacelli), beginning in 1939 and ending in 1958, immediately preceded that of John XXIII.

that relations between States, as between individuals, must be regulated not by armed force, but in accordance with the principles of right reason: the principles, that is, of truth, justice and vigorous and sincere co-operation.

115.   Secondly, it is an objective which We maintain is most earnestly to be desired. For who is there who does not feel the craving to be rid of the threat of war, and to see peace preserved and made daily more secure?

116.   And finally it is an objective which is rich with possibilities for good. Its advantages will be felt everywhere, by individuals, by families, by nations, by the whole human race. The warning of Pope Pius XII still rings in our ears: "Nothing is lost by peace; everything may be lost by war."

A Call to Unsparing Effort

117.   We therefore consider it Our duty as the vicar on earth of Jesus Christ—the Saviour of the world, the Author of peace—and as interpreter of the most ardent wishes of the whole human family, in the fatherly love We bear all mankind, to beg and beseech mankind, and above all the rulers of States, to be unsparing of their labor and efforts to ensure that human affairs follow a rational and dignified course.

• • •

Inadequacy of Modern States to Ensure the Universal Common Good

132.   No era will ever succeed in destroying the unity of the human family, for it consists of men who are all equal by virtue of their natural dignity. Hence there will always be an imperative need—born of man's very nature—to promote in sufficient measure the universal common good; the good, that is, of the whole human family.

133.   In the past rulers of States seem to have been able to make sufficient provision for the universal common good through the normal diplomatic channels, or by top-level meetings and discussions, treaties and agreements; by using, that is, the ways and means suggested by the natural law, the law of nations, or international law.

134.   In our own day, however, mutual relationships between States have undergone a far-reaching change. On the one hand, the universal common good gives rise to problems of the utmost gravity, complexity and urgency—especially as regards the preservation of the security and peace of the whole world. On the other hand, the rulers of individual nations, being all on an equal footing, largely fail in their efforts to achieve this, however much they multiply their meetings and their endeavors to discover more fitting instruments of justice. And this is no reflection on their sincerity and enterprise. It is merely that their authority is not sufficiently influential.

135.   We are thus driven to the conclusion that the shape and structure of political life in the modern world, and the influence exercised by public authority in all the nations of the world are unequal to the task of promoting the common good of all peoples.

Connection between the Common Good and Political Authority

136.   Now, if one considers carefully the inner significance of the common good on the one hand, and the nature and function of public authority on the other, one cannot fail to see that there is an intrinsic connection between them. Public authority, as the means of promoting the common good in civil society, is a postulate of the moral order. But the moral order likewise requires that this authority be effective in attaining its end. Hence the civil institutions in which such authority resides, becomes operative and promotes its ends, are endowed with a certain kind of structure and efficacy: a structure and efficacy which make such institutions capable of realizing the common good by ways and means adequate to the changing historical conditions.

137.   Today the universal common good presents us with problems which are world-wide in their dimensions; problems, therefore, which cannot be solved except by a public authority with power, organization and means co-extensive with these problems, and with a world-wide sphere of activity. Consequently the moral order itself demands the establishment of some such general form of public authority.

*Public Authority Instituted by Common Consent and Not
Imposed by Force*

138.   But this general authority equipped with world-wide power
and adequate means for achieving the universal common good cannot be imposed by force. It must be set up with the consent of all nations. If its work is to be effective, it must operate with fairness,
absolute impartiality, and with dedication to the common good of all
peoples. The forcible imposition by the more powerful nations of a
universal authority of this kind would inevitably arouse fears of its
being used as an instrument to serve the interests of the few or to
take the side of a single nation, and thus the influence and effectiveness of its activity would be undermined. For even though nations may differ widely in material progress and military strength,
they are very sensitive as regards their juridical equality and the excellence of their own way of life. They are right, therefore, in their
reluctance to submit to an authority imposed by force, established
without their co-operation, or not accepted of their own accord.

The Universal Common Good and Personal Rights

139.   The common good of individual States is something that
cannot be determined without reference to the human person, and
the same is true of the common good of all States taken together.
Hence the public authority of the world community must likewise
have as its special aim the recognition, respect, safeguarding and
promotion of the rights of the human person. This can be done by
direct action, if need be, or by the creation throughout the world of
the sort of conditions in which rulers of individual States can more
easily carry out their specific functions.

The Principle of Subsidiarity

140.   The same principle of subsidiarity which governs the relations between public authorities and individuals, families and intermediate societies in a single State, must also apply to the relations
between the public authority of the world community and the public
authorities of each political community. The special function of this

universal authority must be to evaluate and find a solution to economic, social, political and cultural problems which affect the universal common good. These are problems which, because of their extreme gravity, vastness and urgency, must be considered too difficult for the rulers of individual States to solve with any degree of success.

141.   But it is no part of the duty of universal authority to limit the sphere of action of the public authority of individual States, or to arrogate any of their functions to itself. On the contrary, its essential purpose is to create world conditions in which the public authorities of each nation, its citizens and intermediate groups, can carry out their tasks, fulfil their duties and claim their rights with greater security. . . .

Modern Developments

145.   It is therefore Our earnest wish that the United Nations Organization may be able progressively to adapt its structure and methods of operation to the magnitude and nobility of its tasks. May the day be not long delayed when every human being can find in this organization an effective safeguard of his personal rights; those rights, that is, which derive directly from his dignity as a human person, and which are therefore universal, inviolable and inalienable. This is all the more desirable in that men today are taking an ever more active part in the public life of their own nations, and in doing so they are showing an increased interest in the affairs of all peoples. They are becoming more and more conscious of being living members of the universal family of mankind.

Duty of Taking Part in Public Life

146.   Here once more We exhort Our sons to take an active part in public life, and to work together for the benefit of the whole human race, as well as for their own political communities. It is vitally necessary for them to endeavor, in the light of Christian faith and with love as their guide, to ensure that every institution, whether economic, social, cultural or political, be such as not to ob-

struct but rather to facilitate man's self-betterment, both in the natural and in the supernatural order. . . .

Relations Between Catholics and Non-Catholics in Social and Economic Affairs

157. The principles We have set out in this document take their rise from the very nature of things. They derive, for the most part, from the consideration of man's natural rights. Thus the putting of these principles into effect frequently involves extensive co-operation between Catholics and those Christians who are separated from the Apostolic See. It even involves the co-operation of Catholics with men who may not be Christians but who nevertheless are reasonable men, and men of natural moral integrity. "In such circumstances they must, of course, bear themselves as Catholics, and do nothing to compromise religion and morality. Yet at the same time they should show themselves animated by a spirit of understanding and unselfishness, ready to co-operate loyally in achieving objects which are good in themselves, or conducive to good." [2]

Error and the Errant

158. It is always perfectly justifiable to distinguish between error as such and the person who falls into error—even in the case of men who err regarding the truth or are led astray as a result of their inadequate knowledge, in matters either of religion or of the highest ethical standards. A man who has fallen into error does not cease to be a man. He never forfeits his personal dignity; and that is something that must always be taken into account. Besides, there exists in man's very nature an undying capacity to break through the barriers of error and seek the road to truth. God, in His great providence, is ever present with His aid. Today, maybe, a man lacks faith and turns aside into error; tomorrow, perhaps, illumined by God's light, he may indeed embrace the truth.

[2] A quotation from *Mater et Magistra* (1961), the other major encyclical by Pope John XXIII.

Catholics who, in order to achieve some external good, collaborate with unbelievers or with those who through error lack the fullness of faith in Christ, may possibly provide the occasion or even the incentive for their conversion to the truth.

Philosophies and Historical Movements

159.   Again it is perfectly legitimate to make a clear distinction between a false philosophy of the nature, origin and purpose of men and the world, and economic, social, cultural, and political undertakings, even when such undertakings draw their origin and inspiration from that philosophy. True, the philosophic formula does not change once it has been set down in precise terms, but the undertakings clearly cannot avoid being influenced to a certain extent by the changing conditions in which they have to operate. Besides, who can deny the possible existence of good and commendable elements in these undertakings, elements which do indeed conform to the dictates of right reason, and are an expression of man's lawful aspirations?

160.   It may sometimes happen, therefore, that meetings arranged for some practical end—though hitherto they were thought to be altogether useless—may in fact be fruitful at the present time, or at least offer prospects of success.

But whether or not the moment for such co-operation has arrived, and the manner and degree of such co-operation in the attainment of economic, social, cultural and political advantages—these are matters for prudence to decide; prudence, the queen of all the virtues which rule the lives of men both as individuals and in society.

As far as Catholics are concerned, the decision rests primarily with those who take a leading part in the life of the community, and in these specific fields. They must, however, act in accordance with the principles of the natural law, and observe the Church's social teaching and the directives of ecclesiastical authority. For it must not be forgotten that the Church has the right and duty not only to safeguard her teaching on faith and morals, but also to exercise her authority over her sons by intervening in their external affairs whenever a judgment has to be made concerning the practical application of this teaching. . . .

An Immense Task

163.   Hence among the very serious obligations incumbent upon men of high principles, We must include the task of establishing new relationships in human society, under the mastery and guidance of truth, justice, charity and freedom—relations between individual citizens, between citizens and their respective States, between States, and finally between individuals, families, intermediate associations and States on the one hand, and the world community on the other. There is surely no one who will not consider this a most exalted task, for it is one which is able to bring about true peace in accordance with divinely established order.

164.   Considering the need, the men who are shouldering this responsibility are far too few in number, yet they are deserving of the highest recognition from society, and We rightfully honor them with Our public praise. We call upon them to persevere in their ideals, which are of such tremendous benefit to mankind. At the same time We are encouraged to hope that many more men, Christians especially, will join their cause, spurred on by love and the realization of their duty. Everyone who has joined the ranks of Christ must be a glowing point of light in the world, a nucleus of love, a leaven of the whole mass. He will be so in proportion to his degree of spiritual union with God.

165.   The world will never be the dwelling-place of peace, till peace has found a home in the heart of each and every man, till every man preserves in himself the order ordained by God to be preserved. That is why St. Augustine[3] asks the question: "Does your mind desire the strength to gain the mastery over your passions? Let it submit to a greater power, and it will conquer all beneath it. And peace will be in you—true, sure, most ordered peace. What is that order? God as ruler of the mind; the mind as ruler of the body. Nothing could be more orderly."

The Prince of Peace

166.   Our concern here has been with problems which are causing men extreme anxiety at the present time; problems which are inti-

---

[3] A Christian theologian and one of the fathers of the early Church (A.D. 354–430).

mately bound up with the progress of human society. Unquestionably, the teaching We have given has been inspired by a longing which We feel most keenly, and which We know is shared by all men of good will: that peace may be assured on earth.

167.   We who, in spite of Our inadequacy, are nevertheless the vicar of Him whom the prophet announced as the *Prince of Peace,* conceive of it as Our duty to devote all Our thoughts and care and energy to further this common good of all mankind. Yet peace is but an empty word, if it does not rest upon that order which our hope prevailed upon Us to set forth in outline in this encyclical. It is an order that is founded on truth, built up on justice, nurtured and animated by charity, and brought into effect under the auspices of freedom. . . .

Finally, may Christ inflame the desires of all men to break through the barriers which divide them, to strengthen the bonds of mutual love, to learn to understand one another, and to pardon those who have done them wrong. Through His power and inspiration may all peoples welcome each other to their hearts as brothers, and may the peace they long for ever flower and ever reign among them.

172.   And so, dear brothers, with the ardent wish that peace may come upon the flocks committed to your care, for the special benefit of those who are most lowly and in the greatest need of help and defense, lovingly in the Lord We bestow on you, on Our priests both secular and regular, on religious[4] both men and women, on all the faithful and especially those who give wholehearted obedience to these Our exhortations, Our Apostolic Blessing. And upon all men of good will, to whom We also address this encyclical, We implore from God health and prosperity.

173.   Given at Rome, at St. Peter's, on Holy Thursday, the eleventh day of April, in the year 1963, the fifth of Our Pontificate.

JOHN PP. XXIII

[4]Members of Catholic religious orders.

VI
The New Consciousness

30

Jerry Farber

The Student as Nigger

✷

In the late 1960s a general rejection of traditional values was the dominant attitude among young people in the Western world. In the United States, especially because of the divisive effects of the Vietnam War, the mood was often one of fierce alienation. Educational—as well as political—institutions were blown by the unsettling winds of change. Students, and their activist allies off campus, demanded changes in the established structures of colleges and universities. Direct participatory democracy, often directed ideologically by an articulate and forceful minority, was the keynote in matters of academic curriculum, just as it was in social and political issues.

One typically unrestrained expression of the "new" educational philosophy was The Student as Nigger *(1969), a collection of essays and stories by Jerry (Gerald Howard) Farber (1935–   ). Born in El Paso, Texas, Farber reflected the geographical mobility of many in his generation by moving as a youth to southern California. There he received a bachelor's degree from the University of California at Los Angeles in 1958, a master's degree from California State University at Los Angeles in 1962, and a doctorate in comparative literature from Occidental College in 1970. Currently, he is a member of the faculty at San Diego State University, where he teaches contemporary literature.*

The following selection, the title essay from The Student as Nigger, *first appeared in the "underground"* Los Angeles Free Press *in 1967. Its vulgarity of language is a device used by some educated literary critics to indicate their radical contempt for traditionally polite and submissive language.*

Ultimately, Farber's sentiments go back to the wandering eighteenth-century French-Swiss philosopher Jean Jacques Rousseau, an originator of literary romanticism noted for his doctrine of "the noble savage." Man's natural feelings—including the sexual—are happy and good, says Rousseau; organized society corrupts the feelings of "natural man." Rousseau's cure for human depravity is, therefore, a radical reconstruction of society into a primitive, communal, non-repressive model. In Émile *(1762), Rousseau's educational treatise, a youth is protected from the harmful artifices of civilization and raised amid the moral influence of unspoiled nature.*

In its emphasis on learning only by seeking what the heart desires to know, Émile *is a "father" influence on twentieth-century "progressive" education and on radical manifestoes such as this one by Farber. The call for elimination of the barriers between schools and life, for free expression of uncorrupted natural feelings, and for a general liberation of communal consciousness—although expressed by Farber in relation to the contemporary social environment—is clearly part of the romantic expression that began with Rousseau.*

Students are niggers. When you get that straight, our schools begin to make sense. It's more important, though, to understand why they're niggers. If we follow that question seriously enough, it will lead us past the zone of academic bullshit, where dedicated teachers pass their knowledge on to a new generation, and into the nitty-gritty of human needs and hangups. And from there we can go on to consider whether it might ever be possible for students to come up from slavery.

First let's see what's happening now. Let's look at the role students play in what we like to call education. At Cal State L.A., where I teach,[1] the students have separate and unequal dining facilities. If I take them into the faculty dining room, my colleagues get uncomfortable, as though there were a bad smell. If I eat in the student cafeteria, I become known as the educational equivalent of a niggerlover. In at least one building there are even rest rooms which students may

---

[1] Make that "taught." [Farber's note. *Ed.*]

not use. At Cal State, also, there is an unwritten law barring student-faculty lovemaking. Fortunately, this anti-miscegenation law, like its Southern counterpart, is not 100 percent effective.

Students at Cal State are politically disenfranchised. They are in an academic Lowndes County.[2] Most of them can vote in national elections—their average age is about 26—but they have no voice in the decisions which affect their academic lives. The students are, it is true, allowed to have a toy government run for the most part by Uncle Toms[3] and concerned principally with trivia. The faculty and administrators decide what courses will be offered; the students get to choose their own Homecoming Queen. Occasionally when student leaders get uppity and rebellious, they're either ignored, put off with trivial concessions, or maneuvered expertly out of position.

A student at Cal State is expected to know his place. He calls a faculty member "Sir" or "Doctor" or "Professor"—and he smiles and shuffles some as he stands outside the professor's office waiting for permission to enter. The faculty tell him what courses to take (in my department, English, even electives have to be approved by a faculty member); they tell him what to read, what to write, and, frequently, where to set the margins on his typewriter. They tell him what's true and what isn't. Some teachers insist that they encourage dissent but they're almost always jiving and every student knows it. Tell the man what he wants to hear or he'll fail your ass out of the course.

When a teacher says "jump," students jump. I know of one professor who refused to take up class time for exams and required students to show up for tests at 6:30 in the morning. And they did, by God! Another, at exam time, provides answer cards to be filled out—each one enclosed in a paper bag with a hole cut in the top to see through. Students stick their writing hands in the bags while taking the test. The teacher isn't a provo;[4] I wish he were. He does it to prevent cheating. Another colleague once caught a student reading

---

[2] A county in Alabama that was notorious in the mid 1960s for the resistance shown by some of its white officials to voting and office-holding by its black citizens.

[3] Uncle Tom is an old black slave, devoted to his white master, in the famous abolitionist novel *Uncle Tom's Cabin* (1852), by Harriet Beecher Stowe. In recent usage "Uncle Tomism" is a derisive term referring to undue subservience by Afro-Americans toward Americans of European ancestry.

[4] Possibly, a reference to the "provos," who were youthful radicals of the 1960s in Holland. They often participated in absurd political behavior, which included the use of masks and other satirical devices made of paper bags.

during one of his lectures and threw her book against the wall. Still another lectures his students into a stupor and then screams at them in a rage when they fall asleep.

Just last week during the first meeting of a class, one girl got up to leave after about ten minutes had gone by. The teacher rushed over, grabbed her by the arm, saying, "This class is NOT dismissed!" and led her back to her seat. On the same day another teacher began by informing his class that he does not like beards, mustaches, long hair on boys, or capri pants on girls, and will not tolerate any of that in his class. The class, incidentally, consisted mostly of high school teachers.

Even more discouraging than this master-slave approach to education is the fact that the students take it. They haven't gone through twelve years of public school for nothing. They've learned one thing and perhaps only one thing during those twelve years. They've forgotten their algebra. They've grown to fear and resent literature. They write like they've been lobotomized. But, Jesus, can they follow orders! Freshmen come up to me with an essay and ask if I want it folded, and whether their name should be in the upper right hand corner. And I want to cry and kiss them and caress their poor tortured heads.

Students don't ask that orders make sense. They give up expecting things to make sense long before they leave elementary school. Things are true because the teacher says they're true. At a very early age we all learn to accept "two truths," as did certain medieval churchmen. Outside of class, things are true to your tongue, your fingers, your stomach, your heart. Inside class things are true by reason of authority. And that's just fine because you don't care anyway. Miss Wiedemeyer tells you a noun is a person, place or thing. So let it be. You don't give a rat's ass; she doesn't give a rat's ass.

The important thing is to please her. Back in kindergarten, you found out that teachers only love children who stand in nice straight lines. And that's where it's been at ever since. Nothing changes except to get worse. School becomes more and more obviously a prison. Last year I spoke to a student assembly at Manual Arts High School and then couldn't get out of the goddamn school. I mean there was NO WAY OUT. Locked doors. High fences. One of the inmates was trying to make it over a fence when he saw me coming and froze in panic. For a moment I expected sirens, a rattle of bullets, and him clawing the fence.

Then there's the infamous "code of dress." In some high schools, if your skirt looks too short, you have to kneel before the principal in a brief allegory of fellatio. If the hem doesn't reach the floor, you go home to change while he, presumably, jacks off. Boys in high school can't be too sloppy and they can't even be too sharp. You'd think the school board would have been delighted to see all the black kids trooping to school in pointy shoes, suits, ties and stingy brims. Uh-uh. They're too visible.

What school amounts to, then, for white and black alike, is a 12-year course in how to be slaves. What else could explain what I see in a freshman class? They've got that slave mentality: obliging and ingratiating on the surface but hostile and resistant underneath.

As do black slaves, students vary in their awareness of what's going on. Some recognize their own put-on for what it is and even let their rebellion break through to the surface now and then. Others—including most of the "good students"—have been more deeply brainwashed. They swallow the bullshit with greedy mouths. They honest-to-God believe in grades, in busy work, in General Education requirements. They're pathetically eager to be pushed around. They're like those old grey-headed house niggers you can still find in the South who don't see what all the fuss is about because Mr. Charlie[5] "treats us real good."

College entrance requirements tend to favor the Toms and screen out the rebels. Not entirely, of course. Some students at Cal State L.A. are expert con artists who know perfectly well what's happening. They want the degree or the 2-S[6] and spend their years on the old plantation alternately laughing and cursing as they play the game. If their egos are strong enough, they cheat a lot. And, of course, even the Toms are angry down deep somewhere. But it comes out in passive rather than active aggression. They're unexplainably thickwitted and subject to frequent spells of laziness. They misread simple questions. They spent their nights mechanically outlining history chapters while meticulously failing to comprehend a word of what's in front of them.

The saddest cases among both black slaves and student slaves are the ones who have so thoroughly introjected their masters' values that their anger is all turned inward. At Cal State these are the kids

[5] The white employer.
[6] A deferment from military service (during the early years of the Vietnam War), based on one's status as a college student.

for whom every low grade is torture, who stammer and shake when they speak to a professor, who go through an emotional crisis every time they're called upon during class. You can recognize them easily at finals time. Their faces are festooned with fresh pimples; their bowels boil audibly across the room. If there really is a Last Judgment, then the parents and teachers who created these wrecks are going to burn in hell.

So students are niggers. It's time to find out why, and to do this we have to take a long look at Mr. Charlie.

The teachers I know best are college professors. Outside the classroom and taken as a group, their most striking characteristic is timidity. They're short on balls. Just look at their working conditions. At a time when even migrant workers have begun to fight and win, most college professors are still afraid to make more than a token effort to improve their pitiful economic status. In California state colleges, the faculties are screwed regularly and vigorously by the Governor and Legislature and yet they still won't offer any solid resistance. They lie flat on their stomachs with their pants down, mumbling catch phrases like "professional dignity" and "meaningful dialogue."

Professors were no different when I was an undergraduate at UCLA during the McCarthy era; it was like a cattle stampede as they rushed to cop out. And in more recent years, I found that my being arrested in demonstrations brought from my colleagues not so much approval or condemnation as open-mouthed astonishment. "You could lose your job!"

Now, of course, there's the Vietnamese war. It gets some opposition from a few teachers. Some support it. But a vast number of professors who know perfectly well what's happening, are copping out again. And in the high schools, you can forget it. Stillness reigns.

I'm not sure why teachers are so chickenshit. It could be that academic training itself forces a split between thought and action. It might also be that the tenured security of a teaching job attracts timid persons and, furthermore, that teaching, like police work, pulls in persons who are unsure of themselves and need weapons and the other external trappings of authority.

At any rate teachers ARE short on balls. And . . . the classroom offers an artificial and protected environment in which they can exercise their will to power. Your neighbors may drive a better car; gas station attendants may intimidate you; your wife may dominate you; the State Legislature may shit on you; but in the classroom, by God, students do what you say—or else. The grade is a hell of a weapon. It may not rest on your hip, potent and rigid like a cop's gun, but in the long run it's more powerful. At your personal whim—any time you choose—you can keep 35 students up for nights and have the pleasure of seeing them walk into the classroom pasty-faced and red-eyed carrying a sheaf of typewritten pages, with title page, MLA footnotes[7] and margins set at 15 and 91.

The general timidity which causes teachers to make niggers of their students usually includes a more specific fear—fear of the students themselves. After all, students are different, just like black people. You stand exposed in front of them, knowing that their interests, their values and their language are different from yours. To make matters worse, you may suspect that you yourself are not the most engaging of persons. What then can protect you from their ridicule and scorn? Respect for authority. That's what. It's the policeman's gun again. The white bwana's pith helmet. So you flaunt that authority. You wither whisperers with a murderous glance. You crush objectors with erudition and heavy irony. And worst of all, you make your own attainments seem not accessible but awesomely remote. You conceal your massive ignorance—and parade a slender learning.

The teacher's fear is mixed with an understandable need to be admired and to feel superior—a need which also makes him cling to his "white supremacy." Ideally, a teacher should minimize the distance between himself and his students. He should encourage them not to need him—eventually or even immediately. But this is rarely the case. Teachers make themselves high priests of arcane mysteries. They become masters of mumbo-jumbo. Even a more or less conscientious teacher may be torn between the need to give and the need to hold back, between the desire to free his students and the desire to hold them in bondage to him. I can find no other explanation that accounts for the way my own subject, literature, is generally taught. Literature, which ought to be a source of joy, solace and enlightenment, often becomes in the classroom nothing more than a source of

---

[7] The MLA (Modern Language Association of America) publishes a "Style Sheet" dealing with matters of form in the writing of scholarly papers.

anxiety—at best an arena for expertise, a ledger book for the ego. Literature teachers, often afraid to join a real union, nonetheless may practice the worst kind of trade-unionism in the classroom; they do to literature what Beckmesser does to song in Wagner's "Meistersinger."[8] The avowed purpose of English departments is to teach literature; too often their real function is to kill it.

Finally, there's the darkest reason of all for the master-slave approach to education. The less trained and the less socialized a person is, the more he constitutes a sexual threat and the more he will be subjugated by institutions, such as penitentiaries and schools. Many of us are aware by now of the sexual neurosis which makes white men so fearful of integrated schools and neighborhoods, and which make the castration of Negroes a deeply entrenched Southern folkway. We should recognize a similar pattern in education. There is a kind of castration that goes on in schools. It begins before school years with parents' first encroachments on their children's free unashamed sexuality and continues right up to the day when they hand you your doctoral diploma with a bleeding, shriveled pair of testicles stapled to the parchment. It's not that sexuality has no place in the classroom. You'll find it there but only in certain perverted and vitiated forms.

How does sex show up in school? First of all, there's the sadomasochistic relationship between teachers and students. That's plenty sexual, although the price of enjoying it is to be unaware of what's happening. In walks the teacher in his Ivy League equivalent of a motorcycle jacket. In walks the teacher—a kind of intellectual rough trade—and flogs his students with grades, tests, sarcasm and snotty superiority until their very brains are bleeding. In Swinburne's England, the whipped school boy frequently grew up to be a flagellant. With us the perversion is intellectual but it's no less perverse.

Sex also shows up in the classroom as academic subject matter—sanitized and abstracted, thoroughly divorced from feeling. You get "sex education" now in both high school and college classes: everyone determined not to be embarrassed, to be very up to date, very contempo. These are the classes for which sex, as Feiffer puts it, "can

---

[8] Beckmesser, the pedantic town clerk and unsuccessful suitor in Wagner's comic opera *The Mastersingers of Nuremberg* ("Meistersinger," 1868), respects only the established customs of music and has no understanding of the freedom, passion, and genius of natural musicians.

be a beautiful thing if properly administered." And then, of course there's still another depressing manifestation of sex in the classroom: the "off-color" teacher who keeps his class awake with sniggering sexual allusions, obscene titters and academic innuendo. The sexuality he purveys, it must be admitted, is at least better than none at all. . . .

So you can add sexual repression to the list of causes, along with vanity, fear and will to power, that turn the teacher into Mr. Charlie. You might also want to keep in mind that he was a nigger once himself and has never really gotten over it. And there are more causes, some of which are better described in sociological than in psychological terms. Work them out, it's not hard. But in the meantime what we've got on our hands is a whole lot of niggers. And what makes this particularly grim is that the student has less chance than the black man of getting out of his bag. Because the student doesn't even know he's in it. That, more or less, is what's happening in higher education. And the results are staggering.

For one thing damn little education takes place in the schools. How could it? You can't educate slaves; you can only train them. Or, to use an even uglier and more timely word, you can only program them.

I like to folk dance. Like other novices, I've gone to the Intersection or to the Museum and laid out good money in order to learn how to dance. No grades, no prerequisites, no separate dining rooms; they just turn you on to dancing. That's education. Now look at what happens in college. A friend of mine, Milt, recently finished a folk dance class. For his final, he had to learn things like this: "The Irish are known for their wit and imagination, qualities reflected in their dances, which include the jig, the reel and the hornpipe." And then the teacher graded him, A, B, C, D, or F, while he danced in front of her. That's not education. That's not even training. That's an abomination on the face of the earth. It's especially ironic because Milt took that dance class trying to get out of the academic rut. He took crafts for the same reason. Great, right? Get your hands in some clay? Make something? Then the teacher announced a 20-page term paper would be required—with footnotes.

At my school we even grade people on how they read poetry. That's like grading people on how they fuck. But we do it. In fact, God help me, I do it. I'm the Commandant of English 323. Simon

Legree[9] on the poetry plantation. "Tote that iamb! Lift that spon-dee!"[10] Even to discuss a good poem in that environment is poten-tially dangerous because the very classroom is contaminated. As hard as I may try to turn students on to poetry, I know that the desks, the tests, the IBM cards, their own attitudes toward school, and my own residue of UCLA method are turning them off.

Another result of student slavery is equally serious. Students don't get emancipated when they graduate. As a matter of fact, we don't let them graduate until they've demonstrated their willingness—over 16 years—to remain slaves. And for important jobs, like teaching, we make them go through more years just to make sure. What I'm getting at is that we're all more or less niggers and slaves, teachers and students alike. This is a fact you might want to start with in try-ing to understand wider social phenomena, say, politics, in our country and in other countries.

Educational oppression is trickier to fight than racial oppression. If you're a black rebel, they can't exile you; they either have to intimi-date you or kill you. But in high school or college they can just bounce you out of the fold. And they do. Rebel students and ren-egade faculty members get smothered or shot down with devastating accuracy. Others get tired of fighting and voluntarily leave the sys-tem. This may be a mistake though. Dropping out of college for a rebel is a little like going North for a Negro. You can't really get away from it so you might as well stay and raise hell.

How do you raise hell? That's a whole other article. But just for a start, why not stay with the analogy? What have black people done? They have, first of all, faced the fact of their slavery. They've stopped kidding themselves about an eventual reward in that Great Watermelon Patch in the sky. They've organized; they've decided to get freedom now, and they've started taking it.

Students, like black people, have immense unused power. They could, theoretically, insist on participating in their own education. They could make academic freedom bilateral. They could teach their teachers to thrive on love and admiration, rather than fear and re-spect, and to lay down their weapons. Students could discover com-munity. And they could learn to dance by dancing on the IBM cards.

---

[9]In Stowe's *Uncle Tom's Cabin,* the cruel slave-owner who caused the death of Uncle Tom by severely beating him.

[10]*Iamb* and *spondee* are terms indicating different poetic rhythms.

They could make coloring books out of the catalogs and they could put the grading system in a museum. They could raze one set of walls and let life come blowing into the classroom. They could raze another set of walls and let education flow out and flood the streets. They could turn the classroom into where it's at—a "field of action" as Peter Marin describes it. And believe it or not, they could study eagerly and learn prodigiously for the best of all possible reasons— their own reasons.

They could. Theoretically. They have the power. But only in a very few places, like Berkeley, have they even begun to think about using it. For students, as for black people, the hardest battle isn't with Mr. Charlie. It's with what Mr. Charlie has done to your mind.

31

Robert Brustein

The Case for Professionalism

*The intense rejection of traditional values by young people during the late
1960s eventually provoked a strong conservative reaction. By the late 1970s
the reassertion of the old standards—in politics, education, and society in
general—had become a dominant national theme. At a time when revolutionary rhetoric was at is peak, a strong case for the need to restore standards
in American universities was made by Robert Brustein (1927–   ), Dean of
the School of Drama at Yale University.*

*Born in Brooklyn, New York, Brustein attended local elementary schools
and the High School of Music and Art. Later, he attended Amherst College,
receiving a bachelor's degree in medieval history in 1948, and the Yale
School of Drama. Feeling that the program there lacked intellectual depth,
Brustein completed only one year at Yale, then transferred to Columbia
University for the study of drama as literature. He received a master's degree
from Columbia in 1950 and a doctorate in 1957.*

*Torn between academic life and the theatre, Brustein continued to act and
direct in summer theatres and off-Broadway productions while earning his
graduate degrees. He began his teaching career at Cornell University, in
1955, and soon afterwards returned to Columbia as a professor. In 1966,
Brustein became Dean of the School of Drama at Yale, the very institution
that had disappointed him as a student. There, he developed a rigorous "professional" curriculum of training in basic dramatic skills and created the outstanding Yale Repertory Company, composed of professionals and interning
students. He combined at Yale a demanding professionalism with an openness to experimental theatre.*

A prolific writer, Brustein for many years wrote regularly for The New Republic *as its theatre critic. In an early book,* The Theatre of Revolt *(1964), he analyzes the works of eight modern playwrights and concludes that the theme of rebellion—with roots in romanticism and Nietsche's philosophy of power—is an inevitable development of modern drama. In* The Third Theatre *(1969) Brustein describes the emergence of radically innovative theatrical companies and, qualifying the admiration for radical theatre expressed in* The Theatre of Revolt, *indicates his growing disillusionment with characteristics of the new drama: ". . . its anti-intellectualism, its sensationalism, its sexual obsessiveness, its massacre of language, . . . its indifference to artistry, craft and skill, its violence, and, above all, its mindless tributes to Love and Togetherness. . . ." Continuing to widen his differences with the radical theatre, Brustein chastises the militant counter-culture even more severely in* Revolution as Theatre: Notes on the New Radical Style *(1971).*

"The Case for Professionalism," the following selection, is typical of the quest by Brustein for what he considers to be the highest standards in theatre, literature, and teaching. Published first in The New Republic *(1969), the essay is part of his series on the "eroding effects of student radicalism on the function of education." Placing his views squarely against the Rousseauistic romanticism of such new radicals as Jerry Farber,* Brustein looks back to the unchanging ideals of Plato, the ancient Greek philosopher. Only those universities, Brustein asserts, that judge their students and faculty by genuinely "professional standards" are performing their essential intellectual function and, thereby, making possible a society of democratic excellence.*

In such a state of society [*a state of democratic anarchy*]*, the master fears and flatters his scholars, and the scholars despise their masters and tutors; young and old are alike; and the young man is on a level with the old, and is ready to compete with him in word and deed; and old men condescend to the young and are full of pleasantry and gaiety; they are loth to be thought morose and authoritative, and therefore they adopt the manners of the young. . . .*

PLATO, *The Republic,* BOOK VIII

*See selection 30.

Among the many valuable things on the verge of disintegration in
contemporary America is the concept of professionalism—by which
I mean to suggest a condition determined by training, experience,
skill, and achievement (by remuneration, too, but this is secondary).
In our intensely Romantic age, where so many activities are being
politicized and objective judgments are continually colliding with
subjective demands, the amateur is exalted as a kind of democratic
culture hero, subject to no standards or restrictions. This development has been of concern to me because of its impact upon my immediate areas of interest—the theater and theater training—but its
consequences can be seen everywhere, most conspicuously in the
field of liberal education. If the amateur is coequal—and some would
say, superior—to the professional, then the student is coequal or superior to the professor, and "the young man," as Plato puts it in his
discourse on the conditions that lead to tyranny, "is on a level with
the old, and is ready to compete with him in word and deed."

As recently as five years ago, this proposition would have seemed
remote; today, it has virtually become established dogma, and its
implementation is absorbing much of the energy of the young. Although student unrest was originally stimulated, and rightly so, by
such external issues as the war in Vietnam and the social grievances
of the blacks and the poor, it is now more often aroused over internal issues of power and influence in the university itself. Making an
analogy between democratic political systems and the university
structure, students begin by demanding a representative voice in the
"decisions that affect our lives," including questions of faculty ten-
ure, curriculum changes, grading, and academic discipline. As universities begin to grant some of these demands, thus tacitly accepting
the analogy, the demands escalate to the point where students are
now insisting on a voice in electing the university president, a role in
choosing the faculty, and even a place on the board of trustees.

I do not wish to comment here on the validity of individual student demands—certainly, a student role in university affairs is both
practical and desirable, as long as that role remains advisory. Nor
will I take the time to repeat the familiar litany of admiration for the
current student generation—it has, to my mind, already been sufficiently praised, even overpraised, since for all its intrinsic passion,
intelligence, and commitment, the proportion of serious, gifted,
hardworking students remains about what it always was (if not actually dwindling, for reasons I hope soon to develop). I do want, how-

ever, to examine the analogy, which is now helping to politicize the university, and scholarship itself, because it seems to me full of falsehood.

Clearly, it is absurd to identify electoral with educational institutions. To compare the state with the academy is to assume that the primary function of the university is to govern and to rule. While the relationship between the administration and the faculty does have certain political overtones, the faculty and administration can no more be considered the elected representatives of the student body than the students—who were admitted after voluntary application on a selective and competitive basis—can be considered freeborn citizens of a democratic state: The relationship between teacher and student is strictly tutorial. Thus, the faculty member functions not to represent the student's interests in relation to the administration, but rather to communicate knowledge from one who knows to one who doesn't. That the reasoning behind this analogy has not been more frequently questioned indicates the extent to which some teachers are refusing to exercise their roles as professionals. During a time when all authority is being radically questioned, faculty members are becoming reluctant to accept the responsibility of their wisdom and experience and are, therefore, often willing to abandon their authoritative position in order to placate the young.

The issue of authority is a crucial one here, and once again we can see how the concept of professionalism is being vitiated by false analogies. Because *some* authority is cruel, callow, or indifferent (notably the government in its treatment of certain urgent issues of the day), the Platonic *idea* of authority comes under attack. Because some faculty members are remote and pedantic, the credentials of distinguished scholars, artists, and intellectuals are ignored or rejected, and anyone taking charge of a classroom or a seminar is open to charges of "authoritarianism." This explains the hostility of many students toward the lecture course—where an "authority" communicates the fruits of his research, elaborating on unclear points when prodded by student questioning (still a valuable pedagogical technique, especially for beginning students, along with seminars and tutorials). Preferred to this, and therefore replacing it in some departments, is the discussion group or "bull session," where the student's opinion about the material receives more attention than the material itself, if indeed the material is still being treated. The idea—so central to scholarship—that there is an inherited body of knowledge to be transmitted from one generation to another loses favor because it puts the student in an unacceptably subordinate position, with the result that the learning process gives way to a general free-for-all in which one man's opinion is as good as another's.

The problem is exacerbated in the humanities and social sciences with their more subjective criteria of judgment; one hardly senses the same difficulties in the clinical sciences. It is unlikely (though anything is possible these days) that medical students will insist on making a diagnosis through majority vote, or that students entering surgery will refuse anesthesia because they want to participate in decisions that affect their lives and, therefore, demand to choose the surgeon's instruments or tell him where to cut. Obviously, some forms of authority are still respected, and some professionals remain untouched by the incursions of the amateur. In liberal education, however, where the development of the individual assumes such weight and importance, the subordination of mind to material is often looked on as some kind of repression. One begins to understand the current loss of interest in the past, which offers a literature and history verified to some extent by time, and the passionate concern with the immediate present, whose works still remain to be objectively evaluated. When one's educational concerns are contemporary, the material can be subordinated to one's own interests, whether political or aesthetic, as the contemporary literary journalist is often more occupied with his own ideas than with the book he reviews.

Allied to this problem, and compounding it, is the problem of the black students, who are sometimes inclined to reject the customary university curriculum as "irrelevant" to their interests, largely because of its orientation toward "white" culture and history. In its place, they demand courses dealing with the history and achievements of the black man, both in Africa and America. Wherever history or anthropology departments have failed to provide appropriate courses, this is a serious omission and should be rectified. Such an omission is an insult not only to black culture but to scholarship itself. But when black students begin clamoring for courses in black law, black business, black medicine, or black theater, then the university is in danger of becoming the instrument of community hopes and aspirations rather than the repository of an already achieved culture. It is only one more step before the university is asked to serve propaganda purposes, usually of an activist nature: A recent course, demanded by black law students at Yale, was to be called something like "white capitalist exploitation of the black ghetto poor."

On the one hand, the demand for "relevance" is an effort to make the university undertake the reparations that society should be paying. On the other, it is a form of solipsism,* among both black students and white. And such solipsism is a serious threat to that "disinterestedness" that Matthew Arnold claimed to be the legitimate function of the scholar and the critic. The proper study of mankind becomes contemporary for future man; and the student focuses not on the outside world, past or present, so much as on a parochial corner of his own immediate needs. But this is childish, in addition to being Romantic, reflecting as it does the student's unwillingness to examine or conceive a world beyond the self. And here, the university seems to be paying a debt not of its own making—a debt incurred in the permissive home and the progressive school, where knowledge was usually of considerably less importance than self-expression.

In the schools, particularly, techniques of education always seemed to take precedence over the material to be communicated; lessons in democracy were frequently substituted for training in subjects; and everyone learned to be concerned citizens, often at the sacrifice of a solid education. I remember applying for a position many years ago in such a school. I was prepared to teach English literature, but was told no such subject was being offered. Instead, the students had a course called *Core*, which was meant to provide the essence of literature, history, civics, and the like. The students sat together at a round table to dramatize their essential equality with their instructor; the instructor—or rather, the coordinator, as he was called— remained completely unobtrusive; and instead of determining answers by investigation or the teacher's authority, they were decided upon by majority vote. I took my leave in haste, convinced that I was witnessing democracy totally misunderstood. That misunderstanding has invaded our institutions of higher learning.

For the scholastic habits of childhood and adolescence are now being extended into adulthood. The graduates of the *Core* course, and courses like it, are concentrating on the development of their "life styles," chafing against restrictions of all kinds (words like "co-

---

*The concept that one can know only one's own self—that the external world is beyond verifiable knowledge.

ercion" and "co-option" are the current jargon), and demanding that all courses be geared to their personal requirements and individual interests. But this is not at all the function of the university. As Paul Goodman has observed, in *The Community of Scholars,* when you teach the child, you teach the person; when you teach the adolescent, you teach the subject through the person; *but when you teach the adult, you teach the subject.* Behind Goodman's observation lies the assumption that the university student is, or should already be, a developed personality, that he comes to the academy not to investigate his "life style" but to absorb what knowledge he can, and that he is, therefore, preparing himself, through study, research, and contemplation, to enter the community of professional scholars. In resisting this notion, some students reveal their desire to maintain the conditions of childhood, to preserve the liberty they enjoyed in their homes and secondary schools, to extend the privileges of a child- and youth-oriented culture into their mature years. They wish to remain amateurs.

One can see why Goodman has concluded that many of the university young do not deserve the name of students: They are creating conditions in which it is becoming virtually impossible to do intellectual work. In turning their political wrath from the social world, which is in serious need of reform (partly because of a breakdown in professionalism), to the academic world, which still has considerable value as a learning institution, they have determined, on the one hand, that society will remain as venal, as corrupt, as retrogressive as ever, and, on the other hand, that the university will no longer be able to proceed with the work of free inquiry for which it was founded. As an added irony, students, despite their professed distaste for the bureaucratic administration of the university, are now helping to construct—through the insane proliferation of student-faculty committees—a far vaster network of bureaucracy than ever before existed. This, added to their continual meetings, confrontations, and demonstrations—not to mention occupations and sit-ins—is leaving precious little time or energy either for their intellectual development, or for that of the faculty. As a result, attendance at classes has dropped drastically; exams are frequently skipped; and papers and reports are either late, underresearched, or permanently postponed. That the university needs improvement goes without saying. And students have been very helpful in breaking down its excesses of impersonality and attempting to sever its ties with the military-industrial complex. But students need improvement too, which they are hardly receiving through all this self-righteous bustle over power. That students should pay so much attention to this activity creates an even more serious problem: The specter of an ignorant, uninformed group of graduates or dropouts who (when they finally leave the academic sanctuary) are incompetent to deal with society's real evils or to function properly in professions they have chosen to enter.

It is often observed that the word *amateur* comes from the Latin verb "to love"—presumably because the amateur is motivated by passion rather than money. Today's amateur, however, seems to love not his subject but himself. And his assault on authority—on the application of professional standards in judgment of his intellectual development—is a strategy to keep this self-love unalloyed. The permanent dream of this nation, a dream still to be realized, has been a dream of equal opportunity—the right of each man to discover wherein he might excel. But this is quite different from that sentimental egalitarianism which assumes that each man excels in everything. There is no blinking the fact that some people are brighter than others, some more beautiful, some more gifted. Any other conclusion is a degradation of the democratic dogma and promises a bleak future if universally insisted on—a future of monochromatic amateurism in which everybody has opinions, few have facts, nobody has an idea.

32

Simone de Beauvoir
The Second Sex

Among the more significant aspects of "the new consciousness" in recent decades is the transformed self-image of many women, the changing perceptions
of their sexual, social, and economic roles. Obviously, men have also been
affected by the women's struggle for liberation, most of them being previously
unmindful of many women's feelings of repression. The mid-century's first
important statement of the need for change in the traditional roles of men
and women was The Second Sex (1952), by Simone de Beauvoir
(1908–   ), a French existential philosopher, novelist, and social critic.

Born in Paris into a middle-class family, de Beauvoir was educated in
Catholic schools and at the University of Paris, where, in 1929, she earned
a degree in philosophy. While at the university, she became acquainted with
a fellow student named Jean-Paul Sartre, whose emerging philosophy of individualist atheistic existentialism was to become the dominating influence on
her life. Her intimate, non-contractual personal association with Sartre also
proved to be enduring.

In 1931 de Beauvoir went to Marseilles to teach philosophy at a college
preparatory school; later, she taught in Rouen and in Paris. In 1943 she
gave up teaching in order to devote more time to writing, and in 1945 joined
Sartre in editing the monthly review Les Temps Modernes (The Modern
Age).

During the years of world war and German occupation of France
(1939–45), de Beauvoir dropped her academic detachment and, like Sartre,
became politically involved. In The Blood of Others (1948), for example,

a novel written during the occupation, she endorses the existential thesis that each person is solely responsible for the consequences of his or her own actions — in this case, participation in the Resistance. In a later philosophical essay, The Ethics of Ambiguity *(1949), de Beauvoir, avoiding absolute individualism, writes that the individual's freedom "can be achieved only through the freedom of others. He justifies his existence by a movement which, like freedom, springs from his heart but which leads outside of him." Questions of free moral choice, thus, dominate in de Beauvoir's writings. In her 1945 play* The Useless Mouths, *the hungry citizens of a town have to decide whether or not to feed the "useless mouths" of women and children.*

In 1947, de Beauvoir made a lecture tour of the United States. Her observations on that tour were later published here as America Day by Day *(1953), a book whose critical reception was overshadowed by the furor created by the concurrent publication of* The Second Sex. *The latest of de Beauvoir's major works — which include more than twenty volumes of fiction, drama, social philosophy, and autobiography — is* The Coming of Age *(1972), a book that severely criticizes the cruel neglect of the elderly in Western society.*

In The Second Sex, *from which the following selection is taken, de Beauvoir asserts that social custom — created by men — has relegated women to a secondary, dependent, inferior position. She further argues that there is no essentially "feminine" nature, the traditional "clinging" female personality being a construct of a male-dominated society. Much of de Beauvoir's analysis, though it shocked middle-class European society only decades ago, may now seem tame — at least to many educated American women. Nevertheless, it should be remembered that this manifesto of "complete economic and social equality" contributed to the philosophical base from which the postwar women's movement shaped its ultimate goal — total equality in a society of free, self-determining individuals.*

INTRODUCTION

. . . first we must ask: what is a woman? *"Tota mulier in utero,"* says one, "woman is a womb." But in speaking of certain women, connoisseurs declare that they are not women, although they are equipped with a uterus like the rest. All agree in recognizing the fact that females exist in the human species; today as always they make up about one half of humanity. And yet we are told that femininity is in danger; we are exhorted to be women, remain women, become women. It would appear, then, that every female human being is not necessarily a woman; to be so considered she must share in that mysterious and threatened reality known as femininity. Is this attribute something secreted by the ovaries? Or is it a Platonic essence, a product of the philosophic imagination? Is a rustling petticoat enough to bring it down to earth? Although some women try zealously to incarnate this essence, it is hardly patentable. It is frequently described in vague and dazzling terms that seem to have been borrowed from the vocabulary of the seers, and indeed in the times of St. Thomas[1] it was considered an essence as certainly defined as the somniferous virtue of the poppy.

But conceptualism has lost ground. The biological and social sciences no longer admit the existence of unchangeably fixed entities that determine given characteristics, such as those ascribed to woman, the Jew, or the Negro. Science regards any characteristic as a reaction dependent in part upon a *situation*. If today femininity no longer exists, then it never existed. But does the word *woman,* then, have no specific content? This is stoutly affirmed by those who hold to the philosophy of the enlightenment, of rationalism, of nominalism; women, to them, are merely the human beings arbitrarily designated by the word *woman.* Many American women particularly are prepared to think that there is no longer any place for woman as such; if a backward individual still takes herself for a woman, her friends advise her to be psychoanalyzed and thus get rid of this obsession. In regard to a work, *Modern Woman: The Lost Sex,* which in other respects has its irritating features, Dorothy Parker has written: "I cannot be just to books which treat of woman as woman. . . . My idea is that all of us, men as well as women, should be regarded as human beings." But nominalism is a rather inadequate doctrine, and the antifemininists have had no trouble in showing that women simply *are not* men. Surely woman is, like man, a human being; but such a declaration is abstract. The fact is that every concrete human being is always a singular, separate individual. To decline to accept such notions as the eternal feminine, the black soul, the Jewish character, is not to deny that Jews, Negroes, women exist today—this

---

[1] Thomas Aquinas (1225–74), the leading philosopher of medieval Christianity.

denial does not represent a liberation for those concerned, but rather a flight from reality. Some years ago a well-known woman writer refused to permit her portrait to appear in a series of photographs especially devoted to women writers; she wished to be counted among the men. But in order to gain this privilege she made use of her husband's influence! Women who assert that they are men lay claim none the less to masculine consideration and respect. I recall also a young Trotskyite standing on a platform at a boisterous meeting and getting ready to use her fists, in spite of her evident fragility. She was denying her feminine weakness; but it was for love of a militant male whose equal she wished to be. The attitude of defiance of many American women proves that they are haunted by a sense of their femininity. In truth, to go for a walk with one's eyes open is enough to demonstrate that humanity is divided into two classes of individuals whose clothes, faces, bodies, smiles, gaits, interests, and occupations are manifestly different. Perhaps these differences are superficial, perhaps they are destined to disappear. What is certain is that right now they do most obviously exist.

If her functioning as a female is not enough to define woman, if we decline also to explain her through "the eternal feminine," and if nevertheless we admit, provisionally, that women do exist, then we must face the question: what is a woman?

To state the question is, to me, to suggest, at once, a preliminary answer. The fact that I ask it is in itself significant. A man would never get the notion of writing a book on the peculiar situation of the human male. But if I wish to define myself, I must first of all say: "I am a woman"; on this truth must be based all further discussion. A man never begins by presenting himself as an individual of a certain sex; it goes without saying that he is a man. The terms *masculine* and *feminine* are used symmetrically only as a matter of form, as on legal papers. In actuality the relation of the two sexes is not quite like that of two electrical poles, for man represents both the positive and the neutral, as is indicated by the common use of *man* to designate human beings in general; whereas woman represents only the negative, defined by limiting criteria, without reciprocity. In the midst of an abstract discussion it is vexing to hear a man say: "You think thus and so because you are a woman"; but I know that my only defense is to reply: "I think thus and so because it is true," thereby removing my subjective self from the argument. It would be out of the question to reply: "And you think the contrary because you are a man," for it is understood that the fact of being a man is no peculiarity. A man is in the right in being a man; it is the woman who is in the wrong. It amounts to this: just as for the ancients there was an absolute vertical with reference to which the oblique was defined, so there is an absolute human type, the masculine. Woman has ovaries, a uterus; these peculiarities imprison her in her subjectivity, circumscribe her within the limits of her own nature. It is often said that she thinks with her glands. Man superbly ignores the fact that his anatomy also includes glands, such as the testicles, and that they secrete hormones. He thinks of his body as a direct and normal connection with the world, which he believes he apprehends objectively, whereas he regards the body of woman as a hindrance, a prison, weighed down by everything peculiar to it. "The female is a female by virtue of a certain *lack* of qualities," said Aristotle; "we should regard the female nature as afflicted with a natural defectiveness." And St. Thomas for his part pronounced woman to be an "imperfect man," an "incidental" being. This is symbolized in Genesis where Eve is depicted as made from what Bossuet[2] called "a supernumerary bone" of Adam.

Thus humanity is male and man defines woman not in herself but as relative to him; she is not regarded as an autonomous being. Michelet writes: "Woman, the relative being. . . ." And Benda is most positive in his *Rapport d'Uriel:* "The body of man makes sense in itself quite apart from that of woman, whereas the latter seems wanting in significance by itself. . . . Man can think of himself without woman. She cannot think of herself without man." And she is simply what man decrees; thus she is called "the sex," by which is meant that she appears essentially to the male as a sexual being. For him she is sex—absolute sex, no less. She is defined and differentiated with reference to man and not he with reference to her; she is the incidental, the inessential as opposed to the essential. He is the Subject, he is the Absolute—she is the Other.

The category of the *Other* is as primordial as consciousness itself. In the most primitive societies, in the most ancient mythologies, one finds the expression of a duality—that of the Self and the Other. This duality was not originally attached to the division of the sexes; it was not dependent upon any empirical facts. It is revealed in such

---

[2] Jacques Bossuet (1627–1704), a prominent French Catholic bishop and conservative theologian.

works as that of Granet on Chinese thought and those of Dumézil on the East Indies and Rome. The feminine element was at first no more involved in such pairs as Varuna-Mitra,[3] Uranus-Zeus,[4] Sun-Moon, and Day-Night than it was in the contrasts between Good and Evil, lucky and unlucky auspices, right and left, God and Lucifer. Otherness is a fundamental category of human thought.

Thus it is that no group ever sets itself up as the One without at once setting up the Other over against itself. If three travelers chance to occupy the same compartment, that is enough to make vaguely hostile "others" out of all the rest of the passengers on the train. In small-town eyes all persons not belonging to the village are "strangers" and suspect; to the native of a country all who inhabit other countries are "foreigners"; Jews are "different" for the anti-Semite, Negroes are "inferior" for American racists, aborigines are "natives" for colonists, proletarians are the "lower class" for the privileged.

Lévi-Strauss,[5] at the end of a profound work on the various forms of primitive societies, reaches the following conclusion: "Passage from the state of Nature to the state of Culture is marked by man's ability to view biological relations as a series of contrasts; duality, alternation, opposition, and symmetry, whether under definite or vague forms, constitute not so much phenomena to be explained as fundamental and immediately given data of social reality." These phenomena would be incomprehensible if in fact human society were simply a *Mitsein* or fellowship based on solidarity and friendliness. Things become clear, on the contrary, if, following Hegel,[6] we find in consciousness itself a fundamental hostility toward every other consciousness; the subject can be posed only in being opposed—he sets himself up as the essential, as opposed to the other, the inessential, the object.

---

[3] Varuna and Mitra are brothers, gods of universal power, in the ancient Hindu religion. Varuna, the Moon, sees and shines during the night; Mitra, the Sun, during the day.

[4] Uranus, a male deity, was the first god of the sky in the pre-Olympian Greek religion. Eventually, after much struggle, his grandson Zeus, reigning from Mount Olympus, became the new god of the sky and lord of the universe.

[5] Claude Lévi-Strauss (1908–   ), a French founder of structural anthropology, which attempts to discover the underlying intellectual and behavioral principles upon which all societies operate. The quotation is from *The Elementary Structures of Kinship* (trans., 1969).

[6] Georg Wilhelm Friedrich Hegel (1770–1831), a German dialectical philosopher.

But the other consciousness, the other ego, sets up a reciprocal claim. The native traveling abroad is shocked to find himself in turn regarded as a "stranger" by the natives of neighboring countries. As a matter of fact, wars, festivals, trading, treaties, and contests among tribes, nations, and classes tend to deprive the concept *Other* of its absolute sense and to make manifest its relativity; willy-nilly, individuals and groups are forced to realize the reciprocity of their relations. How is it, then, that this reciprocity has not been recognized between the sexes, that one of the contrasting terms is set up as the sole essential, denying any relativity in regard to its correlative and defining the latter as pure otherness? Why is it that women do not dispute male sovereignty? No subject will readily volunteer to become the object, the inessential; it is not the Other who, in defining himself as the Other, establishes the One. The Other is posed as such by the One in defining himself as the One. But if the Other is not to regain the status of being the One, he must be submissive enough to accept this alien point of view. Whence comes this submission in the case of woman?

There are, to be sure, other cases in which a certain category has been able to dominate another completely for a time. Very often this privilege depends upon inequality of numbers—the majority imposes its rule upon the minority or persecutes it. But women are not a minority, like the American Negroes or the Jews; there are as many women as men on earth. Again, the two groups concerned have often been originally independent; they may have been formerly unaware of each other's existence, or perhaps they recognized each other's autonomy. But a historical event has resulted in the subjugation of the weaker by the stronger. The scattering of the Jews, the introduction of slavery into America, the conquests of imperialism are examples in point. In these cases the oppressed retained at least the memory of former days; they possessed in common a past, a tradition, sometimes a religion or a culture.

The parallel drawn by Bebel[7] between women and the proletariat is valid in that neither ever formed a minority or a separate collective unit of mankind. And instead of a single historical event it is in both cases a historical development that explains their status as a class and accounts for the membership of *particular individuals* in that class. But proletarians have not always existed, whereas there have always been

[7] August Bebel (1840–1913), a German socialist thinker and activist.

women. They are women in virtue of their anatomy and physiology. Throughout history they have always been subordinated to men, and hence their dependency is not the result of a historical event or a social change—it was not something that *occurred*. The reason why otherness in this case seems to be an absolute is in part that it lacks the contingent or incidental nature of historical facts. A condition brought about at a certain time can be abolished at some other time, as the Negroes of Haiti and others have proved; but it might seem that a natural condition is beyond the possibility of change. In truth, however, the nature of things is no more immutably given, once for all, than is historical reality. If woman seems to be the inessential which never becomes the essential, it is because she herself fails to bring about this change. Proletarians say "We"; Negroes also. Regarding themselves as subjects, they transform the bourgeois, the whites, into "others." But women do not say "We," except at some congress of feminists or similar formal demonstration; men say "women," and women use the same word in referring to themselves. They do not authentically assume a subjective attitude. The proletarians have accomplished the revolution in Russia, the Negroes in Haiti, the Indo-Chinese are battling for it in Indo-China; but the women's effort has never been anything more than a symbolic agitation. They have gained only what men have been willing to grant; they have taken nothing, they have only received.

The reason for this is that women lack concrete means for organizing themselves into a unit which can stand face to face with the correlative unit. They have no past, no history, no religion of their own; and they have no such solidarity of work and interest as that of the proletariat. They are not even promiscuously herded together in the way that creates community feeling among the American Negroes, the ghetto Jews, the workers of Saint-Dènis, or the factory hands of Renault. They live dispersed among the males, attached through residence, housework, economic condition, and social standing to certain men—fathers or husbands—more firmly than they are to other women. If they belong to the bourgeoisie, they feel solidarity with men of that class, not with proletarian women; if they are white, their allegiance is to white men, not to Negro women. The proletariat can propose to massacre the ruling class, and a sufficiently fanatical Jew or Negro might dream of getting sole possession of the atomic bomb and making humanity wholly Jewish or black; but woman cannot even dream of exterminating the males.

The bond that unites her to her oppressors is not comparable to any other. The division of the sexes is a biological fact, not an event in human history. Male and female stand opposed within a primordial *Mitsein,* and woman has not broken it. The couple is a fundamental unity with its two halves riveted together, and the cleavage of society along the line of sex is impossible. Here is to be found the basic trait of woman: she is the Other in a totality of which the two components are necessary to one another.

One could suppose that this reciprocity might have facilitated the liberation of woman. When Hercules sat at the feet of Omphale and helped with her spinning, his desire for her held him captive; but why did she fail to gain a lasting power? To revenge herself on Jason, Medea killed their children; and this grim legend would seem to suggest that she might have obtained a formidable influence over him through his love for his offspring. In *Lysistrata* Aristophanes gaily depicts a band of women who joined forces to gain social ends through the sexual needs of their men; but this is only a play. In the legend of the Sabine women, the latter soon abandoned their plan of remaining sterile to punish their ravishers. In truth woman has not been socially emancipated through man's need—sexual desire and the desire for offspring—which makes the male dependent for satisfaction upon the female.

Master and slave, also, are united by a reciprocal need, in this case economic, which does not liberate the slave. In the relation of master to slave the master does not make a point of the need that he has for the other; he has in his grasp the power of satisfying this need through his own action; whereas the slave, in his dependent condition, his hope and fear, is quite conscious of the need he has for his master. Even if the need is at bottom equally urgent for both, it always works in favor of the oppressor and against the oppressed. That is why the liberation of the working class, for example, has been slow.

Now, woman has always been man's dependent, if not his slave; the two sexes have never shared the world in equality. And even today woman is heavily handicapped, though her situation is beginning to change. Almost nowhere is her legal status the same as man's, and frequently it is much to her disadvantage. Even when her rights are legally recognized in the abstract, long-standing custom prevents their full expression in the mores. In the economic sphere men and women can almost be said to make up two castes; other things being equal, the former hold the better jobs, get higher wages, and have more opportunity for success than their new competitors. In industry and politics men have a great many more positions and they monopolize the most important posts. In addition to all this, they enjoy a traditional prestige that the education of children tends in every way to support, for the present enshrines the past—and in the past all history has been made by men. At the present time, when women are beginning to take part in the affairs of the world, it is still a world that belongs to men—they have no doubt of it at all and women have scarcely any. To decline to be the Other, to refuse to be a party to the deal—this would be for women to renounce all the advantages conferred upon them by their alliance with the superior caste. Man-the-sovereign will provide woman-the-liege with material protection and will undertake the moral justification of her existence; thus she can evade at once both economic risk and the metaphysical risk of a liberty in which ends and aims must be contrived without assistance. Indeed, along with the ethical urge of each individual to affirm his subjective existence, there is also the temptation to forgo liberty and become a thing. This is an inauspicious road, for he who takes it—passive, lost, ruined—becomes henceforth the creature of another's will, frustrated in his transcendence and deprived of every value. But it is an easy road; on it one avoids the strain involved in undertaking an authentic existence. When man makes of woman the *Other,* he may, then, expect her to manifest deep-seated tendencies toward complicity. Thus, woman may fail to lay claim to the status of subject because she lacks definite resources, because she feels the necessary bond that ties her to man regardless of reciprocity, and because she is often very well pleased with her role as the *Other.*

But it will be asked at once: how did all this begin? It is easy to see that the duality of the sexes, like any duality, gives rise to conflict. And doubtless the winner will assume the status of absolute. But why should man have won from the start? It seems possible that women could have won the victory; or that the outcome of the conflict might never have been decided. How is it that this world has always belonged to the men and that things have begun to change only recently? Is this change a good thing? Will it bring about an equal sharing of the world between men and women?

These questions are not new, and they have often been answered. But the very fact that woman *is the Other* tends to cast suspicion upon all the justifications that men have ever been able to provide for it. These have all too evidently been dictated by men's interest. A little-known feminist of the seventeenth century, Poulain de la Barre, put it this way: "All that has been written about woman by men should be suspect, for the men are at once judge and party to the lawsuit." Everywhere, at all times, the males have displayed their satisfaction in feeling that they are the lords of creation. "Blessed be God . . . that He did not make me a woman," say the Jews in their morning prayers, while their wives pray on a note of resignation: "Blessed be the Lord, who created me according to His will." The first among the blessings for which Plato thanked the gods was that he had been created free, not enslaved; the second, a man, not a woman. But the males could not enjoy this privilege fully unless they believed it to be founded on the absolute and the eternal; they sought to make the fact of their supremacy into a right. "Being men, those who have made and compiled the laws have favored their own sex, and jurists have elevated these laws into principles," to quote Poulain de la Barre once more.

Legislators, priests, philosophers, writers, and scientists have striven to show that the subordinate position of woman is willed in heaven and advantageous on earth. The religions invented by men reflect this wish for domination. . . .

. . . If we survey some of the works on woman, we note that one of the points of view most frequently adopted is that of the public good, the general interest; and one always means by this the benefit of society as one wishes it to be maintained or established. For our part, we hold that the only public good is that which assures the private good of the citizens; we shall pass judgment on institutions according to their effectiveness in giving concrete opportunities to individuals. But we do not confuse the idea of private interest with that of happiness, although that is another common point of view. Are not women of the harem more happy than women voters? Is not the housekeeper happier than the working-woman? It is not too clear just what the word *happy* really means and still less what true values it may mask. There is no possibility of measuring the happiness of others, and it is always easy to describe as happy the situation in which one wishes to place them.

In particular those who are condemned to stagnation are often pronounced happy on the pretext that happiness consists in being at rest. This notion we reject, for our perspective is that of existentialist ethics. Every subject plays his part as such specifically through exploits or projects that serve as a mode of transcendence; he achieves liberty only through a continual reaching out toward other liberties. There is no justification for present existence other than its expansion into an indefinitely open future. Every time transcendence falls back into immanence, stagnation, there is a degradation of existence into the *"en-soi"*—the brutish life of subjection to given conditions—and of liberty into constraint and contingence. This downfall represents a moral fault if the subject consents to it; if it is inflicted upon him, it spells frustration and oppression. In both cases it is an absolute evil. Every individual concerned to justify his existence feels that his existence involves an undefined need to transcend himself, to engage in freely chosen projects.

Now, what peculiarly signalizes the situation of woman is that she—a free and autonomous being like all human creatures—nevertheless finds herself living in a world where men compel her to assume the status of the Other. They propose to stabilize her as object and to doom her to immanence since her transcendence is to be overshadowed and forever transcended by another ego (*conscience*) which is essential and sovereign. The drama of woman lies in this conflict between the fundamental aspirations of every subject (ego)—who always regards the self as the essential—and the compulsions of a situation in which she is the inessential. How can a human being in woman's situation attain fulfillment? What roads are open to her? Which are blocked? How can independence be recovered in a state of dependency? What circumstances limit woman's liberty and how can they be overcome? These are the fundamental questions on which I would fain throw some light. This means that I am interested in the fortunes of the individual as defined not in terms of happiness but in terms of liberty.

• • •

CONCLUSION

. . . The fact is that today neither men nor women are satisfied with each other. But the question is to know whether there is an original curse that condemns them to rend each other or whether the conflicts in which they are opposed merely mark a transitional moment in human history.

We have seen that in spite of legends no physiological destiny imposes an eternal hostility upon Male and Female as such; even the famous praying mantis devours her male only for want of other food and for the good of the species: it is to this, the species, that all individuals are subordinated, from the top to the bottom of the scale of animal life. Moreover, humanity is something more than a mere species: it is a historical development; it is to be defined by the manner in which it deals with its natural, fixed characteristics, its *facticité*. Indeed, even with the most extreme bad faith in the world, it is impossible to demonstrate the existence of a rivalry between the human male and female of a truly physiological nature. Further, their hostility may be allocated rather to that intermediate terrain between biology and psychology: psychoanalysis. Woman, we are told, envies man his penis and wishes to castrate him; but the childish desire for the penis is important in the life of the adult woman only if she feels her femininity as a mutilation; and then it is as a symbol of all the privileges of manhood that she wishes to appropriate the male organ. We may readily agree that her dream of castration has this symbolic significance: she wishes, it is thought, to deprive the male of his transcendence.

But her desire, as we have seen, is much more ambiguous: she wishes, in a contradictory fashion, *to have* this transcendence, which is to suppose that she at once respects it and denies it, that she intends at once to throw herself into it and keep it within herself. This is to say that the drama does not unfold on a sexual level; further, sexuality has never seemed to us to define a destiny, to furnish in itself the key to human behavior, but to express the totality of a situation that it only helps to define. The battle of the sexes is not immediately implied in the anatomy of man and woman. The truth is that when one evokes it, one takes for granted that in the timeless realm of Ideas a battle is being waged between those vague essences the Eternal Feminine and the Eternal Masculine; and one neglects the fact that this titanic combat assumes on earth two totally different forms, corresponding with two different moments of history.

The woman who is shut up in immanence endeavors to hold man in that prison also; thus the prison will be confused with the world, and woman will no longer suffer from being confined there: mother, wife, sweetheart are the jailers. Society, being codified by man, decrees that woman is inferior: she can do away with this inferiority only by destroying the male's superiority. She sets about mutilating, dominating man, she contradicts him, she denies his truth and his values. But in doing this she is only defending herself; it was neither a changeless essence nor a mistaken choice that doomed her to immanence, to inferiority. They were imposed upon her. All oppression creates a state of war. And this is no exception. The existent who is regarded as inessential cannot fail to demand the re-establishment of her sovereignty.

Today the combat takes a different shape; instead of wishing to put man in a prison, woman endeavors to escape from one; she no longer seeks to drag him into the realms of immanence but to emerge, herself, into the light of transcendence. Now the attitude of the males creates a new conflict: it is with a bad grace that the man lets her go. He is very well pleased to remain the sovereign subject, the absolute superior, the essential being; he refuses to accept his companion as an equal in any concrete way. She replies to his lack of confidence in her by assuming an aggressive attitude. It is no longer a question of a war between individuals each shut up in his or her sphere: a caste claiming its rights goes over the top and it is resisted by the privileged caste. Here two transcendences are face to face; instead of displaying mutual recognition, each free being wishes to dominate the other.

This difference of attitude is manifest on the sexual plane as on the spiritual plane. The "feminine" woman in making herself prey tries to reduce man, also, to her carnal passivity; she occupies herself in catching him in her trap, in enchaining him by means of the desire she arouses in him in submissively making herself a thing. The emancipated woman, on the contrary, wants to be active, a taker, and refuses the passivity man means to impose on her. . . .

It must be admitted that the males find in woman more complicity than the oppressor usually finds in the oppressed. And in bad faith they take authorization from this to declare that she has *desired* the destiny they have imposed on her. We have seen that all the main features of her training combine to bar her from the roads of revolt and adventure. Society in general—beginning with her respected parents—lies to her by praising the lofty values of love, devotion, the gift of herself, and then concealing from her the fact that neither lover nor husband nor yet her children will be inclined to accept the burdensome charge of all that. She cheerfully believes these lies because they invite her to follow the easy slope: in this others commit their worst crime against her; throughout her life from childhood on, they damage and corrupt her by designating as her true vocation this submission, which is the temptation of every existent in the anxiety of liberty. If a child is taught idleness by being amused all day long and never being led to study, or shown its usefulness, it will hardly be said, when he grows up, that he chose to be incapable and ignorant; yet this is how woman is brought up, without ever being impressed with the necessity of taking charge of her own existence. So she readily lets herself come to count on the protection, love, assistance, and supervision of others, she lets herself be fascinated with the hope of self-realization without *doing* anything. She does wrong in yielding to the temptation; but man is in no position to blame her, since he has led her into the temptation. When conflict arises between them, each will hold the other responsible for the situation; she will reproach him with having made her what she is: "No one taught me to reason or to earn my own living"; he will reproach her with having accepted the consequences: "You don't know anything, you are an incompetent," and so on. Each sex thinks it can justify itself by taking the offensive; but the wrongs done by one do not make the other innocent.

The innumerable conflicts that set men and women against one another come from the fact that neither is prepared to assume all the consequences of this situation which the one has offered and the other accepted. The doubtful concept of "equality in inequality," which the one uses to mask his despotism and the other to mask her cowardice, does not stand the test of experience: in their exchanges, woman appeals to the theoretical equality she has been guaranteed, the man the concrete inequality that exists. The result is that in every association an endless debate goes on concerning the ambiguous meaning of the words *give* and *take:* she complains of giving her all, he protests that she takes his all. Woman has to learn that exchanges—it is a fundamental law of political economy—are based on the value the merchandise offered has for the buyer, and not for the seller: she has been deceived in being persuaded that her worth is priceless. The truth is that for man she is an amusement, a pleasure, company, an inessential boon; he is for her the meaning, the justification of her existence. The exchange, therefore, is not of two items of equal value.

This inequality will be especially brought out in the fact that the time they spend together—which fallaciously seems to be the same time—does not have the same value for both partners. During the evening the lover spends with his mistress he could be doing something of advantage to his career, seeing friends, cultivating business relationships, seeking recreation; for a man normally integrated in society, time is a positive value: money, reputation, pleasure. For the idle, bored woman, on the contrary, it is a burden she wishes to get rid of; when she succeeds in killing time, it is a benefit to her: the man's presence is pure profit. In a liaison what most clearly interests the man, in many cases, is the sexual benefit he gets from it: if need be, he can be content to spend no more time with his mistress than is required for the sexual act; but—with exceptions—what she, on her part, wants is to kill all the excess time she has on her hands; and— like the storekeeper who will not sell potatoes unless the customer will take turnips also—she will not yield her body unless her lover will take hours of conversation and "going out" into the bargain. A balance is reached if, on the whole, the cost does not seem too high to the man, and this depends, of course, on the strength of his desire and the importance he gives to what is to be sacrificed. But if the woman demands—offers—too much time, she becomes wholly in- trusive, like the river overflowing its banks, and the man will prefer to have nothing rather than too much. Then she reduces her de- mands; but very often the balance is reached at the cost of a double tension: she feels that the man has "had" her at a bargain, and he thinks her price is too high. This analysis, of course, is put in some- what humorous terms; but—except for those affairs of jealous and exclusive passion in which the man wants total possession of the woman—this conflict constantly appears in cases of affection, desire, and even love. He always has "other things to do" with his time; whereas she has time to burn; and he considers much of the time she gives him not as a gift but as a burden. . . .

In daily life we meet with an abundance of these cases which are incapable of satisfactory solution because they are determined by un- satisfactory conditions. A man who is compelled to go on materially and morally supporting a woman whom he no longer loves feels he is victimized; but if he abandons without resources the woman who has pledged her whole life to him, she will be quite as unjustly vic- timized. The evil originates not in the perversity of individuals—and bad faith first appears when each blames the other—it originates rather in a situation against which all individual action is powerless. Women are "clinging," they are a dead weight, and they suffer for it; the point is that their situation is like that of a parasite sucking out the living strength of another organism. Let them be provided with

living strength of their own, let them have the means to attack the
world and wrest from it their own subsistence, and their dependence
will be abolished—that of man also. There is no doubt that both
men and women will profit greatly from the new situation. . . .

If the little girl were brought up from the first with the same
demands and rewards, the same severity and the same freedom, as
her brothers, taking part in the same studies, the same games, promised the same future, surrounded with women and men who seemed
to her undoubted equals, the meanings of the castration complex and
of the Œdipus complex would be profoundly modified. Assuming on
the same basis as the father the material and moral responsibility of
the couple, the mother would enjoy the same lasting prestige; the
child would perceive around her an androgynous[8] world and not a
masculine world. Were she emotionally more attracted to her
father—which is not even sure—her love for him would be tinged
with a will to emulation and not a feeling of powerlessness; she
would not be oriented toward passivity. Authorized to test her powers in work and sports, competing actively with the boys, she would
not find the absence of the penis—compensated by the promise of a
child—enough to give rise to an inferiority complex; correlatively,
the boy would not have a superiority complex if it were not instilled
into him and if he looked up to women with as much respect as to
men. The little girl would not seek sterile compensation in narcissism and dreaming, she would not take her fate for granted; she
would be interested in what she was *doing,* she would throw herself
without reserve into undertakings.

I have already pointed out how much easier the transformation of
puberty would be if she looked beyond it, like the boys, toward a
free adult future: menstruation horrifies her only because it is an
abrupt descent into femininity. She would also take her young eroticism in much more tranquil fashion if she did not feel a frightened
disgust for her destiny as a whole; coherent sexual information
would do much to help her over this crisis. And thanks to coeduca-
tional schooling, the august mystery of Man would have no occasion
to enter her mind: it would be eliminated by everyday familiarity
and open rivalry.

Objections raised against this system always imply respect for sexual taboos; but the effort to inhibit all sex curiosity and pleasure in

[8]Having both masculine and feminine characteristics.

the child is quite useless; one succeeds only in creating repressions, obsessions, neuroses. The excessive sentimentality, homosexual fervors, and platonic crushes of adolescent girls, with all their train of silliness and frivolity, are much more injurious than a little childish sex play and a few definite sex experiences. It would be beneficial above all for the young girl not to be influenced against taking charge herself of her own existence, for then she would not seek a demigod in the male—merely a comrade, a friend, a partner. Eroticism and love would take on the nature of free transcendence and not that of resignation; she could experience them as a relation between equals. There is no intention, of course, to remove by a stroke of the pen all the difficulties that the child has to overcome in changing into an adult; the most intelligent, the most tolerant education could not relieve the child of experiencing things for herself; what could be asked is that obstacles should not be piled gratuitously in her path. . . .

I shall be told that all this is utopian fancy, because woman cannot be "made over" unless society has first made her really the equal of man. Conservatives have never failed in such circumstances to refer to that vicious circle; history, however, does not revolve. If a caste is kept in a state of inferiority, no doubt it remains inferior; but liberty can break the circle. Let the Negroes vote and they become worthy of having the vote: let woman be given responsibilities and she is able to assume them. The fact is that oppressors cannot be expected to make a move of gratuitous generosity; but at one time the revolt of the oppressed, at another time even the very evolution of the privileged caste itself, creates new situations; thus men have been led, in their own interest, to give partial emancipation to women: it remains only for women to continue their ascent, and the successes they are obtaining are an encouragement for them to do so. It seems almost certain that sooner or later they will arrive at complete economic and social equality, which will bring about an inner metamorphosis.

However this may be, there will be some to object that if such a world is possible it is not desirable. When woman is "the same" as her male, life will lose its salt and spice. This argument, also, has lost its novelty: those interested in perpetuating present conditions are always in tears about the marvelous past that is about to disappear, without having so much as a smile for the young future. It is quite true that doing away with the slave trade meant death to the great plantations, magnificent with azaleas and camellias, it meant ruin to the whole refined Southern civilization. The attics of time have received its rare old laces along with the clear pure voices of the Sistine *castrati*,[9] and there is a certain "feminine charm" that is also on the way to the same dusty repository. I agree that he would be a barbarian indeed who failed to appreciate exquisite flowers, rare lace, the crystal-clear voice of the eunuch, and feminine charm. . . .

. . . And it is true that the evolution now in progress threatens more than feminine charm alone: in beginning to exist for herself, woman will relinquish the function as double and mediator to which she owes her privileged place in the masculine universe; to man, caught between the silence of nature and the demanding presence of other free beings, a creature who is at once his like and a passive thing seems a great treasure. The guise in which he conceives his companion may be mythical, but the experiences for which she is the source or the pretext are none the less real: there are hardly any more precious, more intimate, more ardent. There is no denying that feminine dependence, inferiority, woe, give women their special character; assuredly woman's autonomy, if it spares men many troubles, will also deny them many conveniences; assuredly there are certain forms of the sexual adventure which will be lost in the world of tomorrow. But this does not mean that love, happiness, poetry, dream, will be banished from it.

Let us not forget that our lack of imagination always depopulates the future; for us it is only an abstraction; each one of us secretly deplores the absence there of the one who was himself. But the humanity of tomorrow will be living in its flesh and in its conscious liberty; that time will be its present and it will in turn prefer it. New relations of flesh and sentiment of which we have no conception will arise between the sexes; already, indeed, there have appeared between men and women friendships, rivalries, complicities, comradeships—chaste or sensual—which past centuries could not have conceived. To mention one point, nothing could seem to me more debatable than the opinion that dooms the new world to uniformity

[9]Italian: castrated males, eunuchs. [*Ed.*] Eunuchs were long used in the male choirs of the Sistine Chapel in Rome, until the practice was forbidden by Pope Leo XIII in 1880. The operation of castration caused the boy's soprano voice to be retained into adulthood, and it was performed for this purpose. [Translator's note. *Ed.*]

and hence to boredom. I fail to see that this present world is free from boredom or that liberty ever creates uniformity.

To begin with, there will always be certain differences between man and woman; her eroticism, and therefore her sexual world, have a special form of their own and therefore cannot fail to engender a sensuality, a sensitivity, of a special nature. This means that her relations to her own body, to that of the male, to the child, will never be identical with those the male bears to his own body, to that of the female, and to the child; those who make much of "equality in difference" could not with good grace refuse to grant me the possible existence of differences in equality. Then again, it is institutions that create uniformity. Young and pretty, the slaves of the harem are always the same in the sultan's embrace; Christianity gave eroticism its savor of sin and legend when it endowed the human female with a soul; if society restores her sovereign individuality to woman, it will not thereby destroy the power of love's embrace to move the heart. . . .

33

Frantz Fanon

Black Skin, White Masks

Letter to the
Resident Minister (1956)

The Wretched of the Earth

⚛

*Frantz Fanon (1925–1961), a psychiatrist, was born and raised on the
island of Martinique in the West Indies, educated in France, and radicalized
in the colonial struggle in Algeria. His writings—of greatest influence among
black militants of the 1960s in the United States, rather than in his adopted
Algeria—present a poetic combination of existentialism and Marxism, not a
systematic theoretical structure. His theories, although sometimes vaguely
defined, grow out of his personal experiences of racism and colonial repression. Fanon's general sensitivity to the miseries of the human condition may
be attributable to his changing but ever-present sense of his own alienation:
he was, at various times, an African (by descent) in a West Indian culture, a
Martinican in a French culture, a black man in an Arab culture, a Euro-
pean-educated humanist in an Islamic world.*

Brought up among the black middle class of an "overseas France," Fanon initially thought of himself as totally French. During the Second World War he fought with the French forces against the Germans and, wounded in battle, was decorated for gallantry. Upon his return to Martinique, he renewed his studies and pursued them with sufficient distinction to win a scholarship to study further in France. He received a medical degree from the University of Lyons in 1951 and, two years later, passed the examinations that certified him to practice psychiatry.

In 1952 Fanon published his first book, Black Skin, White Masks, *in which he set out to examine the psychological origins and effects of racism. The book shows no commitment to a revolutionary cause but rather seems to be the author's attempt to analyze his own feelings of alienation as a black. He parallels white racism to European anti-Semitism and states that, in both cases, the identity problem is created by the dominant group's exploitative stereotypes, for they are eventually assimilated by the repressed group (as "white masks"). But Fanon also expresses hope for a change in these relationships, closing his book with a lyrical passage of reconciliation: ". . . I can already see a white man and a black man hand in hand." The first of the three excerpts in the following selection is taken from the concluding part of* Black Skin, White Masks. *In it Fanon rejects white and black racism, as well as the rigid categories of a closed "middle-class" society; in their stead he affirms "authentic" human freedom.*

Appointed director of psychiatric services in an Algerian hospital in 1953, Fanon soon found himself treating the psychic casualties of the Arab population's armed revolution against the colonial French government. He now saw colonialism, based on economic and technological power, as the cause of much human misery. Fanon's letter of resignation from the hospital is the second item in the selection. The French bureaucracy's reaction to the resignation came in the form of an official "Letter of Expulsion": leave Algeria or face arrest. Clearly, the physician had dropped his "mask."

As a member of the Algerian nationalist movement Fanon survived severe injuries from a land mine and several assassination attempts only to discover that he was suffering from a fatal leukemia. His masterwork, The Wretched of the Earth *(1961), was written in a heroic burst of energy by a dying man. Among its major themes are: the absolute necessity of violence by the colonized masses, the role of the poorest peasants as the primary force of revolution, the betrayal of the masses by a native middle class that merely replaces and imitates the old colonial power, the emergence of a new national culture after the therapy of violence. Although Fanon took his book's title from "The Internationale," a traditional communist anthem, he deviates from orthodox Marxism in such basic matters as the psychic necessity of de-*

colonializing violence and the near-dismissal of a revolutionary role for the urban proletariat.

The conclusion of Fanon's The Wretched of the Earth, *the final excerpt in the selection, calls for the creation of a "new man," free of the old exploitations, who will effect those solutions that have previously existed in some lines of European thought. Rejecting the European pattern of development, Fanon sees "the Third World starting a new history of Man" for the sake of all humanity. As he died soon after writing these words, Fanon did not live to see the new nations of the 1960s and 70s and to judge the accuracy or inaccuracy of his intense vision.*

BLACK SKIN, WHITE MASKS

It is obvious—and I will never weary of repeating this—that the quest for disalienation by a doctor of medicine born in Guadeloupe [1] can be understood only by recognizing motivations basically different from those of the Negro laborer building the port facilities in Abidjan. [2] In the first case, the alienation is of an almost intellectual character. Insofar as he conceives of European culture as a means of stripping himself of his race, he becomes alienated. In the second case, it is a question of a victim of a system based on the exploitation of a given race by another, on the contempt in which a given branch of humanity is held by a form of civilization that pretends to superiority.

I do not carry innocence to the point of believing that appeals to reason or to respect for human dignity can alter reality. For the Negro who works on a sugar plantation in Le Robert, [3] there is only one solution: to fight. He will embark on this struggle, and he will pursue it, not as the result of a Marxist or idealistic analysis but quite simply because he cannot conceive of life otherwise than in the form of a battle against exploitation, misery, and hunger.

It would never occur to me to ask these Negroes to change their conception of history. I am convinced, however, that without even

---

[1] An island group in the West Indies. Fanon was actually born in nearby Martinique.
[2] A city on the west coast of Africa, capital of the Ivory Coast.
[3] A settlement on the island of Martinique. The dominant crop of the entire island is sugar.

knowing it they share my views, accustomed as they are to speaking and thinking in terms of the present. The few working-class people whom I had the chance to know in Paris never took it on themselves to pose the problem of the discovery of a Negro past. They knew they were black, but, they told me, that made no difference in anything. In which they were absolutely right.

In this connection, I should like to say something that I have found in many other writers: Intellectual alienation is a creation of middle-class society. What I call middle-class society is any society that becomes rigidified in predetermined forms, forbidding all evolution, all gains, all progress, all discovery. I call middle-class a closed society in which life has no taste, in which the air is tainted, in which ideas and men are corrupt. And I think that a man who takes a stand against this death is in a sense a revolutionary.

The discovery of the existence of a Negro civilization in the fifteenth century confers no patent of humanity on me. Like it or not, the past can in no way guide me in the present moment.

The situation that I have examined, it is clear by now, is not a classic one. Scientific objectivity was barred to me, for the alienated, the neurotic, was my brother, my sister, my father. I have ceaselessly striven to show the Negro that in a sense he makes himself abnormal; to show the white man that he is at once the perpetrator and the victim of a delusion.

There are times when the black man is locked into his body. Now, "for a being who has acquired consciousness of himself and of his body, who has attained to the dialectic of subject and object, the body is no longer a cause of the structure of consciousness, it has become an object of consciousness."

The Negro, however sincere, is the slave of the past. None the less I am a man, and in this sense the Peloponnesian War[4] is as much mine as the invention of the compass. Face to face with the white man, the Negro has a past to legitimate, a vengeance to exact; face to face with the Negro, the contemporary white man feels the need to recall the times of cannibalism. A few years ago, the Lyon branch of the Union of Students From Overseas France asked me to reply to an article that made jazz music literally an irruption of cannibalism into the modern world. Knowing exactly what I was doing, I rejected the

---

[4] A war fought among the ancient Greek city-states (431– 404 B.C.), ending in the defeat of Athens, once the leading city-state.

premises on which the request was based, and I suggested to the defender of European purity that he cure himself of a spasm that had nothing cultural in it. Some men want to fill the world with their presence. A German philosopher described this mechanism as *the pathology of freedom*. In the circumstances, I did not have to take up a position on behalf of Negro music against white music, but rather to help my brother to rid himself of an attitude in which there was nothing healthful.

The problem considered here is one of time. Those Negroes and white men will be disalienated who refuse to let themselves be sealed away in the materialized Tower of the Past. For many other Negroes, in other ways, disalienation will come into being through their refusal to accept the present as definitive.

I am a man, and what I have to recapture is the whole past of the world. I am not responsible solely for the revolt in Santo Domingo.[5]

Every time a man has contributed to the victory of the dignity of the spirit, every time a man has said no to an attempt to subjugate his fellows, I have felt solidarity with his act.

In no way should I derive my basic purpose from the past of the peoples of color.

In no way should I dedicate myself to the revival of an unjustly unrecognized Negro civilization. I will not make myself the man of any past. I do not want to exalt the past at the expense of my present and of my future.

It is not because the Indo-Chinese has discovered a culture of his own that he is in revolt.[6] It is because "quite simply" it was, in more than one way, becoming impossible for him to breathe. When one remembers the stories with which, in 1938, old regular sergeants described the land of piastres[7] and rickshaws,[8] of cut-rate boys and

[5] In 1791, the black slaves of Santo Domingo (now Haiti and the Dominican Republic) revolted against French colonial rule. The bloody war lasted twelve years. It ended with the independence of Haiti, ruled initially by ex-slaves who had originally been imported from Africa.

[6] After the Second World War, the Indo-Chinese—specifically, the Vietnamese, Laotians, and Cambodians—revolted against their French colonial rulers. They achieved full independence in 1954 (two years after the original French publication of *Black Skin, White Masks*).

[7] A piastre was a unit of Vietnamese paper money, equal in value to about one U.S. cent.

[8] Small two-wheeled "taxicabs," each pulled by one man.

women, one understands only too well the rage with which the men of the Viet-Minh[9] go into battle.

An acquaintance with whom I served during the Second World War recently returned from Indo-China. He has enlightened me on many things. For instance, the serenity with which young Vietnamese of sixteen or seventeen faced firing squads. "On one occasion," he told me, "we had to shoot from a kneeling position: The soldiers' hands were shaking in the presence of those young 'fanatics.'" Summing up, he added: "The war that you and I were in was only a game compared to what is going on out there."

Seen from Europe, these things are beyond understanding. There are those who talk of a so-called Asiatic attitude toward death. But these basement philosophers cannot convince anyone. This Asiatic serenity, not so long ago, was a quality to be seen in the "bandits" of Vercors[10] and the "terrorists" of the Resistance.

The Vietnamese who die before the firing squads are not hoping that their sacrifice will bring about the reappearance of a past. It is for the sake of the present and of the future that they are willing to die.

If the question of practical solidarity with a given past ever arose for me, it did so only to the extent to which I was committed to myself and to my neighbor to fight for all my life and with all my strength so that never again would a people on the earth be subjugated. It was not the black world that laid down my course of conduct. My black skin is not the wrapping of specific values. It is a long time since the starry sky that took away Kant's[11] breath revealed the last of its secrets to us. And the moral law is not certain of itself.

As a man, I undertake to face the possibility of annihilation in

---

[9] The communist-led native forces which fought the French (and later the Americans) in Vietnam.
[10] A thickly wooded Alpine area of France. It was a center of the French resistance to German occupation during the Second World War. Vercors is also the pen name of Jean Bruller (1902–   ), who founded a clandestine publishing venture of the Resistance. His *The Silence of the Sea* (1942) was translated into thirty languages and generally aroused anti-Nazi sentiment.
[11] Immanuel Kant (1724–1804), a German philosopher whose work is epitomized in his famous comment that "two things fill the mind with ever new and increasing admiration and awe . . . the starry heavens above and the moral law within."

order that two or three truths may cast their eternal brilliance over the world.

Sartre [12] has shown that, in the line of an unauthentic position, the past "takes" in quantity, and, when solidly constructed, *informs* the individual. He is the past in a changed value. But, too, I can recapture my past, validate it, or condemn it through my successive choices.

The black man wants to be like the white man. For the black man there is only one destiny. And it is white. Long ago the black man admitted the unarguable superiority of the white man, and all his efforts are aimed at achieving a white existence.

Have I no other purpose on earth, then, but to avenge the Negro of the seventeenth century?

In this world, which is already trying to disappear, do I have to pose the problem of black truth?

Do I have to be limited to the justification of a facial conformation?

I as a man of color do not have the right to seek to know in what respect my race is superior or inferior to another race.

I as a man of color do not have the right to hope that in the white man there will be a crystallization of guilt toward the past of my race.

I as a man of color do not have the right to seek ways of stamping down the pride of my former master.

I have neither the right nor the duty to claim reparation for the domestication of my ancestors.

There is no Negro mission; there is no white burden.

I find myself suddenly in a world in which things do evil; a world in which I am summoned into battle; a world in which it is always a question of annihilation or triumph.

I find myself—I, a man—in a world where words wrap themselves in silence; in a world where the other endlessly hardens himself.

No, I do not have the right to go and cry out my hatred at the white man. I do not have the duty to murmur my gratitude to the white man.

---

[12] Jean-Paul Sartre (1905–   ), a French existential philosopher who affirmed that a man achieves the value of "authentic" personal existence only through freely acting upon his own choices.

My life is caught in the lasso of existence. My freedom turns me back on myself. No, I do not have the right to be a Negro.

I do not have the duty to be this or that. . . .

If the white man challenges my humanity, I will impose my whole weight as a man on his life and show him that I am not that "sho' good eatin' " that he persists in imagining.

I find myself suddenly in the world and I recognize that I have one right alone: That of demanding human behavior from the other.

One duty alone: That of not renouncing my freedom through my choices.

I have no wish to be the victim of the *Fraud* of a black world.

My life should not be devoted to drawing up the balance sheet of Negro values.

There is no white world, there is no white ethic, any more than there is a white intelligence.

There are in every part of the world men who search.

I am not a prisoner of history. I should not seek there for the meaning of my destiny.

I should constantly remind myself that the real *leap* consists in introducing invention into existence.

In the world through which I travel, I am endlessly creating myself.

I am a part of Being to the degree that I go beyond it.

And, through a private problem, we see the outline of the problem of Action. Placed in this world, in a situation, "embarked," as Pascal[13] would have it, am I going to gather weapons?

Am I going to ask the contemporary white man to answer for the slave-ships of the seventeenth century?

Am I going to try by every possible means to cause Guilt to be born in minds?

Moral anguish in the face of the massiveness of the Past? I am a Negro, and tons of chains, storms of blows, rivers of expectoration flow down my shoulders.

But I do not have the right to allow myself to bog down. I do not have the right to allow the slightest fragment to remain in my existence. I do not have the right to allow myself to be mired in what the past has determined.

[13] Blaise Pascal (1623–62), a French man of science and literature.

I am not the slave of the Slavery that dehumanized my ancestors.

To many colored intellectuals European culture has a quality of exteriority. What is more, in human relationships, the Negro may feel himself a stranger to the Western world. Not wanting to live the part of a poor relative, of an adopted son, of a bastard child, shall he feverishly seek to discover a Negro civilization?

Let us be clearly understood. I am convinced that it would be of the greatest interest to be able to have contact with a Negro literature or architecture of the third century before Christ. I should be very happy to know that a correspondence had flourished between some Negro philosopher and Plato.[14] But I can absolutely not see how this fact would change anything in the lives of the eight-year-old children who labor in the cane fields of Martinique or Guadeloupe.

No attempt must be made to encase man, for it is his destiny to be set free.

The body of history does not determine a single one of my actions.

I am my own foundation.

And it is by going beyond the historical, instrumental hypothesis that I will initiate the cycle of my freedom.

The disaster of the man of color lies in the fact that he was enslaved.

The disaster and the inhumanity of the white man lie in the fact that somewhere he has killed man.

And even today they subsist, to organize this dehumanization rationally. But I as a man of color, to the extent that it becomes possible for me to exist absolutely, do not have the right to lock myself into a world of retroactive reparations.

I, the man of color, want only this:

That the tool never possess the man. That the enslavement of man by man cease forever. That is, of one by another. That it be possible for me to discover and to love man, wherever he may be.

The Negro is not. Any more than the white man.

Both must turn their backs on the inhuman voices which were those of their respective ancestors in order that authentic communication be possible. Before it can adopt a positive voice, freedom requires an effort at disalienation. At the beginning of his life a man

[14] A Greek idealistic philosopher (*ca.* 427–348 B.C.).

is always clotted, he is drowned in contingency. The tragedy of the man is that he was once a child.

It is through the effort to recapture the self and to scrutinize the self, it is through the lasting tension of their freedom that men will be able to create the ideal conditions of existence for a human world.

Superiority? Inferiority?

Why not the quite simple attempt to touch the other, to feel the other, to explain the other to myself?

Was my freedom not given to me then in order to build the world of the *You?*

At the conclusion of this study, I want the world to recognize, with me, the open door of every consciousness.

My final prayer:
O my body, make of me always a man who questions!

LETTER TO THE RESIDENT MINISTER (1956)

Monsieur le Docteur Frantz Fanon
Médecin des Hôpitaux Psychiatriques
Médecin-Chef de Service à
l'Hôpital Psychiatrique de
BLIDA–JOINVILLE

à Monsieur le Ministre Résident,
Gouverneur Général de l'Algérie
ALGER

Monsieur le Ministre,

At my request and my decree under date of October 22, 1953, the Minister of Public Health and Population was good enough to put me at the disposal of the Governor-General of Algeria to be assigned to a Psychiatric Hospital in Algeria.

Having been given a post at the Psychiatric Hospital of Blida-Joinville on November 23, 1953, I have since that date performed the duties of medical director here.

Although the objective conditions under which psychiatry is practiced in Algeria constituted a challenge to common sense, it appeared to me that an effort should be made to attenuate the viciousness of a system of which the doctrinal foundations are a daily defiance of an authentically human outlook.

For nearly three years I have placed myself wholly at the service of this country and of the men who inhabit it. I have spared neither my efforts nor my enthusiasm. There is not a parcel of my activity that has not had as its objective the unanimously hoped-for emergence of a better world.

But what can a man's enthusiasm and devotion achieve if everyday reality is a tissue of lies, of cowardice, of contempt for man?

What good are intentions if their realization is made impossible by the indigence of the heart, the sterility of the mind, the hatred of the natives of this country?

Madness is one of the means man has of losing his freedom. And I can say, on the basis of what I have been able to observe from this point of vantage, that the degree of alienation of the inhabitants of this country appears to me frightening.

If psychiatry is the medical technique that aims to enable man no longer to be a stranger to his environment, I owe it to myself to affirm that the Arab, permanently an alien in his own country, lives in a state of absolute depersonalization.

What is the status of Algeria? A systematized de-humanization.

It was an absurd gamble to undertake, at whatever cost, to bring into existence a certain number of values, when the lawlessness, the inequality, the multi-daily murder of man were raised to the status of legislative principles.

The social structure existing in Algeria was hostile to any attempt to put the individual back where he belonged.

Monsieur le Ministre, there comes a moment when tenacity becomes morbid perseverance. Hope is then no longer an open door to the future but the illogical maintenance of a subjective attitude in organized contradiction with reality.

Monsieur le Ministre, the present-day events that are steeping Algeria in blood do not constitute a scandal for the observer. What is happening is the result neither of an accident nor of a breakdown in the mechanism.

The events in Algeria are the logical consequence of an abortive attempt to decerebralize a people.

One did not have to be a psychologist to divine, beneath the apparent good-nature of the Algerian, behind his stripped humility, a fundamental aspiration to dignity. And nothing is to be gained, with respect to non-simplifiable manifestations, by appealing to some form of civic conscience.

The function of a social structure is to set up institutions to serve man's needs. A society that drives it members to desperate solutions is a non-viable society, a society to be replaced.

It is the duty of the citizen to say this. No professional morality, no class solidarity, no desire to wash the family linen in private, can have a prior claim. No pseudo-national mystification can prevail against the requirement of reason.

Monsieur le Ministre, the decision to punish the workers who went out on strike on July 5th, 1956, is a measure which, literally, strikes me as irrational.

Either the strikers have been terrorized in their flesh and that of their families, in which case there was an obligation to understand their attitude, to regard it as normal, in view of the atmosphere.

Or else their abstention expressed a unanimous current of opinion, an unshakable conviction, in which case any punitive attitude was superfluous, gratuitous, inoperative.

I owe it to the truth to say that fear has not struck me as being the dominant mood of the strikers. Rather, there was the inevitable determination to bring about, in calm and silence, a new era of peace and dignity.

The worker in the commonwealth must cooperate in the social scheme of things. But he must be convinced of the excellence of the society in which he lives. There comes a time when silence becomes dishonesty.

The ruling intentions of personal existence are not in accord with the permanent assaults on the most commonplace values.

For many months my conscience has been the seat of unpardonable debates. And their conclusion is the determination not to despair of man, in other words, of myself.

The decision I have reached is that I cannot continue to bear a responsibility at no matter what cost, on the false pretext that there is nothing else to be done.

For all these reasons I have the honor, Monsieur le Ministre, to ask you to be good enough to accept my resignation and to put an end to my mission in Algeria.

Yours sincerely

THE WRETCHED OF THE EARTH

Come, then, comrades; it would be as well to decide at once to change our ways. We must shake off the heavy darkness in which we were plunged, and leave it behind. The new day which is already at hand must find us firm, prudent, and resolute.

We must leave our dreams and abandon our old beliefs and friendships from the time before life began. Let us waste no time in sterile litanies and nauseating mimicry. Leave this Europe where they are never done talking of Man, yet murder men everywhere they find them, at the corner of every one of their own streets, in all the corners of the globe. For centuries they have stifled almost the whole of humanity in the name of a so-called spiritual experience. Look at them today swaying between atomic and spiritual disintegration.

And yet it may be said that Europe has been successful in as much as everything that she has attempted has succeeded.

Europe undertook the leadership of the world with ardor, cynicism, and violence. Look at how the shadow of her palaces stretches out ever further! Every one of her movements has burst the bounds of space and thought. Europe has declined all humility and all modesty; but she has also set her face against all solicitude and all tenderness.

She has only shown herself parsimonious and niggardly where men are concerned; it is only men that she has killed and devoured.

So, my brothers, how is it that we do not understand that we have better things to do than to follow that same Europe?

That same Europe where they were never done talking of Man, and where they never stopped proclaiming that they were only anxious for the welfare of Man: today we know with what sufferings humanity has paid for every one of their triumphs of the mind.

Come, then, comrades, the European game has finally ended; we must find something different. We today can do everything, so long as we do not imitate Europe, so long as we are not obsessed by the desire to catch up with Europe.

Europe now lives at such a mad, reckless pace that she has shaken off all guidance and all reason, and she is running headlong into the abyss; we would do well to avoid it with all possible speed.

Yet it is very true that we need a model, and that we want blueprints and examples. For many among us the European model is the most inspiring. . . . European achievements, European techniques, and the European style ought no longer to tempt us and to throw us off our balance.

When I search for Man in the technique and the style of Europe, I see only a succession of negations of man, and an avalanche of murders.

The human condition, plans for mankind, and collaboration between men in those tasks which increase the sum total of humanity are new problems, which demand true inventions.

Let us decide not to imitate Europe; let us combine our muscles and our brains in a new direction. Let us try to create the whole man, whom Europe has been incapable of bringing to triumphant birth.

Two centuries ago, a former European colony decided to catch up with Europe. It succeeded so well that the United States of America became a monster, in which the taints, the sickness, and the inhumanity of Europe have grown to appalling dimensions.

Comrades, have we not other work to do than to create a third Europe? The West saw itself as a spiritual adventure. It is in the name of the spirit, in the name of the spirit of Europe, that Europe has made her encroachments, that she has justified her crimes and legitimized the slavery in which she holds the four-fifths of humanity.

Yes, the European spirit has strange roots. All European thought has unfolded in places which were increasingly more deserted and more encircled by precipices; and thus it was that the custom grew up in those places of very seldom meeting man.

A permanent dialogue with oneself and an increasingly obscene narcissism never ceased to prepare the way for a half delirious state, where intellectual work became suffering and the reality was not at all that of a living man, working and creating himself, but rather words, different combinations of words, and the tensions springing from the meanings contained in words. Yet some Europeans were found to urge the European workers to shatter this narcissism and to break with this unreality.

But in general, the workers of Europe have not replied to these calls; for the workers believe, too, that they are part of the prodigious adventure of the European spirit.

All the elements of a solution to the great problems of humanity have, at different times, existed in European thought. But the action of European men has not carried out the mission which fell to them, and which consisted of bringing their whole weight violently to bear upon these elements, of modifying their arrangement and their nature, of changing them and finally of bringing the problem of mankind to an infinitely higher plane.

Today we are present at the stasis of Europe. Comrades, let us flee from this motionless movement where gradually dialectic is changing into the logic of equilibrium. Let us reconsider the question of mankind. Let us reconsider the question of cerebral reality and of the cerebral mass of all humanity, whose connections must be increased, whose channels must be diversified and whose messages must be re-humanized.

Come, brothers, we have far too much work to do for us to play the game of rearguard. Europe has done what she set out to do and on the whole she has done it well; let us stop blaming her, but let us say to her firmly that she should not make such a song and dance about it. We have no more to fear; so let us stop envying her.

The Third World today faces Europe like a colossal mass whose aim should be to try to resolve the problems to which Europe has not been able to find the answers.

But let us be clear: what matters is to stop talking about output, and intensification, and the rhythm of work.

No, there is no question of a return to Nature. It is simply a very concrete question of not dragging men toward mutilation, of not imposing upon the brain rhythms which very quickly obliterate it and wreck it. The pretext of catching up must not be used to push man around, to tear him away from himself or from his privacy, to break and kill him.

No, we do not want to catch up with anyone. What we want to do is to go forward all the time, night and day, in the company of Man, in the company of all men. The caravan should not be stretched out, for in that case each line will hardly see those who precede it; and men who no longer recognize each other meet less and less together, and talk to each other less and less.

It is a question of the Third World starting a new history of Man, a history which will have regard to the sometimes prodigious theses which Europe has put forward, but which will also not forget Europe's crimes, of which the most horrible was committed in the heart of man, and consisted of the pathological tearing apart of his functions and the crumbling away of his unity. And in the framework of the collectivity there were the differentiations, the stratification, and the bloodthirsty tensions fed by classes; and finally, on the immense scale of humanity, there were racial hatreds, slavery, exploitation, and above all the bloodless genocide which consisted in the setting aside of fifteen thousand millions of men.

So, comrades, let us not pay tribute to Europe by creating states, institutions, and societies which draw their inspiration from her.

Humanity is waiting for something from us other than such an imitation, which would be almost an obscene caricature.

If we want to turn Africa into a new Europe, and America into a new Europe, then let us leave the destiny of our countries to Europeans. They will know how to do it better than the most gifted among us.

But if we want humanity to advance a step further, if we want to bring it up to a different level than that which Europe has shown it, then we must invent and we must make discoveries.

If we wish to live up to our peoples' expectations, we must seek the response elsewhere than in Europe.

Moreover, if we wish to reply to the expectations of the people of Europe, it is no good sending them back a reflection, even an ideal reflection of their society and their thought with which from time to time they feel immeasurably sickened.

For Europe, for ourselves, and for humanity, comrades, we must turn over a new leaf, we must work out new concepts, and try to set afoot a new man.

34

André Breton

Manifesto of Surrealism

The "new consciousness" that began early in the century affected the arts in the same liberating, often disturbing, way that it affected politics, education, and other basic human activities. In literature and the visual arts, the "surrealists" sought to liberate artistic expression from all conscious rational, aesthetic, or moral controls; their leading spokesman was the French writer André Breton (1896–1966).

Breton was born the son of a shopkeeper in the Norman village of Tinchebray. Drafted into the French army in 1915, while he was studying to become a doctor, Breton was assigned as a medical assistant in the military psychiatric wards. His experiences there and elsewhere during the First World War became extremely important in the shaping of his ideas. In the army he met the rebellious young writers Louis Aragon and Philippe Soupault, with whom he later collaborated. Influenced also by meetings with poets Guillaume Apollinaire and Paul Valéry, Breton became interested in the impact of revolution upon the arts and upon society. Jacques Vaché, a nihilist who committed suicide for a joke, was a further influence on Breton. The mental patients he observed in the military wards were, like his personal encounters, significant in forming his artistic and social theories.

In 1919—the war concluded—Breton, together with Aragon and Soupault, brought out the first issue of the review Littérature. *Breton later continued its editorial supervision alone and eventually founded other surrealist journals. In 1921, he visited Sigmund Freud in Vienna, after having utilized Freud's techniques of free association and psychoanalysis. Growing increasingly more interested in dreams and "psychic automatism," Breton soon thereafter organized a group that was dedicated to surrealism. He also wrote the first of three manifestoes intended to explain its principles.*

As the surrealist movement moved away from purely artistic concerns toward social action, Breton joined the Communist Party. However, the incompatibility of surrealism's emphasis on total personal freedom with the party's call for submission to a collectivist ideology at last became clear to Breton. He withdrew from membership in 1935.

In 1938 Breton journeyed to Mexico, where he worked with Leon Trotsky—exiled Russian revolutionary—in establishing The International Federation of Independent Revolutionary Art. Soon afterwards, with the German occupation of France during the Second World War and censorship of his works by the collaborationist French government, Breton, too, became an exile. He went to the United States, where he lectured on surrealism and studied art and ritual among the American and Caribbean Indians. Returning to France after the war, Breton revived the European surrealist movement and participated in international humanitarian causes.

Breton is the author of countless works of poetry, fiction, and criticism. His novel Nadja *(1928) tells of his chance encounters in Paris with an extraordinary woman—and her intuitive, liberating, irrational, "mad" imagination. Like many of his other works it is characterized by streams of images—often deliberately bizarre, illogical, and contradictory. Breton believed that rational ideas were ineffectual, compared to the sudden force of an unexpected image. Even in translation the titles of his poems—such as "Soluble Fish," "The Whitehaired Revolver," and "Fertile Eyes"—show the fascinating contradictions of his images. (A visual counterpart to Breton's literary images can be seen in the surrealist paintings of Salvador Dali, with whom Breton was sometimes associated.)*

The first Manifesto of Surrealism *(1924), the source of the following selection, "officially" inaugurated and defined the surrealist movement. It includes Breton's explicit thanks to Freud for bringing to light the unconscious psychic world, especially the world of dreams. The technique of "psychic automatism," by which Breton proposes to express "the actual functioning of thought," is the literary equivalent of Freud's clinical technique of free association. Under Breton's leadership, surrealism became not merely an aesthetic movement but a way of life. In its "modernity," it rejected the "proper," stable bourgeois values and embraced the rediscovery of the disordered and irrational.*

The mere word "freedom" is the only one that still excites me. I deem it capable of indefinitely sustaining the old human fanaticism. It doubtless satisfies my only legitimate aspiration. Among all the many misfortunes to which we are heir, it is only fair to admit that we are allowed the greatest degree of freedom of thought. It is up to us not to misuse it. To reduce the imagination to a state of slavery— even though it would mean the elimination of what is commonly called happiness—is to betray all sense of absolute justice within oneself. Imagination alone offers me some intimation of what *can be,* and this is enough to remove to some slight degree the terrible injunction; enough, too, to allow me to devote myself to it without fear of making a mistake (as though it were possible to make a bigger mistake). Where does it begin to turn bad, and where does the mind's stability cease? For the mind, is the possibility of erring not rather the contingency of good?

There remains madness, "the madness that one locks up," as it has aptly been described. That madness or another. . . . We all know, in fact, that the insane owe their incarceration to a tiny number of legally reprehensible acts and that, were it not for these acts, their freedom (or what we see as their freedom) would not be threatened. I am willing to admit that they are, to some degree, victims of their imagination, in that it induces them not to pay attention to certain rules—outside of which the species feels itself threatened—which we are all supposed to know and respect. But their profound indifference to the way in which we judge them, and even to the various punishments meted out to them, allows us to suppose that they derive a great deal of comfort and consolation from their imagination, that they enjoy their madness sufficiently to endure the thought that its validity does not extend beyond themselves. And, indeed, hallucinations, illusions, etc., are not a source of trifling pleasure. The best controlled sensuality partakes of it, and I know that there are many evenings when I would gladly tame that pretty hand which, during the last pages of Taine's *L'Intelligence,*[1] indulges in some curious misdeeds. I could spend my whole life prying loose the secrets of the insane. These people are honest to a fault, and their na-

[1] A treatise on experimental psychology by Hippolyte Taine (1828–93), who rigorously applied the scientific method to criticism of literature and art. He believed that heredity, environment, and the historical moment totally determine the character of writers and artists and their work. Obviously, Taine's mechanistic, "naturalistic" principles annoyed Breton.

iveté has no peer but my own. Christopher Columbus should have set out to discover America with a boatload of madmen. And note how this madness has taken shape, and endured.

It is not the fear of madness which will oblige us to leave the flag of imagination furled.

The case against the realistic attitude demands to be examined, following the case against the materialistic attitude. The latter, more poetic in fact than the former, admittedly implies on the part of man a kind of monstrous pride which, admittedly, is monstrous, but not a new and more complete decay. It should above all be viewed as a welcome reaction against certain ridiculous tendencies of spiritualism. Finally, it is not incompatible with a certain nobility of thought.

By contrast, the realistic attitude, inspired by positivism,[2] from Saint Thomas Aquinas[3] to Anatole France,[4] clearly seems to me to be hostile to any intellectual or moral advancement. I loathe it, for it is made up of mediocrity, hate, and dull conceit. It is this attitude which today gives birth to these ridiculous books, these insulting plays. It constantly feeds on and derives strength from the newspapers and stultifies both science and art by assiduously flattering the lowest of tastes; clarity bordering on stupidity, a dog's life. The activity of the best minds feels the effects of it; the law of the lowest common denominator finally prevails upon them as it does upon the others. . . .

We are still living under the reign of logic: this, of course, is what I have been driving at. But in this day and age logical methods are applicable only to solving problems of secondary interest. The absolute rationalism that is still in vogue allows us to consider only facts relating directly to our experience. Logical ends, on the contrary, escape us. It is pointless to add that experience itself has found itself increasingly circumscribed. It paces back and forth in a cage from which it is more and more difficult to make it emerge. It too leans for support on what is most immediately expedient, and it

---

[2] The philosophical position that all earlier forms of philosophy were based on inadequate knowledge, and that — in the modern age — complete or "positive" knowledge can be based only upon those "facts" which have been verified by the physical sciences.

[3] A leading medieval philosopher (1225–74).

[4] A French satirical writer (1844–1924); he was awarded a Nobel Prize in 1921.

is protected by the sentinels of common sense. Under the pretense of civilization and progress, we have managed to banish from the mind everything that may rightly or wrongly be termed superstition, or fancy; forbidden is any kind of search for truth which is not in conformance with accepted practices. It was, apparently, by pure chance that a part of our mental world which we pretended not to be concerned with any longer—and, in my opinion, by far the most important part—has been brought back to light. For this we must give thanks to the discoveries of Sigmund Freud.[5] On the basis of these discoveries a current of opinion is finally forming by means of which the human explorer will be able to carry his investigations much further, authorized as he will henceforth be not to confine himself solely to the most summary realities. The imagination is perhaps on the point of reasserting itself, of reclaiming its rights. If the depths of our mind contain within it strange forces capable of augmenting those on the surface, or of waging a victorious battle against them, there is every reason to seize them—first to seize them, then, if need be, to submit them to the control of our reason. The analysts themselves have everything to gain by it. But it is worth noting that no means has been designated a priori for carrying out this undertaking, that until further notice it can be construed to be the province of poets as well as scholars, and that its success is not dependent upon the more or less capricious paths that will be followed.

Freud very rightly brought his critical faculties to bear upon the dream. It is, in fact, inadmissible that this considerable portion of psychic activity (since, at least from man's birth until his death, thought offers no solution of continuity, the sum of the moments of dream, from the point of view of time, and taking into consideration only the time of pure dreaming, that is the dreams of sleep, is not inferior to the sum of the moments of reality, or, to be more precisely limiting, the moments of waking) has still today been so grossly neglected. I have always been amazed at the way an ordinary observer lends so much more credence and attaches so much more importance to waking events than to those occurring in dreams. It is because man, when he ceases to sleep, is above all the plaything of his memory, and in its normal state memory takes pleasure in weakly retrac-

[5] An Austrian physician who became the founder of clinical psychoanalysis (1856–1939). Freud demonstrated the importance of unconscious, irrational drives.

ing for him the circumstances of the dream, in stripping it of any real importance, and in dismissing the only *determinant* from the point where he thinks he has left it a few hours before: this firm hope, this concern. He is under the impression of continuing something that is worthwhile. Thus the dream finds itself reduced to a mere parenthesis, as is the night. And, like the night, dreams generally contribute little to furthering our understanding. This curious state of affairs seems to me to call for certain reflections:

1. Within the limits where they operate (or are thought to operate) dreams give every evidence of being continuous and show signs of organization. Memory alone arrogates to itself the right to excerpt from dreams, to ignore the transitions, and to depict for us rather a series of dreams than the *dream itself.* By the same token, at any given moment we have only a distinct notion of realities, the coordination of which is a question of will.[6] What is worth noting is that nothing allows us to presuppose a greater dissipation of the elements of which the dream is constituted. I am sorry to have to speak about it according to a formula which in principle excludes the dream. When will we have sleeping logicians, sleeping philosophers? I would like to sleep, in order to surrender myself to the dreamers, the way I surrender myself to those who read me with eyes wide open; in order to stop imposing, in this realm, the conscious rhythm of my thought. Perhaps my dream last night follows that of the night before, and will be continued the next night, with an exemplary strictness. *It's quite possible,* as the saying goes. And since it has not been proved in the slightest that, in doing so, the "reality" with which I am kept busy continues to exist in the state of dream, that it does not sink back down into the immemorial, why should I not grant to dreams what I occasionally refuse reality, that is, this value of certainty in itself which, in its own time, is not open to my repudiation? Why should I not expect from the sign of the dream more than I expect from a degree of consciousness which is daily more acute? Can't the dream also be used in solving the fundamental questions of life? Are these questions the same in one case as in the other and, in the dream, do these questions already exist? Is the dream any

---

[6] Account must be taken of the *depth* of the dream. For the most part I retain only what I can glean from its most superficial layers. What I most enjoy contemplating about a dream is everything that sinks back below the surface in a waking state, everything I have forgotten about my activities in the course of the preceding day, dark foliage, stupid branches. In "reality," likewise, I prefer to *fall.* [Breton's note. *Ed.*]

less restrictive or punitive than the rest? I am growing old and, more than that reality to which I believe I subject myself, it is perhaps the dream, the difference with which I treat the dream, which makes me grow old.

2. Let me come back again to the waking state. I have no choice but to consider it a phenomenon of interference. Not only does the mind display, in this state, a strange tendency to lose its bearings (as evidenced by the slips and mistakes the secrets of which are just beginning to be revealed to us), but, what is more, it does not appear that, when the mind is functioning normally, it really responds to anything but the suggestions which come to it from the depths of that dark night to which I commend it. However conditioned it may be, its balance is relative. It scarcely dares express itself and, if it does, it confines itself to verifying that such and such an idea, or such and such a woman, has made an impression on it. What impression it would be hard pressed to say, by which it reveals the degree of its subjectivity, and nothing more. This idea, this woman, disturb it, they tend to make it less severe. What they do is isolate the mind for a second from its solvent and spirit it to heaven, as the beautiful pre-cipitate it can be, that it is. When all else fails, it then calls upon chance, a divinity even more obscure than the others to whom it ascribes all its aberrations. Who can say to me that the angle by which that idea which affects it is offered, that what it likes in the eye of that woman is not precisely what links it to its dream, binds it to those fundamental facts which, through its own fault, it has lost? And if things were different, what might it be capable of? I would like to provide it with the key to this corridor.

3. The mind of the man who dreams is fully satisfied by what happens to him. The agonizing question of possibility is no longer pertinent. Kill, fly faster, love to your heart's content. And if you should die, are you not certain of reawaking among the dead? Let yourself be carried along, events will not tolerate your interference. You are nameless. The ease of everything is priceless.

What reason, I ask, a reason so much vaster than the other, makes dreams seem so natural and allows me to welcome unreservedly a welter of episodes so strange that they would confound me now as I write? And yet I can believe my eyes, my ears; this great day has ar-rived, this beast has spoken.

If man's awaking is harder, if it breaks the spell too abruptly, it is because he has been led to make for himself too impoverished a notion of atonement.

4. From the moment when it is subjected to a methodical examination, when, by means yet to be determined, we succeed in recording the contents of dreams in their entirety (and that presupposes a discipline of memory spanning generations; but let us nonetheless begin by noting the most salient facts), when its graph will expand with unparalleled volume and regularity, we may hope that the mysteries which really are not will give way to the great Mystery. I believe in the future resolution of these two states, dream and reality, which are seemingly so contradictory, into a kind of absolute reality, a *surreality*, if one may so speak. It is in quest of this surreality that I am going, certain not to find it but too unmindful of my death not to calculate to some slight degree the joys of its possession.

A story is told according to which Saint-Pol-Roux,[7] in times gone by, used to have a notice posted on the door of his manor house in Camaret, every evening before he went to sleep, which read: THE POET IS WORKING.

A great deal more could be said, but in passing I merely wanted to touch upon a subject which in itself would require a very long and much more detailed discussion; I shall come back to it. At this juncture, my intention was merely to mark a point by noting the *hate of the marvelous* which rages in certain men, this absurdity beneath which they try to bury it. Let us not mince words: the marvelous is always beautiful, anything marvelous is beautiful, in fact only the marvelous is beautiful. . . .

One evening, therefore, before I fell asleep, I perceived, so clearly articulated that it was impossible to change a word, but nonetheless removed from the sound of any voice, a rather strange phrase which came to me without any apparent relationship to the events in which, my consciousness agrees, I was then involved, a phrase which seemed to me insistent, a phrase, if I may be so bold, *which was knocking at the window*. I took cursory note of it and prepared to move on when its organic character caught my attention. Actually, this phrase astonished me: unfortunately I cannot remember it ex-

---

[7] Pseudonym of Paul Roux (1861–1940), a French poet known for his use of vivid images; he spent his entire life in the rural village of Camaret in Brittany.

actly, but it was something like: "There is a man cut in two by the window," but there could be no question of ambiguity, accompanied as it was by the faint visual image[8] of a man walking cut half way up by a window perpendicular to the axis of his body. Beyond the slightest shadow of a doubt, what I saw was the simple reconstruction in space of a man leaning out a window. But this window having shifted with the man, I realized that I was dealing with an image of a fairly rare sort, and all I could think of was to incorporate it into my material for poetic construction. No sooner had I granted it this capacity than it was in fact succeeded by a whole series of phrases, with only brief pauses between them, which surprised me only slightly less and left me with the impression of their being so gratuitous that the control I had then exercised upon myself seemed to me illusory and all I could think of was putting an end to the interminable quarrel raging within me.

Completely occupied as I still was with Freud at that time, and familiar as I was with his methods of examination which I had had some slight occasion to use on some patients during the war, I resolved to obtain from myself what we were trying to obtain from them, namely, a monologue spoken as rapidly as possible without any intervention on the part of the critical faculties, a monologue consequently unencumbered by the slightest inhibition and which was, as closely as possible, akin to *spoken thought*. It had seemed to me, and still does—the way in which the phrase about the man cut in two had come to me is an indication of it—that the speed of thought is no greater than the speed of speech, and that thought does

---

[8] Were I a painter, this visual depiction would doubtless have become more important for me than the other. It was most certainly my previous predispositions which decided the matter. Since that day, I have had occasion to concentrate my attention voluntarily on similar apparitions, and I know that they are fully as clear as auditory phenomena. With a pencil and white sheet of paper to hand, I could easily trace their outlines. Here again it is not a matter of drawing, but *simply of tracing*. I could thus depict a tree, a wave, a musical instrument, all manner of things of which I am presently incapable of providing even the roughest sketch. I would plunge into it, convinced that I would find my way again, in a maze of lines which at first glance would seem to be going nowhere. And, upon opening my eyes, I would get the very strong impression of something "never seen." The proof of what I am saying has been provided many times by Robert Desnos: to be convinced, one has only to leaf through the pages of issue number 36 of *Feuilles libres* which contains several of his drawings (*Romeo and Juliet, A Man Died This Morning*, etc.) which were taken by this magazine as the drawings of a madman and published as such. [Breton's note. *Ed.*]

not necessarily defy language, nor even the fast-moving pen. It was in this frame of mind that Philippe Soupault[9]—to whom I had confided these initial conclusions—and I decided to blacken some paper, with a praiseworthy disdain for what might result from a literary point of view. The ease of execution did the rest. By the end of the first day we were able to read to ourselves some fifty or so pages obtained in this manner, and begin to compare our results. All in all, Soupault's pages and mine proved to be remarkably similar: the same overconstruction, shortcomings of a similar nature, but also, on both our parts, the illusion of an extraordinary verve, a great deal of emotion, a considerable choice of images of a quality such that we would not have been capable of preparing a single one in longhand, a very special picturesque quality and, here and there, a strong comical effect. The only difference between our two texts seemed to me to derive essentially from our respective tempers, Soupault's being less static than mine, and, if he does not mind my offering this one slight criticism, from the fact that he had made the error of putting a few words by way of titles at the top of certain pages, I suppose in a spirit of mystification. On the other hand, I must give credit where credit is due and say that he constantly and vigorously opposed any effort to retouch or correct, however slightly, any passage of this kind which seemed to me unfortunate. In this he was, to be sure, absolutely right. It is, in fact, difficult to appreciate fairly the various elements present; one may even go so far as to say that it is impossible to appreciate them at a first reading. To you who write, these elements are, on the surface, *as strange to you as they are to anyone else,* and naturally you are wary of them. Poetically speaking, what strikes you about them above all is their *extreme degree of immediate absurdity,* the quality of this absurdity, upon closer scrutiny, being to give way to everything admissible, everything legitimate in the world: the disclosure of a certain number of properties and of facts no less objective, in the final analysis, than the others.

• • •

Those who might dispute our right to employ the term SURREAL-ISM in the very special sense that we understand it are being extremely dishonest, for there can be no doubt that this word had no

[9] Until 1926 Philippe Soupault (1897–   ), a poet, novelist, and critic, took an active part with Breton in the surrealist movement. Their collaborative experiment in "automatic writing" was published in 1921 as *Magnetic Fields.*

currency before we came along. Therefore, I am defining it once and for all:

SURREALISM, *n.* Psychic automatism in its pure state, by which one proposes to express—verbally, by means of the written word, or in any other manner—the actual functioning of thought. Dictated by thought, in the absence of any control exercised by reason, exempt from any aesthetic or moral concern. . . . Surrealism is based on the belief in the superior reality of certain forms of previously neglected associations, in the omnipotence of dream, in the disinterested play of thought. It tends to ruin once and for all all other psychic mechanisms and to substitute itself for them in solving all the principal problems of life. . . .

35

Wassily Kandinsky
Concerning the Spiritual in Art

The art of painting was, by the early twentieth century, no longer regarded by many painters as essentially the imitation of nature. Among the leaders of the movement away from strict copying of the natural world was the Russian artist Wassily Kandinsky (1866–1944).

Born in Moscow, Kandinsky studied law and economics at the University of Moscow, earning an advanced degree in 1893. While a student he was particularly impressed by a showing of paintings by Rembrandt, the seventeenth-century Dutch master. After seeing an exhibition of works by Monet and others in the new group of French Impressionists, Kandinsky abandoned a promising career as a professor of law and in 1896 traveled to Munich to study painting.

Settling in Germany, after extensive travels in Europe and North Africa, Kandinsky began to make his influence felt as a teacher and as a spokesman for new artistic movements. He was a founding member, for example, of the important "Blue Rider" movement in Munich. The members of this group, although diverse in their artistic interests, shared a desire to break loose from the confines of traditionalism.

By 1910 Kandinsky had painted the first totally non-representational works in Western art. They depended entirely on the emotional significance of colors and had no suggestions of human figures or other objects in nature. In Kandinsky's work, color dominates over any recognizable form and creates a sensual pleasure and emotional intensity that the artist himself compared to modern music.

With the outbreak of the First World War, Kandinsky returned to his native Moscow. After the Bolsheviks seized power in 1917, and as revolutionary Soviet culture emerged, he assumed important official posts. For example, he became Professor at the Moscow Academy of Fine Arts (1918), Director of the Moscow Museum of Pictorial Culture (1919), Professor at the University of Moscow (1920), and founder of the Russian Academy of Artistic Sciences (1921). However, as the artistic possibilities of the Russian Revolution became increasingly narrowed by the tastes of the new bureaucracy—especially by the imposition of propagandistic "socialist realism"—Kandinsky returned to Germany. There, from 1922 to 1933, he taught at the famous Bauhaus (House of Building). The most influential art school of the modern age, it combined the talents of architects, painters, designers, engineers, and craftsmen to solve the aesthetic problems of machine production. With the coming of the Nazis to power in 1933 and the closing of the Bauhaus by Hitler, Kandinsky moved to France, where he spent his remaining years.

Kandinsky's painting after 1910 was expressively "abstract"—showing color and form independent of the world of nature; the Bauhaus years moved Kandinsky toward the mathematical purity of geometrical forms: points, bundles of lines, circles, and triangles. During his last decade, however, he achieved a synthesis between the unrestrained, intuitive images of his early period and the more technically precise ones of his Bauhaus years.

In Concerning the Spiritual in Art *(1914, rev. trans. 1947), the source of the following selection, Kandinsky expresses his lofty conception of the spiritual power of the independent artist. Not yet influenced by the technological synthesis of the Bauhaus, Kandinsky maintains that the artist must create out of his own internal needs, released by his spiritual mission from imitating the "impure" forms of the material world. Through such statements and the example of his own works, Kandinsky became known as the founder of abstract expressionism, the artistic style based on the liberation of the artist's feelings and the expression of those feelings in "pure"—not imitative—forms and colors.*

A work or art is born of the artist in a mysterious and secret way. Detached from him it acquires autonomous life, becomes an entity. Nor is its existence casual and inconsequent: it has a definite and purposeful strength, alike in its material and spiritual life. It exists and has power to create spiritual atmosphere; and from this internal standpoint alone can one judge whether it is a good work of art or bad. If its form is "poor," it is too weak to call forth spiritual vibration.[1] Likewise a picture is not necessarily "well painted" if it possesses the "values"[2] of which the French so constantly speak. It is only well painted if its spiritual value is completed and satisfying. "Good drawing" is drawing that cannot be altered without destruction of this inner value, quite irrespective of its correctness as anatomy, botany or any other science. This is not a question of a violation of natural form, but of the need of the artist for such a form. Similarly, colors are not used because they are true to nature but because they are necessary to the particular picture. The artist is not only justified in using, but is under a moral obligation to use, only those forms which fulfill his *own need*. Absolute freedom from anatomy or anything else of the kind must be given to the artist in his choice of means. Such spiritual freedom is as necessary in art as it is in life.[3]

But blind following of scientific precept is less blameworthy than its blind and purposeless rejection. At least the former produces an imitation of material objects which may have some use.[4] The latter is an artistic fraud, bringing confusion in its train. The former leaves the spiritual atmosphere empty; the latter poisons it.

Painting is an art; and art is not vague production, transitory and isolated, but a power which must be directed to the development and refinement of the human soul, to raising the triangle of the spirit.[5]

---

[1] So-called "immoral" pictures either are not capable of causing vibrations of the soul (in which case they are not art), or are capable. In the latter case they are not to be spurned, even though they produce purely aphrodisiac vibrations. [Kandinsky's note. *Ed.*]

[2] Gradations of tone from light to dark in any solid object.

[3] This absolute liberty must be based on internal necessity, which might be called honesty. The principle holds good in life and in art. It is the most effective weapon against Philistines. [Kandinsky's note. *Ed.*]

[4] Plainly, an imitation of nature, if made by the hand of a true artist, is not a mere reproduction. The voice of the soul will in some degree make itself heard. . . . [Kandinsky's note. *Ed.*]

[5] In an earlier passage of the same work, Kandinsky defined "the triangle of the spirit":

The life of the spirit may be graphically represented as a large acute-angled triangle, divided horizontally into unequal parts, with the narrowest segment uppermost. The lower the segment, the greater it is in breadth, depth and area.

The whole triangle moves slowly, almost invisibly forward and upward. Where

If art rejects this work, a pit remains unbridged; no other power can take the place of art in this activity.[6] And sometimes when the human soul is gaining greater strength, art also grows in power, for the two are inextricably connected and complementary. Conversely, at those times when the soul tends to be choked by materialist lack of belief, art becomes purposeless, and it is said that art exists for art's sake alone.[7] The relation between art and the soul is, as it were, doped into unconsciousness. The artist and the public drift apart, until at last the public turns its back, or regards the artist as a juggler whose skill and dexterity alone are worthy of applause. It is important for the artist to gauge his position correctly, to realize that he has a duty to his art and to himself, that he is not a king but a servant of a noble end. He must search his soul deeply, develop it and guard it, so that his art may have something on which to rest and does not remain flesh without bones.

The artist must have something to communicate, since mastery over form is not the end but, instead, the adapting of form to internal significance.[8]

The artist's life is not one of pleasure. He must not live irresponsibly; he has a difficult work to perform, one which often proves a crown of thorns. He must realize that his acts, feelings and thoughts are the imponderable but sound material from which his work is to rise; he is free in art, but not in life.

Compared with non-artists the artist has a triple responsibility: (1) he must return the talent which he has; (2) his actions, feelings and thoughts, like those of every man, create a spiritual atmosphere which is either pure or infected; (3) his actions and thoughts are the material for his creations, which in turn influence the spiritual atmo-

the apex was today, the second segment will be tomorrow; what today can be understood only by the apex, is tomorrow the thought and feeling of the second segment.

At the apex of the highest segment often stands one man.

[6] This pit can easily be filled by poison and plague. [Kandinsky's note. *Ed.*]

[7] This phrase "art for art's sake" is really the best ideal such an age can attain. It is an unconscious protest against materialism, against the demand that everything should have a use and practical value. It is proof of the indestructibility of art and the human soul, which can never be killed, but only temporarily dazed. [Kandinsky's note. *Ed.*]

[8] This does not mean that the artist is to instill forcibly and deliberately into his work a meaning. The generation of a work of art is a mystery. If artistry exists, there is no need of theory or logic to direct the painter's activity. The inner voice tells him what form he needs, whether inside or outside nature. Every artist who works with feeling knows how suddenly the right form comes. . . . [Kandinsky's note. *Ed.*]

sphere. The artist is a king, as Péladan[9] says, not only because he has great powers, but also because he has great obligations.

If the artist be guardian of beauty, beauty can be measured only by the yardstick of internal greatness and necessity.

That is beautiful which is produced by internal necessity, which springs from the soul.[10] . . .

[9] Joseph Péladan (1858–1918), a French mystic and novelist.

[10] By this "beauty" we do not mean the contemporary external or even inner morality, but that quality which, itself imponderable, enriches and refines the soul. In painting any color is intrinsically beautiful, for each color causes a spiritual vibration. Each vibration, in turn, enriches the soul. Thus any outward ugliness contains potential beauty. [Kandinsky's note. *Ed.*]

36

Igor Stravinsky

Poetics of Music

❈

Music, like the other arts, has experienced a startling degree of change during the twentieth century—both in style and in content. A composer whose varied works exemplify many of the era's significant musical trends and cultural traditions is Igor Stravinsky (1882–1971).

Born near St. Petersburg (now Leningrad), Russia, Stravinsky studied law—at his parents' insistence—at St. Petersburg University. Becoming acquainted with the established composer Nikolay Rimsky-Korsakov, Stravinsky began to study music privately with him and eventually abandoned the legal profession. Thus he regularly discussed his new compositions with Rimsky-Korsakov, and the older man's orchestral mastery and distinctively Russian musical style had an enduring effect on Stravinsky.

After attending a performance of several early symphonic works by Stravinsky, Sergei Diaghilev, founder and director of the Russian Ballet, commissioned him to compose the scores for a number of ballets. Thus began Stravinsky's explosive rise to prominence among modern composers. The Firebird *(1910), the first of these ballets, combines elements of the Russian nationalist tradition with all the exotic orientalism and orchestral sensuality typical of the music of Stravinsky's teacher, Rimsky-Korsakov. The second,* Petrushka *(1911), is a brashly colorful ballet about puppets come to life. While completing* The Firebird, *Stravinsky had a daydream about a pagan ritual in which a young girl danced herself to death. This image was the genesis of the third ballet for Diaghilev,* The Rite of Spring *(1913), subtitled* Pictures of Pagan Russia—*a score that represents the culmination of sophisticated primitivism in modern music. Its dynamic opening performance in Paris caused one of the wildest riots in the history of music. The profoundly disturbing effects of the ballet stem from unusual rhythms, dissonant combinations of chords, and, especially, from an elemental power that implacably sweeps the music to a shattering conclusion.*

Seeing his native Russia changed by the First World War and the Bolshevik Revolution, Stravinsky eventually moved to France, where he abandoned the romantic Russian features of his earlier compositions and adopted an austere "neoclassical" style. Among his outstanding works of this period are the opera-oratorio Oedipus Rex *(1927), the choral* Symphony of Psalms *(1930), and the full-length opera* The Rake's Progress *(1951), which deliberately re-created Mozart's eighteenth-century style. Deprived of his private income in Russia, Stravinsky began a performing career as pianist and conductor.*

The third major phase of the composer's work was as impressively startling in its results as the earlier two. Stravinsky untiringly moved from the world of musical harmonies derived from traditional scales and modes to the new twelve-note scale or "tone-row" devised by Arnold Schoenberg, his Austro-American contemporary. Stravinsky, around 1955, became a twelve-tone composer who based each work on a series of notes stated as a tone-row in the opening measures. This new technique can be observed, for example, in the ballet Agon *(1957), the orchestral* Variations *(1964), and the choral* Requiem Canticles *(1966).*

In the Poetics of Music *(1947), the book from which the following selection is taken, Stravinsky acknowledges his debt to the great musical tradition. The book is actually a translation of six lectures delivered by him in French at Harvard University during 1939 and 1940. The rapid fall of France to the Germans while Stravinsky was away from Europe for these lectures necessitated the composer's stay in the United States for the duration of the war. (Eventually, he was to live more than a quarter of a century in Hollywood, California.) Stravinsky in these lectures criticizes the vulgarization of music—through commercialization, excessive desire for novelty, and propagandistic requirements. He pleads for order and discipline, for the limitations imposed by cultural forms and the living force of tradition. Although usually regarded as an innovator, Stravinsky reveals himself as a creator who has absorbed the lessons of the past—and who affirms his cultural heritage by building upon it.*

In truth, I should be hard pressed to cite for you a single fact in the history of art that might be qualified as revolutionary. Art is by essence constructive. Revolution implies a disruption of equilibrium. To speak of revolution is to speak of a temporary chaos. Now art is the contrary of chaos. It never gives itself up to chaos without immediately finding its living works, its very existence, threatened.

The quality of being revolutionary is generally attributed to artists in our day with a laudatory intent, undoubtedly because we are living in a period when revolution enjoys a kind of prestige among yesterday's elite. Let us understand each other: I am the first to recognize that daring is the motive force of the finest and greatest acts; which is all the more reason for not putting it unthinkingly at the service of disorder and base cravings in a desire to cause sensation at any price. I approve of daring; I set no limits to it. But likewise there are no limits to the mischief wrought by arbitrary acts.

To enjoy to the full the conquests of daring, we must demand that it operate in a pitiless light. We are working in its favor when we denounce the false wares that would usurp its place. Gratuitous excess spoils every substance, every form that it touches. In its blundering it impairs the effectiveness of the most valuable discoveries and at the same time corrupts the taste of its devotees—which explains why their taste often plunges without transition from the wildest complications to the flattest banalities.

A musical complex, however harsh it may be, is legitimate to the extent to which it is genuine. But to recognize genuine values in the midst of the excesses of sham one must be gifted with a sure instinct that our snobs hate all the more intensely for being themselves completely deprived thereof.

Our vanguard elite, sworn perpetually to outdo itself, expects and requires that music should satisfy the taste for absurd cacophony.

• • •

We are living at a time when the status of man is undergoing profound upheavals.[1] Modern man is progressively losing his understanding of values and his sense of proportions. This failure to understand essential realities is extremely serious. It leads us infallibly to the violation of the fundamental laws of human equilibrium. In

[1] The Second World War was in its first year when Stravinsky delivered his lectures; they were later published as the *Poetics of Music* (1947). The war caused him to remain in the United States.

the domain of music, the consequences of this misunderstanding are these: on one hand there is a tendency to turn the mind away from what I shall call the higher mathematics of music in order to degrade music to servile employment, and to vulgarize it by adapting it to the requirements of an elementary utilitarianism—as we shall soon see on examining Soviet music. On the other hand, since the mind itself is ailing, the music of our time, and particularly the music that calls itself and believes itself *pure,* carries within it the symptoms of a pathologic blemish and spreads the germs of a new original sin. The old original sin was chiefly a sin of knowledge; the new original sin, if I may speak in these terms, is first and foremost a sin of non-acknowledgement—a refusal to acknowledge the truth and the laws that proceed therefrom, laws that we have called fundamental. What then is this truth in the domain of music? And what are its repercussions on creative activity?

Let us not forget that it is written: "Spiritus ubi vult spirat"[2] (St. John, 3:8). What we must retain in this proposition is above all the word WILL. The Spirit is thus endowed with the capacity of willing. The principle of speculative volition is a fact.

Now it is just this fact that is too often disputed. People question the direction that the wind of the Spirit is taking, not the rightness of the artisan's work. In so doing, whatever may be your feelings about ontology[3] or whatever your own philosophy and beliefs may be, you must admit that you are making an attack on the very freedom of the spirit—whether you begin this large word with a capital or not. If a believer in Christian philosophy, you would then also have to refuse to accept the idea of the Holy Spirit. If an agnostic or atheist, you would have to do nothing less than refuse to be a *free-thinker* . . .

It should be noted that there is never any dispute when the listener takes pleasure in the work he hears. The least informed of music-lovers readily clings to the periphery of a work; it pleases him for reasons that are most often entirely foreign to the essence of music. This pleasure is enough for him and calls for no justification. But if it happens that the music displeases him, our music-lover will ask you for an explanation of his discomfiture. He will demand that we explain something that is in its essence ineffable.

[2] Latin: The Spirit [or wind] blows where it wills.
[3] The branch of philosophy that studies the ultimate nature of reality.

By its fruit we judge the tree.[4] Judge the tree by its fruit then, and do not meddle with the roots. Function justifies an organ, no matter how strange the organ may appear in the eyes of those who are not accustomed to see it functioning. Snobbish circles are cluttered with persons who, like one of Montesquieu's characters, wonder how one can possibly be a Persian.[5] They make me think unfailingly of the story of the peasant who, on seeing a dromedary in the zoo for the first time, examines it at length, shakes his head and, turning to leave, says, to the great delight of those present: "It isn't true."

It is through the unhampered play of its functions, then, that a work is revealed and justified. We are free to accept or reject this play, but no one has the right to question the fact of its existence. To judge, dispute, and criticize the principle of speculative volition which is at the origin of all creation is thus manifestly useless. In the pure state, music is free speculation. Artists of all epochs have unceasingly testified to this concept. For myself, I see no reason for not trying to do as they did. Since I myself was created, I cannot help having the desire to create. What sets this desire in motion, and what can I do to make it productive?

The study of the creative process is an extremely delicate one. In truth, it is impossible to observe the inner workings of this process from the outside. It is futile to try and follow its successive phases in someone else's work. It is likewise very difficult to observe one's self. Yet it is only by enlisting the aid of introspection that I may have any chance at all of guiding you in this essentially fluctuating matter.

Most music-lovers believe that what sets the composer's creative imagination in motion is a certain emotive disturbance generally designated by the name of *inspiration.*

I have no thought of denying to inspiration the outstanding role that has devolved upon it in the generative process we are studying; I simply maintain that inspiration is in no way a prescribed condition of the creative act, but rather a manifestation that is chronologically secondary.

[4] Compare the Gospel of Matthew 12:33: ". . . for the tree is known by its fruit."
[5] In the fictitious *The Persian Letters* (1721) of the French political philosopher Montesquieu (1689–1755), a Persian letter-writer in Paris exchanges his Persian clothes for European ones. Immediately, he ceases to be an exotic celebrity among the Parisians. "However, if someone chanced to inform them that I was a Persian, I soon heard a murmur all around me: 'Ah! Indeed! He is a Persian? How extraordinary! How can anyone be a Persian?' " (Letter XXX)

Inspiration, art, artist—so many words, hazy at least, that keep us from seeing clearly in a field where everything is balance and calculation through which the breath of the speculative spirit blows. It is afterwards, and only afterwards, that the emotive disturbance which is at the root of inspiration may arise—an emotive disturbance about which people talk so indelicately by conferring upon it a meaning that is shocking to us and that compromises the term itself. Is it not clear that this emotion is merely a reaction on the part of the creator grappling with that unknown entity which is still only the object of his creating and which is to become a work of art? Step by step, link by link, it will be granted him to discover the work. It is this chain of discoveries, as well as each individual discovery, that give rise to the emotion—an almost physiological reflex, like that of the appetite causing a flow of saliva—this emotion which invariably follows closely the phases of the creative process.

All creation presupposes at its origin a sort of appetite that is brought on by the foretaste of discovery. This foretaste of the creative act accompanies the intuitive grasp of an unknown entity already possessed but not yet intelligible, an entity that will not take definite shape except by the action of a constantly vigilant technique.

This appetite that is aroused in me at the mere thought of putting in order musical elements that have attracted my attention is not at all a fortuitous thing like inspiration, but as habitual and periodic, if not as constant, as a natural need.

This premonition of an obligation, this foretaste of a pleasure, this conditioned reflex, as a modern physiologist would say, shows clearly that it is the idea of discovery and hard work that attracts me.

The very act of putting my work on paper, of, as we say, kneading the dough, is for me inseparable from the pleasure of creation. So far as I am concerned, I cannot separate the spiritual effort from the psychological and physical effort; they confront me on the same level and do not present a hierarchy.

The word *artist* which, as it is most generally understood today, bestows on its bearer the highest intellectual prestige, the privilege of being accepted as a pure mind—this pretentious term is in my view entirely incompatible with the role of the *homo faber*. [6]

At this point it should be remembered that, whatever field of en-

---

[6] Literally (in Latin), skillful man; usually translated as man the maker or man the creator.

deavor has fallen to our lot, if it is true that we are *intellectuals,* we are called upon not to cogitate, but to perform.

The philosopher Jacques Maritain[7] reminds us that in the mighty structure of medieval civilization, the artist held only the rank of an artisan. "And his individualism was forbidden any sort of anarchic development, because a natural social discipline imposed certain limitative conditions upon him from without." It was the Renaissance that invented the artist, distinguished him from the artisan and began to exalt the former at the expense of the latter.

At the outset the name artist was given only to the Masters of Arts: philosophers, alchemists, magicians; but painters, sculptors, musicians, and poets had the right to be qualified only as artisans.

> Plying divers implements,
> The subtile artizan implants
> Life in marble, copper, bronze,

says the poet Du Bellay.[8] And Montaigne[9] enumerates in his *Essays* the "painters, poets and other artizans." And even in the seventeenth century, La Fontaine[10] hails a painter with the name of *artisan* and draws a sharp rebuke from an ill-tempered critic who might have been the ancestor of most of our present-day critics.

The idea of work to be done is for me so closely bound up with the idea of the arranging of materials and of the pleasure that the actual doing of the work affords us that, should the impossible happen and my work suddenly be given to me in a perfectly completed form, I should be embarrassed and nonplussed by it, as by a hoax.

We have a duty towards music, namely, to invent it.

• • •

The faculty of observation and of making something out of what is observed belongs only to the person who at least possesses, in his particular field of endeavor, an acquired culture and an innate taste. A dealer, an art-lover who is the first to buy the canvases of an unknown painter who will be famous twenty-five years later under the

---

[7] A French Catholic philosopher (1882–1973); like Stravinsky, he remained in America because of the fall of France during his American lecture tour.

[8] Joachim Du Bellay (1522–60), a French satirical poet.

[9] Michel de Montaigne (1533–92), a French moralist and creator of the personal essay as a literary form.

[10] Jean de La Fontaine (1621–95), a prolific French scholar, poet, and author of satirical fables.

name of Cézanne[11]—doesn't such a person give us a clear example of this innate taste? What else guides him in his choices? A flair, an instinct from which this taste proceeds, a completely spontaneous faculty anterior to reflection.

As for culture, it is a sort of upbringing which, in the social sphere, confers polish upon education, sustains and rounds out academic instruction. This upbringing is just as important in the sphere of taste and is essential to the creator who must ceaselessly refine his taste or run the risk of losing his perspicacity. Our mind, as well as our body, requires continual exercise. It atrophies if we do not cultivate it.

It is culture that brings out the full value of taste and gives it a chance to prove its worth simply by its application. The artist imposes a culture upon himself and ends by imposing it upon others. That is how tradition becomes established.

Tradition is entirely different from habit, even from an excellent habit, since habit is by definition an unconscious acquisition and tends to become mechanical, whereas tradition results from a conscious and deliberate acceptance. A real tradition is not the relic of a past that is irretrievably gone; it is a living force that animates and informs the present. In this sense the paradox which banteringly maintains that everything which is not tradition is plagiarism, is true . . .

Far from implying the repetition of what has been, tradition presupposes the reality of what endures. It appears as an heirloom, a heritage that one receives on condition of making it bear fruit before passing it on to one's descendants.

Brahms was born sixty years after Beethoven.[12] From the one to the other, and from every aspect, the distance is great; they do not dress the same way, but Brahms follows the tradition of Beethoven without borrowing one of his habiliments. For the borrowing of a method has nothing to do with observing a tradition. "A method is replaced: a tradition is carried forward in order to produce something new." Tradition thus assures the continuity of creation. The example that I have just cited does not constitute an exception but is one proof out of a hundred of a constant law. This sense of tradition which is a natural need must not be confused with the desire which

[11] Paul Cézanne (1839–1906), a French Post-Impressionist painter who was a pivotal figure in the redirection of painting away from mere imitation of nature.
[12] Johannes Brahms (1833–97) and Ludwig van Beethoven (1770–1827), two of the great composers of romantic orchestral music.

the composer feels to affirm the kinship he finds across the centuries with some master of the past.

·   ·   ·

. . . A mode of composition that does not assign itself limits becomes pure fantasy. The effects it produces may accidentally amuse but are not capable of being repeated. I cannot conceive of a fantasy that is repeated, for it can be repeated only to its detriment.

Let us understand each other in regard to this word fantasy. We are not using the word in the sense in which it is connected with a definite musical form, but in the acceptation which presupposes an abandonment of one's self to the caprices of imagination. And this presupposes that the composer's will is voluntarily paralyzed. For imagination is not only the mother of caprice but the servant and handmaiden of the creative will as well.

The creator's function is to sift the elements he receives from her, for human activity must impose limits upon itself. The more art is controlled, limited, worked over, the more it is free.

As for myself, I experience a sort of terror when, at the moment of setting to work and finding myself before the infinitude of possibilities that present themselves, I have the feeling that everything is permissible to me. If everything is permissible to me, the best and the worst; if nothing offers me any resistance, then any effort is inconceivable, and I cannot use anything as a basis, and consequently every undertaking becomes futile.

Will I then have to lose myself in this abyss of freedom? To what shall I cling in order to escape the dizziness that seizes me before the virtuality of this infinitude? However, I shall not succumb. I shall overcome my terror and shall be reassured by the thought that I have the seven notes of the scale and its chromatic intervals at my disposal, that strong and weak accents are within my reach, and that in all of these I possess solid and concrete elements which offer me a field of experience just as vast as the upsetting and dizzy infinitude that had just frightened me. It is into this field that I shall sink my roots, fully convinced that combinations which have at their disposal twelve sounds in each octave and all possible rhythmic varieties promise me riches that all the activity of human genius will never exhaust.

What delivers me from the anguish into which an unrestricted freedom plunges me is the fact that I am always able to turn immediately to the concrete things that are here in question. I have no use for a theoretic freedom. Let me have something finite, definite— matter that can lend itself to my operation only insofar as it is commensurate with my possibilities. And such matter presents itself to me together with its limitations. I must in turn impose mine upon it. So here we are, whether we like it or not, in the realm of necessity. And yet which of us has ever heard talk of art as other than a realm of freedom? This sort of heresy is uniformly widespread because it is imagined that art is outside the bounds of ordinary activity. Well, in art as in everything else, one can build only upon a resisting foundation: whatever constantly gives way to pressure, constantly renders movement impossible.

My freedom thus consists in my moving about within the narrow frame that I have assigned myself for each one of my undertakings.

I shall go even further: my freedom will be so much the greater and more meaningful the more narrowly I limit my field of action and the more I surround myself with obstacles. Whatever diminishes constraint, diminishes strength. The more constraints one imposes, the more one frees one's self of the chains that shackle the spirit. . . .

37

Sidney Bechet

It's the Music and It's the People

Jazz, a uniquely American contribution to the art of music, developed in the early twentieth century. Growing out of tribal African rhythms, this new music also drew upon aspects of American experience, such as nineteenth-century minstrel music, early brass bands, string bands, ragtime, and blues. As the century progressed, jazz moved rapidly upstream from its legendary birthplace in New Orleans to all parts of the United States and the world.

In early jazz the leader tapped his foot to indicate the tempo and the group then played a refrain somewhat faithful to some original melody. Then each soloist was allowed a refrain for individual *expression. In conclusion, the entire band returned to a joyous musical excursion within the original composition's harmonic framework. The jazz band thus presented a vivid contrast to the traditional orchestra's European cultural inheritance and carefully prescribed composition. Jazz was a new world of improvised spontaneity and flexibility. One of the "old masters" of jazz was New Orleans-born Sidney Bechet (1897–1959), whose principal instruments were the soprano saxophone and the clarinet.*

At age eight, using a borrowed clarinet, Bechet began to "sit in" with local bands. By age seventeen he had left home to become one of the many traveling players and creators of the new music. Although his career had its phases of poverty, Bechet eventually traveled with his music throughout the world and was the featured performer with many of the leading jazz groups. The French became especially appreciative of his talents, and for some years he chose to live in France. Bechet was the only jazz musician to

From *Treat It Gentle* by Sidney Bechet. Copyright © 1960 by Twayne Publishers Inc. and Cassell & Company, Ltd. Reprinted by permission of Hill and Wang (a division of Farrar, Straus & Giroux, Inc.) [Pp. 201–207, 209–14, 214, 217, 218–19.]

achieve fame primarily through the use of the soprano saxophone; his emo-
tional, aggressive playing was heightened by the inclusion of heavy and wide
vibrato. One of his early European tours (1919–20) was reviewed by the
distinguished classical musician and conductor Ernest Ansermet. Bechet thus
became one of the first jazz artists to be taken seriously by the musical es-
tablishment.

In his later years, as a sort of crowning commentary upon his scores of
masterful recordings, Bechet told his life story. Recorded on tape and edited,
it became a book called Treat It Gentle *(1960). This autobiography's*
concluding chapter, "It's the Music and It's the People," is excerpted in the
following selection. It shows Bechet's deep feeling for his African heritage
and his sorrow and longing for it. Also apparent is his annoyance with the
novelty-seeking sellers and consumers of the music business, who often de-
stroy true musical freedom and feeling. Above all, the autobiography suggests
the intuitive, spontaneous, joyous nature of Bechet's jazz creation: "Life
isn't just a question of time; it's a way you have of talking back and forth to
the music."

I wouldn't tell all this in a story about the music, except that all I
been telling, it's part of the music. That man there in the grocery
store, the Mexican, the jail—they're all in the music.[1] Whatever kind
of thing it was, whenever it happened, the music put it together.
That boy having to play for those people to dance there in his own
house; that man wanting to scare me down by the railroad tracks,
getting a pleasure out of wanting to scare me; and when I was in jail,
playing the blues, really finding out about the blues—it was always
the music that explained things. What it is that takes you out of
being just a kid and thinking it's all adventure, and you find there's a
lesson underneath all that adventure—that lesson, it's the music.
You come into life alone and you go out of it alone, and you're
going to be alone a lot of time when you're on this earth—and what
tells it all, it's the music. You tell it to the music and the music tells it
to you. And then you know about it. You know what it was happened to you.

---

[1] In this paragraph Bechet refers to events previously described in his narration.

I guess all of us in some way or another learn that way when we're young. The only difference is most people don't have something they're travelling along with, that's just going on. They just stop being a kid; that's all they know. They never know why. They just know something's happened.

But with something like the music though, you can be stupid or wise or a kid, or anything at all, but you've always *got* it. And as long as you've got it, you haven't got any time, so to speak. Life isn't just a question of time; it's a way you have of talking back and forth to the music.

You tell it to the music, and the music tells it to you. That's the life there is to a musicianer. I guess I've known about all of them. Some of them was good, and some of them was real good, and some of them was just nothing. But if they was real good, that's what their life was; it was a way of telling, a way of remembering something that has to be remembered.

It was Omar [2] started the song. Or maybe he didn't start it exactly. There was somebody singing and playing the drums and the horns behind Omar, and there was somebody behind that. But it was Omar began the melody of it, the new thing. Behind Omar there was the rhythm and after Omar there was the melody. He started the song and all the good musicianers have been singing that song ever since, changing it some, adding parts, finding the way it has to go. But if you're a musicianer, if you're any good musicianer, it's Omar's song you're singing.

I met many a musicianer in many a place after I struck out from New Orleans, but it was always the same: if they was any good, it was Omar's song they were singing. It was the long song, and the good musicianers, they all heard it behind them. They all had an Omar, somebody like an Omar, somebody that was *their* Omar. It didn't need just recollecting somebody like that: it was the feeling of someone back there—hearing the song like it was coming up from somewhere.

A musicianer could be playing it in New Orleans, or Chicago, or New York; he could be playing it in London, in Tunis, in Paris, in Germany. I heard it played in all those places and a many more. But no matter where it's played, you gotta hear it starting way behind

[2] Bechet's grandfather, a black slave.

you. There's the drum beating from Congo Square[3] and there's the song starting in a field just over the trees. The good musicianer, he's playing *with* it, and he's playing *after* it. He's finishing something. No matter what he's playing, it's the long song that started back there in the South.

It's the remembering song. There's so much to remember. There's so much wanting, and there's so much sorrow, and there's so much waiting for the sorrow to end. My people, all they want is a place where they can be people, a place where they can stand up and be part of that place, just being natural to the place without worrying how someone may be coming along to take that place away from them.

There's a pride in it, too. The man singing it, the man playing it, he makes a place. For as long as the song is being played, *that's* the place he's been looking for. And when the piece is all played and he's back, it may be he's feeling good; maybe he's making good money and getting good treatment and he's feeling good—or maybe he starts missing the song. Maybe he starts wanting the place he found while he was playing the song. Or maybe it just troubles back at him. The song, it takes a lot out of a man, and when it's over it can trouble him. Because there's misery in the song too. He can remember the trouble the song was making all that time. And a man, he can get mean when he's troubled.

I met many musicianers and there was none of them hadn't found himself some trouble sometime. Many a one, he just had this trouble stored up inside him, and it was bound to have him. Just like all those old musicianers in New Orleans—Buddy Bolden, Armand J. Piron, Manuel Perez, all those that ended up so bad. I met a many another and there was always that trouble waiting to go bad in them. Some of them, they were strong enough and the trouble didn't take them: they were stronger than the trouble. And some of them, they had the trouble too strong and it took them. But I don't care how strong they were, they all of them had a piece of this trouble in them.

There was all this feuding between musicianers, and there was a whole lot of meanness at times. There was all kinds of bad things.

---

[3] The place in New Orleans where, according to Bechet, slaves gathered freely on Sundays to socialize, make music, and dance.

Bessie Smith, she was the best blues singer there was, but that trouble was inside her and it wouldn't let her rest.

But what I mean is that when a musicianer made a bad end, it was never a surprise. Sometimes you got the feeling that a musicianer was *looking* for a bad end like it was something he had to have. So many of them had something inside them and it wouldn't let them rest. It was like there was something in that song deeper than a man could bear, something he could hear calling from the bottom of his dreams so that he'd wake up all in a terrible hurry to get up and go there, but then not knowing where to go. It was that stirring, all that night sound there was at the bottom of the song all that long way back making itself heard.

People come up to me and they say, "What's Negro music? What is it really being?" I have to tell them there's no straight answer to that. If I could give them a straight answer, just in one sentence like, I wouldn't have to say all this I'm saying. You can't say that just out straight. There's no answer to that question, not just direct. You could come up to me and say, "What's an American? What's a Frenchman?" How do you answer a thing like that?

But it's coming to an understanding; people are learning it. And when you get so you really hear it, when you can listen to the music being itself—then you don't have to ask that question. The music gives you its own understanding of itself.

But first, you have to like it; you have to be wanting to hear it. I read many a thing written by this critic and that critic, but it all comes to that one thing: if you're interested to hear the music, if it's a pleasure to you, then you can understand it; but if you're only writing to be a critic, to be saying what's a fashionable thing to say, then there's nothing to it.

I talked before about meeting Ernest Ansermet[4] in London. Well, when we were in Paris in 1926 he was there: I ran into him in the street and he reminded me of the first review he'd written back in 1919, and how he had foreseen that the world would swing along this highway. And there it was: it had all come about in seven years. There's a man, you see, a classic musicianer, but his feeling for music could show him what it was going to mean to people. He had felt

---

[4] A Swiss symphonic conductor (1883–1969), distinguished for his authoritative interpretations of twentieth-century composers, especially Stravinsky.

that right off. And I know what that means, because I can remember back in New Orleans when people who first heard our music just didn't know what to think. They'd never heard anything like it in their lives; they didn't even know how to dance to it. And in New York later, it was the same thing: people didn't know how to listen to it, they didn't know how to sing to it, they didn't know how to dance to it. But they learned the music, it made itself important enough to them; it made them want to learn.

But that doesn't really say what Negro music is. That's just to illustrate that it can be understood and it can be misunderstood. It's a way of feeling. It's a way of listening too, and that complicates it because there's so much difference that can be listened to. For instance, there's people come up to me, they still think Jazz, it's that whorehouse music. They say, "What about barrel house? Where's all that vaudeville I hear about being part of the music? What's this about redlight music?" Well, all I can answer is it's like I've already said about Freddie Keppard; it was just that pleasure music. A man, he's got all kinds of things in him and the music wants to talk to all of him. The music is everything that it wants to say to a man. Some of it came up from jokes and some of it came up from sorrow, but all of it has a man's feelings in it. How that came about, that's my real story. The music has come a long way, and it's time for it now to come out from around a corner; it's got to come up and cross the street. If I could believe it would do that, I wouldn't worry. For me, all there is to life aside from the music, it's not the things you'd expect people to say. All I want is to eat, sleep, and don't worry. Don't *worry*, that's the big thing. And that's what's holding back the music from this step it has to take. It's still worried. It's still not sure of itself. It's still in the shade, and it's time it just stood up and crossed the street to the sunny side.

But that's not yet. It won't happen yet. It has a way to go, and I'm not ready to say what that way is. All I say is, it's my people. The worry has to be gotten out of them and *then* it will be gotten out of the music.

I suppose most people would think right away of that show *Porgy and Bess*. [5] But what do you call a thing like that—symphonic Jazz? That's not real Jazz. There's some feeling there, it's a nice show; but that's about the closest it comes. There's one or two nice pieces to it:

[5] A "folk opera," first performed, with Afro-American cast and setting, in 1933.

Summertime, that's one, that's nice, in that you get just about the closest to the mood of Negro music. But listen to it, listen to it real careful—you get a feeling of *St. Louis Blues*[6] there. It's a borrowed feeling.

Gershwin,[7] I've got a lot of respect for him. He's a hell of a fine writer. All his music you can listen to, there's a whole lot of beauty to it and a whole lot of feeling. It really tells a story inside itself. But it still isn't Negro music. It still isn't saying what the black man, he'd say.

There's one thing about Negro music that hasn't really been put on yet, and that's how hard it can be to get Negro music performed, the trouble there is to getting it staged and listened to. Let me tell you about a show once in New York. Just for an example. This show was called *Shuffle Along,* and it was put on by coloured people and it was acted by coloured people. The music was written by Noble Sissle[8] and Eubie Blake.[9] That show had troubles you wouldn't have in the regular kind of production. The writers had to be awful clever about what they wrote because everything had to be done on what you call a limited budget. There were costumes they had a hell of a time finding and sets they had to go out after, God knows where, and there were even things for props that couldn't be come by. Noble and Eubie had to write their songs to what they *could,* to the kind of budget they had for getting them produced. They weren't free to do it how they wanted: they just had to work it whatever way it was possible. But they made real numbers of them. It was really music: you couldn't help it being that. Some of those numbers are still famous: *I'm Wild About Harry* was one of them; and *Dear Old Southland,* that was from that show too. But if you could have seen the trouble they had to go to just to see that the songs could be produced in any real manner of a show—I don't mean just

[6] The *blues* are an early ingredient of jazz, containing both vocal and instrumental parts. The form is derived mainly from Afro-American work songs and spirituals.

[7] George Gershwin (1898–1937), the American composer who created *Porgy and Bess.* His *Rhapsody in Blue* (1924), for piano and jazz orchestra, was the first major attempt to bring jazz themes into the symphonic concert repertoire.

[8] Jazz band leader, vocalist, and composer (1889–1975). Sissle employed Sidney Bechet in Sissle's traveling orchestra in Europe, Chicago, and New York—with various interruptions—from 1928 to 1938.

[9] Composer and ragtime pianist (1883–   ). Blake worked with Noble Sissle for many years; together they wrote the musical revues *Shuffle Along* (1921) and *Chocolate Dandies* (1924). A 1978 Broadway musical, *Eubie,* was based on the life and music of this creative musician.

the worry of when you're having a show and hoping it will go over, but just the trouble of getting it together with just about no budget at all—all that changing that had to be done to save money, all the good things that had to be left out, all the ideas that couldn't be made to work because of expense. If you could have seen some of that, you'd have an understanding of what it is with Negro music, how hard it is to get it really performed.

And that show, it was a really beautiful thing. They could bring it out again right now and you'd still find it was a hell of a fine show. But every Negro show had this same trouble. There was never enough to do it with. It's like having a hundred verses you want to write down and all you can find is one scrap of paper: there's so much of it that gets lost.

I remember another time when I was in England back in the early 'twenties. I'd written a play and I had the music to it, a lot of singing and melody. It had a story too, but nothing complicated, nothing so involved that you couldn't see it for what it was, just a show with music. I called it *Voice of the Slaves*. I've got it with me still. Well, back there in England I took it to this director and he told me, "It's very beautiful. I'd like to put it on but I don't think the public is interested enough in coloured people to put out the kind of money it needs for getting produced." That's what he said. I'm not trying to say the white-man-this and conditions-that and change-how: I'm just telling you the story, how the fact of it was, and I'm not saying what interpreting you can find to put around the fact, because I don't know myself for sure. I do know for sure, though, that music—a melody, a story—if it's to be at home on the stage it has to be simple enough to tell you about itself. After that there's no importance in who's written it so long as it's good. I'm trying to say there's so much Negro music *waiting*. It hasn't been heard yet. *Conditions* haven't been right. . . .

There's some of Scott Joplin's numbers, too—they're still waiting. And they're just as beautiful. Scott had a show once, *Treemonisha* it was called. The numbers he had in that were really fine. You could look a long time to find something as fine as that.[10]

---

[10] Scott Joplin (1868–1917) was one of the originators of ragtime music, another early ingredient of jazz. Unlike most jazz, ragtime is carefully composed and metrically regular; it was an outgrowth of minstrel show bands and the dance music at bordellos. Joplin wrote two operas in the ragtime style—one was *Treemonisha*. In the 1970s there was a revival of interest in Joplin's "rags," nurtured by their inclusion in the popular movie *The Sting* and by a revival of *Treemonisha*.

And it's all waiting. All these numbers and many more. They're just listened to mostly by themselves, the way you wind up one of those little music boxes once in a while when you step into your own room. If they could be heard, if they could get out of that room, they could really add a whole lot of understanding to what Negro music really is.

But still, you know, there wouldn't ever be any straight answer. Like I said before, you could ask me, "What's classical music?" I couldn't answer that. It's not a thing that could be answered straight out. You have to tell it the long way. You have to tell about the people who make it, what they have inside them, what they're doing, what they're waiting for. Then you can begin to have an understanding.

This story of what's happening to Jazz, there's a whole lot to it, a whole lot of changes; but one thing, it's still the same that it was when the musicianers first began to come North. Right away then, this *presenting* began to take over the music. The men who are doing the business part of the presenting, they won't let the music be. They give the public what *they* want them to hear. They don't care about the music; just so it's something different, something a little bit more novelty like from what's being played the next dial down—just so long as they can get that, they don't care about nothing else.

Some band leader gets himself a reputation for being a personality, and that's it. From there on out it has to be his personality first and *then* the music. He's busy doing every kind of thing *but* the music. "Here's another saxophone," he says. Maybe you don't need that extra sax, it doesn't belong, but that's no matter to him. "Here, here's another bass," he says. Well there's no reason for it, but there it is. And before you know it, you've got eighteen pieces, you've got a whole lot of noise, you've got a whole lot of something that hasn't got any spirit. All you've got, it's something like running a ball through a pinball machine and watching all the lights come on. You've got a hell of a lot of lights showing themselves off.

These personality boys don't ask the musicianer what *he* thinks is best: they arrange it for him. "Here," they say, "you play it *this* way." They've got themselves a great big band. They've got themselves a kind of machine. And so to make sense out of whatever it is the machine is doing, they get a whole lot of composers and arrangers to write it all down, just the way the machine is supposed to run—every note of it.

And all that freedom, all that feeling a man's got when he's playing next to you—they take that away. They give you *his* part to play
and they give him your part, and that's how it's to be: they've got a
trumpet taking the clarinet part and a clarinet taking the trombone
part, and every man doing any damn' thing but the one thing he
should be doing if he's really to find the music. All that closeness of
speaking to another instrument, to another man—it's gone. All that
waiting to get in for your own chance, freeing yourself, all that holding back, not rushing the next man, not bucking him, holding back
for the right time to come out, all that pride and spirit—it's gone.
They take away your dignity and they take away your heart and
after they've done that there's nothing left.

You know, a lot of musicianers, they drop their playing. "Well,
I'm going to become a clerk," they say, "or I'll drive a taxi, or I'll
shine shoes." And they try that for a while. And then pretty soon
they're back at their instrument.[11] Lots of times that's a thing I don't
understand. Why do they come back? It's not because they love their
music, or because they cared too much and dropped the music because they didn't want to see what was happening to it. It's not like
going back home when you can't stay away any longer. Because
they keep coming back to play *any* old way. Like it doesn't matter at
all *what* they're playing so long as they *are* playing. Some of them get
their jobs playing again and they get paid less, maybe, than what
they were making doing something else. But still they come back
and there they are playing without any kind of ideas or soul or respect for the music. They come back and they fit themselves into any
kind of a combination that comes along, playing any which way
they're told to play.

And that's what I can't understand. I can guess maybe it's how the
life is, how they like being in front of people, wearing dress clothes,
making the night-time over into daytime, being known as a musicianer. Maybe it's some of all those things. But you put that all
together and it's still no music.

And what they're playing . . . well, it *was* New Orleans. A long
time ago it had a memory of being that. But what it is today, it's
nothing. It's no music. *New Orleans,* well it just stopped back there
in New Orleans. These new musicianers, they lack the memory of

---

[11] Bechet, himself, left full-time work in music temporarily in 1934 to open his own
"Southern Tailor Shop" in New York City.

it. They don't know where the music comes from and they don't know where it's going. So how do you expect someone to know that that foundation, that *real* foundation, is capable of saying sincere things? And if the musicianers don't know that, how can you expect the audience to know it? You say *Jazz,* you say *ragtime* and right away they're thinking, *"Royal Garden Blues,* give me that, that's it." Or *Maple Leaf Rag;*[12] they'll name that. It's like they believed the music stopped way back there. "Give me some of that old-time stuff," they say. You could take some new piece and play it in that rhythm, you could make a real rendition, but that's not what they'll listen to. *Give me some of that old stuff:* that's all they want. And then they want to know about barrel house[13] and honky-tonks.[14] That's what's supposed to be New Orleans. That's where it's supposed to have been born.

But those things don't exist today. They're gone. But the people won't let them *be* gone. That's what they're wanting, and so a musicianer who knows his music, a man who's had his training, he's always under this necessity to give a spectacle. He gets up there to play, but they won't let him be a musicianer: they haven't got him up there to be a musicianer, he's an *attraction.* Look at him, they say, he composed *Maple Leaf Rag,* or *Royal Garden,* or any damn' number of that time. Look at him, they say, he's still around: why he can *still* play!

But ragtime, that's no history thing. It's not dead. Ragtime, it's the musicianers. *Rag it up,* we used to say. You take any piece, you make it so people can dance to it, pat their feet, move around. You make it so they can't help themselves from doing that. You make it so they just can't sit still. And that's all there is to it. It's the rhythm there. The rhythm *is* ragtime. That's still there to be done. You could do that to all kinds of numbers still being played, still being composed today.

That rhythm goes all the way back. In the spirituals the people clapped their hands—that was their rhythm. In the blues it was further down; they didn't need the clapping, but they remembered it, it

---

[12] Scott Joplin's most famous composition (1899).
[13] A vigorous, unpolished, loud style of jazz originating in the disreputable bars (barrelhouses) of New Orleans early in this century.
[14] A style of ragtime performed in a cheap dance hall (honkytonk) on a piano whose strings have been muffled to give a tinny sound.

was still there. And both of them, the spirituals and the blues, they was a prayer. One was praying to God and the other was praying to what's human. It's like one was saying, "Oh, God, let me go," and the other was saying, "Oh, Mister, let me be." And they were both the same thing in a way; they were both my people's way of praying to be themselves, praying to be let alone so they could be human. The spirituals, they had a kind of trance to them, a kind of forgetting. It was like a man closing his eyes so he can see a light inside him. That light, it's far off and you've got to wait to see it. But it's there. It's waiting. The spirituals, they're a way of seeing that light. It's a far off music; it's a going away, but it's a going away that takes you with it. And the blues, they've got that sob inside, that awful lonesome feeling. It's got so much remembering inside it, so many bad things to remember, so many losses.

But both of them, they're based on rhythm. They're both of them leading up to a rhythm. And they're both coming up from a rhythm. It's like they're going and coming at the same time. Going, coming—inside the music that's the same thing, it's the rhythm. And that rhythm and that feeling you put around it, always keeping the melody, that's all there is to it. That's nothing that's dead. That's nothing that could die: 1910, 1923, 1950—there's no difference in that. And to give you what this Jazz is—all you need is a few men who can hear what the man next him is doing at the same time that you know your instrument and how you can say on it what you gotta say to keep the next man going with you, leading one another on to the place the music has to go.

Back in New Orleans when I was young, back there before all this personality stuff, all this radio and contracts and "attraction"—the music, it was free. It was all different then. We were always having contests—those "bucking contests."[15] There were always people out listening to us play. Wherever there was music, a whole lot of people would be there. And those people, they were just natural to the music. The music, it was all they needed. They weren't there to ask for "attractions."

And that left the music natural to be itself. It could have a good time; it was free to. And that spirit there was to it, that was a won-

---

[15] Contests in which one jazz group attempted to outplay the other, the winner determined by audience applause.

derful thing, there was a happiness in it. It was there to be enjoyed, a whole lot of spirit.

The musicianers in those good bands, they could really play; they'd come out of a bucking contest just as sweet as they went in. But what made that possible, in one way at least, it was the people. The people knew what they wanted to hear and the musicianers gave it to them. The musicianers could be sure the people would know what they were hearing. If the music was being played right, the people would know it, and if it was being played wrong, they'd know that too. And because the musicianers knew they were being *listened* to by people who cared for the music, that made it all different. They could want to play then; they could want to have those people cheering them.

In some ways it's like a play. The actors come out on the stage and there's an audience. That audience has a feeling for the play. They want to see it, they have an understanding for it. And those actors feel that, and they play their best; they *want* to give what they can. But you take those same actors and bring them out somewhere with no audience, or with some audience that just don't care. You have them act their play in front of some crowd of people who don't know why they've come. And there's just no performance then; the play it just dies down inside itself. . . .

New Orleans, that was a place where the music was natural as the air. The people were ready for it like it was sun and rain. A musicianer, when he played in New Orleans, was home; and the music, when he played it, would go right to where he sent it. The people there were waiting for it, they were wanting it.

The bucking contests were one way the people had of coming toward the music, but it never stopped there. The next day there was bound to be some picnic out at Milneberg Lake. There was a big park there with all kinds of walks, a saloon, wharves, open spaces. And there'd be these different camps where the people would be and the musicianers would go there to play. In those days there wasn't anything you could do without music—holidays, funerals, pleasurements, it was all done to music, the music had all that to say.

At these camps there'd be a big square hall with a porch at one end and the sun would be beating on one side. We'd come to play there, but a musicianer, you know, he wouldn't care to be playing in the strong sun, so right off as soon as your band got together, you'd have a big bucking contest with whatever other band there was. And that was the real thing then: we'd play at them until finally we'd beat that other band right out into the sun. The way it was, they'd have to back out or stop playing because they weren't able to play against us. . . .

That music, it was like where you lived. It was like waking up in the morning and eating, it was that regular in your life. It was natural to the way you lived and the way you died. Like when the band, it started back from the cemetery; that band, it would change the music. It would start playing something like *Oh, Didn't He Ramble*. They'd play that and it was like saying good-bye for the dead man: that band it would go back all through the town seeing the places where that man had liked to be before he died. The music it was rambling for him one last time. It was seeing the world for him again.

And that's the way I want to remember the music. That's the way I'd like to have it remembered: the way it came back from the man's burying and spoke for him to the world, and spoke the world to him once more.

I've been telling you this story, and maybe you're asking, "How's it going to end?" There's ways I could make a fiction to give you an ending. But that won't do. What I got to say has to be as natural as the music. There's no fiction to it. What I have to say, it's what the music has been saying to me and what I've been saying to it as far back as I can remember. The music makes a voice, and, no matter what happens, the man that cares to hear that voice, he *can* hear it. I don't mean there's any end to the things that make it hard for the people to hear the real voice the music has got in it. All I mean is the music is still there for any who want it.

Really, all I been saying, it comes down to something as simple as that, something that's just waiting for its own happiness. A way of speaking. . . .

I'm an old man now; I can't keep hanging on. I'm even wanting to go; I'm waiting, longing to hear my peace. And all I've been waiting for is the music. All the beauty that there's ever been, it's moving inside that music. Omar's voice, that's there, and the girl's voice,[16] and the voice the wind had in Africa, and the cries from Congo Square,

---

[16] The girl was Bechet's enslaved grandmother, Marie, who first met Omar at Congo Square and then was separated from him by the false accusation of her owner. She took her owner's family name, Bechet.

and the fine shouting that came up from Free Day.[17] The blues, and the spirituals, and the remembering, and the waiting, and the suffering, and the looking at the sky watching the dark come down—that's all inside the music.

And somehow when the music is played right it does an explaining of all those things. Me, I want to explain myself so bad. I want to have myself understood. And the music, it can do that. The music, it's my whole story. . . .

I'd like to hear it all one more time. I'd like to sit in a box at some performance and see all I saw years ago and hear all I heard way back to the start. I want to sit there and you could come in and find me in that box and I'd have a smile on my face. What I'd be feeling is "the music, it has a home." As long as I got a heart to be filled by it, the music has a place that's natural to it. I could sit there and listen, and I'd smile. And when I've got to go I could go that way. I could remember all the richness there is, and I could go smiling.

[17] January 1, 1863, the date of President Lincoln's Emancipation Proclamation, which declared free all the slaves within the rebellious Confederate States.

38

Ralph J. Gleason

Like a Rolling Stone

⊗

Marking the emergence of a distinctive youth culture in the United States of the 1950s was a new musical form called "rock-and-roll." Its strong, sensual beat excited throngs of young people who idolized such early performers as Chuck Berry and Elvis Presley. The roots of rock music grew from the "rhythm and blues" of black jazz musicians and the country folk music of white hillbillies. By the mid 1960s the new music was the primary expression of a new life-style. Led by rock groups with strange names, such as the Beatles and the Rolling Stones, many young Americans protested their country's military involvement in Vietnam and generally rejected the middle-class attitudes and manners of their parents' generation.

Some of the new lyrics were openly political, such as Bob Dylan's antiwar ballad, "Masters of War"; some were more subtly subversive of traditional morality, such as the Beatle's "Strawberry Fields Forever." Many of the songs pointed toward a frankly pleasure-seeking "new morality."

Some commentators criticized the music as savagely obscene; some found its frequent electronic amplification of sound physically unbearable; others regarded the new music as a cultural blossoming. One consistently admiring commentator was Ralph J. Gleason (1917–1975), a music critic and columnist for the San Francisco Chronicle.

Born in New York City, Gleason attended Columbia University from 1934 to 1938. Even then much of his life was devoted to music. He had discovered jazz on the radio while in high school, and he never recovered from the effects of first hearing the broadcasts of Louis Armstrong, Earl Hines,

From "Like a Rolling Stone" by Ralph J. Gleason. Reprinted from *The American Scholar* (Autumn, 1967), pp. 555–63. Copyright © 1967 by the United Chapters of Phi Beta Kappa. Reprinted by permission of Mrs. Ralph Gleason.

and Fletcher Henderson. As a student at Columbia, he haunted the jazz halls downtown on 52nd Street.

Gleason was a founder in 1939 of the first jazz periodical, Jazz Information, *which lasted two years. After overseas service in the Second World War, he moved to San Francisco because he considered it a better city for listening to jazz. When he joined the* San Francisco Chronicle *in 1950, Gleason set a precedent by reviewing the concerts of folk groups, popular singers, and jazz bands with the same seriousness and in the same column previously devoted only to classical music. Eventually his reviews grew into a daily column in the* Chronicle, *and Gleason became the first internationally syndicated newspaper columnist on jazz and popular music.*

In 1957 Gleason founded a scholarly periodical, Jazz: A Quarterly of American Music, *which also lasted two years. He was an editor of* Ramparts *magazine and a founding editor, in 1967, of* Rolling Stone. *His musical activities also went beyond the print media. Gleason was a radio disc jockey in San Francisco and the producer of a television series, "Jazz Casual" (1960–70), for National Educational Television. His documentary television program on Duke Ellington was nominated for an Emmy award. Gleason was the first jazz critic to take seriously the new rock music, as can be seen in his book* The Jefferson Airplane and the San Francisco Sound *(1969).*

In "Like a Rolling Stone" (1967), the source of the following selection, Gleason shows his affection for the new music and its values of "love and truth and beauty and interpersonal relationships." (The title of this essay has, perhaps, five references: (1) the title of a "folk rock" ballad of 1965 by Bob Dylan, (2) a commentary, like Dylan's ballad, on the vagrant nature of the new generation, (3) a pun on the slang meaning of "stoned," (4) a reference to the Rolling Stones *rock group, and (5) to* Rolling Stone *magazine, which Gleason helped to found.) Gleason's own early discovery of jazz through his home radio doubtless helped him to understand the enthusiasm of "a new generation . . . weaned on a transistor radio." Using the penetrating insights of the philosopher Nietzsche, Gleason relates rock music to those powerful, primitive movements in human history in which people have expressed their deepest, most honest feelings and, thereby, "liberated" their minds.*

*Forms and rhythms in music are never changed without
producing changes in the most important political
forms and ways.*
Plato [1] said that.

*There's something happenin' here.
What it is ain't exactly clear.
There's a man with a gun over there
tellin' me I've got to beware.
I think it's time we STOP,
children, what's that sound?
Everybody look what's goin' down.*
The Buffalo Springfield said that.

For the reality of politics, we must go to the poets, not the politicians.
Norman O. Brown [2] said that.

*For the reality of what's happening today in
America, we must go to rock 'n roll, to popular
music.*
I said that.

For almost forty years in this country, which has prided itself on individualism, freedom and nonconformity, all popular songs were written alike. They had an eight-bar opening statement, an eight-bar repeat, an eight-bar middle section or bridge, and an eight-bar reprise. Anything that did not fit into that framework was, appropriately enough, called a novelty.

Clothes were basically the same whether a suit was double-breasted or single-breasted, and the only people who wore beards were absentminded professors and Bolshevik bomb throwers. Long hair, which was equated with lack of masculinity—in some sort of subconscious reference to Samson, I suspect—was restricted to painters and poets and classical musicians, hence the term "long-hair music" to mean classical.

Four years ago a specter was haunting Europe, one whose fundamental influence, my intuition tells me, may be just as important,

[1] An ancient Greek philosopher (427–348 B.C.) whose work *The Republic* deals extensively with the potentially disturbing effect of the arts on political order.
[2] An American scholar (1913–   ) who—in *Life Against Death* (1959) and *Love's Body* (1966)—asserts the Freudian thesis that civilization is based upon rationalist psychic repression. He also calls for an anti-rationalist psychic liberation.

if in another way, as the original of that line.[3] The Beatles,[4] four long-haired Liverpool teen-agers, were busy changing the image of popular music. In less than a year, they invaded the United States and almost totally wiped out the standard Broadway show-Ed Sullivan TV program[5] popular song. No more were we "flying to the moon on gossamer wings," we were now articulating such interesting and, in this mechanistic society, unusual concepts as "Money can't buy me love" and "I want to hold your hand."

"Societies, like individuals, have their moral crises and their spiritual revolutions," R. H. Tawney says in *Religion and the Rise of Capitalism*. And the Beatles appeared ("a great figure rose up from the sea and pointed to me and said 'you're a Beatle with an "a" ' "—Genesis, according to John Lennon).[6] They came at the proper moment of a spiritual cusp as the martian in Robert Heinlein's *Stranger in a Strange Land*[7] calls a crisis.

Instantly, on those small and sometimes doll-like figures was focused all the rebellion against hypocrisy, all the impudence and irreverence that the youth of that moment was feeling vis-a-vis his elders.

Automation, affluence, the totality of instant communication, the technology of the phonograph record, the transistor radio, had revolutionized life for youth in this society. The population age was lowering. Popular music, the jukebox and the radio were becoming the means of communication. Huntley and Brinkley[8] were for mom and dad. People now sang songs they wrote themselves, not songs written *for* them by hacks in grimy Tin Pan Alley[9] offices.

The folk music boom paved the way. Bob Dylan's poetic polemics, "Blowin' in the Wind" and "The Times They Are A-

---

[3] A reference to the opening sentence of the Preface to *The Communist Manifesto* (1848), by Karl Marx and Friedrich Engels: "A spectre is haunting Europe — the spectre of Communism."

[4] An English "rock" group that first recorded in 1961 and first toured the United States in 1964; they are considered the most creative and most influential of the hundreds of vocal-instrumental groups of the period.

[5] The "Ed Sullivan Show" on CBS-TV (1948–71) introduced a wide range of talent, including Elvis Presley and the Beatles, to the American television audience.

[6] One of the four Beatles.

[7] Popular science-fiction novel (1961).

[8] Chet Huntley and David Brinkley, anchormen on NBC's "Huntley-Brinkley Report," a nightly television newscast (1956–70).

[9] The district in New York City where most popular music used to be published.

Changin'," had helped the breakthrough.[10] "Top-40" radio made Negro music available everywhere to a greater degree than ever before in our history.

This was, truly, a new generation—the first in America raised with music constantly in its ear, weaned on a transistor radio, involved with songs from its earliest moment of memory.

Music means more to this generation than it did even to its dancing parents in the big-band swing era of Benny Goodman. It's natural, then, that self-expression should find popular music so attractive.

The dance of the swing era, of the big bands, was the fox-trot. It was really a formal dance extended in variation only by experts. The swing era's parents had danced the waltz. The fox-trot was a ritual with only a little more room for self-expression. Rock 'n roll brought with it not only the voices of youth singing their protests, their hopes and their expectations (along with their pathos and their sentimentality and their personal affairs from drag racing to romance), it brought their dances.

"Every period which abounded in folk songs has, by the same token, been deeply stirred by Dionysiac currents," Nietzsche points out in *The Birth of Tragedy*.[11] And Dionysiac is the word to describe the dances of the past ten years, call them by whatever name from bop to Twist to the Frug, from the Hully Gully to the Philly Dog.

In general, adult society left the youth alone, prey to the corruption the adults suspected was forthcoming from the song lyrics ("All of me, why not take all of me," from that hit of the thirties, of course, didn't mean *all* of me, it meant, well . . . er . . .) or from the payola-influenced disc jockeys. (Who ever remembers about the General Electric scandals of the fifties, in which over a dozen officials went to jail for industrial illegalities?)

The TV shows were in the afternoon anyway and nobody could stand to watch those rock 'n roll singers; they were worse than Elvis Presley.[12]

---

[10] Bob Dylan, an American folksinger and composer (1941–), was born Robert Zimmerman; his adopted surname is taken from the name of the twentieth-century Welsh romantic poet Dylan Thomas.

[11] *The Birth of Tragedy from the Spirit of Music* (1872), by German philosopher Friedrich Wilhelm Nietzsche (1844–1900), traced the roots of drama to primitive orgiastic festivals in honor of Dionysus, god of fertility and wine in the ancient Greek religion. Nietzsche also identified music as a predominantly Dionysiac art.

[12] American popular singer (1935–77), known as the "king of rock 'n roll."

But all of a sudden the *New Yorker* joke about the married couple dreamily remarking, when a disc jockey played "Houn' Dog" by Elvis, "they're playing our song," wasn't a joke any longer. It was real. That generation had suddenly grown up and married and Elvis was real memories of real romance and not just kid stuff.

All of a sudden, the world of music, which is big business in a very real way, took another look at the music of the ponytail and chewing gum set, as Mitch Miller [13] once called the teenage market, and realized that there was one helluva lot of bread to be made there.

In a short few years, Columbia and R.C.A. Victor and the other companies that dominated the recording market, the huge publishing houses that copyrighted the music and collected the royalties, discovered that they no longer were "kings of the hill." Instead, a lot of small companies, like Atlantic and Chess and Imperial and others, had hits by people the major record companies didn't even know, singing songs written in Nashville and Detroit and Los Angeles and Chicago and sometimes, but no longer almost always, New York.

It's taken the big ones a few years to recoup from that. First they called the music trash and the lyrics dirty. When that didn't work, as the attempt more recently to inhibit songs with supposed psychedelic or marijuana references has failed, they capitulated. They joined up. R.C.A. Victor bought Elvis from the original company he recorded for—Sun Records ("Yaller Sun records from Nashville" as John Sebastian sings it in "Nashville Cats")—and then bought Sam Cooke, and A.B.C. Paramount bought Ray Charles and then Fats Domino. And Columbia, thinking it had a baby folk singer capable of some more sales of "San Francisco Bay," turned out to have a tiny demon of a poet named Bob Dylan.

So the stage was set for the Beatles to take over—"with this ring I can—dare I say it?—rule the world!" And they did take over so thoroughly that they have become the biggest success in the history of show business, the first attraction ever to have a coast-to-coast tour in this country sold out before the first show even opened.

With the Beatles and Dylan running tandem, two things seem to me to have been happening. The early Beatles were at one and the same time a declaration in favor of love and of life, an exuberant

---

[13] An American oboist, band leader, television personality, and musical recording director for several major companies (1911–   ).

paean to the sheer joy of living, and a validation of the importance of American Negro music.

Dylan, by his political, issue-oriented broadsides first and then by his Rimbaudish nightmare visions [14] of the real state of the nation, his bittersweet love songs and his pure imagery, did what the jazz and poetry people of the fifties had wanted to do—he took poetry out of the classroom and out of the hands of the professors and put it right out there in the streets for everyone.

I dare say that with the inspiration of the Beatles and Dylan we have more poetry being produced and more poets being made than ever before in the history of the world. Dr. Malvina Reynolds—the composer of "Little Boxes"—thinks nothing like this has happened since Elizabethan times. I suspect even that is too timid an assessment.

Let's go back to Plato, again. Speaking of the importance of new styles of music, he said, "The new style quietly insinuates itself into manners and customs and from there it issues a greater force . . . goes on to attack laws and constitutions, displaying the utmost impudence, until it ends by overthrowing everything, both in public and in private."

That seems to me to be a pretty good summation of the answer to the British rock singer Donovan's question, "What goes on? I really want to know."

The most immediate apparent change instituted by the new music is a new way of looking at things. We see it evidenced all around us. The old ways are going and a new set of assumptions is beginning to be worked out. I cannot even begin to codify them. Perhaps it's much too soon to do so. But I think there are some clues—the sacred importance of love and truth and beauty and interpersonal relationships. . . .

Among the effects of "what's goin' on" is the relinquishing of belief in the sacredness of logic. "I was a prisoner of logic and I still am," Malvina Reynolds admits, but then goes on to praise the new music. And the prisoners of logic are the ones who are really suffering most—unless they have Mrs. Reynolds' glorious gift of youthful vision.

[14] Arthur Rimbaud (1854–1901), a French symbolist poet, was the author of *A Season in Hell*.

The first manifestation of the importance of this outside the music—I think—came in the works of Ken Kesey and Joseph Heller. *One Flew Over the Cuckoo's Nest,* [15] with its dramatic view of the interchangeability of reality and illusion, and *Catch-22,* [16] with its delightful utilization of crackpot realism (to use C. Wright Mills's phrase) as an explanation of how things are, were works of seminal importance.

No one any longer really believes that the processes of international relations and world economics are rationally explicable. Absolutely the very best and clearest discussion of the entire thing is wrapped up in Milo Minderbinder's explanation, in *Catch-22,* of how you can buy eggs for seven cents apiece in Malta and sell them for five cents in Pianosa and make a profit. Youth understands the truth of this immediately, and no economics textbook is going to change it.

Just as—implying the importance of interpersonal relations and the beauty of being true to oneself—the under-thirty youth immediately understands the creed patiently explained by Yossarian in *Catch-22* that everybody's your enemy who's trying to get you killed, even if he's your own commanding officer. . . .

In almost every aspect of what is happening today, this turning away from the old patterns is making itself manifest. As the formal structure of the show business world of popular music and television has brought out into the open the Negro performer—whose incredibly beautiful folk poetry and music for decades has been the prime mover in American song—we find a curious thing happening.

The Negro performers, from James Brown to Aaron Neville to the Supremes and the Four Tops, are on an Ed Sullivan trip, striving as hard as they can to get on that stage and become part of the American success story, while the white rock performers are motivated to escape from that stereotype. Whereas in years past the Negro performer offered style in performance and content in song—the messages from Leadbelly to Percy Mayfield to Ray Charles were important messages—today he is almost totally style with very little content. And when James Brown sings, "It's a Man's World," or

---

[15] A novel (1962) by Ken Kesey (1935–   ) that deals with rebellious inmates in a state insane asylum.

[16] A novel (1961) by Joseph Heller (1923–   ) that portrays the life of combat aviators in the Second World War as an absurdity.

Aaron Neville sings, "Tell It Like It Is," he takes a phrase and only a phrase with which to work, and the Supremes and the Tops are choreographed more and more like the Four Lads and the Ames Brothers and the McGuire Sisters.[17]

I suggest that this bears a strong relationship to the condition of the civil rights movement today in which the only truly black position is that of Stokely Carmichael,[18] and in which the N.A.A.C.P.[19] and most of the other formal groups are, like the Four Tops and the Supremes, on an Ed Sullivan-TV-trip to middle-class America. And the only true American Negro music is that which abandons the concepts of European musical thought, abandons the systems of scales and keys and notes, for a music whose roots are in the culture of the colored peoples of the world.

The drive behind all American popular music performers, to a greater or lesser extent, from Sophie Tucker and Al Jolson, on down through Pat Boone and as recently as Roy Head and Charlie Rich, has been to sound like a Negro. The white jazz musician was the epitome of this.

Yet an outstanding characteristic of the new music of rock, certainly in its best artists, is something else altogether. This new generation of musicians is not interested in being Negro, since that is an absurdity.

The clarinetist Milton Mezzrow, who grew up with the Negro Chicago jazzmen in the twenties and thirties, even put "Negro" on his prison record and claimed to be more at home with his Negro friends than with his Jewish family and neighbors.

Today's new youth, beginning with the rock band musician but spreading out into the entire movement, into the Haight-Ashbury[20] hippies, is not ashamed of being white.

He is remarkably free from prejudice, but he is not attempting to join the Negro culture or to become part of it, like his musical predecessor, the jazzman, or like his social predecessor, the beatnik. I find this of considerable significance. For the very first time in decades, as far as I know, something important and new is happening artistically and musically in this society that is distinct from the

[17] Three white vocal groups of the 1950s and early 1960s.
[18] A radical black civil-rights activist (1941–   ).
[19] The National Association for the Advancement of Colored People.
[20] A district of San Francisco that served, in the late 1950s and 1960s, as a refuge for young people abandoning middle-class society for a new life-style.

Negro and to which the Negro will have to come, if he is interested in it at all, as in the past the white youth went uptown to Harlem or downtown or crosstown or to wherever the Negro community was centered because there was the locus of artistic creativity.

Today the new electronic music by the Beatles and others (and the Beatles' "Strawberry Fields" is, I suggest, a three-minute master-piece, an electronic miniature symphony) exists somewhere else from and independent of the Negro. This is only one of the more easily observed manifestations of this movement. . . .

Implicit in the very names of the business organizations that these youths form is an attack on the traditional, serious attitude toward money. It is not only that the groups themselves are named with beautiful imagery: the Grateful Dead, the Loading Zone, Blue Cheer or the Jefferson Airplane—all dating back to the Beatles with an A—it is the names of the nonmusical organizations: Frontage Road Productions (the music company of the Grateful Dead), Faithful Virtue Music (the Lovin' Spoonful's publishing company), Ashes and Sand (Bob Dylan's production firm—his music publishing company is Dwarf Music). A group who give light shows is known as the Love Conspiracy Commune, and there was a dance recently in Marin County, California, sponsored by the Northern California Psychedelic Cattlemen's Association, Ltd. And, of course, there is the Family Dog, which, despite *Ramparts,* was never a rock group, only a name under which four people who wanted to present rock 'n roll dances worked.

Attacking the conventional attitude toward money is considered immoral in the society of our fathers, because money is sacred. The reality of what Bob Dylan says—"money doesn't talk, it swears"—has yet to seep through.

A corollary of the money attack is the whole thing about long hair, bare feet and beards. "Nothing makes me sadder," a woman wrote me objecting to the Haight-Ashbury scene, than to see beautiful girls walking along the street in bare feet." My own daughter pointed out that your feet couldn't get any dirtier than your shoes.

Recently I spent an evening with a lawyer, a brilliant man who is engaged in a lifelong crusade to educate and reform lawyers. He is interested in the civil liberties issue of police harassment of hippies. But, he said, they wear those uniforms of buckskin and fringe and beards. Why don't they dress naturally? So I asked him if he was born in his three-button dacron suit. It's like the newspaper descriptions of Joan Baez's[21] "long stringy hair." It may be long, but *stringy?* Come on!

To the eyes of many of the elder generation, all visible aspects of the new generation, its music, its lights, its clothes, are immoral. The City of San Francisco Commission on Juvenile Delinquency reported adversely on the sound level and the lights at the Fillmore Auditorium,[22] as if those things of and by themselves were threats (they may be, but not in the way the Commission saw them). A young girl might have trouble maintaining her judgment in that environment, the Commission chairman said.

Now this all implies that dancing is the road to moral ruin, that young girls on the dance floor are mesmerized by talent scouts for South American brothels and enticed away from their happy (not hippie) homes to live a life of slavery and moral degradation. It ought to be noted, parenthetically, that a British writer, discussing the Beatles, claims that "the Cycladic fertility goddess from Amorgos dates the guitar as a sex symbol to 4800 years B.C."

During the twenties and the thirties and the forties—in other words, during the prime years of the Old Ones of today—dancing, in the immortal words of Bob Scobey, the Dixieland trumpet player, "was an excuse to get next to a broad." The very least effect of the pill on American youth is that this is no longer true.

The assault on hypocrisy works on many levels. The adult society attempted to chastise Bob Dylan by economic sanction, calling the line in "Rainy Day Woman," "everybody must get stoned" (although there is a purely religious, even biblical, meaning to it, if you wish), an enticement to teen-agers to smoke marijuana. But no one has objected to Ray Charles's "Let's Go Get Stoned," which is about gin, or to any number of other songs, from the Kingston Trio's "Scotch and Soda" on through "One for My Baby and One More [ONE MORE!] for the Road." Those are about alcohol and alcohol is socially acceptable, as well as big business, even though I believe that everyone under thirty now knows that alcohol is worse for you than marijuana, that, in fact, the only thing wrong about marijuana is that it is illegal. . . .

---

[21] Joan Baez (1941–   ), an American folksinger, was also an activist against the war in Vietnam.

[22] The site of many early rock concerts.

There's another side to it, of course, or at least another aspect of it. The Rolling Stones,[23] who came into existence really to fight jazz in the clubs of London, were against the jazz of the integrated world, the integrated world arrived at by rational processes. Their songs, from "Satisfaction" and "19th Nervous Breakdown" to "Get Off of My Cloud" and "Mother's Little Helper," were antiestablishment songs in a nonpolitical sort of way, just as Dylan's first period was antiestablishment in a political way. The Stones are now moving, with "Ruby Tuesday" and "Let's Spend the Night Together," into a social radicalism of sorts; but in the beginning, and for their basic first-thrust appeal, they hit out in rage, almost in blind anger and certainly with overtones of destructiveness, against the adult world. It's no wonder the novel they were attracted to was David Wallis' *Only Lovers Left Alive,* that Hell's Angels[24] story of a teen-age, future jungle. And it is further interesting that their manager, Andrew Loog Oldham, writes the essays on their albums in the style of Anthony Burgess' violent *A Clockwork Orange.*[25]

Nor is it any wonder that this attitude appealed to that section of the youth whose basic position was still in politics and economics (remember that the Rolling Stone Mick Jagger[26] was a London School of Economics student, whereas Lennon and McCartney[27] were artists and writers). When the Stones first came to the West Coast, a group of young radicals issued the following proclamation of welcome:

> Greetings and welcome Rolling Stones, our comrades in the desperate battle against the maniacs who hold power. The revolutionary youth of the world hears your music and is inspired to even more deadly acts. We fight in guerrilla bands against the invading imperialists in Asia and South America, we riot at rock n' roll concerts everywhere. We burned and pillaged in Los Angeles and the cops know our snipers will return.
>
> They call us dropouts and delinquents and draftdodgers and punks and hopheads and heap tons of shit on our heads. In Viet Nam they drop bombs on us and in America they try to make us make war on our

[23] An internationally-known English rock group that made its first recording in 1964; notorious for its image of disheveled, aggressive sexuality.
[24] A notorious motorcycle gang.
[25] An English novel (1962) in which the narrator is a maniacally violent adolescent who deliberately rejects a conventional life-style, even to the point of inventing his own "language."
[26] The lead vocalist of the Rolling Stones.
[27] Two of the Beatles.

own comrades but the bastards hear us playing you on our little transistor radios and know that they will not escape the blood and fire of the anarchist revolution.

We will play your music in rock 'n roll marching bands as we tear down the jails and free the prisoners, as we tear down the State schools and free the students, as we tear down the military bases and arm the poor, as we tatoo BURN BABY BURN! on the bellies of the wardens and generals and create a new society from the ashes of our fires.

Comrades, you will return to this country when it is free from the tyranny of the State and you will play your splendid music in factories run by the workers, in the domes of emptied city halls, on the rubble of police stations, under the hanging corpses of priests, under a million red flags waving over a million anarchist communities. In the words of Breton,[28] THE ROLLING STONES ARE THAT WHICH SHALL BE! LYNDON JOHNSON—THE YOUTH OF CALIFORNIA DEDICATES ITSELF TO YOUR DESTRUCTION! ROLLING STONES—THE YOUTH OF CALIFORNIA HEARS YOUR MESSAGE! LONG LIVE THE REVOLUTION!!!

But rhetoric like that did not bring out last January to a Human Be-In on the polo grounds of San Francisco's Golden Gate Park twenty thousand people who were there, fundamentally, just to see the other members of the tribe, not to hear speeches. . . .

The New Youth is finding its prophets in strange places—in dance halls and on the jukebox. It is on, perhaps, a frontier buckskin trip after a decade of Matt Dillon and Bonanza and the other TV folk myths, in which the values are clear (as opposed to those in the world around us) and right is right and wrong is wrong. The Negro singers have brought the style and the manner of the Negro gospel preacher to popular music, just as they brought the rhythms and the feeling of the gospel music, and now the radio is the church and Everyman carries his own walkie-talkie to God in his transistor.

Examine the outcry against the Beatles for John Lennon's remark about being more popular than Jesus. No radio station that depended on rock 'n roll music for its audience banned Beatles records, and in the only instance where we had a precise measuring rod for the contest—the Beatles concert in Memphis where a revival meeting ran day and date with them—the Beatles won overwhelmingly. Something like eight to five over Jesus in attendance, even though the

---

[28] André Breton (1896–1966), a French surrealist writer of manifestoes. (See selection 34.) Obviously, the "words of Breton" have been changed to suit the writers of the "proclamation."

Beatles charged a stiff price and the Gospel according to the revival preacher was free. Was my friend so wrong who said that if Hitler were alive today, the German girls wouldn't allow him to bomb London if the Beatles were there?

"Nobody ever taught you how to live out in the streets," Bob Dylan sings in "Like a Rolling Stone." You may consider that directed at a specific person, or you may, as I do, consider it poetically aimed at plastic uptight America, to use a phrase from one of the Family Dog Founders. . . .

Let's go back again to Nietzsche.

> Orgiastic movements of a society leave their traces in music [he wrote].
> Dionysiac stirrings arise either through the influence of those narcotic
> potions of which all primitive races speak in their hymns [—dig
> that!—] or through the powerful approach of spring, which penetrates
> with joy the whole frame of nature. So stirred, the individual forgets
> himself completely. It is the same Dionysiac power which in medieval
> Germany drove ever increasing crowds of people singing and dancing
> from place to place; we recognize in these St. John's and St. Vitus'
> dancers[29] the bacchic choruses of the Greeks,[30] who had their precur-
> sors in Asia Minor and as far back as Babylon and the orgiastic Sacea.[31]
> There are people who, either from lack of experience or out of sheer stu-
> pidity, turn away from such phenomena, and strong, in the sense of
> their own sanity, label them either mockingly or pityingly "endemic
> diseases." These benighted souls have no idea how cadaverous and
> ghostly their "sanity" appears as the intense throng of Dionysiac
> revelers sweeps past them.

And Nietzsche never heard of the San Francisco Commission on Juvenile Delinquency or the Fillmore and the Avalon ballrooms.

---

[29] Grotesque dances were performed by a fanatical wandering sect of men and women in parts of northern Europe from the fourteenth to the sixteenth centuries. The religious frenzy of these wild dancers may have had its roots in the old pagan Germanic dances celebrating the summer solstice. When the Germanic tribes became Christian the festival was changed in form and meaning to honor the birth of John the Baptist. These "St John's dancers" were regarded as being possessed by the devil; the cure was exorcism and pilgrimage to churches dedicated to St. Vitus. (Thus, the term "St. Vitus's Dance" is still used to describe chorea, a disease of the nervous system characterized by uncontrollable bodily movements.)

[30] In ancient Greek drama, there was a chorus, which provided song and dance. This chorus was descended from the frenzied choric singing and dancing of the older spring festival of Dionysus (Bacchus).

[31] A wild and licentious festival in ancient Babylon, perhaps in celebration of the New Year. It lasted five days during which slaves ruled their masters and criminals were granted royal rights before being put to death.

"Believe in the magic, it will set you free," the Lovin' Spoonful sing. "This is an invitation across the nation," sing Martha and the Vandellas, and the Mamas and the Papas, "a chance for folks to meet, there'll be laughin', singin' and music swingin', and dancin' in the street!"

Do I project too much? Again, to Nietzsche. "Man now expresses himself through song and dance as the member of a higher community; he has forgotten how to walk, how to speak and is on the brink of taking wing as he dances . . . no longer the *artist,* he has himself become *a work of art.*"

"Hail hail rock 'n roll," as Chuck Berry sings. "Deliver me from the days of old!"

I think he's about to be granted his wish.

39

Henry Moore
On Sculpture

✵

Sculpture, like painting, has moved toward abstraction in the twentieth century. Henry Moore (1898–   ), one of the century's major sculptors, is noted for massive wood, stone, or bronze figures whose abstract yet organic forms evoke primitive natural forces.

Moore was born in Castleford, a small coal-mining town near Leeds, Yorkshire, in northern England. The seventh child of a self-educated coal miner, he followed his father's advice in first training to be a schoolteacher. Dutifully, he earned scholarships to the local private schools, although he had known since childhood that he really wanted to be a sculptor.

The First World War interrupted Moore's career plans—as it did those of so many others. Moore became a soldier and, on the battlefield in 1917, was overcome by poison gas; he spent the next several months convalescing. After the war he received a veteran's grant that enabled him to attend the Leeds School of Art, his two years there providing him with his first formal instruction in sculpture. Upon winning a scholarship to the Royal College of Art in 1921, Moore moved to London. Academic instruction in the metropolis proved less important to him, however, than the individual study possible in the great museums. He discovered there the strange power of archaic and primitive carvings, especially in Mexican art of the pre-Columbian periods. Even in these early years of his career, Moore reacted against the dominant sculptural tradition—"the realistic ideal of physical beauty in art which sprang from fifth-century [B.C.] Greece." In contrast, in primitive art— whether Mexican, or African, or Viking, for example—he found an expression of the "common world-language of form."

After he completed his formal training in 1924, Moore began to carve the subjects that were to make him famous: the reclining figure (usually a woman) and the mother and child. In 1933 he joined with a group of young artists to form the influential "Unit One" group, an attempt to make the English public aware of the modern international movement in art and architecture.

By this time Moore was working sometimes with purely abstract forms, sometimes with abstract forms that resembled the human figure, and increasingly with abstract sculptures that resembled organic forms, such as driftwood, trees, pebbles, rocks, shells, and—especially—bones. In attempting to apply nature's "principles of form and rhythm," Moore gave his sculptures irregular concavities and unexpected holes that allow light to penetrate through the forms. Viewers initially found this technique shocking, especially when the sculptures resembled human beings, as it disturbed their classical sense of the heroic human form.

With the outbreak of the Second World War in 1939, Moore experienced a temporary shortage of his usual large sculptural materials and thus turned, for a time, to drawing. Among the drawings he created during this period is a compelling series that shows the people of London seeking shelter from German bombardment: they crowd the underground railway station, forming long rows of helpless recumbent figures. His wartime experiences caused Moore to reassess the role of the artist in society. Feeling a new need to affect the lives of common people, he moved to positions of public leadership in artistic institutions, accepted a commission for a "Madonna and Child" in a church, and began to carve the first of his many family groups. Moore thus helped to revive the great "humanist" tradition of sculpture, enriching it with the experimental forms of his earlier work.

In the years after the Second World War, Moore showed no diminution of creative energy. Two particularly notable massive, bronze outdoor sculptures of his postwar period are the two-part Reclining Figure *(1965) at New York's Lincoln Center and* Nuclear Energy *(1966) at the University of Chicago.*

The following selection presents excerpts gleaned from written and spoken comments made by Moore over the last five decades. In his words we see, among other major themes, an early rejection of realistic representation, a "feeling for organic form," an awareness of the unconscious meanings of sculptural forms, and a sensitivity to the honesty and "intense vitality" of primitive art.

THE NATURE OF SCULPTURE

In sculpture the later Greeks worshipped their own likeness, making realistic representation of much greater importance than it had been at any previous period. The Renaissance revived the Greek ideal and European sculpture since then, until recent times, has been dominated by the Greek ideal.

The world has been producing sculpture for at least some thirty thousand years. Through modern development of communication much of this we now know and the few sculptors of a hundred years or so of Greece no longer blot our eyes to the sculptural achievements of the rest of mankind. Palaeolithic and Neolithic sculpture, Sumerian, Babylonian and Egyptian, Early Greek, Chinese, Etruscan, Indian, Mayan, Mexican and Peruvian, Romanesque, Byzantine and Gothic, Negro, South Sea Island and North American Indian sculpture; actual examples or photographs of all are available, giving us a world view of sculpture never previously possible.

This removal of the Greek spectacles from the eyes of the modern sculptor (along with the direction given by the work of such painters as Cézanne[1] and Seurat[2]) has helped him to realise again the intrinsic emotional significance of shapes instead of seeing mainly a representation value, and freed him to recognise again the importance of the material in which he works, to think and create in his material by carving direct, understanding and being in sympathy with his material so that he does not force it beyond its natural constructive build, producing weakness; to know that sculpture in stone should look honestly like stone, that to make it look like flesh and blood, hair and dimples is coming down to the level of the stage conjuror.

A limitless scope is open to him. His inspiration will come, as always, from nature and the world around him, from which he learns such principles as balance, rhythm, organic growth of life, attraction and repulsion, harmony and contrast. His work may be comparatively representational or may be as Music and Architecture are, non–representational, but mechanical copying of objects and surrounding life will leave him dissatisfied—the camera and cameo-

---

[1] Paul Cézanne (1839–1906), a French Post-Impressionist painter who reintroduced a sense of solid form into painting in reaction to the Impressionist focus upon surface tones.

[2] Georges Seurat (1859–91), a French painter who used small dots of pure color, mixed only in the eye of the viewer, creating a strict, formal composition.

graph[3] have nullified this as his aim. He will want his works to be creations, new in themselves, not merely feats of copying nor of memory, having only the second-hand life of realistic waxworks.

Each sculptor differs in his aims and ideals according to his different character, personality and point of development. The sculpture which moves me most is full blooded and self-supporting, fully in the round, that is, its component forms are completely realised and work as masses in opposition, not being merely indicated by surface cutting in relief; it is not perfectly symmetrical, it is static and it is strong and vital, giving out something of the energy and power of great mountains. It has a life of its own, independent of the object it represents.

Sculpture, for me, must have life in it, vitality. It must have a feeling for organic form, a certain pathos and warmth. Purely abstract sculpture seems to me to be an activity that would be better fulfilled in another art, such as architecture. That is why I have never been tempted to remain a purely abstract sculptor. Abstract sculptures are too often but models for monuments that are never carried out, and the works of many abstract or "constructivist" sculptors suffer from this frustration in that the artist never gets around to finding the real material solution to his problems. But sculpture is different from architecture. It creates organisms that must be complete in themselves. An architect has to deal with practical considerations, such as comfort, costs and so on, which remain alien to an artist, very real problems that are different from those which a sculptor has to face. . . . A sculpture must have its own life. Rather than give the impression of a smaller object carved out of a bigger block, it should make the observer feel that what he is seeing contains within itself its own organic energy thrusting outwards—if a work of sculpture has its own life and form, it will be alive and expansive, seeming larger than the stone or wood from which it is carved. It should always give the impression, whether carved or modelled, of having grown organically, created by pressure from within.

You see, I think a sculptor is a person who is interested in the shape of things. A poet is somebody who is interested in words; a musician

---

[3] Moore is actually referring to the pantograph, an instrument for the mechanical copying of drawings on any desired scale.

is someone who is interested in or obsessed by sounds. But a sculptor is a person obsessed with the form and the shape of things, and it's not just the shape of any one thing, but the shape of anything and everything: the growth in a flower; the hard, tense strength, although delicate form of a bone; the strong, solid fleshiness of a beech tree trunk. All these things are just as much a lesson to a sculptor as a pretty girl—as a young girl's figure—and so on. They're all part of the experience of form and therefore, in my opinion, everything, every shape, every bit of natural form, animals, people, pebbles, shells, anything you like are all things that can help you to make a sculpture. And for me, I collect odd bits of driftwood—anything I find that has a shape that interests me—and keep it around in that little studio so that if any day I go in there, or evening, within five or ten minutes of being in that little room there will be something that I can pick up or look at that would give me a start for a new idea. This is why I like leaving all these odds and ends around in a small studio—to start one off with an idea.

One of the things I would like to think my sculpture has is a force, is a strength, is a life, a vitality from inside it, so that you have a sense that the form is pressing from inside trying to burst or trying to give off the strength from inside itself, rather than having something which is just shaped from outside and stopped. It's as though you have something trying to make itself come to a shape from inside itself. This is, perhaps, what makes me interested in bones as much as in flesh because the bone is the inner structure of all living form. It's the bone that pushes out from inside; as you bend your leg the knee gets tautness over it, and it's there that the movement and the energy come from. If you clench a knuckle, you clench a fist, you get in that sense the bones, the knuckles pushing through, giving a force that if you open your hand and just have it relaxed you don't feel. And so the knee, the shoulder, the skull, the forehead, the part where from inside you get a sense of pressure of the bone outwards—these for me are the key points.

You can then, as it were, between those key points have a slack part, as you might between the bridge of a drapery and the hollow of it, so that in this way you get a feeling that the form is all inside it, and this is what also makes me think that I prefer hard form to soft form. For me, sculpture should have a hardness, and because I think sculpture should have a hardness fundamentally I really like carving better than I like modelling. Although I do bronzes, I make the orig-

inal which is turned into bronze in plaster, and although anyone can
build a plaster up as soft mixture, that mixture hardens and I then file
it and chop it and make it have its final shape as hard plaster, not as
a soft material.

Sculpture should always at first sight have some obscurities, and further meanings. People should want to go on looking and thinking; it
should never tell all about itself immediately. Initially both sculpture
and painting must need effort to be fully appreciated . . . all art
should have some more mystery and meaning to it than is apparent
to a quick observer. In my sculpture explanations often come afterwards. I do not make a sculpture to a programme or because I
have a particular idea I am trying to express. While working, I
change parts, because I do not like them, in such a way that I hope I
am going to like them better. The kind of alteration I make is not
thought out; I do not say to myself, this is too big, or too small. I
just look at it and, if I do not like it, I change it. I work from likes
and dislikes, and not by literary logic! Not by words, but by being
satisfied with form. Afterwards I can explain or find reasons for it,
but that is rationalisation after the event. I can even look at old
sculptures and find meanings in them and explanations which at the
time were not in my mind at all—not consciously anyway.

THE SCULPTOR SPEAKS

• • •

The violent quarrel between the abstractionists and the surrealists [4] seems to me quite unnecessary. All good art has contained
both abstract and surrealist elements, just as it has contained both
classical and romantic elements—order and surprise, intellect and
imagination, conscious and unconscious. Both sides of the artists's
personality must play their part. And I think the first inception of a
painting or a sculpture may begin from either end. As far as my own
experience is concerned, I sometimes begin a drawing with no pre-
conceived problem to solve, with only the desire to use pencil on

[4] A reference to the dispute between those who believe that art should concern itself
only with pure non-representational form (the "abstractionists") and those who believe that art's primary purpose is to express the irrational creative energy of the unconscious mind (the "surrealists"). For a discussion of the latter, see selection 34.

paper, and make lines, tones and shapes with no conscious aim; but as my mind takes in what is so produced, a point arrives where some idea becomes conscious and crystallises, and then a control and ordering begin to take place.

Or sometimes I start with a set subject; or to solve, in a block of stone of known dimensions, a sculptural problem I've given myself, and then consciously attempt to build an ordered relationship of forms, which shall express my idea. But if the work is to be more than just a sculptural exercise, unexplainable jumps in the process of thought occur; and the imagination plays its part.

It might seem from what I have said of shape and form that I regard them as ends in themselves. Far from it. I am very much aware that associational, psychological factors play a large part in sculpture. The meaning and significance of form itself probably depends on the countless associations of man's history. For example, rounded forms convey an idea of fruitfulness, maturity, probably because the earth, women's breasts, and most fruits are rounded, and these shapes are important because they have this background in our habits of perception. I think the humanist organic element will always be for me of fundamental importance in sculpture, giving sculpture its vitality. Each particular carving I make takes on in my mind a human or occasionally animal character and personality, and this personality controls its design and formal qualities, and makes me satisfied or dissatisfied with the work as it develops.

My own aim and direction seems to be consistent with these beliefs, though it does not depend upon them. My sculpture is becoming less representational, less an outward visual copy, and so what some people would call more abstract; but only because I believe that in this way I can present the human psychological content of my work with the greatest directness and intensity.

UNIT ONE[5]

Each sculptor through his past experience, through observation of natural laws, through criticism of his own work and other sculpture,

[5] In 1933 Moore was one of a group of eleven painters, sculptors, and architects who wished to bring awareness of modern artistic movements to the English public. The name of the group combines the idea of unity ("Unit") with that of individuality ("One").

through his character and psychological make-up, and according to his stage of development, finds that certain qualities in sculpture become of fundamental importance to him. For me these qualities are:

Truth to material. Every material has its own individual qualities. It is only when the sculptor works direct, when there is an active relationship with his material, that the material can take its part in the shaping of an idea. Stone, for example, is hard and concentrated and should not be falsified to look like soft flesh—it should not be forced beyond its constructive build to a point of weakness. It should keep its hard tense stoniness.

Full three-dimensional realisation. Complete sculptural expression is form in its full spatial reality.

Only to make relief shapes on the surface of the block is to forego the full power of expression of sculpture. When the sculptor understands his material, has a knowledge of its possibilities and its constructive build, it is possible to keep within its limitations and yet turn an inert block into a composition which has a full form-existence, with masses of varied size and section conceived in their air-surrounded entirety, stressing and straining, thrusting and opposing each other in spatial relationship—being static, in the sense that the centre of gravity lies within the base (and does not seem to be falling over or moving off its base)—and yet having an alert dynamic tension between its parts.

Sculpture fully in the round has no two points of view alike. The desire for form completely realised is connected with asymmetry. For a symmetrical mass being the same from both sides cannot have more than half the number of different points of view possessed by a non-symmetrical mass.

Asymmetry is connected also with the desire for the organic (which I have) rather than the geometric.

Organic forms, though they may be symmetrical in their main disposition, in their reaction to environment, growth and gravity, lose their perfect symmetry.

Observation of Natural Objects. The observation of nature is part of an artist's life, it enlarges his form-knowledge, keeps him fresh and from working only by formula, and feeds inspiration.

The human figure is what interests me most deeply, but I have found principles of form and rhythm from the study of natural objects such as pebbles, rocks, bones, trees, plants, etc.

Pebbles and rocks show nature's way of working stone. Smooth, sea-worn pebbles show the wearing away, rubbed treatment of stone and principles of asymmetry.

Rocks show the hacked, hewn treatment of stone, and have a jagged nervous block rhythm.

Bones have marvellous structural strength and hard tenseness of form, subtle transition of one shape into the next and great variety in section.

Trees (tree trunks) show principles of growth and strength of joints, with easy passing of one section into the next. They give the ideal for wood sculpture, upward twisting movement.

Shells show nature's hard but hollow form (metal sculpture) and have a wonderful completeness of single shape.

There is in nature a limitless variety of shapes and rhythms (and the telescope and microscope have enlarged the field) from which the sculptor can enlarge his form-knowledge experience.

But besides formal qualities there are qualities of vision and expression:

Vision and expression. My aim in work is to combine as intensely as possible the abstract principles of sculpture along with the realisation of my idea.

All art is an abstraction to some degree (in sculpture the material alone forces one away from pure representation and towards abstraction).

Abstract qualities of design are essential to the value of a work, but to me of equal importance is the psychological, human element. If both abstract and human elements are welded together in a work, it must have a fuller, deeper meaning.

Vitality and power of expression. For me a work must first have a vitality of its own. I do not mean a reflection of the vitality of life, of movement, physical action, frisking, dancing figures and so on, but that a work can have in it a pent-up energy, an intense life of its own, independent of the object it may represent. When a work has this powerful vitality we do not connect the word Beauty with it.

Beauty, in the later Greek or Renaissance sense, is not the aim of my sculpture.

Between beauty of expression and power of expression there is a difference of function. The first aims at pleasing the senses, the second has a spiritual vitality which for me is more moving and goes deeper than the senses.

Because a work does not aim at reproducing natural appearances it is not, therefore, an escape from life—but may be a penetration into reality, not a sedative or drug, not just the exercise of good taste, the provision of pleasant shapes and colours in a pleasing combination, not a decoration to life, but an expression of the significance of life, a stimulation to a greater effort in living.

PRIMITIVE ART

The term "Primitive Art" is generally used to include the products of a great variety of races and periods in history, many different social and religious systems. In its widest sense it seems to cover most of those cultures which are outside European and the great Oriental civilisations. This is the sense in which I shall use it here, though I do not much like the application of the word "primitive" to art, since, through its associations, it suggests to many people an idea of crudeness and incompetence, ignorant gropings rather than finished achievements. Primitive art means far more than that; it makes a straightforward statement, its primary concern is with the elemental, and its simplicity comes from direct and strong feeling, which is a very different thing from that fashionable simplicity-for-its-own-sake which is emptiness. Like beauty, true simplicity is an unselfconscious virtue; it comes by the way and can never be an end in itself.

The most striking quality common to all primitive art is its intense vitality. It is something made by people with a direct and immediate response to life. Sculpture and painting for them was not an activity of calculation or academism, but a channel for expressing powerful beliefs, hopes, and fears. It is art before it got smothered in trimmings and surface decorations, before inspiration had flagged into technical tricks and intellectual conceits. But apart from its own enduring value, a knowledge of it conditions a fuller and truer appreciation of the later developments of the so-called great periods, and shows art to be a universal continuous activity with no separation between past and present.

All art has its roots in the "primitive," or else it becomes decadent, which explains why the "great" periods, Pericles' Greece and the Renaissance for example, flower and follow quickly on primitive periods, and then slowly fade out. The fundamental sculptural principles of the Archaic Greeks[6] were near enough to Phidias'[7] day to carry through into his carvings a true quality, although his conscious aim was so naturalistic; and the tradition of early Italian art was sufficiently in the blood of Masaccio[8] for him to strive for realism and yet retain a primitive grandeur and simplicity. The steadily growing appreciation of primitive art among artists and the public today is therefore a very hopeful and important sign.

---

[6] The sculptural period lasting from the seventh century B.C. to about 480 B.C. was characterized by increasing naturalism in the treatment of the human body combined with firm, quasi-abstract formal design.

[7] Phidias was a master sculptor (500–432 B.C.) of the classical period in Athens, which was also known as "the Golden Age" and "the Age of Pericles."

[8] An Italian painter (1401–28) who was the first of the great masters in fifteenth–century Florence and one of the founders of "modern" painting.

40

Aldous Huxley

The Doors of Perception

AND

Heaven and Hell

*Drugs, known in all ages but more widely available since the advent of mod-
ern chemistry, have had varied functions in the twentieth century. Some
have been used to relieve pain, some to combat depression or mental illness,
and some simply to produce pleasurable sensations. In addition, many people
contend, certain drugs can be employed to expand the consciousness of the
user. An intellectually distinguished advocate of such psycho-chemical exploration was the writer Aldous Huxley (1894–1963).*

*Throughout his exceptionally productive literary career (see selection 10),
Huxley was interested in the idea of psychological liberation. In his later
years, considering the failure for many of religious worship, Huxley began to
view biochemistry as a means of escaping the confinement of the rational-
izing, verbalizing ego. Much of his personal experimentation toward this
end is carefully and eloquently recorded in* The Doors of Perception
(1954) and Heaven and Hell *(1956), the sources of the following selection.*

*In 1953, under the supervision of a psychiatrist who had written exten-
sively on the biochemistry of schizophrenia (a form of mental disturbance),
Huxley swallowed four-tenths of a gram of mescalin. (Mescalin is the active
ingredient of peyote, the root of a desert cactus plant that is eaten in religious*

From pp. 67–79, 85–89, and 96–101 in *The Doors of Perception* and *Heaven and Hell* by
Aldous Huxley. Copyright © 1954, 1955, 1956 by Aldous Huxley. Reprinted by permission of Harper & Row, Publishers, Inc.

ceremonies by the Indians of Mexico and the American Southwest. It is also chemically related to LSD, widely known as a hallucinogen—an inducer of false perceptions of the external world.) Within a half-hour, as Huxley relates in The Doors of Perception, he began to experience "visionary" effects—not in the subjective, internalized sense that he had initially expected, but rather in the outward "realm of objective fact." Previously a verbalizer who visualized very poorly, he now saw the objects of his everyday world with an intensity of light and color that revealed their "true Being." It was as if he had walked through the "Door in the Wall" of normal consciousness and returned "wiser but less cocksure, happier but less self-satisfied, humbler . . . yet better equipped to understand the relationship of words to things, of systematic reasoning to the unfathomable Mystery."

In Heaven and Hell, the sequel to The Doors of Perception, Huxley describes the features of the visionary world and the methods by which the visions may be gained. He traces the correspondence between the visions made possible by mescalin and those consistently recorded in religious literature, in folklore and legend, and in certain works of art. Through mescalin and similar drugs, Huxley suggests, "the efficiency of the brain as an instrument for focusing the mind on the problems of life" is lowered. The lowering of the efficiency of the "cerebral reducing valve" permits the "intrusions of biologically useless, but aesthetically and sometimes spiritually valuable material."

As Huxley indicates in his title, however, there is a visionary hell as well as a visionary paradise. ("The schizophrenic is like a man permanently under the influence of mescalin and therefore unable to shut off the experience of a reality which he is not holy enough to live with, . . . it never permits him to look at the world with merely human eyes.") Since, as Huxley notes, the effect of such drugs is always conditional on the nature of the individual user, it seems doubtful that any "ideal drug" is possible or even desirable.

Huxley, nevertheless, advocates the search for a new drug, which— unlike alcohol and tobacco—"will relieve and console our suffering species without doing more harm in the long run than it does good in the short." (Huxley's "ideal drug" should not be identified with the "soma" of his fictional Brave New World; soma anesthetizes the user to reality, rather than aiding him in penetrating to another level of reality.) It is a sad commentary on contemporary society that some individuals mistakenly point to Huxley's disciplined aesthetic and spiritual searching as justification for their own undisciplined and self-destructive addictions.

THE DOORS OF PERCEPTION

The urge to transcend self-conscious selfhood is, as I have said, a principal appetite of the soul. When, for whatever reason, men and women fail to transcend themselves by means of worship, good works and spiritual exercises, they are apt to resort to religion's chemical surrogates—alcohol and "goof pills" in the modern West, alcohol and opium in the East, hashish in the Mohammedan world, alcohol and marijuana in Central America, alcohol and coca in the Andes, alcohol and the barbiturates in the more up-to-date regions of South America. In *Poisons Sacrés, Ivresses Divines* [*Holy Poisons, Heavenly Frenzies*] Philippe de Félice has written at length and with a wealth of documentation on the immemorial connection between religion and the taking of drugs. Here, in summary or in direct quotation, are his conclusions. The employment for religious purposes of toxic substances is "extraordinarily widespread. . . . The practices studied in this volume can be observed in every region of the earth, among primitives no less than among those who have reached a high pitch of civilization. We are therefore dealing not with exceptional facts, which might justifiably be overlooked, but with a general and, in the widest sense of the word, a human phenomenon, the kind of phenomenon which cannot be disregarded by anyone who is trying to discover what religion is, and what are the deep needs which it must satisfy."

Ideally, everyone should be able to find self-transcendence in some form of pure or applied religion. In practice it seems very unlikely that this hoped for consummation will ever be realized. There are, and doubtless there always will be, good churchmen and good churchwomen for whom, unfortunately, piety is not enough. The late G. K. Chesterton,[1] who wrote at least as lyrically of drink as of devotion, may serve as their eloquent spokesman.

The modern churches, with some exceptions among the Protestant denominations, tolerate alcohol; but even the most tolerant have

---

[1] An English essayist, novelist, poet, and convert to Roman Catholicism (1874–1936).

made no attempt to convert the drug to Christianity, or to sacramen-
talize its use. The pious drinker is forced to take his religion in one
compartment, his religion-surrogate in another. And perhaps this is
inevitable. Drinking cannot be sacramentalized except in religions
which set no store on decorum. The worship of Dionysos[2] or the
Celtic god of beer was a loud and disorderly affair. The rites of
Christianity are incompatible with even religious drunkenness. This
does no harm to the distillers, but is very bad for Christianity.
Countless persons desire self-transcendence and would be glad to
find it in church. But, alas, "the hungry sheep look up and are not
fed."[3] They take part in rites, they listen to sermons, they repeat
prayers; but their thirst remains unassuaged. Disappointed, they turn
to the bottle. For a time at least and in a kind of way, it works.
Church may still be attended; but it is no more than the Musical
Bank of Butler's *Erewhon*.[4] God may still be acknowledged; but He
is God only on the verbal level, only in a strictly Pickwickian sense.[5]
The effective object of worship is the bottle and the sole religious experience is that state of uninhibited and belligerent euphoria which
follows the ingestion of the third cocktail.

We see, then, that Christianity and alcohol do not and cannot mix.
Christianity and mescalin seem to be much more compatible. This
has been demonstrated by many tribes of Indians, from Texas to as
far north as Wisconsin. Among these tribes are to be found groups
affiliated with the Native American Church, a sect whose principal
rite is a kind of Early Christian agape, or love feast, where slices of
peyote take the place of the sacramental bread and wine. These Native Americans regard the cactus as God's special gift to the Indians,
and equate its effects with the workings of the divine Spirit.

Professor J. S. Slotkin, one of the very few white men ever to
have participated in the rites of a Peyotist congregation, says of his
fellow worshipers that they are "certainly not stupefied or drunk.
. . . They never get out of rhythm or fumble their words, as a

[2] The ancient Greek god of wine and fertility.
[3] A quotation from John Milton's *Lycidas* (1637).
[4] A utopian satire (1872) by the English novelist and essayist Samuel Butler
(1835–1902). *Erewhon* is an anagram of *nowhere*. The Musical Bank is Butler's satirical
depiction of a commercially corrupted and ineffectual church where people exchange
coins for music.
[5] Understood in an unusual or non-traditional way, like the peculiar meanings given
to common words by Mr. Pickwick in Charles Dickens' novel *The Pickwick Papers*
(1837).

drunken or stupefied man would do. . . . They are all quiet, courteous and considerate of one another. I have never been in any white man's house of worship where there is either so much religious feeling or decorum." And what, we may ask, are these devout and well-behaved Peyotists experiencing? Not the mild sense of virtue which sustains the average Sunday churchgoer through ninety minutes of boredom. Not even those high feelings, inspired by thoughts of the Creator and the Redeemer, the Judge and the Comforter, which animate the pious. For these Native Americans, religious experience is something more direct and illuminating, more spontaneous, less the homemade product of the superficial, self-conscious mind. Sometimes (according to the reports collected by Dr. Slotkin) they see visions, which may be of Christ Himself. Sometimes they hear the voice of the Great Spirit. Sometimes they become aware of the presence of God and of those personal shortcomings which must be corrected if they are to do His will. The practical consequences of these chemical openings of doors into the Other World seem to be wholly good. Dr. Slotkin reports that habitual Peyotists are on the whole more industrious, more temperate (many of them abstain altogether from alcohol), more peaceable than non-Peyotists. A tree with such satisfactory fruits cannot be condemned out of hand as evil.

In sacramentalizing the use of peyote, the Indians of the Native American Church have done something which is at once psychologically sound and historically respectable. In the early centuries of Christianity many pagan rites and festivals were baptized, so to say, and made to serve the purposes of the Church. These jollifications were not particularly edifying; but they assuaged a certain psychological hunger and, instead of trying to suppress them, the earlier missionaries had the sense to accept them for what they were, soul-satisfying expressions of fundamental urges, and to incorporate them into the fabric of the new religion. What the Native Americans have done is essentially similar. They have taken a pagan custom (a custom, incidentally, far more elevating and enlightening than most of the rather brutish carousals and mummeries adopted from European paganism) and given it a Christian significance.

Though but recently introduced into the northern United States, peyote-eating and the religion based upon it have become important symbols of the red man's right to spiritual independence. Some Indians have reacted to white supremacy by becoming Americanized, others by retreating into traditional Indianism. But some have tried to make the best of both worlds, indeed of all the worlds—the best of Indianism, the best of Christianity, and the best of those Other Worlds of transcendental experience, where the soul knows itself as unconditioned and of like nature with the divine. Hence the Native American Church. In it two great appetites of the soul—the urge to independence and self-determination and the urge to self-transcendence—were fused with, and interpreted in the light of, a third—the urge to worship, to justify the ways of God to man, to explain the universe by means of a coherent theology.

> Lo, the poor Indian, whose untutored mind
> Clothes him in front, but leaves him bare behind.[6]

But actually it is we, the rich and highly educated whites, who have left ourselves bare behind. We cover our anterior nakedness with some philosophy—Christian, Marxian, Freudo-Physicalist—but abaft we remain uncovered, at the mercy of all the winds of circumstance. The poor Indian, on the other hand, has had the wit to protect his rear by supplementing the fig leaf of a theology with the breechclout of transcendental experience.

I am not so foolish as to equate what happens under the influence of mescalin or of any other drug, prepared or in the future preparable, with the realization of the end and ultimate purpose of human life: Enlightenment, the Beatific Vision. All I am suggesting is that the mescalin experience is what Catholic theologians call "a gratuitous grace," not necessary to salvation but potentially helpful and to be accepted thankfully, if made available. To be shaken out of the ruts of ordinary perception, to be shown for a few timeless hours the outer and the inner world, not as they appear to an animal obsessed with survival or to a human being obsessed with words and notions, but as they are apprehended, directly and unconditionally, by Mind at Large—this is an experience of inestimable value to everyone and especially to the intellectual. For the intellectual is by definition the man for whom, in Goethe's[7] phrase, "the word is

---

[6] A parody of lines from Alexander Pope's long philosophical poem *An Essay on Man* (1733):

> Lo! the poor Indian, whose untutor'd mind
> Sees God in clouds, or hears him in the wind.

[7] Johann Wolfgang von Goethe (1749–1832), a German poet and dramatist, was, for much of his life, a romantic concerned with the direct relationship of the human being to external nature.

essentially fruitful." He is the man who feels that "what we perceive by the eye is foreign to us as such and need not impress us deeply." And yet, though himself an intellectual and one of the supreme masters of language, Goethe did not always agree with his own evaluation of the word. "We talk," he wrote in middle life, "far too much. We should talk less and draw more. I personally should like to renounce speech altogether and, like organic Nature, communicate everything I have to say in sketches. That fig tree, this little snake, the cocoon on my window sill quietly awaiting its future—all these are momentous signatures. A person able to decipher their meaning properly would soon be able to dispense with the written or the spoken word altogether. The more I think of it, there is something futile, mediocre, even (I am tempted to say) foppish about speech. By contrast, how the gravity of Nature and her silence startle you, when you stand face to face with her, undistracted, before a barren ridge or in the desolation of the ancient hills." We can never dispense with language and the other symbol systems; for it is by means of them, and only by their means, that we have raised ourselves above the brutes, to the level of human beings. But we can easily become the victims as well as the beneficiaries of these systems. We must learn how to handle words effectively; but at the same time we must preserve and, if necessary, intensify our ability to look at the world directly and not through that half opaque medium of concepts, which distorts every given fact into the all too familiar likeness of some generic label or explanatory abstraction.

Literary or scientific, liberal or specialist, all our education is predominantly verbal and therefore fails to accomplish what it is supposed to do. Instead of transforming children into fully developed adults, it turns out students of the natural sciences who are completely unaware of Nature as the primary fact of experience, it inflicts upon the world students of the humanities who know nothing of humanity, their own or anyone else's.

Gestalt psychologists, such as Samuel Renshaw, have devised methods for widening the range and increasing the acuity of human perceptions. But do our educators apply them? The answer is, No.

Teachers in every field of psycho-physical skill, from seeing to tennis, from tightrope walking to prayer, have discovered, by trial and error, the conditions of optimum functioning within their special fields. But have any of the great Foundations financed a project for co-ordinating these empirical findings into a general theory and practice of heightened creativeness? Again, so far as I am aware, the answer is, No.

All sorts of cultists and queer fish teach all kinds of techniques for achieving health, contentment, peace of mind; and for many of their hearers many of these techniques are demonstrably effective. But do we see respectable psychologists, philosophers and clergymen boldly descending into those odd and sometimes malodorous wells, at the bottom of which poor Truth is so often condemned to sit? Yet once more the answer is, No.

And now look at the history of mescalin research. Seventy years ago men of first-rate ability described the transcendental experiences which come to those who, in good health, under proper conditions and in the right spirit, take the drug. How many philosophers, how many theologians, how many professional educators have had the curiosity to open this Door in the Wall? The answer, for all practical purposes, is, None.

In a world where education is predominantly verbal, highly educated people find it all but impossible to pay serious attention to anything but words and notions. There is always money for, there are always doctorates in, the learned foolery of research into what, for scholars, is the all-important problem: Who influenced whom to say what when? Even in this age of technology the verbal humanities are honored. The non-verbal humanities, the arts of being directly aware of the given facts of our existence, are almost completely ignored. A catalogue, a bibliography, a definitive edition of a third-rate versifier's *ipsissima verba*,[8] a stupendous index to end all indexes—any genuinely Alexandrian project is sure of approval and financial support. But when it comes to finding out how you and I, our children and grandchildren, may become more perceptive, more intensely aware of inward and outward reality, more open to the Spirit, less apt, by psychological malpractices, to make ourselves physically ill, and more capable of controlling our own autonomic nervous system—when it comes to any form of non-verbal education more fundamental (and more likely to be of some practical use) than Swedish drill,[9] no really respectable person in any really respectable university or church will do anything about it. Verbalists are suspicious of the non-verbal; rationalists fear the given, non-rational fact; intellectuals

---

[8] Latin: the very words.
[9] A system of exercising the body's muscles and joints.

feel that "what we perceive by the eye (or in any other way) is foreign to us as such and need not impress us deeply." Besides, this matter of education in the non-verbal humanities will not fit into any of the established pigeonholes. It is not religion, not neurology, not gymnastics, not morality or civics, not even experimental psychology. This being so the subject is, for academic and ecclesiastical purposes, non-existent and may safely be ignored altogether or left, with a patronizing smile, to those whom the Pharisees[10] of verbal orthodoxy call cranks, quacks, charlatans and unqualified amateurs.

"I have always found," Blake[11] wrote rather bitterly, "that Angels have the vanity to speak of themselves as the only wise. This they do with a confident insolence sprouting from systematic reasoning."

Systematic reasoning is something we could not, as a species or as individuals, possibly do without. But neither, if we are to remain sane, can we possibly do without direct perception, the more unsystematic the better, of the inner and outer worlds into which we have been born. This given reality is an infinite which passes all understanding and yet admits of being directly and in some sort totally apprehended. It is a transcendence belonging to another order than the human, and yet it may be present to us as a felt immanence, an experienced participation. To be enlightened is to be aware, always, of total reality in its immanent otherness—to be aware of it and yet to remain in a condition to survive as an animal, to think and feel as a human being, to resort whenever expedient to systematic reasoning. Our goal is to discover that we have always been where we ought to be. Unhappily we make the task exceedingly difficult for ourselves. Meanwhile, however, there are gratuitous graces in the form of partial and fleeting realizations. Under a more realistic, a less exclusively verbal system of education than ours, every Angel (in Blake's sense of that word) would be permitted as a sabbatical treat, would be urged and even, if necessary, compelled to take an occasional trip through some chemical Door in the Wall into the world of transcendental experience. If it terrified him, it would be unfortunate but probably salutary. If it brought him a brief but timeless illumination, so much the better. In either case the Angel might lose a

[10] Self-righteous, hypocritical people.
[11] William Blake (1757–1827), an English visionary poet and artist. The titles of both of the books by Huxley excerpted here were taken from Blake's revolutionary work *The Marriage of Heaven and Hell* (1790): "If the doors of perception were cleansed every thing would appear to man as it is, infinite."

little of the confident insolence sprouting from systematic reasoning and the consciousness of having read all the books.

Near the end of his life Aquinas [12] experienced Infused Contemplation. Thereafter he refused to go back to work on his unfinished book. Compared with *this,* everything he had read and argued about and written—Aristotle and the Sentences, the Questions, the Propositions, the majestic Summas—was no better than chaff or straw. For most intellectuals such a sit-down strike would be inadvisable, even morally wrong. But the Angelic Doctor had done more systematic reasoning than any twelve ordinary Angels, and was already ripe for death. He had earned the right, in those last months of his mortality, to turn away from merely symbolic straw and chaff to the bread of actual and substantial Fact. For Angels of a lower order and with better prospects of longevity, there must be a return to the straw. But the man who comes back through the Door in the Wall will never be quite the same as the man who went out. He will be wiser but less cocksure, happier but less self-satisfied, humbler in acknowledging his ignorance yet better equipped to understand the relationship of words to things, of systematic reasoning to the unfathomable Mystery which it tries, forever vainly, to comprehend.

HEAVEN AND HELL

Some people never consciously discover their antipodes. Others make an occasional landing. Yet others (but they are few) find it easy to go and come as they please. For the naturalist of the mind, the collector of psychological specimens, the primary need is some safe, easy and reliable method of transporting himself and others from the Old World to the New, from the continent of familiar cows and horses to the continent of a wallaby and the platypus.

Two such methods exist. Neither of them is perfect; but both are sufficiently reliable, sufficiently easy and sufficiently safe to justify their employment by those who know what they are doing. In the first case the soul is transported to its far-off destination by the aid of a chemical—either mescalin or lysergic acid. [13] In the second case,

[12] St. Thomas Aquinas (1225–74), the most influential medieval philosopher—known as the "Angelic Doctor"; his *Summa Theologica* sought to reconcile the truths of reason with those of faith.

[13] An extremely potent hallucinogen (inducer of false perceptions of the external world) chemically similar to mescalin and to adrenalin; used in the synthesis of LSD.

the vehicle is psychological in nature, and the passage to the mind's antipodes is accomplished by hypnosis.[14] The two vehicles carry the consciousness to the same region; but the drug has the longer range and takes its passengers further into the *terra incognita*.[15]

How and why does hypnosis produce its observed effects? We do not know. For our present purposes, however, we do not have to know. All that is necessary, in this context, is to record the fact that some hypnotic subjects are transported, in the trance state, to a region in the mind's antipodes, where they find the equivalent of marsupials—strange psychological creatures leading an autonomous existence according to the law of their own being.

About the physiological effects of mescalin we know a little. Probably (for we are not yet certain) it interferes with the enzyme system that regulates cerebral functioning. By doing so it lowers the efficiency of the brain as an instrument for focusing the mind on the problems of life on the surface of our planet. This lowering of what may be called the biological efficiency of the brain seems to permit the entry into consciousness of certain classes of mental events, which are normally excluded, because they possess no survival value. Similar intrusions of biologically useless, but aesthetically and sometimes spiritually valuable material may occur as the result of illness or fatigue; or they may be induced by fasting, or a period of confinement in a place of darkness and complete silence.

A person under the influence of mescalin or lysergic acid will stop seeing visions when given a large dose of nicotinic acid. This helps to explain the effectiveness of fasting as an inducer of visionary experience. By reducing the amount of available sugar, fasting lowers the brain's biological efficiency and so makes possible the entry into consciousness of material possessing no survival value. Moreover, by causing a vitamin deficiency, it removes from the blood that known inhibitor of visions, nicotinic acid. Another inhibitor of visionary experience is ordinary, everyday, perceptual experience. Experimental psychologists have found that, if you confine a man to a "restricted environment," where there is no light, no sound, nothing to smell and, if you put him in a tepid bath, only one, almost imperceptible thing to touch, the victim will very soon start "seeing things," "hearing things" and having strange bodily sensations.

[14] In an appendix Huxley also mentions the use of carbon dioxide and the stroboscopic lamp as "two other, less effective aids to visionary experience."
[15] Latin: unknown territory.

Milarepa, in his Himalayan cavern, and the anchorites [16] of the Thebaid followed essentially the same procedure and got essentially the same results. A thousand pictures of the Temptations of St. Anthony bear witness to the effectiveness of restricted diet and restricted environment. Asceticism, it is evident, has a double motivation. If men and women torment their bodies, it is not only because they hope in this way to atone for past sins and avoid future punishments; it is also because they long to visit the mind's antipodes and do some visionary sightseeing. Empirically and from the reports of other ascetics, they know that fasting and a restricted environment will transport them where they long to go. Their self-inflicted punishment may be the door to paradise. (It may also—and this is a point which will be discussed in a later paragraph—be a door into the infernal regions.)

From the point of view of an inhabitant of the Old World, marsupials are exceedingly odd. But oddity is not the same as randomness. Kangaroos and wallabies may lack verisimilitude; but their improbability repeats itself and obeys recognizable laws. The same is true of the psychological creatures inhabiting the remoter regions of our minds. The experiences encountered under the influence of mescalin or deep hypnosis are very strange; but they are strange with a certain regularity, strange according to a pattern.

What are the common features which this pattern imposes upon our visionary experiences? First and most important is the experience of light. Everything seen by those who visit the mind's antipodes is brilliantly illuminated and seems to shine from within. All colors are intensified to a pitch far beyond anything seen in the normal state, and at the same time the mind's capacity for recognizing fine distinctions of tone and hue is notably heightened. . . .

The typical mescalin or lysergic-acid experience begins with perceptions of colored, moving, living geometrical forms. In time, pure geometry becomes concrete, and the visionary perceives, not patterns, but patterned things, such as carpets, carvings, mosaics. These give place to vast and complicated buildings, in the midst of landscapes, which change continuously, passing from richness to more intensely colored richness, from grandeur to deepening grandeur. Heroic figures, of the kind that Blake called "The Seraphim," may make their appearance, alone or in multitudes. Fabulous animals

[16] Hermits.

move across the scene. Everything is novel and amazing. Almost never does the visionary see anything that reminds him of his own past. He is not remembering scenes, persons or objects, and he is not inventing them; he is looking on at a new creation.

The raw material for this creation is provided by the visual experiences of ordinary life; but the molding of this material into forms is the work of someone who is most certainly not the self, who originally had the experiences, or who later recalled and reflected upon them. They are (to quote the words used by Dr. J. R. Smythies in a recent paper in the *American Journal of Psychiatry*) "the work of a highly differentiated mental compartment, without any apparent connection, emotional or volitional, with the aims, interests, or feelings of the person concerned."

Here, in quotation or condensed paraphrase, is Weir Mitchell's account of the visionary world to which he was transported by peyote, the cactus which is the natural source of mescalin.

At his entry into that world he saw a host of "star points" and what looked like "fragments of stained glass." Then came "delicate floating films of color." These were displaced by an "abrupt rush of countless points of white light," sweeping across the field of vision. Next there were zigzag lines of very bright colors, which somehow turned into swelling clouds of still more brilliant hues. Buildings now made their appearance, and then landscapes. There was a Gothic tower of elaborate design with worn statues in the doorways or on stone brackets. "As I gazed, every projecting angle, cornice and even the faces of the stones at their joinings were by degrees covered or hung with clusters of what seemed to be huge precious stones, but uncut stones, some being more like masses of transparent fruit. . . . All seemed to possess an interior light." The Gothic tower gave place to a mountain, a cliff of inconceivable height, a colossal bird claw carved in stone and projecting over the abyss, an endless unfurling of colored draperies, and an efflorescence of more precious stones. Finally there was a view of green and purple waves breaking on a beach "with myriads of lights of the same tint as the waves."

Every mescalin experience, every vision arising under hypnosis, is unique; but all recognizably belong to the same species. The landscapes, the architectures, the clustering gems, the brilliant and intricate patterns—these, in their atmosphere of preternatural light, preternatural color and preternatural significance, are the stuff of which the mind's antipodes are made. Why this should be so, we have no idea. It is a brute fact of experience which, whether we like it or not, we have to accept—just as we have to accept the fact of kangaroos.

From these facts of visionary experience let us now pass to the accounts preserved, in all the cultural traditions, of Other Worlds—the worlds inhabited by the gods, by the spirits of the dead, by man in his primal state of innocence.

Reading these accounts, we are immediately struck by the close similarity between induced or spontaneous visionary experience and the heavens and fairylands of folklore and religion. Preternatural light, preternatural intensity of coloring, preternatural significance—these are characteristic of all the Other Worlds and Golden Ages. And in virtually every case this preternaturally significant light shines on, or shines out of, a landscape of such surpassing beauty that words cannot express it.

Thus in the Greco-Roman tradition we find the lovely Garden of the Hesperides, the Elysian Plain, and the fair Island of Leuke, to which Achilles was translated. Memnon went to another luminous island, somewhere in the East. Odysseus and Penelope traveled in the opposite direction and enjoyed their immortality with Circe in Italy. Still further to the west were the Islands of the Blest, first mentioned by Hesiod and so firmly believed in that, as late as the first century B.C., Sertorius planned to send a squadron from Spain to discover them.

Magically lovely islands reappear in the folklore of the Celts and, at the opposite side of the world, in that of the Japanese. And between Avalon in the extreme West and Horaisan in the Far East, there is the land of Uttarakuru, the Other World of the Hindus. "The land," we read in the *Ramayana*,[17] "is watered by lakes with golden lotuses. There are rivers by thousands, full of leaves of the color of sapphire and lapis lazuli; and the lakes, resplendent like the morning sun, are adorned by golden beds of red lotus. The country all around is covered by jewels and precious stones, with gay beds of blue lotus, golden-petalled. Instead of sand, pearls, gems and gold form the banks of the rivers, which are overhung with trees of fire-bright gold. These trees perpetually bear flowers and fruit, give forth a sweet fragrance and abound with birds."

Uttarakuru, we see, resembles the landscapes of the mescalin expe-

---

[17] An ancient Indian epic poem (*ca.* 1000 B.C.).

rience in being rich with precious stones. And this characteristic is common to virtually all the Other Worlds of religious tradition. Every paradise abounds in gems, or at least in gemlike objects resembling, as Weir Mitchell puts it, "transparent fruit." Here, for example, is Ezekiel's version of the Garden of Eden. "Thou hast been in Eden, the garden of God. Every precious stone was thy covering, the sardius, topaz and the diamond, the beryl, the onyx and the jasper, the sapphire, the emerald and the carbuncle, and gold. . . . Thou art the anointed cherub that covereth . . . thou hast walked up and down in the midst of the stones of fire." The Buddhist paradises are adorned with similar "stones of fire.". . .

41

Abraham Maslow

Peak Experiences in
Education and Art

Humanistic psychology has emerged in the past three decades as a counter-force to the reigning orthodoxies of Sigmund Freud and behaviorists such as B. F. Skinner.* Indeed the label "third-force psychology" has often been applied to the humanistic school, which, in the words of its main founder, Abraham Maslow (1908–1970), seeks to help people achieve "the goal of becoming as fully human as possible, . . . to be self-actualized."

Born in Brooklyn, New York, the son of uneducated immigrants, Maslow earned a doctorate in psychology from the University of Wisconsin in 1934. As might be expected of the curriculum offered in psychology departments of the 1930s, Maslow's educational experience was entirely in scientific behaviorism. The study of psychology, as Skinner would assert, was entirely a matter of conditioned responses and mathematically predictable behavior. Maslow's early interest in behaviorism was reflected in his doctoral dissertation, an observational study of reproduction in monkeys. His enthusiasm began to wane, however, as he sensed the oversimplifications that often occur when behavioral models gained from scientific study of rats and monkeys are applied to humans. Maslow began to read the works of Henri Bergson and Alfred North Whitehead, early twentieth-century philosophers who asserted the uniqueness of human nature and rejected the dominant mechanistic, scientific mode of thought as the sole, comprehensive road to knowledge. To

*See selections 24 and 9.

Abraham H. Maslow, "Peak Experiences in Education and Art." This article first appeared in *The Humanist* September/October 1970 and is reprinted by permission. [Pp. 29–31.]

Maslow, even more important in his redirection of thought were his personal experiences of marriage, fatherhood, and psychoanalysis: "I'd say that anyone who had a baby couldn't be a behaviorist."

In the search for knowledge that would clearly be of benefit to humanity, Maslow turned to study of the most creative, "self-actualized" individuals, rather than to study of the typical (emphasized by the behaviorists) or the pathological (emphasized by the Freudians). He discovered that the most creative people had "peak experiences," an almost mystical ecstatic state that results in a higher knowledge of reality.

Maslow's work toward understanding the healthy, creative personality is described in such influential volumes as New Knowledge in Human Values *(1959),* Toward a Psychology of Being *(1962),* Religions, Values, and Peak-Experiences *(1964),* The Psychology of Science *(1966), and* The Farther Reaches of Human Nature *(1971). Much respected as a teacher, notably at Brooklyn College (1937–51) and Brandeis University (1951–69), Maslow was also a president of the American Psychological Association and a founder of the sensitivity training movement in group psychotherapy.*

The following selection presents an essay first published just after Maslow's death. In it, Maslow reiterates the central thesis of his life's work: the goal of education is ultimately "self-actualization, . . . helping the person to become the best that he is able to become." To Maslow, the acquisition of external skills is secondary to the purpose of a genuinely humanistic education. He repudiates the impersonal, neutral model of science for education, and asserts the value of "learning to be a human being." The genuinely humanistic curriculum, he suggests, makes possible a peak experience of excellence in mathematics just as it does in music, and such an education can lead to a higher knowledge of reality ("cognition of being") and to "the growth of full-humanness." Effective education in the arts is essential to Maslow's curricular goal of "learning one's identity." He contends that people can use their "peak experiences," which the arts especially make possible, "as models by which to reevaluate all kinds of teaching."

Something big is happening. It's happening to everything that concerns human beings. Everything the human being generates is involved, and certainly education is involved. A new *Weltanschauung* [1] is in the process of being developed, a new *Zeitgeist,* [2] a new set of values and a new way of finding them, and certainly a new image of man. There is a new kind of psychology—presently called the humanistic, existential, third-force psychology—that at this transitional moment is certainly different in many important ways from the Freudian and behavioristic psychologies, which have been the two great comprehensive, dominating psychologies.

There are new conceptions of interpersonal relationships. There is a new image of society. There is a new conception of the goals of society, of all the social institutions, and of all the social sciences. There is a new economics, a new conception of politics, and revolutions in religion, in science, in work. There is a newer conception of education, and this forms the background for my ideas of music and creativity.

First of all, most psychologies of learning are beside the point; that is, beside the "humanistic" point. Most teachers and books present learning as the acquisition of associations, of skills, and of capacities that are *external* and not *intrinsic* to the human character, to the human personality, to the person himself. Picking up coins or keys or possessions or something of the sort is like picking up reinforcements and conditioned reflexes that are in a certain very profound sense expendable. It does not really matter if one has a conditioned reflex: If I salivate to the sound of a buzzer and then this extinguishes, nothing has happened to me; I have lost nothing of any consequence whatever. We might almost say that those extensive books on the psychology of learning are of no consequence—at least to the human center, to the human soul, to the human essence.

Generated by the new humanistic philosophy is a new conception of learning, teaching, and education. Such a conception holds that the goal of education—the human goal, the humanistic goal—is ultimately the "self-actualization" of a person, the development of the fullest height that the human species or a particular individual can come to. In a less technical way, it is helping the person to become the best that he is able to become. Such a goal involves very serious shifts in learning strategies.

Associative learning is certainly useful: for learning things that are

[1] German: a conception of the universe and of the human relationship to it.
[2] German: spirit of the age.

of no real consequence, or for learning techniques that are interchangeable. And many of the things we must learn are like that. If one needed to memorize the vocabulary of another language, he would learn it by sheer rote memory. Here the laws of association can be a help. Whereas if one wants to learn automatic habits in driving, like responding to a red signal light or something of the sort, then conditioning is of consequence. It is important and useful, especially in a technological society.

In terms of becoming a better person, of self-development, self-fulfillment, or "becoming fully human," the greatest learning experiences are very different. In my life, such experiences have been far more important than listening, memorizing, and organizing data for formal courses.

More important for me have been such experiences as having a child. Our first baby changed me as a psychologist. It made the behaviorism I had been so enthusiastic about look so foolish that I could not stomach it any more. It was impossible. Having a second baby, and learning how profoundly different people are even before birth, made it impossible for me to think in terms of the kind of learning psychology in which one can teach anybody anything. I could no longer think in terms of the John B. Watson theory, "Give me two babies and I will make one into this and one into the other." It is as if he never had any children. We know only too well that a parent cannot make his children into anything. Children make themselves into something. The best we can do, and frequently the most effect we can have, is to serve as something to react against if the child presses too hard.

Another profound learning experience that I value far more highly than any particular course or any degree is my personal psychoanalysis: discovering my own identity, my own self. Yet another basic experience—far more important—was getting married; that was certainly more instructive than my Ph.D.

Thus if one thinks in terms of developing the kinds of wisdom, understanding, and life skills that he would want, he must think of what I call *intrinsic* education, *intrinsic* learning; that is, first, learning to be a human being in general, and second, learning to be *this* particular human being. Once you start thinking in terms of becoming a good human being, and then ask about your high school courses— "How did trigonometry help me to become a better human being?"—an echo answers, "By gosh, they didn't work!" In a certain sense, trigonometry was for me a waste of time. My early music education was also unsuccessful because it taught a child who had a profound feeling for music and a great love for the piano *not* to learn it. My piano teacher taught me in effect that music is something to stay away from. And I had to relearn music as an adult.

I am talking about ends: This is a revolutionary repudiation of 19th-century science and contemporary professional philosophy, which is essentially a technology and not a philosophy of ends. I reject thereby, as theories of human nature, positivism, behaviorism, and objectivism. I reject thereby the whole model of science, and all its works derived from the historical accident that science began with the study of nonpersonal, nonhuman things that in fact had no ends. The development of physics, astronomy, mechanics, and chemistry was impossible until they had become value-free, value-neutral, so that pure descriptiveness was possible. The great mistake that we are now learning about is that this model, developed from the study of objects and of things, has been illegitimately used for the study of human beings. It is a terrible technique. It has not worked.

Most of the psychology on this positivistic, objectivistic, associationistic, value-free, value-neutral model of science, as it piles up like a coral reef of small facts about this and that, is certainly not false, but merely trivial. I do not want to sell my own science short; we know a great deal about things that *do* matter to the human being. But I would maintain that what has mattered most has been learned mainly by nonphysicalistic techniques, by the humanistic science of which we have become more conscious.

In the social sciences many are discovering that the physicalistic, mechanistic model was a mistake, leading us . . . to where? To atom bombs. To a beautiful technology of killing, as in the concentration camps. To Eichmann.[3] An Eichmann cannot be refuted with a positivistic philosophy or science. He just cannot. He didn't know what was wrong. As far as he was concerned, nothing was wrong; he had done a good job. He *did* do a good job, if you forget about ends and values. I have pointed out that professional science and professional philosophy are dedicated to the proposition of forgetting about values, excluding them. This, therefore, must lead to Eichmanns, to atom bombs, and to who knows what! The tendency to

[3] Adolf Eichmann (1906–62), a Nazi bureaucrat who participated in the mass extermination of civilian populations. (See selection 2.)

separate good style or talent from content and ends can lead to this kind of danger.

We can now add to the great discoveries Freud[4] made. His one big mistake, which we are correcting now, is that he thought of the unconscious merely as undesirable evil. But unconsciousness also carries in it the roots of creativeness, of joy, of happiness, of goodnness, of its own ethics and values. There is a healthy unconscious as well as an unhealthy one. And the new psychologies are studying this at full tilt. The existential psychiatrists and psychotherapists are putting it into practice. New kinds of therapies are being practiced. We have a good conscious and a bad conscious, a good unconscious and a bad unconscious. Furthermore, the good is real in a non-Freudian sense. Freud was committed by his own positivism. He was a neurologist. And a sworn oath called for a project to develop a psychology that could be reduced to physical and chemical statements. This is what he dedicated himself to, though he himself disproved his point!

And how do we explain this higher nature that I claim we have discovered? The Freudian explanation has been reductive. Explain it away. If I am a kind man, this is a reaction formation against my rage to kill. Somehow, the killing is more basic than the kindness. And the kindness is a way of trying to cover up, repress, and defend myself against realizing the fact that I am truly a murderer. If I am generous, this is a reaction formation against stinginess. I am really stingy inside. This is a very peculiar thing. Somehow there is a begging of the question that is now so obvious. Why did he not say, for instance, that maybe killing people was a reaction formation against loving them? It is just as legitimate a conclusion and, as a matter of fact, more true for many people.

But, to return to this exciting new development in science, I have a very strong sense of being in the middle of a historical wave. One hundred and fifty years from now, what will the historians say about this age? What was really important? What was going on? What was finished? My belief is that much of what makes the headlines is finished, and the growing tip of mankind is what is now developing and will flourish in 100 or 200 years if we manage to endure. Historians will be talking about this movement as the sweep of history;

[4] Sigmund Freud (1856–1939), an Austrian physician and founder of psychoanalysis, who postulated, within each person's psyche, an unconscious *id* as the repository of repressed instinctual desires. (See selection 24.)

they will say that as Whitehead pointed out, when you get a new model, a new paradigm, a new way of perceiving, new definitions of the old words, suddenly you have an insight. You see things in a different way.

One consequence generated by what I have been talking about is a flat denial, an *empirical* denial (not pious, or arbitrary, or a priori, or wishful) of the Freudian contention of a necessary, intrinsic, constant opposition between the needs of the individual and the needs of society and civilization. It just is not so. We now know something about how to set up the conditions in which the needs of the individual become synergistic with, not opposed to, the needs of society and in which they both work to the same ends.

Another empirical statement can be made about what we call "peak experiences." We have made studies of peak experiences by asking groups of people and individuals such questions as, "What was the most ecstatic moment of your life?" or "Have you experienced transcendent ecstasy?" One might think that in a general population, such questions might get only blank stares. But there were many answers. Apparently the transcendent ecstasies had been kept private because there are few if any ways of speaking about them in public. They are sort of embarrassing, shameful, not "scientific"—which many believe is the ultimate sin.

But we found many trippers to set them off. Almost everybody seems to have peak experiences or ecstasies. The question might be asked in terms of the single most joyous, happiest, most blissful moment of your whole life. You might ask questions of the kind I asked: "How did you feel different about yourself at that time?" "How did the world look different?" "What did you feel like?" "What were your impulses?" "How did you change if you did?" I want to report that the two easiest ways of getting peak experiences (in terms of simple statistics in empirical reports) are through music and through sex. I will push aside sex education, as such discussions are premature—although I am certain that one day we will not giggle over it, but will take it quite seriously and teach children that like music, like love, like insight, like a beautiful meadow, like a cute baby, or whatever, there are many paths to heaven. And sex is one of them. And music is one of them. These happen to be the easiest ones to understand.

For purposes of identifying and studying peak experiences, a list of triggers can be made. The list gets so long, however, that it becomes necessary to make generalizations. It looks as if any experience of real excellence, of real perfection, of any moving toward perfect justice or toward perfect values, tends to produce a peak experience. Not always. But it's a generalization I would make for the many kinds of things that we can concentrate on. Remember, I am talking here as a scientist. This doesn't sound like scientific talk, but this is a new kind of science.

We know that from this new humanistic science has come one of the real childbearing improvements since Adam and Eve; that is, natural childbirth, a potent source of peak experiences. We know just how to encourage peak experiences; how women can have children in such a fashion as to have a great and mystical experience, a religious experience if you wish—an illumination, a revelation, an insight. That is what women say in interviews. They become a different kind of person because there ensues what I have called "the cognition of being."

We must make a new vocabulary for all these untilled, unworked problems. "Cognition of being" really means the cognition that Plato and Socrates[5] were talking about; almost, you could say, a technology of happiness, of pure excellence, pure truth, pure goodness, and so on. Well, why *not* a technology of joy, of happiness?

Let's proceed to music in this relation. So far, peak experiences are reported only from what we might call "classical music." I have not found a peak experience from John Cage[6] (or from an Andy Warhol movie, from abstract expressionist painting, etc.). I just haven't. The peak experiences that have been reported as great joy, ecstasy, visions of another world or another level of living, have come from the great classics. On the other hand, music also melts over and fuses into dancing and rhythm. So far as this realm of research is concerned, there really isn't much difference; they melt into each other. Music as a path to peak experiences includes dancing. It also includes the rhythmic experience, even very simple rhythmic experience— the good dancing of a rumba, or the kinds of things that the

---

[5] Ancient Greek "idealistic" philosophers who believed in the knowable reality of pure "Forms," or "Ideas."
[6] An American composer (1912–   ) whose avant-garde music employs novel effects such as silence, random noise, and electronic sounds.

kids can do with drums. (I don't know whether to call the latter music, dancing, rhythm, athletics, or something else.)

Love, awareness, and reverence of the body are clearly good paths to peak experiences. These in turn are good paths (not guaranteed, but statistically likely) to the "cognition of being," to the perceiving of the Platonic essences, intrinsic values, the ultimate of being. And these paths are a therapeutic-like help toward both the curing-of-sicknesses kind of therapy and toward the growth of full-humanness. In other words, peak experiences often have consequences, very important consequences.

Music and art can have the same kinds of consequences; there is a certain overlap. They can do the same thing as psychotherapy if one keeps his goals right, knows just what he is about, and is conscious of what he is going toward. We can talk of the breaking up of symptoms like the breaking up of clichés, anxieties, and the like; *or* we can talk about the development of spontaneity, courage, Olympian or godlike humor, sensory awareness, body awareness, and the like. Music and art and rhythm and dancing are excellent ways of moving toward that second means of discovering identity.

Such triggers tend to do all kinds of things to our autonomic nervous systems, endocrine glands, feelings, and emotions. They just do. We do not know enough about physiology to understand why they do. But they do, and these are unmistakable experiences. They are a little like pain, which is also an unmistakable experience. For experientially empty people, including a tragically large proportion of the population, for people who do not know what is going on inside themselves and who live by clocks, schedules, rules, laws, hints from the neighbors (i.e., other-directed people), this kind of trigger provides a way of discovering what the self is like. There are signals from inside; there are voices that yell out, "By gosh this is good, don't ever doubt it!" We use these signals as a path to teach the discovery of the self and self-actualization. The discovery of identity comes via the impulse voices, via the ability to listen to your own guts and what is going on inside of you.

This discovery is also an experimental kind of education that may eventually lead us into a parallel educational establishment, into another *kind* of school, where mathematics can be just as beautiful, just as peak-producing, as music. Of course there are mathematics teachers who have devoted themselves to preventing this. I had no glimpse of mathematics as a study in aesthetics until I was 30 years old, when I read some books about it. And one can find the same kind of experience with history or anthropology (in the sense of learning another culture), social anthropology, palaeontology, or the study of science.

Here again I want to talk data. If one works with great creators, great scientists, the creative scientists, *that* is the way they talk. The picture of the scientist—his image as one who never smiles, who bleeds embalming fluid rather than blood—must change. Such conceptions must yield to an understanding of the creative scientist who lives by peak experiences, who lives for the moments of glory when a problem is solved and when suddenly through a microscope he gets a new perception, a moment of revelation, of illumination, insight, understanding, ecstasy. These are vital for him. Scientists are very shy and embarrassed about this. They refuse to talk about it in public. It takes a delicate kind of midwifery to extract it; but it is there, and I have got it out. If one manages to convince a creative scientist that he is not going to be laughed at for these things, then he will blushingly admit the fact of having a high emotional experience at the moment in which the crucial correlation turns out right. They just don't talk about it. As for the usual textbook on how you do science, it is total nonsense.

My point is that if we are conscious enough of what we are doing and are philosophically insightful in doing it, we may be able to use those experiences that most easily produce ecstasies and revelations, peaks and illumination, bliss and rapture. We may be able to use them as models by which to reevaluate all kinds of teaching.

The final impression that I want to try to work out is that effective education in music, art, dancing, and rhythm is intrinsically far closer to the kind of education I think necessary than is the usual "core curriculum"; that is, it is closer to the goal of learning one's identity as an essential part of his education. And if education doesn't do that, it is useless. Education is learning to grow, learning what to grow toward, learning what is good and bad, learning what is desirable and undesirable, learning what to choose and what not to choose. In this realm of intrinsic learning, intrinsic teaching, and intrinsic education, I think that the arts are so close to our psychological and biological core, so close to this identity, this biological identity, that rather than think of these courses as a sort of whipped cream or luxury, we must let them become basic experiences in our education. They could very well serve as a model; the glimpse into the infinite that they provide might well serve as the means by which we might rescue the rest of the school curriculum from the value-free, value-neutral, goal-lacking meaninglessness into which it has fallen.

VII
Prospects
and
Portents

42

Daniel Bell

The Year 2000 . . .

Predictions about the future of the world have been a continual human preoccupation. The ancient Greeks and Romans consulted the oracles; the Christians of the Middle Ages looked to the clergy and its assurances of the Second Coming of Christ; the intellectuals of the Enlightenment read the optimistic volumes of their rationalist philosophers. In modern times, people tend to ask the scientists. One particularly distinguished group of "experts on the future" is that assembled by the American Academy of Arts and Sciences for its Commission on the Year 2000. Nearly all of the forty members of the Commission are social or natural scientists; missing from its ranks are the sorts of people who dealt with such matters in earlier cultures—poets, soothsayers, clergymen, and philosophers. Intellectual and administrative leadership for the Commission is provided by its chairman, sociologist Daniel Bell (1919–).

Born into a poor immigrant family from Poland, Bell developed his early political insights in the culturally mixed neighborhoods of New York's lower East Side. In the late 1930s he attended the City College of New York, where he earned a bachelor's degree in sociology and became committed to socialist ideals. (In recent years, however, Bell has moved cautiously from the political "left" to a non-ideological "centrist" position.) He received a doctorate in sociology from Columbia University in 1960.

His strong social interest moved Bell initially toward publishing, and he became an editor of such varied publications as The New Leader, Fortune, *and* The Public Interest. *He also developed a career as a professor of soci-*

From Daniel Bell, "The Year 2000—The Trajectory of an Idea." Reprinted by permission of *Daedalus,* the Journal of the American Academy of Arts and Sciences, Boston, Massachusetts. Summer, 1967, *Toward the Year 2000: Work in Progress.* [Pp. 639–46.]

ology, teaching mainly at Columbia University (1959–69) and, since, at Harvard University. Bell's move to Harvard was prompted by a desire to work with scholars there on the problems of social prediction, problems closely linked to the continuing work of the Commission on the Year 2000. Bell's book The Coming of Post-Industrial Society *(1973), an outgrowth of his work with the Commission, is his own "venture in social forecasting." His other provocative works include* The End of Ideology *(1960), in which he argues that the traditional ideological systems of the West—including both communism and capitalism—have lost their power to persuade; and* The Reforming of General Education *(1966), in which he asserts the enduring value of interdisciplinary liberal-arts education.*

The following essay by Bell is the introduction to the first publication of the Commission, Toward the Year 2000: Work in Progress *(1967). This volume, written by experts in numerous fields under Bell's editorial direction, forecasts many of the grave problems that will soon confront humanity; but it is, nevertheless, fundamentally optimistic. Its authors set out to "indicate now the future consequences of present public-policy decisions, to anticipate future problems, and to begin the design of alternative solutions. . . ." The assumption that desirable solutions to social problems can be rationally designed by experts and then carried out by political leaders marks the intellectual confidence—perhaps even arrogance—of the Commission's work.*

Time, said St. Augustine,[1] is a three-fold present: the present as we experience it, the past as a present memory, and the future as a present expectation. By that criterion, the world of the year 2000 has already arrived, for in the decisions we make now, in the way we design our environment and thus sketch the lines of constraints, the future is committed. Just as the gridiron pattern of city streets in the nineteenth century shaped the linear growth of cities in the twentieth, so the new networks of radial highways, the location of new towns, the reordering of graduate-school curricula, the decision to create or not to create a computer utility as a single system, and the

---

[1] One of the "fathers" of the Roman Catholic Church (A.D. 354–430); his *City of God* is an inspired Christian view of the past, present, and future.

like will frame the tectonics of the twenty-first century. The future is not an overarching leap into the distance; it begins in the present.

This is the premise of the Commission on the Year 2000.[2] It is an effort to indicate now the future consequences of present public-policy decisions, to anticipate future problems, and to begin the design of alternative solutions so that our society has more options and can make a moral choice, rather than be constrained, as is so often the case when problems descend upon us unnoticed and demand an immediate response.

But what began a few years ago as a serious academic enterprise—along with the Commission on the Year 2000, there is the *Futuribles* project in Paris, directed by Bertrand de Jouvenel, and the Committee on the Next Thirty Years (named with characteristic British understatement), of the English Social Science Research Council, under Michael Young and Mark Abrams—has been seized, predictably, by the mass media and the popular imagination. The Columbia Broadcasting System has revamped its documentary program, "The Twentieth Century," into "The Twenty-First Century," to depict the marvels of the future. *The Wall Street Journal* has been running an intermittent series on expected social and technological changes. *Time* has published a compact essay on "The Futurists: Looking Toward A.D. 2000." The theme of the year 2000 now appears repeatedly on lecture circuits and in the feature pages of newspapers. Dr. Glenn T. Seaborg, chairman of the U. S. Atomic Energy Commission, in a speech to the Women's National Democratic Club, holds out a promising future for women. "By the year 2000, housewives . . . will probably have a robot 'maid' . . . shaped like a box [with] one large eye on the top, several arms and hands, and long narrow pads on each side for moving about." Dr. Isaac Asimov foretells in a Sunday-supplement interview in *The New York Post* that by the year 2000 man will be exploring the limits of the solar system and living underground. Even the beauty industry has clambered aboard. An article on *The New York Times* women's page carries the headline: "In the Year 2000: Push-Button Beauty." The article begins enchantingly: "The chic woman of the year 2000 may have live butterflies fluttering around her hairdo . . . attracted by a specially scented hair spray. The same woman, according to predictions made at a cosmetics industry luncheon, will control her body meas-

[2] A study group established by the American Academy of Arts and Sciences.

urements by reclining on a chaise longue with electronic bubbles that massage away problem areas. . . . She will have available silicones for filling in frown lines and wrinkles on aging faces."

All of this was probably to be expected. Much of the attention given the year 2000 is due, clearly, to the magic of the millennial number. Men have always been attracted by the mystical lure of the *chiloi,* the Greek word for a thousand from which we get our religious term *chiliasm,* the belief in a coming life free from the imperfections of human existence. Plato, in the Myth of Er which concludes *The Republic,* foretold that departed souls would return to earth after spending a thousand years in the netherworld. And the early Christian expectation of a *parousia*[3] (prophesied in Revelation 20) placed its hopes for a Second Coming at the end of a thousand-year period. The millennial point is only thirty-three years away and within the lifetime expectation of more than three fourths of all Americans now alive.

A good deal of today's interest in the future arises also from the bewitchment of technology and the way it has transformed the world. *Time* writes portentously: "A growing number of professionals have made prophecy a serious and highly organized enterprise. They were forced into it by the fact that technology has advanced more rapidly in the past 50 years than in the previous 5000." And most of the images of the future have concentrated on dazzling technological prospects. The possibility of prediction, the promise of technological wizardry, and the idea of a millennial turning point make an irresistible combination to a jaded press that constantly needs to ingest new sensations and novelties. The year 2000 has all the ingredients for becoming, if it has not already become, a hoola-hoop craze.

All of this has its good side and its bad. What is bad, to begin with, is that a serious and necessary effort is in danger of being turned into a fad, and any fad trivializes a subject and quickly wears it out. A second evil is that many more expectations are aroused than can be fulfilled. There do not exist today any reliable methods of prediction or forecasting (even in technology), but some spectacular predictions are often encouraged or demanded in order to enhance the game and attract attention. As is shown in these pages, the serious effort is devoted not to making predictions, but to the more

---

[3] Greek: The Second Coming of Christ.

complicated and subtle art of defining alternatives. The third draw-back in all this is that our major attention, reflecting an aspect of our culture, becomes concentrated on "gadgets," and breezy claims are made that such gadgets will transform our lives. (Thus, Marshall McLuhan predicts that by the year 2000 the wheel and the highway will be obsolete, having given way to hovercraft that will ride on air—a case, perhaps, of the medium creating his own medium.) Not only do people forget the predicted gadgets that failed to appear— for example, the replacement of the daily newspaper by facsimile that would come out of the television set—but the startling claims of yesterday quickly become the prosaic facts of today. Twenty-five years ago the technology magazines were filled with the coming wonders of "fractional horsepower," which would lighten all our burdens and transform our lives. And although small motors with fractions of horsepower have been developed, they have also resulted in such things as electric toothbrushes and electric carving knives.

The simple point is that a complex society is not changed by a flick of the wrist. Considered from the viewpoint of gadgetry, the United States in the year 2000 will be more *like* the United States in the year 1967 than *different*. The basic framework of day-to-day life has been shaped in the last fifty years by the ways the automobile, the airplane, the telephone, and the television have brought people together and increased the networks and interactions among them. It is highly unlikely that in the next thirty-three years (if one takes the year 2000 literally, not symbolically) the impending changes in tech-nology will radically alter this framework. Supersonic transport will "tighten" the network and bring the world more directly into the domestic frame. The major challenges and problems already con-fronting our society, however—a livable physical environment, ef-fective urban planning, the expansion of post-graduate education, the pressures of density and the reduction of privacy, the fragility of po-litical institutions beset by many pressure groups—will extend to the end of the century. Predicting the *social* future is relatively easy, for in the Augustinian sense it is already "present expectation," just as the expectations about urbanization, education, and medical care in the volume *Recent Social Trends*,[4] written thirty-four years ago, are "present memory."

---

[4] A landmark study of the United States, commissioned by President Herbert Hoover and published in 1933.

This is not to say that substantial changes will not take place as they have been doing in the past thirty-three years. But one has to be clear about the character of such changes. In general, there are four sources of change in society, and they can be charted with differential ease. The first source of change is technology. Technology opens up many possibilities of mastering nature and transforming resources, time, and space; it also, in many ways, imposes its own constraints and imperatives. In the next thirty-three years we are likely to see great changes growing out of the new biomedical engineering, the computer, and, possibly, weather modification. Biomedical engineering, particularly its possibilities of organ transplant, genetic modification, and control of disease, promises a substantial increase in human longevity. Previous steps, principally the control of infant mortality, raised the average life expectancy; now the prolongation of life by the control of aging may be at hand. This may accentuate a tendency, already visible, in which the chief concern of a person (particularly in middle age) is not death from disease but staying young, thus strengthening the hedonistic elements in our culture. The impact of the computer will be vast. We will probably see a national information-computer-utility system, with tens of thousands of terminals in homes and offices "hooked" into giant central computers providing library and information services, retail ordering and billing services, and the like. But while the social and economic consequences will be huge, the effect will be greater on the structure of intellectual life and the character of organizations, than on the day-to-day life of the person. Weather modification, still only on the horizon, would shape a control of environment men have dreamed of for thousands of years, but the working out of the economic and social arrangements, if the technology were possible, would pose some difficult problems for human civilization. In all this, one should note that "technology" is itself changing, and this may be one of the more important kinds of change in the next thirty-three years. Technology is not simply a "machine," but a systematic, disciplined approach to objectives, using a calculus of precision and measurement and a concept of system that are quite at variance with traditional and customary religious, aesthetic, and intuitive modes. Instead of a machine technology, we will have, increasingly, an "intellectual technology" in which such techniques as simulation, model construction, linear programming, and operations research will be hitched to the computers and will become the new tools of decision-making.

The second source of change, one of the most powerful engines in American society, represents the *diffusion* of existing goods and privileges in society, whether they be tangible goods or social claims on the community. This, in effect, is the realization of the promise of equality which underlies the founding of this country and the manifestation of Tocqueville's summation of American democracy: What the few have today, many will demand tomorrow.

When diffusion begins to take rapid sway (as has recently been seen in higher education), it changes the size and scale of the servicing institution and, consequently, that institution's character. Dealing with such problems of size and scale and planning for the kind of institution we want become the urgent task of *anticipating*, not predicting, the future; for example, the university should not become a corporate entity because of the pressure of size.

A third kind of change involves structural developments in society. The centralization of the American political system in the last thirty years has marked an extraordinary transformation of American life. It is the result, in part, of our becoming a national society through the new transportation and the mass media. But it also grew out of the need for central instrumentalities first to mediate the conflicts between large functional groups and later to mobilize the society because of the demands of war. A different, more subtle structural change has been the transformation of the economy into a "postindustrial" society. The weight of the economy has shifted from the product sector to services; more importantly, the sources of innovation are becoming lodged in the intellectual institutions, principally the universities and research organizations, rather than in the older, industrial corporations.

The consequences of such a change are enormous for the modes of access to place and privilege in the society. They make the universities the "gatekeepers" of society. They make more urgent the husbanding of "human capital," rather than financial capital, and they raise crucial sociological questions about the relationship of the new technocratic modes of decision-making to the political structures of society.

The fourth source of change—perhaps the most important and certainly the most refractory to prediction—is the relationship of the

United States to the rest of the world. In the last twenty-five years, our lives have been transformed most drastically by our participation in World War II, by our military and political posture in the Cold War, and by our relationship to the extraordinary number of new states that have emerged since 1945. The problem of *détente*[5] in a nuclear age, the gap between rich and poor nations, the threatening role of "color" as a divisive political force, the changing balance of forces—both technological and moral—are all questions that reach from the present into the distant future.

We have begun to realize—and this is the positive side of the current interest in the year 2000—that it is possible to direct some of this change consciously, and because a normative[6] commitment underlies any humanistic approach to social policy, we can try to widen the area of choice. Looking ahead, we realize that the rebuilding of American cities, for example, entails a thirty-five-year cycle, and one can rebuild cities only by making long-range commitments. In the process we are also forced to consider the adequacy of our political mechanisms, since Congress neither has a capital budget nor budgets money for long-range commitments. Furthermore, one must question whether a national society can sensibly be structured according to the present crazy-quilt pattern of fifty states and thousands of unwieldy municipalities.

In short, what matter most about the year 2000 are not the gadgets that might, on the serious side, introduce prosthesis in the human body or, on the lighter side, use silicones to lift wrinkles, but the kinds of social arrangements that can deal adequately with the problems we shall confront. More and more we are becoming a "communal society" in which the public sector has a greater importance and in which the goods and services of the society—those affecting cities, education, medical care, and the environment—will increasingly have to be purchased jointly. Hence, the problem of social choice and individual values—the question of how to reconcile conflicting individual desires through the political mechanism rather than the market—becomes a potential source of discord. The relation of the individual to bureaucratic structures will be subject to even greater strain. The increasing centralization of government creates a need for new social forms that will allow the citizenry

[5] French: A relaxation of political tensions between nations.
[6] Based on prescribed *values*.

greater participation in making decisions. The growth of a large, educated professional and technical class, with its desire for greater autonomy in work, will force institutions to reorganize the older bureaucratic patterns of hierarchy and detailed specialization. The individual will live longer and face the problem of renewed education and new careers. The family as the source of primordial attachment may become less important for the child, in both his early schooling and his emotional reinforcement. This will be a more mobile and more crowded world, raising problems of privacy and stress. The new densities and "communications overload" may increase the potentiality for irrational outbursts in our society. Finally, there is the growing disjunction between the "culture" and the "social structure." Society becomes more functionally organized, geared to knowledge and the mastery of complex bodies of learning. The culture becomes more hedonistic, permissive, expressive, distrustful of authority and of the purposive, delayed-gratification of a bourgeois, achievement-oriented technological world. This tension between the "technocratic" and the "apocalyptic" modes, particularly among the intellectuals, may be one of the great ruptures in moral temper, especially in the universities.

The only prediction about the future that one can make with certainty is that public authorities will face more problems than they have at any previous time in history. This arises from some simple facts: Social issues are more and more intricately related to one another because the impact of any major change is felt quickly throughout the national and even the international system. Individuals and groups, more conscious of these problems as problems, demand action instead of quietly accepting their fate. Because more and more decisions will be made in the political arena than in the market, there will be more open community conflict. The political arena is an open cockpit where decision points are more visible than they are in the impersonal market; different groups will clash more directly as they contend for advantage or seek to resist change in society.

For all these reasons, the society of the year 2000, so quickly and schematically outlined, will be more fragile, more susceptible to hostilities and to polarization along many different lines. Yet to say this is not to surrender to despair, for the power to deal with these problems is also present. It resides, first, in the marvelous productive capacity of our system to generate sufficient economic resources for meeting most of the country's social and economic needs. It is latent in the flexibility of the American political system, its adaptability to change, and its ability to create new social forms to meet these challenges — public corporations, regional compacts, nonprofit organizations, responsive municipalities, and the like. The problem of the future consists in defining one's priorities and making the necessary commitments. This is an intention of the Commission on the Year 2000. . . .

43

Robert L. Heilbroner

An Inquiry into
the Human Prospect

As far back as the days of the Old Testament, many have warned of wide-spread doom—unless sinners reform their ways. Others have foreseen a paradise on earth. Among those more suggestive of the first group than of the latter is Robert L. Heilbroner (1919–), who, in disagreement with Daniel Bell's optimistic scientism, has brooding doubts as to whether there is "hope for man."

Born and raised on the upper West Side of New York, Heilbroner was educated in private schools. He has stated that he "was reared during the Great Depression and never knew there was one." Apparently the family's chauffeur, who had a close relationship with young Heilbroner after his father's death, helped shape his political liberalism. After graduation from Harvard University in 1940, Heilbroner worked briefly in a federal regulatory agency and then in one of his family's clothing stores. During the Second World War he was drafted into the Army, where he served in military intelligence.

After the war Heilbroner began to write magazine articles on economics, while taking graduate courses at the New School for Social Research in New York City. His first book, The Worldly Philosophers *(1953), grew out of one of his magazine articles. Now published in more than twenty languages, it is a popular historical account of the lives and thoughts of the world's great economists since Adam Smith.*

The range of economic thought traversed by Heilbroner in The Worldly Philosophers *foreshadowed the breadth of his subsequent work. In* The Future As History *(1960), for example, he challenges America's traditionally optimistic assumptions about progress toward universal prosperity, enlightenment, and democracy.* The Making of Economic Society *(1962), his long delayed doctoral thesis, is a study of the "economics of the past," beginning with that of ancient Rome. Since 1972 he has been a professor of economics at the New School for Social Research.*

In An Inquiry into the Human Prospect *(1974)—whose opening paragraphs and concluding chapter are presented in the following selection— Heilbroner warns of some possible human catastrophes, catastrophes that could be caused, for example, by the use of military weapons, the depletion of natural resources, the growth of population, or by climatic changes resulting from industrialization. In any case, industrial expansion, central to both capitalistic and socialistic economies, will decline, Heilbroner declares; and thus a drastic reorientation to a "stationary" economic structure and a change in life-style will be necessary. He suggests, further, that traditional human traits will cause the change to occur in a convulsive manner, rather than in a calculated, peaceful way. Indeed, he speculates that the powerful central authority, ultimately required to allocate rationally the diminished resources of a "no-growth" world, will create a society closer to the grim totalitarian prophecy of Aldous Huxley's* Brave New World* *than to any ecological Eden.*

There is a question in the air, more sensed than seen, like the invisible approach of a distant storm, a question that I would hesitate to ask aloud did I not believe it existed unvoiced in the minds of many: "Is there hope for man?"

In another era such a question might have raised thoughts of man's ultimate salvation or damnation. But today the brooding doubts that it arouses have to do with life on earth, now, and in the relatively few generations that constitute the limit of our capacity to imagine the future. For the question asks whether we can imagine that future other than as a continuation of the darkness, cruelty, and disorder of

---

* See selection 10.

the past; worse, whether we do not foresee in the human prospect a deterioration of things, even an impending catastrophe of fearful dimensions.

•   •   •

What is needed now is a summing up of the human prospect, some last reflections on its implications for the present and future alike.

The external challenges can be succinctly reviewed. We are entering a period in which rapid population growth, the presence of obliterative weapons, and dwindling resources will bring international tensions to dangerous levels for an extended period. Indeed, there seems no reason for these levels of danger to subside unless population equilibrium is achieved and some rough measure of equity reached in the distribution of wealth among nations, either by great increases in the output of the underdeveloped world or by a massive redistribution of wealth from the richer to the poorer lands.

Whether such an equitable arrangement can be reached—at least within the next several generations—is open to a serious doubt. Transfers of adequate magnitude imply a willingness to redistribute income internationally on a more generous scale than the advanced nations have evidenced within their own domains. The required increases in output in the backward regions would necessitate gargantuan applications of energy merely to extract the needed resources. It is uncertain whether the requisite energy-producing technology exists, and, more serious, possible that its application would bring us to the threshold of an irreversible change in climate as a consequence of the enormous addition of man-made heat to the atmosphere.

It is this last problem that poses the most demanding and difficult of the challenges. The existing pace of industrial growth, with no allowance for increased industrialization to repair global poverty, holds out the risk of entering the danger zone of climatic change in as little as three or four generations. If that trajectory is in fact pursued, industrial growth will then have to come to an immediate halt, for another generation or two along that path would literally consume human, perhaps all, life. That terrifying outcome can be postponed only to the extent that the wastage of heat can be reduced, or that technologies that do not add to the atmospheric heat burden—for example, the use of solar energy—can be utilized. The outlook can also be mitigated by redirecting output away from heat-creating material outputs into the production of "services" that add only trivially to heat.

All these considerations make the designation of a timetable for industrial deceleration difficult to construct. Yet, under any and all assumptions, one irrefutable conclusion remains. The industrial growth process, so central to the economic and social life of capitalism and Western socialism alike, will be forced to slow down, in all likelihood within a generation or two, and will probably have to give way to decline thereafter. To repeat the words of the text, "whether we are unable to sustain growth or unable to tolerate it," the long era of industrial expansion is now entering its final stages, and we must anticipate the commencement of a new era of stationary total output and (if population growth continues or an equitable sharing among nations has not yet been attained) declining material output per head in the advanced nations.

These challenges also point to a certain time frame within which different aspects of the human prospect will assume different levels of importance. In the short run, by which we may speak of the decade immediately ahead, no doubt the most pressing questions will be those of the use and abuse of national power, the vicissitudes of the narrative of political history, perhaps the short-run vagaries of the economic process, about which we have virtually no predictive capability whatsoever. From our vantage point today, another crisis in the Middle East, further Vietnams or Czechoslovakias, inflation, severe economic malfunction—or their avoidance—are sure to exercise the primary influence over the quality of existence, or even over the possibilities for existence.

In a somewhat longer time frame—extending perhaps for a period of a half century—the main shaping force of the future takes on a different aspect. Assuming that the day-to-day, year-to-year crises are surmounted in relative safety, the issue of the relative resilience and adaptive capabilities of the two great socio-economic systems comes to the fore as the decisive question. Here the properties of industrial socialism and capitalism as ideal types seem likely to provide the parameters within which and by which the prospect for man will be formed. We have already indicated what general tendencies seem characteristic of each of these systems, and the advantages that may accrue to socialist—that is, planned and probably authoritarian social orders—during this era of adjustment.

In the long run, stretching a century or more ahead, still a different facet of the human prospect appears critical. This is the transformational problem, centered in the reconstruction of the material basis of civilization itself. In this period, as indefinite in its boundaries but as unmistakable in its mighty dimensions as a vast storm visible on the horizon, the challenge devolves upon those deep-lying capabilities for political change whose roots in "human nature" have been the subject of our last chapter.

It is the challenges of the middle and the long run that command our attention when we speculate about the human prospect, if only because those of the short run defy our prognostic grasp entirely. It seems unnecessary to add more than a word to underline the magnitude of these still distant problems. No developing country has fully confronted the implications of becoming a "modern" nation-state whose industrial development must be severely limited, or considered the strategy for such a state in a world in which the Western nations, capitalist and socialist both, will continue for a long period to enjoy the material advantages of their early start. Within the advanced nations, in turn, the difficulties of adjustment are no less severe. No capitalist nation has as yet imagined the extent of the alterations it must undergo to attain a viable stationary socio-economic structure, and no socialist state has evidenced the needed willingness to subordinate its national interests to supra-national ones.

To these obstacles we must add certain elements of the political propensities in "human nature" that stand in the way of a rational, orderly adaptation of the industrial mode in the directions that will become increasingly urgent as the distant future comes closer. There seems no hope for rapid changes in the human character traits that would have to be modified to bring about a peaceful, organized reorientation of life styles. Men and women, much as they are today, will set the pace and determine the necessary means for the social changes that will eventually have to be made. The drift toward the strong exercise of political power—a movement given its initial momentum by the need to exercise a much wider and deeper administration of both production and consumption—is likely to attain added support from the psychological insecurity that will be sharpened in a period of unrest and uncertainty. The bonds of national identity are certain to exert their powerful force, mobilizing men for the collective efforts needed but inhibiting the international sharing of burdens and wealth. The myopia that confines the present vision of men to the short-term future is not likely to disappear overnight, rendering still more difficult a planned and orderly retrenchment and redivision of output.

Therefore the outlook is for what we may call "convulsive change"—change forced upon us by external events rather than by conscious choice, by catastrophe rather than by calculation. As with Malthus's much derided but all too prescient forecasts,[1] nature will provide the checks, if foresight and "morality" do not. One such check could be the outbreak of wars arising from the explosive tensions of the coming period, which might reduce the growth rates of the surviving nation-states and thereby defer the danger of industrial asphyxiation for a period. Alternatively, nature may rescue us from ourselves by what John Platt has called a "storm of crisis problems."[2] As we breach now this, now that edge of environmental tolerance, local disasters—large-scale fatal urban temperature inversions, massive crop failures, resource shortages—may also slow down economic growth and give a necessary impetus to the piecemeal construction of an ecologically and socially viable social system.

Such negative feedbacks are likely to exercise an all-important dampening effect on a crisis that would otherwise in all probability overwhelm the slender human capabilities for planned adjustment to the future. However brutal these feedbacks, they are apt to prove effective in changing our attitudes as well as our actions, unlike appeals to our collective foresight, such as the exhortations of the Club of Rome's *Limits to Growth,* or the manifesto of a group of British scientists calling for an immediate halt to growth.[3] The problem is that the challenge to survive still lies sufficiently far in the future, and the inertial momentum of the present industrial order is still so great, that no substantial voluntary diminution of growth, much less a planned reorganization of society, is today even remotely imaginable. What leader of an underdeveloped nation, particularly one caught up in the exhilaration of a revolutionary restructuring of society, would call a halt to industrial activity in his impoverished land? What capitalist or socialist nation would put a ceiling on material

[1] Thomas Malthus (1766–1834) was a British economist whose *Essay on Population* stated that population—tending to increase more rapidly than the food supply—is held in check mainly by war, famine, vice, and disease.
[2] John Platt, "What We Must Do," *Science,* Nov. 28, 1969, p. 1115. [Heilbroner's note. *Ed.*]
[3] "Blueprint for Survival," *The Ecologist,* Jan. 1972. [Heilbroner's note. *Ed.*]

output, limiting its citizens to the well-being obtainable from its present volume of production?

Thus, however admirable in intent, impassioned polemics against growth are exercises in futility today. Worse, they may even point in the wrong direction. Paradoxically, perhaps, the priorities for the present lie in the temporary encouragement of the very process of industrial advance that is ultimately the mortal enemy. In the backward areas, the acute misery that is the potential source of so much international disruption can be remedied only to the extent that rapid improvements are introduced, including that minimal infrastructure needed to support a modern system of health services, education, transportation, fertilizer production, and the like. In the developed nations, what is required at the moment is the encouragement of technical advances that will permit the extraction of new resources to replace depleted reserves of scarce minerals, new sources of energy to stave off the collapse that would occur if present energy reservoirs were exhausted before substitutes were discovered, and, above all, new techniques for the generation of energy that will minimize the associated generation of heat.

Thus there is a short period left during which we can safely continue on the present trajectory. It is possible that during this period a new direction will be struck that will greatly ease the otherwise inescapable adjustments. The underdeveloped nations, making a virtue of necessity, may redefine "development" in ways that minimize the need for the accumulation of capital, stressing instead the education and vitality of their citizens. The possibilities of such an historic step would be much enhanced were the advanced nations to lead the way by a major effort to curtail the enormous wastefulness of industrial production as it is used today. If these changes took place, we might even look forward to a still more desirable redirection of history in a diminution of scale, a reduction in the size of the human community from the dangerous level of immense nation-states toward the "polis" [4] that defined the appropriate reach of political power for the ancient Greeks.

All these are possibilities, but certainly not probabilities. The revitalization of the polis is hardly likely to take place during a period in which an orderly response to social and physical challenges will require an increase of centralized power and the encouragement of

---

[4] The ancient Greek city-state.

634   **Robert L. Heilbroner**

national rather than communal attitudes. The voluntary abandonment of the industrial mode of production would require a degree of
self-abnegation on the part of its beneficiaries—managers and consumers alike—that would be without parallel in history. The re-
definition of development on the part of the poorer nations would
require a prodigious effort of will in the face of the envy and fear that
Western industrial power and "affluence" will arouse.

Thus in all likelihood we must brace ourselves for the consequences of which we have spoken—the risk of "wars of redistribution" or of "preemptive seizure," the rise of social tensions in the
industrialized nations over the division of an ever more slow-grow-
ing or even diminishing product, and the prospect of a far more coercive exercise of national power as the means by which we will
attempt to bring these disruptive processes under control.

From that period of harsh adjustment, I can see no realistic escape.
Rationalize as we will, stretch the figures as favorably as honesty will
permit, we cannot reconcile the requirements for a lengthy continuation of the present rate of industrialization of the globe with the capacity of existing resources or the fragile biosphere to permit or to
tolerate the effects of that industrialization. Nor is it easy to foresee a
willing acquiescence of humankind, individually or through its existing social organizations, in the alterations of lifeways that foresight
would dictate. If then, by the question "Is there hope for man?" we
ask whether it is possible to meet the challenges of the future without
the payment of a fearful price, the answer must be: No, there is no
such hope.

At this final stage of our inquiry, with the full spectacle of the
human prospect before us, the spirit quails and the will falters. We
find ourselves pressed to the very limit of our personal capacities, not
alone in summoning up the courage to look squarely at the dimensions of the impending predicament, but in finding words that can
offer some plausible relief in a situation so bleak. There is now nowhere to turn other than to those private beliefs and disbeliefs that
guide each of us through life, and whose disconcerting presence was
the first problem with which we had to deal in appraising the prospect before us. I shall therefore speak my mind without any pretense
that the words I am about to write have any basis other than those
subjective promptings from which I was forced to begin and in

which I must now discover whatever consolation I can offer after the analysis to which they have driven me.

At this late juncture I have no intention of sounding a call for moral awakening or for social action on some unrealistic scale. Yet, I do not intend to condone, much less to urge, an attitude of passive resignation, or a relegation of the human prospect to the realm of things we choose not to think about. Avoidable evil remains, as it always will, an enemy that can be defeated; and the fact that the collective destiny of man portends unavoidable travail is no reason, and cannot be tolerated as an excuse, for doing nothing. This general admonition applies in particular to the intellectual elements of Western nations whose privileged role as sentries for society takes on a special importance in the face of things as we now see them. It is their task not only to prepare their fellow citizens for the sacrifices that will be required of them but to take the lead in seeking to redefine the legitimate boundaries of power and the permissible sanctuaries of freedom, for a future in which the exercise of power must inevitably increase and many present areas of freedom, especially in economic life, be curtailed.

Let me therefore put these last words in a somewhat more "positive" frame, offsetting to some degree the bleakness of our prospect, without violating the facts or spirit of our inquiry. Here I must begin by stressing for one last time an essential fact. The human prospect is not an irrevocable death sentence. It is not an inevitable doomsday toward which we are headed, although the risk of enormous catastrophes exists. The prospect is better viewed as a formidable array of challenges that must be overcome before human survival is assured, before we can move *beyond doomsday*. These challenges can be overcome—by the saving intervention of nature if not by the wisdom and foresight of man. The death sentence is therefore better viewed as a contingent life sentence—one that will permit the continuance of human society, but only on a basis very different from that of the present, and probably only after much suffering during the period of transition.

What sort of society might eventually emerge? As I have said more than once, I believe the long-term solution requires nothing less than the gradual abandonment of the lethal techniques, the uncongenial lifeways, and the dangerous mentality of industrial civilization itself. The dimensions of such a transformation into a "post-industrial" society[5] have already been touched upon, and cannot be greatly elaborated here: in all probability the extent and ramifications of change are as unforeseeable from our contemporary vantage point as present-day society would have been unimaginable to a speculative observer a thousand years ago.

Yet I think a few elements of the society of the post-industrial era can be discerned. Although we cannot know on what technical foundation it will rest, we can be certain that many of the accompaniments of an industrial order must be absent. To repeat once again what we have already said, the societal view of production and consumption must stress parsimonious, not prodigal, attitudes. Resource-consuming and heat-generating processes must be regarded as necessary evils, not as social triumphs, to be relegated to as small a portion of economic life as possible. This implies a sweeping reorganization of the mode of production in ways that cannot be foretold, but that would seem to imply the end of the giant factory, the huge office, perhaps of the urban complex.

What values and ways of thought would be congenial to such a radical reordering of things we also cannot know, but it is likely that the ethos of "science," so intimately linked with industrial application, would play a much reduced role. In the same way, it seems probable that a true post-industrial society would witness the waning of the work ethic that is also intimately entwined with our industrial society. As one critic has pointed out, even Marx, despite his bitter denunciation of the alienating effects of labor in a capitalist milieu, placed his faith in the presumed "liberating" effects of labor in a socialist society, and did not consider a "terrible secret"—that even the most creative work may be only "a neurotic activity that diverts the mind from the diminution of time and the approach of death."[6]

It is therefore possible that a post-industrial society would also turn in the direction of many pre-industrial societies—toward the exploration of inner states of experience rather than the outer world of fact and material accomplishment. Tradition and ritual, the pillars of life in virtually all societies other than those of an industrial char-

[5] Heilbroner uses the term developed by Daniel Bell in his *The Coming of Post-Industrial Society* (1973). Bell, however, meant a society in which industrial production is subordinated to theoretical knowledge.
[6] John Diggins, "Thoreau, Marx, and the Riddle of Alienation," *Social Research*, Winter 1973, p. 573. [Heilbroner's note. *Ed.*]

acter, would probably once again assert their ancient claims as the guide to and solace for life. The struggle for individual achievement, especially for material ends, is likely to give way to the acceptance of communally organized and ordained roles.

This is by no means an effort to portray a future utopia. On the contrary, many of these possible attributes of a post-industrial society are deeply repugnant to my twentieth-century temper as well as incompatible with my most treasured privileges. The search for scientific knowledge, the delight in intellectual heresy, the freedom to order one's life as one pleases, are not likely to be easily contained within the tradition-oriented, static society I have depicted. To a very great degree, the public must take precedence over the private—an aim to which it is easy to give lip service in the abstract but difficult for someone used to the pleasures of political, social, and intellectual freedom to accept in fact.

These are all necessarily prophetic speculations, offered more in the spirit of providing some vision of the future, however misty, than as a set of predictions to be "rigorously" examined. In these half-blind gropings there is, however, one element in which we can place credence, although it offers uncertainty as well as hope. This is our knowledge that some human societies have existed for millennia, and that others can probably exist for future millennia, in a continuous rhythm of birth and coming of age and death, without pressing toward those dangerous ecological limits, or engendering those dangerous social tensions, that threaten present-day "advanced" societies. In our discovery of "primitive" cultures, living out their timeless histories, we may have found the single most important object lesson for future man.

What we do not know, but can only hope, is that future man can rediscover the self-renewing vitality of primitive culture without reverting to its levels of ignorance and cruel anxiety. It may be the sad lesson of the future that no civilization is without its pervasive "malaise," each expressing in its own way the ineradicable fears of the only animal that contemplates its own death, but at least the human activities expressing that malaise need not, as is the case in our time, threaten the continuance of life itself.

All this goes, perhaps, beyond speculation to fantasy. But something more substantial than speculation or fantasy is needed to sustain men through the long trials ahead. For the driving energy of modern man has come from his Promethean spirit,[7] his nervous will, his intellectual daring. It is this spirit that has enabled him to work miracles, above all to subjugate nature to his will, and to create societies designed to free man from his animal bondage.

Some of that Promethean spirit may still serve us in good stead in the years of transition. But it is not a spirit that conforms easily with the shape of future society as I have imagined it; worse, within that impatient spirit lurks one final danger for the years during which we must watch the approach of an unwanted future. This is the danger that can be glimpsed in our deep consciousness when we take stock of things as they now are: the wish that the drama run its full tragic course, bringing man, like a Greek hero, to the fearful end that he has, however unwittingly, arranged for himself. For it is not only with dismay that Promethean man regards the future. It is also with a kind of anger. If, after so much effort, so little has been accomplished; if, before such vast challenges, so little is apt to be done—then let the drama proceed to its finale, let mankind suffer the end it deserves.

Such a view is by no means the expression of only a few perverse minds. On the contrary, it is the application to the future of the prevailing attitudes with which our age regards the present. When men can generally acquiesce in, even relish, the destruction of their living contemporaries, when they can regard with indifference or irritation the fate of those who live in slums, rot in prison, or starve in lands that have meaning only insofar as they are vacation resorts, why should they be expected to take the painful actions needed to prevent the destruction of future generations whose faces they will never live to see? Worse yet, will they not curse these future generations whose claims to life can be honored only by sacrificing present enjoyments; and will they not, if it comes to a choice, condemn them to nonexistence by choosing the present over the future?

The question, then, is how we are to summon up the will to survive—not perhaps in the distant future, where survival will call on those deep sources of imagined human unity, but in the present and near-term future, while we still enjoy and struggle with the heritage of our personal liberties, our atomistic existences.

---

[7] In the ancient Greek religion, Prometheus was a Titan (god), who, against the will of supreme Zeus, stole fire from heaven and showed humans its many uses. Although he was cruelly punished for his offense, Prometheus has come to represent the boldly original and creative spirit.

At this last moment of reflection another figure from Greek mythology comes to mind. It is that of Atlas, bearing with endless perseverance the weight of the heavens in his hands.[8] If mankind is to rescue life, it must first preserve the very will to live, and thereby rescue the future from the angry condemnation of the present. The spirit of conquest and aspiration will not provide the inspiration it needs for this task. It is the example of Atlas, resolutely bearing his burden, that provides the strength we seek. If, within us, the spirit of Atlas falters, there perishes the determination to preserve humanity at all cost and any cost, forever.

But Atlas is, of course, no other but ourselves. Myths have their magic power because they cast on the screen of our imaginations, like the figures of the heavenly constellations, immense projections of our own hopes and capabilities. We do not know with certainty that humanity will survive, but it is a comfort to know that there exist within us the elements of fortitude and will from which the image of Atlas springs.

---

[8] Atlas, brother of Prometheus, was compelled by Zeus to support the heavens on his head and untiring hands.

44

Alvin Toffler

Future Shock

In addition to the cheerful optimists and gloomy doomsayers who survey the future, there are those who focus primarily on the process *by which society will arrive at that uncertain circumstance. Prominent among them is Alvin Toffler (1928–   ), a writer who considers the now constantly accelerating rate of social change to be the critical new experience of the present age. Since people are not infinitely adaptable, Toffler maintains, they are not able to cope with the rapid and continuous changes forced upon them in modern life. Thus they suffer from what he calls "future shock"—a psychic disorientation caused by premature arrival of the future.*

Toffler was born in New York City to immigrants from Poland. Aspiring to be a writer, he majored in English literature at New York University and in 1949 received a bachelor's degree. He then spent about twelve years as— successively—laborer, Army private, editor of various industry and labor journals, free-lance magazine writer, and labor columnist for Fortune *magazine. An article Toffler wrote for* Fortune *on the rise of mass interest in the arts became the seed of his first book,* The Culture Consumers *(1964). In that book he documented the explosion of general interest and participation in the arts—and their financial plight. His recommendations for greater state and private support of artistic efforts had some measurable results.*

Toffler coined the term "future shock" in a magazine article written in 1965. His book Future Shock, *a fuller study of severe stress due to the constant changes of contemporary culture, was published in 1970. The following selection is the first half of a condensation of the book that appeared in*

From *Future Shock* by Alvin Toffler. Copyright © 1970 by Alvin Toffler. Reprinted by permission of Random House, Inc. Originally appeared in *Playboy* in a slightly different form. [Pp. 94, 97–98, 202–204, 206, 208 in February, 1970 *Playboy*.]

Playboy magazine in February and March 1970. In the book's introduction Toffler clearly states his principal aims: "to help us cope more effectively with both personal and social change by deepening our understanding of how men respond to it; . . . to show that the rate of change has implications . . . more important than the directions of change; . . . and . . . to increase the future-consciousness" of the reader.

In The Eco-Spasm Report *(1975), Toffler continues his exploration of the inadequacy of traditional policies in dealing with the rapidly arriving future. He describes current economic upheavals as "the breakdown of industrial civilization . . . and the first fragmentary appearance of a wholly new and drastically different social order."*

In the three short decades between now and the turn of the next millennium, millions of psychologically normal people will experience an abrupt collision with the future. Affluent, educated citizens of the world's richest and most technically advanced nations, they will fall victim to tomorrow's most menacing malady: the disease of change. Unable to keep up with the supercharged pace of change brought to the edge of breakdown by incessant demands to adapt to novelty, many will plunge into future shock. For them, the future will have arrived too soon.

Future shock is more than an arresting phrase. It may prove to be the most obstinate and debilitating social problem of the future. Its symptoms range from confusion, anxiety and hostility to helpful authority, to physical illness, seemingly senseless violence and self-destructive apathy. Future-shock victims manifest erratic swings in interest and life style, followed by a panicky sense that events are slipping out of their control and, later, a desperate effort to "crawl into their shells" through social, intellectual and emotional withdrawal. They feel continuously harassed and attempt to reduce the number of changes with which they must cope, the number of decisions they must make. The ultimate casualties of future shock terminate by cutting off the outside world entirely—dropping out, spiraling deeper and deeper into disengagement.

In the decades immediately ahead, we face a torrent of change—in our jobs, our families, our sexual standards, our art, our politics, our values. This means that millions of us, ill prepared by either past experience or education, will be forced to make repeated, often painful adaptations. Some of us will be simply unable to function in this social flux and, unless we learn to treat—or prevent—future shock, we shall witness an intensification of the mass neurosis, irrationalism and violence already tearing at today's change-wracked society.

The quickest way to grasp the idea of future shock is to begin with a parallel term—culture shock—that has begun to creep from anthropology texts into the popular language. Culture shock is the queasy physical and mental state produced in an unprepared person who is suddenly immersed in an alien culture. Peace Corps volunteers suffer from it in Ethiopia or Ecuador. Marco Polo probably suffered from it in Cathay. Culture shock is what happens when a traveler suddenly finds himself surrounded by newness, cut off from meaning—when, because of a shift of culture, a yes may mean no, when to slap a man's back in friendly camaraderie may be to offer a mortal insult, when laughter may signify not joy but fury. Culture shock is the bewilderment and distress—sometimes culminating in blind fury or bone-deep apathy—triggered by the removal of the familiar psychological cues on which all of us must depend for survival.

The culture-shock phenomenon accounts for much of the frustration and disorientation that plague Americans in their dealings with other societies. It causes a breakdown in communication, a misreading of reality, an inability to cope. Yet culture shock is relatively mild in comparison with future shock. This malady will not be found in *Index Medicus* or in any listing of psychological abnormalities. Yet, unless intelligent steps are taken to combat it, millions of human beings will find themselves increasingly incompetent to deal rationally with their environments. A product of the greatly accelerated rate of change in society, future shock arises from the superimposition of a new culture on an old one. It is culture shock in one's own society. But its impact is far worse. For most Peace Corps men—in fact, most travelers—have the comforting knowledge that the culture they left behind will be there to return to. The victim of future shock does not.

Take an individual out of his own culture and set him down suddenly in an environment sharply different from his own, with a wholly novel set of cues to react to, different conceptions of time, space, work, love, religion, sex and everything else; then cut him off from any hope of retreat to a more familiar social landscape and the dislocation he suffers is doubly severe. Moreover, if this new culture is itself rife with change, and if, moreover, its values are incessantly changing, the sense of disorientation will be even further intensified. Given few clues as to what kind of behavior is rational under the radically new circumstances, the victim may well become a hazard to himself and others. Now, imagine not merely an individual but an entire society, an entire generation—including its weakest, least intelligent and most irrational members—suddenly transported into this new world. The result is mass disorientation, future shock on a grand scale.

This is the prospect man now faces. For a new society—superindustrial, fast-paced, fragmented, filled with bizarre styles, customs and choices—is erupting in our midst. An alien culture is swiftly displacing the one in which most of us have our roots. Change is avalanching upon our heads, and most people are unprepared to cope with it. Man is not infinitely adaptable, no matter what the romantics or mystics may say. We are biological organisms with only so much resilience, only a limited ability to absorb the physiological and mental punishment inherent in change. In the past, when the pace of change was leisurely, the substitution of one culture for another tended to stretch over centuries. Today, we experience a millennium of change in a few brief decades. Time is compressed. This means that the emergent superindustrial society will, itself, be swept away in the tidal wave of change—even before we have learned to cope adequately with it. In certain quarters, the rate of change is already blinding. Yet there are powerful reasons to believe that we are only at the beginning of the accelerative curve. History itself is speeding up.

This startling statement can be illustrated in a number of ways. It has been observed, for example, that if the past 50,000 years of man's existence were divided into lifetimes of approximately 62 years each, there have been about 800 such lifetimes. Of these 800, fully 650 were spent in caves. Only during the past 70 lifetimes has it been possible to communicate effectively from one lifetime to another—as writing made it possible to do. Only during the past six lifetimes have masses of men ever seen a printed word. Only during the past four has it been possible to measure time with any precision. Only in the past two has anyone anywhere used an electric motor. And the overwhelming majority of all the material goods we use in daily life today have been developed within the present, the 800th, lifetime.

Painting with the broadest of brush strokes, biologist Sir Julian Huxley informs us that "The tempo of human evolution during recorded history is at least 100,000 times as rapid as that of prehuman evolution." Inventions or improvements of a magnitude that took perhaps 50,000 years to accomplish during the early Paleolithic era were, he says, "run through in a mere millennium toward its close; and with the advent of settled civilization, the unit of change soon became reduced to the century." The rate of change, accelerating throughout the past 5000 years, has become, in his words, "particularly noticeable during the past 300 years." Indeed, says social psychologist Warren Bennis, the throttle has been pushed so far forward in recent years that "No exaggeration, no hyperbole, no outrage can realistically describe the extent and pace of change. . . . In fact, only the exaggerations appear to be true."

What changes justify such supercharged language? Let us look at a few—changes in the process by which man forms cities, for example. We are now undergoing the most extensive and rapid urbanization the world has ever seen. In 1850, only four cities on the face of the earth had a population of 1,000,000 or more. By 1900, the number had increased to 19. But by 1960, there were 141; and today, world urban population is rocketing upward at a rate of 6.5 percent per year, according to Egbert de Vries and J. T. Thijsse of the Institute of Social Studies in The Hague. This single stark statistic means a doubling of the earth's urban population within 11 years.

One way to grasp the meaning of change on so phenomenal a scale is to imagine what would happen if all existing cities, instead of expanding, retained their present size. If this were so, in order to accommodate the new urban millions, we would have to build a duplicate city for each of the hundreds that already dot the globe. A new Tokyo, a new Hamburg, a new Rome and Rangoon—and all within 11 years. This explains why Buckminster Fuller has proposed building whole cities in shipyards and towing them to coastal moorings adjacent to big cities. It explains why builders talk more and more about "instant" architecture—an "instant factory" to spring up here, an "instant campus" to be constructed there. It is why French urban planners are sketching subterranean cities—stores, museums, warehouses and factories to be built under the earth—and why a Japanese architect has blueprinted a city to be built on stilts out over the ocean.

The same accelerative tendency is instantly apparent in man's consumption of energy. Dr. Homi Bhabha, the late Indian atomic scientist, once analyzed this trend. "To illustrate," he said, "let us use the letter Q to stand for the energy derived from burning some 33 billion tons of coal. In the 18½ centuries after Christ, the total energy consumed averaged less than ½ Q per century. But by 1850, the rate had risen to one Q per century. Today, the rate is about 10 Q per century." This means, roughly speaking, that half of all the energy consumed by man in the past 2000 years has been consumed in the past 100.

Also dramatically evident is the acceleration of economic growth in the nations now racing toward superindustrialism. Despite the fact that they start from a large industrial base, the annual percentage increases in production in these countries are formidable. And the rate of increase is itself increasing. In France, for example, in the 29 years between 1910 and the outbreak of World War Two, industrial production rose only five percent. Yet between 1948 and 1965, in only 17 years, it increased by more than 220 percent. Today, growth rates of from 5 to 10 percent per year are not uncommon among the most industrialized nations. Thus, for the 21 countries belonging to the Organization for Economic Cooperation and Development—by and large, the "have" nations—the average annual rate of increase in gross national product in the years 1960–1968 ran between 4.5 and 5 percent. The U.S., despite a series of ups and downs, grew at a rate of 4.5 percent, and Japan led the rest with annual increases averaging 9.8 percent.

What such numbers imply is nothing less revolutionary than a doubling of the total output of goods and services in the advanced societies about every 15 years—and the doubling times are shrinking. This means that the child reaching his teens in any of these societies is literally surrounded by twice as much of everything newly man-made as his parents were at the time he was an infant. It means that by the time today's teenager reaches the age of 30, perhaps earlier, a second doubling will have occurred. Within a 70-year lifetime, perhaps five such doublings will take place—meaning, since the increases are compounded, that by the time the individual reaches old age, the society around him will be producing 32 times as much as when he was born. Such changes in the ratio between old and new have, as we shall show, an electric impact on the habits, beliefs and self-images of millions. Never in history has this ratio been transformed so radically in so brief a flick of time.

Behind such prodigious economic facts lies that great, growling engine of change—technology. This is not to say that technology is the only source of change in society. Social upheavals can be touched off by a change in the chemical composition of the atmosphere, by alterations in climate, by changes in fertility and many other factors. Yet technology is indisputably a major force behind the accelerative thrust. To most people, the term technology conjures up images of smoky steel mills and clanking machines. Perhaps the classic symbol of technology is still the assembly line created by Henry Ford half a century ago and transformed into a potent social icon by Charlie Chaplin in *Modern Times*.* This symbol, however, has always been inadequate—indeed, misleading—for technology has always been more than factories and machines. The invention of the horse collar in the Middle Ages led to major changes in agricultural methods and was as much a technological advance as the invention of the Bessemer furnace centuries later. Moreover, technology includes techniques as well as the machines that may or may not be necessary to apply them. It includes ways to make chemical reactions occur, ways to breed fish, plant forests, light theaters, count votes or teach history.

The old symbols of technology are even more misleading today, when the most advanced technological processes are carried out far from assembly lines or open hearths. Indeed, in electronics, in space technology, in most of the new industries, relative silence and clean surroundings are characteristic—sometimes even essential. And the assembly line—the organization of armies of men to carry out simple repetitive functions—is an anachronism. It is time for our symbols of technology to change—to catch up with the fantastic changes in technology itself.

This acceleration is graphically dramatized by a thumbnail account of the progress in transportation. It has been pointed out, for example, that in 6000 B.C. the fastest transportation over long distances available to man was the camel caravan, averaging eight miles per hour. It was not until about 3000 B.C., when the chariot was in-

---

*A classic cinematic satire of the demands placed upon workers by the organization and machinery of the factory system. Chaplin (1889–1977) was the director and comic star of the film.

vented, that the maximum speed was raised to roughly 20 mph. So impressive was this invention, so difficult was it to exceed this speed limit that nearly 5000 years later, when the first mail coach began operating in England in 1784, it averaged a mere ten mph. The first steam locomotive, introduced in 1825, could muster a top speed of only 13 mph, and the great sailing ships of the time labored along at less than half that speed. It was probably not until the 1880s that man, with the help of a more advanced steam locomotive, managed to reach a speed of 100 mph. It took the human race millions of years to attain that record. It took only 50 years, however, to quadruple the limit; so that by 1931, airborne man was cracking the 400-mph line. It took a mere 20 years to double the limit again. And by the 1960s, rocket planes approached speeds of 4000 mph and men in space capsules were circling the earth at 18,000 mph. Plotted on a graph, the line representing progress in the past generation would leap vertically off the page.

Whether we examine distances traveled, altitudes reached, minerals mined or explosive power harnessed, the same accelerative trend is obvious. The pattern, here and in a thousand other statistical series, is absolutely clear and unmistakable. Millenniums or centuries go by, and then, in our own times, a sudden bursting of the limits, a fantastic spurt forward. The reason for this is that technology feeds on itself. Technology makes more technology possible, as we can see if we look for a moment at the process of innovation. Technological innovation consists of three stages, linked together into a self-reinforcing cycle. First, there is the creative, feasible idea. Second, its practical application. Third, its diffusion through society. The process is completed, the loop closed, when the diffusion of technology embodying the new idea, in turn, helps generate new creative ideas. There is evidence now that the time between each of the steps in this cycle has been shortened.

It is not merely true, as frequently noted, that 90 percent of all the scientists who ever lived are now alive and that new scientific discoveries are being made every day. These new ideas are put to work much more quickly than ever before. The time between original concept and practical use has been radically reduced. This is a striking difference between ourselves and our ancestors. Apollonius of Perga discovered conic sections, but it was 2000 years before they were applied to engineering problems. It was literally centuries between the time Paracelsus discovered that ether could be used as an anesthetic and the time it began to be used for that purpose. Even in more recent times, the same pattern of delay prevailed. In 1836, a machine was invented that mowed, threshed, tied straw into sheaves and poured grain into sacks. This machine was itself based on technology at least 20 years old at the time. Yet it was not until a century later, in the 1930s, that such a combine was actually marketed. The first English patent for a typewriter was issued in 1714. But a century and a half elapsed before typewriters became commercially available. A full century passed between the time Nicolas Appert discovered how to can food and the time when canning became important in the food industry.

Such delays between idea and application are almost unthinkable today. It isn't that we are more eager or less lazy than our ancestors, but that, with the passage of time, we have invented all sorts of social devices to hasten the process. We find that the time between the first and second stages of the innovative cycle—between idea and application—has been radically shortened. Frank Lynn, for example, in studying 20 major innovations, such as frozen food, antibiotics, integrated circuits and synthetic leather, found that since the beginning of this century, more than 60 percent has been slashed from the average time needed for a major scientific discovery to be translated into a useful technological form. William O. Baker, vice-president of Bell Laboratories, itself the hatchery of such innovations as sound movies, computers, transistors and Telstar, underscores the narrowing gap between invention and application by noting that while it took 65 years for the electric motor to be applied, 33 years for the vacuum tube and 18 years for the X-ray tube, it took only 10 for the nuclear reactor, 5 for radar and only 3 for the transistor and the solar battery. A vast and growing research-and-development industry is working now to reduce the lag still further.

If it takes less time to bring a new idea to the market place, it also takes less time for it to sweep through society. The interval between the second and third stages of the cycle—between application and diffusion—has likewise been cut, and the pace of diffusion is rising with astonishing speed. This is borne out by the history of several familiar household appliances. Robert A. Young, at the Stanford Research Institute, has studied the span of time between the first commercial appearance of a new electrical appliance and the time the industry manufacturing it reaches peak production of the item. He found that for a group of appliances introduced in the United States before 1920—including the vacuum cleaner, the electric range and the refrigerator—the average span between introduction and peak production was 34 years. But for a group that appeared in the 1939–1959 period—including the electric frying pan, television and the washer-dryer combination—the span was only eight years. The lag had shrunk by more than 76 percent.

The stepped-up pace of invention, exploitation and diffusion, in turn, accelerates the whole cycle even further. For new machines or techniques are not merely a product, but a source, of fresh creative ideas. Each new machine or technique, in a sense, changes all existing machines and techniques, by permitting us to put them together into new combinations. The number of possible combinations rises exponentially as the number of new machines or techniques rises arithmetically. Indeed, each new combination may, itself, be regarded as a new supermachine. The computer, for example, made possible a sophisticated space effort. Linked with sensing devices, communications equipment and power sources, the computer became part of a configuration that, in aggregate, forms a single new supermachine—a machine for reaching into and probing outer space. But for machines or techniques to be combined in new ways, they have to be altered, adapted, refined or otherwise changed. So that the very effort to integrate machines into supermachines compels us to make still further technological innovations.

It is vital to understand, moreover, that technological innovation does not merely combine and recombine machines and techniques. Important new machines do more than suggest or compel changes in other machines—they suggest novel solutions to social, philosophical, even personal problems. They alter man's total intellectual environment, the way he thinks and looks at the world. We all learn from our environment, scanning it constantly—though perhaps unconsciously—for models to emulate. These models are not only other people. They are, increasingly, machines. By their presence, we are subtly conditioned to think along certain lines. It has been observed, for example, that the clock came along before the Newtonian image of the world as a great clocklike mechanism, a philosophical notion that has had the utmost impact on man's intellectual development. Implied in this image of the cosmos as a great clock were ideas about cause and effect and about the importance of external, as against internal, stimuli that shape the everyday behavior of all of us today. The clock also affected our conception of time, so that the idea that a day is divided into 24 equal segments of 60 minutes each has become almost literally a part of us.

Recently the computer has touched off a storm of fresh ideas about man as an interacting part of larger systems, about his physiology, the way he learns, the way he remembers, the way he makes decisions. Virtually every intellectual discipline, from political science to family psychology, has been hit by a wave of imaginative hypotheses triggered by the invention and diffusion of the computer—and its full impact has not yet struck. And so the innovative cycle, feeding on itself, speeds up.

If technology, however, is to be regarded as a great engine, a mighty accelerator, then knowledge must be regarded as its fuel. And we thus come to the crux of the accelerative process in society. For the engine is being fed a richer and richer fuel every day.

The rate at which man has been storing up useful knowledge about himself and the universe has been spiraling upward for 10,000 years. That rate took a sharp leap with the invention of writing; but even so, it remained painfully slow over centuries of time. The next great leap in knowledge acquisition did not occur until the invention of movable type in the 15th Century by Gutenberg and others. Prior to 1500, by the most optimistic estimates, Europe was producing books at a rate of 1000 titles per year. This means that it would take a full century to produce a library of 100,000 titles. By 1950, four and a half centuries later, the rate had accelerated so sharply that Europe was producing 120,000 titles a year. What once took a century now took only ten months. By 1960, a single decade later, that awesome rate of publication had made another significant jump, so that a century's work could be completed in seven and a half months. And by the mid-Sixties, the output of books on a world scale approached the prodigious figure of 1000 titles per *day*.

One can hardly argue that every book is a net gain for the advancement of knowledge, but we find that the accelerative curve in book publication does, in fact, roughly parallel the rate at which man has discovered new knowledge. Prior to Gutenberg, for example, only 11 chemical elements were known. Antimony, the 12th, was discovered about the time he was working on the printing press. It had been fully 200 years since the 11th, arsenic, had been discovered. Had the same rate of discovery continued, we would by now have added only two or three additional elements to the periodic table since Gutenberg. Instead, in the 500 years after his time, 73 additional elements were discovered. And since 1900, we have been isolating the remaining elements at a rate not of one every two centuries but of one every three years.

Furthermore, there is reason to believe that the rate is still rising sharply. The number of scientific journals and articles and the number of known chemical compounds are both doubling about every 15 years, like industrial production in the advanced countries. The doubling time for the number of asteroids known, the literature on non–Euclidean geometry, on experimental psychology and on the theory of determinants is only ten years. According to biochemist Philip Siekevitz, "What has been learned in the last three decades about the nature of living beings dwarfs in extent of knowledge any comparable period of scientific discovery in the history of mankind." The U.S. Government alone generates over 300,000 reports each year, plus 450,000 articles, books and papers. On a world-wide basis, scientific and technical literature mounts at a rate of some 60,000,000 pages a year.

The computer burst upon the scene around 1950. With its unprecedented power for analysis and dissemination of extremely varied kinds of data in unbelievable quantities and at mind-staggering speeds, it has become a major force behind the latest acceleration in knowledge acquisition. Combined with other increasingly powerful analytical tools for observing the invisible universe around us, it has raised the rate of knowledge acquisition to dumfounding speeds.

Francis Bacon told us that knowledge is power. This can now be translated into contemporary terms. In our social setting, knowledge is change—and accelerating knowledge acquisition, fueling the great engine of technology, means accelerating change.

Discovery. Application. Impact. Discovery. We see here a chain reaction of change, a long, sharply rising curve of acceleration in human social development. This accelerative thrust has now reached a level at which it can no longer, by any stretch of the imagination, be regarded as "normal." The established institutions of industrial society can no longer contain it, and its impact is shaking up all our social institutions. Acceleration is one of the most important and least understood of all social forces.

This, however, is only half the story. For the speed-up of change is more than a social force. It is a *psychological* force as well. Although it has been almost totally ignored by psychologists and psychiatrists, the rising rate of change in the world around us disturbs our inner equilibrium, alters the very way in which we experience life. The pace of life is speeding up.

Most of us, without stopping to think too deeply about it, sense this quickening of the pace of events. For it is not just a matter of explosive headlines, world crises and distant technological triumphs. The new pace of change penetrates our personal lives as well. No matter where we are, even the *sounds* of change are there. Cranes and concrete mixers keep up an angry clatter on the Champs Elysées and on Connecticut Avenue. I happen to live in mid-Manhattan, where the noise level created by traffic and the incessant jackhammering is virtually intolerable. Recently, to escape the frenetic pace of New York and do some writing, I flew to a remote beach in Venezuela. At the crack of dawn on the first morning after arrival, I was awakened by the familiar sound of a jackhammer: The hotel was building an addition.

Other symptoms of change abound. In a 17th Century convent in a suburb of Paris, I walked through a long, sun-dappled cloister, up several flights of rickety wooden stairs, in a mood of silent reverie— until I turned a corner and found the man I had come to see: a Berkeley-trained operations researcher with a desktop computer, busy studying long-range change in the French education system and economy. In Amsterdam and Rotterdam, streets built only five years ago are already ridiculously narrow; no one anticipated the rapidity with which automobiles would proliferate. As I can attest from unpleasant personal experience, change is also present in the form of bumper-to-boot traffic hang-ups on Stockholm's once-peaceful Strandvägen. And in Japan, the pace is so swift that an American economist says wryly: "Stepping off a plane in San Francisco after arriving from Tokyo gives one the feeling of having returned to the 'unchanging West.' "

In Aldous Huxley's *Point Counter-Point,* Lucy Tantamount declared that "Living modernly is living quickly." She should have been here now. Eating, once a leisurely semisocial affair, has become for millions a gulp-and-go proposition, and an enormous "fast-food" industry has arisen to purvey doughnuts, hamburgers, French fries, milk shakes, *tacos* and hot dogs, not to mention machine-vended hot soup, sandwiches, packaged pies and a variety of other quasi-edibles intended to be downed in a hurry. The critic Russell Lynes once attended a convention of fast-food executives. "I am not quite sure," he wrote, "whether the fast-food industry gets its name from the speed with which the food is prepared, served and eaten, or on the other hand, from the fact that it is consumed by feeders of all ages on the run and, quite literally, on the wing." It was significant, he observed, that the convention was jointly held with a group of motelkeepers, whose prime passion in life is to keep the rest of us moving around.

As the pace accelerates, we seem to be always en route, never at our destination. The search for a place to stop, at least temporarily, is unwittingly symbolized by our increasingly hectic pursuit of that vanishing commodity—a parking place. As the number of autos grows and the number of places diminishes, so, too, does the allowable parking time. In New York and other major cities, what used to be one-hour meters have been converted to half-hour or 15-minute meters. The world awaits that crowning innovation: the 30-second parking slot. On the other hand, we may be bypassing that stage altogether by simply multiplying those disquieting signs that say NO STANDING.

Unconsciously, through exposure to a thousand such situations, we are conditioned to move faster, to interact more rapidly with other people, to expect things to happen sooner. When they don't, we are upset. Thus, economist W. Allan Beckett of Toronto recently testified before the Canadian Transport Commission that the country needed faster telephone service. Sophisticated young people, he declared, would not be willing to wait six seconds for a dial tone if it were technically possible to provide it in three.

* * *

Much of this might sound like subjective grousing based on impressionistic evidence—except that such facts fall into a vigorously definable, scientifically verifiable and historically significant pattern. They add up to a powerful trend toward transience in the culture: and unless this is understood, we cannot make sense of the contemporary world. Indeed, trying to comprehend the politics, economics, art or psychology of the present—let alone of the future—without the concept of transience is as futile as trying to write the history of the Middle Ages without mentioning religion.

If acceleration has become a primal social force in our time, transience, its cultural concomitant, has become a primal psychological force. The speed-up of change introduces a shaky sense of impermanence into our lives, a quality of transience that will grow more and more intense in the years ahead. Change is now occurring so rapidly that things, places, people, organizations, ideas all pass through our lives at a faster clip than ever before. Each individual's relationships with the world outside himself become foreshortened, compressed. They become transient. The throwaway product, the nonreturnable bottle, the paper dress, the modular building, the temporary structure, the portable playground, the inflatable command post are all examples of *things* designed for short-term, transient purposes, and they require a whole new set of psychological responses from man. In slower-moving societies, man's relationships were more durable. The farmer bought a mule or a horse, worked it for years, then put it out to pasture. The relationship between man and beast spanned a great many years. Industrial-era man bought a car, instead, and kept it for several years. Superindustrial man, living at the new accelerated pace, generally keeps his car a shorter period before turning it in for a new one, and some never buy a car at all, preferring the even shorter-term relationships made possible by leases and rentals.

Our links with *place* are also growing more transient. It is not simply that more of us travel more than ever before, by car, by jet and by boat, but more of us actually change our place of residence as well. In the United States each year, some 36,000,000 people change homes. This migration dwarfs all historical precedent, including the surge of the Mongol hordes across the Asian steppes. It also detonates a host of "micro-changes" in the society, contributing to the sense of transience and uncertainty. Example: Of the 885,000 listings in the Washington, D.C., telephone book in 1969, over half were different from the year before. Under the impact of this highly accelerated nomadism, all sorts of once-durable ties are cut short. Nothing stays put—especially us.

Most of us today meet more people in the course of a few months than a feudal serf did in his lifetime. This implies a faster *turnover* of people in our lives and, correspondingly, shorter-term relationships. We make and break ties with people at a pace that would have astonished our ancestors. This raises all kinds of profound questions about personal commitment and involvement, the quality of friendship, the ability of humans to communicate with one another, the function of education, even of sex, in the future. Yet this extremely significant shift from longer to shorter interpersonal ties is only part of the larger, more encompassing movement toward high-transience society.

This movement can also be illustrated by changes in our great corporations and bureaucracies. Just as we have begun to make temporary products, we are also creating temporary *organizations*. This explains the incredible proliferation of *ad hoc* committees, task forces and project teams. Every large bureaucracy today is increasingly honeycombed with such transient organizational cells that require, among other things, that people migrate from department to department, and from task to task, at ever faster rates. We see, in most large organizations, a frenetic, restless shuffling of people. The rise of temporary organizations may spell the death of traditional bureaucracy. It points toward a new type of organization in the future—one I call Ad-Hocracy. At the same time, it intensifies, or hastens, the foreshortening of human ties.

Finally, the powerful push toward a society based on transience can be seen in the impermanence of knowledge—the accelerating pace at which scientific notions, political ideologies, values and life-organizing concepts are turning over. This is, in part, based on the heavier loads of information transmitted to us by the communications media. In the U.S. today, the median time spent by adults reading newspapers is 52 minutes per day. The same person who commits nearly an hour to the newspaper also spends some time reading other things as well—magazines, books, signs, billboards, recipes, instructions, etc. Surrounded by print, he "ingests" between 10,000 and 20,000 edited words per day of the several times that many to which he is exposed. The same person also probably spends an hour and a quarter per day listening to the radio—more if he owns an FM set. If he listens to news, commercials, commentary or other such programs, he will, during this period, hear about 11,000 preprocessed words. He also spends several hours watching television—add another 10,000 words or so, plus a sequence of carefully arranged, highly purposive visuals.

Nothing, indeed, is quite so purposive as advertising, and the average American adult today is assaulted by a minimum of 560 advertising messages each day. The verbal and visual bombardment of advertising is so great that of the 560 to which he is exposed, he notices only 76. In effect, he blocks out 484 advertising messages a day to preserve his attention for other matters. All this represents the press of engineered messages against his nervous system, and the pressure is rising, for there is evidence that we are today tampering with our communications machinery in an effort to transmit even richer image-producing messages at an even faster rate. Communications people, artists and others are consciously working to make each instant of exposure to the mass media carry a heavier informational and emotional freight.

In this maelstrom of information, the certainties of last night become the ludicrous nonsense of this morning and the individual is forced to learn and relearn, to organize and reorganize the images that help him comprehend reality and function in it. The trend toward telescoped ties with things, places, people and organizations is matched by an accelerated turnover of information.

What emerges, therefore, are two interlinked trends, two driving forces of history: first, the acceleration of change itself: and, second, its cultural and psychological concomitant, transience. Together, they create a new ephemeralized environment for man—a high-transience society. Fascinating, febrile but, above all, fast, this society is racing toward future shock.

One of the astonishing, as-yet-unpublicized findings of medical research, for example, bears directly on the link-up between change and illness. Research conducted at the University of Washington Medical School, at the U.S. Navy Neuropsychiatric Unit at San Diego, as well as in Japan, Europe and elsewhere, documents the disturbing fact that individuals who experience a great deal of change in their lives are more prone to illness—and the more radical and swift the changes, the more serious the illness. These studies suggest strongly that we cannot increase the rate at which we make and break our relationships with the environment without producing marked physiological changes in the human animal.

This is, of course, no argument against change. "There are worse things than illness," Dr. Thomas Holmes, a leader in life-change research, reminds us, dryly. Yet the notion that change can be endlessly accelerated without harm to the individual is sharply challenged by the work of Holmes and many others. There are distinct limits to the speed with which man can respond to environmental change.

These limits, moreover, are psychological as well as physiological. The neural and hormonal responses touched off in the human body when it is forced to adapt to change may well be accompanied by a deterioration of mental functioning as well. Research findings in experimental psychology, in communications theory, in management science, in human-factors engineering and in space biology all point to the conclusion that man's ability to make sound decisions—to adapt—collapses when the rate at which he must make them is too fast. Whether driving a car, steering a space capsule or solving intellectual problems, we operate most efficiently within a certain range of response speeds. When we are insufficiently stimulated by change, we grow bored and our performance deteriorates. But, by the same token, when the rate of responses demanded of us becomes too high, we also break down.

Thus we see people who, living in the midst of the most turbulent change, blindly deny its existence. We meet the world-weary executive who smiles patronizingly at his son and mouths nonsense to the effect that nothing ever really changes. Such people derive comfort from the misleading notions that history repeats itself or that young people were always rebellious. Focusing attention exclusively on the continuities in experience, they desperately attempt to block out evidence of discontinuities, in the unconscious hope that they will therefore not have to deal with them. Yet change, roaring through the social order, inevitably overtakes even those who blind themselves to it. Censoring reality, blocking out important warning signals from the environment, the deniers set themselves up for massive maladaptation, virtually guaranteeing that when change catches up with them, it will come not in small and manageable steps but in the form of a single overwhelming crisis.

Others respond to future shock by burrowing into a specialty—a job, a hobby, a social role—and ignoring everything else. We find the electronics engineer who tries manfully to keep in touch with the latest work in his field. But the more world strife there is, the more outbreaks there are in the ghetto, the more campuses erupt into violence, the more compulsively he focuses on servomechanisms and integrated circuits. Suffering from tunnel vision, monitoring an extremely narrow slice of reality, he becomes masterful at coping with a tightly limited range of life situations—but hopeless at everything else. Any sudden shift of the external environment poses for him the threat of total disorientation.

Yet another response to future shock is reversion to previously successful behavioral programs that are now irrelevant. The reversionist clicks back into an old routine and clings to it with dogmatic desperation. The more change whirls around him, the more blindly he attempts to apply the old action patterns and ideologies. The Barry Goldwaters and George Wallaces of the world appeal to his quivering gut through the politics of nostalgia. Police maintained order in the past; hence, to maintain order, we need only supply more police. Authoritarian treatment of children worked in the past; hence, the troubles of the present spring from permissiveness. The middle-aged, right-wing reversionist yearns for the simple, ordered society of the small town—the slow-paced social environment in which his old routines were appropriate. Instead of adapting to the new, he continues automatically to apply the old solutions, growing more and more divorced from reality as he does so.

If the older reversionist dreams of reinstating a small-town past, the youthful, left-wing reversionist dreams of reviving an even older social system. This accounts for some of the fascination with rural communes, the bucolic romanticism that fills the posters and poetry of the hippie and post-hippie subcultures, the deification of Ché Guevara (identified with mountains and jungles, not with urban or post-urban environments), the exaggerated veneration of pre-technological societies and the exaggerated contempt for science and technology. The left reversionist hands out anachronistic Marxist and Freudian clichés as knee-jerk answers for the problems of tomorrow.

Finally, there is the future-shock victim who attempts to cope with the explosion of information, the pulsing waves of data, the novelty and change in the environment, by reducing everything to a single neat equation. Complexity terrifies him. The world slips from control when it is too complex. This helps explain the intellectual faddism that seizes on a McLuhan or a Marcuse or a Maharishi to explain all the problems of past, present and future. Upset by the untidiness of reality, the supersimplifier attempts to force it into an overneat set of dogmas. He then invests these with tremendous emotional force and clings to them with total conviction—until the next new world-explaining concept is merchandised by the media.

In the field of action and activism, the passionate pursuit of the supersimple leads to supersimple solutions—such as violence. For the older generation and the political establishment, police truncheons and military bayonets loom as attractive remedies, a way to end dissent once and for all. The vigilantes of the right and the brick-throwing cults of the left, overwhelmed by the onrushing complexities of change, employ violence to narrow their options and clarify their lives. Terrorism substitutes for thought.

These all-too-familiar forms of behavior can be seen as modes of response to future shock. They are the ways used by the future-shock victim to get through the thickening tangle of personal and social problems that seem to hit him with ever-increasing force and velocity. To the information scientist, these four responses—blocking-out, overspecialization, reversion and supersimplification—are instantly recognizable, for they are classical ways of coping with overload. But classical or not, these tactics, pushed beyond a reasonable point, flower into full-blown pathology, endangering not merely the individual who employs them but the people around him as well.

Asked to adapt too rapidly, increasing numbers of us grow confused, bewildered, irritable and irrational. Sometimes we throw a tantrum, lashing out against friends or family or committing acts of senseless violence. Pressured too hard, we fall into profound lethargy—the same lethargy exhibited by battle-shocked soldiers or by change-hassled young people who, even without the dubious aid of drugs, all too often seem stoned and apathetic. This is the hidden meaning of the dropout syndrome, the stop-the-world-I-want-to-get-off attitude, the search for tranquillity or nirvana in a host of moldy mystical ideas. Such philosophies are dredged up to provide intellectual justification for an apathy that is essentially unhealthy and anti-adaptive, and that is often a symptom not of intellectual profundity but of future shock.

For future shock is what happens to men when they are pushed beyond their adaptive tolerances. It is the inevitable and crushing consequence of a society that is running too fast for its own good—without even having a clear picture of where it wants to go.

Change is good. Change is life itself. The justifications for radical changes in world society are more than ample. The ghetto, the campus, the deepening misery in the Third World all cry out for rapid change. But every time we accelerate a change, we need to take into account the effect it has on human copability. Just as we need to accelerate some changes, we need to decelerate others. We need to design "future-shock absorbers" into the very fabric of the emergent society. If we don't, if we simply assume that man's capacity for change is infinite, we are likely to suffer a rude awakening in the form of massive adaptive breakdown. We shall become the world's first future-shocked society.